西方经典英汉提要
（卷二）

(奥) 雷立柏 (Leopold Leeb) 著

# 古代晚期经典100部

English-Chinese Summaries of Western Classics Volume II
100 Classics of Late Antiquity

（公元150年到650年）

世界图书出版公司
北京·广州·上海·西安

# 目 录
## CONTENTS

《西方经典英汉提要》总序 / 1
序 / 4
大事年表 / 7

## 第一篇 / CHAPTER 1
罗马帝国的转型时期（公元150年到313年）
The Transformation Period of the Roman Empire (150—313 AD)

|  |  |
|---|---|
| 阿里安 ..................................2 | Flavius Arrianus ..................................3 |
| 001.《亚历山大远征记》..................2 | 001. *Alexandrou Anabasis* ..................3 |
| 犹斯丁 ..................................6 | Iustinos ..................................7 |
| 002.《护教篇》..................6 | 002. *Apologia* ..................7 |
| 托勒密 ..................................10 | Klaudios Ptolemaios ..................................11 |
| 003.《天文学大成》..................10 | 003. *Mathēmatikē syntaxis* ..................11 |
| 保萨尼阿斯 ..................................12 | Pausanias ..................................13 |
| 004.《希腊志》..................12 | 004. *Periēgēsis tēs Hellados* ..................13 |
| 塔提安努斯 ..................................14 | Tatianos ..................................15 |
| 005.《四部福音合参》..................14 | 005. *Diatessarōn* ..................15 |
| 006.《驳希腊人》..................14 | 006. *Logos pros Hellēnas* ..................15 |
| 卢奇安 ..................................16 | Loukianos ..................................17 |
| 007.《真实的故事》..................16 | 007. *Alēthē dihēgēmata* ..................17 |
| 008.《诸神对话》..................18 | 008. *Theōn dialogoi* ..................19 |
| 009.《拍卖诸生命》..................18 | 009. *Biōn prasis* ..................19 |
| 马可·奥勒留 ..................................22 | Marcus Aurelius ..................................23 |
| 010.《沉思录》..................22 | 010. *Ta eis heauton* ..................23 |
| 阿普列乌斯 ..................................26 | Lucius Apuleius ..................................27 |
| 011.《变形记》..................26 | 011. *Metamorphosae* ..................27 |

1

| 盖伦 | 32 | Galēnos | 33 |
| --- | --- | --- | --- |
| 012.《本人著作目录》 | 32 | 012. *Peri tōnidiōn bibliōn* | 33 |

| 格利乌斯 | 34 | Aulus Gellius | 35 |
| --- | --- | --- | --- |
| 013.《雅典之夜》 | 34 | 013. *Noctes Atticae* | 35 |

| 依勒内 | 36 | Irenaeus | 37 |
| --- | --- | --- | --- |
| 014.《驳斥异端》 | 36 | 014. *Adversus haereses* | 37 |

| （亚历山大的）克雷芒 | 42 | Clemens Alexandrinus | 43 |
| --- | --- | --- | --- |
| 015.《教导者》 | 42 | 015. *Paidagōgos* | 43 |
| 016.《劝说》 | 42 | 016. *Protreptikos* | 43 |
| 017.《杂论》 | 44 | 017. *Strōmateis* | 45 |

| 塞克斯都·恩披里柯 | 48 | Sextos Empeirikos | 49 |
| --- | --- | --- | --- |
| 018.《怀疑学派》 | 48 | 018. *Skeptika* | 49 |

| 德尔图良 | 50 | Tertullianus | 51 |
| --- | --- | --- | --- |
| 019.《护教篇》 | 50 | 019. *Apologeticum* | 51 |
| 020.《论斗兽场的表演》 | 52 | 020. *De spectaculis* | 53 |
| 021.《灵魂的见证》 | 54 | 021. *De testimonio animae* | 55 |

| 米努其乌斯 | 56 | Minucius | 57 |
| --- | --- | --- | --- |
| 022.《奥大维乌斯》 | 56 | 022. *Octavius* | 57 |

| 培培图阿 | 60 | Perpetua | 61 |
| --- | --- | --- | --- |
| 023.《培培图阿与菲里契塔斯遇难录》 | 60 | 023. *Passio Perpetuae et Felicitatis* | 61 |

| 奥利金 | 62 | Ōrigenēs | 63 |
| --- | --- | --- | --- |
| 024.《六文本合参》 | 62 | 024. *Hexapla* | 63 |
| 025.《驳凯尔索》 | 62 | 025. *Kata Kelsou* | 63 |
| 026.《论基本的原理》 | 64 | 026. *Peri archōn* | 65 |

| 朗格斯 | 68 | Longos | 69 |
| --- | --- | --- | --- |
| 027.《达夫尼斯和赫洛亚》 | 68 | 027. *Poimenika ta kata Daphnin kai Chloēn* | 69 |

| 赫利奥多鲁斯 | 72 | Hēliodōros | 73 |
| --- | --- | --- | --- |
| 028.《埃塞俄比亚故事》 | 72 | 028. *Aithiopika* | 73 |

| 西普里安 | 76 | Caecilius Cyprianus | 77 |
| --- | --- | --- | --- |
| 029.《书信集》 | 76 | 029. *Epistulae* | 77 |

| 普罗提诺 | 78 | Plōtinos | 79 |

| | |
|---|---|
| 030.《九章集》..............78 | 030. *Enneades* ..............79 |

**第欧根尼·拉尔修** ..............80

031.《著名哲学家的生平和学说》..............80

**Diogenēs Laertios**..............81

031. *Philosophōn biōn kai dogmatōn synagōgē* ...81

# 第二篇

教父学的全盛时期
（公元 313 年到 410 年）

# CHAPTER 2

The Golden Age of Patristic Literature
(313—410 AD)

**拉克坦提乌斯** ..............84
- 032.《凤凰之诗》..............84
- 033.《论上主之愤怒》..............86
- 034.《论迫害者之死》..............86
- 035.《神圣教规》..............88

**Lactantius** ..............85
- 032. *Carmen de ave phoenice* ..............85
- 033. *De ira Dei* ..............87
- 034. *De mortibus persecutorum* ..............87
- 035. *Institutiones divinae* ..............89

**优西比乌斯** ..............92
- 036.《教会历史》..............92

**Eusēbios Pamphili** ..............93
- 036. *Ekklēsiastikē Historia* ..............93

**亚大纳西** ..............96
- 037.《反驳外邦人》..............96
- 038.《圣安托尼传》..............98

**Athanasios** ..............97
- 037. *Logos kata tōn Hellēnōn* ..............97
- 038. *Vita Sancti Antonii* ..............99

**诺尼乌斯** ..............102
- 039.《教育手册》..............102

**Nonius Marcellus** ..............103
- 039. *De compendiosa doctrina* ..............103

**奥索尼乌斯** ..............104
- 040.《书信集》..............104

**Ausonius** ..............105
- 040. *Epistulae* ..............105

**基里洛斯** ..............106
- 041.《教理讲授》..............106

**Kyrillos** ..............107
- 041. *Katēchēseis* ..............107

**多纳图斯** ..............110
- 042.《拉丁语法基础》/《拉丁语法中级》....110

**Aelius Donatus** ..............111
- 042. *Ars minor / Ars maior* ..............111

**阿米阿努斯** ..............112
- 043.《历史》..............112

**Ammianus** ..............113
- 043. *Rerum gestarum libri* ..............113

**（大）巴西略** ..............114
- 044.《修道生活教导》..............114
- 045.《论六天创造》..............116

**Basileios** ..............115
- 044. *Askētika* ..............115
- 045. *Hexaemeron* ..............117

3

| 中文 | 页码 | 原文 | 页码 |
|---|---|---|---|
| 格列高利 | 120 | Grēgorios Nazianzos | 121 |
| 046.《诗集》 | 120 | 046. *Carmina* | 121 |
| 047.《讲道文集》 | 122 | 047. *Logoi* | 123 |
| (尼撒的) 格列高利 | 124 | Grēgorios Nyssēnos | 125 |
| 048.《论人的准备》 | 124 | 048. *Peri kataskeuēs anthrōpou* | 125 |
| 049.《论贞洁》 | 126 | 049. *Peri parthenias* | 127 |
| 050.《关于灵魂和复活的对话》 | 126 | 050. *Peri psychēs kai anastaseōs* | 127 |
| 安博罗修斯 | 128 | Ambrosius | 129 |
| 051.《论圣职人员的职务》 | 128 | 051. *De officiis ministrorum* | 129 |
| 052.《信集》 | 130 | 052. *Epistulae* | 131 |
| 053.《赞美诗集》 | 132 | 053. *Hymni* | 133 |
| 西马克斯 | 134 | Symmachus | 135 |
| 054.《报告》 | 134 | 054. *Relationes* | 135 |
| 金口若望 | 138 | Iōannēs Chrysostomos | 139 |
| 055.《讲道稿》 | 138 | 055. *Logoi* | 139 |
| 056.《论贞洁》 | 140 | 056. *Peri Parthenias* | 141 |
| 热罗尼摩 | 142 | Eusebius Hieronymus | 143 |
| 057.《诸名人传》 | 142 | 057. *De viris illustribus* | 143 |
| 058.《信集》 | 144 | 058. *Epistulae* | 145 |
| 059.《圣经通行译本》 | 150 | 059. *Vulgata* | 151 |
| 普鲁登蒂乌斯 | 154 | Prudentius | 155 |
| 060.《殉道士行传》 | 154 | 060. *Peristephanon* | 155 |
| 061.《灵魂之战》 | 154 | 061. *Psychomachia* | 155 |
| 奥古斯丁 | 158 | Aurelius Augustinus | 159 |
| 062.《忏悔录》 | 158 | 062. *Confessiones* | 159 |
| 063.《论幸福生活》 | 164 | 063. *De beata vita* | 165 |
| 064.《上帝/天主之城》 | 166 | 064. *De civitate Dei* | 167 |
| 065.《论基督宗教的教导》 | 180 | 065. *De doctrina Christiana* | 181 |
| 066.《论真实的宗教》 | 182 | 066. *De vera religione* | 183 |
| 067.《独语》 | 184 | 067. *Soliloquia* | 185 |
| 克劳狄安 | 188 | Claudius Claudianus | 189 |
| 068.《珀尔塞福涅的掠夺》 | 188 | 068. *De raptu Proserpinae* | 189 |

## 第三篇
外族的入侵与隐修院文化的开始
（公元 410 年到 529 年）

## CHAPTER 3
Foreign Intrusions and the Beginnings of Monasticism (410—529 AD)

塞维鲁斯 ..................................................192
 069.《圣马丁传》....................................192

卡西安 ......................................................194
 070.《隐修者教规》................................194

斯托拜乌斯 ..............................................196
 071.《文摘》............................................196

卡佩拉 ......................................................198
 072.《梅库利乌斯和语文学的婚姻》.........198

马克罗比乌斯 ..........................................202
 073.《评注〈西皮欧的梦〉》....................202
 074.《农神节说》....................................202

聂斯托里乌斯 ..........................................206
 075.《赫拉克勒伊德斯之书》................206

奥罗修斯 ..................................................210
 076.《反驳异教徒的世界史》................210

利奥 ..........................................................212
 077.《致佛拉维安的信》........................212

普洛克鲁斯 ..............................................216
 078.《论柏拉图的神学》........................216

欧基皮乌斯 ..............................................218
 079.《圣塞维林传》................................218

小狄奥尼修斯 ..........................................222
 080.《复活节日期查订表》....................222

波伊提乌 ..................................................224
 081.《哲学的慰藉》................................224

（伪）狄奥尼修斯 ..................................232

Sulpicius Severus ...................................193
 069. *Vita Sancti Martini* ......................193

Johannes Cassianus .................................195
 070. *De institutis monachorum* ..........195

Iōannēs Stobaios ....................................197
 071. *Eklogai* ........................................197

Capella ....................................................199
 072. *De nuptiis Philologiae et Mercurii* ........199

Macrobius ...............................................203
 073. *Commentarii in Somnium Scipionis* ........203
 074. *Saturnalia* ....................................203

Nestorios .................................................207
 075. *Pragmateia Herakleidou Damaskenou* ....207

Orosius ....................................................211
 076. *Historiae adversus paganos* .......211

Leo Magnus ............................................213
 077. *Tomus ad Flavianum* ..................213

Proklos ....................................................217
 078. *Eis tēn Platōnos theologian* ........217

Eugippius ................................................219
 079. *Vita Sancti Severini* ....................219

Dionysius Exiguus ..................................223
 080. *Liber de paschale* .......................223

Boethius ..................................................225
 081. *De consolatione philosophiae* ....225

Dionysios Areiopagita ............................233

| 082.《教阶体系》..........232 | 082. *Peri tēs ekklēsiastikēs hierarchias*..........233 |
| 083.《天阶体系》..........234 | 083. *Peri tēs ouranias hierarchias*..........235 |

## 本笃 ..........236
### 084.《会规》..........236

## Benedictus ..........237
### 084. *Regula* ..........237

# 第四篇
拜占庭的崛起与西欧的新型文人
（公元 529 年到 650 年）

# CHAPTER 4
The Rise of Byzantium and the Emerging Scholars of Western Europe (529—650 AD)

## 优士丁尼 ..........242
### 085.《民法大全》..........242

## Flavius Iustinianus ..........243
### 085. *Corpus Iuris Civilis* ..........243

## 菲洛普诺斯 ..........246
### 086.《世界的创造》..........246

## Iōannēs Philoponos ..........247
### 086. *De creatione mundi* ..........247

## 卡西奥多鲁斯 ..........248
### 087.《宗教文学与世俗文学的教学》..........248

## Cassiodorus ..........249
### 087. *Institutiones* ..........249

## 罗曼努斯·梅洛多斯 ..........254
### 088.《圣歌》..........254

## Romanos Melodos ..........255
### 088. *Kontakia* ..........255

## 马丁 ..........256
### 089.《论纠正农民》..........256

## Martinus de Bracara ..........257
### 089. *De correctione rusticorum* ..........257

## 维南蒂乌斯 ..........258
### 090.《诗集》..........258

## Venantius Fortunatus ..........259
### 090. *Carmina* ..........259

## 格列高利 ..........260
### 091.《法兰克人史》..........260

## Gregorius Turonensis ..........261
### 091. *Historia Francorum* ..........261

## （大）格列高利 ..........264
### 092.《对话集》..........264
### 093.《约伯伦理记》..........266
### 094.《牧民守则》..........268

## Gregorius Magnus ..........265
### 092. *Dialogi* ..........265
### 093. *Moralia in Job* ..........267
### 094. *Regula pastoralis* ..........269

## 科伦班 ..........272
### 095.《隐修士会规》..........272

## Columban ..........273
### 095. *Regula coenobialis* ..........273

## 伊西多尔 ..........274
### 096.《语源学》..........274

## Isidorus de Sevilla ..........275
### 096. *Etymologiae* ..........275

| | | | |
|---|---|---|---|
| **梯子约翰** | 278 | **Iōannēs Klimakos** | 279 |
| 097.《天堂之梯》 | 278 | 097. *Klimax tou paradeisou* | 279 |
| **马克西摩斯** | 280 | **Maximos Homologētēs** | 281 |
| 098.《警句集》 | 280 | 098. *Capita* | 281 |
| 099.《引入神秘》 | 282 | 099. *Mystagōgia* | 283 |

## 附录　Appendix

| | | | |
|---|---|---|---|
| **无名作者** | 286 | **Anonymus** | 287 |
| 100.《十二使徒/宗徒遗训》 | 286 | 100. *Didachē* | 287 |
| 101.《谈论自然者》 | 286 | 101. *Physiologos* | 287 |
| 102.《爱笑者》 | 288 | 102. *Philogelōs* | 289 |
| 103.《艾格瑞亚的游记》 | 290 | 103. *Itinerarium Egeriae* | 291 |

拉—希—英—汉索引 Latin–Greek–English–Chinese Index / 292
出版后记 / 380

# 西方经典英汉提要
## 总 序

就早期的来龙去脉而言,欧洲文化的根源在埃及、巴勒斯坦、叙利亚和波斯地区,因此"西方文化"和"西方经典"是有争论的概念。然而从文学和思想来看,古希腊的传统在人类思想史上形成了一种很关键的新开端。因此,本系列从荷马开始梳理欧洲经典的悠久传统,其目标是提供关于一些重要著作及其作者的基本知识。当然,仅仅轮廓性地描述一部经典的内容是远远不够的,应该还要鉴定每一部经典在文学史及思想史上的位置和影响,又要提供一些分析和解释,以及关于该著作的研究书目。不过,这一切都超出本系列的范围。

欧洲文化以及西方思想史应该被视为一个整体。这就意味着人们应该研究每一个时代的作者以及前后著作之间的关联。一种比较全面的角度也应该注意到不同的知识领域,因为一些作者可能通过诗歌表达一些哲学理念或他们会将神话与历史结合起来。因此,文学、历史、哲学、法律和宗教在很多古代经典中是分不开的。比如奥古斯丁的《上帝之城》谈论历史、伦理、政治、神话学、宗教信仰以及解释学的问题。

本系列分为五卷:《古希腊罗马经典100部》(公元前800年到公元150年)、《古代晚期经典100部》(公元150年到650年)、《中世纪经典100部》(650年到1450年)、《文艺复兴和巴罗克时期经典100部》(1450到1750年)、《近现代经典100部》(1750年到1950年)。每一卷都可以充当一部独立的文集,因此在每一卷附加索引,其中罗列作者、著作和重要概念的原名、英语及汉语的翻译。本系列的经典主要属于文学、历史学、哲学、法学和宗教学的领域,但也包括一些著名的自然科学著作和百科全书式的著作。在选择经典时我们优先收录那些形成比较完整叙事的著作,因此残片式的著作、"诗歌集"、"信集"和"讲演集"类型的著作比较少。一些重要的作者在正文中被忽略,但在索引中仍然有关于他们的基本资料。因为本系列特别注重经典的原文,在汉语的叙述中仍然使用ABC写出西文的人名、地名和书名。"关于专名,除有惯译者外,一般均不译成汉语对音。因为单是《荷马史诗》中的英雄Achilleus就有阿喀琉斯、阿基琉斯、阿戏留、阿溪里等许多译名,难定取舍,所以都不采用,一概使用原文。"(参见罗念生,《古希腊语汉语词典》,商务印书馆,2004年,前言)。西文专名的汉译能在索引中查获。

希望本系列能够帮助读者更好地了解和欣赏西方文学及思想的高度、深度和广度!

编者雷立柏
2009年于北京

# The Series of "English–Chinese Summaries of Western Classics"

## General Preface

The more ancient origins of European culture are in Egypt, Palestine, Syria and Persia, and thus the expressions "western culture" and "western classics" are debatable. However, as far as literature and thought are concerned, the tradition of ancient Greece forms a decisive new beginning in the intellectual history of mankind. Thus this series starts with Homer and from there follows the long stream of European classics. The purpose of the collection is to provide basic knowledge about some important classical works and about their authors. Of course, a simple summary of the contents of a classic is not enough, it would also be necessary to assess the position and influence of each work in the history of literature and thought, to offer analysis and possible interpretations, and to add a short bibliography of the studies on each of the classics. However, this exceeds the scope of this series.

European culture and the intellectual history of the West should be understood as a whole. This implies that we should be acquainted with the scholars of every period and with the continuity that links earlier and later works. A more wholistic approach will also pay attention to different fields of knowledge, because many authors may use poetry to express philosophical ideas or combine myth and history. Thus literature, history, philosophy, law, and religion are intertwined in many of the classical writings. For example, Augustine's The City of God discusses questions of history, ethics, politics, mythology, religious faith, and hermeneutical questions.

This series is divided into five volumes: "100 Classics of Ancient Greece and Rome" (800 BC —150 AD), "100 Classics of Late Antiquity" (150 AD—650 AD), "100 Classics of the Middle Ages" (650—1450 AD), "100 Classics of Renaissance and Baroque" (1450—1750), "100 Classics of the Modern Age" (1750—1950). Each volume is designed as an independent collection and thus has an index which contains the original names of the authors, important works and ideas, and the English and Chinese transcriptions. The classical works chosen in this series are mainly taken from the areas of literature, history, philosophy, law, and religion, but there are also some famous scientific works and encyclopedic collections. Preference was given to those works who present a complete narrative, thus collections of fragments, poems, letters, and speeches have been somewhat neglected. Some important authors may not be mentioned in the text, but they appear in the index. Since this series pays special attention to the original languages of the classics, the Chinese text uses the ABC for western personal names, place names, and book titles. "Proper names are generally not transliterated into Chinese, except for commonly used translations. Take for example the different Chinese translations for the hero Achilles in Homer's epic, it will be hard to choose between 'A-ka-liu-si', 'A-ji-liu-si', 'A-xi-liu','A-xi-li' and many other different translations. Thus we do not use any of these transliterations and keep the original way of writing." (Luo Niansheng, Classical Greek - Chinese Dictionary, Shangwu, 2004, preface). The Chinese transliterations of western names can be found in the index.

May this series help the reader to better understand and enjoy the height, depth, and width of western literature and thought!

**Leopold Leeb, Beijing 2009**

# 序

大约于公元150年罗马帝国在军事和经济方面开始走向衰弱,而文化上的转型也带来了文学上的种种变化,尤其是向宗教哲学的发展趋势。当时出现了一些新型的思想家,他们利用希腊哲学来说明基督信仰的合理性。这些"护教士"在某种程度上肯定古希腊罗马的文化传统,但又从一个新的角度来解释它,甚至攻击它,而这种张力催促了很多作者去思考和重新评价传统文学和思想的真实贡献。这些基督教学者中最有权威性的人物被称为"教父",因为古代晚期最杰出的著作来自教父们的创造力,整个时代也被称为"教父时期"或"教父的时代"。早期教父的著作大多是希腊文写的,但一些翻译者和学者在3、4世纪开始创造具有深远影响的拉丁语文献,其中最著名的经典出自Augustinus之手。在古代晚期也出现了一些百科全书式的学者,他们想尽可能完整地保存前人的种种成就或编写教科书来传授最核心的宗教知识和世俗学问,这样他们在很多方面为中世纪文学的新时代做好了准备。

《古代晚期经典100部》仅仅介绍最重要的作者及其著作,很多作者被忽略,这是难免的缺陷。每一部经典的提要尽可能是根据原文写的。参考的德语和英语工具书主要是Herwig Goergemanns, ed., *Die griechische Literatur in Text und Darstellung*, (5 vols.), Reclam, Stuttgart 1998; M. v. Albrecht, ed., *Die roemische Literatur in Text und Darstellung*, (5 vols.), Reclam, 1991; Rainer Nickel, *Lexikon der antiken Literatur*, Patmos 1999; *Kindlers Literaturlexikon*, (12 vols.), Zuerich, 1970; Hornblower, Spawforth, ed. *The Oxford Classical Dictionary*, 1996; Howatson, Chilvers, ed., *Oxford Dictionary of Classical Literature*, 1993。

在希腊语名称方面,本书使用拉丁语的ABC,而不使用希腊字母,但因为希腊语有长短音之别,本书采用上划线来表达长e(即Eta)和长o(即Omega),这样区分短e和长ē,短o和长ō。另外,在英语中,外国人的名称使用英语的写法(比如荷马=Homer),但在古代的文献中,希腊人称荷马Homēros,而拉丁语则为Homerus。为了提高本书的学术价值,我在汉语的部分都用原文的写法(即希腊语的著作使用Homēros,拉丁语的著作使用Homerus)。一般来说,希腊语和拉丁语之间的差别很小,只把后缀-os改成-us,或希腊语的k改成c。书后的"拉—希—英—汉"索引也许能够澄清这些问题。

在此特别感谢黄星女士、赵林先生以及Rob Pattison先生帮助我改进汉、英语的稿子。我也谢谢世界图书出版公司的编辑们在各方面给予的杰出支持与协助。

如果本书能吸引更多的人学习古希腊罗马语言(古希腊语、拉丁语)进而阅读原著,将是本人所付努力之最好偿报。

雷立柏<br>
2009 年于北京

# Preface

Around the year 150 AD the Roman Empire entered a period of military and economic decline, and the cultural changes that happened in the same era brought about many changes in the field of literature and thought, most notably the turn to a philosophy of religion. At that time there emerged a new type of scholars who tried to use Greek philosophy in order to explain the rationality of the Christian faith. Those "apologists" to some extent reconfirmed the value of the ancient Greek and Roman traditions, but they interpreted them from a new perspective or even attacked these traditions. This tension induced many authors to reassess the true value of traditional literature and thought. The more authoritative among these Christian scholars were called "Fathers of the Church", and because the most outstanding works from the period are fruits of the creativity of these "Fathers" ("patres" in Latin), the whole period is also named "Patristic Period" or "Age of the Fathers of the Church". Most works of the early Fathers were written in Greek, but some translators and scholars of the 3rd and 4th centuries produced Latin works of great influence, the most outstanding of them being Augustine. Late antiquity also saw the emergence of some encyclopedic scholars who tried to preserve the achievements of the past or wrote textbooks in order to transmit the most important religious knowledge and secular learning to the next generation, thus preparing the way for the literary developments of the Middle Ages.

This volume entitled "100 Classics of Late Antiquity" can only present outlines of the most important authors and their works. It is a regrettable necessity that many authors must be neglected. Wherever possible the summaries are based on a study of the original works. The German and English reference books that have been consulted are mainly the following:

Herwig Goergemanns, ed., *Die griechische Literatur in Text und Darstellung*, (5 vols.), Reclam, Stuttgart 1998; M. v. Albrecht, ed., *Die roemische Literatur in Text und Darstellung*, (5 vols.), Reclam, 1991; Rainer Nickel, *Lexikon der antiken Literatur*, Patmos 1999; *Kindlers Literaturlexikon*, (12 vols.), Zuerich, 1970;Hornblower, Spawforth, ed. *The Oxford Classical Dictionary*, 1996;Howatson, Chilvers, ed., *Oxford Dictionary of Classical Literature*, 1993.

As to the writing of Greek names, the Latin transcription is used instead of the Greek alphabet. Greek vowels are divided into short and long ones, and so the macron signifies the long "e" (eta) and the long "o" (omega). In the English text the common English transcription is used (for example "Homer"), but in Greek texts the writing would be "Homeros", and in the Latin texts it would be "Homerus". In order to enhance the academic value of this collection, we used the original spelling in the Chinese text (for example "Homeros" if it is a Greek text, and "Homerus" if it is a Latin text). As a general rule, the difference between the Greek and Latin spelling is very small, often it is just the ending "-os" instead of the ending "-us", or the Greek "k" instead of the Latin "c". Maybe the "Latin-Greek-English-Chinese Index" at the end of the book can clarify these questions.

I would like to thank Miss Xing Huang, Mr. Lin Zhao and Mr. Rob Pattison for helping me to improve the Chinese and English manuscripts. I also thank the editors of the World Publishing Corporation for their excellent cooperation and support.

May this book induce more people to learn the ancient languages (classical Greek and Latin) and in a next step inspire them to read the original works, this would be the best reward for my humble efforts.

**Leopold Leeb, Beijing 2009**

# Table of Important Events
# 大事年表

| | | |
|---|---|---|
| 前 3000 | 克里特岛弥诺斯文化的起源 | Beginnings of Minoan culture in Crete |
| 前 1600—前 1200 | 希腊迈锡尼文化的兴衰 | Rise and Fall of Mycenaean culture in Greece |
| 前 1230 | 以色列人在迦南定居 | Settlement of the Israelites in Canaan |
| 前 1200 | 特洛伊被毁 | Fall of Troy |
| 前 1100—前 1000 | 多里斯人侵入希腊地区 | Dorians invade Greece |
| 前 776 | 第一次有记载的奥林匹克运动会 | First recorded Olympian Games |
| 前 753 | 传统认为罗马建城的年份 | Traditional date of the Founding of Rome |
| 前 750—前 550 | 希腊城邦和殖民地的兴起 | Emergence of the Greek polis and colonies |
| 前 621 | 德拉孔颁布雅典第一部法典 | Draco promulgates Athens' first law code |
| 前 539 | 波斯人占据巴比伦，犹太人流亡期结束 | Persians seize Babylon, end of the Jewish exile |
| 前 509 | 罗马共和制的开端 | Foundation of the Roman republic |
| 前 480 | 希腊人在撒拉米斯战胜波斯海军 | Greeks defeat the Persian navy at Salamis |
| 前 480—前 430 | 雅典文化的黄金时代 | Golden Age of Athenian culture |
| 前 431—前 404 | 伯罗奔尼撒战争 | Peloponnesian War |
| 前 387 | 柏拉图创立雅典学园 | Plato founds the Academy in Athens |
| 前 333 | 亚历山大在伊索斯战胜波斯人 | Alexander defeats the Persians at Issos |
| 前 218—前 201 | 第二次普尼克战争，罗马崛起 | Second Punic War, the rise of Roman power |
| 前 146 | 罗马人毁灭迦太基和科林斯 | Romans destroy of Carthage and Corinth |
| 前 31 | 奥古斯都时代的开始 | Beginning of the Augustan Age |
| 50—150 | 在很多城市出现基督徒团体 | Christian communities appear in many cities |
| 70 | 耶路撒冷圣殿被毁 | Destruction of the Temple at Jerusalem |
| 165 | 瘟疫的爆发开始罗马帝国的逐渐衰落 | Plague ushers in the decline of the Roman Empire |
| 250 | 对基督徒的系统迫害开始 | Systematic persecutions of Christians begin |
| 313 | 君士坦丁皇帝支持基督宗教 | Constantine the Great supports Christianity |
| 324 | 新首都君士坦丁堡建立 | Founding of Constantinople, the new capital |
| 410 | 西哥特人劫掠罗马城 | Sack of Rome by the Visigoths |
| 476 | 西罗马帝国的终结 | End of the Roman Empire in the West |
| 497 | 法兰克人和他们的王克洛维接受洗礼 | The Franks under King Clovis are baptized |
| 527—565 | 拜占庭在优士丁尼皇帝时代的兴起 | Rise of Byzantium under Emperor Justinian |
| 529 | 柏拉图学园被关闭，本笃会被创立 | Closure of the Academy, founding of Benedictines |
| 597 | 格列高利的传教士到达英国 | Gregory's missionaries arrive in England |
| 633—655 | 阿拉伯人征服叙利亚、埃及等地区 | Arab conquest of Syria, Egypt and other regions |

第一篇

# 罗马帝国的转型时期
## The Transformation Period of the Roman Empire
(150 — 313 AD)

• *Romans of the Decadence*

# 阿里安(约 90—160 AD)

希腊人,来自 Bithynia 的 Nikomēdia,曾在 Nikopolis 当 Epiktētos 的学生并记录了 Epiktētos 的讲演;后来成为罗马公民,在罗马军队中担任军官,131—137 年任 Kappadokia 的总督,140 年后到 Athēnai(雅典),在其著作中他模仿了 Xenophōn。

著作:《亚历山大远征记》、《论打猎》、《论集》(见 Epiktētos)、《手册》(见 Epiktētos)、《印度》、《环游黑海》(包括东方地理学的宝贵资料)、《军事策略》

## 001.《亚历山大远征记》

本著作成书于 130 年后,甚至可能是在 160 年以后。它是 Alexandros 大帝的传记,分为 7 卷,与 Xenophōn 的《远征记》一样,因为 Arrianos 力图模仿 Xenophōn 的著作。Arrianos 的目标是提供关于 Alexander 生平和成就的一种实际的、可靠的描绘,他遵守 Thoukydidēs 提出来的历史学标准。

第 1 卷叙述在巴尔干半岛上的早期交战(公元前 336 年)以及希腊军队为东征所做的准备。Arrianos 描述了征服小亚细亚的过程(公元前 334—前 333 年)。第 2 卷记载波斯人的保卫措施。Arrianos 叙述了关于 nodus Gordianus(格尔迪之结)的著名故事:在小亚细亚 Phrygia 地区的 Gordium 城中有一辆牛车,一条绳子连结其辕和轭,但没有人能解开这条绳子的结。根据神谕的说法,谁能解开这个结,谁就将成为亚细亚的统治者。Alexandros 用自己的剑切断了这个结并说他自己就是要实现该神谕的人。在 Issos 的交战中(公元前 333 年),波斯人被打败,Dareios III 的家族被擒获,而这个国王求和。

第 3 卷叙述对埃及的征服(公元前 332 年年底)以及 Alexandria 城的奠基。在 Gaugamēla 的交战中(即 Tigris 河附近的地区),Alexander 获得了对 Dareios 王战役的最终胜利(公元前 331 年秋天)。在公元前 330 年秋天,Philōtas 的阴谋被揭露,而那些叛徒被处死。第 4 卷报告了一些发生在北方地区 Skythēs 的战争。此时 Alexandros 逐渐成为一个典型的东方式的独裁统治者。部分人反对他的独断作风,但他们因此被处死,首先是他的骑兵将军 Kleitos——他曾经在一次交战中救过 Alexandros 的性命。另一个被处死的人是哲学家 Kallisthenēs——他反对 Alexandros 要求一切臣民在面见他时要在他面前跪下的提议(即所谓的 proskynēsis)。Alexandros 与 Roxana 结婚,她是 Baktria 地区的某位贵族人士的女儿(公元前 327 年春天)。此后他启程,前往印度(公元前 327 年夏天)。

# Flavius Arrianus / Arrianos

**Opera:** *Alexandrou Anabasis, Cynegeticus (=Kynēgetikos), Diatribai, Encheiridion, Indikē, Periplous, Technē taktikē*

**Works:** *Expedition of Alexander (the Great), On hunting, Lectures (of Epiktetos), Manual (of Epiktetos), Indics, Circumnavigation (of the Black Sea), Military Strategy*

## 001. *Alexandrou Anabasis / Expedition of Alexander*

This work in 7 books was written after 130 AD, possibly even after 160 AD. It is a history of Alexander the Great and it is divided into seven books like Xenophon's *Anabasis*, which Arrian takes as his model. Arrian's aim is to present a factual and authentic picture of Alexander's life and achievements according to the standards of historiography set up by Thucydides.

The first book describes the early battles on the Balkans (336 BC) and the preparations of the Greek army to move to the east. Thereafter Arrian gives an account of the conquest of Asia Minor (334—333 BC). Book 2 records the defense efforts of the Persians. Arrian narrates the famous story of the Gordian Knot: At Gordium in Phrygia (Asia Minor), the pole of an ox-cart is fastened to the yoke by a knot no one could untie. An oracle said that whoever could untie this knot would reign over Asia. Alexander cuts the knot with his sword and applies the oracle to himself. At the battle of Issos (333 BC) the Persians are defeated, the family of king Darius III is captured and the king asks for peace.

Book 3 narrates the invasion of Egypt (end of 332 BC) and the foundation of the city of Alexandria. The battle of Gaugamela (a place east of the river Tigris in Assyria) marks the final victory of Alexander over Darius in the fall of 331 BC. In autumn 330 BC the conspiracy of Philotas is exposed and the rebels are annihilated. Book 4 gives an account of the fights against the Skythes in the north. Alexander develops into an oriental autocratic ruler now. Some people oppose his despotism, but they are put to death, first his cavalry commander Cleitus who saved Alexander in a previous battle, then the philosopher Callisthenes who objected against the plan to demand all subjects to kneel down when greeting Alexander (the so-called proskynēsis). Alexander marries Roxana, the daughter of a Bactrian noble, in spring 327 BC. Then he departs for India (summer 327 BC).

第 5 卷：Alexander 跨越 Indus 河并在最后的大规模交战中于 Hydaspes 河畔打败印度人（公元前 326 年夏天）。始终陪同他的爱马——名为 Boukephalas（"牛头"）——受伤并死去。Alexandros 继续迈进，但到达 Hyphasis 河后他的士兵们拒绝继续前行。Alexandros 尽力鼓励他们，但他被迫后退。第 6 卷：他的军队乘船，顺 Indus 河而下。在一次小战役中，Alexandros 受伤。到达 Indus 河三角洲后，他们开始向西行军（公元前 325 年秋天）。

最后一卷提到 Alexandros 对将来怀有的种种伟大计划，他与犬儒派哲学家 Diogenēs 的相遇以及与印度哲人的对话。一万 Makedonia 士兵在 Susa 取波斯妇女为妻，他们举行了一个巨大的"集体婚礼"（公元前 324 年夏天）。Alexander 自己穿波斯人的衣服并推动他的朋友接受波斯人的生活习俗；他想融合希腊因素和东方文化。在他的理想中，Makedonia 人、希腊人和波斯人在一个普遍的帝国中——在 Makedonia 贵族的领导下——应该享受平等的权利。在 Ōpis 地区，Makedonia 的士兵们发动了一场叛乱，所以 Alexandros 必须在一次讲演中对该事件作出回应。虽然一些神谕警告他不要进入 Babylon，他仍然在公元前 323 年年初进入该城市。在 Babylon 时他在一次宴席中突然生病，并于 10 天后去世，年仅 32 岁。Arrianos 提出关于他的死因的一些猜测（中毒或发烧）并对这位伟大国王的人格作出评价。

Book 5: Alexander crosses the river Indus and in a last big battle defeats the Indians at the river Hydaspes (summer 326 BC). His beloved horse Bucephalas ("bull's head"), which has always accompanied him is wounded and dies. Alexander advances further, but after reaching the river Hyphasis the soldiers refuse to continue the march. Alexander tries to encourage his men, but he is nevertheless forced to retreat. Book 6: The army travels down the Indus by boat. During a minor campaign Alexander is injured. Having arrived in the Indus delta they begin to march to the west (fall of 325 BC).

The last book mentions Alexander's great plans for the future, his encounter with the Cynic Diogenes and with Indian sages. Ten thousand Macedonian soldiers are married to Persian women at a big celebration at Susa (summer 324 BC). Wearing Persian garments and promoting Persian customs among his friends Alexander wants to blend Greek and Oriental elements and envisages a new universal empire where Macedonians, Greeks and Persians enjoy the same rights under a Macedonian leadership. The Macedonian soldiers stage a mutiny at Opis, and Alexander has to respond to the event in a speech. Although oracles warn him not to enter Babylon, Alexander marches into the city in the beginning of 323 BC. In Babylon he suddenly falls ill at a drinking party and dies after ten days, aged only 32. Arrian makes several guesses as to the cause of his death (poison or fever) and adds a final assessment of the personality of the great king.

# 犹斯丁(查士丁)（约 100—165 AD）

来自 Samaria（巴勒斯坦）的 Flavia Neapolis 地区（=Sichem）的希腊人，受具有宗教倾向的 Platōn 学派的教育影响，但因阅读《旧约》并目睹了一些基督徒殉道者的事迹而皈依基督信仰。他接受了基督宗教的教育（大概在小亚细亚地区）并于 135 年后在罗马传播基督信仰，约于 165 年因有人控诉而被审判，并因信仰在罗马被斩首（因此他被称为 Justinus Martyr "殉道者 Iustinos"）。他是公元 2 世纪最杰出的护教士，试图使用 Platōn 和 Philōn 的观点来说明基督信仰。

**著作**：《护教首篇》、《护教次篇》、《与犹太人特里风的对话》（内容：《旧约》，耶稣为天主之子，他是救世主，外邦人的救恩）

## 002. 《护教篇》

本《护教篇》分为两个部分（《首篇》和《次篇》）；第二部分可能是第一部分的结尾。两部著作约于 150 年到 155 年间写成于罗马，目的是在教会受镇压的时期替基督宗教辩护。本著作被提交给 Antoninus Pius 皇帝；这些论文第一次从哲学的角度谈论基督信仰。

本护教著作反驳那些控诉基督徒的不公平说法，但更大的部分致力于描述基督宗教的信仰和生活，也包括一些关于早期基督宗教的重要细节（比如洗礼、感恩祭等）。作者试图说明，基督徒是更好的公民，他们很诚恳、努力劳动、按时纳税并且热爱和平。他们的伦理学概念比那些属于多神论传统的人更高级。那些针对基督徒是无神论者的指控没有根据；他们朝拜唯一的真神，他是永恒的大父，不是被造物，他是正义之父，以及一切其他美德的根源；没有什么不体面的故事降低他的道德要求。基督徒们尊敬上主的儿子，即逻各斯，他降生成人，但仍然是神。同时，他们也尊敬圣神/圣灵，他曾经通过先知们的口说过话（pneuma prophētikon）。对于创造宇宙的神的崇拜完全符合理性。犹太人的经典非常古老，这也是对其真实性的旁证，而耶稣的降生成人也应验了《旧约》的种种预言。

因为降生成人的"逻各斯"包含一切真理，所以在其他文化中的真实因素或理性因素也都与基督信仰有关。根据该原则，一切伟大的哲学家和思想家都可视为基督徒，包括那些生活在基督教之前的人。"基督是上主的首生者，他是逻各斯，一切民族都分享这个逻各斯。而那些按照逻各斯生活的人都是基督徒，虽然他们被视为无信仰的人，比如在希腊传统中的 Sōkratēs 和 Hērakleitos……"（I,46）根据这种"种子式的逻各斯"（logos spermatikos）的理论，在其他文化传统中的人们也能够部分地认识真理。

# Iustinos / Justinus / Justin

**Opera:** *Apologia* I, *Apologia* II, *Dialogus cum Tryphone Iudaeo*
**Works:** *Apology* I, *Apology* II, *Dialogue with the Trypho the Jew*

## 002. *Apologia / Apology*

This apology of Christianity is divided into two parts (*Apologia* I and II) with the shorter second part possibly being the final part of the first one. Both treatises were written in Rome, ca. 150—155 AD and aim at the defense of Christianity in the face of persecutions. They are addressed to Emperor Antoninus Pius and form the first effort to argue for Christianity on a philosophical basis.

The apology refutes unjust accusations against the Christians, but the bigger part is a description of the Christian faith and religion and includes important details about early Christian life (baptism, the eucharist, etc). The author tries to show that Christians are better citizens, since they are honest, hard-working, pay their taxes and love peace. Their ethical concepts are superior to those of the polytheist traditions. The accusation that Christians are atheists is unfounded, since they adore and worship the one true God who is eternal and not created, the Father of justice and all virtues, whose ethical standards are not stained by any depraving narratives. Christians revere God's son, the Logos, who became man and still is God. Likewise, Christians adore the Spirit who has spoken through the prophets (pneuma prophētikon). The worship of God who created the universe is in perfect harmony with reason. The old age of the Jewish scriptures witnesses to the truth of these scriptures, and Jesus' incarnation fulfilled the great prophecies of the Old Testament.

Since the incarnated Logos is the fullness of truth, all true and reasonable elements in other cultures are Christian. According to this principle all great philosophers and poets are Christians, including those who lived before the Christian era. "Christ is the First-born of God, the Logos of whom every race of men were partakers. And they who lived with the Logos are Christians, even though they have been thought to be atheists, among the Greeks some of these were Socrates and Heraclitus⋯"(I, 46)This "logos sper-

除此之外,很多那些"基督之前的基督徒"(包括古希腊思想家)也依赖于 Mōyses 的法律而获得智慧。Iustinos 也是第一个将《旧约》*Gen*(《创世记》)和 Platōn 关于世界的创造叙述(*Tim* 30a ff)联结起来的人。

因为 Iustinos 在皈依之前曾在雅典读书,Platōn 思想的痕迹也能够在他的著作中找到:神的超越性、创造论、物质和精神之间的张力、天佑和自由意志、灵魂的不朽。依他的想法,世界是由一种无形但永恒的原始质料(amorphos hylē)创造的。上主的恩典使得人的灵魂成为不死的。人的自由使他们有选择的能力,可以相信神或拒绝他的恩典。只有那些过着神圣的、有德性生活的人才能够获得永恒的赏报。生活堕落的人将要受到永不熄灭的火的惩罚。

matikos" ("seed-like logos") made it possible that people in other cultures could have a partial knowledge of the truth. Besides that, many of those "Christians before Christ" relied on the knowledge of the Mosaic law for their wisdom (including the Greek thinkers). Justin is also the first to link *Genesis* 1 with the account of the creation of the world found in Plato's *Timaeus* (30a ff).

Justin had studied in Athens before his conversion, and some traces of Plato's thought can be found in his work: God's transcendence, creation, the tension between matter and spirit, providence and free will, the immortality of the soul. According to him the world was created from a kind of formless but eternal matter (amorphos hylē). God's grace has made the human soul immortal. Human beings are free to believe in God or to refuse His graces. Only those who lead a life in holiness and virtue are rewarded with eternal bliss. Those who lead a depraved life will be punished with everlasting fire.

# 托勒密(约 100—170 AD)

古代最后一位伟大的自然科学家，在 Alexandreia 研究数学、天文学、地理学和物理学，总结了前人的研究，再一次肯定了地心说。

**著作**：《地理学指南》(8 卷，包括绘图的理论和世界地图，以及 8000 个地点的经纬度)、《和音》、《行星的行动》、《能测定的城市的目录》(提供各地城市的经纬度)、《天文学大成》(曾被译成阿拉伯文，在中世纪有重大影响)、《光学》(现只存拉丁译本)、《恒星的轨道》、《行星算法》、《占星术四卷》

## 003. 《天文学大成》

本著作亦称 *Megalē syntaxis*《大综合》或 *Megistē syntaxis*《最大综合》(阿拉伯语的 *Almagest*"最大的")。它是第一部全面讲述数学天文学的大作，共 13 卷。它成为天文学的标准著作和教科书，不论是在希腊语地区、阿拉伯语世界还是中世纪的欧洲。

第 1 卷和第 2 卷提供了很多对于地心说观点的证明：大地是球形的，而天界也是球形的，地球处于宇宙的中心，静止不动，一切天体顺着圆圈形的轨道围绕地球移动。对星星的位置的预测也必须符合几何学的种种原则。

第 3 卷试图测定太阳年的长短。作者的思想基础是 Hipparchos (喜帕恰斯，约公元前 160—前 125 年) 的著作，但 Ptolemaios 改进了后者关于太阳轨道的理论。

第 4、5、6 卷谈论月球、其轨道以及一个月的长度。作者也描述了那些用来计算月球位置的天文学仪器。他解释月蚀的成因并提供了一些预测月蚀的规则，也提出一些对于地球和月球之间的距离以及地球和太阳之间的距离的讨论。

第 7、8 卷涉及恒星的位置和大小，其中详细描写了 1022 颗恒星 (共 48 个星座) 以及它们的位置。

第 9 卷到 13 卷的描述被现代人称为"托勒密世界观"：静止不动的地球处于宇宙的中心，而行星在不同的圆圈形轨道上围绕着这个中心，同时沿着一些小型的圆圈 (epikykloi) 运行。行星与恒星都围绕着一个由北极和南极构成的轴心。它们每 24 个小时完成一个循环，而它们的圆圈形转动也是非常规律的，这样就能够很准确地预测及计算各个星星的位置。

# Klaudios Ptolemaios / Claudius Ptolemaeus / Ptolemy

**Opera:** *Geōgraphias hyphēgēsis, Harmonika, Hypothesis tōn planomenon, Kanōn episēmon poleōn, Mathēmatikē syntaxis (Megalē syntaxis), Optica, Phaseis, Procheiroi kanones, Tetrabiblos*

**Works:** *Geography, Harmony, Hypotheses of the Planets, List of marked Cities, System of Mathematics (Almagest), Optics, Phases (of Stars), Lists (for the computation of star constellations), Handbook of Astrology*

## 003. *Mathēmatikē syntaxis / System of Mathematics*

This work is also known as "*Megale syntaxis*" or "*Megiste syntaxis*" (in Arabic "*Almagest*"). It is the first comprehensive sum of mathematical astronomy in 13 books and became the standard work on astronomy, not only for the Greeks, but also in the Arab world and in medieval Europe.

Books 1 and 2 present arguments for the geocentric world view: the earth and the sky is a sphere, the earth is in the immovable center of the cosmos, and all heavenly bodies move in a circular orbit. The calculation of stellar positions must follow the principles of geometry.

Book 3 tries to determine the length of the solar year. The author bases his theory on the writings of Hipparchos (ca. 160—125 BC) and improves the latter's theory of the orbit of the sun.

Books 4, 5 and 6 deal with the moon, its orbit and the length of a month and the instruments used in measuring the position of the moon. The author explains the causes of a lunar eclipse and gives rules for predicting and calculating future eclipses. He also presents some data concerning the distances between earth and moon and earth and sun.

Books 7 and 8 are concerned with the position and size of the stars. 1022 single stars and their positions in 48 constellations are given a thorough description.

Books 9 to 13 describe what has been called the "Ptolemaic world view" in modern times: the immovable earth is the center of the cosmos, and around this center the different planets move in excentric circles, revolving around epicycles. The planets and the stars rotate around an axis formed by the earthly and celestial poles. Their rotation within 24 hours is a matter of utmost regularity and allows the precise calculation and prediction of their positions.

# 保萨尼阿斯（约 112—180 AD）

希腊作者，生平不详。

**著作：**《希腊志》（10卷，古代的"游览指南"，介绍当时的重要地点，对许多宗教及其他文物作了详细的描述）

## 004. 《希腊志》

这部长达10卷的"旅行导游"大约成书于160年到180年间。在早期的文献中可能有更多此类的"文化地理学著作"，但本书是最后的且唯一保存的样本。

有关希腊的描述是从雅典开始的（Attika 地区，第1卷），此后有 Argolis（即 Mykēnai 周围的地区，第2卷）、Lakōnia（即 Sparta 地区，第3卷）、Messēnia（即 Peloponnēsos 半岛的西南地区，第4卷）、Ēlis（西北地区，包括最著名的城市 Olympia，第5、6卷）、Achaia（即 Peloponnēsos 的北部地区，第7卷）、Arkadia（即 Peloponnēsos 的中部地区，第8卷）、Boiōtia（在 Attika 的西北地区，第9卷）以及 Phōkis（包括 Delphoi 地区，第10卷）。

作者很详细地根据当时游览的具体情况描绘了所有著名的城市、乡村、建筑物和神庙，包括废墟、残片、已被破坏的或在古代已经消失的东西。Pausanias 对宗教崇拜和神庙有特别的关注，他说明相关的故事和神话或一些与某个文物有关的地方性习俗。因此，本著作也包含很多轶事与一些英雄、政治家或艺术家的简短传记。一个比较有名的章节是对 Olympia 神庙中的 Zeus 雕像的描述。这座威严的立像（高度大约12米）是由 Pheidias（公元前490—前432年）设计的——他曾是古希腊最杰出的艺术家之一。Zeus 的塑像被称为古代世界的七大奇迹之一，但不幸的是，它业已遗失，只能根据一些硬币和宝石上的图像来了解它。

# Pausanias

**Opera:** *Periēgēsis tēs Hellados*
**Works:** *Description of Greece*

### 004.  *Periēgēsis tēs Hellados / Description of Greece*

This "tour-guide" in 10 volumes was written between 160 and 180. It is the last and the only extant example of this kind of cultural geography.

The description of Greece starts with the area around Athens (Attica, book 1), then follow Argolis (the province in the periphery of Mycenae, book 2), Lakonia (the region around Sparta, book 3), Messenia (the south-west region of the Peloponnese, book 4), Elis (the north-west area with the most famous town of Olympia, books 5~6), Achaea (the northern part of the Peloponnese, book 7), Arcadia (the central part of the Peloponnese, book 8), Boeotia (central Greece, in the north-west of Attica, book 9), and Phocis (the area containing Delphi, book 10).

The author describes in detail all of the famous cities, villages, buildings and temples as he found them during his visits. He even describes ruins, fragments or things that were already destroyed or missing in antiquity. As Pausanias is particularly interested in religious cults and temples, he explains the stories and myths or local customs and how they are connected with certain buildings or monuments. Therefore the work also contains many anecdotes and short biographies of heroes, politicians or artists. The description of the statue of Zeus in the temple of Olympia is well-known. This majestic statue (height ca. 12 meters) was designed by Pheidias (490—432 BC), one of the most outstanding artists of classical Greece. It counted as one of the Seven Wonders of the Ancient World, but unfortunately it is lost and otherwise only known from images on coins and gems.

# 塔提安努斯（约 120—190 AD）

约于 120 年生于"叙利亚"（美索不达米亚地区），曾经去过很多地方旅游并寻求真理，也曾经参与一些神秘宗教团体。他在罗马结识了 Iustinos，向他求学，皈依基督宗教并建立了自己的（哲学）学校。因为他的教导非常严格（他受 Markion、Valentinos 等人的影响），他和罗马信徒团体有了冲突并于 172 年离开，回到东方，在那里过着严格的克修生活。他的著作很多，但保存下来的很少。根据后人的记载，他在一篇谈论完美生活的文章中说耶稣曾经禁止信徒们结婚。

著作：《四部福音合参》、《驳希腊人》

## 005. 《四部福音合参》

本书已失传，全名为 *To dia tessarōn euangelion*（"根据四部福音书写的福音书"）。它是最早的"耶稣传"类型的著作，旨在协调四部《福音书》的记载，使之成为一个完整的故事，大约成书于 180 年。作者很可能使用 Iōannēs（约翰）的福音书作为基础并在这个框架中加入了其他三个福音的资料。这就意味着他必须省略部分章节。也许原文是叙利亚文，但在 223 年以前有一个希腊译本，而根据保存的其他版本（亚美尼亚文、阿拉伯文和拉丁文的译本）能够恢复原文。德国的 Fulda 隐修院保存了一个 6 世纪的拉丁版本，而那里的学者 Hrabanus Maurus 和他的隐修者们大约在 830 年将它译成古德语。

## 006. 《驳希腊人》

这部讽刺性讲演稿是对古希腊哲学与宗教的全面否定和抨击，也是一位基督徒学者彻底批评希腊文化的最早先例。作者可能是想回应那些控诉基督信仰的作者们（如 Kelsos）。成书时间大约在 150—170 年。

非基督徒的哲学家不去过一个良好的或值得赞扬的生活，他们的生活方式有违他们的教导和理想（第 2、3、26 章）。非基督宗教的神灵是一些鬼怪，他们引诱人、败坏道德价值，而从象征意义来解释古代神话也是没有意义的（第 8、21 章）。非基督宗教的神灵等于是某些世俗事物的神化，但这种升华是可笑的（第 4、18 章）。戏剧性表演和希腊人的艺术经常描述神明们，但其中包含很多无耻的话语和情节（第 22、23 章）。第 33 和 34 章描述和批评了作者在罗马所看到的一些艺术品。对他而言，《旧约》的纯正一神论比古希腊那种神明济济的万神庙更有意义（第 29 章）。

# Tatianos / Tatian

**Opera:** *Diatessarōn, Logos pros Hellēnas (=Oratio ad Graecos)*
**Works:** *Diatessaron, Oration to the Greeks*

## 005. *Diatessarōn*

The full title of this lost work was *To dia tessarōn euangelion* ("The Gospel based on four"). It is the earliest "Life of Jesus", probably written around 180 AD, which tries to harmonize the accounts of the four gospels into one single narrative. The author may have used John's Gospel as the foundation and fitted the three synoptic gospels into this frame, omitting certain passages out of necessity. Perhaps the original text was written in Syriac, but before the year 223 AD a Greek translation was made, and from the study of Armenian, Arab and Latin texts it is possible to reconstruct the original version. A Latin translation from the 6th century is kept in the monastery of Fulda (Germany) and was again translated into Old High German by Hrabanus Maurus and his monks (ca. 830 AD).

## 006. *Logos pros Hellēnas / Oration to the Greeks*

This satirical oration is the earliest full-fledged attack on Greek philosophy and religion by a Christian thinker, probably inspired by authors like Celsus who fought against the Christian faith. It was written between 150 and 170 AD.

The pagan philosophers do not lead a good or morally laudable life; their life style contradicts their teachings and ideals (chapters 2, 3 and 26). The pagan gods are demonic seducers of men, they corrupt morality. The allegorical understanding of the old mythology is to be rejected (chapters 8, 21). The pagan gods imply the divinization of earthly things, which is ridiculous (chapters 4, 18). Theatrical performances and pagan arts often depict gods but at the same time are full of shameless stories and expressions (chapters 22, 23). Chapters 33 and 34 describe and criticize some artifacts the author had seen in Rome. For him the simple monotheism of the Old Testament is more rewarding than the crowded Greek pantheon (chapter 29).

# 卢奇安(或译琉善、路吉阿诺斯)(约 120—180 AD)

来自 Samosata (Syria) 的希腊诗人,生平不详。他用讽刺文学来揭露人们的迷信和虚伪。

**著作:**《真实的故事》、《卡润》、《如何写历史》、《德莫纳克斯》、《诸神的商议》、《诸形象》、《伊卡若梅尼普斯》、《到阴间的旅途》、《诸海神的对话》、《梅尼普斯》、《死者的对话》、《尼格里努斯》、《梦》、《诸神对话》、《拍卖诸生命》、《宙斯的审问》

## 007.《真实的故事》

这部长达两卷的著作也被称为 *Alēthēs historia*,大约写成于 160 年,是一部讽刺希腊人的传奇式游记。这些游记从 Homēros 的 *Odysseia* 和 Hērodotos 的 *Histories apodexis* 以来已有,但在 Alexandros 的征服后,这类故事更为流行。

作者在开头就说,读者不应该相信他的话,因为只有当他说"我现在在说谎"时,他才说的是实话。他从向"世界尽头"(到 Hēraklēs 的柱子)的旅途开始叙述。他和他那 50 个水手想知道大海的尽头在哪里,居住在那里的人是谁。航海 80 天后,他们来到一个海岛,在那里他们发现了 Hēraklēs 的巨大脚印。此后他们发现一条流着葡萄酒的河——这个事实似乎证明酒神 Dionysos 已经来过这里。当他们继续他们的旅程时,巨大的风暴捉住了他们的船并使他们越云腾空。这样,他们到达了月亮和星星(1,9~29)。在月亮里有一些奇怪的"马鹰"人,它们马上认出他们是希腊人(Hellēnes),而在太阳上他们则被拘留了一段时间。此后,他们进入了一条巨大的鲸鱼的腹中,在那里他们又发现了一个新天地(1,30~42; 2,1~2)。

第 2 卷叙述到"干酪岛"的旅途,后来他们到达"幸福灵魂之岛"(Elysium, 2,4~29),以及受惩罚的灵魂的海岛。在那些为一生的罪行而受苦的人中也有那些说谎的人和没有说真话的历史学家,其中就有 Ktēsias(公元前 5 世纪末的一位作者)及 Hērodotos(2,31)。此后,希腊人来到"梦岛"和 Ōgygia。在 Ōgygia 他们向 Kalypsō 提交了 Odysseus 的信——他原来是她的爱人,但现在他生活在"幸福灵魂之岛"。在这些探索之后,航海者安全地到达地中海(oikoumenē)对岸的那个地区,就是在大海那边的地方。Loukianos 承诺将来要叙述在那些地方所发生的事(这句话大概是讽刺那些写连续故事的作者)。

# Loukianos / Lucian of Samosata

**Opera:** *Alēthē Dihēgēmata (=Verae historiae), Charōn, De historia conscribenda, Dēmōnax, Deorum concilium, Eikones, Icaromenippus, Kataplous, Marinorum dialogi, Menippus (Necyomantia), Mortuorum dialogi, Nigrinus, Somnium (Vita Luciani), Theōn dialogoi (=Deorum dialogi), Vitarum auctio (=Biōn prasis), Zeus confutatus*
**Works:** *True Stories, Charon, The Way to Write History, Demonax, Meeting of the Gods, Images, Icaromenippus, The Voyage to the Underworld, Dialogues of the Sea Gods, Menippus, Dialogues of the Dead, Nigrinus, Vision (Life of Lucian), Dialogues of the Gods, The Sale of Lives, The Cross-examination of Zeus*

## 007. *Alēthē dihēgēmata / Verae historiae / True Stories*

Probably written around 160 AD, this work of two books is also quoted as *Alethes historia* and is a humorous parody of fabulous Greek itineraries. These stories about journeys to distant lands were well known since the time of Homer's *Odyssey* and Herodotus' *History*, but they became even more popular after Alexander's conquest.

The narrator starts with a warning not to believe his words, since he is only telling the truth when he says that he lies. He starts with the journey to the end of the world (to the Pillars of Hercules). He and his fifty companions in the ship want to know where the ocean ends and what kind of people are living on the other side of the ocean. Sailing for 80 days, the seamen reach an island where they find a giant footprint of Hercules. Then they discover a river with streams of wine instead of water, which hints to the fact that Dionysus, the god of wine had been here before. As they continue their journey, the ship is seized by a hurricane and carried over the clouds. In this way they reach the moon and the stars (1,9~29). On the moon the strange race of "horse-vultures" immediately recognizes the travellers as "Greeks" (Hellēnes), and at the Sun they are held captive for some time. Then they enter the stomach of a huge whale and find another world there (1,30~42; 2,1~2).

The second book tells of the journeys to the "Island of Cheese", to the Elysian Fields (the island of the blissful souls, 2,4~29), and to the island of the condemned souls. Among those who must suffer for their sinful lives are the liars and historians who sinned against truth, among them Ctesias (an author from late fifth century BC) and Herodotus (2,31). Then the Greeks arrive at the island of dreams, and at Ogygia. At Ogygia they hand over a letter to Calypso; the letter was written by Calypso's former lover Odysseus who is now at the island of the blessed. After all these adventures the travellers arrive safely at the continent which lies opposite the Mediterranean world (oikoumenē), behind the great ocean. Lucianus promises to tell in future volumes about what happened there (this remark probably is a parody on the writers of never-ending stories).

## 008. 《诸神对话》

Loukianos 利用古老的并始终受欢迎的"对话"形式来讽刺传统的多神论神话。这26篇对话失去了一切严肃的或悲剧性的思想。早期的诗人对于神明们都表现出某种尊敬和诚肯的敬畏,但 Loukianos 仅仅想作一个开玩笑式的、娱乐性的和讽刺一切的描述。

在第一个对话中,Promētheus 被铁链捆绑,而 Zeus 深深地憎恨他,但当 Promētheus 预言 Zeus 将会有一个新的爱人时,他马上获得了释放。Hēra 将 Zeus 的一个爱人——Iō——变成了一头母牛并继续骚扰这头牛,因此 Zeus 派遣 Hermēs 去帮助这头母牛(3)。Zeus 爱上了一个来自 Phrygia 的少年——他的名字是 Ganymēdē(拉丁语 Catamites)——Zeus 就带他回到 Olympos 山上,在那里这个年轻人先得熟悉他的种种新任务(4)。因此,Hēra 抱怨 Zeus 有很奇怪的爱好和倾向(5)。Ixiōn 试图引诱 Hēra,为此 Zeus 和 Hēra 决定要形成一个具有 Hēra 外貌的云彩(6)。Apollōn 和 Hēphaistos 很气愤,因为婴儿时期的 Hermēs 已经在各地偷东西(7)。Hēphaistos 必须进行一项艰难的工作:他要劈开 Zeus 的头,以使 Athēna 出生(8)。Hermēs 想见 Zeus 但被拒绝,因为此时 Zeus 正好要从他的大腿生出 Dionysos(9)。太阳神 Hēlios 被要求停止工作两天,这样使 Zeus 享受很长的夜晚,因为"众人众神之父"将要去找 Amphitryon 的妻子,以成为大力士英雄 Hēraklēs 的父亲(10)。

此后,Aphroditē 和 Selēnē 分享她们与那个无耻的小 Erōs(爱神)的种种经验(11)。Asklēpios 和 Hēraklēs 争论这样的问题:他们中谁可以在天堂中享受更大的荣耀。因此,Zeus 必须介入评定情况(13)。Apollōn 和 Artemis 的母亲 Lētō 嫉妒 Hēphaistos 的母亲 Hēra(16)。Hermēs 叙述了一个古老的故事:Hēphaistos 如何用一张网来捕捉 Aphroditē 和他的情人 Arēs(参见 *Odysseia*)。Aphroditē 迫使 Erōs 说明他为什么从来没有骚扰 Athēna 和 Artemis(19)。Paris 最终认为在所有的女神当中 Aphroditē 是最美丽的(20)。Pan 告诉 Hermēs 为什么 Zeus 是他的父亲并且 Maia 是他的母亲(22)。Hermēs 向母亲 Maia 抱怨说,他在 Olympos 山上的生活充满劳苦(24)。Zeus 谴责太阳神 Hēlios,因为他有一次允许他的儿子 Phaetōn 驾驶"太阳车",但因此几乎烧毁了大地(25)。最后 Apollōn 请 Hermēs 告诉他一个秘诀来分辨 Lēda 的儿子 Kastōr 和 Polydeukēs (=Pollux) 这一对双胞胎兄弟(26)。

## 009. 《拍卖诸生命》

这部深具讽刺性且幽默的著作的希腊书名是 *Biōn prasis*。商神 Hermēs 试图在一个奴隶市场拍卖各个希腊哲学派的主要代表人物,即 Pythagoras、Diogenēs、Dēmokritos、Hērakleitos、Sōkratēs(他代表 Platōn 的学派)、属于 Stoa 派的 Chrysippos 以及一位

## 008. *Theōn dialogoi / Deorum dialogi / Dialogues of the Gods*

Lucian uses the old and popular form of the dialogue to ridicule the traditional polytheist mythology. These 26 dialogues have lost any trace of seriousness or tragic thought. Where the old poets showed piety and sincere reverence for the gods, Lucian only wants to be witty, entertaining, ironic.

The first dialogue shows Prometheus in chains, hated bitterly by Zeus; but as he foretells that Zeus will have a future love affair, he is immediately freed. Hera has changed one of the women loved by Zeus—Io—into a cow and continues to harass this cow, therefore Zeus sends Hermes to Io in order to help her (3). Zeus has fallen in love with a youth from Phrygia, whose name is Ganymede (Catamites in Latin); Zeus abducts him to Mount Olympus, where he is shown around to get acquainted with his new tasks (4). This again leads to Hera's complaints about Zeus' strange inclinations (5). Ixion tries to seduce Hera, therefore Zeus and Hera decide to form a cloud in the likeness of Hera (6). Apollo and Hephaestus are indignant because the infant Hermes already cheats and steals (7). Hephaestus must help to perform a difficult operation: he is asked to split open the head of Zeus so that Athena can be born (8). Hermes cannot get an audience with Zeus, because at this time Dionysus is being born from Zeus' thigh (9). Helios is ordered to stop work for two days so that Zeus might have a long night, because the "Father of gods and men" is about to go to Amphitryon's wife to father Heracles, the giant hero (10).

Aphrodite and Selene share their experiences with the impudent little Eros (11). Asclepius and Heracles have a quarrel about who should enjoy greater honors in heaven; Zeus must interfere and pacify them (13). Leto, the mother of Apollo and Artemis, envies Hera, the mother of Hephaestus (16). Hermes tells the old story (cf. *Odyssey*) how Hephaestus caught his wife Aphrodite and her lover Ares in a net (17). Eros is asked to explain to Aphrodite why he never harassed Athena and Artemis (19). Paris decides that Aphrodite is the most beautiful goddess (20). Pan tells Hermes how it came about that Zeus is his father and Maia his mother (22). Hermes complains to his mother Maia, since his life at Mount Olympus is hard and laborious (24). Zeus scolds Helios because he allowed his son Phaeton to drive the sun-chariot for one day and in this way almost burned the earth (25). Finally, Apollo asks Hermes for a trick to distinguish the twin-brothers Castor and Polydeuces (=Pollux), the sons of Leda (26).

## 009. *Biōn prasis / Vitarum auctio / The Sale of Lives*

The Greek title of this satirical and entertaining piece is *Biōn prasis*. Hermes tries to sell the main proponents of the Greek philosophical schools like an auctioneer on a slave market. Those going to be sold are Pythagoras, Diogenes, Democritus, Heraclitus, Socrates (identified with Platonic philosophy), the Stoic Chrysippus and a sceptic from Pyrrhon's school. Since some of his contemporaries felt this mockery went too far, Lu-

来自Pyrrhōn学派的怀疑主义者。因为一些人感觉到这种嘲弄太过分,Loukianos后来又写了一篇文章,其中说明他的讽刺只是针对那些为数众多的假哲学家,而不是针对各个学派的创始人;这些创始人仍然是受尊敬的。

  一开始Hermēs宣布和介绍了Pythagoras,因此一个有兴趣购买他的人开始与Pythagoras谈话。此时这位哲学家有机会表现自己的技巧和他的理论的基本教导。在Pythagoras售出后,Hermēs转向犬儒派哲学家Diogenēs,但似乎无法将他售出。最后有一个人以非常低的价格(两个银币)买走了他,使他将来当一个"家犬"。Dēmokritos与Hērakleitos是不能卖出去的,但Syrakousai的Dion以两个talanton(塔伦托)的巨款买下那位解释Platōn理念论的Sōkratēs。然而,Sōkratēs那种同性恋倾向也被嘲笑。在Epikouros和Chrysippos被售出后,那个来自Pyrrhōn学派的怀疑论者也找到了一个新主人。他始终不愿意作任何判断(所谓的epochē),甚至在他被领走以后他也不敢断定他是否已经被卖掉。

cian had to explain in a later treatise that his ridicule was directed at the crowds of pseudo-philosophers, not at the respected founders of the different philosophical schools.

In the beginning Hermes announces and introduces Pythagoras whereupon an interested man starts a conversation with Pythagoras, and now the philosopher can show his special skills and the basic tenets of his teaching. After Pythagoras has been sold, Hermes turns to the Cynic philosopher Diogenes, but it is difficult to find a buyer for him. Finally he goes for a ridiculously low price (two obols) and will serve as a kind of house dog. Democritus and Heracleitus are unsellable, but Dion of Syracuse purchases Socrates who expounds the Platonic ideas for the huge sum of two talents. Socrates' homosexual inclinations are also held up to ridicule. After Epicurus and Chrysippus have been sold, a sceptic from Pyrrhon's school finds a buyer. He tries to abstain from all judgment (epochē) and even after walking off with his new master he is still doubtful as to whether he has been sold or not.

# 马可·奥勒留（121—180 AD）

原名为 Marcus Annius Verus，他生于罗马贵族家庭，获得了良好的文学教育，受 Hadrianus 和 Antoninus Pius 皇帝的支持。他于 145 年和 Antoninus 的女儿 Faustina 结婚，161 年成为皇帝；他喜爱学术和哲学，被称为 Stoa 派哲学的最后的伟大代表。他曾和北方的民族进行战争，在军营中写下了他的《沉思录》。

**著作**：《沉思录》

## 010. 《沉思录》

这部格言集（共 12 卷）包含很多自传性的或哲学的谚语。成书时间大约在 170 年和 178 年之间，即在抵抗 Marcomanni 和 Quadi 等部落的战争期间，Marcus Aurelius 当时在 Carnuntum 城（在今日的奥地利地区，维也纳东部）。皇帝亲自撰写了这部著作，他使用希腊语，并仅仅为自己记载这些事，但不想出版这部书（希腊文的书名是"那些为自己写的东西"）。在这位皇帝的任期内（161—180 年）发生了一些预示罗马帝国衰落的征兆：反对 Parthia 的持久战争（162—166 年），此后又爆发了一场瘟疫，而 Germani 人的部落侵入了 Danubius（多瑙河）地区。

唯独第 1 卷具有一定的安排与写作结构。皇帝在这里表达了他对亲戚、老师和朋友们的感激之情。然而，他并没有直接对某一个人说话，始终保持着自言自语的风格："从我的祖父 Verus 那里我应该学习优美的风度和温和的性格。从别人关于我父亲的说法以及我自己的回忆中，我应该向他学习谦虚和骨气。从我母亲那里我应该学习虔敬和慷慨，不仅要远离恶行，而且要放弃任何邪恶的观念；要单纯、简朴并蔑视财富和奢侈……"（1,1~3）

这位作者的基本问题可能是："我怎样处理对于生命与死亡的深层恐惧？"由希腊的思想家来看，哲学能帮助人们克服这种恐惧，因为哲学教导我们接受我们现时存在的特殊条件。哲学应教导我们如何看待死亡（参见 Platōn 的 *Phaidōn*）。做人意味着拥有某种精神性的自主权，但同时在身体上受到限制以及面对死亡。Marcus Aurelius 寻求这种面对毁灭的生命的意义。他相信一切理性的存在者构成一个普遍的兄弟般的契约，他们会很自然地彼此相爱，所以每一个人应该耐心地对待别人，应该宽恕他们，谅解他们的错误和缺点或引导他们改进他们的恶习。然而，应该完全忽视别人的评价（赞美或谴责），因为这些评价没有意义。最好的方式是耐心地接受别人的人性，但同时也应与他们保持距离。人们也应该以类似的态度面对荣誉、欲望以及权力的诱惑。Stoa 派的思想家说最好要"坚持和保持距离"（anechou kai apechou）。这个要求是一种挑战，但

# Marcus Aurelius / Marc Aurel

**Opera:** *Ta eis heauton*
**Works:** *Meditations*

### 010. *Ta eis heauton / Meditations*

This is a collection of autobiographical and philosophical aphorisms in 12 books, written between 170 AD and 178 AD during the war against the Marcomanni and Quadi, when the author was in Carnuntum (today's Austria, east of Vienna). The Roman emperor Marc Aurel himself wrote this work in Greek and for his own use, not for publication (the Greek title means "things for oneself"). In his reign (161—180 AD) fell the first symptoms of the future crisis of the Roman Empire: the long war against the Parthians (162—166 AD) was followed by a plague and then by the invasion of the Germanic tribes in the Danube area.

The first book is the only one which shows signs of a composition. Here the emperor expresses his gratefulness towards his relatives, teachers and friends. However, always leading his monologue, he does not address anyone in particular: "From Verus, my grandfather, I should learn this beauty of character and meekness of temper; From my father's repute and my recollections of him, modesty and manliness; From my mother piety and liberality; abstention not merely from ill-doing, but from the very thought of evil; simplicity and frugality and contempt for the luxuries of wealth…" (1,1~3)

The basic question of the author might be: "How to deal with my deep-seated fear of life and death?" According to the Greek thinkers, philosophy can overcome this fear, because philosophy teaches us how to accept our specific being. Philosophy should teach us how to die (cf. Plato's *Phaedo*). To be human is to have a kind of mental sovereignty and at the same time to be physically limited, to face death. Marc Aurel searches for the meaning of human life that is threatened by destruction. He believes that all rational beings form a universal brotherhood and love each other naturally, so that one should be patient with one's neighbor. One should forgive others their mistakes or teach them to correct their vices. However, one should completely ignore the judgment (praise or criticism) of others since it is meaningless. It is the best to patiently accept the humanity of one's neighbor, but also to keep distance to them. In a similar way one should face the temptations of fame, desires, power. The Stoics suggest that you "endure and stay away"

其中也有一个包含这一切矛盾的观念——大自然和宇宙是理性的;神圣的造物者不会允许任何不理性的事情发生。因此,没有无意义的事,因为整个宇宙是具有意义的。

  本著作中的许多格言是从 Epiktētos 和 Seneca 抄写而来。作者的思想也受了 Hērakleitos、Sōkratēs、Platōn、Epikouros 和犬儒派思想家,比如 Diogenēs 的影响。Marcus Aurelius 忽视基督宗教的教导、柏拉图主义以及当时流行的其他思想传统(比如跨越文化的宗教混合主义、占星术和算命、诺斯替派、神秘宗教)。他想恢复"古代的传统",即强调理性、清醒,以及对于那些能够理解的事物的掌握。整部书是一种自我劝勉,一种作为自我教育的独语。作者提醒自己要保持这样的理想:不怀任何幻想,要有谦虚的、谦逊的、不引起人们反感的、严肃的以及警醒的态度。作者对于自己始终坦然无欺(Hadrianus 皇帝曾经称他为 Verissimus "最诚实的",因为他原名是 M. Annius Verus)。甚至当他作为皇帝时,他也始终意识到,与几百年历史的漫长时期比较,个人的名誉根本算不了什么。这种诚心与坦白精神使许多后来的统治者视他为楷模,比如 Julianus、Justinianus 和德国的 Friedrich der Grosse 都很敬佩他。

(anechou kai apechou). This challenge is encompassed by the conviction that nature and the cosmos are reasonable: the divine creator cannot admit of anything that would be nonsensical. Nothing can be meaningless, because the cosmos as a whole is meaningful.

The author copied many of his aphorisms from Epictetus and Seneca. His thinking was also influenced by Heraclitus, Socrates, Plato, Epicurus and Cynics like Diogenes. He ignored the Christian teachings, Platonism, and the other trends of his time—cross-cultural syncretism, astrology and divination, gnosticism, mystery religions—and went back to the "old tradition" with its emphasis on reason, sobriety and insight into those things that are intelligible. The whole book is a self-exhortation, a monologue written as a means of self-education. The author reminds himself of the ideals of having no illusions, of modesty, unassuming humility, and sober earnestness. He is always honest to himself. (Emperor Hadrian punningly calls Marc Aurel "Verissimus"—"most truthful"—in allusion to his name "Verus".) Even as an emperor he is aware that a person's fame is nothing in comparison with the long spans of the centuries. This modesty and candour later made him a model for rulers like Julian, Justinianus, and Frederick the Great.

# 阿普列乌斯（约 125—190 AD）

来自 Madauros(Africa)的修辞学家和思想家；他生在 Carthago，后在雅典学习柏拉图的哲学，曾在罗马任律师，后回到 Carthago 并成为一位著名的修辞学老师；他与一位很富裕的寡妇结婚，曾因遭受亲戚的控告而必须为自己进行辩护，最终被宣布无罪，后在 Carthago 等地担任哲学老师。

**著作**：《辩护》《苏格拉底的神》《论柏拉图及其学说》《论世界》《荟萃》《变形记》（又名《金驴》）

## 011.《变形记》

这部长达 11 卷的拉丁语小说约成书于 180 年或 190 年。作者可能利用了被归于 Loukianos 的希腊语小说 *Loukios ē onos*（《卢克欧斯或驴》），并参考了另外一些希腊小说集。本小说对欧洲文学产生了深远的影响，比如《变形记》直接影响了 Boccaccio（薄伽丘）的 *Decamerone*（《十日谈》）。

Lucius 要从 Corinthus 前往希腊东北地区的 Thessalia（该地区在传统上与巫术及魔法有关）。在路上已经有一些人向他叙述了各种奇特的故事。在 Hypata 城附近，Lucius 居住在一个很吝啬的人(Milo)的家中。Lucius 参加一个酒会，其后他刺杀了三个强盗并被送到法院。法院的调查表明，这三个强盗并不是人，只是一些酒袋。Lucius 对 Milo 的美丽女仆 Photis 有兴趣，他们悄悄地在夜晚相会。有一个晚上，Lucius 和 Photis 偷偷看到 Milo 的妻子是怎样在身上涂了某种神秘的膏药，并变成一只猫头鹰从窗户飞出去的。Lucius 求 Photis 也为他弄到这样的神秘膏药，因为他也想变成一只鸟。然而，女仆错误地拿来另一种膏药，Lucius 变成了一头驴。他发现自己身体的变化并感到恐惧，但他已无法表达他的感受，因为他失去了说话的能力，虽然他仍保持一个人的思想和理解能力。Photis 说他只需要吃一些玫瑰花，就能恢复原来的样子并承诺第二天就带来一些玫瑰花，但一些强盗带走了驴子。这样开始小说的核心部分，也就是驴子经历的一系列冒险。

驴遭受了各式各样的压力和侮辱，他幸运地逃脱了许多危险，但他也窃听了很多故事，因为在他周围的人认为他只是一头驴，所以很随便地在他面前说话。其中最著名的故事是关于 Cupido 和 Psyche 的叙述，这是一个古老的民间传说——没有第二个希腊语或拉丁语文献记载过这个故事（第 4~6 卷）。一个老妇人向一个被强盗绑架的女孩子叙述了这个故事（这篇童话经常被理解为暗示心灵经受人生的种种考验，在

# Lucius Apuleius

**Opera:** *Apologia, De deo Socratis (=De genio Socratis), De dogmate Platonis, De mundo, Florida, Metamorphosae (=Metamorphoseon libri XI)*

**Works:** *Apology, On the god of Socrates, On the Beliefs of Plato, On the Cosmos, Anthology, Metamorphoses (=The Golden Ass)*

## 011. *Metamorphosae / Metamorphoses*

This novel in 11 books (Latin) was written between 180 and 190 AD. The author probably used the Greek novel *Loukios ē onos (Lucius or the Ass)* attributed to Lucian and some other Greek novel collections. The *Metamorphoses* had a far-reaching influence on later European literature, for example Boccaccio's *Decamerone* was directly inspired by them.

Lucius is on the way from Corinth to Thessaly, a region in north-eastern Greece traditionally associated with sorceries and enchantments. On the way people tell him all kinds of miraculous stories. Close to the city of Hypata he stays at the house of a very stingy man, Milo. Lucius joins a drinking party, but after the party he stabs three robbers and is brought to court where the investigations reveal that the three victims were not human beings but simply bags of wine. Lucius is interested in Milo's attractive maidservant Photis, and they secretly meet at night. One night Lucius and Photis observe how Milo's wife applies some magic ointment, turns into an owl and flies away through the window. Lucius asks Photis to obtain a magic ointment for him, since he also wants to become a bird. However, the girl gets the wrong ointment for him, and he is changed into an ass. He is terrified as he sees how his body is changing, but he cannot express his feelings, as he loses his ability to speak though still retaining human understanding. Photis says the only thing he has to do is to eat some roses so as to recover his human shape. She promises that she will get roses for him the next day, but the donkey Lucius is stolen by a band of robbers, and now starts a series of adventures that form the main content of the novel.

As a donkey, he suffers all kinds of mistreatment, survives many dangers, and also overhears a number of stories, since the people around him speak freely in his presence, thinking him but an ass. The most famous of these stories is the narrative of Cupid and Psyche, an ancient folk tale found nowhere else in Greek or Latin literature (books 4~6). An old woman tells the story to a girl captured by robbers. (This fairy-tale has often

死亡后能够与神结合)。

　　Psyche 是一个国王的女儿,人们因她的美丽而敬仰她,甚至尊奉她为人间的第二个 Venus。因此 Venus 非常愤怒并派遣 Cupido(=Amor)让他使 Psyche 爱上最可怜的、难看的和穷的男人。通过一个神谕,Psyche 离开了她的父母并被带到一个神奇的、非常豪华的宫殿。晚上 Cupido 来宫殿看她,但他自己爱上了 Psyche。每当他来,他温柔地爱抚 Psyche 并对她说话,但他不允许 Psyche 看见他。Psyche 感到孤独,她希望她的姐妹们能够来宫殿拜访她,而 Amor 允许了这一点,但他警告 Psyche 不要与姐妹们说话,也不要相信她们的话。然而,Psyche 不仅仅与姐妹们谈话,她还告诉她们自己有一个情人。根据她的描述,姐妹们认为她始终没有看见过她所爱的情人。因为 Psyche 的姐妹们很嫉妒,她们就对她说她的情人实际上是一条可怕的巨龙,他将会吃掉她,所以她们建议 Psyche 晚上用一把刀杀死这条巨龙。当 Amor 下次来临时,他和以往一样在 Psyche 身边睡觉,但这次 Psyche 悄悄起来,手拿着灯并偷偷地观看睡着的 Cupido。他的优美外貌使她的手发抖,而油灯的一滴热油滴到了 Amor 的身上,使他醒来。被烫伤的 Amor 很生气,他直接飞走了。此后,Psyche 非常悲伤与孤独,她到处寻找她的情人,但无法找到他。

　　Venus 责备了她的儿子 Amor 并将他关入她的宫殿,因为他爱上了 Psyche。此后 Venus 派遣 Mercurius 神寻觅并逮捕 Psyche,又命令 Sollicitudo(忧虑)和 Tristities(悲伤)来折磨她。Venus 辱骂和拷打 Psyche 并要求她完成一些超过人的能力所及的工作。首先,她必须在一天内将一个很大的谷子堆中的不同种类的谷物予以分类。因为一些蚂蚁同情 Psyche 并帮助她,所以她能够完成这个任务。此后她必须得到一束金羊毛并从山区水泉的危险激流中得到一杯水。因为芦苇和一只老鹰帮助她,她再次完成了 Venus 命令的事务。最后的任务是要求她从阴间女王 Proserpina(Persephonē)那里带来一篮美丽。走了很长的路后 Psyche 来到阴间,她从 Proserpina 那里获得这个篮子,但当她再次回到光明来,她感到好奇并打开了篮子。她发现篮子里没有"美丽",只有致死的长眠——她马上陷入了睡眠。然而,Cupido 这时已经恢复了健康,他从他的监狱里飞出来,找到了 Psyche,用他的箭轻轻地刺她并向她说她的好奇心再次陷害了她。后来 Psyche 将这个美丽的篮子带给 Venus。Cupido 飞到天界,请求 Jupiter 同意他与 Psyche 的婚姻。Psyche 被迎接到天界,她喝下了 ambrosia(不死汁),而诸神庆祝这两个人的婚礼。

　　老妇人一说完关于 Amor 和 Psyche 的故事,强盗们就回来了并开始殴打可怜的驴。后来他得以与那个被绑架的女孩(她的名字是 Charite)逃跑。女孩子的新郎解救了他们,但结果是驴必须为他劳动。驴经过几个主人的转手。有一次甚至有一个老妇人爱上了他,但他感到羞耻并且逃走。在这些危险中,Lucius 始终找不到那些能够改变他外貌的玫瑰花。在第 11 卷中,他在午夜醒来并见到了 Isis 女神向他辉煌显现。她

been understood as an allegory of the soul's challenging journey through life until final union with the divine after death.)

Psyche, the daughter of a king, is so beautiful that the people venerate her as a second Venus living on earth. That enrages Venus so much that she sends Cupid (= Amor) to make her fall in love with the most miserable, ugly, and poor man. Through an oracle Psyche is taken away from her parents and lives in a miraculous luxurious palace. At night Cupid visits her in the palace but he himself falls in love with her. Whenever he comes he caresses Psyche and talks to her but does not allow Psyche to see him. In her loneliness Psyche wants her sisters to come and visit her, which Amor allows, but at the same time he warns her not to talk to them or to believe their words. Psyche talks to her sisters and finally tells them that she has a lover whom she describes in a way that her sisters suspect she has never really seen the man. Since Psyche's sisters are jealous, they tell Psyche that her mysterious lover is in fact a terrible dragon who would devour her, and they advise her to kill this dragon at night with a knife. When Amor comes as usual the next night and sleeps at her side in the darkness, Psyche secretly gets up and takes an oil lamp to look at the sleeping Cupid. Trembling at the sight of his beauty a drop of her lamp's hot oil falls on him and he wakes up. Amor, wounded and angry, flies away. After this, Psyche is sad and lonely, and she looks for her lover everywhere but cannot find him.

Venus scolds her wounded son Amor bitterly for loving Psyche and locks him up in her palace. She sends Mercury to find and arrest Psyche and orders Sorrow and Sadness to torture her. Then Venus scolds and beats Psyche and demands that she perform several superhuman tasks. First she has to sort out different kinds of grain from a huge heap within one day. Ants take pity on Psyche and help her, so she can accomplish the task. Then she has to obtain a lock of wool from a golden sheep and get a cup of water from the dangerous torrent of a mountain spring. Aided by the advice of reeds and a helpful eagle, Psyche fulfulls Venus's orders. The last task is to bring a casket of beauty from Persephone, the queen of the Underworld. After a long journey Psyche reaches the Underworld, obtains the casket from Persephone, but as she returns to the sunlight again she is curious and opens the casket. Instead of beauty she only finds a deadly sleep inside and falls asleep at once. However, Cupid has recovered from his wound and, flying out of his prison, finds Psyche. He wakes her up with a soft cut of his arrow, telling her that curiosity has trapped her again. Psyche brings the beauty casket to Venus, and Cupid flies up to Jupiter, asking him to agree to his marriage with Psyche. Now Psyche is welcomed to heaven, she drinks ambrosia, and the gods celebrate their wedding.

As the old woman finishes the story of Amor and Psyche, the robbers return and club Lucius, the poor donkey. Later he tries to escape with the kidnapped girl, Charite. The girl's bridegroom frees her, but the result is that the donkey has to toil for him. Lucius passes through the hands of several masters. Once an elderly woman even falls in love with him, but he runs away from that shameful situation. Through all his adventures, Lucius searches in vain for roses, the one food that can restore his original human form. In book 11 he wakes up at midnight, and in a vision of great beauty and power, the god-

告诉他如何获得玫瑰花：他必须参与 Isis 的节庆，在那时他要走到 Isis 的祭司那里，从祭司的手中吃玫瑰花。几天后，当驴子在节庆游行中走近祭司并吃下玫瑰花后，他恢复了原来的人的形貌。他朝拜这个女神并深入学习她的秘密仪式，此后也学习她的兄弟 Osiris 的仪式。也许最后的部分包含一些自传因素，因为 Apuleius 曾经是东方神秘宗教的信徒。整个故事的教训可能是两方面的：人如果被欲望控制住，他和野兽就几乎没有区别，并且人们的好奇心就是灾难的源头。

dess Isis appears to him. She shows him the way to the roses: the ass must attend Isis' festival and there approach her priest, who will be expecting him. Then the donkey should eat the roses from the hand of the priest. Some days later he makes his way through the festival procession, approaches the priest, and as he eats the roses, the miracle occurs and he is restored to human shape again. He adores the goddess, is initiated into her rites and later also into the rites of her brother, Osiris. Perhaps the final passage has some autobiographical meaning, because Apuleius was a devotee of the Eastern mystery cults. The morale seems to be twofold: man enslaved by lust is little better than the brute animal, and curiosity is the mother of calamity.

# 盖伦（129—199 AD）

希腊医生，杰出的医学著述者；他来自 Pergamum，曾在许多地方学习，后在罗马当医生，曾为罗马皇帝 Marcus Aurelius, Commodus, Septimius Severus 服务。他几乎在所有的医学领域都著有具有影响力的希腊语著作，9世纪后，他的书被译成阿拉伯语和拉丁语，成为西方医学的标准资料。

**著作**：《论解剖学的做法》(15卷)、《诸器官的功能》(17卷，一种功能性的解剖学)、《本人著作目录》、《治疗方法》(14卷)；Galēnos 共有100多部著作。

## 012. 《本人著作目录》

Galēnos 的著作目录包括153部书，共分为500卷。作者将自己的书分为3类：(1)哲学著作；(2)谈论语法和修辞学的书(大部分失传)以及(3)医学著作。Galēnos 强调说，一个伟大的医生也需要哲学教育。一个书名是 *Hoti ho aristos iatros kai philosophos*（《最好的医生也是哲学家》）。在一些著作中，他分析不同医学流派的思想。他自己并没有加入任何哲学派别或医学流派，而是一个选择性的汇编者。他最流行的著作之一是 *Technē iatrikē*（《医学技术》，在中世纪以 *Mikrotechni* 的书名流传）。他的文集 *Therapeutikē methodos*（《医疗方法》，共14卷）展示了各种临床医疗法。*Peri chreias moriōn*（《论诸器官的功能》，17卷）是一部关于功能解剖学的著作。*Anatomikai encheireseis*（《论解剖学的做法》，15卷）则是一部介绍描述性的解剖学著作，其中提供了一些关于手术的指南。Galēnos 也有一些心理学方面的著作。

# Galēnos / Claudius Galenus

**Opera:** *Anatomikai encheireseis, Peri chreias moriōn, Peri tōn idiōn bibliōn, Therapeutikē methodos*

**Works:** *On Anatomical Procedures, On the Faculties of the Organs, On My Books, Therapeutical Method*

## 012. *Peri tōnidiōn bibliōn / On My Books*

Galen's catalogue of the books he wrote enlists 153 works in 500 volumes. The author himself divides his works into three groups: (1) philosophical works, (2) books on grammar and oratory (most of them are lost) and (3) medical works. Galen emphasizes that a good physician also needs philosophical education. One of his works is entitled: *Hoti ho aristos iatros kai philosophos (The best physician also is a philosopher)*. In some of his books he analyzed different medical schools. He himself did not belong to any philosophical or medical school but was an eclectic compiler. One of his most popular books is entitled *Technē iatrikē (The Art of Medicine*, also known under the title *Mikrotechni* in the Middle Ages). The compilation *Therapeutikē methodos (Therapeutical Method*, 14 vols.) presents ways of clinical treatment. The book *Peri chreias moriōn (On the Faculties of the Organs*, 17 vols.) is a functional anatomy. The *Anatomikai encheireseis (On Anatomical Procedures*, 15 vols) contains a descriptive anatomy and directions to perform surgical operations. Galen also wrote on psychology.

# 格利乌斯(约 130—180 AD)

拉丁文作家,曾在罗马和雅典学习,生平不详。

著作:《雅典之夜》

## 013. 《雅典之夜》

这部长达 20 卷的"荟萃"包含来自大约 280 位希腊、罗马作者(尤其是 Varro 和 Cicero)的警句和短文,因此保存了许多有关这些人物的知识。书名来自雅典冬天的长夜,因为作者是在那里开始记载这些故事的(大概在 170 年左右)。第 8 卷失传,但其他 19 卷都保存了下来。

作者致力于用短小的文章或故事来提供一切资料。整部书没有明显的结构,但因为 Gellius 的文笔好、叙述灵活有趣,这部文集成了后世最流行的资料书之一。它包含关于奇怪事件或值得回忆的故事的叙述、对话、哲学探讨、代表某种格言的历史人物或文学英雄、来自生物学、物理学、医学、数学或法律领域的观察、文学评论、语法规则、谜语、某些语词的用法和语源学分析,而且作者经常比较希腊文化和罗马文化。这部书也保存了无数来自别的、业已失传的著作的引言。

其中一个比较著名的故事是关于奴隶 Androclus 的叙述(参见 5,14)。他是一位执政官的奴隶,从家里逃跑并在森林中隐藏了起来。一头狮子走近他,使 Androclus 感到非常恐惧。然而,这头狮子并没有攻击他,只是伸出他的爪子,而奴隶看到有一根很大的刺插在他的爪子中。他以抖动的手拔出了这根刺后,狮子就离开了他。几天后 Androclus 被逮捕,而他获得的惩罚就是在斗兽场中死去。他进入斗兽场,准备被杀,但那头本应撕裂他的狮子跑到他那里,在他的脚前躺下并开始舔他的手。原来这是 Androclus 在森林中遇到的那头狮子。因为狮子表现了如此明显的感恩态度,所有的人都感到非常惊讶,Androclus 也被释放。

# Aulus Gellius / Gellius

**Opera:** *Noctes Atticae*
**Works:** *Attic Nights*

## 013. *Noctes Atticae / Attic Nights*

This anthology in 20 books contains quotations and excerpts from 280 Greek and Roman authors (especially from Varro and Cicero) and is therefore a rich source of information on these authors. The title of the collection is derived from the long winter nights in Athens, when the author started to write the stories down (probably around 170 AD). Only book 8 is lost, all other books are extant.

The author tries to present all the pieces of information in short essays or narratives. There is no obvious structure, but the skilled and entertaining style made the collection one of the most popular source books of later ages. It contains short narratives of strange or remarkable events, dialogues, philosophical discussions, historical or literary figures who exemplify a proverb, observations from the areas of biology, physics, medicine, mathematics or law, literary criticism, grammar rules, riddles, the use and etymology of certain words, and quite often the author compares Greek and Roman culture. The work also preserves innumerable passages from works no longer extant.

One of the more well-known stories is the narrative of the slave Androclus who escapes from his master (a consul) and hides in the forest (5,14). A lion approaches him, and Androclus is terribly scared. However, the animal does not attack him but stretches out its paw, and the slave notices the big thorn in it. With trembling hands he pulls out the thorn from the lion's paw, and the animal trods away. Some time later Androclus is caught and his punishment will be to die in the arena. Awaiting death he enters the arena, but the lion supposed to tear him to pieces runs over to him, lies down at the slave's feet and licks his hands. It is the same lion which Androclus had met in the forest. As everyone is amazed at the lion's gratitude, Androclus is set free.

# 依勒内（135—202 AD）

这位教父来自小亚细亚的 Smyrna，他曾听 Polykarpos（约于 155 年殉道）的讲道，而根据 Irenaeus 的说法，Polykarpos 又是 Iōannēs（约翰，即耶稣的门徒）的学生。Irenaeus 也曾在 Iustinos 的学校进修，但他不接受 Iustinos 的柏拉图主义，更多地倾向于 Polykarpos 对《圣经》的推崇。164 年后，他在今属法国南部地区的 Lugdunum（=Lyon 里昂）传教，在那里被祝圣为 presbyter（长老）。当地的教会团体曾经派遣他到罗马，给当时的罗马主教 Eleutherius（175—189 年）送一些信件。当时任 Lugdunum 主教的 Pothinus 因教难被处死，而 Irenaeus 在 178—202 年作为其继承人，担任 Lugdunum 的主教。他曾经就复活节时间的问题向 Victor 教宗（189—199 年）写信，信中说不应因这个问题而使教会分裂。关于他晚年的生活并没有可靠的资料。根据 Gregorius Turonensis 约于 576 年写成的报告，他在 Lugdunum 殉道，为信仰牺牲了生命。

著作：《驳斥异端》（希腊原文只保存了残篇，但拉丁译文被保存了下来，这是历史上第一部系统地说明基督信仰的著作）、《宗徒论证》（包括基督论等教义）

## 014.《驳斥异端》

这部分为 5 卷的著作仅仅有一些早期的拉丁译本保存，原来的希腊本只有残篇，部分章节还有一些叙利亚和亚美尼亚译文。原来的书名是 *Elenchos kai anatropē tēs pseudonymou gnōseōs*（《揭露和反驳虚假的知识》），作者应一个朋友的要求约于 185 年撰写了这部书。它是关于当时异端的最丰富资料，同时也是第一部全面论述基督宗教教义的著作。一些早期的译本表明，这部著作对下一代的神学家（如 Hippolytos、Tertullianus、Clemens Alexandrinus）具有重大的影响。

第 1 卷描述一切违背大公教会教义的异端，即 Valentinos 和他的学生 Ptolemaios、Markosianus 学派、Simōn Magus（他是最早的异端人物，参见 *Acts* 8:9）、Menander、Saturninus、Basilidēs、Karpokrates、Kerinthos、Ebionitai、Nikolaitani、Kerdo、Markion、Tatianus 和 Enkratitai、Barbeliobai、Ophitai、Sethiani 以及 Kainitai。作者特别注意 Valentinos，因为他的思想体系似乎包含了一切其他异端。Valentinos 曾经于 140—155 年间在罗马地区活动，他传播的教义受了柏拉图主义的影响。在他的异端学说中，人是由天使创造的，而人类从被创造以来就存在很多缺陷。

在第 2 卷中，作者一步步详细地反驳 Valentinos 并很理性地指出其教导中的矛盾。诺斯替派思想对《圣经》所作的解释意味着不断有新的时期（aiōnes）和新的世界出

# Irenaeus de Lugduno / Eirenaios of Lyon

**Opera:** *Adversus haereses (Elenchos kai anatropē tēs pseudonymou gnōseōs), Demonstratio apostolica (Epideixis tou apostolikou kerygmatos)*
**Works:** *Against Heresies (Unmasking and Refutation of the False Gnosis), Demonstration of the Apostolic Preaching*

## 014. *Adversus haereses / Against Heresies*

This work in 5 books is only extant in an old Latin translations, but there are small fragments of the original Greek version and parts of Syrian and Armenian translations. The original title was *Elenchos kai anatropē tēs pseudonymou gnōseōs* (*Unmasking and Refutation of the False Gnosis*). It was written at the request of a friend and is dated at ca. 185. It is the richest source-book for heresies of that period and also the first comprehensive work on Christian dogmatic teachings. Old translations prove that the book had great impact on the next generation of theologians (Hippolytus, Tertullian, Clement of Alexandria).

Book 1 outlines the heretical gnostic teachings of all schools that are opposed to the catholic church's teaching: Valentinos and his pupil Ptolemaeus, the Markosians, Simon Magus (the arch-heretic, cf. *Acts* 8:9), Menander, Saturninus, Basilides, Carpocrates, Cerinthos, the Ebionites, Nicolaitans, Cerdo, Marcion, Tatian and the Encratites, Barbeliobes, Ophites, Sethians and Cainites. The author pays special attention to Valentinos, whose system of thought somehow contains all other heresies. Valentinos was active in Rome ca. 140—155 and propagated a doctrine inspired by Platonism. In his heresy man was created by angels, and human beings were created with many imperfections.

In book 2 the author undertakes a detailed rational refutation of the gnostic system of Valentinos and exposes the contradictions of these teachings. The gnostic way of inter-

现。诺斯替派还把人类分为三种人：物质人(physikoi)、那些拥有灵魂的人(psychikoi)以及充满灵性的人(pneumatikoi)。然而，这一切教导都是错误的。人生的目标是肉身、灵魂和灵性(pneuma)的复活。上主成为人，以使人成为神圣的并且有全部的生命，人应该在各方面获得救恩。

在第 3 卷中，Irenaeus 说公教会的教义必须符合《圣经》以及教会的传统。《圣经》必须是真理的标准，它是"真理的正经"。《旧约》和《新约》的书卷是权威性的文本。《福音书》只有四部。在另一方面，主教们的圣传确保了纯正的使徒传统没有中断。没有任何异端邪说具有这种权威性。Irenaeus 以罗马主教为例并列出历代的罗马主教：在 Petros 和 Paulos 后有 Linus、Anencletus、Clemens、Euaristos、Alexander、Xystos、Telesphoros、Hyginos、Pius、Anicetos、Soter、Eleutheros(3,3)。Irenaeus 说他能够指出所有的由使徒们在各地指定的主教的名字，但他仅仅以罗马的 successio（传承，希腊语的 diadochē）为例。这些罗马主教的名单表明，与使徒/宗徒们的密切接触能够确保正统的信仰、正统的教导与对《圣经》的解释。在"圣传"（或"传承"）中最重要的因素是主教们(episkopos)和长老们(presbyteros)。一个著名的章节谈论了罗马教会的关键地位："ad hanc enim ecclesiam propter potiorem principalitatem necesse est omnem convenire ecclesiam"。它曾经被译为"一切地方教会必须与这个教会（即罗马教会）达成共识，因为它的权威性更大"（或译"它更古老"）。

根据 *Eph* 1:10,22 的记载 Irenaeus 发展其著名的 "总归基督论"（希腊语：anakephalaiosis，拉丁语：recapitulatio / instauratio in Christo)：耶稣是一切的元首。为了补修亚当的罪，耶稣过一种与亚当一样的生活，他也体验到了人生的每一个过程（婴儿时期、孩提时代、青春期、成熟的壮年时期)，但耶稣因服从而圣化了每一个阶段，这样他克服了那些控制人类的种种力量：罪恶、死亡和魔鬼。耶稣补修并消除了亚当的罪，他带给人活力，在他内使所有的人类统一，他引导人类历史走向一个高峰并被高举为万物之元首，尤其为教会的元首。通过他的复活，耶稣表现了这样一个观点：救恩历史的目标是不死与永恒的生命(3,16~19)。

第 4 卷发展了关于"依赖《圣经》"的论点，主要是为了反驳 Markion（约于 160 年去世）——他仅仅接受《新约》的部分文献为《圣经》并完全拒绝了《旧约》那位"充满愤怒的上主"。然而，基督和先知们的见证表明，《旧约》的神和在 Nazareth 的 Iēsous 启示自己的神就是同一个上主。基督的到来并不是为了宣布一个新的"时代"(aiōn) 的来临，而是他要成为万代人类的救世主。通过他的"双手"（即"圣言"基督和"智慧"圣灵）神直接进行创造，因此当他创造人时，他并没有借助于一些"中间力量"（精神体、天使)。上主继续给予某些人灵感或启示自己，他充满动力地引导世界逐渐实现他的救恩计划。

preting the scriptures seems to hold that ever new eras (aiōnes) and worlds are coming into being ("emanating"). The Gnostics also divide humanity into three types: physical people (physikoi); people with a soul (psychikoi) and the elect who are inspired (pneumatikoi). All of these theories are wrong. Man's aim is the resurrection of body, soul and spirit (pneuma). God became man so that man might become divine and be fully alive and redeemed in every respect.

In book 3 Irenaeus develops the influential argument that catholic teaching must be based on the Scriptures and on tradition. The Bible must be the standard of theology, it is the "canon of truth". The books of the Old Testament and the New Testament are the normative Scriptures. There are only four gospels. On the other hand, the succession of bishops guarantees the authenticity of the unbroken apostolic tradition. No heresy can claim this kind of authority. Irenaeus demonstrates this point by listing up the bishops of Rome: After Peter and Paul there came Linus, Anencletus, Clemens, Euaristus, Alexander, Xystus, Telesphorus, Hyginus, Pius, Anicetus, Soter, Eleutherus (3,3). Irenaeus claims that he could name all of the bishops that were appointed in the different churches by the apostles, but he limits himself to the example of Rome's succession ("diadochē" in Greek). This list of bishops shows that the authentic faith, teaching, and interpretation of the Scriptures is guaranteed by personal contact with the apostles. Essential in the succession are the bishops (episkopos) and eldest (presbyteros). The famous passage concerning the church in Rome "ad hanc enim ecclesiam propter potiorem principalitatem necesse est omnem convenire ecclesiam" has been variously translated as "it is necessary that every church agree with this church on account of its more powerful authority" or "of its greater antiquity."

Based on *Eph* 1:10, 22, Irenaeus develops the famous theory of recapitulation (Greek: anakephalaiosis, Latin: recapitulatio, instauratio in Christo): Jesus is the head of all. In order to reverse Adam's sin, Jesus lived a similar life as Adam and experienced every phase of human life (infancy, childhood, youth, mature adulthood), but he sanctified each by obedience and so overcame the powers that enslave humankind: sin, death, and the devil. Jesus reverses and obliterates Adam's sin, He revives man, brings together all mankind in himself, leads human history to a climax and is raised to be the head of all things—in particular of the church—, showing through His resurrection that immortality and eternal life is the aim of the history of salvation (3, 16~19).

Book 4 elaborates the argument from Scripture in order to refute Marcion (died ca. 160 AD) who only accepted parts of the New Testament and rejected the "wrathful God" of the Old Testament altogether. However, the witness of Christ and the prophets show that the God of the Old Testament and the one who revealed Himself in Jesus of Nazareth are one and the same. Christ did not come to inaugurate another new era (aiōn), but to be the Saviour of mankind for all ages. Through His "two hands" (the word = Christ, and wisdom = Spirit), God acted directly in creation and did therefore not need intermediaries (spirits, angels) when He created man. God continues to act in inspiration or revelation and dynamically leads creation to the realization of His salvific plan.

最后的书卷谈论耶稣"降生成人"的事件和他的复活以及"最终的事"（eschatologia）。与 Iustinos 一样，作者强调"普遍复活"的概念并坚持肉身的复活，以此反驳诺斯替派的二元论。根据 Irenaeus 相当奇特的看法，在人类和众堕落天使的普遍复活与最终审判后，基督将要开始他的千年统治（参见 Rev 20:6）。Irenaeus 引用 Hierapolis 的 Papias（大约 60—130 年）来强调他的另一种教导：魔鬼和他的天使（鬼神）将要进入永久的火，但基督与他的圣徒将要统治一千年。

Irenaeus 不仅仅依赖于 Polykarpos 和 Papias 的权威性，他也了解早期教会的重要文献（比如 Clemens 的书信、*Hermas* 和 Iustinos 的著作）。天主教和新教的神学家都曾经强调了 Irenaeus 的思想，因为他的著作能够说明罗马教会的主席权，但他也指出了《圣经》的重要性。东方教会继承了他的另一个主要思想：Christus Victor（"胜利者基督"，"作为万物之首的基督"），以及人性能够达到完善和永生的观点。Tertullian 那种比较重视法律的教导、Clemens Alexandrinus 的智慧思想以及 Irenaeus 那种比较历史性的、动态的以及重视经验的神学共同构成了早期基督宗教思想的三大基本模式。

The last book examines Jesus' incarnation and resurrection as well as the "last things" (eschatology). Following Justin the Martyr, the author emphasizes the idea of a general resurrection and insists on the resurrection of the flesh, thereby countering Gnostic dualism. According to Irenaeus' somewhat special view, the general resurrection and Last Judgment of both human beings and fallen angels will precede the chiliastic reign of Christ (from "chilias" = thousand years, cf. *Rev.* 20:6). Irenaeus quotes Papias of Hierapolis (ca. 60—130 AD) to support his teaching that the devil and his angels (demons) would enter eternal fire, whereas Christ and His saints would reign during the millennium.

Irenaeus did not only rely on the authority of Polycarp and Papias but also knew the important documents of the early Church (i.e. the first letter of Clement, Justin's works, and the *Hermas*). Both Catholics and Protestants have claimed Irenaeus as their mentor, be it as authority for the primacy of the Church of Rome or as Biblical theologian. His "Christus Victor" motif (Christ—the Head of all) and the view that human nature can be perfected and consummated in immortality was adopted by the Eastern Church. The more legalistic teaching of Tertullian, the wisdom-oriented thought of Clement of Alexandria, and Irenaeus' more historical, dynamic and experience-oriented type of theology, form the three basic approaches of early Christian thought.

# （亚历山大的）克雷芒（约 150—215 AD）

关于他生平的资料很少。他大概出生在雅典，来自外教人的家庭，后在 Alexandreia 创办一所道理学校（catechetical school）；他在 202 或 203 年的教难中离开了埃及，此后再也没有回去。他和希腊思想进行对话，对 Ōrigenēs 有重要的影响。

**著作**：《教导者》（亦译《导师》，内容：基督是"Logos—导师"）、《劝说》（向外教人介绍"真正的哲学"，即基督信仰，同时反驳一些希腊思想）、《杂论》（或译《杂记》，强调"真正的 gnōsis"）、《富人能得救吗？》（讲演）

## 015. 《教导者》

这部介绍基督徒生活方式的导论（共 3 卷）大约成书于 195 年，他面向非基督徒读者。本书很可能构成了一个"三部曲"的第二部分：Protreptikos（《劝说》）劝勉人们放弃异教信仰并认真考虑转向基督信仰，Paidagōgos（《教导者》）等于是基督徒生活的具体介绍，而最后的部分（Didaskalikos《教导》，并没有成书，但 Strōmateis《杂论》可能准备了第三部分）则提供了《圣经》的一种象征性的解释方式、将神和万物本源的知识建立在一些科学性的论述之上。

第 1 卷阐述永恒的 Logos（即基督），他有教导者和教育者的角色，不仅仅教导人们具体的美德，也治疗内心的种种情绪和创伤（参见 Stoa 的教导）。通过教导，基督拯救人们，使他们脱离罪恶。神的惩罚只是一种拯救灵魂的工具。第 2、3 卷包含一些具体的人生方面的建议，涉及吃、喝、服装、财富的使用和生活方式。作者记载了很多有趣的关于早期基督教文化和道德的观察。他的重点不在克修和刻苦方面，更多的是古代哲学的种种理想，即符合自然的生活、在一切事上的节制，以及让理性统治一切欲望和情绪。这种思想也出现在 Tis ho sōzomenos plousios（《富人能得救吗？》）这篇短小的讲道稿中。他谈论 Mk 10:17-31 的《新约》章节并指出财富并不是得救的绝对障碍，但是不公正地使用人间财富却是救恩的障碍。任何正义的人都有升天的机会，而基督将会把他引领到父那里。

## 016. 《劝说》

这篇文章（亦称 Protreptikos pros Hellēnas《劝勉希腊人》）呼吁那些有修养的异教徒放弃他们的多神论传统。成书时间大约是在 190 年。

在头 5 章中，Clemens 揭露多神论传统及神话的不道德和无用。他使用古典哲学家曾经用过的论点来谴责民间的宗教。异教徒应该放弃他们的多神论崇拜并接受基

# Titus Flavius Clemens / Clemens Alexandrinus / Clement

**Opera:** *Paidagōgos, Protreptikos(pros Hellēnas), Strōmateis, Tis ho sōzomenos plousios (=Quis dives salvetur)*
**Works:** *Paedagogus (The Instructor), Protrepticus (Exhortation to the Greeks), Stromateis, Who is the Rich Man Being Saved?*

## 015. *Paidagōgos / Paedagogus / The Instructor*

This introduction to a Christian way of life in 3 books was written for non-Christians around the year 195 AD. It probably forms the second part of a trilogy: the *Protrepticus* was meant as an exhortation to turn away from paganism and to seriously consider the Christian faith. The *Paidagōgos* instructs on leading a practical Christian life, and the last part (*Didaskalikos*, "Teaching", unfinished but perhaps prepared in the *Strōmateis*) would have presented a symbolic interpretation of the Scriptures, knowledge of God and the origin of all things based on scientific arguments.

The first book presents the eternal Logos (=Christ) as an educator and instructor who not only teaches practical virtues but also heals the harmful passions that are wounding the heart (confer Stoic teaching). Christ's education leads to the redemption from sins. God's punishments are a means to save the soul. Books 2 and 3 contain concrete practical suggestions concerning eating, drinking, dress, use of wealth and way of living, whereby the author presents an interesting glimpse on many details of the early Christian culture and morality. His standard is not so much an ascetic life of abstinence, but rather, the old philosophical ideals of a life according to nature, moderation in all things, and the reign of reason over all desires and emotions. This way of reasoning also recurs in the short homily *Tis ho sōzomenos plousios* (=*Who is the Rich Man Being Saved?*) on Mk 10:17–31: wealth does not exclude from salvation, it is only the unjust use of earthly goods that is harmful; any just person may go to Heaven, and Christ will lead him to the Father.

## 016. *Protreptikos / Protrepticus / Exhortation*

The treatise (also known as *Protreptikos pros Hellēnas, Exhortation to the Greeks*) is an appeal to cultured pagans to turn away from their polytheistic traditions. It was written around 190 AD.

In the first 5 chapters, Clement exposes the immorality and futility of polytheistic cults and their mythology. He makes use of the same arguments that classical philoso-

督信仰。然而,第 6 章到第 9 章却又肯定希腊哲学的价值,肯定犹太人的法律和先知。神的召唤是普遍的,而一切智慧指向上主在耶稣基督内的完满启示——他是 Logos 并与一切民族分享他的智慧。尤其那些认真寻求真理的哲学家(比如 Platōn)达到"唯一的神"的概念,将神视为宇宙的起源和目标(6,68~72)。Clemens 使用 Orpheus 的形象来描述福音:Orpheus 的音乐如此迷人,他使野兽陶醉,而上主的圣言也以一种类似的方式引导那些没有文化的人过着有德性的生活。福音书是一种"新歌",它影响整个宇宙的秩序与和谐。基督是一种"新的 Orpheus"。

## 017. 《杂论》

这部分为 8 卷的、没有明确体系的文集包含各个知识领域中的资料,创作于 208—211 年,但没有最终完成。

创作这部文集的目标大概是为一个"三部曲"的第三部著作作准备,即 *Protreptikos*(一部劝人放弃异教传统的书)、*Paidagōgos*(关于基督伦理教育的书)以及 *Didaskalikos*(关于信仰教条和《圣经》的象征性解释)。作者讨论了很多影响教会生活的问题,但没有系统的安排。Clemens 摘录一些来自古希腊哲学的——根据他的理解——"真实"观点。Paulos 曾经谴责"世俗的智慧"(hē sophia tou kosmou, 1 *Cor* 1:20),但在 Clemens 的眼中,这种说法仅仅针对 Epikouros 的享乐主义。他认为,一切其他的哲学家都曾因神圣的逻各斯而被照亮。因此,那些哲学家是异教徒们中的"先知"。哲学本来就是"上帝赐给希腊人的礼物"(1,2,20),而"正如法律/律法引导了希伯来人走向基督,哲学引导了希腊人走向救世主"(1,5,28)。人的思想(phronēsis, noēsis)的目标既是信仰,又是知识;哲学能够为信仰提供一些证据,能够在诡辩派面前保卫信仰。在另一方面,信仰(pistis)又超过知识,信仰是真理的标准(1,98,4)。为了说明这一点,Clemens 引用 *Is* 7:9("如果你们不相信,你们无法存在"),即后来的说法 credo ut intelligam("我信是为了理解")的基础。

任何基督徒都应有关于自己信仰的理论性理解,他应该成为一个真正的"诺斯替者",而在这个过程中,哲学是一个必要的工具。这一进程的不同阶段是: prolēpsis(预先掌握,预感)、epistēmē(知识)、pistis(信仰)和 gnōsis(领悟、智慧,这是基督徒生活的最高领域)。每一个人必须自己作决定要成为一个好的信徒,这样他将获得 gnōsis(领悟、智慧)。信仰不是最后的目标,他只是获得理想基督徒生活("领悟")的基础。只有一个有"悟性"的基督徒才是一个完美的信徒,他才能认识神、爱神、在神面前生活。与那些神秘宗教相类似,基督宗教也有一种深层的信仰结构,不是所有信徒都能认识到这个深层智慧,而且不能够(也不应该)向所有的人都说明这些内容(5, 9, 57, 2)。

在其著作中,Clemens 引用了大约 360 个古代作者,这样他保存了很多在别的地

phers had brought in against popular religion. The pagans should turn away from their cults and accept Christianity. Chapters 6~9 however, confirm the value of Greek philosophy, the Jewish law and the prophets. God's call is universal, and all wisdom points to the full revelation of God in Jesus Christ—the Logos who shares His wisdom with all peoples. Especially philosophers (like Plato) who earnestly searched for the truth arrived at the concept of one God who is origin and aim of the world (6, 68~72). Clement uses the figure of Orpheus as a parable for the gospel: Orpheus' music could enchant wild beasts, and in a similar way the word of God can lead uncultured people to a virtuous life. The gospel is a "new song" which effects order and harmony in the whole cosmos. Christ is a kind of new Orpheus.

## 017. *Strōmateis*

This unsystematic collection of interesting details from all areas of knowledge in 8 books was written from 208 to 211 AD and remains unfinished.

This collection of notes was possibly intended to prepare the third book of Clement's trilogy: (1) *Protrepticus* (aimed at the rejection of paganism),(2) *Paidagogus* (a work on Christian moral education),(3) *Didascalicus* (Christan doctrine, symbolic interpretation of the Bible). The author discusses many problems that became an obstacle to Church life. The book does not show any obvious system or order. Clement picks out "true" insights—according to his understanding—from the Greek philosophers. Paul had condemned the "wisdom of this world" (hē sophia tou kosmou, cf. 1 *Cor* 1:20), but in Clement's opinion this expression only refers to Epicurus' hedonism (1,1). He thinks that all other philosophers were enlightened by the divine Logos. The philosophers were the prophets of the pagans. Philosophy is a "gift from God given to the Greeks" (1,2,20), and "just like the law led the Hebrew people towards Christ, philosophy led the Greeks to the redeemer" (1,5,28). Human thought (phronēsis, noēsis) aims at both, faith and knowledge; philosophy can provide arguments for the faith and can help to defend the faith against the sophists. On the other hand, faith (pistis) is higher than knowledge and faith is the standard of truth (1,98,4). In this context Clemens quotes *Is* 7:9 (si non credideritis non permanebitis), the basis of the later mottoe "credo ut intelligam".

Any Christian must have a theoretical understanding of their faith and should become a true "gnostic". Philosophy is a necessary tool in this process. The different stages of progressing are: prolēpsis (anticipation), epistēmē (science), pistis (faith), gnōsis (insight, highest stage of insight and of a Christian life). Every person must decide for himself to become a good Christian, so he can attain gnosis (insight). Faith is not the last aim, it is only the basis for attaining gnosis, the ideal of Christian life. Only the insightful ("gnostic") Christian is a perfect believer who recognizes God, loves God and lives before God. Similar to the mystery religions Christianity has a deeper faith structure which is not obvious to all believers, and this deeper wisdom can not and should not be revealed to all (5, 9, 57, 2).

Clement quotes around 360 authors and in this way preserves many texts that would

方失传的文献（比如一些来自 Hērakleitos、Empedoklēs、Parmenidēs、Xenophanēs、Dēmokritos 的话）。Clemens 曾经受过良好的文学和哲学教育，他认为希腊的世俗思想传统本来就是神预先安排的工具。然而，他也了解一些基督徒认为哲学是无用的，甚至是有害的看法。他们认为"只应该学习信仰需要的那些最基本的知识，放弃一切其他的多余思想——那些仅仅消耗人们的精力并让人们投入于那些对终极目标无用的东西"(1,15,2)。针对那些"只要有信仰"的基督徒，Clemens 想表达这样的观点：哲学来自神，并在救恩的历史进程中具有一种积极的功能。

otherwise have been lost (for example words from Heraclitus, Empedocles, Parmenides, Xenophanes, Democritus). Clement has a thorough literary and philosophical schooling, and he thinks that the secular philosophical tradition of Greece was an instrument of divine providence. However, he also realizes that some Christians consider philosophy as useless and even dangerous. They think "one should only study those basic things that are most necessary for the faith and do away with all other superfluous speculations, which only waste away our energies and restrict us to those things that are not conducive to the final goal." (1,15,2). In answer to these "faith-only" Christians, Clement tries to show that philosophy comes from God and has a positive function in the process of salvation.

# 塞克斯都·恩披里柯(约 160—220 AD)

希腊医生,曾在 Alexandria 活动;他的著作是关于古代怀疑论学派的重要资料。

**著作:**《反对独断论者》(5 卷)、《反对教授们》(6 卷)、《皮朗主义纲要》(3 卷)、《怀疑学派》

## 018. 《怀疑学派》

本文集前 6 卷称 *Pros mathēmatikous*(《反对教授们》),而第 7 卷到 11 卷被称为 *Pros dogmatikous*(《反对独断论者》)。

第 1 到第 6 卷主要反驳了 6 种学科的代表,即那些学习语文学、修辞学、几何学、算术学、天文学和音乐理论的人。第 7 到 11 卷则谈论传统哲学的三部分,即逻辑学、物理学(宇宙论)和伦理学。那些 dogmatikoi(独断论者)是谁呢?就是那些认为在某种领域中可以获得可靠的、有证据的、不可辩驳的知识的人。这种怀疑论的理论基础记载在 Sextos Empeirikos 的另一部著作(即 *Pyrrhōneioi hypōtheseis*《皮朗主义纲要》,大部分失传)。Pyrrhōn 曾经使用 10 种辩论方式(tropai)来怀疑科学研究的成果,其中包括这样的论点:人们都是不一样的,他们的性情和感官认识都不同。感官或思想的印象经常是互相矛盾的,而这些格格不入的因素具有同样的力度和有效性,所以人们应该放弃任何判断(epochē)并且不要相信自己已经掌握了真理。然而,这种怀疑论的态度在日常生活中仍然容许人有所行动,因为它可以带来一种精神上的坚定(ataraxia)以及在一切事物上的节制。

# Sextos Empeirikos / Sextus Empiricus

**Opera:** *Pros dogmatikous* (=*Adversus dogmaticos*), *Pros mathēmatikous* (=*Adversus mathematicos*), *Pyrrhōneioi hypotheseis*, *Skeptika* (= *Pros dogmatikous*, *Pros mathēmatikous*)

**Works:** *Against the Dogmatists, Against the Professors, Outlines of Pyrrhonism, Outline of the Skeptical School*

## 018. *Skeptika / Outline of the Skeptical School*

The first 6 books of this collection are also quoted as "*Against the Professors*" (*Pros mathēmatikous, Adversus mathematicos*), whereas the books 7~11 are known under the title "*Against the Dogmatists*" (*Pros dogmatikous, Adversus dogmaticos*).

Books 1 to 6 argue against the representatives of the six academic sciences, namely: grammar, rhetoric, geometry, arithmetics, astrology and musical theory. Books 7 to 11 discuss the three traditional parts of philosophy, namely logic, physics (cosmology) and ethics. But who are the "dogmatists"?—Those philosophers who presume that it is possible to obtain reliable, provable and irrefutable knowledge in their field of study. The theoretical basis of this scepticism is presented in another work of Sextus Empiricus (*Outlines of Pyrrhonism*—most of it lost). The school of Pyrrho used 10 ways of argumentation (tropai) to doubt the results of scientific research, among them the arguments based on the differences between human beings, and also the differences between their dispositions and sensual perception. Since contradictory sensual or mental impressions have equal strength and validity, one should refrain from any judgment (epochē) and should not believe that one has understood the truth. However, this skeptical attitude still allows practical action in daily life, since it should bring about a spiritual firmness (ataraxia) and moderation in all things.

# 德尔图良（约 160—230 AD）

曾被称为"拉丁神学之父"，因为他创造了一些重要的拉丁语神学概念；他生于 Carthago 的一个军官家庭，学习修辞学和法律并且掌握希腊语。他曾经在罗马当过律师，大约于 193 年皈依基督信仰，编写了许多护教的、教义的、伦理学和灵修学的书，但晚年（207 年）加入了一个很严格的教派（Montanistae）并脱离了正统的教导。

**著作：**《致殉道者》、《向万民》（亦译《致异教徒》）、《致斯卡普拉》、《致妻子》、《反驳赫莫格内斯》（亦译《反赫谟根尼》）、《反驳犹太人》、《驳斥马西翁》（亦译《反马其翁》）、《反驳普拉克西亚》、《反驳瓦冷丁派》（《反瓦伦廷派》）、《护教篇》（亦译《申辩书》，为基督信仰辩护）、《论灵魂》、《论洗礼》、《论基督的肉身》、《论肉体的复活》、《论花冠》、《论妇女的服饰》、《劝贞洁》、《论遭受迫害时的逃跑》、《论拜偶像》、《论守斋》、《论一夫一妻》、《论祈祷》、《论补赎》、《论大披肩》、《论耐心》、《论关于异端的规定》、《论羞愧》、《论斗兽场的表演》、《灵魂的见证》、《关于贞女的头纱》、《毒蝎》

## 019.《护教篇》

这篇杰出的护教论文（亦称 *Apologeticus*）针对省的总督们，写成于 197 年；其目标是为那些因信仰而被控告的基督徒辩护。

作者辩论说，反对基督宗教的法律（所谓的 Institutum Neronianum）是不合适且不公平的，所以那些优秀的皇帝们（比如 Traianus、Hadrianus 等）始终没有执行它。Tertullianus 是一位律师，他揭露对于法律的歪曲，而他的语气相当自信（与比他早 50 年的 Justinus 的谦逊说法有相当大的差距）。Tertullianus 指明那些控诉基督徒的奇异控告都是没有根据的，都是虚构的：基督宗教的礼仪不包括"牺牲人"，不包括淫秽的事或"吃人"的礼拜。这些东西更多地属于多神教。基督徒的道德生活非常纯洁，与异教徒的道德败坏形成明显的对比。实际上，基督徒从来没有因他们是强盗、凶手或犯了其他罪行而被控诉，控告他们的唯一理由恰恰是他们的"名字"（即"基督徒"nomen Christianum）。针对基督徒的其他控告（比如说他们是"无神论者"、"冒犯君主罪"、"不忠于祖国"）也都是虚构的罪名。

作者攻击异教徒的宗教。异教的神明们是空虚的，他们不存在。这些"神明"仅仅是一些杰出的人物，在他们去世后他们被尊奉为"神"。（Tertullianus 可能利用了 Euhemerus 对宗教的解释，因为他要影响那些有比较高的教育水平的官员。）异教徒并不严肃地相信他们的神明，他们的多神论必然会导致一种"不敬神"的态度（irreli-

# Quintus Septimius Tertullianus Florens / Tertullian

**Opera:** *Ad martyres, Ad nationes, Ad Scapulam, Ad uxorem, Adversus Hermogenem, Adversus Iudaeos, Adversus Marcionem, Adversus Praxean, Adversus Valentinianos, Apologeticum, De anima, De baptismo, De carne Christi, De carnis resurrectione, De corona, De cultu feminarum, De exhortatione castitatis, De fuga in persecutione, De idolatria, De ieiunio adversus psychicos, De monogamia, De oratione, De paenitentia, De pallio, De patientia, De praescriptione haereticorum, De pudicitia, De spectaculis, De testimonio animae, De virginibus velandis, Scorpiace*

**Works:** *To the Martyrs, To the Nations (To the Heathen), To Scapula, To the Wife, Against Hermogenes, Against the Jews, Against Marcion, Against Praxeas, Against the Valentinians, Apology, On the Soul, On Baptism, On the Flesh of Christ, On the Resurrection of the Body, On the Crown, On the Dress of Women, Exhortation to Chastity, On Flight in Persecution, On Idolatry, On Sobriety against the Psychists, On Monogamy, On Prayer, On Penitence, On the Pallium, On Patience, On the Persecution of Heretics, On Modesty, On the Games, The Testimony of the Soul, On the Veiling of Virgins, Scorpiace*

## 019. *Apologeticum / Apology*

This brilliant apologetic treatise (also known as *Apologeticus*) is addressed to the provincial governors and was written in 197 AD in order to defend Christians who are only accused because of their name.

The author argues that the anti-Christian law ("Institutum Neronianum") is inadequate and unfair; the "good emperors" (like Trajan, Hadrian) have never enforced it. The advocate Tertullian exposes the distortion of the law in a very self-confident way (quite different from the polite formulations of Justinus fifty years earlier). Tertullian shows the bizarre accusations against the Christians to be unfounded and false: Christian worship does not include human sacrifices, cannibalism or immodest and insolent actions. All these things rather belong to pagan customs. The pure moral life of Christians forms a bright contrast to the moral corruption of the pagans. In fact, Christans are never accused of robbing, murdering or other crimes, but only because of their name (nomen Christianum) and because of their faith are they accused at all. Also the other accusations trumped up against the Christians (atheism, laesio maiestatis and lack of loyalty to the state) are without merit.

Tertullian attacks pagan religion. The pagan gods are nothing, they do not exist. These "gods" are only outstanding humans who were deified after death. (Tertullian probably uses this explanation of Euhemerus to appeal to the more educated officials.) Since the pagans do not seriously believe in their gods, their polytheism must lead to a lack of piety

giositas)。反过来,基督徒们诚恳地相信唯一的神,他是宇宙的创造者。宇宙的美妙和人的灵魂都为这个神的存在作见证。在一些自然的说法当中,每一个人的心灵都表明自己是一个"自然的基督徒的心灵"(anima naturaliter Christiana, 17)。基督徒们尊敬圣父和他永恒的儿子,即"逻各斯"。他们向唯一的真神祈祷,但异教徒仅仅激起真神的愤怒。传统的哲学家(比如 Xenophanēs 公元前 550—前 470 年)也类似于基督徒,他们拒绝了多神论的宗教传统,但国家并没有迫害那些哲学家。

由于他们的信仰,基督徒们活出一种优越的道德生活。他们的伦理标准是神圣的。基督徒诚实地纳税,他们是更好的公民。上主的审判和他的永恒惩罚比任何人间的法院更有效。如果基督徒们面对一些虚假的控告或遭受审判,他们会欢乐地接受并殉道,将它当做一种胜利,而他们的殉道又会增加他们的人数("殉道者的血是新基督徒的种子",sanguis martyrum semen Christianorum, 49, 13~14)。即使人间的法院审判他们,上主也会宣布他们为无罪。因为基督徒们的信仰是如此坚定,省的总督们应该意识到,任何对于这个信仰的镇压是没有意义的,因为没有任何力量能够阻碍这个信仰的传播。

### 020. 《论斗兽场的表演》

这篇道德性文章(共 30 卷)成书于公元 196 年或 202 年。

作者 Tertullianus 警告每一位基督徒不要去看罗马斗兽场中的表演,因为这些表演违背基督信仰(1)。上主创造了万物,而万物都是美善的;上主创造了钢铁,但他不容忍凶杀。同理,神不允许人们滥用或罪恶地使用自己的器官。不可以用眼睛充满欲望地窥伺别人,不能用舌头来诅咒别人,也不能用心思来欺骗他人(2)。《圣经》在关于斗兽场的表演上并没有清楚的规定,但"不参与恶人聚会的人是幸福的"(《诗篇》Ps 1:1)这句话可以这样理解:不去斗兽场的人是幸福的(3)。

因为那些表演(spectacula)源于异教传统,他们等于是偶像崇拜(4)。在以前,他们被称为 liberalia,因为他们是献给葡萄酒的神 Bacchus(亦称 Liber)的。赛马活动则奉献给 Mars(战神),即 Romulus 的父亲。早期的王 Numa Pompilius 和其他的圣王规定了那些节庆与其中的表演来敬拜的诸神(5)。另一些习俗性的节庆则奉献给 Apollo、Magna Mater、Ceres、Neptunus 等等(6)。那些在斗兽场举行游行的人经常抬着一些神明的塑像,因此这些教派是偶像崇拜(7)。这些神灵的名称和象征也处处出现,"魔鬼和他的天使充满一切"(totum saeculum satanas et angeli eius repleverunt, 8)。马戏与马车赛也都与一些神有关系(Castor、Pollux、Neptunus, 9)。剧院中的表演(ludi)献给 Venus 和 Bacchus,即"沉醉与情欲的邪魔"(daemonia ebrietatis et libidinis),舞台上的表演都模仿爱神 Venus(即 sexus 情欲的象征)和酒神 Liber(即 luxus 奢侈浪费的象征,10)。那些体育比赛也同样献给某些神明,Olympia 的竞赛属于 Jupiter,在 Neme 的

(irreligiositas). Christians, in contrast, sincerely believe in the one God who created the cosmos. The beauty of the universe and the human soul give witness to His existence. In natural expressions every human soul manifests itself as "anima naturaliter Christiana" (17). Christians revere the Father and His eternal Son, the Logos. Christians pray to the one true God, whereas the pagan worship only provokes His wrath. The old philosophers (for example Xenophanes, 570—480 BC) rejected the polytheist traditions in a way similar to the Christians, and the state did not persecute these philosophers.

Because of their faith, Christians try to live out a superior morality, since their ethical standards are divine. Christians are honest tax-payers, they are better citizens. God's judgment and His eternal punishment surpass any earthly court. If Christians face false accusations and are sentenced, they will gladly accept martyrdom as a victory, and their martyrdom will only increase their number (sanguis martyrum semen Christianorum, 49,13~14). If earthly courts sentence Christians, God will acquit them. Because of the steadfastness of the Christians, the provincial governors should realize that any persecution is simply meaningless; nothing can stop the spread of this new faith.

## 020. *De spectaculis / On the Games*

This moral treatise in 30 chapters was written either in 196 or in 202 AD.

Tertullian warns any Christian against watching the performances of the Roman amphitheaters because the games are incompatible with their faith (1). God has created all things, and they are good; he created iron but does not tolerate murder. Likewise he does not allow the perverted or sinful use of our organs. Eyes are not made for lustful glances, the tongue is not meant for cursing others, and the mind is not for deceiving other people (2). The Bible has no clear commandment concerning performances at the circus, but the sentence "blessed the man who does not sit in the assembly of the wicked" (*Ps* 1:1) can be applied in this way: blessed is he who does not go to the circus (3).

Since the performances (spectacula) have a pagan origin, they are idolatrous (4). At some time the games were called "liberalia", since they were dedicated to Bacchus (=Liber), the god of wine. The horse races were sacred to Mars, father of Romulus. Numa Pompilius and the other kings instituted festivals and games in honor of certain gods (5). Other customary celebrations were dedicated to Apollo, the Great Mother, Ceres, Neptune, etc. (6). Circus processions usually carry idols of gods and are therefore idolatrous (7). Names and symbols of the gods appear in many places, "Satan and his angels are everywhere" (totum saeculum satanas et angeli eius repleverunt, 8). Horse riding and charioteering are inseparably linked to the gods (Castor, Pollux, Neptune, 9). Theatrical performances (ludi) are dedicated to Venus and Bacchus, the "demons of drunkenness and lust" (daemonia ebrietatis et libidinis), and scenical presentations imitate the licentiousness of Venus (sexus) or Liber (luxus) (10). Athletic games are dedicated to the gods, Olympia to Jupiter, Neme to Heracles, Isthmia to Neptune (11).

运动会属于 Hercules,而在 Isthmia 的比赛是献给 Neptunus 的(11)。

最著名的表演被称为 munus("为亡者做的事"),就是牺牲一些奴隶或战俘,而这种习俗演变成某种娱乐活动,这就是角斗士表演的来源(12)。正如我们不吃不洁净的食品,我们也应该保护我们的耳朵和眼睛不受偶像崇拜的污染(13)。为什么要说,那些娱乐性的享受(voluptates)是邪恶的呢?(14)它们激起人们的种种情绪(争吵、愤怒、嫉妒、痛苦),但这些情绪都违背着圣神/圣灵的平安(15)。因为人们观看这些表演,他们成为不理性的、狂妄的群众。很多表演是无耻的,它们违背贞洁和纯洁的要求(16、17)。人们受伤本来是对上主肖像的歪曲,但在斗兽场中的人喜欢看到残暴、不敬和野蛮的事(18、19)。

在正常生活中被认为是无耻的事在斗兽场中不可能成为好的(20)。看了表演后,甚至是一些有修养的人也会变得残忍(21)。剧院中的假面具和伪装的情绪不是真实的,因而是邪恶的,而基督徒不可以去看这些表演(22、23)。很多人去斗兽场仅仅是为了受尊敬或表现自己的地位,但表演的地方也是种种恶鬼的居所(25、26)。因为基督宗教的被镇压也与斗兽场有关,所以信徒们应该远离斗兽场(27)。

基督徒们不应该追求世俗的享受,他们不应该爱好"美味"和"精品",他们甚至愿意放弃这个世俗的世界,因为他们希望主将来会接受他们(exire de saeculo et recipi apud Dominum,28)。基督徒们也追求喜乐与享受(voluptates),但他们的爱好是精神性的价值:与神和好,真理的启示,真正的自由,良心平安等等。基督徒们观察时代不断改变的记号,这是他们的"斗兽场"。基督徒的著作表明,基督信仰的教导具有吸引力,他是"戏剧性的教导"(scaenica doctrina)。那些基督徒也参与一些"摔跤运动"(pugilatus, agones):他们的对手是不洁与淫秽(29)。最终,基督和新耶路撒冷的到来将成为一场非常庞大的凯旋游行(triumphus,30)。

## 021. 《灵魂的见证》

这篇护教性的文章大约是在 197—200 年间撰写的。

根据作者的说法,灵魂是对于神的存在的证据,因为她是"神的气息",而灵魂的权威性(auctoritas)建立在伟大的人性之上(maiestas naturae, 5,1)。人们很自然地发出一些叹息或呼吁天神(如"我的天"或"以 Jupiter 的名义")。人们也诅咒那些邪恶的力量或恶鬼,这些都说明古代的非基督徒作者已经隐约地意识到了神的存在。这样,"异教"(非基督宗教)的传统获得一个新的维度,因为可以视它为基督信仰的一种准备或铺路。根据这种思想态度,基督徒思想家能够第一次对罗马传统进行一种"文艺复兴运动"。

The most famous spectacles are called "munus" ("service to the dead"), as slaves or captives were sacrificed, and this custom was turned into entertainment—the origin of the gladiatorial games (12). Just as we do not eat impure and dirty food, we should keep our eyes and ears clean from idolatrous sacrifices (13). Why are entertainments (voluptates) bad? (14) They excite people's passions (contention, fury, envy, pain), but all these passions are contrary to the peacefulness of the Holy Spirit (15). By watching the performances, people turn into an irrational frenzied crowd, and many games are shameless, they offend against chastity and purity (16, 17). Injuries are a deformation of the image of God, but at the games people indulge in watching cruelties, impiety and savageness (18, 19).

What is shameless in real life cannot be considered good in the circus (20). Even refined and good people turn cruel when watching the games (21). The masks and pretended emotions of the theater are not truthful and therefore evil, therefore Christians must not go to the games (22, 23). Many people only go to the circus in order to be seen and respected in society, but the theater is also the place of demons (25, 26). The persecution of Christians is connected to the games, therefore Christians should stay far away from the circus (27).

Christians should not strive for worldly pleasures, they must not be fastidious, they even desire to leave this secular world behind, because they want to be received by the Lord (exire de saeculo et recipi apud Dominum, 28). However, Christians also strive for joy and pleasure (voluptates), but they delight in spiritual values: reconciliation with God, the revelation of the truth, real freedom, a pure conscience etc. Christians look at the changing signs of the time, this is their "circus". The attractive and "colourful" teaching (scaenica doctrina) of Christianity is to be found in books of Christian authors, and Christians also take part in a kind of wrestling competition (pugilatus, agones): they fight against impurity and licentiousness (29). Finally the advent of Christ and the New Jerusalem will be a monumental victory parade (triumphus, 30).

## 021. *De testimonio animae* / *On the Witness of the Soul*

This apologetic treatise was written ca. in the years 197—200 AD.

According to the author the soul is a witness to God's existence because she is "God's breath", and her authority (auctoritas) is based on the greatness of human nature (maiestas naturae, 5,1). The spontaneous interjections and invocations (like "my God", "by Jove") or curses against evil forces or demons are a proof that even non-Christian authors of antiquity had a glimpse of the existence of God. In this way the "heathen" (non-Christian) tradition gains a new perspective, since it can be interpreted as preparing the way for Christianity. This attitude lays the foundation for a first "Renaissance" of the Roman tradition under Christian auspices.

# 米努其乌斯（约 170—240 AD）

早期的基督宗教护教士，生平不详。

**著作**：《奥大维乌斯》（基督徒和教会以外人的对话，受了 Tertullianus 的 *Apologeticum* 的影响）

## 022. 《奥大维乌斯》

本著作是基督徒 Octavius 和非基督徒 Caecilius 之间的对话，共分为 40 章，大约成书在 Tertullianus 的 *Apologeticum*（《护教篇》，197 年成书）以后，但一些学者曾说，Tertullianus 的著作反过来受了 Minucius 对话篇的影响。这部著作要证明两点：基督徒们掌握高水平的世俗知识，而且他们能够在哲学一神论和他们的一神论信仰之间搭起一座桥梁。

两主角 Caecilius 和 Octavius 在 Roma 的港口 Ostia 城的海边上谈论宗教和信仰的问题。Caecilius 怀疑关于神的 providentia（眷顾，天命）的任何确切知识，因此最好要继续遵守罗马的传统宗教，因为罗马的伟大文明就建立在这个基础之上。Caecilius 的论点在很大程度上受了 Cicero 的 *De natura deorum* 的影响。此后他针对基督宗教提出三方面的批评：基督徒们认为人的理性无法掌握宇宙的奥秘，因此他们的思想很独断；他们坚决拒绝传统的罗马宗教；而且，他们过着一种不道德的生活。Octavius 简短地谈论口才和信用之间的关系，此后开始为唯一的神的存在及他的眷顾提出一些证据。

他使用 Tertullianus 的 *Apologeticum* 以及 Stoa 关于 providentia 的说法。他说明宇宙的秩序需要一种指导和一个统治者，并指出普通的民众都尊敬一个最高的神。部分的古典诗人（比如 Homerus, Hesiodus）关于最高的神的论述也应该被尊重。在第19、20 章中 Octavius 列出很多非基督徒哲学家的观点；他们的教导虽然不同，但都指向某一个最高的神的存在：Miletus 的 Thales、Anaximenes、Anaxagoras、Xenophanes、Aristoteles、属于 Stoa 学派的 Zeno、Chrysippus 和 Cleanthes，最终还有 Plato——他的 *Timaeus* 很清楚地谈到一个"创造世界的神"（mundi parens）。"我提到了几乎所有的著名哲学家的名字；他们虽然使用了不同的名称，但都指向同一个神（deum unum multis licet designasse nominibus）。某人也许会想，今天的基督徒是哲学家，或者说过去的哲学家曾是基督徒（aut philosophos fuisse iam tunc Christianos）"（20, 1）。

Octavius 接着指出异教的缺点并反驳那些针对基督宗教的控诉。这种支持基督信仰并劝勉人们放弃异教习俗的做法效法了早期的作者（参见 Tatianus 的 *Logos* 和 Clemens 的 *Protrepticus*）。最终 Octavius 试图反驳哲学怀疑论的观点（参见 Sextus

# Marcus Minucius Felix / Minucius

**Opera:** *Octavius*
**Works:** *Octavius*

### 022. *Octavius*

This dialogue in 40 chapters between the Christian Octavius and the pagan Caecilius was probably written shortly after Tertullian's *Apologeticum* (written in 197 AD), although some scholars have argued that Tertullian's work was in turn influenced by Minucius' dialogue. The aim of the work is to show that Christians command a high level of secular education, and that they are able to form a bridge between philosophical monotheism and their monotheist faith.

At the beach of Ostia near Rome, Caecilius and Octavius debate the question of religion and faith. Caecilius doubts any certain knowledge concerning divine providence, and therefore it would be the best to cling to traditional Roman religion, since the greatness of Roman civilization is built on this foundation. Much of Caecilius' reasoning is based on Cicero's *De natura deorum*. Then he adds a critique of Christianity containing three accusations: Christians deny that human intelligence can grasp the mystery of the universe and thus are dogmatists; Christians reject the ancient religion of Rome; and they lead an immoral life. Following a short discussion concerning eloquence and truthfulness, Octavius undertakes the proof of the existence of the only God and His providence.

He uses Tertullian's *Apologeticum*, and the Stoic arguments concerning providence. Having shown that the order of the universe needs guidance and a ruler, he argues that the common people have always revered one highest god. Also some of the classical poets (Homer, Hesiod and others) are to be respected as witnesses to monotheist faith. In the chapters 19 and 20 Octavius presents many pagan philosophers whose different teachings in a way pointed to the existence of a highest god: Thales of Milet, Anaximenes, Anaxagoras, Xenophanes, Aristotle, the Stoics Zenon, Chrysippus, and Cleanthes, and finally Plato, whose *Timaius* clearly talks about a god who is the creator of the world (mundi parens). "I have mentioned the tenets of almost all of the famous philosophers; all of them pointed to the same god albeit under different names (deum unum multis licet designasse nominibus). One could even think that the Christians of our day are philosophers, or that the philosophers of the past were Christians (aut philosophos fuisse iam tunc Christianos)." (20,1)

Octavius argues against paganism and refutes the objections against Christianity. This argumentation supporting the Christian faith and persuading others to abandon pa-

Empeiricus)。基督徒们应该感觉到很自豪，因为他们所掌握的真理是前人无法找到的,虽然他们曾经"全力以赴地"(summa intentione)寻求了这个真理。因此"我们不要成为忘恩负义的人。如果关于神的真理在我们这个时代变得很成熟的话，我们何必拒绝它呢？(quid nobis invidemur, si veritas divinitatis nostri temporis aetate maturuit)。让我们享受我们的幸福并作出公平的判断：应该限制迷信,应该为不虔敬的态度作补赎,应该保护真正的宗教(cohibeatur superstitio, inpietas expietur, vera religio reservetur)"(38, 7)。在对话篇的结尾部分(39、40章),Caecilius 说他愿意接受那些支持基督信仰的论点。

gan polytheism is an imitation of Tatian's *Logos* and Clement's *Protrepticus*. Finally Octavius refutes the claims of philosophical skepticism (cf. Sextus Empiricus). Christians can be proud to have arrived at a truth which others tried to find with greatest fervor (summa intentione) but which they could not obtain. Therefore "let us not be ungrateful. Why should we deny this to ourselves, now that the true knowledge about God has matured in our day? (quid nobis invidemur, si veritas divinitatis nostri temporis aetate maturuit). Let us enjoy our happiness and make a balanced judgment: may superstition be banned, may impiety find atonement, may the true religion be preserved (cohibeatur superstitio, inpietas expietur, vera religio reservetur)" (38, 7). At the end of the dialogue (chapters 39, 40), Caecilius announces that he accepts the arguments in favor of Christianity.

# 培培图阿（182—202 AD）

Vibia Perpetua 是一位罗马贵族女士，也是一名基督徒，因此她被捕并于 Geta 王子的生日（202 年 3 月 7 日）在 Carthago（迦太基）的斗兽场殉道。与她一起去世的基督徒是她的女仆 Felicitas，她的弟弟 Saturus，还有另外一些基督徒。Perpetua 和 Felicitas 很早就被视为"圣徒/圣人"（sanctus），而天主教也有传统的节日来纪念她们。

**著作：**《培培图阿与菲里契塔斯遇难录》

## 023.《培培图阿与菲里契塔斯遇难录》

本著作（亦简称 Passio Perpetuae）属于"遇难录"的文学类型，就是关于某一个殉道者的死亡的报告，一般都描述这些殉道者如何被处死或在斗兽场中的死亡。Perpetua 这种纯正的神视等于是一个妇女写的现存最早的拉丁语文献。她的《遇难录》不久后被译成希腊语，它始终是一个广为流行的文献并影响了后人为殉道者的死亡所写的报告。

叙述者加上了一个导论（第 1、2 章）以及关于 Perpetua 殉道的报告。她、她的仆婢 Felicitas 以及另一些基督徒曾在斗兽场被一些野兽撕裂（第 14~21 章）。著作的核心（第 3~10 章）是 Perpetua 在牢狱中体验到的 visio（神视）。因为她是一个来自罗马贵族的、受过教育的女基督徒，她写下她那种具有鼓励作用的神视。她看到自己要走上一个梯子，而在梯子下有一条龙（draco），它伸出它的头并威胁着 Perpetua。到达了梯子的顶点后，她遇到了基督："我看见了一个庞大的花园，而在中间有一个高大的、白头发的男人，看来他是一个牧人并给一些羊挤奶。周围有几千个人，都穿着白衣。他抬头看着我说：孩子，你来了，欢迎你（Et levavit caput et aspexit me et dixit mihi: Bene venisti tegnon）。"基督甚至给她一块干酪吃并安慰她。第 11 章到第 13 章叙述 Perpetua 的弟兄 Saturus 所看到的神视。

# Perpetua

**Opera:** *Passio Perpetuae et Felicitatis*
**Works:** *The Passion of Perpetua and Felicitas*

### 023. *Passio Perpetuae et Felicitatis / The Passion of Perpetua and Felicitas*

This literary work (also known as *Passio Perpetuae*) belongs to the type of "passio", which is a report about the death of a martyr, usually his or her execution or violent death in the amphitheater. The authentic vision of Perpetua is the earliest extant Latin text from the hand of a woman. Her *Passio* was soon translated into Greek, it was always a popular text and influenced later reports about the death of martyrs.

The narrator adds an introduction (chapters 1 and 2) and a report concerning Perpetua's martyrdom. She, her maid Felicitas, and the other Christians were devoured by wild animals in the amphitheater (chapters 14 to 21). The core of the work (chapters 3 to 10) is the vision which Perpetua had in her prison. Being an educated Christian from Roman nobility, she wrote down her edifying vision. She saw how she had to climb up a ladder, under which a dragon (draco) stretched out its head threatening her. After reaching the top of the ladder, she encountered Christ: "And I saw a huge garden, and in the center of it a tall white-haired man sitting there like a shepherd and milking sheep; and many thousand of people in white clothes were standing around him. He looked up, saw me and said: Child, good that you have come." (Et vidi spatium immensum horti et in medio sedentem hominem canum, in habitu pastoris, grandem, oves mulgentem; et circumstantes candidati milia multa. Et levavit caput et aspexit me et dixit mihi: Bene venisti, tegnon). Christ even gives her a piece of cheese to eat and consoles her. Chapters 11 to 13 contain the vision of Perpetua's brother Saturus.

# 奥利金(欧瑞根尼斯)（约 185—254 AD）

第一位伟大的希腊教父学者,科学性神学研究的奠基人,曾在 Alexandreia 继续 Clement 的教育工作,除了护教式的和解释教义的著作之外还有许多圣经学方面的书。他开创了《圣经》文本分辨(textual criticism)的研究,230 年被祝圣司铎,但与其主教有冲突,因此来到 Caesarea,在 249 年以后的教难中殉道而去世。他的著作对希腊的教父有很深远的影响,但一些太接近某些希腊哲学的观点因引起争论而没有被主流教会所接受。他的著作仅保存了三分之一,有的只存有拉丁语的译本。

**著作：**《六文本合参》(《六种经文合璧》)、《驳凯尔索》、《论基本的原理》(第一本信理学手册)、《论祈祷》、《论殉道》、《讲演》(关于基督信仰的讲演稿,共 574 篇,现存有 200 篇)、《简短注解》、《圣经注解》(留存的关于 *Mt, Jn,* 1 *Cor, Eph, Rom* 的诠注)

## 024. 《六文本合参》

这部用希伯来文和希腊文写的学术性强的《旧约》版本大约成书于 228—245 年间。

这部《旧约》版本包括六种不同的文本,这六个文本并排在六个平行的栏中。Ōrigenēs 的目标是创造一个符合希伯来原文的希腊语版本。第一栏是希伯来原文,用"方块"字体书写。第二栏用希腊字母写出希伯来语的发音。第三栏是 Aquila 的希腊语翻译,第四栏是 Symmachus 的希腊语翻译,第六栏是 Theodotion 的希腊语翻译。第五栏是 LXX(《七十贤士译本》)的希腊译文。这个(第五个)栏是最重要的,它曾多次被抄写并在古代基督宗教的圈子里有广泛的影响。整个著作大约有 6000 页。Ōrigenēs 又编写了一个"简缩本",即所谓的 Tetrapla (《四栏本》),它只包括 Aquila、Symmachus、LXX 和 Theodotion 的翻译。两部著作的原稿都保存在 Caesarea(巴勒斯坦)的图书馆,但都在第 7 世纪失踪,大概是因为阿拉伯人于 638 年的入侵。

## 025. 《驳凯尔索》

这部护教论文分为 8 卷,大约于 246—248 年间写成(希腊文)。Ōrigenēs 的反驳之所以被视为整个古代最优秀的护教论文,主要是因为作者非常渊博及其所具有的洞察力。

本著作大概是 Ōrigenēs 最重要的护教论文,幸亏它被保存,但作者的众多其他著作都没有被保存。本书反驳 Kelsos 的著作《真实的话》(*Logos alēthēs*)。那位折中主义的柏拉图主义思想家 Kelsos 大约于公元 178 年(或早在 150 年?)写过他那种攻击基

# Ōrigenēs / Origen

**Opera:** *Hexapla, Kata Kelsou, Peri archōn, Peri euchēs, Peri martyriou; homiliai, scholia, tomoi*

**Works:** *Hexapla, Against Celsus (Contra Celsum), On the Principal Doctrines (De principiis, On First Principles), On prayer (De oratione), On martyrdom; Homilies, Scholia, Commentaries (to Mt, Jn, 1 Cor, Eph, Rom)*

## 024. *Hexapla / Sixfold Bible*

This scholarly edition of the Old Testament in Hebrew and Greek was written around 228—245 AD.

This edition of the Old Testament contains six different versions of the text in six parallel columns. Origen wanted to create a Greek translation that matched the Hebrew original. The first column presents the Hebrew text written in the quadrata ("square script"). The second column reproduces the pronunciation of the Hebrew text in Greek letters. The third column contains the Greek translation of Aquila, the fourth the Greek translation of Symmachus, and the sixth the Greek translation of Theodotion. The fifth column is a Greek version of the Septuagint. This fifth column was the most important, it was frequently copied and spread far in the Christian circles of antiquity. The whole work was written on 6000 pages. Origen also made a shorter version, the "Tetrapla", which only contains Aquila, Symmachus, the Septuagint and Theodotion. The originals of both books were kept in the library of Caesarea (Palestine) but they were lost in the 7th century, probably during the Arab invasion of 638.

## 025. *Kata Kelsou / Contra Celsum / Against Celsus*

This apologetic treatise in 8 books was written in Greek, in the years 246—248 AD. Origen's refutations were seen as the best apologetic treatise of antiquity, mainly because of the scholarship and the penetrating insight of the author.

By a fortunate coincidence the most important of all apologetic books of Origen has been preserved, whereas all of his other numerous writings have disappeared. This work is a refutation of the polemic treatise *Logos alēthēs* (*The True Word*) by Celsus. The eclectic Platonist Celsus wrote his attack on Christianity around the year 178 (or already in 150?). The original is lost, but Origen preserved 70% of the text in form of quotations. Celsus tried to prove that seen from the perspective of Judaism, Christianity could

督信仰的著作。原著不可考，但 Ōrigenēs 在他的著作中以引用的形式保存了原著的 70%。Kelsos 先想证明说，从犹太教的角度来看，基督宗教无法说服任何人，此后他进而辩论说，犹太人关于弥赛亚的想法是无根据的。Ōrigenēs 近乎逐句谈论 Kelsos 的论文并一一反驳他。

Kelsos 说耶稣和他的使徒/宗徒本来想欺骗他们的随从者。他也从理性主义的角度着手辩论：基督宗教仅仅要求信仰，它不愿意面对任何理性的探讨。理性必须让步于信仰。Ōrigenēs 指出说，信仰是必要的，因为 Kelsos 所要求的"理性的探讨"需要很多时间，这就超过人的寿限和人的能力。然而，信仰与自然和理性相符合。信仰的道德效果都表明这一点。Ōrigenēs 说《旧约》，尤其是《摩西五书》，是一些非常古老的文献，实际上它们比异教世界的任何著作都早。

第 3 卷包含基督信仰教导的详细纲要，首先说明基督的位格和他的神性。第 4 卷讨论"创造"和"善恶"的问题。第 5 卷论述天使、复活、世界的终结，但他也指出《旧约》和《新约》之间的种种联系。

第 6 卷比较 Platōn 的引语和《福音书》的一些语句。作者想澄清关于魔鬼、圣灵（圣神）和"降生成人"的疑问。第 7 卷谈论各种预言、复活和关于神的认识。第 8 卷试图反驳 Kelsos 提出的另一个论点：基督信仰看起来很无力，这就削弱了它的可信度。如果这个宗教是真的，它为什么没有赢得更广泛的成功呢？

## 026. 《论基本的原理》

这部哲学和神学论文分为 4 卷（希腊文），在 220—230 年间成书。Ōrigenēs 的思辨引起了很多争论。主流的教会权威后来谴责了他关于"灵魂在生前已经存在"、"受造界的永恒性"的说法，尤其反对他的 apokatastasis pantōn（"万有复兴论"）观点。然而，他的思想对历代希腊神学家产生深远的影响，也影响了早期的经院思想（比如 Johannes Scotus Eriugena）。

第 1 卷谈论关于神、天使和星星之精灵的教导。Ōrigenēs 强调神的独特地位和他的统一性，这一点与多神论及诺斯替派有很大的差异——诺斯替派分裂了《旧约》的神（他仅仅是正义的但不是仁慈的）和《新约》的神（他只是慈祥的，但不是正义的）。异教徒认为 Logos（逻各斯）是一个没有人格的概念，而基督徒们因为肯定 Logos 的人格性，他们能够坚持救世主与唯一真神之间的联系。与 Philōn 和自己的老师 Clemens Alexandrinus 一样，Ōrigenēs 认为我们无法充分适当地谈论神。我们的一切称呼及言语上的表达要么是否定性的（比如"非物质的"、"无限的"）要么是"最高级式的"（如"全知的"、"最有爱心的"等）。

为了解释神证论的问题（即恶的问题，参见 Boethius, *De consolatione phil.*），

not convince anyone, and in a second step he wanted to show that the Jewish idea of the Messiah itself was unfounded. Origen follows Celsus's treatise almost sentence for sentence and refutes him.

Celsus says that Jesus and his apostles had the intention to deceive their followers. He also argues from the point of rationalism: Christianity only demands faith and is not willing to face any intellectual inquiry. The intellect has to be sacrificed to faith. Origen argues that faith is absolutely necessary, because the kind of thorough rational inquiry that Celsus demands would surpass human limitations in terms of time and of intellectual capacity. However, faith is in accordance with nature and with reason. The moral effects of the faith show this. Origen argues that the Old Testament, especially the books of Moses, are very old scriptures, in fact they are older than any other scriptures of the pagan world.

Book 3 contains a detailed outline of Christian doctrine, starting with the person of Christ and His divinity. Book 4 talks about the themes of creation and the nature of good and evil. Book 5 discusses angels, the resurrection, the end of the world, and also looks at the connections between the Old and the New Testaments.

Book 6 contains comparisons of quotations from Plato with words from the Gospels. The author tries to explain questions concerning satan, the Holy Spirit, and the incarnation. Book 7 discusses prophecies, the resurrection and the knowledge of God. Book 8 tries to counter the argument of Celsus that the apparent weakness of Christianity itself undermines its credibility. If that religion should be true, why does it not have more success?

## 026. *Peri archōn / De principiis / On First Principles*

This philosophical and theological treatise in 4 books in Greek was written between 220—230 AD. Origen's speculations caused much debate. His views of the pre-existence of the soul, the eternity of creation and especially his theory of the apokatastasis pantōn ("return of all things") were rejected by the official Church. However, he deeply influenced the Greek theologians of later ages and also early scholasticism (e.g. Johannes Scotus Eriugena).

The first book discusses the doctrine about God, the angels and the spirits of the stars. Origen emphasizes the uniqueness and unity of God in opposition to polytheism and in opposition to those Gnostics who separated the God of the Old Testament (a God only just but not merciful) and the God of the New Testament (a God merciful but not just). The pagan concept of Logos is an impersonal idea, but the personal understanding of the Logos enables Christians to maintain the unity of the Redeemer with the one God. Like Philo and his own teacher Clement of Alexandria, Origen holds that we cannot adequately talk about God. All our terms and verbal expressions concerning God are either negative (like: "not material", "un-ending") or superlative (like: "all-knowing", "most loving", etc.).

In order to solve the theodicy-problem (the problem of the existence of evil, see

Ōrigenēs 发展了一种关于神灵的理论(pneumatologia)。这种理论回应了一些错误的主张：Markion、Valentinos 和 Basilidēs 说，恶的存在来自理性存在物之间的差等，而这种差等又起源于一个邪恶的原则，就是《旧约》的创造主。根据 Ōrigenēs 的想法，创造主创造一切精神体(理性存在物)为同样美善的存在。他们的差等来自他们远离神的自由决定。他们对神的爱慕变得越来越软弱，所以他们都犯了罪，一些犯了比较轻微的罪，另一些犯了严重的罪。那些犯下了比较轻微的罪的天使获得了一种"天空式的"(aitherios)身体，对那些恶魔的惩罚是让他们获得一种物质性的、很沉重的身体。在天使和恶魔中间有人类，担负着他们的肉身。

第 2 卷描述物质性的世界，就是在受造界中那种比较不高尚的部分。因为神是永恒的，同时也是创造主，世界也同样是永恒的，但我们看到的现世并不是永恒的。现在的世界被创造是因为神想惩罚这种精神体，而身体(肉身)就是这种惩罚的表现。因为神是完美完全的，所以世界不可能在某一个时刻有一个固定的开头。这种想法要避免一种悖论：如果世界是永恒的，它就不属于神的预先眷顾，但如果说世界在某个时刻被创造以及在某个时刻将要结束，这就意味着神有变化，神也有局限性。Ōrigenēs 加上一篇关于人的灵魂的论文，始终引用《圣经》的语句来证明自己的说法。第 2 卷的结尾部分谈论复活以及终末论的种种问题。

第 3 卷谈论种种精神体的自由以及神的正义。魔鬼和"敌对的势力"威胁人类。人们又面对一些纯粹属于人性的诱惑。此后 Ōrigenēs 描述一切万有最终的和谐状态，就是所谓的 apokatastasis pantōn("万有复兴论")。上主要惩罚种种天神和精神体并给予他们一个身体，但这同时也是改变和提升他们的第一个步骤，因为这样神就限制了他们的邪恶。在第二个阶段，神将要毁灭这个世界的秩序，将要实现一个新的时代和新的世界(aiōn, saeculum)。最终，神是 panta en pasin("万物中的一切"，参见 1 *Cor* 15: 27–28)。那时，一切有理性的存在物将会恢复它们那种"非物质的状态"，他们将会恢复原先与神的合一以及彼此之间的和谐。那时一切邪恶将会消失，而精灵们都要回到原来的美善状态中去。

第 4 卷谈论作为启示的《圣经》。Ōrigenēs 强调整部《圣经》是充满灵性(inspiratio "灵感"、"默感")的，是神的话语。然而，如果仅仅从字面上来理解《圣经》，人们无法领会神的启示的全部涵义，所以需要一种灵性的解释和说明(exēgēsis)。Ōrigenēs 认为只有为数不多的信徒有机会掌握《圣经》的真正意义。第 4 卷的最后部分总结了作者关于三位一体、作为创造者与救世主的 Logos(逻各斯)、物质世界和精神体的观点——这些有理性的精神体是不可毁灭的，而他们的命运是在将来恢复与神以及彼此之间的合一。

Boethius, *De consolatione philosophiae*), Origen developed a pneumatology (doctrine of spirits). This was necessary because Marcion, Valentinus and Basilides taught that the existence of evil originated in the inequality of rational beings, and this inequality derived from an evil principle, coming from the creator God of the Old Testament. According to Origen, the Creator created all spirits (rational beings) equally good. The inequality was due to their free decision to turn away from God. Their love to God grew weak, and so they all sinned, some graver than others. Those angels who sinned less gravely were given an ethereal body, the devils were punished with a dense and heavy body. Between angels and demons are humans, burdened with their earthly bodies.

The second book presents the material world, i.e. the less noble part of creation. Because God is eternal and Creator at the same time, the world is also eternal, but our present world might not be eternal. The present world was created because God wanted to punish the spirits by giving them a body. God's perfection does not allow a beginning of the world in time. This view tries to avoid an impasse: either the world is eternal and does not belong to God's providential care, or the world was created in time and ends at some point, which would imply God's changeability and imperfection. Origen adds a treatise about the human soul, always basing his speculations on Biblical quotations. The second book ends with a discussion of the resurrection and the meaning of the eschatological promises.

The third book examines the freedom of the spirits and divine justice. Satan and hostile powers threaten human beings. Man also faces purely human temptations. Then Origen envisions the final harmony of all things in the "apocatastasis panton", the return of all things. God punished the spirits by giving them a body, but this was also the first step to convert them, since He limited their maliciousness in this way. The second step will be that God destroys this world in order to bring about a new age (aiōn, saeculum). In the end, God will be "panta en pasin" ("all in all", cf. 1 *Cor* 15:27–28), the rational beings will return to their state of immateriality, they will find a way back to their unity with God and each other. Then all evil will disappear and the spirits will return to their original state of goodness.

The fourth book discusses the understanding of the Bible as revelation. Origen emphasizes that the whole Bible is an inspired scripture (inspiratio), the Word of God. However, a literal interpretation will not be able to show the whole meaning of God's revelation, therefore it needs a kind of spiritual commentary and interpretation (exēgēsis). Origen thinks that the true meaning of the Bible will only be accessible for very few believers. The last chapter of book four sums up the author's views of the Trinity, the Logos being Creator and Redeemer, the material creation and the indestructible rational beings (souls, spirits) whose destiny is to restore the original unity with God and with one another.

# 朗格斯(约 200—250 AD)

生平不详。

著作:《达夫尼斯和赫洛亚》

## 027.《达夫尼斯和赫洛亚》

这部长达 4 卷的浪漫著作是来自 Lesbos 岛的 Longos 的唯一现存作品,是古代唯一的以浪漫情绪为主题的爱情小说。Longos 第一个描述了热切爱情的萌芽和发展过程,虽然牧人生活与爱情之间的关系早在荷马那里就被提到(参见 Ilias 5,313: Aphroditē 恋慕牧人 Anchisēs)。Longos 描写两个年轻人的青梅竹马和他们的天真相处,但恰恰是这种纯朴的叙述创造了一种充满情欲的氛围。

男孩 Daphnis 和女孩 Chloē 本来是两个弃婴,被他们的父母抛弃。一些牧人将他们养大。在牧人 Dryas 的照顾下,他们生活在 Lesbos 岛的乡村地区,离 Mytilēnē 城不远。春天这两个天真的少年一起玩耍,但当他们共同吃饭、共同放羊时,他们感觉到彼此之间有某种吸引力,也是一种很痛苦的感受和激情,但他们不知道这种莫明其妙的现象是什么。在夏天的时候,他们的渴望进一步加深。突然出现一些海盗并绑架了 Daphnis,但一个牧人和勇敢的 Chloē 拯救了 Daphnis,使他逃离危险。

第 2 卷描述秋季。一个老牧人(Philetas)愿意向两个青年解释他们这种莫明其妙的渴望和痛苦的来源。他说两个人的"疾病"被称为 eros(爱情),而这位老牧人也告诉他们治疗这种痛苦的"良药",即"亲吻"与"拥抱"。然而,Daphnis 和 Chloē 并没有充分理解他的说法。不久后他们再次遇到一个很危险的情况:Chloē 被一些海盗绑架,但通过牧人的保护神 Pan 的帮助,她能够安全地回来。

第 3 卷包含关于冬天状况的描述。此时的情人被分开,他们无法去外面的牧场。他们伤感地回忆春天和夏天时的种种经验,即他们如何一起吃饭,如何一起玩耍。当春天再来时,他们充满喜悦地再次相逢,但春天也恢复了他们爱情的渴望和痛苦。一个住在附近的善良妇女(名为 Lykainion)向 Daphnis 提示了更多关于爱情的秘密,但 Daphnis 不愿意伤害 Chloē 并继续和她玩一些无害的、孩童般的游戏。当地的仙女们使 Daphnis 发现一个宝藏,这样他能够向 Dryas 提供这些钱,借此向 Chloē 求婚。然而,这必须先获得牧人们的主人 Dionysophanēs 的同意。

# Longos / Longus

**Opera:** *Poimenika ta kata Daphnin kai Chloēn* (=*Daphnis kai Chloē*)
**Works:** *Shepherd Stories about Daphnis and Chloe* (=*Daphnis and Chloe*)

## 027. *Poimenika ta kata Daphnin kai Chloēn* / *Shepherd Stories about Daphnis and Chloe*

This romance in four books is the only extant work of a certain Longos from the island of Lesbos, and it is the only love novel of antiquity where tender feelings are the main theme. Longos was the first to describe the awakening of passionate love, although the connection between bucolic life (the life of shepherds) and love had already been set forth in the *Iliad* (compare *Iliad* 5,313: Aphrodite loves the Shepherd Anchises). Longos' seemingly innocent description of the naive interaction of the lovers produces a sublime atmosphere of erotic longings.

The boy Daphnis and the girl Chloe are two foundlings who were exposed by their parents as infants and reared together by shepherds. Under the guidance of the shepherd Dryas, they live on a countryside estate near Mytilene on the island of Lesbos. In spring the two innocent youths play together, but as they eat with each other and tend the sheep together they feel a certain attraction for the other and a painful passion for which they have no name. In the summer their desire grows. Suddenly pirates arrives and kidnap Daphnis, but a shepherd and the courageous Chloe manage to save him.

The second book describes the season of autumn. An old shepherd (Philetas) tries to explain to the young people the origin of their desires and pains: the name of their "ailment" is love (eros). The shepherd also tells them about the "remedies" for this kind of suffering: hugging and kissing. However, Daphnis and Chloe do not yet fully understand his advice. And soon they face a dangerous situation once more: Chloe is abducted by pirates, but with the help of the shepherd-god Pan, she comes back unharmed.

The third book contains the description of the winter season, in which the lovers are separated and cannot go out to the pastures. They remember in a nostalgic mood how they ate together and played together in the season of warmth. As soon as spring returns, they joyfully reunite, but spring brings back the old longings and pains of love as well. A benevolent woman (Lykainion) from the neighborhood tells Daphnis more about the secrets of love, but he prefers not to hurt Chloe and continues to play harmless and childlike games with her. The nymphs arrange it that Daphnis discovers a treasure, so that he can now offer it to Dryas in order to get Chloe's hand. However, the lord of the shepherds, Dionysophanes, has to agree to the marriage.

在第 4 卷的叙述中，Dionysophanēs 来参观他的农场并认出 Daphnis 是自己的儿子。他同意两个人的婚姻。当他们都在城市中参加一个宴席时，Chloē 也找到了她的父亲，即富有的 Megaklēs。此后，两个情人在农场那里庆祝他们的婚姻，最终双方成为丈夫和妻子。现在 Chloē 也意识到，他们早期的来往仅仅是"牧人的游戏"。整个叙述的结构是一种渐进式的发展，其中有一些对称的情节（即 Daphnis 遇到的事不久后也是 Chloē 所经历的事）。

In book 4 Dionysophanes visits the estate and recognizes Daphnis as his own son. He agrees to the marriage. At a meal in the city Chloe discovers her father, the rich Megakles. The wedding celebration takes place on the countryside estate, and finally the lovers can unite as man and woman. Now also Chloe realizes that their former interactions were only "shepherd's games". The narrative is constructed as a gradual progress with several symmetrical parallelisms (i.e., whatever happens to Daphnis soon also happens to Chloe).

# 赫利奥多鲁斯(约 200—250 AD)

生平不详。

著作:《埃塞俄比亚故事》

## 028. 《埃塞俄比亚故事》

保存下来的古希腊语小说不多，而 Hēliodōros 的十卷本 *Aithiopika ta peri Theagenēn kai Charikleian*(《关于特亚根尼斯及卡瑞克雷亚的埃塞俄比亚故事》)是其中之一。本著作大约成书在公元 232—250 年之间。

小说的基本主题是两个情人的分离。只有在经历许许多多困境和奇妙的危险后，两个人才重逢。Hēliodōros 很巧妙地使用故事中的一个环节作为叙述的开端：一帮强盗黎明时在尼罗河口的海岸发现一只搁浅的船。他们感到非常惊讶，因为船员都被杀死，沙滩铺满尸体和货物。只有一个年轻的女孩子(名叫 Charikleia)和一个男青年(Theagenēs)幸存。这个男青年受伤了，他慢慢地醒过来。他睁开眼睛并看到坐在他旁边的女青年，就说:"甜心(ō glykeia)你真的活着？"因为这个女孩子看来非常高贵和美丽，强盗们认为她是一个女神或一个女祭司。强盗的酋长将这两个年轻人交给 Knēmōn，一个希腊奴隶。两个人开始向 Knēmōn 叙述自己的故事，但 Knēmōn 打断他们的话并讲说自己的经历，所以读者后来才知道 Charikleia 和 Theagenēs 到底是谁。

故事的主人翁是埃塞俄比亚女王的女儿 Charikleia。因为她出生时被发现有白皮肤，她的母亲丢弃她。一个来埃塞俄比亚的希腊人发现 Charikleia 并将这个小孩子带到希腊的 Delphoi，在那里给予她良好的希腊教育。她在 Delphoi 成为 Artemis 的女祭司，而在一个 Artemis 节庆活动中，她爱上一位来自 Thessalia 的贵族青年，即 Theagenes。Charikleia 的母亲，即埃塞俄比亚的女王，请 Kalasiris，一位来自 Memphis 的祭司，去寻找她的女儿。在一定时间后，Kalasiris 在 Delphoi 找到了 Charikleia。他帮助两个年轻人一起从希腊逃走，但这位祭司不久后又与他们分开。在埃及他们的船遭受海盗的袭击，而 Knēmōn 奴隶照顾他们两个人。在 Knēmōn 的家中 Kalasiris 再次找到 Charikleia，但 Theagenēs 早已被另一些强盗带走，所以需要去寻找他。整个叙述错综复杂，两个人必须经历很多危险的情况——海盗、强盗、充满淫欲的求婚者——，最后两个人来到埃塞俄比亚的 Meroe 城，就是 Charikleia 的出生地。在那里他们差点被残酷地作为祭牲，但人们认出 Charikleia 是国王的女儿，而两个人准备他们的婚姻，这就是这部小说的结局。

# Hēliodōros / Heliodorus

**Opera:** *Aithiopika*
**Works:** *Ethiopian Stories*

## 028. *Aithiopika / Ethiopian Stories*

Heliodorus' ten-book *Aithiopika ta peri Theagenēn kai Charikleian* (*Ethiopian Stories of Theagenes and Charicleia*) is one of the few Greek novels of antiquity that have been preserved. It was probably written between 232 and 250 AD.

The basic theme of the novel is the separation of two lovers who can only reunite after many sufferings and fantastic adventures. Heliodorus masterfully starts with an event in the middle of the story: At sunrise a group of brigands find a stranded ship in the Nile delta. The robbers are perplexed as they find out that the crew has been killed. Bloody corpses and booty lie on the beach, only a young girl (Charicleia) and a young man (Theagenes) have survived. The man is wounded and regains consciousness. As he openes his eyes and looks at the young woman sitting at his side, he says: "O my sweetheart (ō glykeia), are you really alive?" Since the girl is extremely dignified and beautiful, the robbers think that she is a goddess or a priestess. The chieftain of the brigands assigns Cnemon, a Greek slave, to care for the girl and the young man. The couple starts to reveal their story to Cnemon, but Cnemon interrupts them and tells his own tale, and only much later the reader gets to know who Charicleia and Theagenes actually are.

The central figure of the novel is Charicleia, the daughter of the Ethiopian queen. Since she is born white she is exposed by her mother. A Greek traveller finds the girl and brings her from Ethiopia to Delphi, where she gets a good Greek education. In Delphi she becomes a priestess of Artemis, and at the festival of Artemis she falls in love with Theagenes, a young man from Thessalian nobility. Charicleia's mother, the queen of Ethiopia, asks Calasiris, a priest from Memphis, to search for her daughter, and after some time Calasiris finds Charicleia in Delphi. He helps the couple to elope from Greece, but soon the priest loses sight of them. In Egypt their ship is attacked by pirates, and Cnemon the slave cares for the couple. At the house of the slave Cnemon Calasiris finds Charicleia again, but in the meantime Theagenes has been kidnapped by another band of brigands, and so they go to search for him. The complex narrative leads through many dangers and adventures—pirates, brigands, lustful suitors—and finally the couple reaches the city of Meroe in Ethiopia, where Charicleia was born. There they are in danger of being cruelly sacrificed, but Charicleia is recognized as being the daughter of the king, and the novel ends with the two lovers preparing their marriage.

作者和故事中的人物多次肯定神明们的权力和命运在宇宙中的安排。因此，种种危险经验都被视为一种严肃的考验。经过这些考验的人应该表现他们对于神明们的依赖。在古代的希腊语小说传统中，这种兴趣是很独特的。作者的名字 Hēliodōros（即"太阳神之礼物"）也与叙述中具有核心地位的太阳神 Hēlios 有关系。本故事几次提到两个情人在很多危险的情况当中能够保持他们的贞洁和纯净的爱；这就意味着这部小说首次将贞洁描述为个人的高贵理想。

The author and the characters in the novel repeatedly confirm the power of the gods and the ordinances of Fate that govern the universe. Thus the adventures are understood as serious tests in which the persons involved have to prove their piety and trust in the gods. This particular religious interest of the author is unique within the Greek novel literature of antiquity. His name Heliodorus ("gift of Helios") is associated with the god of the sun (Hēlios) who enjoys a central place in the pagan pantheon of the narrative. This narrative repeatedly mentions that in all dangerous situations the two lovers struggle successfully to keep their virginity and chastity; thus chastity is for the first time presented as an ennobling ideal of a person.

# 西普里安（约 200—258 AD）

他来自非基督徒的上层家庭，皈依了基督信仰，领洗后不久成为 Carthago 教会的主教（248 年），并且很快面对 Decius 皇帝对基督徒的镇压；他的著作是当时教难的主要历史资料。在 Valerianus 皇帝的教难时期（257 年），他被流放到 Curubis，但他回到 Carthago，并于 258 年 9 月 14 日在那里被处死，为信仰殉道。他的执事 Pontius 曾给他写了一篇传记，这是最早的基督徒传记。

**著作**：《致 Donatus》、《致 Fortunatus，劝殉道》、《论耐心的价值》、《论主的祈祷》、《论教会的合一》、《论贞女的地位》、《论背教的人》（谈论当时在教难中离开教会，但后来又想入教的人）、《论死亡》、《论善功和施舍》、《书信》、《偶像不是神》、《为 Quirinus 写的证论，三卷》（包括很多古拉丁语《圣经》的语句）

## 029.《书信集》

本《书信集》包含 81 封信，其中有 16 封不是 Carthago 主教 Cyprianus 写的，而是别人写给他的。

大部分书信涉及教会在受到严厉镇压时面对的种种难题。一些信包括伦理学问题或礼仪问题。很多文献来自 249 年到 251 年间的教难时期，当时的 Decius 皇帝致力于系统地清除基督信仰。在那个时期，Cyprianus 只能在地下活动，他无法公开当主教。通过这些书信，他和当地那些属于他照顾的信徒保持联系。他在种种困境中鼓励信徒们并给予他们一些忠告。Cyprianus 也抄写了 13 封信并将这些复印件寄到罗马，以表明他忠于自己的职责，虽然当时无法当公开的主教。

当时教会的主要难题之一是如何对待那些曾经在教难的压力之下放弃了基督信仰但后来又想进入基督徒团体的人（他们被称为 lapsi，即"堕落者"）。根据 Novatianus（第 30、36 封信）的说法，只能以最严格的态度对待这些"跌倒的"基督徒，他们不能再次进入教会的团体。在 251 年，Novatianus 自己在罗马被祝圣为主教，这样他组织了在罗马的与正规主教 Cornelius 对立的教会团体。他的追随者自称为 katharoi（"洁净者"），而这种分裂的教派在 Carthago 也有很多拥护者。Cyprianus 认为那些曾经背教的人（lapsi）必须经过一段作严格补赎的时期，才能够再次进入教会团体（参见他的 *De lapsis*《论背教的人》）。

# Caecilius Cyprianus / Cyprian

**Opera:** *Ad Donatum, Ad Fortunatum de exhortatione martyrii, De bono patientiae, De dominica oratione, De ecclesiae unitate, De habitu virginum, De lapsis, De mortalitate, De opere et elemosynis, Epistulae, Quod idola dii non sint, Testimoniorum libri III ad Quirinum*

**Works:** *To Donatus, To Fortunatus on the Encouragement to Martyrdom, On the Value of Patience, On the Lord's Prayer, On the Unity of the Church, On the State of Virgins, On the Apostates, On Mortality, On Good Works and Alms, Letters, Idols are no Gods, Three Books to Quirinus of Scriptural Testimony*

## 029. *Epistulae / Letters*

This collection contains 81 letters, 16 of which were not written by Cyprian, the Bishop of Carthage, but addressed to him.

Most of the letters are concerned with the difficult life of the church in a time of fierce persecutions. Some of the letters deal with ethical questions or liturgical problems. Many of the texts were written during the persecution of 249 to 251 AD, when Emperor Decius tried to systematically wipe out Christianity. During that time Cyprian had to act from the underground and could not be bishop in public. Through the letters the bishop kept contact with the believers in his care. He encouraged them and advised them in their predicaments. Cyprian also sent copies of 13 of his letters to the clergy of Rome in order to show that he was faithful to his duties even as a bishop in the underground church.

One of the main problems of the church at that time was the attitude to those Christians who had renounced Christianity under pressure but later wanted to be readmitted to the Christian community (these apostates were called "lapsi"). According to Novatianus (see letters 30 and 36) these "fallen" Christians were to be treated with utmost rigor and could not be readmitted to the community. Novatianus himself had been consecrated a counter-bishop of Cornelius in Rome in 251 AD and continued to set up a schismatic church. His followers called themselves "katharoi" (the pure ones) and this sectarian church also had many believers in Carthage, where Cyprian was bishop. Cyprian held that the fallen Christians (lapsi) had to undergo a period of severe penitence before they could be readmitted to the church community (cf. his *De lapsis*).

# 普罗提诺（柏罗丁）（约 205—270 AD）

他大概出生于埃及的 Lycopolis，母语是希腊语。28 岁时他转向哲学，232—242 年间于 Alexandreia 在 Ammonius Saccas 的指导下学习，40 岁时在罗马定居并成为哲学老师。他在罗马领导一个相当有影响力的知识分子圈子，晚年退隐到 Campania（意大利南部）。他被视为古代晚期最伟大的哲学家之一，也是新柏拉图主义的主要代表。他的著作重视精神生活、神秘体验和苦修。

**著作**：《九章集》（由他的学生 Porphyrios 收集整理的讲稿）

## 030. 《九章集》

这部哲学论文集（共 6 卷）是由 Plōtinos 的学生 Porphyrios 在 254 年以后编撰的。每一个书卷包含 9 篇论文，因此这部著作被称为《九章集》。

第 1 卷的主题是伦理学。第 2、3 卷涉及到物理学的一些问题。第 4 卷包含一些关于灵魂（psychē）的论文，第 5 卷谈论精神（nous），而第 6 卷的核心概念是"太一"（to hen）——它是最先的、最高的存在原则，同时也是善良和优美的理念。这种神圣的存在是崇高的并超越一切描述。精神（nous, spiritus）曾经是从"太一"流出来的；精神比"太一"低一层，但它自身包含一切万物的理念（kosmos noētos，即拉丁语的 mundus intelligibilis）。灵魂（psychē，即称为宇宙的灵魂）属于第三个层次，而这个层次是精神领域和物质领域之间的中介者。最低的层次属于物质（hylē），它也是邪恶的象征，正如"太一"是至善的象征。

灵魂本来也属于精神的领域，但它与物质的牵连始终限制它的活动。灵魂提升的途径应该是逐渐脱离物质的障碍、远离世俗的事物，这样上升到精神的高度。最终，灵魂能够与精神结合并在激昂的精神超拔体验中默观"太一"（参见 Platōn 的 *Phaidōn*, *Politeia*, *Symposion*）。

# Plōtinos / Plotinus / Plotin

**Opera:** *Enneades*
**Works:** *Enneads*

### 030. *Enneades / Enneadae / Enneads*

This collection of philosophical treatises in 6 books was edited by Plotin's student Porphyry after 254 AD. Each book contains 9 treatises, and therefore the books are called "enneads".

The main theme of the texts in the first ennead is ethics. The second and the third ennead deal with problems of physics. The fourth ennead contains treatises about the soul (psychē), the fifth discusses the spirit (nous), and the central idea of the sixth ennead is "the One" (to hen), which is the first and highest principle of being, and it is also the idea of the good and the beautiful. This divine being is sublime and transcends all description. The nous (spirit) has emerged from this "One"; the nous is one level under the "One", but it contains in itself the ideas of all things (kosmos noētos, or in Latin: mundus intelligibilis). On the third level there is the soul (psychē, also the soul of the universe), which mediates between the spiritual and the material reality. The lowest level is occupied by matter (hylē), which is also the symbol of the evil, just like the "One" is the symbol of highest goodness.

The soul originally belongs to the realm of the spirit, but matter hampers and restricts the activities of the soul. The liberation from material impediments and the detachment from earthly things is the way of the soul that rises to the lofty heights of the spirit (nous). Finally the soul can find union with the spirit and contemplate the "One" in ecstatic vision (cf. Plato's *Phaedo, Republic, Symposium*).

# 第欧根尼·拉尔修(约 220—280 AD)

来自 Sicilia 的 Laerte,生平不详。他根据别人书中的资料编写了他自己的重要著作。

**著作:**《著名哲学家的生平和学说》(或译《名哲言行录》,共 10 卷,全部保存,包含关于古代思想的宝贵资料,有许多资料在别处没有记载)

## 031. 《著名哲学家的生平和学说》

本文集(共 10 卷)大概成书于 250 年左右,它的另一个书名是 *Bioi kai gnōmai tōn en philosophia eudokimēsantōn*(《名哲言行录》),它是关于古典哲学的最重要资料之一,包含 80 多位思想家的传记、他们的著作书目,以及很多来自希腊化时期的手册的资料。

作者将希腊哲学分为两个学派:"伊奥尼亚学派"(从 Thalēs 到 Platōn 和 Stoa 学派)以及"意大利学派"(从 Pythagoras 到 Epikouros)。第 1 卷包含哲学的起源,即"七贤"(比如 Solōn)的具体格言。第 2 卷论述 Iōnia(伊奥尼亚)的哲学家(如 Anaximandros 和 Anaxagoras)、Sōkratēs 以及他的部分学生。第 3、4 卷包含关于 Platōn 和他的学派(学院派)的资料。第 5 卷提供关于 Aristotelēs 的资料,而第 6 卷描述 Antisthenēs 和 Kynikoi(犬儒派)。第 7 卷论述 Stoa 学派(即 Zēnōn、Kleanthēs、Chrysippos)。第 8 卷开始介绍"意大利传统"(Pythagoras、Empedoklēs)。第 9 卷谈论 Hērakleitos、Xenophanēs、Parmenidēs、Elea 的 Zēnōn、Leukippos、Dēmokritos、Prōtagoras 和 Elis 的 Pyrrhōn。第 10 卷保存很多来自 Epikouros 的警句和名言(大部分被认为是可信的)。

# Diogenēs Laertios / Diogenes Laertius

**Opera:** *Philosophōn biōn kai dogmatōn synagōgē*
**Works:** *A Collection of the Lives and Teachings of the Philosophers* (*Opinions of Eminent Philosophers*)

## 031. *Philosophōn biōn kai dogmatōn synagōgē / A Collection of the Lives and Teachings of the Philosophers*

This collection of 10 books was probably written around 250, it is also known under the title *Bioi kai gnōmai tōn en philosophia eudokimēsantōn* (*Lives and Opinions of Eminent Philosophers*) and is one of the most important sources for our knowledge about classical philosophy. The work contains biographies of more than 80 thinkers, lists of works and much information collected from other manuals from the Hellenistic period.

The author divides Greek philosophy into two traditions: the "Ionians" (from Thales to Plato and the Stoa) and the "Italians" (from Pythagoras to Epicurus). Book 1 contains the origins of philosophy, namely the practical sayings of the Seven Sages (for example Solon). Book 2 presents Ionian philosophers (Anaximandros, Anaxagoras), then Socrates and some of his students. Books 3 and 4 contain material concerning Plato and his school, the Academy. Aristotle and his school is presented in book 5, then follow Antisthenes and the Cynics (book 6). Book 7 gives an account of the Stoa (Zeno, Cleanthes, Chrysippus). Book 8 starts with the "Italian tradition" (Pythagoras, Empedocles). Book 9 presents Heraclitus, Xenophanes, Parmenides, Zeno of Elea, Leucippus, Democritus, Protagoras, Pyrrhon of Elis, and book 10 preserves many maxims of Epicurus (most of them are considered to be authentic).

第二篇

# 教父学的全盛时期
## The Golden Age of Patristic Literature
(313 — 410 AD)

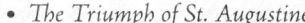
The Triumph of St. Augustine

# 拉克坦提乌斯(约250—325 AD)

来自Africa的拉丁作者和护教士,曾是修辞学家Arnobius的学生,后应Diocletianus皇帝的邀请在Bithynia的Nikomedia(小亚细亚)教授修辞学,并在那里皈依基督信仰。教难爆发(303年)后,他成为一名护教士。在317年,他应Constantinus皇帝的邀请去Gallia(高卢,也许在Trier),担任皇帝儿子Crispus的老师。现在保存的只有他关于基督宗教的著作。因为他的写作风格是一种"演讲式的散文",他也被称为Cicero Christianus("基督宗教的西塞罗")。

**著作**:《凤凰之诗》、《论上主之愤怒》、《论迫害者之死》、《论上主的创造》、《神圣教规纲要》、《神圣教规》(主要著作,7卷,为基督信仰辩护的著作,同时也全面介绍了这个信仰)

## 032. 《凤凰之诗》

这首诗长达170行,它是古老的"凤凰神话"的许多版本之一。根据这个神话,凤凰与太阳有某种联系;它用一些芬芳树枝做一个鸟巢,在其中死去并再次复生。关于复生的过程有两种描述:烧毁自己并从骨灰中复兴,或者在腐烂的尸体中生一个小虫子,而这个虫子蜕变成一只新的凤凰。基督徒们很早就利用这个神话来肯定基督的复活和坚固每一个信徒对复活的希望。

Lactantius先描述凤凰的家乡,即天上乐园中的森林,这就是太阳神的领域。这个地方非常平安,充满光明,那里没有死亡,没有痛苦。在森林中有一口泉源,涌出的是"生命之水"。凤凰是一种很"独特的鸟"(unica avis),它是太阳神Apollo的追随者(satelles Phoebo)。每天早上凤凰在"生命之水"中洗澡,坐在一棵树上并等待着日出。太阳升起时它以一种奇妙的、独特的歌曲迎接太阳神。

在1000年后凤凰鸟感觉到自己已经衰老,它要死去以获得新生命(nam perit ut vivat,78行)。它飞到叙利亚(即Phoinikē,腓尼基人的地区)并在一棵棕榈树上给自己做一个巢窝(棕榈树的希腊语名称是phoinix)。凤凰在巢中躺下并在自己的身体上喷一种液体。一身充满香味的凤凰鸟"交出自己的灵魂"(commendat animam,93行)并死去,但其死亡是带来生命的死亡(morte genitale)。凤凰鸟的死亡导致新的凤凰的诞生,而年轻凤凰的美丽超过一切其他的动物,备受敬仰。一切鸟类都围绕着新出生的凤凰,而当它起飞时,鸟群陪同它。当年轻的凤凰飞向那些更高的空气层时(ad aetheris auras),其他的鸟无法跟着它。凤凰单独回到自己的家乡。在结尾的地方诗人赞美这只无性的鸟,它不遭受爱神纽带的约束(Veneris foedera),这实际上是对贞洁生活的赞美。对凤凰鸟来说,死亡是爱,而它渴望的是死亡,因为通过死亡它进入永恒

# Lucius Caecilius Firmianus Lactantius / Lactantius

**Opera:** *Carmen de ave phoenice, De ira Dei, De mortibus persecutorum, De opificio Dei, Epitome divinarum institutionum, Institutiones divinae*

**Works:** *The Poem of the Phoenix, On God's Wrath, On the Deaths of the Persecutors, On God's Handiwork, Epitome of the Institutions, Divine Institutions*

## 032. *Carmen de ave phoenice / The Poem of the Phoenix*

This poem in 170 verses is one of the many versions of the old myth of the phoenix. According to the myth, this miraculous bird is somehow related to the sun. It builds a nest of aromatic branches, dies in it and resurrects again. The process of rebirth is either depicted as burning and resurgence from the ashes or as death, decay and rebirth as worm which is metamorphosed into a bird. The Christians started very early to use this myth as support for the resurrection of Christ and for the hope of the resurrection of each believer.

Lactantius first describes the home of the phoenix in the grove of a kind of heavenly paradise, the realm of the god of the sun. This place is peaceful and bright, there is no death and no suffering. In the middle of the grove there is a fountain, where the "water of life" wells up. The phoenix is a unique bird (unica avis), it lives in the forest as a follower of Apollo (satelles Phoebo). Early in the morning the phoenix takes a bath in the water of life and sitting on a tree it awaits the sunrise, welcoming the god of the sun with its miraculous and inimitable song.

After one thousand years the phoenix feels that it is getting old and wants to die so as to be reborn (nam perit ut vivat, v. 78). It flies to Syria ("Phoinike", the land of the Phoenicians) and builds a nest for itself on a palm-tree ("phoinix" in Greek). Then the phoenix lies down in the nest and sprays a fluid over its body. Covered in fragrant smells the bird commends its soul (commendat animam, 93) and dies a death which generates new life (morte genitale). The death of the phoenix leads to the birth of a new phoenix whose beauty surpasses all other animals and is much adored. All birds gather around the new-born phoenix, and the crowd accompanies the young phoenix as it flies on high. As the young phoenix flies higher up to aetheric regions (ad aetheris auras), the other birds cannot follow. The phoenix returns to its home. The poem ends with a praise of this asexual bird which is not restricted by the bonds of Venus (Veneris foedera)—in fact a praise of virginity. For the phoenix death is love, and it desires to die since through

的生命(vitam aeternam,170 行)。

### 033. 《论上主之愤怒》

这一论战性的文章反驳了异教哲学关于神的概念,成书时间是 311 年或 312 年。关于该问题的讨论很重要,因为一些异端人物甚至要分裂"旧约中充满愤怒的神"和"新约中充满爱的神"(参见 Marcion 或 Tertullianus 的著作 *Adversus Marcionem*)。

受攻击的是 Epicurus 学派,因为该学派否认神明有任何感觉,所以 Lactantius 说这些人实际上是无神论者。在另一方面,Stoa 学派坚持说神是充满仁慈的,但对他们来说,神没有发怒的能力。这种说法不会在一个愿意敬畏神的人的心中培养一种很虔诚的态度。作者的总结是,无论是 Epicurus 学派或 Stoa 学派的人都无法认识真神,因为如果他们有这种洞见,他们就应该接受唯一的神和他在耶稣基督身上的启示。

Lactantius 很系统地提出四种可能性:(1)神既没有愤怒(ira),又不慈祥(gratia)——这是 Epicurus 学派的观点。(2)神是仁慈的,但他不发怒(即 Stoa 派的思想)。(3)神是充满怒气的,但不能是仁慈的(异教的神明)。(4)神既有表现仁慈,又有发怒的能力(这才符合《圣经》的记载)。根据古代哲学家(Aristoteles、Cicero、Seneca)的说法,愤怒是一种不正义的、毁灭性的情绪,就是寻求报复。但 Lactantius 说,上主的愤怒是一种正义的、不寻求报复的愤怒。上主的愤怒实际上只是对罪恶的控制以及抵抗。人们的罪激怒上主,但通过这种愤怒,罪人可以再次找到正路。因此,神的愤怒不仅仅是正义的和有益的愤怒,它甚至是人类悔改和被纠正的必要条件。上主的愤怒并不是一种不由自主的情绪,而是上主随时作的审判。上主永远反对罪恶,但他的愤怒将不会居留在那些有忏悔意识的罪人身上。

### 034. 《论迫害者之死》

这部历史性的论文大约写于 314 年,就是在 Milano(米兰)敕令(313 年)被宣布后不久(该敕令规定要宽容基督信仰)。当时在东部当皇帝的 Licinius(308—324 年在位)接近一些反对基督信仰的圈子,而 Lactantius 的著作要表明一个同时有神学意识和政治意义的道理:上主始终惩罚那些镇压基督宗教的人。当那些统治者开始迫害新的基督信仰时,他们(和他们的亲属)马上遇到了很多灾难,最终死得很惨。

第一个迫害基督徒的皇帝是 Nero,圣 Petrus 及圣 Paulus 因为他在罗马遇难;然而这个皇帝死得早,他的逝世并不光荣,而人们都不知道他的墓在哪里——这一切可以视为上主的惩罚。同理,Domitianus 的死于非命也算为一种惩罚。激烈镇压基督信仰的 Decius 皇帝阵亡,没有人埋葬他。Valerianus 皇帝最终成为俘虏,而野蛮民族拿着他的皮作为他们胜利的记号。Aurelianus 在实践他的残酷计划之前就已经被杀害。

death it enters eternal life (vitam aeternam, 170).

## 033. *De ira Dei / On God's Wrath*

This polemic treatise against the conceptions of God presented by pagan philosophy was written in 311 or 312 AD. The clarification of the issue was very important, because some heretics even went so far as to separate the "wrathful God of the Old Testament" from the "loving God of the New Testament" (see Marcion, and Tertullian *Adversus Marcionem*).

Lactantius attacks the Epicureans who deny any feelings to divine beings and therefore are practically atheists. The Stoics on the other hand admit that the deity is merciful, but they would not see God as capable of wrath, a tenet which excludes the pious attitude of a god-fearing person. The author concludes that neither Epicureans nor Stoics are able to know the truth about God, because that would imply that they abandon idol-worship, accept the one God and His revelation in Christ Jesus.

Lactantius systematically presents four possibilities: A deity can (1) neither have wrath (ira) nor mercy (gratia) (the Epicurean position), or (2) be merciful but not wrathful (the Stoic position), or (3) be wrathful but not merciful (pagan gods), or (4) be capable of both mercy and wrath (the Biblical account). According to the philosophers (Aristotle, Cicero, Seneca) wrath is an unjust and destructive passion which is seeking revenge. However, Lactantius states that God's wrath is a just wrath which does not pursue vengeance. The meaning of God's wrath is the control and rejection of sin. The sins of men make God angry, but by this wrath the sinner should be brought back to the right course. Therefore, God's wrath is just, useful, and even necessary for the conversion of mankind. God's wrath is not an uncontrollable passion, but His continuous judgment. God is eternally opposed to sin, but His wrath will turn away from a contrite sinner.

## 034. *De mortibus persecutorum / On the Deaths of the Persecutors*

This historical treatise was written around 314 AD, shortly after the Edict of Milan (313 AD) which granted tolerance to Christianity. In a time when Licinius, the ruler of the East (in power 308—324 AD) approached circles that were hostile to Christianity, Lactantius wants to present a truth that is both theological and political: God has always punished those who persecuted Christians. As soon as these rulers started to suppress the new faith they (and even their relatives) faced calamities and finally suffered a terrible death.

The early and inglorious death of Nero and the fact that his tomb cannot be found are a sign of God's punishment, since this emperor caused the first persecution of Christians and had St. Peter and St. Paul killed in Rome. In a similar way, the violent death of emperor Domitian also counts as punishment. Emperor Decius who fiercely suppressed Christianity died in battle and remained unburied, and emperor Valerian ended up in imprisonment, leaving his skin in the hands of the barbarians as a symbol of their victory. Aurelianus was murdered before he could realize his atrocious plans.

大部分的篇幅属于 Diocletianus 时期（284—305 年）以及他的继承人推动的教难。一旦一个人开始"以正义人的血沾染自己的手"，他自己的命运就会转恶。作者也叙述 Constantinus 皇帝在 312 年的关键交战之前见到的神视，即十字架的神视（visio）。Lactantius 最后赞扬 10 年教难（303—313 年）后的和平，他也祈求上主保护充满生命力的教会，不让她受魔鬼的干扰并赐给她永久的平安。因为 Lactantius 的著作比较详细地反映了教难时期的最后几年以及 Constantinus 任期的前几年，它也是一部具有历史学价值的资料书。

### 035.《神圣教规》

这部护教性的宗教手册（共 7 卷，亦称 *Divinarum institutionum libri VII*《神圣教规七卷》）成书于 304—313 年间；当时的基督宗教遭受严厉的镇压。因为该著作篇幅相当大，作者后来撰写了一个比较短的"提要"，即所谓的 *Epitome*（《纲要》）。Lactantius 面向那些有学问的异教徒，因此他使用很理性的论点，很少引用《圣经》的语句。他更多强调罗马诗人是真理的见证人，比如他第一次从基督信仰的角度来解释 Vergilius 的 *Eclogae* 中第 4 首诗（参见 7, 24, 11）。作者的文笔非常优雅，而著作的思想结构也很清晰，所以它成为一部名著，同时这也是第一部用拉丁语全面论述基督信仰的著作。这部著作在很多中世纪的图书馆中都被保存，也是第一部在意大利被印刷的书（1465 年在 Subiaco 印行）。

第 1 卷（标题是 *De falsa religione*《论虚假的宗教》）是针对多神论的反驳。多神论的来源是对于那些逝世的国王或统治者的崇拜（即是 Euhemerus 的理论）。只有一种理性的宗教概念，就是一神论。从宇宙的秩序中，我们能够推论只存在一个神，而他对一切事物都有一个计划。

第 2 卷的标题是 *De origine erroris*（《论错误的来源》）。Lactantius 试图说明古代的异教徒如何陷入种种恶鬼的虚假奇迹和欺骗性的现象。异教徒们看到了这些表面上很奇妙的东西，所以他们开始崇拜不洁的精灵和没有生命的偶像。

第 3 卷（*De falsa sapientia*《论虚假的智慧》）致力于反驳异教徒的哲学，视其为空虚的和无价值的。作者区分纯粹的修辞学和认真的哲学探索。修辞学的目标是华丽的辞藻和世俗的成就，因此根本不值得谈论，但严肃的哲学研究也无法找到真理。哲学家们最多能摸索智慧的一些琐碎的残片，可以组织这些片断，但他们始终没有可靠的、长期的原则。部分哲学家也曾经是善良的人，他们曾很诚心地寻求真理，但这些具有修养的人只能发表一些精美的讲演而已。他们的修辞学技巧并没有引导他们走向真理，因为他们"没有向掌握真理的那一位学习"（3,1,14）。Lactantius 分析传统哲学的三大领域（即物理学、逻辑学和伦理学）并得出结论说，不同的思想体系（比如 Plato 的学院派、Aristoteles 和 Epicurus 的学派）必定是错误的，因为他们彼此之间存在着很

Most of the text documents the persecutions in the period of Diocletian (284—305 AD) and his successors. As soon as anyone started to "stain his hands with the blood of the just", his fortune changed to the worse. The narrative also contains the vision of the cross which emperor Constantine had before the decisive battle at the Milvian bridge in 312 AD. Lactantius closes with a praise of the peace after 10 years of persecutions (303—313 AD) and a prayer to God that the Lord may protect the flourishing Church from the power of the devil and grant her everlasting peace. As this is a more detailed reflection on the last years of persecution and an important sourcebook for the first years of Constantine's reign, the treatise is invaluable for historians.

## 035. *Institutiones divinae / Divine Institutions*

This apologetic handbook of religion in 7 books (also known as *Divinarum institutionum libri VII*) was written during the time of the fierce persecution of Christianity in the years between 304 and 313 AD. Since the work is quite voluminous the author later made a short extract, called *Epitome*. Lactantius addresses educated pagans and thus argues rationally and only seldom quotes the Bible. He rather sees Roman poets as witnesses to the truth, for example he is the first to interpret Vergilius' fourth Eclogue in a Christian way (7, 24, 11). The classical style and the clear structure contributed to the fame of this first comprehensive description of the Christian faith in Latin. The book was present in many medieval libraries and it was the first book to be printed in Italy (1465 in Subiaco).

The first book (*De falsa religione, On the Wrong Religion*) is a refutation of polytheism. The origin of polytheism is the worship of deceased kings or rulers (the theory of Euhemerus). The only rational view of religion is monotheism. From the order of the universe it can be concluded that there is one God who has a plan for all things.

The title of the second book is *De origine erroris* (*On the Origin of Error*). Lactantius tries to explain how the pagans of the ancient world fell prey to the deceiving, false miracles and pseudo-wonders of demons. Seeing these apparent "wonders", the pagans began to worship unclean spirits and dead idols.

Book 3 (*De falsa sapientia, On False Wisdom*) attempts to refute pagan philosophy as empty and worthless. The author distinguishes between mere rhetorical brilliance and serious philosophical research. Eloquence aims at beauty of expression and secular success, and thus it does not deserve any discussion, but even serious philosophy cannot find the fullness of truth. The philosophers at best can collect fragments of wisdom and assemble them without having any reliable and lasting guidelines. Some of the philosophers were virtuous people, and their search for truth was sincere, but all these educated men could do was to hold elaborate speeches. Their rhetorical skills were refined but did not lead to the truth, since they "did not learn from the One who alone commands truth" (3,1,14). Lactantius analyzes the three traditional areas of philosophy (physics, logic, and ethics) and concludes that the different systems of thought—Plato's Academy, the schools of Aristotle and Epicurus—must be wrong since they are mutually contradictory. Even Plato and Socrates are attacked. Socrates supposedly died with the conviction to know nothing except his own ignorance (3,28,17). Epicurus denies divine providence

多矛盾之处。甚至 Plato 和 Socrates 都受到谴责。据说 Sokrates 至死都认为他什么也不知道，他仅仅意识到自己的无知(3,28,17)。Epicurus 否认神明们的眷顾，所以他遭受很多批评(3,17,41)。因此，基督信仰不再被描述为一种新的哲学或更完善的哲学，而被视为真理本身，即一种超越和取缔任何哲学的世界观。

在前 3 卷的护教性论述后，第 4 卷的标题是 *De vera sapientia et religione*（《论真正的智慧与宗教》），而后面几卷呈现出关于基督宗教教导的全面表达。真理与宗教之间不可能存在矛盾，而基督宗教既是真正的智慧，又是真正的信仰。造物主通过他的先知们启示真理，最终他派遣自己的儿子耶稣到人间，使他启示全部的真理。作者反对 Arianismus，所以强调耶稣是真神，又是真人（即 incarnatio"降生成人"的原则）。只有通过耶稣以及在教会内，人们才能真正地朝拜圣父。

第 5 卷被称为 *De iustitia*（《论正义》），并把异教徒诗学中的"黄金时代"解释为一种"原始的一神论"，但后来的人逐渐丢失了这种信仰并沉入了多神论的陷阱。基督曾经想恢复原本的信仰，而唯独这种对一切人的大父的信仰能够成为万民平等的思想基础。男女老少，即一切人的平等概念才构成正义的基石。那些遭受镇压的基督徒的坚定不移以及殉道者的坚忍精神都证明一点：基督宗教的教导是真实的。

第 6 卷（标题为 *De vero cultu*《论真正的朝拜》）强调说，一切爱慕和敬拜神的信徒也必须遵守他的盟约。敬爱神并关爱其他人——这都是纯正朝拜的表现。

最后一卷（*De vita beata*《论幸福生活》）谈论灵魂的不死、信徒们的赏报、肉身的复活、最后的审判以及神对于每一个人的永久赏报或惩罚的决定。

惟独对永生的希望能够在此世提供精神力量："假如死亡将结束一切，保留别人性命而因此损害自己的人是一个傻子。假如死亡将消除灵魂，那么人们应该只追求长寿和舒适的生活。但如果在死亡后有一个新的生命期待着我们，即一种永恒的、幸福的生命，那么一个正直的或明智的人会轻视物质生活和世界上的一切财宝，因为他知道神应该给予他什么样的赏报。虽然不去向那些神灵进行祭献而保全性命却接受折磨和死亡在民众的眼中是愚蠢的事，我们仍然要尽可能忠于上主，要投入全部力量和耐心。死亡不可以使我们感到害怕，而痛苦和折磨不应该使我们屈服。我们必须要坚定不移地保持精神的毅力和忍耐。"

and receives much criticism (3,17,41). Thus Christianity is no longer presented as a kind of new or more perfect philosophy but rather as truth itself, namely a world view that dwarfs and replaces any philosophy.

After the first three apologetic books the fourth title is *De vera sapientia et religione* (*On True Wisdom and True Religion*), and the following volumes present an all-encompassing account of Christian doctrine. Truth and religion cannot be contradictory, and Christianity is true wisdom as well as the true faith. The Creator revealed truth through His prophets and finally sent His son Jesus to mankind to reveal the full truth. Against Arianism Lactantius emphasizes that Jesus was true God and true man (the principle of the incarnation). Only through Jesus and within the Church is the true worship of the Father even possible.

Book 5 is entitled *De iustitia* (*On Justice*) and interprets the "Golden Era" of pagan poetry as a period of a kind of "original monotheism", but this faith was lost in later generations as mankind was trapped by polytheism. Christ tried to restore the original faith, and only this faith in the one Father of all can be the basis on which the equality of all people is recognized. The equality of all men and women is the foundation of justice. The steadfastness of the persecuted Christians and the firmness of the martyrs is a proof that the Christian teachings are true.

Book 6 (*De vero cultu, On True Worship*) emphasizes that all believers who love and adore God must also keep His commandments. Piety towards God and love towards other people are the expressions of authentic adoration.

The last book (*De vita beata, On a Happy Life*) discusses the immortality of the soul, the reward of the faithful, the resurrection of the body, the Last Judgment and God's decision about each person's eternal reward or punishment.

Only the hope for eternal life gives strength in this secular world: "If death would end all things then it would be foolish to spare the life of another to one's own disadvantage. If death wipes out the soul then one should only care for a long and comfortable life; but if after death a new life expects us, a life which is eternal and blessed, then a just and wise person will despise this physical life and all the treasures of the world, because he knows which kind of reward he should be given by God. Even if it is foolish and stupid in the eyes of the people to rather accept torture and death instead of sacrificing to the gods and thus preserving one's life, we should try hard to be faithful to God with all our strength and all our patience. Death must not frighten us, and pain must not bend us. We must be unshaken and abide by the strength of the spirit in steadfastness."

# 优西比乌斯（约 265—339 AD）

这位主教、圣经学家和历史学家曾经在巴勒斯坦的 Caesarea 当过 Pamphilos（310 年被处死）的学生，他与 Pamphilos 一样想确保 Ōrigenēs 的文献遗产和思想传统。在 303—313 年的大教难中，他可能还留在 Caesarea 并目睹了许多殉道事件，大约于 312 年前往 Tyros 城和埃及，而于 313 年（或 314 年）被提名为 Caesarea 的主教，在当时的教会和政治生活中具有很大的影响力。因为他支持 Ōrigenēs 的思想，他也比较友好地面对 Arius 的学说，因此在 325 年的 Antiochia 主教会议上被开除教籍，但在同年的 Nicaea（尼西亚）会议上他能说明自己的观点并恢复了自己的地位。在另一方面，由于他的劝说，有些神学家被审判为异端者，比如 Antiochia 的 Eustathios（327 年）和 Ankyra 的 Marcellus（336 年）。Eusēbios 和 Constantinus 皇帝的关系比较密切。

**著作**：《诸民族的历史》（亦译《编年史》仅保存 Hieronymus 的拉丁译本，从 Abraham 的诞生[=公元前 2016 年]开始，记载许多古代历史事件，也是关于希腊、罗马历史的重要资料）、《教会历史》（323 年以前的教会史，非常重要的著作）、《福音的说明》、《福音的准备》、《圣经地点考》（亦译《奥诺玛斯提肯》）、《神的显示》（亦译《塞奥芳尼》）

## 036. 《教会历史》

Eusēbios 曾经被称为"教会史之父"。他的重要著作共分 10 卷（亦称 *Historia ekklēsiastikē*），写成于 324 年。在那一年，Constantinus 皇帝打败了非基督徒皇帝 Licinius。从 303 年到 324 年，本著作 4 次被扩充，后来由 Rufinus de Aquileia 译成拉丁语（403 年），而一些希腊作者继续补充了一些内容，就是 Sōkratēs（380—439 年）和 Sōzomenos（约于 450 年）。

Eusēbios 的《教会史》的基础是他早期的著作 *Chronikon*（《编年史》），大概在 303 年成书。该书的第二部分（*Chronikoi kanones*）包含很多"同期表"，因此描述一个全球性的世界历史，即从世界的创造和 Abraham 的诞生（被定在公元前 2016 年）一直到公元 324 年。所谓的"同期表"指 Eusēbios 比较很多来自埃及、巴比伦、犹太和希腊历史的年代事件并从中得出一个共同的、普遍的编年标准。在《教会史》中他也使用了这种编年方法，他经常插入某个罗马皇帝或四个大主教城市（Jerusalem、Alexandria、Antiochia、Roma）的主教的即位年代。

教会史的叙述是从 Iēsous（耶稣）开始的，他是拯救者和主，他的出生年代符合先知们的预言，而他在 Pilatus 总督执政时遇难。他的门徒传播福音（第 1 卷）。关于基督

# Eusēbios Pamphili / Eusebius de Caesarea

**Opera:** *Chronikoi kanones* (*Chronographia, Chronikon*), *Ekklēsiastikē historia, Euaggelikē apodeixis, Euaggelikē proparaskeuē, Peri tōn topikōn onomatōn, Theophania*

**Works:** *Chronicles, Church History* (*Ecclesiastical History*), *Demonstratio evangelica, Preparation for the Gospel* (*Praeparatio evangelica*), *Onomasticon, Theophany*

## 036. *Ekklēsiastikē Historia* / *Church History*

Eusebius has been called "Father of Church history". His monumental work in 10 books (also entitled *Historia ekklēsiastikē*) was finished in 324 AD—the year when emperor Constantine defeated the pagan emperor Licinius. The work was enlarged in 4 (?) successive editions from 303 to 324. It was translated into Latin by Rufinus of Aquileia (in 403). Greek authors like Socrates (380—439 AD) and Sozomenos (c. 450 AD) enlarged the work.

Eusebius based his *Church History* on the foundation of an earlier work, the *Chronicles* (*Chronikon*), probably written in 303 AD. The second part of this work (*Chronikoi kanones*) contains many synchronic tables which outline a universal history from the creation of the world and Abraham's birth (supposedly in the year 2016 BC) until the year 324 AD. "Synchronic tables" means that Eusebius compared annual data from the Egyptian, Babylonian, Jewish, and Greek histories and formulated a common, universal chronology from these data. This method he carried over to the *Church History*, where he often inserted the accession of Roman emperors or of the bishops of the four great sees (Jerusalem, Alexandria, Antioch, Rome).

The narrative starts with Jesus, the Savior and Lord, who appears in His time in agreement with prophesy and suffers under Pilate. His disciples spread the gospel (book

的消息很快传到各地。在他们处死基督后，犹太人遇到很多灾难。Iakōbos 在耶路撒冷遇难，Petros 在罗马宣道，而 Markos 在埃及传教。Paulos 被捕并被押送到罗马。在 Nero 皇帝的教难中，Petros 和 Paulos 都成为殉道者（第 2 卷）。第 3 卷论及 apostoloi（宗徒/使徒）的继承人、罗马的主教们、Clemens 主教的书信、耶路撒冷的毁灭、Iosephus Flavius 以及 Domitianus 和 Traianus 皇帝的统治。一些持异端理念的人物传播错误的教导，比如 Menander 和 Kerinthos（第 3 卷）。那些"护教士们"试图保卫基督信仰和教会。Justinus 向 Antoninus 皇帝写了一封信，但他最终和 Polykarpos 一样殉道遇难。Polykarpos 还见过 apostoloi（宗徒/使徒）。第 4 卷记录了 Roma、Alexandria、Jerusalem 和叙利亚的 Antiochia 的主教的姓名。第 5 卷谈论 Marcus Aurelius 时期的教难，以及"上主如何回应基督徒的祈祷并从天上降下雨水给 Marcus Aurelius"（5,5）。作者介绍了 Clemens Alexandrinus、Apollōnios 以及他们的著作。

在其他的基督徒作者和学者当中，对于 Ōrigenēs 的描述是最详细的，包括他受的教育、他的严格精神和《圣经》方面的知识、他的学生和著作。Decius（249—251 年）进行的系统镇压基督徒的运动尤其残酷。一些新的异端（Sabellianismus、Novatianismus、Manichaeismus）威胁教会的统一（第 6、7 卷）。前 7 卷描述教会到 280 年的发展，第 8、9 卷形容 303—313 年间的"大教难"，而第 10 卷加上关于 313 年以后的情况的报告：各地的教堂被归还，皇帝的法令为基督徒提供基本的权利，而圣职人员免于公共税务。作者没有谈论关于 Arianismus、Melitianismus 和 Donatismus 的争论，也没有提到 324 年和 325 年的主教会议。因为 Eusēbios 的信息来源是 Caesarea 和 Jerusalem 的教会档案室，他对西部和许多东部地区的了解很有限。因为作者支持 Ōrigenēs 的学派，他特别注重 Alexandria 的基督徒团体。Eusēbios 记录最重要的城市的主教，但也列出教会作者和他们著作的书名（其中有很多书已失传）。

因为这是第一部教会史，他成为一部里程碑式的著作，而 Eusēbios 也意识到了自己是一位前驱者。他的著作也是一部重要的资料书，因为作为一名真正的历史学家，Eusēbios 多次从他搜集的手抄本中引用了别人的原文。他的研究也依赖于 Constantinus 皇帝的支持——这位皇帝允许他使用朝廷的档案室。作者也曾四次与 Constantinus 见面（在 325 年、327 年、335 年和 336 年）并为皇帝写了一篇赞美文，就是《君士坦丁传》（337 年）文集的一个部分。

1). In a short time the message concerning Christ covers the whole world. The Jews encounter many evils after their crime against Christ. James is martyred in Jerusalem, Peter preaches at Rome, Mark in Egypt. Paul is sent a prisoner to Rome, and during the persecution under Nero, both Peter and Paul die as martyrs (book 2). The third book tells of the first successors of the apostles, the first bishops of Rome, Clement's epistle, the destruction of Jerusalem, the life of Josephus Flavius, and of the reign of Domitian and Traian. Menander, Cerinthus and other heretics spread false teachings (book 3). Apologists try to defend the Christian teaching and the Church. Justin writes a letter to emperor Antoninus, but he is martyred like Polycarp, who knew the apostles. The names of the Bishops of Rome, Alexandria, Jerusalem, and Antioch in Syria are written down (book 4). Book 5 tells of the persecutions under Marcus Aurelius and "how God sent rain from heaven to M. Aurelius in response to the prayers of the Christians" (5,5). The author introduces Clement of Alexandria, Apollonius and their works.

Among other Christian scholars and authors, Origen receives the most detailed treatment, which includes the education he received, his austerity and Biblical scholarship, his pupils and works. The systematic persecution of the emperor Decius (249—251 AD) is particularly cruel. New heresies (Sabellianism, Novatianism, Manicheism) threaten Christian unity (books 6 and 7). The first 7 books follow the growth of the Church from the beginning up to the year 280. Books 8 and 9 describe the "Great Persecution" lasting from 303 to 313 AD, and book 10 adds a report on the situation after the year 313 AD: churches are restored, the imperial laws grant basic rights to Christians, and clerics become exempt from public service. The author does not discuss the conflicts over Arianism, Melitianism and Donatism, nor does he mention the synods (bishops' conferences) of the years 324 and 325 AD. Since Eusebius' main sources come from the church archives at Caesarea and Jerusalem, his knowledge of the developments in the West and many Eastern areas is rather limited. Being an adherent of the Origenist school he pays special attention to the Christian community in Alexandria. Eusebius records the succession of bishops of the most important cities, but also the names of ecclesiastical authors and the titles of their works. (Most of these works are lost.)

Being the first historical record of this kind, the *Church History* is an epoch-making work, and Eusebius is aware of his pioneering role. The work is a chief primary source because Eusebius, being a true historian, often quotes literally from the manuscripts he collected. His comprehensive study also relied on the favors of emperor Constantine who allowed him to use the imperial archives. Therefore the author who personally met Constantine four times (in 325, 327, 335, and 336 AD) wrote a panegyric (praise) on the emperor, which is a part of his collection "Life of Constantine" (written in 337 AD).

# 亚大纳西（295—373 AD）

他生于埃及，比较早就成为圣职人员，于325年以执事和主教秘书的身份陪同他的主教Alexandros参加Nicaea的主教会议，并于328年成为Alexandria的宗主教。他一生反对Arius派的异端主张，又使一些属于Meletios派的人重新皈依公教。部分东方主教335年在Eusebios主教的领导下举行了一个主教会议，其中控诉Athanasios说他的祝圣因年龄太小而无效，又说他用暴力镇压Meletios派的人。Athanasios逃难到Constantinopolis，而首都的皇帝流放他到Trier（德国）。他于337年才能回到Alexandria继续当主教。339年他再次被迫逃难，这次去了罗马。罗马的主教确认他为埃及的正统大主教，使他于346年能凯旋式地回到Alexandria去。因为Constantius皇帝（351-361年在位）反对Athanasios，他于356到361年间被迫在埃及沙漠的隐修院中避难6年之久。Julianus皇帝召回了一切被流放的主教们，包括Athanasios，所以他于362年夏天在Alexandria召开了一次主教会议，在会议中巩固了Nicaea会议的正统信仰。此后Julianus皇帝又流放了他，但皇帝不久后（363年）被暗杀。Athanasios成功地向新皇帝Jovianus提交了他的《信经》，但这位皇帝突然死去（364年）。他的继承人Valens坚定地支持Arius派，所以于365年冬天又想驱逐Athanasios，但于366年2月收回了他的决策。Athanasios前后被流放5次，但始终坚持正统的信仰（基督与圣父"同性同体"，即homoousios，参见Nicaea主教会议），所以成为最有名的埃及主教和教父。

**著作：**《向君士坦提乌斯陈词》、《反驳阿里乌派》、《为逃亡辩护》（在教难时，Athanasios主教在一个隐蔽的地方继续指导他的教区；他为自己的逃难作了说明）、《论降生，反驳阿里乌派》、《关于Nicaea会议规定的信》、《向埃及和北阿富利加各地主教的通信》、《节庆的信》（告诉埃及各地教会每年复活节的日期，其中367年的第39封信包括《圣经》正典诸书卷的目录）、《阿里乌派史》、《反驳外邦人》、《三驳阿里乌派的讲演》、《圣安托尼传》（埃及人安托尼是第一位重要的隐修士，开始了隐修生活的传统；参见Benedictus本笃。）

## 037.《反驳外邦人》

该护教文章在系统护教学的形成过程中具有重要的影响力。他大约写成于作者被流放到Trier（特里尔，即335—337年）的时期。该护教文献的第二个部分是一篇关于"圣言降生成人"的论述（名为 *Logos peri tēs enanthrōpeseos tou logou*《论逻各斯成为人》）。

第一部分根据一些心理学的观察深入地描述异教徒的崇拜。罪恶本身不存在，它是人的思想的产物。人们投入于偶像崇拜，因为他们滥用了他们的自由。他们离开了上主并成为他们身体欲望的奴隶，并且认为他们可以随心所欲。人们崇拜有色有形的

# Athanasios / Athanasius

**Opera:** *Apologia ad Constantium imperatorem, Apologia contra Arianos, Apologia de fuga, De incarnatione contra Arianos, Epistola de decretis Nicaene synodi, Epistola encyclica ad episcopos Aegyptii et Libyae, Epistolē heortastikē, Historia Arianorum ad monachos, Logos kata tōn Hellēnōn* (=*Oratio contra gentes*), *Tres Orationes contra Arianos, Vita S. Antonii*

**Works:** *Apology to the Emperor Constantine, Apology against the Arianists, Apology for My Escape, On Incarnation against the Arianists, Letter on the Decisions of the Synod of Nicaea, Encyclical Letter to the bishops of Egypt and Libya, Festal Letter, History of Arianism, Speech against the Gentiles, Three Sermons against the Arianists, The Life of St. Anthony*

## 037. *Logos kata tōn Hellēnōn / Speech against the Gentiles*

This apology is one of the works that became fundamental for the tradition of systematic apologetics. It was probably written before or during the exile of Athanasius in Trier, Germany (335—337 AD). The second part of the apology is a treatise on the incarnation (*Logos peri tēs enanthrōpeseos tou logou* = *Treatise on the Word Becoming Human*).

The first part is an extensive description of pagan worship, structured according to psychological observations. Evil does not exist, it is a product of human thought. Men adhere to idol worship because they abused their freedom. They turned away from God and became slaves of their bodily desires, thinking that they are allowed to do whatever they can do. The adoration of sensual things has its roots in the perversion of the human heart. Without the intention to do so, the (Greek) poets have described depraved desires and the evil actions of the gods and so exposed the fact that these gods are not real gods at all. No

东西是因为人心的腐败。古希腊的诗人们描述了神明们的邪恶欲望或不良行动,这样他们就无意识地揭露了这样的事实:这些神明根本就不是真正的神灵。宇宙中没有任何一个部分是神圣的,因为一切部分都依赖于另一些部分。另外,整个宇宙也不可称为"神",因为它的各个部分不断地处于冲突和矛盾之中。

在下面的章节中,作者谈论人灵魂的本性和命运,同时充分表现出 Alexandria 教父学中的"基督教柏拉图主义"倾向。真理只能在内心中找到,即是在灵魂(psychē)和心神(nous)之中。作者这样理解《圣经》中的名言"天国在你们中间"。人心既分享理性,又分享永生,正如 Platōn 的论点所证明那样。因此如果灵魂摆脱了各种欲望,它就能转向关于神的原初的知识。因为只有一个宇宙,说只有一个神也符合理性。唯一的神是耶稣基督的父亲,他是永恒的 Logos(圣言、道),而整个世界就是通过他而创造的。因此,这个逻各斯在受造界中启示自己,但他也在耶稣基督降生成人时启示自己。

*Logos peri tēs enanthrōpeseos tou Logou*(《论逻各斯成为人》)的成书时间与 *Logos kata tōn Hellēnōn*(《反驳外邦人》)相同,两部著作有密切关系。人们(和世界一样)是通过逻各斯(圣言)而创造的,但通过罪恶人失去了与圣言的合一,因此人丢失了真正的、精神性的生命。只有上主的圣言能够再次激活人类。逻各斯居住在耶稣内,而通过耶稣的死亡,人类堕落带来的罪责被除掉。面对死亡的人类获得拯救。十字架的胜利表现在两方面:异教徒的神明们逐渐消失,而殉道者们不怕死亡。神圣的逻各斯必须居住在一个人的身体内,因为他需要与那个期待着拯救的受造物合一。因为逻各斯能够在受造界的任何部分中显示它自己,它也能够在一个人的身体内出现。针对犹太人的不信,作者指出说《旧约》(尤其是 *Dan* 9:24)无疑是预告了弥赛亚将会在耶稣的时代出现。

## 038.《圣安托尼传》

这部传记的希腊书名是 *Ho bios kai hē politeia tou hosiou patros hēmon Antoniou*(《我们神圣之父安托尼的生活及其团体》)。这关于一位基督徒圣人的第一个 vita(传记)在 356 年后不久成书。在后来的时期中,它成为古代基督宗教界最流行的著作之一(仅次于《圣经》)。很多中世纪的传记以它为典范。该 vita(传记)保存有 Antiochia 的主教 Evagrios 的拉丁文译本,但也保存了一些非常古老的叙利亚文、科普特文、亚美尼亚文及格鲁吉亚文译本。Athanasios 亲自见过 Antonius,而后者早在有生之年就已经被称为"隐修运动之父"。

Antonius(安托尼)生于公元 251 年,他是埃及中部地区一位比较富有的基督徒的儿子并曾经是一个普通的孩童和青少年。当他 20 岁时,他的父母去世。在参与教会礼仪时他听到福音的教导,尤其因 *Mt* 19:21("如果你渴望做个完全的人,你应该变卖你的一切……")和 *Mk* 6:34 被感动,就决定过一种彻底的 askēsis(克修)生活。一段

part of the universe is divine, because all parts depend on each other. Neither can the universe as a whole be "god" because its parts are in a constant fight and conflict.

The following chapters contain an important discussion of the nature and destination of the human soul, which fully manifests the elements of Christian Platonism which is alive in the Alexandrine tradition. The way of truth is found only within, namely in the soul (psychē) and in its spirit (nous). This is the author's interpretation of the Biblical word "The kingdom of God is among you". The human soul is rational and immortal, as Plato's arguments show. If therefore the soul abandons its desires it can return to the original knowledge of God. Since there is only one universe, it is reasonable to assume that there is only one God. This one God is the Father of Jesus Christ, the eternal Logos (Word), through whom the world was created. Therefore this Word is revealed in creation, but it has also revealed itself through the incarnation of the Logos in Jesus Christ.

The *Logos peri tēs enanthrōpeseos tou Logou* (*Treatise on the Word Becoming Human*) was written at the same time as the *Logos kata tōn Hellēnōn* and is connected with it. Human Beings were created (like the world) through the Logos (Word), but through sin man lost the grace of unity with the Word and therefore forfeited real, spiritual life. Only God's Word can lead mankind back to life. The Logos dwelt in Jesus, and through Jesus' death the guilt of the fall of mankind was taken away. Man is saved from death. The victory of the cross is manifested in two ways: the pagan gods disappear and the martyrs are not afraid of death. The divine Logos had to dwell in a human body because it needed to be united with that part that awaited salvation. Since the Logos can manifest itself in any part of the creation, it is not unreasonable that it appeared in a human body. Addressing the disbelief of the Jews, the author points out that the prophecies of the Old Testament (especially *Daniel* 9:24) doubtless announce the coming of the Messiah in Jesus' time.

## 038. *Vita Sancti Antonii* / *The Life of St. Anthony*

The Greek title of this biography is *Ho bios kai hē politeia tou hosiou patros hēmon Antoniou* (*The Life and the Community of Our Saintly Father Antonius*). This first "vita" (biography) of a Christian saint was written shortly after 356 AD. It subsequently became the second most popular book of Christian antiquity after the Bible. Many medieval biographies are modeled on it. The *Vita* is preserved in a Latin translation made by Bishop Evagrios of Antioch, but there are also very old Syrian, Coptic, Armenian and Georgian versions. Athanasius knew Antonius personally, and the latter was named "Father of Monasticism" already in his lifetime.

Born in 251 in the middle part of Egypt as the son of well-to-do Christian parents, Antonius leads a normal life in his youth. When he is 20 years old, his parents die. Hearing the gospel passages *Mt* 19:21 ("if you want to be perfect, go and sell everything you have") and *Mk* 6:34 as they are read in the church, he is moved and decides to lead a radical life of asceticism. For some time, he lives in a tomb chamber, then for 20 years

时间他生活在一个墓屋中,此后20年生活在沙漠中的旧堡垒的废墟里,他多次遭受一些以野兽形象出现的恶鬼的强烈攻击。魔鬼多次试图引诱他放弃克修生活,甚至在夜间以美女的形象诱惑他。最终他独居在离红海不远的山区(Der Mar Antonios)。在311年的教难时期,他曾经去Alexandria安慰和鼓励那些坐牢或受审判的基督徒。此后他又退隐到沙漠中去。许多人去找他,想要听他的建议或求他治病,而一些人决定要和他一起在沙漠当"隐修者"(monachos)。Athanasios使用很大的篇幅来叙述Antonius的治病能力,他的先知预感,以及他的visiones(神视)。Antonius预先知道自己什么时候要死去,这就是圣人(圣徒)的特征(后来写的许多圣人传也含有同样的因素)。他在356年去世(根据Hieronymus的*Chronicon*),享年105岁。从Antonius的书信中(以阿拉伯文保存的),我们知道他熟悉Ōrigenēs的思想。

in the ruins of a fortress in the desert, often facing the attacks of many fierce demons which appear in the shapes of wild animals. The devil repeatedly tries to lead him away from his strict ascetic life style, even appearing in the shape of a woman at night. Finally Antonius lives in solitude at a mountain not far from the Red Sea (Der Mar Antonios). During the persecution of 311 AD, he travels to Alexandria in order to console and encourage imprisoned and sentenced Christians. Then he retreats to the desert again. Many come to ask him for advice or healing, and some stay with him in the desert to be "monks" (monachos) like him. Athanasius spends much time to narrate many stories that show Antonius' healing powers, his prophetic gifts and his visions. He foretells his own death, which is a sign of holiness (often repeated in subsequent biographies of saints). He dies at the age of 105 in the year 356 AD (according to Jerome's *Chronicle*). From Antonius' letters, extant in the Arabic language, we know that he was acquainted with Origen's ideas.

# 诺尼乌斯（约 300—350 AD）

他来自 Numidia,生平不详,大概生活在第 4 世纪前半叶。

**著作**:《教育手册》(20 卷,除了第 16 卷外都保存,讨论语言、语法和专用名字、术语等,算为一种百科全书,保存 Varro 等人的许多资料)

## 039.《教育手册》

作者为自己的儿子写了这部百科全书式的文集(共 20 卷),只有第 16 卷(谈论鞋子)失传。Nonius 使用了 Gellius 的 *Noctes Atticae* 作为他的资料书。

第一部分(1~12 卷)谈论早期拉丁作者的语法和语言风格问题。尤其重要的是第 4 卷,在其中解释了很多词语涵义的不同层面,并按照 ABC 顺序排列这些词汇。第二部分(13~20 卷)的每一个卷说明一个特殊的知识领域:船只(第 13 卷)、衣服(14)、各种器皿(15)、布料的染料和颜色(17)、饮食(18)、武器(19)以及亲戚关系的种种名称(20)。作者提供很多定义和同义词,他引用了 40 多部拉丁著作。对于早期作者的一些语录,Nonius 的著作是最重要的资料书之一, 尤其保存了 Ennius、Lucilius 和 Varro 的文献残篇。

# Nonius Marcellus

**Opera:** *De compendiosa doctrina*
**Works:** *Handbook of Instruction*

### 039.  *De compendiosa doctrina / Handbook of Instruction*

This encyclopaedic text collection of 20 books was written for the son of the author, only book 16 (concerning shoes) is lost. Nonius used Gellius' *Noctes Atticae* (*Attic Nights*) as a source book.

The first part (books 1~12) is concerned with grammar and diction of the older Latin writers. Book 4 is particularly interesting, since it explains the different layers of the meaning of words. The entries are arranged according to the alphabet. In the second part (books 13~20) each book deals with a certain theme: ships (book 13), dress and clothing (14), all kinds of vessels (15), colours of dresses (17), food and drinks (18), weapons (19), and the names for family relationships (20). The author presents many definitions and synonyms of words, and he quotes from more than 40 works by Latin authors. Nonius is the main source for fragments of early writings, especially for the works of Ennius, Lucilius, and Varro.

# 奥索尼乌斯（约310—393 AD）

法国地区 Burdigala（Bordeaux）的诗人，曾成为 Gratianus（Valentinianus I 皇帝的儿子）的老师，379年担任执政官，后回到高卢；他自己是基督徒，也曾是圣人 Paulinus of Nola 的老师。

**著作：**《一天中所发生的事》（一首诗，内容是诗人普通的一天生活）、《书信集》、《莫萨拉河》（详细地描述了这条德国河流的美丽和河边的文化）

## 040. 《书信集》

这部书信集包含34封信，有散文，也有诗歌。这些信写给 Ausonius 的父亲、他的儿子、孙子、Symmachus（参见 *Relationes*）以及写给 Paulinus——他是作者的学生和朋友，后来成为 Nola 的主教。在古代文献中，这是唯一的描述老师和学生之间的书信对话的例子。Ausonius 尽力劝勉 Paulinus 不要过分严肃地对待基督宗教，但他的学生 Paulinus 回信说他宁可以放弃与 Ausonius 的友情，也不会放弃当隐修者和独身者的计划。

# Decimus Magnus Ausonius / Ausonius

**Opera:** *Ephemeris, Epistulae, Mosella*
**Works:** *A day's events, Letters, The Mosel River*

## 040. *Epistulae / Letters*

This collection of 34 letters in verse and prose contains letters to Ausonius' father, his son, grandson, to Symmachus (conf: *Relationes*), and to Paulinus, student and friend of the author, who later became Bishop of Nola. This is the only example from classical literature which records a literary dialogue between a teacher (Ausonius) and a student (Paulinus). Ausonius tries to persuade Paulinus not to take Christianity too serious, but his student Paulinus answers that he would rather give up the friendship to Ausonius than to retreat from his plan to lead an ascetic and celibate life.

# 基里洛斯（约 313—387 AD）

他约于 348 年（或 350 年）被祝圣为 Jerusalem（耶路撒冷）的主教，但因 Arius 派的影响三次被迫离开该城（357—359 年，360—362 年，367—378 年）。他也长期和 Caesarea 的大主教（metropolita）Akakios 有冲突，因为这位主教不愿意承认耶路撒冷教会及 Kyrillos 主教的特殊地位。Kyrillos 曾向 Constantius II 皇帝写了一封关于十字架的显现的信（351 年）。Julianus 皇帝于 362 年想重建耶路撒冷的圣殿，但 Kyrillos 反对这个计划。虽然早期的 Kyrillos 曾一时倾向于 Arius 派的某些主张（比如"homoiousios"的说法），但在 Constantinopolis 的主教会议上（381 年），他肯定正统的信仰，后来也被承认为一个教父。

**著作**：《教理讲授》

## 041. 《教理讲授》

这 24 篇《教理讲授》是 Kyrillos 最著名的著作。他大约在 348 年或 350 年在耶路撒冷的圣墓教堂（由 Constantinus 皇帝建立）中发表了这些讲演。

前面的 18 篇《教理讲授》——Kyrillos 在四斋期发表它们——面向那些准备领洗的人（即所谓的 phōtizomenoi 或 catechumens）。最后五篇讲演稿（被称为 *katēchēseis mystagōgikoi* 或《神秘的教理讲授》）面向那些刚刚领洗的人（即 neophōtistoi）。第 1 到第 5 篇讲演稿是以罪、忏悔和信仰为核心的。此后的讲演稿解释洗礼仪式中要宣布的信仰经文（"圣洗信经"），即对于三位一体的神的信仰，圣父是造物主，耶稣基督是上主的独生子，他降生成人，由 Maria 诞生，曾在十字架上受苦受难，被埋葬，但第三天复活了。所谓的《神秘的教理讲授》解释那些一般在复活节举行的圣事：第 19 和 20 篇谈论圣洗，21 篇说明坚振，22 篇解释感恩祭，而第 23 篇介绍信徒的仪式。Kyrillos 主教在耶路撒冷的接班人 Iōannēs 可能重新编写了这 5 篇《教理讲授》。

值得注意的是这一点，即 Kyrillos 有意识地回避了 Nicaea 主教会议提出的"homousios"术语（即基督和圣父是"同性同体"的），因为他认为这种说法将会引发 Sabellius 的异端（过分强调三位一体的合一性）。除此之外，在《圣经》中没有"homousios"这个词。然而，Kyrillos 很坚定地拒绝了 Arius 派的一切重要观点并宣认基督是"来自天主的天主"和"真神"。在礼仪史方面，Kyrillos 也有特殊的贡献，因为他培养了耶路撒冷教会的习俗和礼仪。这样他逐渐形成了"圣周"和复活节的礼仪程序。那些来耶路撒冷朝圣的人将 Kyrillos 的复活节礼仪传到整个基督宗教世界。

# Kyrillos / Cyril of Jerusalem

**Opera:** *Katēchēseis*
**Works:** *Catecheses*

## 041. *Katēchēseis* / *Catecheses*

These 24 catechetical lectures are the most famous of Cyril's works. He held most of them in the Church of the Sepulcre (built by emperor Constantine) in Jerusalem in 348 or 350 AD.

The first 18 lectures, which Cyril delivered during the fasting period of Lent, address those who prepare themselves to be baptized (the so-called phōtizomenoi or catechumens). The last five catecheses (*Katēchēseis mystagōgikai*, or "mystagogical catecheses") were held for the newly baptized believers ("neophōtistoi"). The first five orations are focus on sin, penance, and the Christian faith. The following catecheses explain the formulation of the Christian faith that was to be confessed at baptism ("baptismal creed"): the faith in the Triune God, in the Creator, in the only Son of God, Jesus Christ, who became man and was born by Mary, who suffered on the cross, died, and was buried, but rose on the third day. The "mystagogical catecheses" explain the sacraments that are celebrated at Easter: Nr. 19 and 20 are on baptism, 21 on the confirmation, 22 on the eucharist, and 23 on the liturgy of the believers. These last five mystagogical catecheses were possibly rewritten by Cyril's successor, Bishop John of Jerusalem.

It is interesting to note that Cyril consciously avoided the Nicene formula "homousios" (meaning Jesus Christ is "one in being" with the Father), because he thought that this term would lead to the heresy of Sabellianism, which overemphasizes the unity of the three Persons of the Trinity. Besides that, the term "homousios" is not found in the Bible. However, Cyril consistently rejected all the main teachings of Arianism and confessed Christ as "God from God" and "true God". In the history of liturgy Cyril made a special contribution, since he fostered and cultivated the customs and liturgy of the church of Jerusalem. His efforts helped to shape the cycle of the Holy Week and the cel-

Kyrillos 比以前的教父们更清楚地表达了对基督临在于感恩祭的信仰。他使用了"metaballesthai"这个词来描述"体变说",即是说在弥撒中的面饼和葡萄酒真正成为基督的圣体和圣血。他也提到另一个习俗:信徒们在弥撒中为亡者祈祷(所谓"commemoratio mortuorum")。

让我们看看 Kyrillos 如何说明将临期和圣诞节的意义(*Katēchēseis* 15,1~3):"我们宣讲基督的到来,不仅仅是第一次的到来,而且还有第二次的来临,他将光荣辉煌,远远超过第一次。主的第一次来临是痛苦中的来临,但他第二次的降临将会戴上神圣荣耀的冠冕。对于我们的主耶稣基督来说,很多事是双重的:他是两次诞生的,因为他在万世之前由圣父而生,而时期一满,他是由童贞女诞生的。他的来临也是双重的:一次到来是隐藏的、悄悄的,如同 Gideon 羊皮上的露水(参见 *Jgs* 6:36-40);第二次来临将是公开的,在众人眼前的,但这是将来的事。在第一次来临的时候他裹着旧布躺在马槽里,但在第二次来临时光芒将会环照他,就像一件衣服(参见 *Ps* 104:2)。在第一次来临时他背上十字架并且没有抵抗人们的侮辱。在第二次来临时却会有一群天使围绕他并敬拜他。

因此我们不仅仅相信基督的第一次来临,而且也期待他的第二次到来。正如我们曾在他的第一次来临时快乐地呼喊说'奉主名而来的那位是被祝福的'(参见 *Mt* 21:9),我们将来也同样欢迎他的第二次来临。我们将和天使们一同敬拜他并呼喊说:'奉主名而来的那位是被祝福的。'救世主将要来,不是为了要再次受审判,而是为了审判那些曾经判决他的人。在第一次的来临,当他被判刑时他保持缄默,但在将来的那一天他将要向他们指出他们的罪行,就是他们把他钉在十字架上的罪。他将对他们说:'你们做了这些事,而我沉默无言。'(参见 *Ps* 50:21)

因此,我们承受传下来的信条是这样的:'我们信升天并坐在圣父之右边的那位。他还要光荣地再来,将要审判生者和死者,而他的王国将永无终结。'因此我们的主耶稣基督还要降临,在最后的日子在世界的末期,他将光荣地降临。那时这个世界将会达到其终点,它将被更新。"

ebration of Easter. Through pilgrims who came to Jerusalem his liturgy of Easter spread across the world of Christendom. Cyril expressed the faith in the real presence of Christ in the eucharist more clearly than any of theologians before him. He used the word "metaballesthai" to describe the transsubstantiation, namely the view that bread and wine truly become the Body and Blood of Christ during Holy Mass. He also mentions the custom to pray for the dead during the Mass ("commemoratio mortuorum").

Let us see how Cyrillus explains the meaning of the Advent season and of Christmas (*Katēchēseis* 15,1~3): "We proclaim the coming of Christ, and not only the first, but also the second coming, which is far more glorious than the first. That first coming of the Lord was marked by suffering, but this second parousia will be crowned with the diadem of divine glory. For many things are given to our Lord Jesus Christ in a twofold way: His twofold birth, since He was born of God before all time, and he was born of a virgin in the fullness of time. His coming is twofold, too: one advent was hidden and secret like the dew on Gideon's fleece (compare *Jgs* 6:36–40), and the other will be in public before the whole world, though this will be in the future. At His first coming he lay wrapped in swaddling clothes in a crib; at His second coming He will be shrouded in light like in a vestment (compare *Ps* 104:2). At His first coming He carried the cross and did not resist humiliation. At His second coming hosts of angels will surround Him and glorify Him.

Thus we do not only confess His first coming but also expect the second coming of Christ. Just as we have shouted in joy at His first arrival and cried out: 'Blessed is He who comes in the name of the Lord' (compare *Mt* 21:9), so we will also do at His second arrival. Together with the angels we will welcome Him, venerate Him and shout: 'Blessed is He who comes in the name of the Lord.' The Savior will come, not in order to be judged a second time, but in order to judge those who passed judgment on him. At the first time He was silent when He was condemned. But on that day He will make manifest their crime unto them, namely the crime by which they forced him under the cross. And He will tell them: "You have done these things, and I kept silence." (compare *Ps* 50:21).

Thus the doctrine of the faith that has come down to us is like this: 'We believe in Him who ascended to heaven and is seated at the right hand of the Father. He will come again in glory to judge the living and the dead, and His kingdom will have no end.' Thus our Lord Jesus Christ will come again from above. He will come in glory on the Last Day at the end of the world. Then this world will arrive at its end, and when this happens it will be renewed."

# 多纳图斯(约 320—380 AD)

拉丁语语文老师,曾经是 Hieronymus 的教师。

**著作:**《拉丁语法基础》/《拉丁语法中级》、《泰伦斯评论》

## 042. 《拉丁语法基础》/《拉丁语法中级》

这两部拉丁语法书在整个欧洲中世纪都是基本的教科书,并且影响了 Priscianus 的巨著 *Institutio de arte grammatica*（《语法导论》,18 卷,大约成书于 500 年）以及 Isidorus 的 *Etymologiae*（《语源学》）等作者。关于早期的拉丁语法书请参见 Varro 的 *De lingua Latina*（《论拉丁语》）。

*Ars minor* 以问答的方式介绍语言的 8 个"部分"(partes orationis),即 8 种不同类型的词(名词、形容词、代词、动词、副词、介词、连词、感叹词)。*Ars maior* 分为三部分:语音学(phonologia,即音、字母、音节)、形态学(morphologia,即不同类型词的不同变格形式)以及修辞学(stilistica,即介绍语言和隐喻的用法)。

# Aelius Donatus / Donatus

**Opera:** *Ars minor / Ars maior, Commentum Terenti*
**Works:** *Introduction to Grammar / Further Grammar Studies, Commentary on Terence*

## 042. *Ars minor / Ars maior*

These two books of Latin grammar from the 4th century were the basic textbooks for Latin throughout the Middle Ages and also influenced the much larger *Institutio de arte grammatica* (*Introduction to Grammar*, 18 volumes, written by Priscianus in 500 AD) and Isidore's *Etymologies*. For earlier textbooks of Latin grammar, see Varro *De lingua Latina*.

The *Ars minor* uses the question-and-answer style to present the eight "parts of oration" (partes orationis), namely the different kinds of words: noun (nomen), adjective (adiectivum), pronoun (pronomen), verb (verbum), adverb (adverbium), preposition (praepositio), conjunction (coniunctio), interjection (interiectio). The *Ars maior* is divided into three parts: phonology (phonologia, namely: sounds, letters, syllables), morphology (morphologia, namely: the different flective forms of the various types of words), and style (stilistica, an introduction to the rhetorical use of language and metaphorical expressions).

# 阿米阿努斯（约 330—395 AD）

来自 Antiocheia 的拉丁作者，参与了 Ursicius 将军在意大利、高卢和东方的军事活动，后为 Julianus 皇帝服务，晚年居住在罗马。他曾被称作在 Tacitus 之后最伟大的历史学家。

**著作**：《历史》（31卷，记载96年到378年的历史，只保存了14~31卷，即从353年到378年的详细记载）

## 043.《历史》

本著作叙述罗马历史，即从 Nerva 皇帝的登基（96年）到 Valens 皇帝的逝世（378年），成书时间是395年和400年间。全部著作共有31卷，但只有最后18卷被保存（第14到31卷），他们描述从350年到378年的时期，这也包括 Julianus 皇帝（号称"背教者"，360—363年）的时代——Ammianus 认为他是一个具有哲学思想和修养的统治者，他结合了智慧与修辞学的才华。

作者尽可能客观地描述当时的种种事件，他想叙述"真相"（veritas, 31,16,9）。他对基督宗教怀着某种中立的态度并认为这个新的信仰是"绝对的和简朴的"（Christiana religio absoluta et simplex, 21,16,18）。作者是希腊人，因此他很强调希腊文化与罗马文化之间的合一性。他的叙述插入了很多小故事，其中有一些讽刺罗马生活的文献，也有一些涉及地理学知识或科学和技术方面的观察。他也曾描述匈奴等部落的文化。在第14卷中，Ammianus 使用"从童年的老年"成长的比喻来描述罗马城。这座可敬的城市（urbs venerabilis）曾经征服了很多民族并如同一个明智的母亲（parens prudens）为他们提供了种种法律作为自由的基础（fundamenta libertatis, 14, 6, 5）。

# Ammianus Marcellinus

**Opera:** *Rerum gestarum libri*
**Works:** *History*

## 043. *Rerum gestarum libri / History*

This record of Roman history from the year 96 (Emperor Nerva) until the death of Emperor Valens (378) was written between 395 and 400. Of 31 books only the last 18 (books 14~31) are preserved, they cover the years from 350 until 378, which includes the reign of Emperor Julian (the Apostate, 360—363) whom Ammianus depicts as a philosophical and educated ruler who combines wisdom and rhetorical talent.

The author tries to give an objective account of the essential events of his time, he wants to depict the "truth" (veritas, 31,16,9). He is neutral towards Christianity and judges the new faith to be "consequent and simple" (Christiana religio absoluta et simplex, 21,16,18). Being from Greek descent he emphasizes the unity of Greek and Roman culture. The narrative is interspersed with many digressions, some of them are satirical attacks on the city of Rome, other insertions present interesting observations on geography or technical details. The work also contains descriptions of the life of certain tribes in northern Europe, for example of the Huns. In book 14 Ammianus describes the history of Rome using the metaphor of a person growing from childhood to adulthood. The dignified city (urbs venerabilis) has subdued many peoples and like a prudent mother (parens prudens) gave them laws and the foundations of freedom (fundamenta libertatis). (14, 6, 5)

# (大)巴西略（330—379 AD）

他生于 Cappadocia 的 Caesarea 的贵族家庭，生活在一个充满基督精神的环境中；他的母亲是一位殉道者的女儿。他的两个弟兄 Grēgorios Nyssenos 和 Petros 都是主教。Basileios 曾经在 Caesarea、Constantinopolis 和 Athenae 受教育，在那里结识了 Grēgorios Nazianzos，他于 356 年返回家乡，著名的演讲学家 Libanios 曾经赞扬他的口才，但他放弃了修辞学家的光荣并在 Cappadocia 当一个隐修者。他曾去埃及、巴勒斯坦和美索不达米亚以认识最著名的隐修者。不久后，他的隐修生活方式吸引了 Grēgorios Nazianzos 和另外一些人士。在 368 年的饥荒中，他帮助了很多人。370 年他被提名为 Caesarea（在 Cappadocia）的主教。他重视隐修院的文化，也建立了一些照顾病人的慈善机构，曾与 Alexandria 的 Athanasios 主教以及罗马的 Damasus 主教保持书信来往，以之克服教会内部的张力。他也坚定地抵抗 Valens 皇帝（378 年去世）和 Arius 派的压力。

**著作**：(根据近代的研究成果，他写了 362 部著作，这里只能列出最重要的)：《修道生活教导》(亦译《禁欲论》)、《论洗礼》、《信集》、《论六天创造九篇》(亦译《解经九篇》，论述上主的创造工程和宇宙的秩序)、《论圣咏》(《译诗篇》13 篇)、《驳斥欧诺弥书》、《论圣神》(《论圣灵》)、《泛谈伦理》(亦译《道德论》)、《论文集》(Ōrigenēs 著作的选集)、《修道规则》。

## 044. 《修道生活教导》

这部关于隐修生活原则的文集的原文是希腊语，但 Rufinus 将它译成拉丁语，所以 Benedictus de Nursia 在编写自己的 *Regula*（《会规》）时受其影响。

整个文集包括 80 条隐修规则（regulae）。作为一种导论，作者写了两篇论文，第一篇是关于神的审判（*De iudicio Dei*），第二篇是关于信仰（*De fide*）。55 个隐修规则得到比较深入的讨论，作者使用"疑问和回答"的形式澄清这些问题（这个部分被称为 *Regulae fusius tractatae*《深入谈论的规则》）。另外加入的还有 313 条教育性的格言，这个部分被称为 *Regulae brevius tractatae*（《简略谈论的规则》）。

Basileios 在自己的隐修院（koinobion）中（在小亚细亚的 Neokaisareia）写出这些规则。其中的基本灵修概念是这样的：因为世俗的世界很腐败，人们应该爱神，努力寻求与神的合一。人们很自然地追求美善。神是最高的善，所以一切人的努力都指向神。人间的事物没有长久的意义，它们不是永恒的价值，所以我们应该放弃这些，与它们保持距离。只有一个不受物质控制的灵魂才能够接近神。个别灵魂的这种解放不能通过独处性的个人苦修生活而达到，更好的方式是共同的隐修生活（隐修院被称为 koinobion = koinos bios "共同的生活"）。

# Basileios / Basilius Magnus / Basil the Great

**Opera:** *Askētika, De Baptismo, Epistulae, Hexaemeron, Homiliae ad Psalmis, Kata Eunomiou (Adversus Eunomium), Liber de Spiritu Sancto, Moralia, Philokalia, Regulae Fusius tractatae*

**Works:** *Ascetic Admonitions, On Baptism, Letters, Hexaemeron, On the Psalms, Against Eunomios, On the Holy Spirit, Moralia, Philocalia, Rules*

## 044. *Askētika / Ascetic Admonitions*

This collection of rules for monastic life was written in Greek, but Rufinus translated it into Latin, and thus it had some influence on the *Rule (Regula)* of Benedict of Nursia.

The collection comprises 80 rules (regulae) for monks. Basilius wrote two introductory essays, one on the judgement of God (*De iudicio Dei*), and a second on the faith (*De fide*). In an additional treatise the author discusses 55 rules in greater detail in the form of questions and answers under the title *Regulae fusius tractatae*. Another collection of 313 educational proverbs is known as *Regulae brevius tractatae*.

These rules were written in Basilius' own monastery (koinobion) in Neocaesarea. Their basic spirituality is like this: since the world is corrupt, man must strive to find union with God in the love of God. Man searches naturally for good. God is the highest good himself, therefore all human efforts are directed towards God. Earthly matters have no lasting meaning, they are not eternal values. We must leave them behind and detach ourselves from them. Only a soul that is free from the shackles of matter can be close to God. This liberation of the individual soul is not brought about by solitary asceticism, but rather by the life in a monastic community (cf. "koinobion" = koinos bios "common life").

这里有一段来自 *Regulae fusius tractatae*（2,2~4）的原文："当神按照自己的肖像创造了人时,他以自知的能力提升了人,又赋予他理性之光,使他和一切动物有差异。神给予人们能力去欣赏乐园的奇妙美丽,最终使人类成为世上万物的元首。此后人使魔鬼欺骗自己,陷入罪恶,而通过罪恶又走向死亡（参见 *Rom* 5:15）,同时遭受他应受的苦难。上主仍然没有放弃他,但赋予了他律法作为一种帮助。他将人交托于天使们的照顾（参见 *Hebr* 1:14）,又派遣先知们来纠正人们的罪并教导他们追求种种美德。通过严厉惩罚的威胁上主挫败并消除邪恶力量的攻击。借着一些许诺神又激励人们热切追求美善。神曾多次立这双重劝勉的榜样来教训人们。当我们的态度还很顽固时,他仍然没有转面不顾。

神的美善从来没有离开过我们,上主甚至从死亡中将我们叫回来,并通过我们的主耶稣基督再次赋予我们生命。……'我怎样能回报上主赐予我的一切恩惠？'（*Ps* 116:12）然而,神是如此美善的,他不要求任何回报。如果他因他的种种恩赐得到人们的爱,他就满足了。要我说是什么事在这些考虑中使我不安,那就是这个可能性:我害怕并且感到恐惧,因为我有可能因疏忽或空虚的挂虑将会脱离神爱。我将来还会使基督受侮辱或蔑视吗？"

## 045. 《论六天创造》

这部著作由 9 篇（希腊语的）讲演稿构成,主要内容是谈论世界在六天内的创造。作者强调说,上主的圣言是大自然秩序的基础,但同时他也利用早期的非基督宗教作者的著作（尤其是 Aristotelēs）来丰富自己关于自然科学的知识。

Basileios 的著作是关于《圣经》中"上主创造天地万物"的记载的注解。作者坚持一种更"字面上的理解",但同时也使用一些比喻性的解释。《圣经》的目标并不是反驳某些科学的理论,而是启发和激励精神性的生活。他认为,种种自然科学知识无法达到《圣经》的深度,但《圣经》反过来能够为科学研究提供宝贵的观察。外教传统关于宇宙的种种思想都无法达到《圣经》的创造故事的博大精深。

根据 Basileios 的理解,创造的开始并不是在时间之内,而是无时间的,是永恒的（参见 Ōrigenēs 的 *Peri archōn*）。当上主创造时间的本性时,他规定"日"为他的量度,并且规定一周有七日。所有创造物都指向人生的体验,但它们具有一种更深的、象征性的意义:太阳是基督的象征,因为基督是"正义的太阳"。月亮的朔望代表人间一切事物的暂时性,草花的枯萎提醒我们万物的变化无常。莠子是异端邪说的象征。正如在一棵不太高级的树枝上可以嫁接一根很好的树枝,人们也可以有"改过迁善"的机会,这一点对罪人来说应该是一种鼓励。某些动物找对象交配,这指向人的婚姻的不可拆解性。蜜蜂的勤劳和秩序感应该给人们一些灵感,使他们也同样建立社会的秩序或计划未来（参见作者不明的 *Physiologos* 一书）。

Here are some lines from the *Regulae fusius tractatae* (2,2~4): "When God created man according to His image and likeness, He ennobled man with the gift of self-knowledge and, different from the animals, bestowed unto him the gift of reason. He gave human beings the ability to rejoice in the miraculous beauty of the Paradise and finally established them as the head of all earthly things. Then man let himself be deceived by the devil, was caught by sin and through sin entered death (compare *Rom* 5:15) and faced the sufferings which he deserved. Still God did not forsake him, rather gave him the law as a kind of help. He entrusted man to the care and protection of angels (compare *Hebr* 1:14), sent prophets to correct his sins and to teach him the virtues. By way of threatening with punishment God repelled and thwarted the attacks of the evil. Through promises He aroused the zeal for the good. Quite often God has set examples of this twofold exhortation so as to admonish others. When we remained stubborn He still did not turn away from us.

The goodness of the Lord has never forsaken us, He even called us back from death, and through our Lord Jesus Christ He gave us back to life. (…) 'How can I repay the Lord all the good things He has done to me?' (*Ps* 116:12) But He is so good that He does not demand any repay. It is enough for Him if He is loved for His gifts. If I should say what moves my heart in all these considerations, then it is this: I am frightened and a terrible fear overcomes me at the possibility that I may deviate from the love of God through negligence or occupation with vain things. Will I ever be the cause that Christ suffers humiliation or dishonor?"

## 045. *Hexaemeron*

These nine sermons (written in Greek) are about the creation of the world in six days. The author emphasizes that God's word is the basis of the order of nature, but at the same time he used works of earlier non-Christian authors (especially Aristotle) on natural science as source-books for his knowledge about nature.

Basilius' work is a commentary to the Biblical account of God's creation. The author emphasizes a more literal understanding of the Bible, but he also uses allegorical interpretation. The Bible is not contradicting scientific theories but aims at edifying and encouraging spiritual life. Natural sciences cannot comprehend the depth of the Scriptures, but the Bible can provide valuable insights for scientific research. Pagan speculations about the cosmos are dwarfed by the magnificence and depth of the Biblical creation story.

According to Basilius the beginning of creation is not within time, it is timeless and eternal (cf. Origenes' *Peri archōn*). When God created the nature of time, He decreed that the "day" should be its measuring unit, one week having seven days. The created phenomena point to many human experiences, but they also have a deeper, symbolic meaning: the sun is a symbol of Christ, the "Sun of Justice", the waxing and waning of the moon reflects the transitoriness of all earthly things; grass and flowers remind us that all things are subjected to change. Weeds are a symbol of heresies. The possibility of grafting a nobler branch onto an inferior tree should encourage sinners to believe in the real possibility of conversion. The mating of certain animals points to the indissolubility of marriage, and the diligence and orderliness of bees should inspire human efforts to building up society and planning the future (confer the anonymous book *Physiologus*).

上主的话语创造了大自然,而他的命令规定了自然的法则。根据这个神规定的自然法则,水必然要往下流。根据《圣经》的说法,上主先创造了"天和地",而 Basileios 认为,"天"指火(最清净的元素),"地"指土(最低级的元素)。这样,他也能够推断另外两个传统物质元素,即"气"和"水"(参见 Platōn, *Timaios*),在很多科学知识的细节上,Basileios 大量利用了当时的希腊语工具书和手册。比如,在植物学和生物学上,Basileios 的最重要信息来源是 Aristotelēs、Poseidōnios 和 Stoa 学派的作者。

Nature was created by God's word, and His decree brought about the law of nature. The fact that water flows down is based on this law of nature, divinely ordained. According to the Bible, God first created heaven and earth. Basilius equates "heaven" with the purest element of "fire" and "earth" with the most basic element of "soil". In this way he arrives at the four basic elements fire, air, water, earth (cf. Plato's *Timaios*). At the same time, Basilius made extensive use of the Greek science he found in the numerous textbooks and handbooks of his time. For the empirical sciences of botany and zoology, Basilius' most important sources were Aristotle, Poseidonius and the Stoic writers.

# 格列高利（约 331—390 AD）

他是一位主教的儿子，曾在 Cappadocia 的 Caesarea、Palestina 的 Caesarea、Alexandria、Jerusalem 以及 Athenae 学习。他的同学是 Basileios 和后来的皇帝 Julianus。大约于 360 年他离开希腊，回到 Cappadocia 去，支持他的父亲管理 Nazianz 的教会，并被祝圣为司铎。在 370 年他支持 Basileios 当 Caesarea 的主教。为了对付 Arius 派的人，Basileios 于 372 年指定 Grēgorios 为 Sasima（在 Cappadocia）的主教，但 Grēgorios 没有去那里就任。当时 Constantinopolis 的正统派信徒（Nicaea 派）不多，而 Arius 派的圣职人员占多数，所以他们于 379 年请 Grēgorios 去首都。圣职人员和民众都支持他，所以他于 380 年被祝圣为 Constantinopolis 的主教，而 381 年在 Constantinopolis 举行的主教会议也承认他并选举他为会议的主席。此后，他因内部的争论退位，继续管理 Nazianz 教区，并在那里去世。

著作：《诗集》、《铭记》、《书信集》（共保存 240 封信）、《关于逃跑》、《讲演稿》（共保存 47 篇讲演稿）、《关于自己生活的诗》（《诗集》中的诗，是一部自传）、《论文集》（与 Basileios 一起编写的，为了传下 Ōrigenēs 的思想）。

## 046. 《诗集》

这部《诗集》大约包括 400 首诗，长达 16,000 行（即等于《伊利亚特》的篇幅）。它使用的韵律有变化，部分诗歌是伦理道德上的劝勉或教育诗，另一些是赞美诗，还有一些沉思式的诗或叙述性的史诗。

最有名的诗大概是 Grēgorios 写的"自传"（Carmen 2,1,11，亦称 Peri ton heautou bion），即以短长韵律写的、长达 1950 行的与 Augustinus 的 Confessiones 具有对比性的著作。与 Confessiones 一样，这部自传既无"前身"，又无"模仿者"。作者回顾自己一生，但更多地表示一种忧伤的态度，并不是一种很客观的叙述。他表达某些艰难的决定所带来的折磨。他出生在 Cappadocia 的 Nazianz，后来在 Palaestina 的 Caesarea、在 Alexandria 和 Athenae 学习。年轻时，他在雅典与他一生的朋友 Basileios 一起学习，并对自己父亲表示感谢，但在另一方面这两个人劝勉他在教会内任职，他们当时并没有关注他自己的倾向或意愿。Grēgorios 更想当一名隐修士，所以他必须在"入世生活"（vita activa）和"默观式生活"（vita contemplativa）之间找出一种中间的路线。他提到自己在教会任职时遇到的挫折：对敌人或政治对手的怀恨、遭诽谤的体验、恶意对手的阴谋、教会内部也有人滥用权力。

在 379 年，他被派到 Constantinopolis，在那里发表了一些讲演（所谓的《五个神学

# Grēgorios Nazianzos / Gregory of Nazianz

**Opera:** *Carmina, Epigrammata, Epistulae, Logos peri phygēs, Logoi (=Orationes), Peri ton heautou bion (=Eis ton heautou bion, Carmen de se ipso), Philokalia*

**Works:** *Poems, Epigrams, Epistles, On Flight, Orations (Homilies), Song about My Life, Philocalia*

## 046. *Carmina / Poems*

This collection of 400 poems is approximately the length of the *Iliad*, it has more than 16,000 verses. The metrical forms change; some of the poems are moral exhortations, others are didactic, hymnic, meditative or more like epic narratives.

Possibly the most famous poem is Gregory's autobiography (*Carmen* 2,1,11, also entitled *Peri tōn heautou biōn*), which is written in 1950 iambic trimeters and forms an interesting counterpart to Augustine's *Confessions*. Like the *Confessiones*, this autobiography is without precedent and without later imitation. The author looks back at his life, but rather in a melancholic and meditative mood, not in a style of epic objectivity. He expresses the torments of difficult decisions. He was born in Nazianz (Cappadocia) and studied in Caesarea (Palestine), Alexandria and Athens. In Athens he enjoyed studying together with his life-long friend Basil, and he expresses gratefulness for his father, but on the other hand both had urged him to serve in ecclesiastical offices without caring much about his own inclinations. Gregory rather wanted to become a monk, and so he had to find a compromise between active life and contemplative life. He mentions his disappointments in the service of the Church: bitterness against enemies, the experience of being exposed to slander, intrigues of malicious rivals, and the abuse of power by members of the Church.

In 379 AD he was appointed to go to Constantinople and he gave several speeches (the *Five theological Orations*) against the Arianists. On the Council of Constantinople

讲演》)来反驳 Arius 学派的人。在 Constantinopolis 的大公会议上(381 年),他甚至被任命为该会议的主席,而该大公会议肯定他为主教和 Constantinopolis 的宗主教(patriarcha)。然而,关于他个人的一些阴谋出现,所以他主动地退职。在他的《自传》中,他说他愿意牺牲自己,就像 Jonas 也愿意被扔到水里,为了拯救船上的人们(即教会的人)。退位后,他在 Nazianz 生活一段时间,后来退休前往自己父亲的庄园,在那里写了他的书信和诗歌。他的诗表明他非常熟悉古典希腊文学。

## 047. 《讲道文集》

这个讲道文集(共包括 45 篇)针对很多不同的问题。在其中也有 Grēgorios 为自己的父亲、兄弟姐妹以及为其朋友 Basileios 作的诔词(丧礼讲道)。

在讲道文集中最著名的是五篇被称为"神学讲道稿"(*Logoi theologikoi*,第 27 到 31 篇)的演讲。在这些演讲中,Grēgorios 首次清楚地区分神学和哲学的领域。他说不是所有的人都能成为"神学家"(theologos),只有那些通过默想上主圣言(theou logos)而净化自己的人才能做到。他要从一个神学家的角度来说明信仰,但他担心这种思维也许使一些人感到困惑(第 27 篇)。在第 30 篇中他说,如果神是无限的,人就无法为神下定义,因为这就意味着为神设定一些限制。虽然如此,人们仍然需要向神作祈祷并需要知道神的名号。神有两个名称:ho ōn(临在者)与 hē ousia(本有)。神是"存在的庞大海洋,他无始无终"。

皇帝 Julianus Apostata(360—363 年在位)曾经愿意镇压基督宗教并禁止基督徒当古典哲学和修辞学的老师。Grēgorios 的两篇讲道稿(第 4、5 篇)揭露了皇帝的政策。Grēgorios 自己获得了很高级的希腊教育,而他也保卫了基督徒参与古典学术传统的权利。372 年,Grēgorios 被选立为 Sasima 的主教,但在他被祝圣后,他又在上任之前逃跑了,因为他感觉到,别人指定他违背了他的意愿。后来他又写了一篇说明自己想法的著作(*Logos peri phygēs*《关于逃跑》),其中也阐述了司铎职务及作为司铎服务的理想。

(381) he was even appointed president of the council for some time, and the council confirmed him as bishop and patriarch of Constantinople. However, due to some intrigues personally aimed at him he demonstratively resigned from office. In his autobiography he writes that he sacrificed himself like Jonas who wanted to be thrown from the ship in order to save the community (of the Church). After spending some time in Nazianz he retired to his father's estate where he wrote his letters and poems. The poems of Gregory show that he was exceptionally familiar with classical Greek poetry.

## 047. *Logoi / Orationes / Sermons*

This collection of 45 orations (sermons) addresses many different themes. Among the orations are also the funeral orations Gregory held for his father, his brothers and sisters and for his friend Basil.

The five "theological orations" (*Logoi theologikoi*, speeches Nr. 27~31) are most well-known. In these speeches Gregory for the first time clearly distinguishes the fields of theology and philosophy. He says not everyone can become a theologian (theologos), but only those who purify their hearts by contemplating the word of God (theou logos). He tries to talk about the faith from the point of a theologian but is concerned that these speculations might confuse certain people (Oratio Nr. 27). In the sermon Nr. 30, he says that if God is infinite, then man cannot find a definition for God, because that would mean to limit God. Still, men need to pray to God and need to know His name. God has two names: ho ōn (existence) and hē ousia (being). God is the "wide ocean of being, without limit or end".

Emperor Julian Apostata (360—363 AD) tried to suppress Christianity and forbade Christians to teach classical philosophy and rhetoric. Gregory held two sermons (Nr. 4 and 5) in which he exposed the policy of the Emperor. Gregory who had enjoyed an excellent Greek education himself defended the right of Christians to have access to the academic tradition of pre-Christian antiquity. In 372 Gregory was chosen bishop of Sasima, but after his ordination he fled before taking office, because he felt he was appointed bishop against his will. He later wrote the *Logos peri phygēs* (*Sermon about the flight*). In this oration he presented the ideal of priestly ministry.

# (尼撒的)格列高利(约335—394 AD)

他是 Basileios 的弟弟并通过哥哥接受了杰出的哲学和神学教育,成为修辞学家,于371年由 Basileios 指定为 Nyssa(在 Cappadocia)的主教。由于当时的"同性同体论"问题,他于374年被罢免,但在378年后成为"新 Nicaea 派"的神学领袖,参与 Constantinopolis 的主教会议(381年、382年和383年)。他被承认为正统的神学家并恢复他的主教地位。他的神学使用 Platōn 的思想:灵修生活是灵魂一步一步上升到神(即真、善)那里,因为人渴望见到神。

**著作:**《雅歌注解》、《信集》、《基督宗教信仰》(系统地说明基督信仰)、《梅瑟/摩西传》、《论人的准备》、《论贞洁》、《关于灵魂和复活的对话》(与其临终的姐妹 Macrina 的对话)、《反驳 Eunomios 的书》,还有注解《圣经》的著作。

## 048. 《论人的准备》

这篇解经学论文写于379年,其目标是补充作者的弟兄 Basileios 写的 *Hexaemeron*(《论六天创造》)。

根据《圣经·创世记》,人在上主的创造中是最后的项目。人们应该统治和利用其他受造物,也应该在大自然中意识到神的伟大和他的智慧。因为每一个人都是根据上主的肖像而创造的,每一个人都有特殊的尊严,这一点也可以从其精神性的力量看出:人有精神、理性和爱。为了认识整个受造界,人的精神利用种种感官。人的身体结构是不完善的,软弱的,所以人需要统治和利用受造界。人们需要利用动物来丰富自己的生活。

人是按照上主的肖像而创造的。然而,神没有性别,但人分为男女。Grēgorios 这样解释这个问题:上主最早创造了一个"一般的人",后来再加上了性别的区分。除此之外,在复活的时候,性别的差异再次被取消。

下面的段落来自 Gregorios 关于复活的讲演(*Oratio in Christi resurrectionem*)并说明他如何从精神和比喻的维度看待人的身体:"一个新的创造已开始,这是一种新的生命,一种新的生存方式,甚至是我们本性的改变。这是什么样的新受造物呢?这个新的存在是在信仰的母怀中受孕的。通过圣洗的复生他开始见到世界之光。这个新人的奶妈是教会,他喝的奶是教会的教导,而他的食粮是从天降下的食粮。他将成长并获得最完善的形状,而这个完美就是他的神圣生活。这个新人的婚姻是他与智慧的结合。他的孩子是希望,他的家是天国,他的财富和遗产是天堂中的喜乐。他的终结不是死亡,而是为那些堪享受永恒幸福的人准备的永生。"

# Grēgorios Nyssēnos / Gregory of Nyssa

**Opera:** *Commentarius in canticum canticorum, Epistulae, Logos katēchētikos ho megas (=De instituto Christiano), Peri biou Mōyseos, Peri kataskeuēs anthrōpou (=De opificio hominis), Peri parthenias, Peri psychēs kai anastaseōs (=Dialogus de anima et resurrectione), Pros Eunomion logoi antirrhētorikoi*

**Works:** Commentary on the Song of Songs, Letters, Great Catechesis (Address on Religious Instruction), Life of Moses, On the Equipment of Man, On Virginity, Dialog on the soul and the resurrection, Against Eunomios

## 048. *Peri kataskeuēs anthrōpou / On the Equipment of Man*

This exegetical treatise, written in 379 AD, was meant to complement the *Hexaemeron* of Gregory's brother Basil.

According to the Bible (*Genesis*) man was the last part of God's creation. Humans should use and control the creation and perceive in the beauty of creation the greatness and wisdom of God. Being made in the likeness of God, every human person has a special dignity, which is also seen from the use of their mental powers like the power of the spirit, of reason, of love. In order to perceive the whole of reality, the spirit uses the senses. The physical weakness and imperfection of the human body demands that men dominate creation and make use of it. For example, human beings are bound to use animals and animal products to enhance their own life.

Since human beings are created in the likeness of God, there arises a minor problem: God is beyond sexuality, but humans are created as men and women. Gregory tries to explain that God first created a kind of "general" human being, and only later added the sexual differentiation. Besides that, in the day of the resurrection the sexual differences will forever be removed.

The following lines from one of Gregory's sermons on the resurrection (*Oratio in Christi resurrectionem*) show how he looks at the body in a spiritual and metaphorical way: "A new creation has begun, a new life, a new way of existence, even a change of our nature. What kind of new creation? This new being is conceived in the womb of faith. Through the rebirth of baptism it comes to the light of the world. The nurse of this creature is the Church, the ecclesiastical doctrine is milk for it, and heavenly bread is its nourishment. It will grow and reach its perfect form, and this perfection is its holy way of life. The wedding of this being is its union with wisdom. Its descendants are hope, its house is the kingdom, its legacy and wealth are the joys of Paradise. Its end is not death but that blessed eternal life which is prepared for those who deserve it."

### 049. 《论贞洁》

这篇苦修性的论文写于 370 年到 378 年间，在某些方面和 Chrysostomos 的同名论文（大约撰写于 10 年以后）相似。

根据基督宗教的传统，贞洁不仅仅是一个物质性的、身体的理想，更多是一种精神性的、灵性的自由状态，即脱免于世俗的欲望，恒心地、虔敬地朝拜上主。贞洁生活的主要作用是远离种种渴望和欲望，对这些渴望保持一种平衡冷静的态度。种种渴望不是来自于人的本性——这种本性原来是很纯洁的——它们来自于人们败坏的心意。耶稣是"真人"，他应该诞生在每一个基督徒的心中，正如他在童贞女 Maria 的怀里成了人。因此，Maria 是贞洁和忠信生活的榜样和典范。每一个基督徒应该和那位"有生育能力的童贞女"一样在自己的生活中生出"永恒的圣言"。这种"精神性的诞生"影响了中世纪的思想家，比如圣 Bernardus 和 Meister Eckhart。

上主祝福了婚姻生活，而这种生活方式也在人的本性中有着很深的基础，因此不应该蔑视或谴责婚姻生活。但那些无法超越人间忧虑的人们似乎也无法找到通往灵修成全的路。无论谁成了肉身的奴隶或让身体统治精神，这样的人就无法成全。精神应该统治身体，这才是正确的秩序，不是反过来的。另一个支持贞洁生活的理由是这个：贞洁生活突破生育的循环，即死亡的锁链。然而，在通往完满的道路上，人们也不应该采取过分严格的措施或折磨自己的方式，比如通过长期守斋使身体变得虚弱无力也是一种障碍，和一个肥胖的身体一样。

### 050. 《关于灵魂和复活的对话》

这部哲学性的（希腊语的）对话大约写成于 379 年。作者与他的姐妹 Makrina 进行一种（虚构的）对话——当时他的姐妹面临死亡或已经去世了。

在这部对话的开始，一些与死亡有关的问题被讨论。Makrina 担任老师的角色，因为她有一定的"体验"，所以她能够回答作者的种种问题。根据《圣经》教导的解释，灵魂等于上主的肖像。一切离上主很远的因素对灵魂也是陌生的或有害的。古代思想家 Platōn 和 Aristotelēs 关于灵魂的理论无法正确地掌握灵魂的本性。灵魂很自然地知道上主的存在，但需要努力进一步认识神的奥迹。每一个人都有两种本性，即灵魂的精神性和肉身的物质层面。这两种层面的结合总是一个奥迹，因为灵魂可以脱离身体而存在，但身体不能没有灵魂。末日的复活只能是灵魂和身体的再一次结合。那些有罪的人的灵魂需要在死亡后经过一种火焰的净化，直到一切邪恶的因素从灵魂中消除为止。人们希望在漫长的时间后，一切灵魂都会达到完美的状态，都将会成全，换言之，他们将会恢复原来的上主的肖像，会接近神。

## 049. *Peri parthenias / On Virginity*

In some aspects, this ascetic treatise—written between 370 and 378 AD—is similar to Chrysostom's work with the same title which was written about 10 years later.

According to Christian tradition, virginity is not only a physical, bodily ideal, but even more so a spiritual and mental attitude of freedom from earthly passions and perseverance in the pious adoration of God. The main effect of virginity is detachment from and indifference to desires and passions. These desires do not stem from the original pure human nature but rather from the perversions of the human will. The true man Jesus must be spiritually born in the Christian's heart, like He became man in the virgin Mary's womb. Therefore Mary is the model and example of virginity and of faithful life: every Christian should live like this "fruitful virgin", giving birth to the Eternal Word. This "spiritual birth" influenced medieval thinkers like St. Bernhard and Eckhart.

God blessed marital life, which is also deeply rooted in human nature; therefore, marriage and conjugal life should not be despised or condemned. But those who cannot extricate themselves from earthly worries are in danger of losing the way to spiritual perfection. Whoever serves the desires of the flesh and lets the body dominate the mind cannot be perfect. The proper order demands that the spirit leads the body—not the other way round. Another reason to praise the virtues of virginity is that it interrupts the chain of procreation, which is also the chain of death. However, any excessive strictness or self-torment is not a good guide on the way to perfection. Physical emaciation through long fasting is also an obstacle just like obesity.

## 050. *Peri psychēs kai anastaseōs / Dialog on the Soul and Resurrection*

This philosophical dialog in Greek was written in 379 AD, the Latin title is *Dialogus de anima et de resurrectione*. It is a fictive dialogue of the author with his sister Macrina who was close to death at that time.

The dialogue starts with some considerations concerning death. Taking the role of a teacher, Macrina is speaking "from experience", and so she can answer the questions of the author. According to an interpretation of biblical teaching, the soul is the image of God. Whatever is far from God is harmful and alien to the soul. The theories of Plato and Aristotle about the soul cannot properly grasp the true nature of the soul. The soul naturally knows about God's existence but needs to strive for a proper understanding of God's mystery. In every person there are two natures, namely the spiritual level of the soul and the material level of the body. The connection of these two levels is a mystery, since the soul can exist without the body, but not vice versa. The resurrection on the last day can only be a reunification of soul and body. The soul of a sinful person must be purified after death in a kind of fire (the purgatory), until all evil elements are expurged from the soul. There is the hope that after a very long time all the souls will reach perfection, that is to say they will be restored to their original likeness of God and will be similar to the divine.

# 安博罗修斯 (339—397 AD)

339年生于德国Trier的一个基督徒家庭，其父是高官，曾任Gallia的总督。Ambrosius在父亲去世后于罗马长大，获得了全面的教育，开始在Sirmium任职，于370年成为Aemilia和Liguria的总督，374年由Milan(米兰)人民宣布为主教，当时他还是一个慕道生(catechumenus)，遂即被祝圣司铎和主教。他反对意大利北部的Arius派并尽力为社会的基督化工作。由于他的影响，罗马皇帝放弃了Pontifex Maximus(大司祭)的尊称，并下令将Victoria(胜利)女神的像从元老院中拿掉。Ambrosius曾回应Symmachus写的抗议书。在晚年，Ambrosius和Theodosius皇帝有比较密切的合作，但因为Theodosius皇帝在390年下令屠杀一群人，Ambrosius强迫他公开为此作补赎。他强调新信徒的教育，支持克修生活并写了许多著作。他利用Stoa(尤其Cicero)和新柏拉图主义(Plotinos)的思想来丰富他的神学思维，在《圣经》解释方面采纳了Philo和Origenes的allegorical(隐喻式的)诠释方式。他的赞美诗开辟了拉丁圣歌的传统。

**著作**：《David先知的辩论》、《论Abraham》、《论Cain和Abel》、《论信仰》、《论Helia和觉醒》、《论圣体圣事的降生》、《论贞洁的规则》、《论Job和David》、《论Isaac和灵魂》、《论Jacob和幸福的生活》、《论Joseph》、《论诸奥迹》、《论Nabuth》、《论Noah》、《论圣职人员的职务》、《论补赎》、《论乐园》、《论圣祖》、《论诸圣事》(6卷)、《论圣神》(亦译《论圣灵》)、《论Tobias》、《论寡妇》、《论贞女》、《论贞洁》、《12篇圣咏的论述》、《信集》、《对贞洁的劝言》、《向初学者解释信经》、《路加福音诠注》(共10卷)、《信仰概论》、《第118篇圣咏阐释》、《创世六天》(6卷)、《赞美诗》、《讲演集》

## 051. 《论圣职人员的职务》

该著作(亦称 De officiis libri tres《论职务三卷》)是第一部基督宗教伦理学方面的系统论述，在386年后成书，面向意大利米兰的教会，尤其针对圣职人员。正如书名所暗示的那样，作者的思想建立在Cicero的伟大著作 De officiis(《论义务》)之上并偶尔引用该著作的原文。

Cicero曾经用希腊和罗马历史上的英雄人物来说明他的道德原则，但Ambrosius用一些来自《旧约》的人士来代替这些英雄，因为Abraham、Joseph、David和Job很早之前就已经是伦理道德方面的榜样，他们都已经拥有Stoa学派的智慧。作者说犹太—基督宗教的传统在两方面超越世俗思想：第一，犹太人的智慧比希腊的Stoa派更古老；第二，如果伦理道德的行为受了终极目标(永生)的启迪，他将超越任何世俗的道德学说，因为世俗的道德没有希望。因此，只有《旧约》的哲人才能活出完美的德性。Stoa派的人缺乏Moses和Solomon那种来自上天的智慧。

# Ambrosius / Ambrose

**Opera:** *Apologia prophetae David, De Abraham, De Cain et Abel, De fide ad Gratianum, De Helia et ieiunio, De incarnationis dominicae sacramento, De institutione virginis, De interpellatione Job et David, De Isaac et anima, De Jacob et vita beata, De Joseph, De mysteriis, De Nabuthe, De Noe, De officiis ministrorum, De paenitentia, De Paradiso, De Patriarchis, De sacramentis libri VI, De Spiritu Sancto, De Tobia, De viduis, De virginibus ad Marcellinam sororem, De virginitate, Ennarationes in 12 psalmos, Epistulae, Exhortatio virginitatis, Explanatio symboli ad initiandos, Expositio evangelii secundum Lucam, Expositio fidei, Expositio in psalmum 118, Hexaemeron (libri VI), Hymni, Sermones*

**Works:** *Apology of the Prophet David, Abraham, On Cain and Abel, On Faith to Gratianus, On Helia and Sobriety, On the Sacrament of the Incarnation, On the Institution of the Virgins, On Job and David, On Isaac and the Soul, On James and a Blessed Life, On Joseph, On the Mysteries, On Naboth, On Noe, On the Duties of the Clergy, On Penitence, On the Paradise, On the Fathers, On the Sacraments, On the Holy Spirit, On Tobias, On Widows, On Virgins, On Virginity, Commentaries to Psalms, Letters, Exhortation to Virginity, Explanation of the Creed to Novices, Commentary on St. Luke's Gospel, An introduction to the faith, Exposition to Psalm 118, Six days' work, Hymns, Sermons*

## 051. *De officiis ministrorum / On the Duties of the Clergy*

This work (also called *De officiis libri tres*), the first systematic outline of Christian ethics, was written after 386 and is addressed to the Church of Milan, especially to the clergy. As the title suggests, the author bases his considerations on Cicero's great work *De officiis* (*On Duty*) and sometimes quotes from it.

Cicero uses heroes or politicians of Greek or Roman history in order to explain his moral tenets, but Ambrose substitutes those figures with models taken from the Old Testament, since Abraham, Joseph, David and Job were already early examples of the ethical ideals and the wisdom of the Stoic philosophy. The author points out that Jewish–Christian wisdom surpasses the secular tradition in two ways: first, Jewish wisdom is older than the Greek Stoa; secondly, ethical behavior that is inspired by an ultimate aim (eternal life) will surpass and transcend any secular Stoicism that is without such hope. Therefore only the sages of the Old Testament could live out perfect virtue. The Stoics lacked the heavenly inspired wisdom of Moses and King Solomon.

作者澄清 Stoa 派关于"中间的义务"(officium medium)和"完美的义务"(officium perfectum)的理解(参见 Cicero 的著作),此后谈论四枢德(virtutes cardinales),它们是一切其他的道德理想和美德的根源。首先,智慧(明智,prudentia, sapientia)引导人们越来越强烈渴望和研究真理,希望获得更多的知识和智慧。第二个美德是正义(iustitia),它为每一个人提供他应该拥有的东西。根据正义的原则,人们不可以违背公共的利益,也不可以侵犯他人的权利,而正义也要求一切人无私地为公益服务。勇气(fortitudo)是那种帮助人们面对挑战的美德,无论是在战争或在和平的时代。最后的枢德是节制(temperantia),他控制我们的一切言论和行为并建立人生中的正当秩序。

因为司祭们和圣职人员应该过一种体现出近乎完美无缺的道德生活榜样,Ambrosius 多次呼吁司铎们并鼓励他们,使他们的榜样为平信徒提供一些启迪。圣职人员不应该给人们一种庸俗化的印象,因为如果他们完全融入群众,没有人会尊敬他们。

## 052. 《信集》

本《信集》包含 Ambrosius 的 77 封信,但其中有一部分并不是真正的书信,而是一种用书信文体写的论文。这些论文阐明神学的、政治的或私人的问题。

特别值得注意的是第 18 封信,它是针对 Symmachus 第 3 个 *Relatio*(《报告》)的回应。Symmachus 和那些非基督徒元老在公元 384 年请求皇帝再次恢复罗马的古代宗教崇拜。Ambrosius 反驳那种来自新 Plato(柏拉图)主义的模糊观点,即"一切宗教都是相对平等的"。他说,只有当一切人相信真神(deum verum,即基督徒们的神)时,才能够确保和平。根据《圣经》的说法(sicut scriptura dicit),异教中的神明只是鬼怪。Ambrosius 也同样反驳了 Symmachus 的爱国主义论点:罗马成为一个伟大的国度不是因为它的宗教,而是因为罗马人有美德(virtus)。耶稣曾说不能事奉两个主人,因此"我们不可以认同他人的错误"(alieni erroris societatem suscipere non possumus)。Ambrosius 使用一种很亲切的语气与年轻的皇帝交谈,将自己称为皇帝的"弟兄"(germanus tuus)并鼓励皇帝不要把自己的年龄作为一个借口:"对于基督来说,每一个年龄都是完满的,每一个时代都是成熟的。"(Omnis aetas perfecta Christo est, omnis Deo plena.)同时,米兰的主教也提醒皇帝说,如果他放弃真实的信仰,他将来在教堂那里就不会得到好的接待。

第 51 封信类似表明 Ambrosius 在教会和社会上的强有力的地位。Theodosius 皇帝曾经在 390 年下令在 Thessalonike 屠杀一群人,而 Ambrosius 写信要求皇帝为这个事件作公开的忏悔。如果皇帝不接受这种要求,主教将会把他开除教籍,这样皇帝就不能再进入教堂,不能参与基督徒们的节庆。Theodosius 皇帝听从了 Ambrosius 的要求并在一次教堂的聚会中公开承认了自己的罪过,这样他再次被接受到基督徒们的

After clarifying the Stoic concepts of "middle duty" (officium medium) and "perfect duty" (officium perfectum, cf. Cicero's work), the author discusses the four cardinal virtues which are the source of all other moral ideals and virtues. First of all, prudence (prudentia, sapientia) leads to an ever deeper longing for and investigation of the truth, desiring ever more knowledge and wisdom. The second virtue is justice (iustitia) which grants to each person what she or he deserves. Justice forbids that anyone offends against the common good or infringes upon the rights of others, and it demands selfless service for the good of all. Courage (fortitudo) is the virtue which helps a person to face challenges posed not only in war but also at home and in peaceful times. The last of the cardinal virtues, temperance (temperantia) controls all of our words and actions and brings about the right order in life.

Since the priests and clergymen are supposed to live a lifestyle that represents an almost perfect example of virtue, Ambrose often addresses the priests and exhorts them so that their example may in turn inspire the faithful. Clerics should not give an impression of vulgarity, because if they are not distinct from the crowd they will not command respect.

## 052. *Epistulae / Letters*

The collection contains 77 of Ambrose's letters, some of which are not real letters but rather essays in the form of a letter. These treatises discuss theological, political or private questions.

Special attention should be given to letter 18 which is a reply to the *Relatio* Nr. 3 of Symmachus. In 384 AD Symmachus and the pagan senators asked the emperor to restore the old Roman religious cults. Ambrose argues against the vage Neoplatonist theory concerning the equality of all religions and says peace is only possible if all believe in the true God (deum verum), namely the Christian God. According to the Bible (sicut scriptura dicit), the gods of the pagan religions are demons. The nationalist argument of Symmachus is also refuted: Rome did not become a great empire because of its traditional religion but rather by relying on the virtue (virtus) of the Roman people. Jesus said that it is not possible to serve two masters, and thus "we cannot associate with the error of some other person" (Alieni erroris societatem suscipere non possumus). Ambrose talks in a very familiar tone to the young emperor, calling himself his "brother" (germanus tuus) and encouraging the emperor not to use his young age as an excuse: "Every age is mature for Christ and perfect for God" (Omnis aetas perfecta Christo est, omnis Deo plena.) At the same time, being the bishop of Milan, Ambrose also warns the emperor that he will not be received when going to church if he abandons the true faith.

In a similar way, letter 51 also expresses Ambrose's strong position in church and society. Emperor Theodosius had a crowd of people massacred in Thessalonice in 390 AD, and in his letter Ambrose urges the emperor to do public penitence for this event. If the emperor should not comply with this demand he might be excommunicated and thus would not be allowed to enter the church and participate in Christian celebrations. Theodosius actually obeyed Ambrose and did penitence, openly confessing his sin before a church congregation, and so he was readmitted to the community of Christians. This

团体当中。这个事件表达了第 75 封信所提出的原则:"皇帝在教会之内,不在教会之上。"(imperator intra ecclesiam, non supra ecclesiam est.)

### 053. 《赞美诗集》

Ambrosius 撰写的这部《赞美诗集》共有 12 首诗,基督徒们在他们的团体礼仪中咏唱这些赞美诗。每一首赞美诗都是由四行长的诗句组成的,格律则是短长韵律。这些诗歌为 Ambrosius 带来了"拉丁教会赞美诗的创造者"的美名,这对后来的文学史的影响极其深远。

其中比较有名的赞美诗是 *Ad galli cantum*(《公鸡之歌》)。这首诗有 8 节并反思早上叫醒人们的公鸡。头两节呼吁上主,他是"永恒的造物主"(Aeterne rerum conditor)。下面两节则赞美公鸡,因为它的叫声使罪人悔改并给那些受压力的人以新的力量。第 5 和第 6 节鼓励人们要起来,并要怀着新的希望(Gallo canente spes redit)。最后两节比较世俗的世界和精神性的世界。正如公鸡早上叫醒我们,基督也将从睡眠和死亡中唤醒人类。公鸡宣布早晨的时刻,而上主则是白天和夜晚的主人,他是时间和永恒的主。基督驱逐灵魂的睡眠(mentisque somnum discute),这样公鸡就成为更深奥的实在的象征。

event exemplifies the principle expressed in letter 75: "The emperor is within the Church, not above the Church" (imperator intra ecclesiam, non supra ecclesiam est).

## 053. *Hymni / Hymns*

Ambrose wrote this collection of 12 songs for the liturgical celebrations of the Christian community. All hymns consist of stanzas in the length of four iambic verses. These songs made Ambrosius the "creator of Latin ecclesiastical hymns" and had a lasting influence on the subsequent centuries.

One of the more famous hymns in entitled *Ad galli cantum* (*Song of the Cock*). The hymn has 8 stanzas and reflects on the cock-crow that calls the people to get up in the morning. The first two stanzas invoke God the eternal Creator (Aeterne rerum conditor) as the cock crows. The next two stanzas are an appraisal of the cock, since its crowing calls sinners to repentance and strengthens those who toil. Stanzas 5 and 6 are an exhortation to rise from sleep with new hope (Gallo canente spes redit). The last two stanzas compare the secular and the spiritual world. Just like the cock wakes us up in the morning, Christ raises mankind from sleep and death. The cock announces the time of the day, and God is the master of day and night, He is the Lord of time and eternity. Christ banishes the slumber of the souls (mentisque somnum discute), thus the cock becomes a symbol of a deeper, spiritual reality.

# 西马克斯（约 340—402 AD）

这位罗马元老、讲演家和学者是反对基督信仰并护卫传统宗教的主要代表人物。他曾任 Africa（阿富利加）省的总督，又任罗马市长（官名 praefectus urbi，383—384 年），并于 391 年当选执政官。在 Alaric 王第一次占领意大利北部时，他率领一个使团前往 Ravenna 的朝廷。

**著作**：《信集》、《讲演集》、《报告》

## 054. 《报告》

这些报告是罗马市长 Symmachus 在 384 年和 385 年向 Valentinianus II（375—392 年）提出的建议、请求和申请，其中涉及到当时的法律和政治问题。

第 3 篇 *Relatio* 是一种特殊的申请，作者建议恢复罗马元老院旁边的位于 Victoria 女神像前面的祭坛。Augustus 皇帝曾在公元前 29 年建立了这个神像和祭坛，而元老院的人员则习惯性地在这个祭坛上奉献葡萄酒或上香；然而，当时的基督徒反对这种习俗，所以 Constantinus 皇帝的儿子 Constantius II 于 357 年移走了该神像。Julianus 皇帝于 361 年恢复了它，而在 Gratianus 皇帝的时代保留了女神像，但没有祭坛。Symmachus 建议恢复该祭坛并且也要恢复那些属于古罗马异教徒宗教的祭司们的特权："我们要求恢复宗教的原先形式，这种宗教长期以来对国家有利"（Repetimus igitur religionum statum, qui rei publicae diu profuit）。Symmachus 说罗马因传统的罗马宗教才变得如此伟大，但由于人们忽略了旧神明，384 年的收成非常不好，"渎神行为使得这一年变得干燥"（Sacrilegio annus exaruit, ch. 16）。人们应该遵守古老的传统，"我们深爱我们的习俗"（Consuetudinis amor magnus est, ch. 4）。

Symmachus 恳请年轻的皇帝（称他为"您的永恒"aeternitas vestra）要宽容地对待其他宗教，就和以前的几位皇帝一样：他们虽然是基督徒，但并没有毁灭罗马城的种种神庙。一切人的宗教敬拜都应该享有同等的权利，因为"每一个人都有自己的习俗和崇拜方式。为了保护不同的城市，神明为他们分配了不同的宗教"（Suum enim cuique mos, suus cuique ritus est. Varios custodes urbibus cultus mens divina distribuit. ch. 8）。"我们在同一片天空下，生活在一个世界中。为什么需要区分每一个人用什么教义来寻求真理？如此大的奥迹不能仅仅用一条路来到达"（commune caelum est, idem nos mundus involvit. Quid interest, qua quisque prudentia verum requirat? Uno itinere non potest perveniri ad tam grande secretum. ch. 9）。在这里的"神明"和"一与

# Symmachus / Quintus Aurelius Symmachus

**Opera:** *Epistulae, Orationes, Relationes*
**Works:** *Letters, Orations, Reports*

## 054. *Relationes / Reports*

These reports written by Symmachus, prefect of Rome in 384 and 385, are suggestions, inquiries and petitions addressed to Emperor Valentinian II (375—392) concerning certain legal and political matters.

The third *Relatio* is a petition which suggests that the traditional altar of the goddess Victoria at the Curia in Rome should be restored. This altar together with the statue of Victoria was dedicated by Augustus in 29 BC, and the senators used to offer wine and frankincense there, a ceremony that aroused opposition from Christians. Thus Emperor Constantius II, the son of Constantine had the statue removed in 357. Emperor Julian restored it in 361, and under Emperor Gratianus the altar was removed but the statue remained there. Symmachus suggests to restore the altar to the statue and to renew the old privileges of the priests that serve the pagan Roman religion: "We therefore ask to renew the form of religious worship that always has been so useful for the state" (Repetimus igitur religionum statum, qui rei publicae diu profuit). Symmachus argues that the traditional Roman religion is the basis of Rome's greatness. Because of the neglect of the old gods, the harvest was very bad in the year 384. "Sacrilege made the year so dry" (Sacrilegio annus exaruit. chap. 16). The old tradition should be kept, since "we dearly love our old customs" (Consuetudinis amor magnus est, chap. 4).

Symmachus entreats the young emperor ("your eternity" aeternitas vestra) to be tolerant like his predecessors who were Christians but did not destroy the temples in Rome. The religious faith of all people should enjoy equal right, "for each has his own custom and his own form of worship. The divine spirit has granted different cults to different cities to protect them" (Suum enim cuique mos, suus cuique ritus est. Varios custodes urbibus cultus mens divina distribuit. chap. 8). "We live under the same sky and in the same world. Why is it so important to know by which doctrine each one searches for the truth? It is not possible to approach such a great mystery by only one way" (Commune caelum est, idem nos mundus involvit. Quid interest, qua quisque prudentia verum requirat? Uno itinere non potest perveniri ad tam grande secretum. chap. 9). The idea of

多"的问题都来自新 Plato 主义的思维方式。

  为了表达其爱国主义的情绪，Symmachus 使用一种特殊的修辞学方式：他引进"罗马女士"。这位女士今天会说一些什么呢？她说的话就是这些："尊贵的统治者们和元老们！请你们尊敬我的高龄，我仅仅通过虔诚的宗教崇拜（pius ritus）才活了如此长的时间。我要保留那些古老的礼仪，我没有理由因它们而忏悔。我愿意按照我的方式过日子，因为我是自由的。这种传统的崇拜曾经让整个世界都服从于我的法律（hic cultus in leges meas orbem redegit）……"为了应对 Symmachus 的政策，Ambrosius 后来向皇帝写了一封信（第 18 封信），其中也使"罗马女士"说出自己的想法，但在 Ambrosius 心目中罗马仍然是一个比较年轻的妇女，她还有精力学习一些新的东西以及学习新的信仰。

the one "divine spirit" and the "unity in diversity" are obviously inspired by Neoplatonism.

As a special rhetorical tool to express nationalist feelings Symmachus introduces "Lady Rome". What would she say to us today? And these are her words: "Noble rulers and senators, please respect my advanced age, only through pious worship (pius ritus) I could grow so old! I want to keep the old ceremonies and have no reason to feel regret because of them. I want to live in my own way since I am free. This traditional worship has subjected the whole world to my laws (hic cultus in leges meas orbem redegit)…" In order to counteract Symmachus' policies, Ambrose wroter a letter (epistula 18) to the emperor, in which he also used the image of Roma speaking for herself, but in Ambrose's view Roma is not too old to learn new things and a new faith.

# 金口若望（克里索斯托谟）（344—407 AD）

生于 Antiochia 并接受了希腊教育，于 368 年受洗，向 Flavianus 和 Diodōros 求学，被任命为教会学校的老师，但于 372 年进入一所隐修院，当了 4 年的隐修者，此后他也当了 2 年的独修者，但这种刻苦的生活方式影响了他的身体健康，所以他被迫放弃独修生活（378 年）。他被祝圣执事（380 年），又于 386 年被祝圣司铎，不久后因其讲道的口才而美名远扬，因此东方的皇帝 Arkadios 于 397 年命令人绑架他并使他成为 Constantinopolis 的主教。他当主教时要求圣职人员、隐修者和贞女们过一种完美的生活，要为穷人、病者和外国人建立一些客栈，又邀请一些哥特牧者来首都照顾哥特信徒。他也曾批评掌权者，尤其是皇后 Eudokia。他的主要对手却是 Alexandria 的 Theophilos 主教，他于 403 年举行了一次主教会议，其中谴责和罢免不在场的 Chrysostomos。此后，皇帝两次流放了 Chrysostomos，将他押送到小亚细亚，而这位伟大的讲演家就在流放之地去世。

著作：《书信集》（共 240 封信）、《关于玛窦/马太福音的讲道稿》、《讲道集》（共 700 多篇讲道稿）、《反驳犹太人的讲道集》、《论上主不可理解的本性》、《论神圣生活》、《论贞洁》、《论圣像》；共有 16 篇论文，是现存著作最多的东方教父。

## 055.《讲道稿》

圣 Chrysostomos 的讲道文集在著名的 *Patrologia Graeca*（《希腊教父丛书》）系列中占有 18 卷篇幅（PG 47~64），共保存了 700 篇讲道稿。这些都是灵修生活中的重要资源。

这些讲道稿的主要目标是从宗教信仰的角度来理解和解释《旧约》和《新约》。75 篇谈论《创世记》，58 篇说明 *Psalmoi*（《圣咏集/诗篇》），90 篇解释 *Matthaios*（《玛窦/马太福音》），88 篇针对 *Iōannēs*（《若望/约翰福音》）。16 篇讲道稿谈论 *Lukas*（《路加福音》，而 63 篇是以《宗徒大事录/使徒行传》为主题。Chrysostomos 也解释了圣 Paulos（保禄/保罗）的书信，其中特别重视《罗马人书》（32 篇）。

所谓的 *Peri akataleptou*《论上主不可理解的本性》的讲道文集包括 12 篇讲道稿，这些都想说明神的不可理解性以及圣父和圣子在本质上的合一。这类说明针对 Arius（亚略/亚流）派的人，他们否认基督的神性，特别是 Anomoii 派。

另一个文集包括八篇反对犹太人的讲道稿（*Logoi kata Ioudaiōn*）。在当时的 Antiochia 有一个很大的犹太人团体，而一些基督徒既参与基督宗教的节日和礼仪，又参加犹太人的节庆。因此 Chrysostomos 要求那些"亲犹太派"（Ioudaizantes）与犹太人保持距离，要很清楚地支持基督信仰。他也丑化犹太人的习俗和他们的传统。如果这种

# Iōannēs Chrysostomos / John Chrysostom

**Opera:** *Epistulae, Homiliae in Matthaeum, Logoi* (=*Homiliae, Orationes*), *Logoi kata Ioudaiōn, Peri akataleptou* (=*De incomprehensibili Dei natura seu contra Anomoeos*), *Peri hierosynēs, Peri parthenias* (=*De virginitate*), *Peri stēlōn*

**Works:** *Letters, Homilies on Matthew, Homilies* (*Orations*), *Homilies against the Jews, On the Incomprehensibility of God's Nature, On Holiness, On Virginity, On Image Columns*

## 055. *Logoi / Homiliae*

The collection of Chrysostom's homilies fills 18 volumes in the *Patrologia Graeca* (PG 47~64), there are around 700 homilies extant. They are a rich source of spiritual edification.

Chrysostom's homilies mainly serve the purpose of a spiritual understanding and interpretation of the Old and New Testament. 75 homilies deal with the Book of *Genesis*, 58 explain the *Psalms*, 90 interpret the *Gospel of Matthew*, and 88 explain the *Gospel of John*. 16 homilies expound the theology of the *Gospel of Luke*, and 63 homilies are centered on the *Acts of the Apostles*. Chrysostom also interpreted St. Paul's letters, among which the *Letter to the Romans* (32 homilies) has a place of special importance.

The collection *Peri akataleptou* (*On the Incomprehensibility of God's nature*) consists of 12 homilies which try to show the incomprehensibility of God and the essential unity of God the Father and God the Son. It is directed against the Arianist denial of the divinity of Christ, especially against the sect of the "Anomoians".

The eight homilies entitled *Logoi kata Ioudaiōn* (*Against the Jews*) responds to the situation of Antioch, where a big Jewish community attracted Christians who participated in both Jewish and Christian communities and ceremonies. Chrysostom demands that these "Ioudaizantes" (Friends of Jews) detach themselves from the Jews and make a clear decision for Christianity. He also uglifies Jewish custom and tradition. If this "reli-

"过去的宗教"真是可敬的,那么基督信仰就等于是错误的。这些讲道稿是早期基督宗教中最重要的反犹太文献之一。

在387年的一次暴动中,Antiochia城的一些皇帝和皇室成员的石像("柱像",stēlai)遭受损坏,而Antiochia的基督徒们因此非常害怕他们将要受的严厉惩罚。在这种情况下,Chrysostomos想鼓励他的团体,发表了21篇安慰人们的讲道稿(《论石像》,*Peri stēlōn*)。

## 056. 《论贞洁》

这部论文写于381—386年间,作者当时正在Antiochia当执事。

在基督宗教的传统中,圣保禄/保罗(参见 1 *Cor* 7:25–38)的训诫是后来关于贞洁种种论述的基础。为了基督的缘故而不结婚,这种生活方式比婚姻更好,但如果一个人无法过独身的生活,他应该结婚。Chrysostomos认为,贞洁不仅仅是不结婚,也包括精神上的纯洁。贞洁涉及到放弃淫欲,超脱对有吸引力外貌的渴望,克服感官上的好奇心,但也很自由自在地面对世俗的种种忧虑和义务。"如果没有精神性的自由,身体上的自由还有什么意义呢?"因此,贞洁的概念应该是积极的、建设性的和丰富人生的。贞洁和童贞生活的目标是结出精神性的果实。Chrysostomos反对持异端主张的人(比如Markion、Valentinos等人)的极端教导,他们为了赞美贞洁丑化婚姻。

在堕落之前,Adam和Eva生活在完美的贞洁之中,他们也不知道什么是Paulos(保禄/保罗)所说的"肉身中的利刺"(参见 2 *Cor* 12:7),即肉欲的种种诱惑。婚姻自身并不是什么恶事,虽然它是原祖堕落以后的事。因此,最美好的生活方式是守贞。上主命令Adam和Eva"繁殖并充满大地",因此婚姻的首要目标和原初目标是生育子女,但因为人类已经充满着大地的各个角落,而且因为历史的终结已经临近,今天的婚姻的主要目标只是"补救欲望"。婚姻应该引导人们过一种神圣和纯洁的生活。如果没有婚姻,很多人可能会放纵私欲,天天在妓院中寻觅快乐。因此,上主规定了婚姻制度,以扶助人性的软弱。

夫妻两方不应该过一种奢侈或玩世不恭的生活,但他们还是要表达夫妻之爱的。如果妻子违背丈夫的意愿而拒绝夫妻的爱,她就是有罪的,因为这样她也许会使丈夫在婚外有不正当的关系。婚姻基本上是好的,但它没有永恒的价值,它最终只是一场梦。婚姻也带来很多不可避免的困难与挑战:由于财富引起的自高自大、强烈的嫉妒、嫁妆问题、担心自己不能生育、对孩子的照顾等等。因此,当一个人能够过独身的生活而仍然结婚,她/他为自己创造了巨大的损失,因为一个独身的纯洁的人能够更容易进入天国。贞洁生活将会带来真正的幸福,而他在来世的赏报也是很大的。不过,因为过贞洁生活也不太容易,所以不能鼓励所有人都过这种生活。

gion of the past" would be respectable, then Christianity would be wrong. The homilies belong to the most significant anti-Jewish texts of early Christianity.

During some riots in the year 387 several statues of the Roman emperor and of members of the imperial family ("column-monuments", stēlai) in Antioch were overthrown or damaged, and the Christian community of Antioch feared severe punishment. In this situation Chrysostom tries to encourage his community with a series of 21 homilies called *Peri stēlōn*.

## 056. *Peri Parthenias / On Virginity*

This treatise was written between 381 and 386 AD, when the author was a deacon in Antioch.

In the Christian tradition the admonitions of St. Paul (cf. 1 *Cor* 7:25-38) are the basis for later elaborations of the theme of virginity: Unmarried life for Christ's sake is better than marriage, but if someone is unable to lead a solitary life, he should marry. Chrysostom states that virginity is not only to remain unmarried but also to keep a mental chastity. Virginity is not only detachment from immodest desires, freedom from the desire for attractive appearance, and freedom from sensual curiosity, it also means to be free from secular worries and duties. "If there is no spiritual freedom, what is the meaning of bodily chastity?" Therefore the perception of virginity should be positive, constructive and enriching. The purpose of chastity and virginity is to be able to bear spiritual fruit. Chrysostom opposes the extreme teachings of heretics like Marcion and Valentinus who uglify marriage in order to praise virginity.

Before the fall, Adam and Eve lived in perfect virginity and did not know the "thorn in the flesh" which Paul mentions (2 *Cor* 12:7), they were not harrassed by the temptations of sexual desire. Marriage is not evil in itself, even though it stems from the fall of our ancestors. However, the best way of life is virginity. God commanded Adam and Eve "to be fruitful and fill the earth", thus the first and original purpose of marriage was procreation of descendants, but since the earth has been fully populated by now, and because the end of history draws near, the main purpose of marriage is now the "remedy of passion" (cf. 1 *Cor* 7:9). Marriage should be a way to lead a life in holiness and chastity. Without marriage humans would submit to uncontrolled lust and would go to prostitutes. Therefore God instituted marriage as a kind of concession to human weakness.

Spouses must not lead a life in luxury and sensual debauchery, but they should live together in conjugal love. If the wife forces abstinence upon her husband, she is guilty because she might induce her husband to have an extramarital affair. Marriage is basically good, but seen from the perspective of eternity it is not an eternal value. Conjugal life is only a short-lived dream. Marriage also implies inevitable servitude and many hardships: pride because of wealth, bitter envy, dowry problems, the fear of sterility, care for children, etc. If therefore someone could live as a virgin and still marries he or she inflicts grave harm upon himself / herself, since it is easier to reach the kingdom of heaven as a celibate and chaste person. Virginity will lead to true happiness, and the reward for it in the afterlife is great. However, since it is difficult to lead a life in virginity, not all can be encouraged to follow the ideal of chastity.

# 热罗尼摩(哲罗姆)(347—420 AD)

生于 Strido(Dalmatia 地区)的基督徒家庭,曾在罗马获得良好的教育,在那里认识 Rufinus 并受洗入教。他在一次旅途中在 Trier(今天属德国)首次接触到隐修生活并加入 Aquileia 的隐修团体,于 373 年前往 Antiocheia,在那里学习希腊语并阅读 Origenes 的著作,不久后在叙利亚地区(Aleppo 附近)的沙漠当苦修者并学习希伯来语。他和当地的一些隐修者因神学问题发生冲突并于 379 年在 Antiocheia 被祝圣司铎,280 年在 Constantinopolis 结识 Gregorios Nazianzos,于 382 年去罗马参加某次主教会议并成为教宗 Damasus 的神学顾问和秘书。教宗委任他将《圣经》重新译成拉丁语。Hieronymus 成为一些罗马贵族女士的神师,她们是两个寡妇(Marcella 和 Paula)以及 Paula 的两个女儿 Blesilla 和 Eustochium。Damasus 教宗在 384 年去世,但 Hieronymus 并没有当选为他的继承人。因为 Hieronymus 曾经谴责罗马的部分圣职人员的一些世俗化倾向,他被迫离开首都并与 Paula 和 Eustochium 一起去埃及和巴勒斯坦地区旅游,最终于 386 年在 Bethlehem 定居,在那里建立了几所隐修院,此后完全投身于《圣经》研究和神学著作。393 年以后,他和 Jerusalem 的主教 Johannes 有冲突,因此开始谴责 Origenes 的思想并远离多年的友人 Rufinus。他曾被称为"最有学问的拉丁教父"、"古代的人文主义者",他从 8 世纪以来被尊敬为"教父",并于 1295 年被正式宣布为四位拉丁教父之一。他的最重要译著是 *Vulgata*(《通俗拉丁圣经译本》),这个版本在中世纪一直到近代都是教会(尤其是天主教)的权威性《圣经》版本。

**著作**:《反驳赫尔维狄论玛利亚始终童贞》、《反驳约维尼亚》、《争论》、《编年史》(从 Eusebius 的《教会史》翻译的,并加上了 326—379 年的历史和罗马历史的资料)、《注解》、《反驳耶路撒冷的若望》、《反驳维吉兰修》、《论圣经的希伯来地名》(从 Eusebius 的 *Onomasticon* 翻译)、《诸名人传》(135 名作家的材料,第一部基督教文献史著作)、《论依撒意亚的神视》、《反驳贝拉基派》、《信集》、《讲演集》、《创世记中的希伯来文问题》、《拉丁文圣经通行本》

## 057. 《诸名人传》

该著作是关于基督宗教文学的最早研究之一。他在 392 年成书,约 100 年后通过 Gennadius de Massilia(马赛)得到很大的扩充(大约 470—480 年)。Gennadius 的书也被称为 *De viris illustribus*(《诸名人传》),他增添了大约 100 名新的作者,并是第 4、5 世纪教父学的独特资料书。其他作者效法或补充了 Hieronymus 的书,比如 Isidorus de Sevilla 和 Honorius Augustodensis(约 1080—1137 年,参见他的 *De luminaribus ecclesiae*《教会的伟人》)。

在 Hieronymus 的著作中有关于 135 名基督徒作者的描述,其榜样是 Suetonius

# Eusebius Hieronymus / Jerome

**Opera:** *Adversus Helvidium de perpetua virginitate b. Mariae, Adversus Jovinianum, Altercatio Liciferiani et orthodoxi, Chronicum, Commentarioli, Contra Ioannem Hierosolymitanum, Contra Vigilantium, De situ et nominibus locorum hebraicorum (Liber de nominibus Hebraicis), De viris illustribus, De visione Isaiae, Dialogi contra Pelagianos libri III, Epistulae, Orationes, Quaestiones hebraicae in Genesim, Vulgata*

**Works:** *Against Helvidius on the perpetual virginity of Mary, Against Jovinianus, Altercatio, Chronicle, Commentaries, Against John of Jerusalem, Against Vigilantius, On Hebrew Place Names, On the Lives of Famous Men, On the Vision of Isaiah, Against the Pelagians, Letters, Sermons, Questions of Hebrew in Genesis, Vulgate*

## 057. *De viris illustribus / On the Lives of Famous Men*

This work is one of the earliest books on the history of Christian literature. It was written in 392 and one century later was substantially expanded by Gennadius de Massilia (Marseille) in ca. 470—480. Gennadius' *De viris illustribus* contains around 100 new authors and is a unique source for the history of patrology in the fourth and fifth centuries. Other authors who imitated or elaborated Jerome's work are Isidore of Sevilla and Honorius Augustodensis (ca. 1080—1137, confer his *De luminaribus ecclesiae*).

Jerome presents short outlines of 135 Christian authors, taking Sueton's *De viris illustribus* as model. Jerome narrates the life of each author and introduces their works. A fair measure of the material concerning the first three centuries comes from Eusebius'

的 *De viris illustribus*(《诸名人传》)。因此，Hieronymus 介绍每一个人的生平并简单介绍他们的著作。有关第 1、2、3 世纪的部分资料来自 Eusebius 的《教会史》。Hieronymus 的著作也包括一些犹太作者（Philo Judaeus, Flavius Iosephus）以及一些非正统的作者，比如 Tatianus、Novatianus、Eunomios 等人。在序言中 Hieronymus 说明他的目标：那些攻击基督宗教的外教学者说基督徒们是一些"没有修养的农民"(simplicitas rustica)，但他们应该承认在基督徒当中也有很多具有学问的学者、修辞学家和哲学家。

## 058.《信集》

该信集共包括 150 封信（其中有 26 封不是 Hieronymus 写的），Hieronymus 在他去世之前将它编写为两个部分。

部分书信是写给教宗 Damasus 的——他曾经邀请 Hieronymus 翻译《圣经》；一些是写给 Augustinus、Paulinus de Nola 的，而另一些是写给一些罗马贵族妇女的——她们曾经支持 Hieronymus 的克修生活。部分的信包含一些小传记或讣词、个人的安慰或鼓励、对于某些人的推荐或谈论解经学的问题（涉及到对《圣经》文献的解释）。部分的信攻击一些异端或鼓励人们过一种比较刻苦的生活。在一些信中，Hieronymus 哀悼罗马于 410 年的沦陷。

第 22 封信记载了 Hieronymus 的一个著名的梦，在梦中他被谴责为是一个"西塞罗信徒"，而不是基督徒。这个梦后来使 Hieronymus 放弃阅读外教人的文学有好几年之久，但同时也表达了这样的事实：当时的一些（有学问的）基督徒感觉到在他们的信仰和他们的文化传统之间存在着某种张力。虽然 Hieronymus 因为享受 Cicero 著作而感到羞愧，但他的优雅文笔和句句引经据典的风格都表明他是古代最有激情、最有才华的古典语文学家之一。实际上，第 22 封信谈论克修生活和隐修主义。该信是写给 Paula 的女儿 Eustochium 的，标题是 *De virginitate servanda*(《保持贞洁》)。Hieronymus 鼓励 Eustochium 继续过一种克修的、贞洁的生活，因为"人生是一种赛跑"(Stadium est haec vita mortalibus)。

另一封重要的信是第 57 号，标题是 *Ad Pammachium de optimo genere interpretandi*(《给 Pammachius，论最好的翻译方式》)。作者谈论两种翻译方式，即字面上的翻译以及根据某个文献的内容进行类比的翻译。有一次，人们请 Hieronymus 翻译一封 Epiphanios 主教向耶路撒冷的 Joannes 主教写的希腊语的信，但这封信后来引起了激烈的争论，因为涉及到 Origenes 的异端。在第 57 号信中，Hieronymus 试图替自己的翻译方式进行辩护，他指出那种"非字面翻译"的做法在 Cicero 和 Horatius（参见 *Ars poet.* 133）的著作中都能找到，因此是一个悠久的传统。Hieronymus 写出一个经典的定义："不是一字一字地翻译，而是根据原文的意义表达意义"(non verbum e verbo, sed sensum exprimere de sensu, 57,5,2)。Hieronymus 在这方面追随 Cicero，而 Cicero

*Ecclesiastical History*. Jerome also includes some Jewish authors (Philo Judaeus, Flavius Josephus) and unorthodox writers like Tatian, Novatian, Eunomius and others. In the preface Jerome expresses his intention: those pagan scholars who attack Christianity and accuse the Christians of being "unrefined peasants" (simplicitas rustica) should acknowledge that there are many educated scholars, orators and philosophers among the Christians.

## 058. *Epistulae / Letters*

This collection of 150 letters (26 are from other authors) was edited by Jerome in two separate parts some time before his death.

Some of the letters are addressed to Pope Damasus, who had invited Jerome to translate the Bible, others to Augustine, to Paulinus of Nola, and some are written to the patrician women from Rome who supported the ascetic efforts of Jerome. Some of the letters contain biographies or obituaries, personal consolation or exhortations, recommendations of certain people, or they deal with matters from the area of exegesis (the interpretation of Biblical texts). A part of the letters are attacks against heresies or admonitions to lead a more ascetic life style. In several letters Jerome mourns the fall of Rome in the year 410.

The famous dream or vision in which Jerome was accused of being not a Christian but a "Ciceronian" (a lover of Cicero's books) is recorded in letter 22. This dream made Jerome give up reading pagan literature for many years and reflects the tension felt by some (educated) Christians of that time between their faith and their classical heritage. Even if Jerome was somewhat ashamed of enjoying Cicero so much, his fine style and frequent quotations from classical literature show that he was one of the most enthusiastic and talented classicists of antiquity. Letter 22 is actually concerned with ascetic life and monasticism. The letter is adressed to Eustochium, the daughter of St. Paula, and it is entitled *De virginitate servanda* (*On Remaining a Virgin*). Jerome exhorts Eustochium to cling to a life in ascetic chastity, since "our life is like a race" (Stadium est haec vita mortalibus).

Another important letter is Epistula 57, entitled *Ad Pammachium de optimo genere interpretandi* (*Letter to Pammachius on the Best Way of Translation*). Jerome discusses the two ways of translation, namely literal translation and translation according to the meaning of a passage. Jerome once was asked to translate a Greek letter of Bishop Epiphanios addressed to Bishop John of Jerusalem, and this letter evoked fierce debates concerning Origenist heresies. In letter 57 Jerome tries to defend his way of translation by pointing to the long tradition of "non-literal translation" based on texts from Cicero and Horace. Jerome gives the classical formulation: a good translation is "not word for word but sense for sense" (non verbum e verbo, sed sensum exprimere de sensu, 57, 5, 2). Jerome follows Cicero who translated Plato's *Protagoras*, Xenophon's *Oeconomicus*,

曾经翻译了 Plato 的 *Protagoras*、Xenophon 的 *Oikonomikos* 以及 Demosthenes 和 Aeschinos 的讲演。Hieronymus 引用了 Cicero 的著作 *De optimo genere oratorum*(5,13)："我没有像一个翻译者译出这些著作，而像一个讲演家进行翻译。"(nec converti ut interpres, sed ut orator)这样保留了这些作者的理念（sententiae）和比喻（formae, figurae），但使用"符合我们惯用的话语"（verbis ad nostram consuetudinem aptis）。Cicero 两次强调应该保留原文的文笔和话语的感召力（genus omne verborum vimque servavi）。

Hieronymus 也引用 Horatius 的《诗艺》（*Ars poetica*）："你不应该一字一字很拘泥地进行翻译并因此感到忧虑"(*Ars poet.* 133)。早期诗人 Terentius 和 Plautus 曾经翻译希腊人的喜剧，但他们并没有顽固地停留在一些细节上。那些控诉 Hieronymus 的人称为"真实翻译"的东西，那些有修养的人会称之为"恶劣的模仿"（Quam vos veritatem interpretationis, hanc eruditi kakozelian nuncupant）。Hieronymus 说他在 20 年以前曾经将 Eusebius 的 *Chronikon*(《编年史》)译成拉丁语，而在译本的序中他写自己很明白字面翻译和优美及可理解性之间的冲突。"如果我作一种字面的翻译，听起来荒谬。如果我改变词序或表达方式，我似乎没有完成译员的任务。"(si ad verbum interpretor, absurde resonant; si ob necessitatem aliquid in ordine, in sermone mutavero, ab interpretis videbor officio recessisse. 57, 5, 7)。Homerus（荷马）也可以当一个例子：如果逐字地翻译这位"最有口才的诗人"（poeta eloquentissimus），结果只能是一种可笑的词序。Hieronymus 指出他从少年时期致力于翻译有意义的概念，而不是言词（me semper ab adulescentia non verba, sed sententias transtulisse）。此后他引用 Athanasius 的 *Vita Antonii*(《圣安托尼传》)的拉丁译本。译者 Evagrius 说："让其他人捕捉具体的字和音节，你却应该掌握其意义"（Alii syllabas aucupentur et litteras, tu quaere sententias 57, 6, 2）。

Hieronymus 列出一些来自《圣经》的句子，比如来自 *Evangelium secundum Ioannen*(《约翰福音》*Jn* 19:37)的话。Ioannes（约翰）在那里引用《旧约》，但他的希腊译文不符合《七十贤士译本》，而是根据希伯来语的原文（iuxta Hebraicam veritatem）重新译的。因此，《福音书》、《七十贤士译本》与拉丁语的翻译（nostra translatio）都不同，但"在同一的精神内，这些差异仍然彼此相同"（et tamen sermonum varietas spiritus unitate concordat, 57, 7, 5）。Hieronymus 说《七十贤士译本》曾经加上或省略了一些话，而在教会内使用的《圣经》手抄本经常用特殊的标点符号来指示这些词（obelis asteriscisque distincta sunt. 这些标点符号来自公元前 3、2 世纪在 Alexandria 工作的学者，他们曾经使用这些符号来恢复早期希腊诗人的文献。Origenes 和 Hieronymus 类似地使用了这些符号来标出希伯来文和希腊文版本之间的差异。)Hieronymus 多次指出字面翻译的种种问题。最后他说他永远不会谴责一个缺乏口才（sermonis imperitiam）的基督徒，如果人们和 Socrates 一样意识到自己的局限性（Scio, quod nesciam）。"我始终更佩服虔诚的简朴态度，超过有口才的无知。如果有谁想模仿使徒们的话语，应该先

and speeches of Demosthenes and Aeschinus. Jerome quotes Cicero's *De optimo genere oratorum* (5,13): "I did not translate like an interpreter but like an orator" (nec converti ut interpres, sed ut orator), keeping the ideas (sententiae) and metaphors (formae, figurae) of these authors but using "words according to our own usage" (verbis ad nostram consuetudinem aptis). Cicero emphasizes twice the importance of preserving the style and impact of the original wording (genus omne verborum vimque servavi).

Jerome also quotes from Horace's *Ars poetica*: "You should not worry about painstakingly rendering word for word" (nec verbum verbo curabis reddere fidus, Ars. poet. 133). Terence and Plautus translated Greek comedies without stubbornly clinging to certain words. What the attackers of Jerome call "faithful translation" has been termed "bad imitation" by educated people. (Quam vos veritatem interpretationis, hanc eruditi kakozelian nuncupant.) Jerome says that 20 years earlier he translated Eusebius' *Chronikon* into Latin, and in the preface to the translation he explained that he was well aware of the tension between literal translation and preservation of beauty or intelligibility. "If I translate literally it sounds absurd. If I change the word order or the expressions, I seem not to fulfill the task of a translator." (si ad verbum interpretor, absurde resonant; si ob necessitatem aliquid in ordine, in sermone mutavero, ab interpretis videbor officio recessisse." (57, 5, 7). Homer serves as an example: a literal translation of the "most eloquent poet" (poeta eloquentissimus) will lead to a ridiculous order of words. In all humility Jerome points out that since his youth it was his aim to translate meaningful ideas and not words (me semper ab adulescentia non verba, sed sententias transtulisse). Then he quotes from the Latin translation of Athanasius' *Life of St. Anthony* (*Vita Antonii*) a line where the translator Evagrius says "Let other people snatch at syllables and letters, but you should grasp the meaning." (Alii syllabas aucupentur et litteras, tu quaere sententias. 5, 6, 2)

Jerome presents several verses from the Holy Scriptures, for example the passage from the *Gospel of John* (Jn 19:37), where John quotes from the Old Testament not according to the Greek *Septuaginta* but according to the Hebrew original ("iuxta Hebraicam veritatem"). Thus the evangelist, the *Septuaginta*, and the Latin translation ("nostra translatio") are all different, but the "different expressions are nevertheless in harmony through the unity of the Spirit" (et tamen sermonum varietas spiritus unitate concordat, 57, 7,5). Jerome mentions that the translators of the *Septuaginta* have added or omitted certain words, and the Bible manuscripts used in the churches mark these passages with little crosses and stars. (obelis asteriscisque distincta sunt. These diacritical signs were first used by Greek scholars in Alexandria in the 3rd and 2nd century BC in order to reconstruct the texts of early Greek poets. Origen and Jerome used these marks in a similar way to signify differences between the Hebrew and Greek texts.) Repeatedly Jerome points to the absurdities of a literal translation. Finally he says he would never blame a Christian for lacking eloquence (sermonis imperitiam), as long as there is a Socratic attitude of acknowledging one's limitations (Scio, quod nesciam.) "I have always admired pious simplicity more than eloquent boorishness. Whoever wants to imitate

让他模仿使徒们的生活。也许使徒们曾缺乏口才,但他们的神圣生活为他们的简朴言词提供一种辩解(Illorum in loquendo simplicitatem excusabat sanctimoniae magnitudo. 57, 12, 4)。

第70封信回应Magnus的一个问题:为什么Hieronymus在他的著作中经常引用一些来自世俗文学的例子。Hieronymus提出一系列的论点,而他的观点后来在中世纪和文艺复兴时代经常被重复。比如,Solomon曾经鼓励人们学习哲学(参见《箴言篇》*Prov.* 1:1-6)。圣Paulus熟悉希腊的作者并引用过他们中一些人的书(Menander, Aratos)。基督徒们应该理解《申命记》*Dtn* 21:12中的隐喻:如果一个犹太人想与一个外族的被俘虏妇女结婚,他应该先剪她的头发和指甲,才可以接近她。类似,那些爱好世俗智慧的基督徒们也应该净化世俗的知识,才能够接受和拥抱它。作为一个人文学者,Hieronymus认为,如果不了解世俗文学也无法理解《圣经》。

第107号的信(标题是 *Ad Laetam de institutione filiae*《论小女孩的教育》)包括一些以基督徒精神教育子女的内容。"一个基督徒不是被生出来的,而是被教育出来的"(Fiunt, non nascuntur Christiani)。Laeta已将自己的女儿献给基督了,正如《旧约》中的Hannah,她曾奉献了她的儿子Samuel。一个将要成为"上主的圣殿"(templum Domini)的孩子不可以听到愚蠢的话或世俗的歌曲,不应该受粗鲁仆婢的坏影响。要用木头或象牙给他制造一些刻上字母的小块,使孩子以玩耍的方式学习认字(ut et lusus eius eruditio sit)。小女孩要早开始学会用笔。可以用一些小奖品鼓励她学习言辞的正确发音,而练习的单字也要仔细挑选,比如可以让她说出先知们和宗徒/使徒们的名字。一个孩子不应学习一些后来还得摆脱的习惯(quod ei postea dediscendum est)。在某一个时期,小女孩要与成年人一起去教堂,并且要学习节制和克己。然而,对于孩子来说严格的刻苦是危险的,所以可以允许他们去公共的洗浴场,也可以让他们喝一点酒,使他们享受肉食,"以免他们的脚在运动赛开始之前就没有力量"(ne prius deficiant pedes, quam currere incipiant)。小女孩应该每天学习《圣经》的一些章节,同时也应该背"几行希腊语章节"。

一个奉献给精神生活的贞女必须与她的神圣配偶基督保持合一,在成年的时期必须远离那些不遵守贞洁誓愿的贞女们,也不应该参与奴隶们的婚礼。她也不应该去公共浴场,而要通过警醒守夜和守斋控制自己的身体,以消灭欲望的火焰(flammam libidinis)。她不可以爱惜珍珠宝石、"中国人的羊皮"(Serum vellera)和织有金银丝浮花的锦缎,而是要更喜爱《圣经》的手抄本。这样她可以安心地阅读《雅歌》中那些似乎是表达肉欲的话(carnalia verba)。Hieronymus说他将来很愿意当这样的贞女的老师,这样他会感觉到很自豪,甚至比Alexander的老师Aristoteles更自豪,"因为我将不会教导一位马其顿王——他将在Babylon被毒死——而将教导基督的女仆和配偶(ancillam et sponsam Christi)——她将来要奉献给天上的宝座"。

the words of the apostles, let him imitate their life first. Perhaps the apostles lacked eloquence, but their outstanding saintliness excused their simple speech (Illorum in loquendo simplicitatem excusabat sanctimoniae magnitudo. 57, 12, 4).

Letter 70 responds to Magnus' inquiry why Jerome often uses examples from secular literature in his works. Jerome enlists a whole series of arguments, and this kind of argumentation was often repeated in the Middle Ages and in the Renaissance. Solomon recommended the study of philosophy (cf. *Prov.* 1:1-6). St. Paul was aquainted with Greek authors and quoted some of them (Menander, Aratos). Christians should understand the allegory of *Deuteronomy* 21:12, where we read that if a Jew wants to marry a pagan woman who is his captive he should cut her hair and her fingernails before marrying her. Likewise Christians who love secular wisdom should purgate it from errors before accepting and embracing it. Being a humanist, Jerome argues that without the knowledge of secular literature it would be impossible to understand the Bible.

Letter 107 (*Ad Laetam de institutione filiae*, "To Laeta, On a Girl's Education") contains advice concerning the education of children in a Christian spirit. "Christians are not born but made" (Fiunt, non nascuntur Christiani). Laeta has consecrated her baby daughter to Christ, similar to Hannah who consecrated Samuel to God. A child educated to be a "temple of God" (templum domini) should hear no foolish words and know no worldly songs, the child should not be influenced by uncultured maids or servants. A set of letters should be made of wood or ivory so as to make play a road to learning (ut et lusus eius eruditio sit). The girl should learn to write with a pen at an early age. Trifling gifts should encourage her to spell words correctly, but even the words for exercises should be carefully chosen, for example, they could be the names of the prophets and apostles. A child should never learn what it will later have to unlearn (quod ei postea dediscendum est). At a certain age the girl should be taken to church and should learn temperance and self-control. However, since strict abstinence is dangerous for children, she may occasionally visit the baths and take a little wine. She may also have the support of a meat diet "lest her feet fail before the race begins" (ne prius deficiant pedes, quam currere incipiant). Every day she should learn a portion of the Scriptures, and she should also memorize "a number of Greek lines".

In adulthood a virgin dedicated to a life in the Spirit and in union with her Spouse Christ should stay away from those virgins who do not keep their vows of chastity, she should not attend the weddings of slaves, nor go to the baths but rather control her body by vigils and fasting, thus extinguishing the flame of lust (flammam libidinis). She should not love jewels, "Chinese fleeces" (Serum vellera) and gold brocades but rather delight in the manuscripts of the Holy Scriptures. Then she may safely read the somewhat "fleshly language" (carnalia verba) of the Song of Songs. Jerome says in the future that he would enjoy being the tutor of such a virgin, being more proud than Aristotle, the teacher of Alexander, "for I shall not be teaching a Macedonian king, destined to die by poison in Babylon, but a handmaid and bride of Christ (ancillam et sponsam Christi) who one day shall be presented to the Heavenly throne".

### 059. 《圣经通行译本》

本书被称为 Vulgata，而这个称呼指"普遍的"或"通行的"拉丁语《圣经》译本；然而，该名称在中世纪晚期才被使用。在教会历史上，*Vulgata* 译本具有特殊的地位和影响。教宗 Damasus I（达马苏一世，366—384 年）曾经邀请 Hieronymus 开始《圣经》的拉丁语翻译，而 Hieronymus 在 383 年着手修订《新约》的早期译本。他意识到如果要翻译《旧约》就需要学习古希伯来语，从 391 年到 406 年他投身于这项巨大的工程，根据希伯来语的原文翻译了《旧约》的文献。早期的《旧约》译本主要是根据希腊语的版本（所谓的 *Septuaginta*）翻译的。

人们曾经佩服 Hieronymus 如此勤奋地进行翻译工作，但他在一定程度上依赖于 Origenes 的工作，尤其需要参考《旧约》的《六栏本》，即 *Hexapla*（参见 Origenes）。Hieronymus 在 Caesarea 的图书馆中发现了 *Hexapla*，这样他能够更轻易地比较希伯来语的原文和不同的希腊语译本。早期的教会普遍认为 *Septuaginta*（《七十贤士译本》）是《旧约》的标准的并被默启的（inspiratio）版本（参见 Augustinus, *De civ. Dei* 18, 43），但 Hieronymus 强调希伯来语文本（Hebraica veritas, "希伯来语的真理"）的重要性。他更多是一位历史学家和语文学家，而不是一位神学家，所以他一般都优先考虑到希伯来语的版本，但同时他也尊敬希腊语的译文。他发现在希伯来语文本、《七十贤士译本》以及《新约》中的《旧约》引语之间有一些差异。Hieronymus 这样解释这些差异：《福音书》的作者没有提供希伯来文的字面翻译（ad litteram），而是更多地作了意义的翻译（ad sensum）。

随着基督教向罗马帝国西部的扩展，人们从大约 150 年时开始将《圣经》的部分文献译成拉丁语，但这些翻译彼此有差异，没有统一的拉丁语译本。这些早期的拉丁译本通常被称为 *Vetus Latina*（"老拉丁语译本"）。一些教会作者曾经在他们的著作中引用部分译本，这样就保存了这些古老的翻译。那些在欧洲流行的拉丁译本被称为 *Itala*（"意大利译本"），而那些在阿富利加完成的译本则被称为 *Afra*（"阿富利加译本"）；这两个翻译传统之间的差异比较多。基于自己的深入研究，Hieronymus 能够完成一部高质量的、具有古典风格的拉丁译本，而这个译本成为后来几百年的权威译本。

就欧洲部分的传教工作来说，《通行译本》成为一个很有影响力的工具，但在另一方面 Augustinus 曾经反对《圣经》的拉丁译本；他预先看到这会进一步加剧东、西方教会之间的分裂，因为东方的基督徒仅仅接受希腊语的 *Septuaginta*（《七十贤士译本》）为权威性的版本。在拉丁语的教会中，《通行译本》逐渐取代了更早的译本，但在第 8 世纪才成为普遍使用的版本。作为教育改革中的一个部分，查理曼要求每一个堂区都应该有一部《通行译本》。他命令 Alcuinus 再次修订拉丁语的版本，因为在几百年的历史中，一些抄书者又在某些章节中插入了一些来自 *Vetus Latina*（"老拉丁译本"）

## 059. *Vulgata / Vulgate*

The name "Vulgata" means "commonly known version of the Latin Bible", but this name has only been in use since the late Middle Ages. The *Vulgate* has a special place in the history of the Church. Pope Damasus I (366—384 AD) asked Jerome to try a new Latin translation of the Bible, and Jerome started a revision of earlier New Testament translations in 383 AD. He realized that he had to learn Hebrew for the Old Testament, and in the 15 years from 391 to 406 AD he devoted himself to the translation of the Old Testament from the Hebrew text. Earlier Latin Old Testament versions had mainly been translated from the Greek text (*Septuaginta*).

Jerome has been admired for his industry and painstaking efforts, but to some extent he relied on the earlier studies of Origen, especially on the synoptic version of the Old Testament, the *Hexapla* (see Origen). Jerome discovered the *Hexapla* in the library of Caesarea and thus could more easily compare the Hebrew original and different Greek translations. The early Church generally took the *Septuaginta* as the normative and inspired text of the Old Testament (see Augustine, *De civ. Dei* 18, 43), but Jerome emphasizes the importance of the Hebrew original ("Hebraica veritas", the "Hebrew truth"). Being more a historian and philologist than a theologian he generally prefers the Hebrew text to the *Septuaginta* but at the same time respects the Greek translation. He perceives the discrepancies between the Hebrew text, the *Septuaginta*, and quotations from the Old Testament found in the New Testament. Jerome sometimes tries to explain the discrepancies in this way: the evangelists did not attempt to make a literal translation (ad litteram) of Hebrew texts but rather translated according to the meaning (ad sensum).

As Christianity spread to the Western part of the Roman empire, parts of the Bible were translated into Latin since 150 AD, but sometimes the translations differed and there was no unified Latin text. These early Latin Bible versions are usually called *Vetus Latina*. Some ecclesiastical authors quoted them in their works and so preserved some parts of these old versions. The differences between Latin Bible versions made in Europe (the so-called *Itala*, "Italian Bibles") and those translated in Africa (the *Afra*, "African Bibles") were particularly great. By virtue of his solid scholarship Jerome managed to produce a translation of very good quality in a more classical style which became the authoritative version for many centuries to follow.

For the mission work among the tribes of northern Europe the *Vulgate* became an effective tool. On the other hand Augustine opposed the Latin Bible, because he already foresaw that the Latin text would deepen the rift between the Greek and the Latin Churches, since the Christians in the East only accepted the *Septuaginta* as the authoritative version. In the Latin Church the *Vulgate* gradually replaced the earlier versions, and in the 8th century it became the commonly used text. As part of his education program, Charlemagne demanded that each monastery and each parish should have a copy of the *Vulgate*. He ordered Alcuin to revise the Latin text again, because in the course of

的语句。法兰克王在他的王国各地分配拉丁语的《圣经》,这就意味着书法和学术受到鼓励。1546 年,Trento 的大公会议宣布 *Vulgata* 的译文是教会的权威性译本,但该会议没有排除对希腊和希伯来原文的研究。教宗 Clemens VIII(克雷孟八世,1592—1605 年在位)发行了一部修订的《通行译本》,即所谓的 *Vulgata Clementina*。20 世纪的学者继续进行修订的工作。在 20 年的修订工作后,罗马教廷的一个委员会在 1979 年发行了一部《新通行译本》,即 *Nova Vulgata*。该译本的基础仍然是 Hieronymus 的版本,但也考虑了原文和早期的拉丁译本。

the centuries some interpolations from the *Vetus Latina* had been inserted into Jerome's text by some scribes. The dissemination of Latin Bibles across the Frankish kingdom stimulated calligraphy and studies in general. In 1546 the Council of Trient declared the text of the *Vulgate* to be the authentic and authoritative text of the Bible for the Church, but the Council did not exclude the study of the original Greek and Hebrew texts. Pope Clemens VIII (1592—1605) ordered the edition of a revised version of the *Vulgate*, the so-called *Vulgata Clementina*. Scholars of the 20th century continued the work of revision. In 1979 a new version (*Nova Vulgata*) was published by a Papal commission in Rome after 20 years of revision work. The new version is based on Jerome's translation but also takes into account the original texts and older Latin versions.

# 普鲁登蒂乌斯（348—405 AD）

西班牙人，大概来自 Tarracona，曾学习修辞学，当过律师，并两次任总督，后来在 Theodosius 皇帝的朝廷中任高官。在晚年他放弃了一切职位并过着苦修的生活。在古代晚期他是最优秀的基督徒诗人；其诗取材于圣经及殉道者传记。

**著作**：《神化》（论述三位一体的神，基督的神性；人通过信仰"成圣"）、《日课颂诗》（12首诗）、《反驳西马克》、《两约》（即《旧约》和《新约》的格言）、《罪恶之根源》、《殉教士行传》（14首关于罗马和西班牙的殉道士的诗）、《灵魂之战》（《灵魂的奋斗》，欧洲文学史上第一个完全比喻性的诗）

## 060. 《殉道士行传》

本著作包含14首关于殉道者的赞美诗（其中最长的有1140行），而作者将他编为他的"全集"的第7卷（因此也被称为 Liber peristephanon）。当时的教宗 Damasus（366—384年）最早开始记载关于殉道者的故事，他为罗马的殉道者的坟墓写了一些简短的碑文。Prudentius 是第一位叙述殉道者的生活和死亡并且描述他们墓地的诗人。他的赞美诗的文笔、格律和风格都反映出古典的优雅风度。这些诗也对中世纪无数的殉道者传说有着长期的影响。

前面7首诗是关于一些在西班牙去世的殉道者的，第二部分的7首描述一些在意大利或东方牺牲性命的圣徒，即 Hippolytus、Eulalia 和贞女 Agnes、Petrus 和 Paulus（他们在 Tiberis 河两岸的墓地被描述）、Carthago 的 Cyprianus、Antiochia 的 Romanus 以及在罗马死去的 Laurentius，他是慢慢地被烤死的。在去世之前，Laurentius 还作了一次讲演，在这次讲演中他预先看到了皈依于基督宗教的罗马社会。很多殉道者为处死自己的人的皈依祈祷或在死去之前赞美上主，因为他们有殉道的机会。在临终的时候，他们的面容发光，有时候一只白鸽子（象征灵魂）离开他们的躯体飞向天空。

## 061. 《灵魂之战》

该教育诗（长达915六韵步行）是第一首从头到尾使用隐喻的拉丁叙事诗。它对中世纪的文学和艺术产生了深远的影响。

前言简单地介绍了救恩的历史，从 Abraham、Lot 和 Melchisedek 到基督。基督是一切美德的统率（1~20行）。基督徒的种种美德与异教徒的种种恶习交战。首先 Fides（信仰，即"众德之王后"regina virtutum）杀害"偶像崇拜"（Idolatria，即"旧神灵的崇拜"veterum cultura deorum，21~39行）。此后，Pudicitia（贞洁）杀死 Libido（淫欲，40~108行）。Ira（愤怒）攻击 Patientia（忍耐），但因为她无法伤害忍耐的德性，她刺杀了自己

# Aurelius Clemens Prudentius / Prudentius

**Opera:** *Apotheosis, Cathemerinon, Contra Symmachum, Dittochaeon, Hamartigenia, Peristephanon, Psychomachia*

**Works:** *Apotheosis, Book in Accordance with the Hours, Agains Symmachus, The Double Testament, The Origin of Sin, Crowns of Martyrdom, Contest of the Soul*

## 060. *Peristephanon / Crowns of Martyrdom*

This collection of 14 hymns on martyrs (the longest hymn has 1140 verses) was edited by the author as book 7 of his works (also cited as *Liber peristephanon*). Pope Damasus (366–384 AD) had started to write short epigrams for the tombs of martyrs in Rome, but Prudentius was the first to narrate life and death of the martyrs and to describe their burial places. The language, meter, and style of the hymns reflect classical beauty and refinement. They had a lasting influence on innumerable medieval legends of martyrs.

The first seven hymns are dedicated to martyrs who died in Spain, the seven hymns of the second part praise witnesses of the faith who died in Italy or in the East, namely Hippolytus, Eulalia and Agnes the virgin, Peter and Paul (whose tombs on the right and left bank of the Tiber are given a description), Cyprian of Carthage, Romanus of Antioch, and Laurentius who died at Rome, being slowly roasted to death. Before his death Laurentius holds a speech in which he foresees the future of a Christian Rome. Many of the martyrs pray for the conversion of their executors or praise God for their martyrdom before they die. As they die their faces show a radiant beauty, sometimes a white dove (symbolizing their soul) leaves their bodies and soars to the sky.

## 061. *Psychomachia / Contest of the Soul*

This didactic poem in 915 hexameters is the first Latin narrative in which everything is an allegory. It had a far-reaching influence on the arts and literature of the Middle Ages.

The preface gives an outline of the history of salvation from Abraham, Lot, and Melchisedek to Christ. Christ is the commander of all virtues (verses 1~20). The (Christian) virtues encounter the (pagan) vices in a battle. First Fides (faith), the regina virtutum (queen of virtues) kills Idolatry (the "veterum cultura deorum", verses 21~39). Then Pudicitia (Chastity) slays Libido (filthy Lust, v. 40~108). Ira (Wrath) at-

(109~177行)。Superbia(骄傲)针对Mens Humilis(谦卑心灵)作一个宣讲,但因为Fraus(欺骗)挖掘了一个陷阱,骄傲从马背摔下并被Spes(希望)与Humilitas(谦卑)杀死(178~309行)。

通过其华丽的外貌,Luxuria(奢侈邪淫)迷惑一切美德,使诸美德松懈并逐渐变得软弱,但Sobrietas(觉醒)提醒和鼓励他们,她向Luxuria伸出十字架,而Luxuria那辆豪华马车的马立即受惊跑掉,车被拉向一个危险的山坡,而Luxuria这样就死去(310~453行)。第454~628行描述Avaritia(贪婪)与Cura(忧虑)、Famis(饥荒)、Metus(恐惧)、Dolus(欺诈)、Crimina(罪恶)、Amor Habendi(贪财)以及Civilis Discordia(纷争)共同攻击美德的军队。Ratio(理性)保护着那些美德,但Avaritia披着Frugi(节俭)的外衣并迷惑了那些轻信的心灵。然而,Operatio(美功)扼杀Avaritia并宣布了诸美德的胜利。

其他恶习逃跑,而Pax(和平)禁止人们继续作战。Concordia(合一)聚集士兵们(629~663行)。在诸美德的军营中Discordia(分裂,她的另一个名称是Haeresis异端)攻击Concordia(合一)。Fides(信仰)杀死Discordia(664~725行)。现在种种美德聚集在一起,而Concordia开始讲演:"让我们保持合一,就像圣父、圣子、圣灵那样。"此后Fides讲话:"让我们建立一座神圣的殿宇。"(726~821行)最后几行描述"圣城",就是一种精神性的团体。该城的四个方向代表四个时期:童年、青春期、壮年、老年时期。一切美德指向基督并感谢他。人的心灵始终需要奋斗,但Sapientia(智慧)对其予以控制。

tacks Patientia (Long-suffering), but since she cannot hurt the virtue of patience, she stabs herself (v. 109~177). Superbia (Pride) holds a speech against Mens Humilis (Humble Mind), but due to a pit dug by Fraus (Deceit) she falls from the horse and is killed by Spes (Hope) and Humility (178~309).

Luxuria (Indulgence) entices all virtues by her magnificent appearance, she makes them relax and grow weak, but Sobrietas (Soberness) exhorts them, stretches out the cross against Luxuria, and immediately the horses of Luxuria's splendid chariot flee in panic. The chariot is dragged down a steep slope and Luxuria is killed (310~453). The verses 454~628 depict how Avaritia (Greed) together with Cura (Sorrow), Famis (Hunger), Metus (Fear), Dolus (Fraud), Crimina (Crime), Amor Habendi (Love of Possessions) and Civilis Discordia (Social Unrest) attack the virtues, who are protected by Ratio (Reason). However, Greed takes the appearance of Frugi (Frugality) and manages to confuse and cheat credulous hearts. Then Operatio (Good Works) strangles Avaritia (Greed) and announces the victory of the virtues.

The other vices flee, and Pax (Peace) banishes war. Concordia (Unity) collects the army (vv 629~663). In the camp of the virtues Concordia is attacked by Discordia (Discord, her other name is heresy). Faith kills Discordia (vv 664~725). Now the virtues assemble, and Concordia addresses them with the words: "Let us be united like the Trinity of the Father, Son and Spirit.".Then Fides (Faith) holds a speech: "Let a sacred temple arise…".(vv 726~821). The last verses describe the holy city, which is a spiritual civilization; the four sides of the city symbolize the four ages: childhood, youth, maturity, old age. All virtues point to Christ and thank Him. The human soul is fighting forever, but Sapientia (Wisdom) reigns.

# 奥古斯丁（354—430 AD）

于 354 年生于 Africa 的 Thagaste（今天的 Algeria, Souk Ahras），其父 Patricius 是外教人，但母亲 Monica（331—387 年）是基督徒并深深影响了儿子的成长。Augustinus 在 Thagaste 上小学，在 Madaura 入语文学校，16 岁到 Carthago，在那里学习修辞学（参见 Cf. 3,3,6）并与一名女士同居，有私生子 Adeodatus。19 岁时他阅读 Cicero 的 *Hortensius*（失传）并决定要过精神性的生活，因此几天后加入了摩尼教，因为他认为这是更纯正的基督教。376 年后他在 Carthago 当老师，383 年到罗马，不久后获得良好的职位：在米兰当修辞学 magister（教师，参见 Cf. 5,13,23）。在米兰他听著名的讲演家 Ambrosius 的讲道并逐渐脱离摩尼教的影响。386 年 8 月 1 日他阅读 Paulus 书信而获得内心的平安，克服了一切怀疑并皈依了正统的信仰，387 年 4 月 25 日（复活节）接受圣洗，同年回到 Thagaste，与一些朋友过一种隐修者的生活。在 391 年他被要求担任 Hippo Regius 的"长老"（司铎），约于 395 年被祝圣主教，此后领导当地的教会一直到 430 年，专务写作，在恩宠论、原罪论、伦理观和历史观等方面深深地影响了神学和哲学的发展，共有 90 多卷书，还有讲演稿和书信。他抵抗当时的 Donatismus 教派，又在 410 年以后反驳 Pelagius 派的乐观主义。当 Vandales 围攻 Hippo Regius 时，他在城内去世（430 年 8 月 28 日）。

**著作**：《驳犹太人》、《忏悔录》（13 卷，是 Augustinus 的自传）、《驳学院派》、《驳亚略派的言论》、《驳马克西米乌斯》、《论基督徒的奋斗》、《论灵魂及其来源》、《论幸福的人生》、《论婚姻之美》、《上主之城》（亦译《上帝之城》、《天主之城》，22 卷的巨著，从基督信仰的角度谈论古代历史和文化）、《论婚姻和奸淫》、《论福音作者的共同点》、《论贞洁》、《论对于亡者的照顾》、《向 Simplicianus 的杂论》、《杂论》、《论占卜》、《论基督宗教的教导》、《论两个灵魂》、《论信仰和善功》、《论信仰和信经》、《论信无形之事》、《论创世记的言辞》、《论创世记，反驳摩尼教》、《论贝拉基诸行动》、《论语法》、《论基督的恩宠和原罪》、《论新约》、《论异端》、《论自由意志》、《论基督导师》、《论说谎》、《论公教的习俗和摩尼教的习俗》、《论音乐》、《论自然和恩宠》、《论婚姻和欲望》、《论杜尔西提乌斯的八个问题》、《论罪的赦免和婴儿的圣洗》、《论人的正义的成全》、《论美与适宜》、《论灵魂的量》、《论精神和文字》、《论三位一体》、《论信仰的用处》、《论真正的宗教》、《论圣咏》、《信、望、爱的手册》、《关于旧约最初七书的言论》、《关于旧约最初七书的问题》、《订正录》、《独语》（亦译《论灵魂不朽》）

## 062.《忏悔录》

本著作长达 13 卷，大约在 Augustinus 皈依后 10 年成书（397—400 年之间）。这部书在古代和近代的文学史上是独一无二的，因为它是一种"承认自己罪过"的自传，同时也是对上主的赞美（拉丁语的 confessio 可以有这两种意义）。

# Aurelius Augustinus / Augustine

**Opera:** *Adversus Iudaeos, Confessiones, Contra academicos, Contra sermonem Arianorum, Contra Maximinum, De agone christiano, De anima et eius origine, De beata vita, De bono coniugali, De civitate Dei, De coniugiis adulterinis, De consensu evangelistarum, De continentia, De cura gerenda pro mortuis, De diversis quaestionibus ad Simplicianum, De diversis quaestionibus 83 libri, De divinatione daemonum, De doctrina christiana, De duabus animabus, De fide et operibus, De fide et symbolo, De fide rerum quae non videntur, De Genesi ad litteram, De Genesi contra Manichaeos, De gestis Pelagii, De grammatica, De gratia Christi et de peccato originali, De gratia Novi Testamenti, De haeresibus, De libero arbitrio, De magistro, De mendacio, De moribus ecclesiae catholicae et de moribus Manichaeorum, De musica, De natura et gratia, De nuptiis et concupiscentia, De octo Dulcitii quaestionibus, De peccatorum meritis et remissione et de baptismo parvulorum, De perfectione iustitiae hominis, De pulchro et apto, De quantitate animae, De spiritu et littera, De trinitate, De utilitate credendi, De vera religione, Enarrationes in Psalmos, Enchiridion ad Laurentium sive de fide, spe et caritate, Locutiones in Heptateuchum, Quaestiones in Heptateuchum, Retractationes, Soliloquia*

**Works:** *Against the Jews, Confessions (Praises), Against the Academics, Against the Speeches of the Arianists, Against Maximinus, On the Christian Struggle, On the Soul and its Origin, On a Blessed Life, On the Value of Marriage, The City of God, On Marriage and Adultery, On the Consensus of the Evangelists, On Continence, On the Care of the Deceased, On different Questions to Simplicianus, On different Questions, On Divination, On the Christian Doctrine, On two Souls, On Faith and Works, On the Faith and the Creed, On believing invisible things, On the Words of Genesis, On Genesis against the Manichaeans, On the Works of Pelagius, On Grammar, On the Grace of Christ and Original Sin, On the New Testament, On Heresies, On the Free Will, On the Teacher, On Lies, On the Customs of the Catholic Church and of the Manichaeans, On Music, On Nature and Grace, On Marriage and Concupiscence, On the Eight Questions of Dulcitius, On the Forgiving of Sins and the Baptism of Infants, On the Perfection of Human Justice, On the Beautiful and Proper, On the Soul, On Spirit and Letter, On Trinity, On the Use of Faith, On the True Religion, Words on the Psalms, A Handbook to Laurentius or On Faith, Hope and Love, Words on the Heptateuch, Questions concerning the Heptateuch, Retractations, Soliloquia*

## 062. *Confessiones / Confessions*

This autobiography in 13 books was written ca. 10 years after Augustine's conversion, in 397 or 400 AD. The work has no equal neither in antiquity nor in modern literature, because it is an autobiography meant as a confession of sins and at the same time as a praise of God and thanksgiving for the author's conversion (cf. the different meanings of the Latin word "confessio").

这部著作的结构曾经被描写为"过去—现在—未来"。前面9卷叙述作者过去的生活，一直到他离开意大利和他母亲 Monica 去世的时刻。第10卷 Augustinus 反省皈依后的灵性生活（即"现在"）。第11到第13卷根据《创世记》的创世论故事讨论一些神学问题。

第1卷包括一个多次被引用的句子，也是整部书的主题："你创造我们是为了你，而我们的心灵始终不安，直到他在你内获得安息。"（1,1,1）作者描述自己的童年和青春期。他的父亲是外教人，他的母亲 Monica 是基督徒，而母亲给予他一种基督教教育，一直希望她的儿子在信仰中成长。Augustinus 叙述他的童年生活时说他和其他婴孩一样通过学习母语（他的母语是拉丁语）而进入了社会的大团体。他也回顾自己所受的文学教育以及某些外教人的神话的坏影响，比如 Jupiter（天神）用闪电惩罚恶人，但他自己也犯下了奸淫罪。Augustinus 在学习希腊语方面没有成功，虽然他后来非常尊敬 Plato 和 Plotinus 及 Porphyrius 的新柏拉图主义著作（他阅读这些著作的拉丁译文）。

第2卷叙述16岁的 Augustinus 如何去了 Thagaste，其中也描绘年轻的他内心的欲望和渴求。作者具有心理学的洞察力，分析青春期的徘徊和痛苦经验，性欲和孤独。他意识到，年轻人有时候因为要"出风头"而犯罪。他也知道读书在有的情况下等于是逃避自己生活中的实际问题。另一种观察是这个：休闲无事的人会容易陷入性欲之火。在一个晚上 Augustinus 和几个青年一起偷一棵梨树上的果子，这个行动说明人心的邪恶（2,4）。

第3卷描写他如何在 Carthago 有恋爱的经验以及 Cicero 的著作 *Hortensius* 如何在他内心燃烧了对智慧和知识的长期渴望。从此以后，他的一生的最大特点就是对于那种无所不包的真理的追求。同时，他也受了摩尼教的影响，属于这个教派9年之久。摩尼的教导是一种诺斯替教式的基督信仰，它的基础是"光明"与"黑暗"之间的冲突。

在第4卷中的 Augustinus 已经是在 Carthago 任教的修辞学老师，他沉迷于占星术，又与一名妇女同居，就是他私生子 Adeodatus 的母亲。他的朋友的逝世使他感到非常悲伤，所以他在 Carthago 找另一些朋友，在他们那里寻求一些安慰。

第5卷：Augustinus 和一位 Mani（摩尼）派的主教（名为 Faustus）谈论时发现，这种教派的人无法说明确切科学知识和他们教义的关系。他离开家乡并去罗马，开始在那里任教。他被新柏拉图主义吸引，同时逐渐离弃摩尼教。后来，Symmachus 选择他在 Milan（米兰，意大利北部）当修辞学老师，在那里他认识了 Ambrosius，那位具有名气、修养和口才的主教。Ambrosius 的讲道一方面给他留下深刻的印象，但另一方面仍不能使他心服口服。

第6卷的内容包括他在米兰的教学工作以及基督信仰对他的吸引力。他定期去

The structure of the book has been described as: past – present – future. The first 9 books describe the life of the author, ending with his departure from Italy and the death of his mother Monica. The tenth book reflect on the state of Augustine's spiritual life after his conversion (=present). Books 11~13 are speculations about theological problems, based on an interpretation of the narrative of creation of the *Book of Genesis*.

Book 1 opens up with the often-quoted passage of the "restless heart" the theme of the whole book: "You have created us for yourself, and our heart is restless until it rest in you." (Fecisti nos ad te, et inquietum est cor nostrum donec requiescat in te. 1,1,1) The author describes his childhood and youth. He is the son of a pagan father and a Catholic mother, Monica, who educates her son as a Christian and always hopes that he would grow in the faith. Augustine depicts how he, like any infant, grows into the human community by learning his mother tongue (Latin). He also reflects on his literary education and on the bad influence of certain pagan myths: Jupiter punishes the wicked with his thunderbolts but commits adultery himself. Augustine fails to learn Greek well although later on he appreciates Plato and the Neoplatonic writings of Plotinus and Porphyry (in Latin translations) very much.

Book 2 tells of a stay in Thagaste when Augustine is 16 years old, and it describes his youthful passions and desires. With fine psychological insight, the author analyses the aimless wanderings and painful experiences of adolescence, sexual desires and loneliness. The author observes that the will to impress others can induce young people to commit mistakes, that the reading of books may be an escape from existential problems in one's own life, and that a craving for sensual pleasures is usually linked to idleness. One night Augustine and some other little rogues steal the pears from a tree in the neighborhood, an act revealing the sinfulness and malice of the human heart (2,4).

Book 3 narrates how he falls in love in Carthage, and how the lecture of Cicero's book *Hortensius* (now lost) gives him with a lasting love for wisdom and knowledge. His whole life is characterized by the search for an all-encompassing truth. At the same time, he is under the influence of the Manichaean sect, which he accepts for about 9 years. The teaching of Mani expounds a Gnostic form of Christianity, based on a conflict between light and darkness.

Book 4: Augustine as teacher of rhetoric in Carthage is infatuated with astrology. He takes a mistress, the mother of his son Adeodatus. He deplores the death of a friend and looks for consolation in the companionship of other friends at Carthage.

Book 5: After talking to the Manichean bishop Faustus, Augustine finds out that these sectarians are unable to reconcile their doctrines with known scientific facts. He leaves for Rome and starts to teach there. Being attracted by the teaching of Neo-Platonism he turns away from the Manichaeans. He is chosen by Symmachus to be professor of rhetoric at Milan, where he meets the famous, educated and eloquent bishop Ambrose. The sermons of Ambrose impress him without fully convincing him.

Book 6 tells of his teaching activities in Milan, and how he continues to be attracted by Christianity. Listening regularly to Ambrose's sermons, he learns that Scriptural texts are not always to be understood in the literal sense. His worldliness and difficulties con-

听 Ambrosius 的讲道，因此了解到，对《圣经》的解释不一定都要符合字面上的意思。他的世俗精神和关于贞洁生活的困难仍然阻碍他接受信仰。Monica 来到米兰。她劝儿子放弃他的情妇并过正式的婚姻生活。

第 7 卷讨论"恶"的来源这个哲学和神学难题。那些柏拉图主义的著作帮助 Augustinus 理解神为一个精神性的存在以及解释恶的问题。他理解到这一点：恶是意志的颠倒，而不是 Mani 教人所说的"物体"。他开始阅读圣 Paulus（保罗/保禄）的书信。

第 8 卷：Augustinus 听说一些学者和朝廷官员接受了基督信仰，他也愿意皈依。这个强烈的皈依经验发生在他在米兰家中的园子里（作者大概后来又改写了这一段，使它更具戏剧性）。在他内心烦闷和情绪不满时，Augustinus 突然听见了一个小孩子的声音："拿吧！读！"（Tolle, lege, 8,5~12）他拿来一部《圣经》并开始阅读，遇到圣 Paulus 的话："天国不在于吃与喝，而在于正义、喜乐与圣神/圣灵内的平安。"他深深地被感动，决定要开始一种新的生活。作者用这样的比喻来描绘自己的皈依："主啊，你使我转向我自己，因为你从我的背后找回了我。"(8,7)他的母亲因儿子最终的皈依感到非常喜乐。

第 9 卷：辞职之后，他与一些朋友去 Milan（米兰）以北的乡间农院。在第二年的复活节，他在米兰接受洗礼并准备回到 Africa 去。当他在罗马的港口 Ostia 等待船只时，他与母亲 Monica 谈论圣人在天堂的生活。Monica 在 Ostia 去世。

第 10 卷描写 Augustinus 在皈依 10 年后处于什么样的心理状态（就是他写《忏悔录》的时刻）。他无保留地分析自己的弱点。虽然他受洗，于 391 年当司铎，395 年当 Hippo 的主教，但仍然有一些软弱的表现。只有上主的恩宠能够使人有能力抵抗人间的诱惑。关于"记忆力"的讨论预示了最后三卷的内容——以哲学的问题意识谈论宗教和信仰。

第 11、12 卷包括作者著名的"时间理论"：根据《创世记》第 1 章，Augustinus 比较神的"无时间前后的永恒性"与人世的"昨天—今天—明天"。他给"时间"下了一个很现代的定义：时间是人的意识现象。过去、现在和未来都是人心的体验，即"回顾、回忆"，"意识"和"期待"。这些考虑针对斯多亚派的观点：在他们那里，时间是宇宙的运动或一个物体的运动。上主通过他的圣言创造了一切，而在创造之前没有时间；因此，"在创造天和地之前，神做了什么"是一个没有意义的问题。

最后的书卷包含关于《旧约·创世记》第 1 章的象征性解释：上主创造的"光"代表精神界的创造，而"黑暗"代表没有上主的灵魂的黑暗。上天的"苍穹"暗示保护我们的《圣经》。"大海"指远离上主的人类，而"大海中突出的陆地"指善良的灵魂，它产生植物和果子（即仁慈的善行）。天体等于是智慧和知识，而动物是一些象征和圣事——这些圣事帮助人们克服疑惑和诱惑。人们获得了理性的礼物，这就是"上主的

cerning chastity still prevent him from accepting the faith. Monica arrives in Milan. She urges him to leave his concubine and marry.

Book 7 discusses the question of the origin of evil. The Platonist books help Augustine to understand God as a spiritual being and to explain the problem of evil. He understands that evil is a perversion of the will, not a substance as the Manicheans pretend. He starts to read the Pauline epistles.

Book 8: Augustine hears that some scholars and court officers convert to Christianity, and he wants to follow their example. The scene of his powerful conversion experience in the garden of his house in Milan was probably rewritten later so as to make it more dramatic. In his state of mental irritation and dissatisfaction Augustine hears the voice of a child: "take and read!" (Tolle, lege, 8,5~12). As he opens Scripture and starts to read, the words of St. Paul overwhelm him: "the kingdom of God is not eating and drinking, but righteousness, and joy and peace in the Holy Spirit." Deeply moved he decides to start a new life. The author uses this metaphor to depict his conversion: "Tu autem, Domine, ⋯ retorquebas me ad me, auferens me a dorso meo." (8,7) "You, Lord, ⋯ turned me to myself by turning me back from behind myself." His mother is overjoyed at his final conversion.

Book 9: Having resigned his appointment he moves with friends to a country estate north of Milan. At Easter the following year he is baptized at Milan and prepares to return to Africa. While awaiting a ship at Ostia (the harbour of Rome), he has a conversation with his mother Monica about the life of the saints in heaven. Monica dies at Ostia.

Book 10 describes the mental state of Augustine 10 years after his conversion (at the time when he wrote the *Confessions*), mercilessly analysing his weaknesses as a Christian and even after having been ordained priest (391) and bishop of Hippo (395). Only God's grace gives the power to resist temptations. The excursus on the theme of "memory" leads on to the last three books, which contain philosophical considerations about religion and faith.

Books 11 and 12 contain the author's famous theory of time: Starting from the account of the creation in *Genesis* 1, Augustine compares God's timeless eternity with the transience of our worldy "yesterday - today - tomorrow" and arrives at a very modern definition of time as a phenomenon of consciousness. Past, presence and future only exist as an experience of the heart, namely, remembering, perceiving and expecting. These considerations refute the Stoic conception of time as movement of the universe or movement of a physical body. God created everything through His word, and before the creation there was no time; it is therefore nonsense to ask "what God was doing before He created heaven and earth".

The last book contains an allegorical interpretation of *Gen* 1: The light which God created is the spiritual creation, the darkness points to the soul still in need of God's light. The firmament is a symbol of the Scriptures which shield us. The sea resembles the human race estranged from God, and the "dry land standing out from the sea" represents the good soul which produces plants and fruits (=works of mercy). The heavenly lights are

肖像"的意义。人"统治动物界"代表教会在精神界中拥有权柄。植物等于是人的食粮，这就意味着善功是精神的食粮。上主在第七天休息，所以"我们将来也要在你内永远安息"（Sabbato vitae aeternae requiescamus in te, 13,37）。

### 063. 《论幸福生活》

这部对话篇反映了 Augustinus 在他的生日那天（386 年 11 月 12 日）及随后几天进行的对话。他在乡下的庄园（名称 rus Cassiacum，即在米兰以北的 Lago di Como）和他的朋友及亲戚（包括他的母亲和儿子 Adeodatus）相会。在开始，Augustinus 面向 Theodorus（全名 Flavius Manlius Theodorus），一位著名的政治家和基督徒，他有接近新柏拉图主义的倾向。对话的主要内容是幸福——人类一切努力都指向幸福。与 *Contra academicos*（《反驳学院派》）一样，本著作也旨在反驳柏拉图主义者的怀疑论。Augustinus 提到 Cicero 的 *Hortensius*，但他自己的观点超越了 Cicero 的相对主义——Cicero 曾经自称为 magnus opinatur（"大认为者"）。Augustinus 坚持一个终极的、确定的真理，即对于唯一的神的信仰，而只有这个真理才会给人们带来智慧与幸福。

哲学能够"接受"三种人：那些在离海岸不远的浅水地区中行船的人——他们不久后会回到港口那里去；那些航海并出行很远的人——他们追求各种享受及荣誉，经历了一些悲剧或阅读一些哲学著作后，他们也回到港口（portus）那里。第三种人经历很多考验并遇到很多危险情况。在很长时间后，他们才想到家乡并最终平安归家。Augustinus 似乎属于第三种类型的人。他 19 岁时阅读 Cicero 的 *Hortensius*，从此就热爱哲学（amore philosophiae succensus sum）。他也遇到一些考验、云雾、失去了方向并被摩尼教误导。离开了它们后，学院派"指导了我的小船"，但此时他发现了最可靠的北斗星（septentrionem cui me crederem）；他领悟到，神和灵魂是精神性的实体。最后他阅读 Plotinus 的著作并与《圣经》的真理进行比较，这样获得了内心的平安。

在这个导论后，Augustinus 叙述他在他的生日与后来的日子中与他母亲和一些亲戚朋友进行的对话。他们谈论肉身与灵魂（corpus, anima）的结合。身体需要食粮，而灵魂类似地需要默想和思考（theoriae et cogitationes）。精神性的饥渴（fames animorum）或"虚无"（nequitia）是"一切恶习之母"（mater omnium vitiorum）。与这种恶习相反的美德是俭朴（frugalitas）和节制（temperantia）。在他的生日 Augustinus 要为他的灵魂提供一份美好的早餐，所以他们谈论这样的问题：那些渴望某事物的人是否是幸福的？富有的人担心失去他们的财富，而这种忧虑违背真正的幸福。因此，人们应该试图拥有一种永恒的财富（quod semper manet），而这就是神：谁拥有神，谁就是幸福的人（Deum qui habet beatus est）。但是谁"拥有"神呢？那个奉行神旨意的人？Augustinus 准备一种精神性的点心，它由"蜂蜜、面粉与核桃"组成，就是由这三个句子组成的：1）学院派的人始终寻求真理但达不到真理。2）他们必然是悲伤的，因为他们得不到他们所追求的东西。3）因为他们是不幸福的，他们也必然是不明智的，所以学院派的人没

wisdom and knowledge, and the moving creatures are signs and sacraments that help men to overcome doubts and temptations. Human beings are given the gift of reason, which is the meaning of the "likeness of God". Their rule over the animals is a symbol of the spiritual power given to the Church. Plants serving as food means that works of love and charity nourish the soul. On the seventh day God rested, "and we too shall rest in you on the Sabbath of eternal life" (vitae aeternae requiescamus in te, 13,37).

## 063. *De beata vita / On a Happy Life*

This philosophical dialogue reflects conversations at Augustine's birthday on the 12th Nov. of 386 and on the following days. He met his friends and relatives (including his mother and his son Adeodatus) at a countryside villa (rus Cassiacum), close to the Lago di Como north of Milan. In the beginning Augustine adresses Theodorus (Flavius Manlius Theodorus), a well-known politician and Christian who had affinities to Neoplatonism. The main topic is the happiness which is the aim of all human efforts. Like *Contra academicos*, this work too is an attack against the scepticism of the Platonists. Augustine mentions Cicero's *Hortensius*, but his own outlook surpasses the relativism of Cicero, who called himself "magnus opinator" (great opiner). Augustine clings to a last and definitive truth, the faith in the one God, and only this truth will make humans wise and happy.

There are three people whom "philosophy can accept": those who navigate in a shallow area close to the coast and return to the harbor soon; those who sail far away and are motivated by all kinds of pleasures and honors—but after the experience of some tragedies or after reading some philosophical books they return to the harbor (portus). The third group of people undergoes many trials and faces many dangers. Only after a long time do they remember their home and finally arrive back at the harbor in peace. It seems Augustine belongs to this third group. He started to read Cicero's *Hortensius* at the age of 19 and since then was filled with ardent love for philosophy (amore philosophiae succensus sum). He also faced trials, mists, lack of orientation and was misled by the Manicheans. After leaving them the Academy "steered my boat", but then he discovered the reliable polar star (septentrionem cui me crederem) and realized that God and the soul are spiritual entities. Finally, he read Plotin's books and compared them to the truth of the Bible, thus finally obtaining inner peace.

After this introduction Augustine narrates three conversations he had on his birthday and the following days with his mother and some of his relatives. They discuss the unity of body and soul (corpus, anima). The body needs food, and the soul needs meditation and thought (theoriae et cogitationes). Spiritual hunger (fames animorum) or "nothingness" (nequitia) is the "mother of all vices" (mater omnium vitiorum). The virtue opposed to this vice is frugality (frugalitas) and moderation (temperantia). On his birthday Augustine wants to offer a good breakfast to his soul, and so they discuss whether those who desire something are happy. Rich people fear losing their riches, and this fear is opposed to happiness. One should therefore try to possess an eternal good (quod semper manet), and this is God: Who has God is happy (Deum qui habet beatus est). But who "has" God? The one who does His will? Augustine prepares a spiritual delicacy, made of "honey, flour and nuts", namely of three sentences: The adherents of

有智慧。

第二天他们再次聚集并继续进行对话。寻求上主并始终依靠他是真正的贞洁（vere castus）。为了"拥有神"（habere Deum）需要先寻求他（quaerere），而神帮助那些寻求他的人，因此那些寻求他的人已经有一个仁慈的上主（deum propitium），但他们仍然不十分幸福，只当他们找到了（invenire）上主时他们才感到完满的幸福。

第三天的谈话围绕着悲痛（miseria）和匮乏（egestas）。一个很富有的人也许仍然缺少智慧，而这种精神性的匮乏（animi egestas）就是愚蠢（stultitia）。任何一个愚蠢的人都是可怜的。愚蠢的思想则是邪恶的。前面提到的俭朴（节制）和"虚无"（nequitia）等于是"存在"与"不存在"（esse et non esse）。俭朴等于是节制和克己。智慧是精神的平衡状态（modus animi），而基督是上主的智慧（参见 1 Cor 1:24），他曾说："我是真理"。Augustinus 认为，真理（veritas）和智慧（sapientia）也等于尺度（modus），就是说"存在"与"应该"是合一的。一个人如果在真理内达到最高的尺度（summus modus），他就是幸福的，因为他"享受"神：hoc est animis deum habere, id est deo perfrui（"对灵魂来说，拥有神就是享受神"）。最后，所有参与对话的人都赞美上主，而 Augustinus 的母亲引用"我们主教"（sacerdos noster = Ambrosius）的话：Fove precantes Trinitas!（"圣三，协助那些祈祷的人吧！"）

## 064. 《上帝/天主之城》

这部巨著（共22卷）成书于公元413—427年间，其目标是反驳这样的观点：Visigothi（西哥特人）于410年征服了罗马是因为基督宗教，或是因为罗马人放弃了传统的宗教。Augustinus 提供历史的全面解释，他视历史为救恩的历史或灾难和受审判的历史。这是第一部伟大的历史哲学（或更准确地说"历史神学"）著作，在中世纪（自然国度和"上主之城"合一！）以及近代都有深远的影响。

第1到10卷分析那些针对基督信仰的控诉并反驳异教徒的宗教。Augustinus 认为罗马的历史早就发生过一系列灾难，从 Romulus 杀死弟兄 Remus 开始。作者比较罗马的异教徒和那些日耳曼征服者——他们已经是基督徒，因而比较文明，他们的行为相当节制温和。基督宗教并没有带来罗马的衰落，而异教徒的神明在过去也没有协助罗马取得伟大的成就，因为异教徒的神是虚假的。传统的神明们对于历史没有影响。在谈论异教徒的宗教时，Augustinus 利用 Varro 的区分：(1)诗人的宗教（religio fabulosa，即神话），(2)政治性的宗教（religio civilis，即共同的敬拜），以及(3)哲学的宗教（religio naturalis，自然神学）。在古代的哲学家中，Plato 曾经最清楚地表达了一种"有神的信仰"，但 Plato 学派和新柏拉图主义者认为人心需要"中介者"，所以他们保留了一种充满鬼神的世界观。然而，人类和神之间的唯一中介就是耶稣基督，他的最伟大的成就是在人间开创天国。

the Academy always search for truth but don't attain it. Not obtaining what they desire they must be unhappy. If they are unhappy they are not wise, therefore the Academic school is not wise.

On the next day they meet again and continue the conversation. To search for God and to cling to Him is true chastity (vere castus). In order to possess God (habere Deum) one must first search for Him (quaerere), but God favors those who search for Him, therefore those who search have a gracious God (deum propitium), but they are not yet happy, they achieve happiness only if they have found (invenire) God.

On the third day the discussion centers on misery (miseria) and need (egestas). A very rich person may still lack wisdom, and this spiritual lack (animi egestas) is foolishness (stultitia). Any fool is miserable. A foolish mind is vicious. Now the concepts of frugalitas (temperance) and nequitia (nothingness) appear like being and non being (esse et non esse). Frugality is modesty and temperance. Wisdom is the balance of the mind (modus animi). At the same time Christ is the wisdom of God (cf. 1 *Cor* 1:24) and also the one who says "I am the truth." Augustine equals veritas (truth) and sapientia (wisdom) with modus (measure), namely the "is" and the "ought". The one who reaches the highest measure (summus modus) in truth is happy, because he "enjoys" God: "hoc est animis deum habere, id est deo perfrui." At the end, all discussion partners praise God and Augustine's mother quotes "our bishop" (sacerdos noster = Ambrose): "fove precantes Trinitas!" (Help those who pray, Holy Trinity!)

## 064. *De civitate Dei / The City of God*

This monumental work in 22 books was written between 413 and 427 AD in order to counter the arguments that Rome was conquered by the Visigoths in 410 AD because of the rise of Christianity or because the Romans gave up their traditional religion. Augustine provides a comprehensive interpretation of history as being a history of salvation or a history of calamity and damnation. Being the first great book of a philosophy (or better: theology) of history, it was immensely influential in the Middle Ages (unity of natural state and City of God!) and in modern times.

Books 1 to 10 analyse the accusations against Christianity and argue against the pagan religion. Augustine shows that Rome's history was a series of calamities, starting with Romulus murdering his brother Remus. The author compares the pagan Romans with the rather moderate behaviour of the Germanic conquerors who are already ennobled by Christianity. Christianity is not guilty of bringing about the downfall of Rome, and on the other hand the pagan gods or the fate are not the cause of Rome's greatness in the past, because the pagan gods are nothing. The old heathen gods had no effect on history. Discussing pagan religion, Augustine uses Varro's distinction between (1) poetic religion (religio fabulosa, myths), (2) political religion (religio civilis, cult-worship), and (3) philosophical faith (religio naturalis, natural theology). Among the classical philosophers Plato was the one to expound a theistic faith most clearly, but the Platonists and Neoplatonists think the human soul needs "mediators", therefore they retain a world view that includes a host of demons. However, the only mediator between God and humankind is Jesus Christ, and His highest achievement is the founding of the heavenly

第 11 到 22 卷的主题是"上主之城"（civitas Dei 亦称 civitas caelestis "天上之城"）。"天上之城"的核心原则是"爱神"——与"爱自己"是相反的，后者则是世俗之城（civitas terrena）的基本原则。一些天使的堕落引起了这两个无形领域的分裂。当神创造了亚当和夏娃时，他想他们的所有孩子要先居住在地上的"自然之城"并在将来要成为天上之城的居民。在人类堕落之前，"两个人对于神的爱以及彼此之间的爱没有受干扰，他们很平静地回避了一切罪，也没有什么灾难给他们带来悲痛"（14,10）。然而，亚当和夏娃的犯罪行为如此严重，以至于人性变坏，所以他们为后裔传下罪恶的束缚和死亡的命运。因为亚当和夏娃滥用了自己的自由意志，他们失去了自由意志："意志的选择如果受恶习和罪的控制，就不是自由的。"（14,11）在堕落的状态中，自爱主导人们的行为，所以他们依赖于神的恩典。只有那些因恩典而蒙召的圣徒以及天使们才形成上主之城。

人类历史经过六个阶段，在这些历史阶段中"上主之城"和"世俗之城"同时存在，一直到历史的终结——在最后的审判中，两个城市将被分开。在第一个时期（"童年"）出现 Adam 和 Seth，他们代表上主之城，也有 Cain，他是第一位建立城市的人并代表世俗之城。第 4 个阶段（成年时期）包括先知们（Samuel, David，即上天之城的代表），以及罗马城的创立人 Romulus（他代表世俗之城，与 Cain 一样杀害了自己的弟兄）。基督的诞生是在第六个以及最后的阶段，正如亚当也在第六天被创造。基督入世的时刻是历史的高峰及转折点。基督的到来意味着最后的阶段已经开始了。

罗马人始终认为他们的社会代表正义。根据 Cicero 的说法，在每一个社会中都有正义，但 Augustinus 指出，罗马从来不是一个"社会"。如果说"给予每一个人他应得到的"是正义的原则，那么为什么罗马人从来没有尊敬真正的神呢？使人离开真神并崇拜不洁的鬼神，这是什么正义呢？在这种"正义观"的转变中——有的人会说这种转化是不公平的——那些不敬拜真神的人不能是正义的。然而，异教徒的国度也能够达到某种正义的形象，即不完善意义上的正义。每一个社会至少得接受"自然国度"的一些理想原则，所以任何具体的国家可能是比远离神的"世俗之城"更好一些。在 Constantinus 皇帝以后的罗马社会（一种具有基督徒精神的社会）被视为最接近"自然国度"的社会。另一方面，教会仅仅是"上主之城"的具体表现。在教会内也可能存在着一些反对神的倾向，所以我们看到的具体教会并不等同于上主之城。异教徒的国度也许有某些贡献，比如他们确保平安，而这种条件对天上之城的成长也很重要。那些异教徒的统治者和独裁者（比如 Nero 和背教者 Julian）必须完成上主对历史的计划，而在异教徒的社会中也会产生一些美德的榜样（比如 Scaevola, Decii 弟兄等）。除此之外，Augustinus 始终尊敬异教徒的学者，比如 Plato、Varro、Plotinus 和 Porphyrius。

第 1 卷：当 Visigothones 侵略罗马时（410 年 8 月），他们没有杀害那些在城中教堂寻求避难处的人。在历史上没有发生过这样的事，即胜利者因宗教信仰而保留人们

kingdom on earth.

Books 11 to 22 focus on the "City of God" (civitas Dei or civitas caelestis, Heavenly City). The guiding principle within the Heavenly City is the love of God as opposed to self-love, which is the constitutive principle of the Secular City (civitas terrena). The split between these two invisible realms was caused by the fall of some angels. When God created Adam and Eve he planned that all their children should become citizens of the Heavenly City by living in a "natural city" on earth. Before the Fall, "the love of the pair for God and for one another was undisturbed, there was tranquil avoidance of sin, and no evil of any kind intruded from any source to bring them sadness" (14,10). However, the transgression of Adam and Eve was so great that it changed human nature for the worse and transmitted to posterity the bondage to sin and the necessity of death. The abuse of free will by Adam and Eve brought the loss of free will: "The choice of the will is truly free only when it is not the slave of vices and sin." (14,11) In the fallen state of mankind, self-love dominates human beings, so that they depend on the aid of God's grace. Only the community of saints who are chosen by grace (and the angels) form the Heavenly City.

The course of history develops in six periods, in which the City of God and the Secular City exist side by side until the end of history, when they will finally be definitively separated at the Last Judgment. The first epoch ("age of childhood") shows Adam and Seth representing the City of God; and Cain, the first founder of a city, as the representative of the Secular City. The fourth period ("age of manhood") shows the prophets (Samuel, David) on the part of the Heavenly City and on the part of the Secular City the founding of Rome by Romulus (who killed his brother like Cain). Christ is born in the beginning of the sixth and last period, just like Adam was created on the sixth day. Christ's coming to the world is the climax and turning point of history. With the coming of the Church the final stage has started already.

The traditional claim of the Roman people was to be the embodiment of justice. According to Cicero, justice is part of the essence of every society, but Augustine shows that Rome was never a society: If justice is "to give to each his due", why did the Romans never extend proper worship to the true God? "What kind of justice is it, that takes a man away from the true God and subjects him to impure demons?" In this shift within the understanding of "justice"—a shift which some might call "unfair"—, those who do not worship the true God cannot be just. However, pagan states can achieve a semblance of justice, justice in an incomplete sense of the word. As every society must at least accept the framework of the (ideal) "natural state", any historical state may be better than the Secular City of godlessness, and Roman society after Constantine (a Christian society) is seen as the closest approach to the ideal of the "natural state". On the other hand, the Church is only the empirical appearance of the City of God. Within the Church there may be tendencies inimical to God, thus the visible Church is not identical with the City of God. Pagan states may make some good contributions by securing peace, which is important for the growth of the Heavenly City. Pagan and tyrannical rulers (Nero, Julian the Apostate) fulfill God's plan for history, and pagan societies can produce examples of virtue (like Scaevola, the Decii etc). Besides this, Augustine consistently respects the pagan scholars Plato, Varro, Plotinus and Porphyry.

的性命。罗马人原来的宗教是愚蠢的,他们信仰那些无法保护 Troia 的神(比如很多特洛伊人在 Juno 的神庙中被杀)。罗马城被劫掠,暴力行为是无法避免的,但同时也发生了一些仁慈的事件——以基督的名义。对于一个圣徒来说,失去世俗的财富或没有获得正式的葬礼不是一个很大的损失(在罗马的屠杀中有的人没有被埋葬)。那些变成了俘虏的人应该想到圣徒们遭受的灾难并感到安慰。Regulus 也曾被掳。一个基督徒不可以自杀,虽然他可能被殴打或强奸。自杀不是一个伟大灵魂的特征。Lucretia 和 Cato Uticensis 不应该被效法。Regulus 比 Cato 伟大,但基督徒们应该超越 Regulus,因为他们不为人间的祖国奋斗,而是为一个超越国度的家乡奋斗。任何人的谦虚都可能因逆境而被强化。那些因基督教时代而感到不满意的人仅仅是那些渴望过奢侈生活的人。恰恰是奢侈生活和对(希腊的)戏剧的幼稚爱好削弱了罗马人的骨气和美德。在那些外邦人中存在一些将会皈依基督的人,并且有的基督徒可能不会达到永恒的幸福。

第 2 卷:在基督到来之前早就有很多灾难困扰了罗马社会。古罗马的神明们从来没有发表一些禁令或道德规律,这样他们就没有保护他们信徒的心灵不受可恶因素的影响。缺少神圣权威的哲学教导是无用的,因为人们更多效法神明们的榜样,比如一个青年也许会模仿 Jupiter 的奸淫行为。罗马人模仿希腊诗人的放纵并嘲笑神明们,但罗马人不允许对人的讽刺。Plato 谴责过诗人,而他自己也不应该被崇拜为半个神。根据 Sallustius 和 Cicero 的说法,罗马的道德状态是令人担忧的。邪恶的精灵使人做坏事。虽然一些女神对于某些人给予了一些秘密的道德教训,但人们仍然公开地举行一些可耻的礼仪。邪淫的礼仪腐蚀公共道德。基督宗教是礼貌和贞洁的宗教。那些可敬的罗马人——他们是 Regulus、Scaevola、Scipio 的后裔——应该渴望上主的祝福并放弃对古代神灵的崇拜。

第 3 卷:在崇拜鬼怪的时期总是发生灾难。神明们多次犯下奸淫之罪,比如 Mars 和 Venus。Varro 曾经认为,如果一些能干的男人(错误地)相信自己是神灵的后裔,这一点对国家有利。Paris 的奸淫和 Romulus 对弟兄的屠杀都没有被惩罚。罗马本来可以保持一个和平的小国状态。罗马人曾对 Alba 进行不正义的侵略战争。很多罗马王被杀。第一个执政官 Brutus 曾驱逐他的同伴并杀害了自己的儿子们。在执政官制度下,罗马也经历了许多暴动和内战,但神明们并没有提供什么帮助。那些针对迦太基的战争带来了灾难,但神明们没有来协助。罗马人驱逐了他们的拯救者 Scipio。Gracchi 弟兄曾引起了不安和分裂。和谐女神(Concordia)的神庙建立在发生过大屠杀的地方。Marius 和 Sulla 曾经杀害了无数的人。公元 410 年的哥特侵略者保留了很多元老的性命,早期的高卢人曾经屠杀过一些元老(公元前 390 年),但 Sulla 杀害的贵族人士比高卢人多(公元前 82 年)。

Book 1: As the Visigoths invaded Rome in August 410 AD (the famous "Fall of Rome") they spared those who fled to Christian churches in the city. In no war before did the victors ever spare the defeated for the sake of their gods. The Romans were foolish to believe in those gods who could not protect Troy (at Juno's sanctuary in Troy many were killed). The sack of Rome was by necessity cruel, but there were also acts of clemency in the name of Christ. Losing temporal goods or being denied a burial is not a big loss for a saint (not all of the dead could be buried in the massacre). Those led into captivity should be consoled by looking at the calamities which the saints suffered. Also Regulus endured captivity. A Christian is not permitted to commit suicide even if threatened with violence or rape. Suicide is not a sign of the greatness of a soul. Lucretia and Cato Uticensis are not to be imitated. Regulus excelled Cato, but Christians excel Regulus, since they do not defend an earthly fatherland but a supernatural fatherland. Adversity can strengthen the humility of anyone. Those complaining of the Christian age only want to live in luxury. Luxury and a girlish enthusiasm for (Greek) stage plays weakened Roman manliness and virtue. Among the pagans there are some future converts, and some Christians may not attain eternal bliss.

Book 2: Many calamities befell the Roman commonwealth long before Christ's coming. The gods of ancient Rome never issued any prohibitions or moral precepts and therefore did not protect the minds of their believers from detestable evils. Philosophical doctrines not backed up by divine authority are useless, because men are more influenced by the example of the gods, just like a young man who might imitate Jupiter the adulterer. Romans imitated Greek poetic licence and ridiculed gods, but they did not allow the slandering of men. Plato rejected poets, and he himself should not be revered as demigod. According to Sallust and Cicero the moral state of Rome was deplorable. Evil spirits incite men to evil deeds. Even if some godesses give secret moral instructions to certain people, shameful rites are still performed in public. Obscene rites undermine public morality. Christianity is a religion of decency and chastity. The admirable Romans—descendants of the Reguli, Scaevolae, Scipios—should desire God's blessing and abandon the worship of the ancient gods.

Book 3: During the period of demon-worship calamities were always present. The gods often committed adultery, for example Mars and Venus. Varro thought it advantageous for states if brave men falsely believe that they are offspring of the gods. Paris' adultery and Romulus' fratricide remained unpunished. Rome could have remained small and peaceful. The Roman wars against Alba were unjust. Many Roman kings were killed. The first consul, Brutus, expelled his colleague and killed his sons. After the inauguration of the consulate, Rome suffered many riots and civil wars, but the gods did not help. The Punic Wars brought disaster but no help from the gods. Rome expelled her own deliverer Scipio. The Gracchi excited civil discord. The temple of Concord, the goddess of unity, was built on the site of massacres. Marius and Sulla killed innumerable people. The Gothic invaders of 410 AD spared many senators, whereas the Gauls killed many in 390 BC, but in 82 BC Sulla killed many more senators than the Gauls.

第 4 卷：如果人们没有幸福，建立一个庞大的帝国是有益的吗？那些掌握政权的人经常被自己的恶习奴役。如果没有正义，一个王国只是一个庞大的盗贼团伙。神明们影响国家的兴衰吗？如果是这样，神明们经常放弃了自己的人并开始支持敌人。Jupiter 的父亲 Saturnus 为什么没有和 Jupiter、Juno 和 Minerva 一样受到相称的尊敬呢？神是世界的灵魂，而世界是神的身体吗？如果是这样，每当一个动物被宰杀，人们也会杀死神的一个部分。罗马人曾经呼求 Stimula 和 Strenua 这样的女神，使她们激励人们，但 Quies（安静）的庙处于 Collinus 门之外。这种现象暗示罗马人有不爱好安静的心灵。崇拜 Fortuna 和 Felicitas 的人都是坏人吗？Virtus（美德）和 Fides（信用）被视为女神，但节制和勇气为什么没有被尊敬为女神？幸福为什么没有列入 12 个主要的神明（di consentes）——他们的雕像站在罗马市中心。幸福只是神的恩赐而不是神，所以人们应该寻求那个能够给予幸福的真神。异教徒们仅仅崇拜神所给予的恩赐（如 Segetia 女神"庄稼"、Pomona"果子"、Bellona"战争"、Virtus"美德"、Honos"荣誉"、Concordia"合一"）。算命和占卜都是虚假的。Cicero 曾经在他的 *De natura deorum* 中试图区分宗教和迷信，但他没有成功。Varro 曾经谴责民间的信仰。一些民族的领导者曾经利用宗教来控制群众。

第 5 卷："命运"这个词指上主的旨意和他的权力。星星不会决定人的行动。两个双胞胎的生活不会是完全一样的，比如 Jacob 和 Esau 有很大的差异。占星术是一种虚假的知识。Cicero 反对预算未来（在他的 *De divinatione* 中）。基督徒们肯定上主的旨意、权力和他的预先知识，但这都不违背我们人的意志力。上主安排了一切，都符合一定的尺度、数字和重量（《智慧篇》Wisd. 11:20）。罗马人渴望自由，因此他们安排了一些"顾问"（consules），他们渴望荣誉和对别人的统治，而且他们的管理方式很有效。他们迷恋世俗的荣誉和赞美的行为是一种恶习，但这种恶习排除了更大的恶习。基督徒们寻求的是上主的赞美，不是人的赞美。圣徒们为上主之城的缘故受苦受难，而他们也可以从罗马人的道德榜样中学到一些东西，虽然罗马人仅仅为了人间的荣誉而追求美德。纯粹渴望权力将会变成邪恶，但如果人们渴望荣誉，他们将会避免可耻的行为。种种美德不应该因"享受皇后"与"荣誉女王"而被捆绑。上主建立了罗马人的统治，而那些基督徒皇帝（如 Constantinus、Theodosius）是幸福的、成功的且是有德行的。

第 6 卷：有人说，为了来世的生命需要崇拜神明们。Varro 曾经是最有学问的罗马人，但他自己也朝拜了罗马人的神，而他的 *Antiquitates*（41 卷）也提到很多神明和他们的礼仪。Varro 描述三种神学，即诗人的神学（神话与传说）、哲学家的神学（自然的、宇宙论的思想）以及司祭们的社会性神学（有政治功能的宗教）。然而，戏剧表演中那种没有价值的神话神学与具有文化的社会性神学和崇高的自然神学是分不开的。Euhemerus 曾经说一切神本来都是人。如何看待那些关于 Hercules 神的淫秽故事呢？个别神的特殊"职务"是一种可笑的说法。Varro 仅仅谴责神话神学，没有谴责社会性

Book 4: If the people are not happy, is it good to have a huge empire? Those in power were often enslaved by their vices. Without justice kingdoms are just large groups of robbers. Do the gods aid or hinder the rise or fall of kingdoms? If so, they often deserted their own people and went over to the enemy. Why was Saturnus, the father of Jupiter, not adequately honoured together with Jupiter, Juno and Minerva? Is God the soul of the world, and the world the body of God? Then killing an animal implies that a part of God is slaughtered. Romans invoked Stimula and Strenua to stir men to action, but the temple of Quiet was outside the Colline gate. This seems to betray an unquiet mind. Do only wicked people worship Fortune and Felicity? Virtue and Faith are goddesses, but why not temperance and fortitude? Why was Felicity not among the 12 superior gods (di consentes) whose statues stood in the Forum? Felicity is a gift of God and no goddess, so let men seek the true God who can give felicity. Pagans worship the gifts of God (Segetia "harvest", Pomona "fruit", Bellona "war", Virtus "virtue", Honos "honor", Concordia "unity"). Divination and augury are false. Cicero tried unsuccessfully to separate religion from superstition in his *De natura deorum*. Varro condemned popular belief. The kings of the nations used false religions to control the people.

Book 5: Many use the word "fate" and mean the will of God and His power. The stars do not determine human actions. No twins are ever found in whose lives everything is the same, for example, Jacob and Esau were very different from one another (cf. *Gen* 25:25). Astrology is a vain science. In his *De divinatione* (*On Divination*), Cicero opposes the belief of foreknowledge of future events. Christians confirm God's will, power, and foreknowledge, which does not contradict the existence of our human will. God has ordained everything according to a certain measure, number, and weight (*Wisd.* 11:20). The Romans desired freedom and therefore appointed consuls ("counsellors"), they desired glory and dominion over others, and they had an efficient way to rule. Their love of honor and praise was a vice, but it prevented greater vices. Christians seek the praise of God, not of men. The saints who suffer for the sake of the City of God should learn from the Roman examples of virtue, even if those were pursued for the sake of merely human glory. Plain desire to rule turns to wickedness, but the love of glory will turn away from shameful actions. The virtues should not be enslaved by "Queen Pleasure" and "Lady Glory". Roman rule was established by God, and Christian emperors (such as Constantine, Theodosius) were happy, virtuous and successful.

Book 6: Some say that the gods should be worshipped for the sake of the life after death. Varro was considered the most learned man, but he himself worshipped Roman gods, and his 41 books of *Antiquities* speak of many gods and rites. Varro wrote about three kinds of theology, namely the theology of poets (mythical and fabulous), the theology of philosophers (natural, physical) and the civil theology of priests (political). However, the unworthy mythical theology of the theatrical performances is inseparably connected to the (cultivated) civil and (sophisticated) natural theology. Euhemerus concluded that all gods were men originally. What about obscene stories concerning the god Hercules? The offices of individual gods are ridiculous. Varro only reprehends mythical

的神学。Seneca 严厉批评了社会性神学。Seneca 部分地尊敬犹太人。无论如何,神话神学和政治性的神学都无法引导人们走向永生。

第 7 卷:本卷谈论某些神(比如 Jupiter、Janus、Mercurius、Mars)以及 Varro 关于他们的看法。

第 8 卷:意大利哲学派(其创立人是 Pythagoras)以及 Ionia 学派(由 Thales 创立)代表一种自然神学。Socrates 是一位杰出的人物,但他的追随者的看法并不一致,甚至互相矛盾。Plato 结合了这两个学派,而 Plato 学派的观点比一切其他的哲学家都好,无论是在逻辑学或在伦理道德方面。Plato 学派"离我们最近",所以 Plato 的 *Timaeus*("神先结合了土地与火")与《旧约》的 *Genesis*(《创世记》)有一些相似之处。Plato 好像看过《旧约》,但 Plato 学派的人仍然相信一些精灵——这些精灵是神明们的使者。埃及的 Hermes Trismegistos 也曾经说过很多有关创造主的事,似乎也有一些真理因素,但他也相信那些精灵。

第 9 卷:Augustinus 分析 Peripatos 学派、Stoa 学派、Plotinos 以及 Apuleius 的思想。Plato 学派的人认为,在神和人们中间有很多使者,但对基督徒来说耶稣基督是唯一的中间人。

第 10 卷:希腊语和拉丁语的单字有类似的意义:latreia - servitus(崇拜)、threskeia - religio(宗教)、theosebeia - adoratio(朝拜)、eusebeia - pietas(虔敬)。Plotinos 认为理性的灵魂从上面获得照亮,这就符合《约翰福音》*Jn* 1:6ff。Religio("宗教")一词来自 relegere("再次选择")或来自 religare("再次约束")。Plato 学派曾经崇拜天使们,但真正的朝拜只归于上主。Porphyrius 曾经在崇拜精灵中允许了一些不合法的知识(行神迹,净化灵魂)。Porphyrius 无法认出基督的智慧,虽然他正确地拒绝了灵魂的轮回说。Plato 学派的人相信灵魂与神是一样永恒的,但基督徒相信灵魂是被创造的。

第 11 卷:整个著作的第二个部分描述两个城市(天上的和人间的城市)的来源和目的。属于正典的《圣经》书卷都是由圣神/圣灵写的。宇宙是由上主创造的。在世界被创造以前没有时间,而在世界以外没有无限的空间。上主创造了天使们,也创造了那些后来堕落的天使们。基督徒们相信唯一的、不变的圣三,即圣父、圣子、圣神/圣灵。一切受造界都赞美创造主。恶的来源是意志,不是创造主。Origenes 的教导是错误的。关于"我存在"的自我意识是真实的,也是可靠的。我们人具有圣三的肖像,因为记忆力、理解力和意志力(或爱)在一个灵魂中结合为一。

第 12 卷:一切天使在被创造的时候都是善的。恶习会伤害善良的本性。宇宙的秩序和一切事物都赞美神。一个善良的受造物可能怀有一个邪恶的意志,并因此转向恶的行为。一种颠倒的喜好会转向那些易变的事物并放弃不变的价值。世界并不是永恒的,也不存在很多宇宙。历史也不会在一些固定的循环中不断重复自己。上主

theology, not civil theology. Seneca fiercely condemned the civil religion. Seneca's views of the Jews were partly respectful. Mythical and political theology certainly cannot lead to eternal life.

Book 7: This book discusses certain deities (Jupiter, Janus, Mercury, Mars etc.) and Varro's views of them.

Book 8: The Italian school of philosophy (founded by Pythagoras) and the Ionian school (founded by Thales) present a kind of natural theology. Socrates was outstanding, but his followers' opinions were diverse and contradictory. Plato combined the two schools, and the views of the Platonists are preferable to the tenets of all other philosophers, both in the fields of logic and moral thought. The Platonists "come closest to us", and Plato's *Timaeus* ("God first united earth and fire") bears some semblance to the *Book of Genesis*. Plato seems to have known the Old Testament, but the Platonists believe in demons as messengers of the gods. The Egyptian Hermes Trismegistos also said many things concerning the Creator, which have the appearance of truth, but he believed in demons, too.

Book 9: In this book Augustine analyzes the views of the Peripatetics, of the Stoics, of Plotinus and Apuleius. The Platonists presume that there are many messengers between God and men, but for Christians, Jesus Christ is the only Mediator.

Book 10: Greek words and Latin words have similar meanings: latreia – servitus (cult), threskeia – religio (religion), theosebeia – adoratio (worship), eusebeia – pietas (piety). Plotinus holds that the rational soul is illuminated from on high, which is in harmony with *John* 1:6. "Religio" comes from "relegere" ("re-choose") or from "religare" ("bind again"). The Platonists worship angels, but true sacrifice is due only to God. Porphyry approves of unlawful arts (spiritist sessions, purification of the soul) in the worship of demons. Porphyry was unable to recognize the wisdom of Christ, although he rightly rejected reincarnation. Platonists believe in a soul co-eternal with God, Christians in the creation of the soul.

Book 11: The second part of the work demonstrates the origin and end of the two cities, the heavenly and the earthly. The canonical Scriptures were composed by the Holy Spirit. The world was created by God. There is no infinite time before the world nor infinite space outside it. God created the angels, even those who later fell away from the light. Christians believe in the simple and immutable Trinity of the Father, Son and Spirit. All creation pleases the Creator. The cause of sin is the will, not the Creator. Origen's doctrine is wrong. The awareness of the "I do exist" is true and reliable. We bear in ourselves the image of the Trinity, as mind, intellect and will—or love—are united in one soul.

Book 12: All angels were created with a good nature. Vices injure a good nature. The order of the universe and all things praise God. A good creature can have an evil will that turns to evil deeds. A perverse love turns to perishable goods and forsakes the immutable good. The world is neither everlasting nor is there a multiplicity of worlds.

知道一切数字,他根据数字、尺度和重量制定了一切(参见《智慧篇》11:21)。上主创造了人和天使,但天使们无法创造任何东西。

第13卷:最早的人类的堕落带来了死亡的惩罚,而罪恶使人的灵魂变坏。圣徒们经常为真理的缘故遭受第一个死亡,这样就从第二个死亡(永恒的惩罚)中解放出来。亚当的罪等于灵魂的第一个死亡。有的哲学家说,人们的身体不能是不朽的或永恒的。另一些人对于 Gen 1~3 作出了隐喻式的解释。这种象征性的解释也是可取的,但同时还必须相信故事本身的真实性。在复活时,圣徒们将拥有一个精神性的身体。上主曾向人吹入生命的气息,而耶稣也曾经以他的圣神/圣灵(pneuma)激励他的信徒。

第14卷:如果上主的恩典没有拯救很多人,亚当的罪将会给人类带来永久的死亡。罪的根源在灵魂,不在肉身。Plato 对于身体和灵魂的看法是不可取的,但仍然比摩尼教的教导好一些。Stoa 派认为在智者的心灵中有三种态度(eupatheiai),即意志、喜乐、谨慎。基督徒们的感受应该符合《圣经》。那种"不受困扰"的心态(apatheia, impassibilitas)仅仅能在一些没有罪的人那里找到。亚当在犯罪之前曾怀有邪恶的意愿和骄傲。智慧应该控制人们的愤怒和欲望。人们很自然地因自己的欲望感到羞愧,这也是正当的。上主在人犯罪之前制定并祝福了婚姻。在乐园中的夫妻生活不会有欲望和意志之间的冲突。没有可耻的欲望也会有生育的机会。两种爱创造了两个城市:爱自己、爱荣誉和权力属于世俗的城市,而爱上主、爱谦虚、仁慈则属于天上之城。

第15卷:Cain 建立了一座城,但 Abel 曾属于天上之城。人间的城市指向天上之城。天上之城的居民们是由于恩典产生的,不是由于罪恶产生的。Cain 杀死他的弟兄,后来又有 Romulus 的凶杀案。在洪水之前,人们曾经有比较长的寿命。虽然祖先的这种高寿生活听起来似乎不能让人相信,但我们更应该相信希伯来语的版本,胜过希腊语的、拉丁语的或叙利亚语的版本。Henoch 突然被夺走(《创世记》5:24),这就是基督复活的预兆。上主的愤怒是对于罪恶的惩罚,比如在洪水时期。Noah 的方舟是基督和教会的象征。关于洪水的故事既有历史含义,又有象征意义。

第16卷:本卷提供关于以色列祖先的历史解释,即从 Noah 的儿子们 Shem、Ham 和 Japhet 到巴比伦王国,以及人类语言的混乱。Augustinus 谈论天使语言的意义并认为希伯来语曾是巴比伦以前的人类的第一个、共同的语言。从 Abraham 开始,作者叙述 Lot、Hagar、Sarah、Isaac 和 Jacob 的故事。Jacob 曾被称为 Israel("看见神")。Joseph、Moses、Joshuah 和 Saul 也被讨论。

第17卷:在先知们的时期,人间的耶路撒冷是天上之城的预兆。Samuel 的母亲 Hannah 是教会的象征。David 所获得的许诺在他的儿子 Solomon 身上没有应验,但在

History does not repeat itself in fixed cycles of ages. God knows all numbers; He ordered all things in number, measure, and weight (cf. *Wisdom* 11:21). God created man, angels, but angels do not create anything.

Book 13: The fall of the first human beings incurred death as a punishment of sin, and sin vitiated human nature. The saints suffer the first death for the sake of the truth, so that they may be freed from the second death (eternal punishment). Adam's sin was the first death of the soul. Some philosophers hold that earthly bodies cannot be made incorruptible and eternal. Others have an allegorical understanding of *Genesis* 1~3. This symbolic interpretation is admissible, but the truth of the story proper must also be believed. After resurrection the saints will have a spiritual body. God breathed the breath of life into man, and Jesus inspired the faithful with His Spirit (pneuma).

Book 14: The sin of Adam would have brought about an everlasting death to mankind if God's grace had not redeemed many. The cause of sin proceeds from the soul, not from the flesh. The Platonic view of body and soul, though not acceptable, is more tolerable than that of the Manicheans. The Stoics wish to find three dispositions (eupatheiai) in the mind of the wise man (will, gladness, caution). Christians' feelings are consistent with the Holy Scriptures. The condition of apatheia (impassibilitas) will only be found in a sinless man. Adam's sin was preceded by an evil will and by pride. Anger and lust must be restrained by wisdom, and human nature is rightfully ashamed of its lust. God established and blessed marriage before man's sin. Marriage in paradise would not have known the conflict between lust and will. Childbirth might have been possible without shameful desire. The two loves have created two cities: love of self, of glory, of power, belong to the earthly city; and love of God, humility, and charity, belong to the City of God.

Book 15: Cain founded a city, but Abel belonged to the City on High. The Earthly City points towards the Heavenly City, whose citizens are produced by grace, not by sin. The fratricide of Cain preceded Romulus' murder. Before the Flood (cf. *Gen* 6~9) men had a longer life, and even if the high age of the ancestors sounds incredible, we should believe the Hebrew text more than the Greek, Latin or Syriac translations. Enoch was suddenly taken away (cf. *Gen* 5:24), which prefigures Christ's resurrection. God's anger is a judgment for the punishment of sin, like in the case of the Flood. Noah's ark is a symbol of Christ and the Church. The story of the Flood has both historical and symbolic meaning.

Book 16: This book presents an interpretation of the history of the patriarchs of Israel, from Noah's sons Shem, Ham and Japheth to the kingdom of Babylon, and the confusion of the languages. Augustine expounds the meaning of the angelic language and presumes that Hebrew was the first and the common language of mankind before Babylon. From Abraham the narrative leads to Lot, Hagar, Sarah, Isaac, Esau and Jacob. Jacob was given the surname "Israel" ("seeing God"). Joseph, Moses, Joshuah and Saul are discussed.

Book 17: In the age of the prophets the earthly Jerusalem prefigures the Heavenly City. Samuel's mother Hannah is a symbol of the Church. The promises given to David

基督那里实现了。很多 psalmi(《诗篇/圣咏》中的诗歌)都预言了基督或暗示他的苦难和复活。

第 18 卷:本卷包括许多关于古代国王和王国的资料,一直到基督的时代,即关于亚述人、希腊人、埃及人、雅典人等等的资料;作者始终与犹太人的历史进行对比,比如 Aeneas 来意大利时,Labdon 正担任希伯来人的领导。当犹太人从巴比伦解放出来时,罗马人摆脱了国王们的统治。《旧约》先知(如 Hosea、Amos、Isaiah、Micha 等)的预言指向基督和《新约》。教会关于《圣经》正典的规定排除了某些书卷。《圣经》曾被从希伯来语译成希腊语,这是由上主的预先安排而完成的事,并且 72 位犹太学者非常可靠地完成了翻译工作。在圣殿被恢复了以后,犹太人再没有先知。基督的诞生带来了一个新的时代。通过门徒们和讲道者的见证,教会不断扩大,虽然也出现一些异端、教难,甚至在未来也可能会出现"敌基督"。

第 19 卷:根据 Varro 的说法,人们曾提出 288 个关于"至善"的看法。Varro 选择三个有关至善的定义。根据一些哲学家的看法,至善在于人本身。基督徒们要始终满怀希望,要面对悲痛,因为美德并不让人避免痛苦。在社会生活、人们的判断、友谊和沟通中存在着许多缺点。圣徒的真正目标是永恒的平安与幸福。甚至尘世的斗争也旨在获得和平,一种普遍的和平,天上与人间的秩序。人拥有自由意志,但也可能成为自己欲望的奴隶。天上之城是人间的朝圣者和旅游者,但它也会利用人间的和平并使它指向天上的和平。不仅仅罗马人可以称为"人民"(populus),因为人民是很多有理性的人因他们爱好的共识而结合的群体。这样 Augustinus 提出了关于"人民"的新定义(参见 Cicero, *De re publica*)。他们所爱的东西也揭示了每一个民族的特性(19,24)。

种种城市和国度的兴起来自于人们对于统治别人的渴望(libido dominandi)。人们的权力欲和暴力导致战争,因此国度是罪恶的结果,也是罪过的契机,而不是人生的自然部分,如同 Plato 和 Aristoteles 所说的那样。最好的国度也会引起恐惧、死亡和痛苦。良好的裁判官也会用虐待的方式来揭露真相,而最好的审判者偶尔也会犯错误(19,6)。

第 20 卷:上主最后的审判将会解开人事的网络。《新约》和《旧约》都预言了末日的神圣审判。Johannes 的默示录/启示录已经暗示将会有两个复活。关于"基督与他的圣者将统治一千年"(*Rev* 20:4)以及"敌基督的时期"这样的说法都需要解释。魔鬼和他的追随者将受惩罚,而"新天新地"意味着教会永久的光荣。*Petrus*、*Paulus*、*Isaiah*、*Daniel*、*Psalmi*(《诗篇/圣咏》)以及 *Malachi* 都预言了这些最后的事。《旧约》中有关神的审判的章节很明显地指向基督,虽然没有明确提到他。

第 21 卷:关于永恒惩罚的问题包括这样的难题:一个物质的身体是否能永远在

are not fulfilled in his son Solomon, but in Christ. Many psalms prophesy Christ or relate to His passion and resurrection.

Book 18: This book is a collection of the dates of many kings and kingdoms down to the time of Christ, including the Assyrians, Argives, Egyptians, Athenians etc., which is always compared to the history of Israel, e.g. Aeneas came to Italy when Labdon was a judge over the Hebrews. When Jewish captivity in Babylon was ended, the Romans were delivered from the domination of their kings. The prophesies of Hosea, Amos, Isaiah, Micah etc. apply to Christ and the New Covenant. The ecclesiastical canon excludes certain writings. The Holy Scriptures were translated from the Hebrew into Greek, a project ordained by God's providence. 72 Jewish scholars—thus the name *Septuaginta* — most faithfully accomplished the work of translation. After the restoration of the Temple, the Jews ceased to have prophets. The birth of Christ marked a new era. Through the witness of the disciples and preachers the Church grows, even though there are heresies, persecutions and perhaps the coming of the Antichrist in the future.

Book 19: According to Varro there are 288 different opinions concerning the supreme good. Varro selects three definitions of the highest good. Philosophers thought that the supreme good lies in themselves. Christians live in hope and are ready to face misery, because virtue does not protect from sufferings. Social life, human judgment, friendship, and communication are beset with imperfections. Eternal peace and happiness are the true aims of the saints. Even earthly struggles aim at peace, at a universal peace, the order in heaven and on earth. Man has free will, but can become a slave of his own lust. The Heavenly City is a pilgrim on earth but makes use of earthly peace and directs it towards heavenly peace. Not only the Romans, but also other nations can be called "people", since a "people" (populus) is a multitude of rational creatures united by a common agreement as to the objects of love. Augustine thus presents a new definition of a "people" (cf. Cicero *De re publica*). The objects of their love will reveal the character of any people (19,24).

The rise of cities and states originated from the lust of mastery (libido dominandi), the desire to dominate others. Man's lust for power and violence leads to wars, therefore the state is a consequence of sin and an occasion for sin, it is not, as for Plato and Aristotle, a natural part of human life. Even at its best, the state will cause fear, death and pain. Even good judges have to resort to torture in order to obtain the truth, and even the best judges make mistakes (19,6).

Book 20: The last judgment of God will disentangle the web of human affairs. This divine judgment at the end of the world was foretold by the New and Old Testaments. The Revelation of John hints at the two resurrections. The meaning of the "reign of the saints with Christ for a thousand years" (*Rev* 20:4) needs explanation, likewise the "time of the Antichrist". The devil and his followers will be condemned, and the "new heaven and the new earth" mean the unending glory of the Church. *Peter, Paul, Isaiah, Daniel, the Psalms* and *Malachi* foretold the last things. Passages of the Old Testament concerning God's judgment clearly hint at Christ, even if He is not explicitly mentioned.

Book 21: The question of eternal punishment entails these problems: can a material

火中存在或遭受永久的苦痛？很多事情不能靠理性作解释，但这些事情仍然是真实的。有的奇迹来自大自然，有的来自鬼怪或来自人的技巧，但只有神是全能的。地狱的永久火焰将会烧毁恶鬼吗？如果说罪恶的惩罚比罪恶本身还要长，这是公平的吗？由于亚当的罪的严重性，一切不包括在救世主的恩典之内的人将遭受永久的惩罚。人生充满诱惑，因此也算为一种有限度的惩罚。上主对于他的创造物的仁慈是很大的，但不能否认永久惩罚的可能性（如 Origenes）。有的人说，通过圣徒的代祷一切人将获救，但这种说法不符合《圣经》的记载。甚至那些与善功同时发生的罪也有坏的影响。

第22卷：最后的书卷又从天使的创造开始并重复前面的一些话题：关于永久幸福或永久惩罚的诺言、复活的问题、基督和 Romulus 之间的比较、奇迹和殉道者们的奇妙行动、Plato 学派的观点、肉身复活的观点、将来的精神性身体、人间生活中的种种恩典、Plato 和 Porphyrius 关于肉身和灵魂分离的看法、在来世见到神以及在天上城市享受永恒的幸福——圣徒们在那里享有永恒安息日的平安。

## 065. 《论基督宗教的教导》

Augustinus 最有影响的著作之一是他关于基督宗教教导的手册，共分四卷。前三卷成书于397年，第4卷于426年才完成。最后的部分经过 Hrabanus Maurus 改写，以 *De institutione clericorum*（《圣职人员的教育》）的书名发行，后来也成为 Augustinus 第一部被印刷的著作（1465年，书名为 *De arte praedicandi*《讲道的艺术》）。

第1、2卷谈论基本的神学知识和世俗的学科——这些学科为理解《圣经》是有用的。世俗的知识（scientia）应该导致一种有哲学和神学维度的世界观（即 sapientia）。因此，前者要为后者服务，但成为一个既有学问（doctus），又有智慧的人（sapiens）是值得赞美的。这种原则支持和保护传统的学术知识，但要在基督信仰的指导下继承这些知识。Augustinus 提出一种关于"事物"（res）和"符号"（signa）的理论。世界可以区分为两种"事物"：那些要为更高的目标而"使用"（uti）的东西，以及那些本身能够"享受"（frui）的东西。物质性的财富属于前者，爱神和爱人属于后者。如果要了解《圣经》必须从最高的价值（神）的角度来解释一切。因此，爱与理解是分不开的。

第2卷谈论"符号"的理解。这种理解的前提是人们对语言和世俗知识的掌握。然而，只有基督所启示的智慧能够引导读者理解种种象征和言辞的深层意义，这样能够从模仿的形象走向原本的形象。

第3卷分析《圣经》的文本和教导。Augustinus 提供一些解释《圣经》文本的原则。《圣经》使用的符号和言辞具有很多方面的意义，而任何全面的解释必须阐明各种话语的深层意义。作者反对一种太自由的或过于灵性的解释方式。他强调说只有科学

body endure for ever in a burning fire or can it suffer eternal pain? Many things cannot be explained by reason but they might be true. Some wonders are produced by nature, others by demons or by human skill, but only the Creator is omnipotent. Will the eternal fire of hell burn the wicked spirits? Is it just that the punishment of sins lasts longer than sin itself? Due to the seriousness of Adam's first transgression eternal punishment is meted out to all who are outside the Savior's grace. This life is full of temptations and is therefore a temporal punishment. God's grace towards His creation is very great, but one cannot deny the possibility of eternal punishment (like Origen). Some believe that by the intercession of the saints all might be saved, but this is not in accordance with the Scriptures. Even sins accompanied by works of mercy are harmful.

Book 22: This last book starts again with the creation of the angels and repeats former topics: the promise of eternal bliss or punishment, the resurrection, the comparison between Romulus and Christ, miracles, the miraculous deeds of martyrs, Platonist views, considerations concerning the resurrection of the body, the new spiritual body, the blessings of this life, views of Plato and of Porphyry on the separation of body and soul, the vision of God in the world to come and the eternal felicity in the City of God, where the saints enjoy the peace of the perpetual Sabbath.

## 065. *De doctrina Christiana / On Christian Teachings*

One of the most influential of Augustine's works is this manual on Christian learning. It is divided into four books. The first three were written in 397 AD, the last book was finished much later, in 426 AD. The last part was used by Hrabanus Maurus in his *De institutione clericorum* (*On the Education of Clerics*) and later became the first work of Augustine to appear in print (in 1465 under the title *De arte praedicandi, On the Art of Preaching*).

Books 1 and 2 treat basic theological knowledge and secular arts which are useful for the study of the Bible. Secular knowledge (scientia) should lead to a philosophical and theological world view (sapientia). Thus the former is subordinated to the latter, but it is laudable to be educated (doctus) in order to become wise (sapiens). This principle promoted and protected classical scholarship under Christian auspices. Augustine presents a theory of "things" (res) and "signs" (signa). The world of things can be divided into things that are to be used (uti) for a higher purpose and goods that can be enjoyed (frui) as a value. Material goods belong to the former, love of God and love of neighbor belong to the latter. In order to understand the Bible well one must orientate everything to the highest good (God). Thus love and insight are inseparable.

Book 2 discusses the understanding of the "signs", which presupposes the command of language and the familiarity with secular sciences. However, only the wisdom revealed by Christ will allow a reader to understand the deeper meaning of symbols and words and so find the way from the copied images to the original image.

Book 3 analyses text and teaching of the Holy Scriptures. Augustine provides several rules for the interpretation of Biblical texts. The signs and expressions used in the Bible have different layers of meaning, and any comprehensive interpretation must ex-

的解释学能够启发《圣经》文本的真实意义，而这就意味着解释《圣经》的人必须有能力阅读希腊语和希伯来语的文献。

第4卷试图提供一种"讲道学"的系统提纲。正如 Cicero 想训练有能力的演讲家，Augustinus 的目标是培养完善的讲道家（praedicator，布道家）——他应该结合智慧与口才。与 Cicero 的修辞学家一样，基督教的讲道者也面对三个任务：他必须教导人，使听众感到快乐并且影响他们（ut doceat, ut delectet, ut flectat, 4, 27）。来自《圣经》的例子表明，先知们和 Paulus 也曾经使用了修辞学的工具来提高他们教导和讲道的效果。讲道词必须带给人一些快乐，否则他们会感到无聊。更重要的是，讲道的话语应该感动和刺激听众，使他们在心中拥有一种新的态度和信念，虽然他们在理智上也许对某些信条仍然怀疑。在说话和写作时需要有优美的文笔和修辞学的比喻，但这些工具必须为信仰的内容和教导而服务。不应该为修辞学而培养修辞学，华丽的言辞必有目标和意义。因此 Augustinus 反对当时很多作家所爱好的空洞、矫揉造作的风格和华而不实的辞藻。他自己也曾经受了这种华丽文风的训练，而在他的书信中他偶尔使用了这种表达方法，仅仅是为了证明自己掌握优越的言辞和风格。总而言之，Augustinus 继承许多来自古典演讲学的方法，但他改变一些因素，使修辞学服从于内容并且为演讲学提出一个新的目标：更有效地宣布福音。

## 066. 《论真实的宗教》

这篇论战性的文章大约于390年成书，与当时摩尼教的讨论和争论有关系。Augustinus 要阐述一种对哲学家有吸引力的基督信仰，但在他晚年的 *Retractationes*（427年）中，他又对 *De vera religione* 中的一些比较倾向于人文主义和理性主义的因素予以保留。

所谓"真正的宗教"只能在基督和他的教会内找到，因为那些异教徒哲学家虽然意识到异教徒宗教中的迷信与害处，但他们并没有抵抗那种偶像崇拜。第一个部分描述上主对人类的救恩计划。亚当和夏娃有意识地反对了神，这就是"恶"的本质。恶自己并不是一个实体，它不存在（这个论点反驳了摩尼教的二元论）。上主给人类的惩罚表面上是痛苦的，实际上却是一种帮助，因为人类被迫离开乐园，他们必须放弃肉身的享受并寻求永恒的真理。人们可以根据几个步骤转向真理：历史上的权威性人物可以当做一种指南；依靠理性，人心能够达到最高的、永恒不变的原则；灵魂和精神能够达到一种合一。在比较高的阶段，人们必须放弃理性。

第二个部分描述了人的理性如何上升到永恒的真理。"同一性"、"单一性"与"真理"的永恒法则都是在理性的上面，而神本身就是真理。在这种语境中 Augustinus 提供一种"不可怀疑的真理的存在"的论证："无论谁认为他在怀疑，他就真正在思考。"（omnis qui se dubitantem intellegit, verum intellegit, XXXIX，参见 Descartes 的

plore the deeper meaning of the words. The author argues against a too free and spiritual explanation of the Bible. He emphasizes that only scientific exegesis will reveal the true meaning of the Biblical text, and this implies that the exegete must be able to read the original Greek and Hebrew documents.

Book 4 attempts to provide a systematic outline for the "art of preaching" (homiletics). Just as Cicero aims at the training of a good orator, Augustine envisages the education of a perfect preacher (praedicator) who must combine wisdom and eloquence. Similar to Cicero's rhetorician, the Christian preacher must face three tasks: he has to teach, to please and to influence his audience (ut doceat, ut delectet, ut flectat, 4, 27). Examples from the Bible show that the prophets and Paul also used rhetorical devices in order to enhance the effect of their teaching and preaching. A homily must be entertaining so as not to give cause to boredom on the side of the audience. Even more important, a sermon should move and stimulate the listeners, it should foster a new conviction in them even when they are intellectually still doubting some tenets of the faith. In speaking and writing a good style and rhetorical figures are important but they must be subordinated to the contents and to the doctrine of the faith. Eloquence must not be cultivated for its own sake, and literary beauty should have orientation and meaning. Thus Augustine attacks the empty mannerisms and the stylistic brilliance that were cultivated by many writers in his day. Even he himself had been trained along these lines and in his letters he occasionally uses long flourishes just to show his command of superior phrase and style. In one word, Augustine inherits much from the classical tradition of oratory but he changes some elements, subordinates style to content and gives the art of oratory a new purpose: to proclaim the gospel more efficiently.

## 066. *De vera religione / On True Religion*

This polemic treatise was written circa 390 AD and is connected to the debates and quarrels with Manichaeism. Augustine presents a Christian faith appealing to philosophers, but in his *Retractationes* of 427 AD—written 37 years later—he distanced himself from some of the more humanist and rationalist tenets of *De vera religione*.

The "true religion" can only be found with Christ and His Church, since the pagan philosophers did not resist idol worship although they perceived the harmful superstitions of pagan religion. The first part of the treatise describes God's salvific plan for mankind. Adam and Eve have willingly rejected God, and this is the essence of evil. Evil itself is without substance, it does not exist (an argument against Manichaean dualism). God's punishment for humans is a "blessing in disguise", since having lost paradise human beings are forced to abandon the love for bodily pleasures and search for the eternal truth. Man's turn towards truth follows several steps: authoritative people from history can serve as an orientation; relying on reason, the human spirit can reach the highest, immutable law; the soul and the spirit may finally reach a union. At the higher stages reason must be left behind.

The second part of the treatise shows the ascension of reason to eternal truth. The immutable laws of identity, unity and truth are above reason, and God is truth himself. In this context Augustine presents a proof of the existence of indubitable truth: "Whoever

"我思故我在")一层一层的存在物都反映了真理和美,甚至负面的现象也是如此:欺骗和错误是对真理的歪曲,弱点和恶习是真理和道德理想的影子。一切事物指向人心的最后使命:追求真理,寻求神——他是"最高的和最内在的真理"(summa et intima veritas)。

Augustinus 的主要目标之一是表达这个观点:基督教是古典希腊哲学最适当的继承人。以前只有 Socrates、Plato 和他们的圈子才意识到,唯独精神生活才使人享受真正的幸福,但现在这种信念已经成了整个地中海世界的共识。基督宗教是一种"给一般人的柏拉图主义",因为那些 Plato 主义者"仅仅需要改变几个词和说法"就能够成为基督徒(Paucis mutatis verbis et sententiis Christiani fierent, IV.7)。Augustinus 重视古代晚期的柏拉图主义,它排除政治思想和关于大自然的思考。在古代晚期的解体与混乱中,用理性的计划来改变世界根本就是无希望的,所以个人的灵魂的拯救成为更重要的事。"不要向外!回到你的内心去吧;真理在内心深处"(Noli foras ire! In te ipsum redi; in interiore homine habitat veritas. XXXIX.72)。

当基督信仰被理解为一种道德性的和理性的宗教时,基督的生活就成为一种道德榜样(XVI.32)。神的拯救行动,神的言词、比喻、圣事,这都主要是"理性行为的规律"(rationalis disciplinae regula, XVII.33)。在比较早期的历史阶段发生的奇迹不再被需要(XXV.47)。然而,在 Augustinus 的眼中,基督信仰并不是一个人文主义的或世俗化的宗教:人们没有自由,他们应该自愿地接受上主的轭(servi meliores serviunt liberaliter, XIV.27)。统治与服从是一些核心的概念:正如精神必须统治身体,上主必须统治人的精神(rationalis substantia Deo subiecta, XXIII.44)。一个基督徒也应该过一种刻苦的生活(non diligamus mundum, non diligamus voluptatem, LV.107),否则种种欲望将会控制和支配人。

在 395 年后,Augustinus 开始对比性地强调信仰与理性、基督宗教与哲学、神的启示与人的自由之间的张力和冲突。在他的 *Retractationes* 中,他认为 *De vera religione* 也许还能帮助人们反驳摩尼教,虽然这本书过于哲理化,而且排除了神的恩典和召选。Augustinus 指出他早期的思想曾使用一种哲学化的(而非来自《圣经》的)"灵魂"概念。他强调了自由意志的自律性,但在晚年他更多地重视整个人类的罪和堕落状态(原罪)。在早期的书中,Augustinus 曾赞扬耶稣从来没有使用过暴力,但当了主教之后,他曾指着耶稣从圣殿驱逐商人的章节说在某些条件下使用强制性的措施是很合理的。在晚年他试图说明,基督信仰与柏拉图主义有很大的差别,信仰并不能建立在理性之上,而需要建立在权威和人类的原罪之上。

## 067.《独语》

Augustinus 在他皈依后不久(386—387 年)写了这部著作(2 卷)。

thinks that he doubts is truly thinking." (Omnis qui se dubitantem intellegit, verum intellegit. XXXIX; cf. Descartes' Cogito ergo sum, "I think, therefore I am") All levels of being reflect truth and beauty, even negative phenomena: deception and error are a distortion of truth, weaknesses and vices are shadow images of truth and the moral ideal. All things point to the ultimate destiny of the human soul: to strive after truth and search for God who is the "highest and innermost truth" (summa et intima veritas).

One of the main aims of Augustine is to show that Christianity is the perfect heir of classical Greek philosophy. The insight, once limited to the small circle of Socrates and Plato, that only the spirit brings true happiness, has already become the faith of the whole Mediterranean world. Christianity is a kind of Platonism for the common people, for the Platonists only needed to "change a few words and phrases" to become Christians (Paucis mutatis verbis et sententiis Christiani fierent. IV.7). Augustine concentrates on the Platonism of late antiquity which excludes political thought and philosophy of nature. In the dissolving world of late antiquity a rational plan for social change has no hope of success, therefore the salvation of the individual soul becomes more important. "Don't go out! Go back into yourself; the truth dwells in the inner man." (Noli foras ire! In te ipsum redi; in interiore homine habitat veritas. XXXIX.72)

When Christianity is understood as a moral and rational religion, Christ's life can be seen as a moral example (XVI.32). God's saving actions, His words, parables, and sacraments are mainly a "rule of rational behaviour" (rationalis disciplinae regula, XVII.33). The miracles of an earlier stage of history are no longer needed (XXV.47). However, in Augustine's eyes Christianity is not a humanist, secular religion: men are not free, they should voluntarily accept God's yoke (servi meliores serviunt liberaliter, XIV.27). Domination and service are central concepts for Augustine: just like the mind must reign over the body, God must reign over the mind (rationalis substantia Deo subiecta, XXIII.44). The Christian must lead an ascetic life (non diligamus mundum, non diligamus voluptatem, LV.107), otherwise the desires will overwhelm and dominate him.

After the year 395 AD, Augustine started to emphasize the conflict between faith and reason, Christianity and philosophy, divine revelation and human freedom. In his *Retractationes* he judges that *De vera religione* might still serve as a tool to oppose Manichaeism though it was too philosophical and excluded divine grace and election. Augustine observes that his earlier thought used a more philosophical but not a Biblical concept of the "soul". Earlier he emphasized the autonomy of the free will, but in his later years he insists on the sinful condition of all mankind (original sin). In his earlier book, Augustine praised Jesus for never using force, but after he became a bishop he pointed to the passage where Jesus expelled the merchants from the Temple and advocated that it was reasonable to use force under certain conditions. In his later years he tried to show that Christianity is something very different from Platonism, not built on reason, but rather on authority and on the sinfulness of all mankind.

## 067. *Soliloquia / Soliloquies*

Augustine wrote this work in 2 books shortly after his conversion, in 386—387 AD.

Augustinus 谈论的问题是上主面前的灵魂，而这部著作的文学形式是作者与自己的理性(ratio)的对话。他仅仅想了解神和灵魂(Deum et animam scire cupio)，不想知道别的东西。这位新皈依的信徒考察他的内心生活并且似乎达到了某种接近神和接近基督信仰的理想的状态。然而他必须承认，某些诱惑在他的内心仍具有很危险的影响力。他仍然过于恋慕某些人。然而，因为他现在过着一种克修的生活，人间的财富、荣誉、婚姻和肉身上的享受不再是一种严重的挑战。这部书又提到一种非常确定性的知识，"我知道(或:我怀疑)，因此我存在"。这话后来又给 Descartes 提供了一些启迪(参见他的名言 Cogito ergo sum)。"自我"和"理性"的对话又预示后来 Boethius 与哲学的对话以及 Petrarca 的著作 *Secretum*。

Presented in the form of a dialogue with his own ratio (reason), Augustine discusses the problem of the soul before God. He only wants to know God and the soul (Deum et animam scire cupio) and nothing besides that. The convert examines his inner life and seems to have reached a certain level of closeness to God and the Christian ideals. However, he must admit that some temptations are still dangerously powerful in him. He is still too much attached to the love of certain people. But as he now leads an ascetic life, the allurements of wealth, honour, marriage and sensual pleasures are no longer a serious threat. The work mentions a first certainty based on knowledge, "I know (or: I doubt), therefore I am", which inspired later Descartes' famous "Cogito ergo sum". The dialog of the ego with reason is a prefiguration of Boethius' dialogue with philosophy and Petrarch's *Secretum*.

# 克劳狄安（约 370—404 AD）

这位古典拉丁语最后的伟大诗人诞生于埃及的 Alexandria，而他的母语是希腊语。他于 394 年前往意大利并开始拉丁语诗篇的创作，随即成名。在 Honorius 和 Stilicho 时期，他成为宫廷诗人，曾为后者写下了一些赞美诗（panegyrici）和其他有政治宣传作用的诗篇。他的风格倾向于模仿白银时期的拉丁诗人，比如 Statius。他的题材来自古代神话，因此 Augustinus 和 Orosius 认为他不是基督徒。然而，他也写过一首名为 *De salvatore*（《论救世主》）的诗，他可能是基督徒。

**著作**：《诗歌集》《哥特战争》《吉尔多战争》《珀尔塞福涅的掠夺》《反驳欧特若比欧斯》《反驳鲁菲努斯》《赞美诗》

## 068. 《珀尔塞福涅的掠夺》

本部未完成的神话诗共分为 3 卷，成书时间大约在 400 年。

在第 1 卷中，阴间的神 Pluto 因自己没有妻子而抱怨。命运女神之一的 Lachesis 建议他派遣 Mercurius 到 Jupiter 那里，向 Jupiter 求助。为了回应这种要求，众神和众人之父决定 Proserpine 应该成为 Pluto 的妻子。Jupiter 派遣 Venus 前往 Proserpina 的家乡 Sicilia（西西里）。Diana 和 Minerva 陪同 Venus 来到 Proserpina 的家，她们找到具有德性和魅力的 Proserpina，她正坐在织布机前，为她母亲 Ceres 织一块布，在这布上有世界的图画。

第 2 卷：第二天早上三个女神前往西西里岛的旺盛草原上采摘鲜花，而诗人很巧妙地描述了这个景色。很多花是一些源于神话的象征，它们是一些曾被神明们或仙女们爱的英雄，而这些英雄后来变形成花或使某些花产生（参见 Narcissus, Hyacinthus）。（"摘花"的隐喻也暗示着将要发生的悲剧：青春年华的少女 Proserpina 将被夺走，她将前往阴间。）甚至 Minerva 女神——她"掌控战争号角和武器"也放弃她的长矛并开始摘花，用花朵装饰自己的头盔。突然这些妇女听到了大地震动的声音。这场地震是 Pluto 的马车引起的，因为他正从冥府来到人间。他出现并带走了 Proserpina。Minerva 和 Diana 两位女神无法阻碍他夺走 Proserpina。

第 3 卷：Jupiter 聚集神明们并宣布说人类将要通过痛苦和贫乏的体验来学习如何创造和发明新事物。主神想要给予人们丰富的生命和文明；他想在各地传播农业方面的知识。因此他命令 Proserpina 的母亲 Ceres——她也是农业的女神——去世界各地寻找她的女儿。并且不允许任何人告诉她她的女儿被送到哪里。充满悲痛的 Ceres 拿着两个巨大的火炬，在 Sicilia 的火山 Aetna 那里点燃它们并开始自己在各地寻找 Proserpina 的旅程。

# Claudius Claudianus / Claudian

**Opera:** *Carmina, De bello Getico (=Bellum Goticum), De bello Gildonico, De raptu Proserpinae, In Eutropium, In Rufinum, Panegyrici*
**Works:** *Poems, The Gothic War, The War against Gildo, The Rape of Proserpine, Invective against Eutropius, Invective against Rufinus, Panegyrics*

## 068. *De raptu Proserpinae / The Rape of Proserpine*

Claudian's mythological epic in three books was written circa 400 AD and left unfinished.

In the first book Pluto, the god of the Underworld complains about having no wife. Lachesis, one of the Fates advises him to send Mercury to Jupiter and ask Jupiter for help. Responding to the request, Jupiter, the father of gods and men, decides that Proserpine should be given to Pluto in marriage. Jupiter sends Venus to Sicily, the home of Proserpine. Accompanied by Diana and Minerva, Venus enters Proserpine's house where the virtuous and beautiful Proserpine is working at her loom. She is weaving a piece of cloth for her mother Ceres. The embroidery on the linen shows a picture of the world.

Book 2: The next morning the goddesses go out to the blooming meadows of Sicily to pick flowers, a scene which the poet unfolds with great skill. Many of the flowers are mythological symbols, they are heroes loved by gods, goddesses or by nymphs, and these heroes were changed into flowers or made certain flowers grow, e.g. Narcissus, and Hyacinthus. (The symbol of "picking flowers" also alludes to the subsequent sad event: Proserpine, a girl in the bloom of youth will be carried off to Hades.) Even Minerva "in command of war trumpets and weapons" lays down her spear to gather flowers, adorning her helmet with the colorful blossoms. Suddenly the women hear the sound of an earthquake. This quake is caused by Pluto's cart, for the god of Hades makes his way to the upper world. He appears and abducts Proserpine. Minerva and Diana cannot prevent him from taking Proserpine with him to the Underworld.

Book 3: Jupiter assembles the gods and declares that humankind should learn to be creative and inventive by living in need. Thus he wants to grant fertility and civilization and plans to facilitate the spread of agriculture. Therefore he ordains that the harvest goddess Ceres, the sad mother of Proserpine, must transverse the whole earth in the search for her daughter. Nobody is allowed to tell her where her abducted daughter has gone. The sorrowful mother Ceres takes two huge torches, lights them at the volcanic Mt. Aetna in Sicily and starts her long search for Proserpine.

第三篇

# 外族的入侵与隐修院文化的开始
## Foreign Intrusions and the Beginnings of Monasticism

(410 — 529 AD)

• The Temptation of St. Anthony

# 塞维鲁斯（约 360—420 AD）

这位拉丁历史学家来自 Aquitania（法国南部）的贵族家庭，他曾在 Bordeaux（波尔多）学习法学，大约于 389 年他与朋友 Paulinus de Nola 一起皈依基督教。在他的妻子去世后，他在 Martinus de Tours 主教的影响下在自己的家里组织建立了一种隐修院，他自己和一些朋友成为隐修者。

**著作:**《编年史》(一部从基督徒的角度编写的史书)、《圣马丁传》

## 069.《圣马丁传》

生活在 316—397 年间的 Martinus（马丁）主教的传大约写成于这位著名的圣人去世之前。Sulpicius Severus 模仿了 Suetonius 传记的结构和 Sallustius 的风格。Martinus 出生于匈牙利地区的 Savaria（Szombathely）。他的父亲是一名罗马军人，所以 Martinus 有义务当兵。然而，他皈依基督意味着他开始过一种为基督服务的生活（miles Christi，基督的精兵）。在高卢他成为 Hilarius de Poitiers 的学生。他一时过了隐修者的生活并在高卢地区创立了一些隐修院（比如 Marmoutier）——这些是拉丁地区中最早的隐修院。在晚年时他被祝圣为 Tours 城的主教，所以他一般被称为 Martinus de Tours（图尔的马丁）。

早在他还活着的时候，Martinus 因他的奇迹和慈善工作而著名。在他年轻时，有一次在 Amiens（Ambagiensis，法国）的城门见到一个半裸体的乞丐。那时正是冬天的时候，天气很冷，但过路人并没有对这个乞丐表示什么同情心和怜悯（misericordia）。Martinus 应该做什么？他没有可以送给人的东西，仅仅穿一件衣服，即他的军人外套（simplicem militiae vestem，亦称 chlamys）。他只好拿起他的剑将外套劈成两半，一块给乞丐，另一块留给自己。一些周围的人笑他，但大部分的人"唉声叹息"（altius gemere），因为这个动作暴露出他们的自私。第二天 Martinus 在梦中见到基督。他发现基督所穿的衣服就是他送给乞丐的那块外套。Martinus 甚至听到基督向周围的天使们说这样的话："那个准备领洗的 Martinus 曾给予我这块衣服。"在这种神视后，Martinus 很快接受了圣洗。不久后，他离开军队并开始一个新的生活，去当隐修士和传教士。后来的艺术品多次描绘他用剑来分割自己外套的情景。在 Martinus 去世后 100 年，法兰克人的王 Clovis（克洛维）接受洗礼（497 年），而圣 Martinus 成为高卢的主保圣人。

# Sulpicius Severus

**Opera:** *Chronica, Vita Sancti Martini*
**Works:** *Chronicle, Life of Saint Martin*

### 069. *Vita Sancti Martini / Life of Saint Martin*

The biography of the bishop Martin (316—397 AD) was probably written shortly before the death of this popular saint. Sulpicius Severus imitated the formal structure of Sueton's biographies and the style of Sallust. Martin was born in Savaria (Szombathely, Hungary) as the son of a Roman soldier and thus obliged to lead a life in the army. However, his conversion meant for him to enter a life in the service of Christ (miles Christi, "soldier of Christ"). In Gaul he became a student of Hilarius of Poitiers. For some time he lived as a hermit and founded monasteries in Gaul (for example Marmoutier)—the first monasteries in the Latin speaking areas. Towards the end of his life he was made bishop of Tours (in Gaul); thus he is commonly called "Martin of Tours".

Already during his lifetime Martin is famous for his miracles and his charity work. In his youth he once encounters a half-naked beggar at the city gate of Amiens (Ambagienses, modern France). It is winter and very cold, but none of the passers-by shows a sign of mercy (misericordia) to the poor man. What shall Martin do? He has nothing to give and only wears one piece of cloth: a simple military coat (simplicem militiae vestem, the so-called "chlamys"). He takes his sword (ferrum) and cuts his coat into two parts, giving one part to the beggar and keeping the other part for himself. Some of the bystanders laugh at him, but most "draw deep sighs" (altius gemere), since this deed of charity exposes their own egoism. The following night Martin sees Christ in a dream vision, and he observes that Christ wears the part of his coat which he gave to the beggar. Martin even hears Christ saying to some of the angels that surround him: "With this coat Martin the catechumen has clothed me." After this vision Martin hurries to get baptized. Soon he leaves the military to start a new life as monk and missionary. The famous scene of the soldier cutting through his coat with the sword has often been depicted in later artifacts. Hundred years after Martin's death Clovis, King of the Franks, was baptized (in 497 AD), and St. Martin became the patron saint of Gaul.

# 卡西安（约 360—435 AD）

来自一个基督徒家庭，曾学习希腊语和拉丁语文学，约于 380 年在 Bethlehem 进入一所隐修院，此后在埃及大约 10 年之久。他在不同的隐修院生活，399 年由 Ioannes Chrysostomos 祝圣为执事，曾于 405 年在罗马替 Chrysostomos 辩护，后于 415 年在 Marseille 建立一所男修院和一所女修院。

**著作：**《隐修者教规》

## 070. 《隐修者教规》

该隐修会规分为 12 卷，成书时期在 419—426 年间，他在很多方面采取了 Evagrius Ponticus 的一些观点。书名亦作 *De institutis coenobiorum et de octo principalibus vitiis*（《论隐修院的制度和八个主要罪恶》），也是研究隐修传统的关键资料之一。

第一个部分描述巴勒斯坦和埃及诸隐修院中的生活方式。Johannes 谈论隐修者的衣服（第 1 卷）、关于夜间祈祷和歌唱 psalmi（圣咏）的规定（第 2 卷）。第 3 卷谈论白天的祈祷规则以及隐修士们的饮食标准。第 4 卷谈论接受一个新人入隐修院的要求以及介绍初学生要遵守的特殊规则。

第三个部分（第 5 到 12 卷）说明该会规的目标：要抵抗种种恶习。Johannes 是一位杰出的教育家，他有心理学方面的洞见并了解人性的软弱。在这种精神中他谈论八个主要的罪过：贪吃（gula，饕餮罪，第 5 卷）、违背贞洁的罪（luxuria，第 6 卷）、贪婪（avaritia, philargyria，第 7 卷）、愤怒（ira，第 8 卷）、忧郁（tristitia，第 9 卷）、懒惰（acedia，第 10 卷）、虚荣心和渴望人间的荣耀（cenodoxia，第 11 卷），以及骄傲（superbia，第 12 卷）。因为作者认为一个人需要上主的恩典，再加上自己的意志，才能达到完满的状态，他成了所谓的 semi-Pelagianism（半贝拉基主义）的奠基人。在一段时间内，这种思想在高卢有相当多的拥护者，直到 529 年在 Orange 召开的主教会议谴责了 semi-Pelagianism 为止。（Pelagius 是与 Johannes Cassianus 同时代的人，他强调自由和人的意志，这样似乎贬低了神的恩典的关键性。Hieronymus 和 Augustinus 等人拒绝了他的教导。）

# Johannes Cassianus / John Cassian

**Opera:** *De institutis monachorum*
**Works:** *The Life of Monks*

### 070. *De institutis monachorum / The Life of Monks*

This set of monastic rules in 12 books was written from 419—426 AD, and in many respects it follows Evagrius Ponticus. It is also quoted as *De institutis coenobiorum et de octo principalibus vitiis* (*The Life-Style in a Monastery and the Eight Principal Sins*) and is one of the most important sources for the study of monasticism.

The first part describes the way of life in the monasteries of Palestine and Egypt. John discusses the clothes of the monks (book 1), the regular demands concerning night prayers, and the singing of psalms (book 2). Book 3 dwells on the questions concerning prayers offered during the day and the diet of the monks. Book 4 clarifies the conditions for accepting a candidate into a monastery and the special rules that apply to novices.

The third part (books 5~12) shows the rule's intention: to resist vices. An excellent educator with psychological insight, John understands the weaknesses of human beings. In this spirit he treats the eight main sins: gluttony (gula, book 5), sins against chastity (luxuria, book 6), greed (avaritia, philargyria, book 7), wrath (ira, book 8), depression (tristitia, book 9), laziness (acedia, book 10), vanity and desire for earthly glory (cenodoxia, book 11), and pride (superbia, book 12). Since the author believes that a person needs God's grace as well as willpower in order to reach perfection, he became the founder of so-called semi-Pelagianism. This particular view had many adherents in Gaul until the Synod of Orange decided the matter in the year 529 AD and condemned semi-Pelagianism. (Pelagius was a contemporary of John Cassian and emphasized freedom and the human will, thus disparaging the crucial impact of divine grace. His teachings, known as "Pelagianism", were rejected by Jerome and Augustine.)

# 斯托拜乌斯（约 370—440 AD）

生平不详。

**著作:**《文摘》

## 071. 《文摘》

本文摘包含来自大约 500 名希腊作家的引言和短文，成书于第 5 世纪初。Stobaios 将他的著作题赠给他的儿子 Septimius。这部文集本来分为 4 个部分，但中世纪的编者将它分为两个文集，即 *Eklogai*（《文摘》，即第 1、2 卷）和 *Anthologion*（《荟萃》，即第 3、4 卷）。

本文摘是根据多种多样的主题编写而成的，每一个题目都有许多作者的摘录，包括从早期诗人到公元 4 世纪的作者。第 1 卷在序言中赞扬哲学，此后介绍了不同的哲学派别、关于数学和音乐的文献，也有一些涉及形而上学和物理学的短文。从第 2 卷开始，作者主要关切伦理学。在第 4 卷中有一些涉及政治学和家务管理的摘录。因为该文摘包含众多来自早期文学的引言，所以它能够帮助我们更好地理解另一些被保存的手抄本的意义。因为作者没有引用任何基督教作者的文献，所以我们也可以推论说他不是基督徒。

# Iōannēs Stobaios / Stobaeus

**Opera:** *Eklogai*
**Works:** *Selections*

## 071. *Eklogai / Selections*

This anthology contains excerpts and quotations from around 500 Greek authors. It was written in the early 5th century. Stobaeus dedicated the work to his son Septimius. The work was originally divided into four parts, but medieval scribes edited it in two parts entitled *Eklogai* (*Selections*, books 1 and 2) and *Anthologion* (*Anthology*, books 3 and 4).

The anthology is arranged according to a great variety of topics, and each heading is illustrated with excerpts, beginning with the early poets down to the authors of the 4th century after Christ. Book 1 starts with a preface in which a praise of philosophy is found, then follows a presentation of the different philosophical schools, an outline of the mathematical and musical sciences, then some texts pertaining to metaphysics and physics. From Book 2 onwards the main concern is ethics. Book 4 contains texts related to politics and the administration of a household. The value of the collection consists in the huge number of citations from earlier literature. These quotations often help to understand the meaning of other manuscripts that are preserved. The absence of excerpts from Christian authors seems to proof that Stobaeus was a pagan author.

# 卡佩拉（约 380—439 AD）

生平不详，曾在 Carthago 进行研究。

**著作**：《梅库利乌斯和语文学的婚姻》

## 072. 《梅库利乌斯和语文学的婚姻》

该部介绍"七个自由学科"（septem artes liberales）的百科全书式的著作成书在 Vandales 征服 Carthago（439 年）之前。全部著作分为 9 卷。

第 1、2 卷叙述一种隐喻式的故事，包括一部分散文和一些诗。故事的背景是 Olympus 山，即希腊神明的传统居所。主人翁是 Mercurius，他跑得快，思想敏锐，因此在古典神话中经常充当神明们的使者，也是一些爱情问题的谈判者，但他自己仍然还没有对象。获得了 Jupiter 的许可后，Mercurius 要为自己寻找一个妻子。他与几个候选人进行了面谈，比如 Psyche（灵魂）和 Sophia（智慧），但她们都不能满足他的要求。Virtus（美德）请 Apollo 帮忙，这个十个文艺女神的领导者建议 Mercurius 去见 Philologia（语文学，即和语言有关系的学问）。Philologia 对于人间生活、天上的星星，甚至阴间的秘密都有深入的了解。Mercurius 和 Philologia 一见钟情，但 Philologia 仍属于可死的世界，她必须先被提升到神明的地位。因此，Apollo、Virtus 和 Mercurius 经过一层层的高天，最终上升到 Jupiter 的宫殿。他们建议 Philologia 加入神明们的行列。神明们开会决定不仅仅 Philologia 要升天，所有有资格的人都应该被提升到天界。

作出这个决定后，Athanasia（不死）要求 Philologia 必须先从她的肚子中吐出一切书，这样才能够获得永远的生命。当 Philologia 吐出无数的书本和书卷时，文艺女神们站在旁边并很贪婪地夺走一些经典。然后 Philologia 坐轿，她被抬到 Olympus 山。两个小男孩儿——Amor（爱情）和 Labor（劳苦）——，以及两个小女孩——Epimelia（勤劳）和 Agrypnia（不眠）——抬着她的轿子。四枢德（义德、智德、勇德、节德）以及美惠三女神（Euphrosyne, Aglaia, Thalia）陪同他们。Jupiter 的妻子 Juno 欢迎 Philologia 并指导她在 Olympus 山应该遵守什么样的仪式。除了神明们外还有很多古典诗人和哲学家居住在天界，还有某些鬼神和半神。在婚礼中，Apollo 是主礼，Philologia 的母亲 Phronesis（实用的智慧）照顾她的女儿，而 Jupiter 亲自打上夫妻的结。两个人交换一些礼物，而 Apollo 宣布说 Mercurius 要为新娘提供一个特殊的礼物：七个仆婢（即七个自由学科）。Philologia 很热切地欢迎她们。其中每一个仆婢用一卷的篇幅来介绍她的知识（第 3 到第 9 卷）。

# Martianus Minneus Felix Capella / Capella

**Opera:** *De nuptiis Philologiae et Mercurii*
**Works:** *The Marriage of Philology and Mercurius*

### 072. *De nuptiis Philologiae et Mercurii / The Marriage of Philology and Mercurius*

This encyclopedic collection of the "seven liberal arts" (septem artes liberales) was written before the Vandals conquered Carthage in 439 AD. The work is divided into 9 books.

The preface of the work (books 1 and 2) present an allegorical fable, written in alternating sections of prose and verse. The setting of the story is Mount Olympus, the traditional residence of the Greek gods. The main character is Mercury, who by his swift feet and quick intellect often is the messenger of the gods in classical mythology and their negotiator in love affairs. However, he himself is left without a partner. Having obtained Jupiter's permission, Mercury looks for a wife. He interviews several candidates, for example Psyche (soul) and Sophia (wisdom), but none of them fulfills his expectations. Virtus (virtue) asks Apollo for advice, and the leader of the Muses suggests that Mercury meets Philologia (philology, the arts connected with the languages). Philologia knows about worldly affairs, about the stars in the sky and even about the secrets of the Underworld. Mercury and Philologia immediately fall in love with one another, but Philologia belongs to the world of the mortals and first must be raised to divine status. Therefore Apollo, Virtus, and Mercury ascend the heavenly spheres until they reach Jupiter's palace. They suggest that Philologia should join the gods. The gods hold an assembly and decide that not only Philologia should be elevated to divinity, but thenceforth all mortals who deserve it.

After this decision Athanasia (Immortality) demands that Philologia must spit out all the books from her belly so as to gain immortality. As Philologia starts vomiting innumerable manuscripts and papyrus rolls from her stomach, the Muses watch her and greedily steal some of the books. Now Philologia is carried up to Mt. Olympus in a sedan-chair. Two boys, Amor (love) and Labor (hard work), and two girls, Epimelia (diligence) and Agrypnia (sleeplessness), carry the chair. The four cardinal virtues (justice, wisdom, courage, temperance) and the three Graces (Euphrosyne, Aglaia, Thalia) usher them. Juno, the wife of Jupiter, welcomes Philologia and instructs her on the etiquette of Mount Olympus. The inhabitants of heaven do not only include the gods, but also the classical poets and philosophers, and certain demons and demigods. At the wedding Apollo is Master of the Ceremony. Philologia's mother Phronesis (practical wisdom) attends her daughter, and Jupiter ties the knot. The couple then exchange vows, and Apollo announces that Mercury will present a special gift for his bride: seven maidservants (the seven liberal arts), who are enthusiastically accepted by Philologia. Each

第一个仆婢是 Grammatica(语法学),她是一个白头发的老妇女,随身带着一个小刀和一个锉子,她用这些工具来切割或纠正学生的语法错误。她为自己的埃及祖先感到自豪并说她曾经在 Attica 生活很长时间,但现在她穿的是罗马人的衣服。Rhetorica(修辞学)是一个高大美丽的妇女,在她的衣服上有各式各样的修辞学和语言学的比喻。她随身带着她的箭,随时准备攻击她的敌人们。其他仆婢们的衣着、姿态与外貌都表现了这些学科的特征。七个学科的简明介绍也暗示当时的标准性教科书:语法学方面有 Donatus 和 Priscinianus 的书;修辞学的学生用 Cicero 的 *De inventione*;逻辑学用 Aristoteles 的 *Kategoriai*;算术学用 Nikomachos 的书;几何学的标准性著作是 Eukleides,天文学用 Ptolemaios,而 Aristoxenos 的著作是音乐学的教科书。

of the seven servants now presents herself in one book (books 3 to 9).

The first of the liberal arts is Grammatica (grammar), a gray-haired old woman, who carries a knife and a file used to excise and correct the mistakes of schoolchildren. She is proud of her Egyptian ancestry and says that for a long time she lived in Attica (Athens), but now she wears a Roman dress. Rhetorica (rhetoric) is a tall and attractive woman whose colorful appearance shows the different figures of speech and rhetorical exuberance. She carries arrows, ready to shoot at her enemies. The dress, stature and appearance of the other maids in the same manner shows the characteristics of each science. The summaries of the seven arts display the educational standards—school books—of the author's time: Donatus and Priscinianus for grammar; Cicero's *De inventione* for rhetoric; Aristotle's *Categories* for logic; Nicomachus for arithmethic, Euclid for geometry, Ptolemy for astronomy, and Aristoxenus for music theory.

# 马克罗比乌斯（约 380—440 AD）

可能是 Carthago 人，生平不详。

**著作**：《评注〈西皮欧的梦〉》(2 卷，有新柏拉图主义的思想，在中世纪受到重视)、《论希腊文和拉丁文动词之异同》（只保存残篇）、《农神节说》(7 卷，采用《会饮篇》的对话方式，内容涉及到古代宗教、政治、文学——评论 Vergilius 与希腊作者的关系并赞扬他为最深邃的学者和诗人、物理学和医学)

## 073. 《评注〈西皮欧的梦〉》

这部新柏拉图主义式的注解文集共分为两卷，Macrobius 将他题赠给自己的儿子。其内容主要解释了 Cicero 的 *De re publica*（《论国家》），因此保存了这个古代文献的部分原文，而《论国家》的其他部分后来才被发现。中世纪的学者们很熟悉这部著作，并从中学习数学和天文学。

Macrobius 首先分析了 Plato 和 Cicero 之间的关系，进而谈论一些涉及到梦的问题以及用神话来解释哲学问题的可能性。伴随着 Cicero 的原文，他从新柏拉图主义的角度来探讨灵魂和灵魂的命运，又加上当时的天文学及数学知识，这样他就结合了传统哲学的三大领域，即物理学（宇宙论）、伦理学及逻辑学。正如 Cicero 的 *Somnium* 所暗示的那样，Macrobius 认为人的灵魂是不朽的，甚至有神圣的特征，但他的观点属于新柏拉图主义，不属于基督宗教。"这部著作的目标似乎是说明这一点：人的灵魂不仅仅是不朽的，而且它是一个神"（Haec sit praesentis operis consummatio ut animam non solum immortalem sed deum esse clarescat. 2, 12, 5）。

## 074. 《农神节说》

本对话集共分为 7 卷，Macrobius 将它题赠给自己的儿子。它报告在 Saturnalia 的节庆期间（12 月 17 日到 23 日）发生的一些虚构的对话。一些罗马贵族人士，即 Avienus、Symmachus、Servius 和 Euangelus 在 Vettius Praetextatus 的家中参与宴席，其中多数人都是 Symmachus 领导的反基督宗教运动中的杰出知识分子和元老。他们的出发点是对 Vergilius 著作的评论，但他们的谈论涉及很多不同的主题：天文学、修辞学、占卜算命和预言、宗教崇拜和礼仪、神话学、哲学以及历法。

第 1 卷探讨古代的宗教，而 Praetextatus 提出这样的理论：一切神话都来自对太阳神的崇拜，所以一切神明都与太阳有某些关系。这就显示出新柏拉图主义的倾向，即用一种比较统一的一神论式的思想体系来取代传统的多神论。很可能，这种思路

# Ambrosius Theodosius Macrobius

**Opera:** *Commentarii in Somnium Scipionis, De differentiis et societatibus Graeci Latinique verbi, Saturnalia*

**Works:** *Commentary on Cicero's Somnium Scipionis, On the differences and similarities of the Greek and Latin verb, Saturnalia*

## 073. *Commentarii in Somnium Scipionis / Commentary on Cicero's Somnium Scipionis*

This Neoplatonist commentary in two books is dedicated to Macrobius' son. It explains the sixth book of Cicero's *De republica* and thus preserved this text at a time when other parts of *De republica* were still undiscovered. Scholars of the Middle Ages were very familiar with this work, learning from it mathematics and astronomy.

Macrobius first analyzes the connection between Plato and Cicero and continues with some considerations concerning dreams and the possibility of presenting philosophical problems in a myth. Following Cicero's text he discusses the soul and its destiny in the light of Neoplatonism, adducing the astronomical and mathematical sciences as he knew them, thus combining the three traditional parts of philosophy: physics (cosmology), ethics and logic. Just as Cicero's *Somnium* suggests, Macrobius considers the human soul to be immortal and even of divine quality, but his outlook is that of a Neoplatonist and not that of a Christian. "It seems to be the aim of this work to show that the soul is not only immortal but also a god" (Haec sit praesentis operis consummatio ut animam non solum immortalem sed deum esse clarescat. 2, 12, 5).

## 074. *Saturnalia*

Macrobius dedicated this dialogue in seven books to his son. It is a fictive conversation at a banquet during the Saturnalian festival (celebrated from 17th to 23rd of Dec.) between several noble Romans. Avienus, Symmachus, Servius and Euangelus dine and debate at the house of Vettius Praetextatus. Most of these men are leading intellectuals in the anti-Christian movement of senators around Symmachus. Starting from a critique of Virgil's works, the discussion covers many different subjects: astronomy, rhetoric, divination and prophecy, cult and worship, mythology, philosophy and calendar computation.

The first book deals with ancient religion. In this context Praetextatus presents a theory of the solar origin of all mythology. According to this view, all gods are seen as phenomena connected with the sun. Thus a distinct tendency of Neoplatonism becomes apparent, namely to replace the traditional polytheism with a more unified monotheist

是对基督宗教一神论的一种回应。第 2 卷包含一些关于首都罗马的宗教界和政治界中的变化的轶事。

第 3 到第 6 卷谈论 Vergilius 的方方面面，比如他对古罗马及希腊传统习俗和仪式的了解，他在描绘人们的心态和情绪方面的才华，他和 Homerus 及其他古希腊诗人的关系，以及他对早期罗马诗人的熟识。随着这些谈论的深入，Vergilius 的形象逐渐变得越来越伟大，他成为一个先知，他通达各种知识领域，他又是一位似乎有着超人能力的魔术师。对于 Vergilius 的这些描述不仅仅反映出当时对于 Vergilius 的研究水平，也深深影响了中世纪的人对 Vergilius 所采取的态度。

第 7 卷引入一系列的物理学的、心理学的和生理学的问题，其中特别重视有关饮料和食品的分析，又谈论了头脑对身体功能的影响。

system, most probably also in response to Christian monotheism. Book 2 contains several anecdotes on the changes of religion and politics in Rome, the capital of the empire.

Books 3 to 6 discuss Virgil, who is analyzed from many different points of view, including his familiarity with Roman and Greek customs and ceremonies, his ability to describe moods and feelings, his dependence on Homer and other Greek poets, and his familiarity with early Roman authors. In the course of these discussions Virgil is gradually growing into the figure of a prophet, an expert in all fields of knowledge and a magician equipped with almost super-human powers. This description of Virgil not only reflects the level of Virgilian scholarship at that time, it also profoundly influenced the medieval perception of Virgil.

Book 7 introduces a series of physical, psychological, and physiological questions, mainly centering on food and drink and on how the brain influences the functions of the body.

# 聂斯托里乌斯（约 381—451 AD）

生于 Germanicia / Mar'ash（在 Euphrates 地区），曾在 Antiochia 获得了良好的文学教育和哲学培养。他接受了 Diodoros de Tarsos 和 Theodoros de Mopsuestia 等人的思想，被祝圣司铎并在 Antiochia 附近指导一所隐修院。东方的皇帝 Theodosios II 于 428 年将他指定为 Constantinopolis 的宗主教。他对于异端的主张和对于信众的态度比较严格，不愿意容忍种种节庆、隆重的表演、舞蹈和音乐。（这种态度和 Chrysostomos 基本上是一致的。）因为 Nestorios 反对"theotokos"（"天主之母"）的说法，很多人反对他。在 Ephesos（以弗所）的主教会议上（431 年），他的主张被谴责。因此，他退隐到他的隐修院去。皇帝于 436 年才将他正式流放，先送他到 Petra，后到 Libya 的沙漠。因为他的教导受谴责，他的著作没有保存。支持他的信徒后来在东方（叙利亚）形成一个教会团体，他们在 450 年后在波斯地区和中亚地区进行传教（即是于 635 年传入中国的"景教"）。

**著作:**《赫拉克勒伊德斯之书》

## 075.《赫拉克勒伊德斯之书》

本文献是关于 Nestorios 的教导的一种辩护文章，是以叙利亚文的手抄本保存的，大约写于 540 年，在 1910 年才被发现。希腊语的原文大概是 Nestorios 晚年或在流放时期写的。Nestorios 使用一个虚构的对话的形式。他和埃及人 Sophronios 谈话时对于在 Ephesus 会议的规定和 Alexandria 的宗主教 Kyrillos（444 年去世）提出批评。这篇论文也叙述 Nestorios 充满变化的一生。

Nestorios 曾是著名叙利亚神学家 Theodoros de Mopsuestia 的学生并在 Antiochia 获得了良好的修辞学培养。在 428 年 Theodosios II 皇帝使 Nestorios 成为 Constantinopolis 的宗主教。然而，他在此之前充当了一所隐修院的院长，并且对种种异端采取了严格的态度。他也试图镇压一些五光十色的庆祝活动、表演、舞蹈，甚至音乐。这样，他得罪了一部分信徒。《赫拉克勒伊德斯之书》第 150 段开始叙述关于圣母玛利亚的"theotokos"（"天主之母"）尊称的争论。信徒中有两种派别的人，他们要求 Nestorios 作决定。一部分人反对"theotokos"一词，但另一方说虔诚的民众、礼仪的语言以及很多神学家（包括 Ōrigenēs、Athanasios、Jerusalem 的 Kyrillos、Epiphanios、Nazianzus 的 Grēgorios 等）都使用这个尊称来称呼 Maria（玛利亚）。Nestorios 建议要使用 Christotokos（"基督之母"）的尊称并坚定反对"theotokos"这个词。这样他就引发了一个复杂的争论。

# Nestorios / Nestorius

**Opera:** *Pragmateia Herakleidou Damaskenou* (*=Liber Heraclidis*)
**Works:** *The Book of Heracleides*

### 075. *Pragmateia Herakleidou Damaskenou / Liber Heraclidis / Essay of Heracleides*

This justification of Nestorius' doctrine is preserved in a Syrian manuscript which was written around 540 AD and discovered in 1910. The Greek original was probably recorded at the end of Nestorius' life or during his exile. Nestorius uses a fictive dialogue with the Egyptian Sophronios to attack the decisions of the council of Ephesus and the teachings of Cyril of Alexandria (died in 444 AD). The treatise also narrates the turbulent story of Nestorius' life.

Nestorius was a student of the famous Syrian theologian Theodore of Mopsuestia and received excellent rhetorical education at Antioch. In 428 AD emperor Theodosius II made Nestorius patriarch of Constantinople. However, Nestorius had been abbot of a monastery before and adopted a rigid attitude towards heresies. He tried to suppress colourful celebrations, performances, dance and even music, thus alienating some of the believers. The *Pragmateia Herakleidou* (section 150 and following) narrate the beginnings of the controversy concerning the title "theotokos" (Mother of God) for Mary. Two factions of believers approached Nestorius. Some opposed the expression "theotokos", whereas the other side pointed out that popular piety, liturgy and many theologians (like Origen, Athanasius, Cyrill of Jerusalem, Epiphanius, Gregory of Nazianz) had used the title "theotokos" for Mary. Nestorius suggested to keep the term "Christotokos" ("Mother of Christ") and strictly opposed the title "theotokos". This triggered a complicated controversy.

Nestorios 的严格态度伤害了 Constantinopolis 的许多信徒的感情，又激起了 Alexandria 神学学派的反驳。他们的领导人是 Alexandria 的宗主教 Kyrillos；他发行一篇通信给埃及的所有隐修者，其中保卫了"theotokos"的尊称。两个宗主教转向罗马教宗 Coelestinus I(422—432 年)，他支持 Kyrillos 并委任他纠正 Nestorios 的错误，使他归于正统的信仰。Kyrillos 在埃及召开了一次主教会议并在一份信仰文献中拒绝了 Antiochia 神学派用来表达基督人性和神性的典型概念——即"寓居"(inhabitatio, enoikēsis)和"结合"(synapheia)。在罗马和 Antiochia 的代表还没有到来之时，Kyrillos 宗主教就主持 Ephesus 会议的开幕礼(431 年)。然而，甚至 Antiochia 派的人也接受了对于 Nestorios 的谴责。该神学争论的深层原因是两种类型的基督论，即 Antiochia 学派和 Alexandria 学派的基督论。Antiochia 学派强调基督人性的独立性，视人性为"逻各斯"以外的实体(所谓的"区分基督论")。Alexandria 学派在另一方面则认为，sarx(基督的肉身)成了"逻各斯"，这样就与"逻各斯"融为一体。因此，这种"合一学派"要求人们肯定"mia physis"("一个本性")的说法，但 Nestorios 无法接受这个表达。一直到今天东叙利亚教会保持这样的说法："基督内有两个本性，两个自立体，一个位格。"

根据 Kyrillos 宗主教的理解，Nestorios 拒绝"theotokos"的尊称就等于是一种异端。他说 Nestorios 的观点意味着神圣"逻各斯"与耶稣这个人的结合仅仅是一种外在的或道德上的结合。因此，耶稣可能被视为仅仅是"上主的嗣子"("嗣子说"adoptianismus)，耶稣只是"神的圣殿"。然而，20 世纪有许多神学家认为，Kyrillos 误解或歪曲了 Nestorios 的观点。他们强调 Nestorios 的教导仍然保持在正统信仰的界线之内，而他使用了 synapheia("结合")之类的术语是为了抵抗基督内两种性(人性和神性)的一种不恰当的混合。Nestorios 一直到最后都相信他的主张就是正统的信仰，又认为教宗 Leo I 也支持了他的基督论，虽然这个基督论有某些二元论因素。

Nestorius' rigidity offended the feelings of many believers in Constantinople and aroused the protest of the Alexandrine school of theology. Their leader, Cyril, patriarch of Alexandria, published a circular letter to all monks in Egypt, in which he defended the title "theotokos". Both patriarchs—Cyril and Nestorius—turned to Pope Coelestine I (422—432) in Rome who supported Cyril and appointed him to bring Nestorius back to orthodoxy. Cyril held a synod in Egypt and produced a document in which he rejected the typical Antiochenian concepts of "indwelling" (inhabitatio, enoikēsis) and "synthesis" (synapheia) of divine and human nature in Jesus Christ. The Council of Ephesus (431 AD) was opened by Cyril even before the Roman and Antiochian delegations had arrived. However, the condemnation of Nestorius was eventually accepted even by the Antiochenians. The deeper cause of this theological controversy were the two different types of Christology presented by the schools of Antioch and Alexandria. The school of Antioch emphasized the autonomy of the human nature of Christ as a second entity besides the divine Logos (the so-called "Christology of division"). The school of Alexandria on the other hand held that the sarx (human body of Christ) had become Logos and thus is one with the Logos. Therefore this school of unity demanded adherence to the formula "mia physis" ("one nature"), which Nestorius could not accept. Even until today the Nestorian Churches (Church of East Syria) confess the formula "two natures, two hypostaseis, one person in Christ".

Cyril interpreted Nestorius' rejection of the title "theotokos" as heresy. He thought that for Nestorius the unity of the divine Logos with the man Jesus was merely an external or moral unity. Thus Jesus would just be the "adopted Son of God" ("adoptianism") or only the "temple of God". However, many theologians of the 20th century think that Cyril misinterpreted or distorted Nestorius' teaching. They confirm that Nestorius' teaching was within the limits of orthodoxy and that he used terms like "combination" (synapheia) in order to resist an incorrect blending of the two natures of Christ. Nestorius himself believed until the end of his life that he was orthodox and that the teaching of Pope Leo I had confirmed his somewhat dualist Christology.

# 奥罗修斯（约 390—440 AD）

葡萄牙 Bracara（Braga）人，基督徒、司铎，第一位撰写世界历史的基督教人士，曾受 Augustinus 的鼓励。

**著作**：《历史》（《反驳异教徒的世界史》，根据 Suetonius、Livius、Tacitus 的著作写的世界史，目标是证明在基督宗教时代以前的人类也曾遇到很大的灾难；根据《旧约》的 *Daniel* 将世界历史分为四个阶段，对后来的历史观有深远的影响）、《反驳 Pelagius 派的人》

## 076. 《反驳异教徒的世界史》

这部著作分为 7 卷，作者应 Augustinus 的要求撰写了它。

与古代晚期的其他历史文集一样（参见 Julius Africanus［约 200 年］和 Eusebius［约 330 年］的著作），Orosius 的 *Historia* 也结合了不同民族的历史事件，即东方民族的、《圣经》的、希腊人的和罗马人的历史。这些历史著作经常视公元前 5500 年为世界史的元年，因为他们认为世界历史等于是"一周"，其中每一天等于是"一千年"（参见 *Ps* 90:4"在你面前一千年如一日"），而基督的诞生发生在"第六天的中午"。（在拜占庭和东方教会那里，这种以公元前 5500 年为元年的历法一直保存到彼得大帝的时代。）

第 1 卷包括从世界被创造到罗马城成立（公元前 753 年）的阶段。第 2 卷继续叙述到高卢人侵略罗马的过程（约到公元前 390 年）。第 3 卷覆盖到公元前 280 年的种种事件，而第 4 卷包含反对 Pyrrhus 和 Carthago 的战争时期。第 5 卷叙述从 Corinthus 被毁灭（公元前 146 年）到 Spartacus 的奴隶战争（公元前 73—前 71 年）时期。第 6 卷继续描述在公元一世纪初以前发生的事，而第 7 卷谈论后来的事件，一直到公元 417 年。

全书的结构符合《旧约》*Daniel* 书（*Dan* 2:31-45）的记载：一个由黄金（头部）、白银（胸部）、青铜（腰部）、铁与陶土（脚部）做成的雕像被逐渐毁灭。这个形象代表四个世界强国的逐步衰落：先是亚述和巴比伦的王朝，此后有马其顿和希腊化时期、迦太基的时期以及（最终）罗马人的时代。

Orosius 罗列一切发生在这些伟大王朝时期的灾难：战争、传染病、自然灾害与犯罪。他想以之说明人类始终都面对种种灾难和痛苦。所以不能说，因为罗马人放弃了原有的传统宗教并接受了基督信仰，所以罗马帝国才衰弱了，并有目前的灾难与混乱的来临（西哥特人于 410 年劫掠了罗马城，而不久后万达尔人又于 455 年侵略了罗马城）。

# Orosius

**Opera:** *Historiae adversus paganos, Liber apologeticus contra Pelagianos*
**Works:** *Histories against the Pagans, An apologetic Tract against the Pelagians*

## 076. *Historiae adversus paganos / Histories against the Pagans*

This work in 7 books was written in 417 AD in response to Augustine's request.

Like other historical compilations of late antiquity (cf. the works of Julius Africanus ca. 200 AD and Eusebius ca. 330 AD), Orosius' *History* also synchronizes the events of Oriental, Biblical, Greek–Hellenistic and Roman History. These histories often take the year 5500 BC as the beginning of world history, since they perceive world history as one "week", each day lasting "one thousand years" (cf. *Psalm* 90:4 "a thousand years are like yesterday in Your sight"). According to this computation the birth of Christ would occur in the middle of the sixth day. (In the Byzantine and in the Eastern churches, this calendar with the year of 5500 BC as the creation of the world, was followed until the time of Peter the Great, 1672—1725.)

The first book covers the time from the creation of the world until the founding of Rome (753 BC). Book 2 proceeds from there until the invasion of the Gauls in Rome (ca. 390 BC). Book 3 continues the story until 280 BC. Book 4 covers the period of the wars against Pyrrhus and the Carthaginians. Book 5 spans the period from the destruction of Corinth (146 BC) until the the slave wars incited by Spartacus (73—71 BC). Book 6 reaches the beginning of the first century of our era, and book 7 covers the events from there until 417 AD.

The structure follows the account of the *Book of Daniel* (*Dan* 2:31–45): a statue of gold (head), silver (chest), bronze (thighs), iron and clay (feet) is gradually destroyed. This image interprets the successive decline of four world-powers: the Assyrian–Babylonian dynasties, the Macedonian– Hellenist rulers, the Carthaginian Empire, and finally the Romans.

Orosius lists up all the calamities that occurred during these great empires: wars, epidemics, disasters, crimes. In this way he tries to show that throughout history mankind was confronted with all kinds of suffering. Therefore one cannot blame the fact that the Roman Empire gave up its old religion for Christianity as being the reason for the present calamities and disorders (the Visigoths sacked Rome in 410 AD, and some time later—in 455 AD—the Vandals invaded Rome).

# 利奥（约 400—461 AD）

来自 Toscana 地区，于 430 年在罗马任 Archidiakon（总执事），曾影响 Johannes Cassianus 写出一部反对 Nestorianismus 的书，又影响了罗马教宗坚持一种反对 Pelagius 的路线。他于 440 年被祝圣为罗马主教（即教宗），始终重视教会的正统信仰并反对 Pelagius 派、Arius 派、（443 年在罗马被发现的）Manichaeismus（摩尼教）以及西班牙的 Priscilla 派。他的地位很高，而罗马皇帝于 445 年发布的敕令承认罗马主教对西罗马各省的司法权（iurisdictio）。Leo 教宗在 452 年前往意大利北部，与匈奴的领导 Attila 进行谈判，结果匈奴人没有侵略罗马城。Vandales 领导 Geiserich 于 455 年劫掠了罗马城，但 Leo 影响了他，使他没有杀人，没有烧毁城市。在 449 年，Leo 反驳 Eutyches 和 monophysitismus（基督一性论），并向 Constantinopolis 的大主教 Flavianus 写了一封信。451 年在 Chalcedon 召开的主教会议（大公会议）上采纳了他的神学观点。Leo 与东方教会进行对话并肯定了罗马教宗的地位。因为他是第一位个人书信和大量讲演稿得以保存的教宗，所以他成为一位重要的拉丁教父。

著作：《书信集》（143 篇，第 28 封信是 Tomus ad Flavianum）、《讲章》（96 篇）

## 077. 《致佛拉维安的信》

教宗 Leo 于 449 年写了这封信（亦称 Epistola dogmatica ad Flavianum《致 Flavianus 的教义信》）。收信的人是 Constantinopolis 的宗主教 Flavianus。然而，在 Ephesus 的主教会议上（449 年），来自埃及 Alexandria 的宗主教阻碍人们在会议上宣读这封信。Leo 后来曾称该会议为"强盗会议"（latrocinium）。在 451 年，东方的皇帝 Markianos 在 Chalkedon 召开了一次大的主教会议，这次会议接受了 Leo 信中的关键说法，这样便为后来的神学家们权威性地澄清了关于基督论的问题。

在当时的小亚细亚出现了隐修院院长 Eutyches（378—454 年），他反驳 Nestorios 的观点并传播一种"基督一性论"（即在基督内神性与人性结合并似乎消除了基督的人性）。Flavianus 和 Eutyches 都请 Leo 教宗支持他们的观点。在他的信中，Leo 教宗很清楚地反对 Eutyches 的理论并称他为一种邪恶的异端。Leo 的信也拒绝了 Dyophysitismus（基督两性论）的观点（即：在基督内不仅仅有两个本性，也有两个人格）。另外，教宗也谴责了 Theopaschitismus（神受苦论），根据这种主张，在基督受苦时神也一起受苦受难。Leo 的信总结了来自 Tertullianus 和 Augustinus 的正统教导：圣子来到了这个世俗世界，但他并没有放弃圣父的光荣。他由童贞女 Maria 生育并成为一

# Leo Magnus / Leo the Great

**Opera:** *Epistulae, Sermones*
**Works:** *Letters, Homilies*


### 077. *Tomus ad Flavianum / Letter to Flavianus*

In 449 AD Leo wrote this letter (also quoted as *Epistola dogmatica ad Flavianum*) concerning the two natures of Christ to Flavianus, the patriarch of Constantinople. However, at the synod of Ephesus (449 AD) the patriarch of Alexandria prevented the letter from being read. Leo later called that synod a "latrocinium" ("robbers' synod"). In 451 AD Emperor Markianos convoked the Council of Chalcedon which accepted the decisive passage from Leo's letter and therefore clarified the Christological debate for the future in an authoritative way.

At that time an abbot in Asia Minor, Eutyches (378—454 AD), the opponent of Nestorius, propagated monophysitism (the theory that the divine nature of Christ unites with and practically eliminates the human nature of Christ). Flavianus and Eutyches both asked Leo to support their views of the nature of Christ. In his letter Leo clearly opposes Eutyches' theory which he calls an evil heresy. Leo's letter also rejects the view of the Dyophysites who held that in Christ two natures and two persons coexisted. In addition, he condemns Theopaschitism, according to which God suffered in Christ. Leo's letter sums up the orthodox teaching based on Tertullian and Augustine: the Son of God came into this secular world without leaving behind the glory of His Father. He was born by the virgin Mary and became a man of flesh and blood, true man and true God. The two natures of Christ are "not mixed, immutable, undivided, inseparable" (inconfuse, immutabiliter, indivise, inseparabiliter, or in the Greek text: asynchytōs, a-

个有血有肉的人,即真人,同时又是真神。基督这两个性质(神性与人性)是"不混合地、不变地、不分裂地、不离散地"结合在一起的(inconfuse, immutabiliter, indivise, inseparabiliter,参见 *Denzinger* DS 302 条)。"上主的威严接受了谦逊,权力接受了软弱,永恒接受了死亡。为了使我们摆脱压抑我们的罪责,那个不被伤害的神性与一个接受苦难的人性结合。这种补救回应了我们人的处境:上主和人类之间的唯一中介者,耶稣基督,他在一个性体中死去了,但在第二个性体中没有死去……他接受了奴隶的形状,但没有受罪恶的污染。他提升了人性,但没有贬低神性。

treptōs, adiairetōs, achōristōs, confer *Denzinger* DS 302). "God's majesty assumed humility, power assumed weakness, eternity accepted mortality. In order to deliver us from the guilt burdening us down, the invulnerable nature (of God) was united with a nature capable of suffering. This remedy answered the needs of our situation: one and the same mediator between God and mankind, Jesus Christ, was to die in one nature but not in the other… He assumed the form of a slave but was not stained by sin. He elevated the human without diminishing the divine."

# 普洛克鲁斯（约 412—485 AD）

生于 Byzantion（拜占庭）的贵族家庭，曾在 Beirut、Alexandria 和雅典求学，后来留在雅典并于 437 年成为雅典学院的"领导"(diadochos)。他以 Platōn 主义为主线总结了整个非基督宗教的古典哲学和宗教（参见 Plotinos），他的著作很多，涉及很多领域的知识。他被称为古希腊哲学的最后总结者，对中世纪、文艺复兴时期和德国唯心主义都有深远的影响。

**著作**：《论恶的存在》、《论天命和命运》、《论柏拉图的神学》、《论欧几里德著作第一卷》、《天文学导论》、《物理学导论》、《神学导论》

## 078. 《论柏拉图的神学》

该著作（共 6 卷）从一个新柏拉图主义的视角谈论柏拉图的哲学和神学。

Proklos 认为一切存在的根源是"一"。第一个"一"是在任何一个"多"之前；至善也是在任何"善"之前，而第一个原因是在任何事物之前。第一个"一"、至善与第一个原因就是一个，即"太一"，它超越一切，不能被形容但产生一切。"太一"产生宇宙（所谓的 kosmos noētos 可以理解的世界），但从"一"没有直接的、达到宇宙的途径。因此需要一些 henades（"单元"），它们结合世界和"一"。Proklos 结合宗教和形而上学的思想，所以他认为这些"单元"就是传统的神灵。他试图描述宇宙的不同层次，同时也将神明们归类。

# Proklos / Proclus

**Opera:** *De malorum subsistentia, De providentia et fato, Eis ten Platōnos theologian, Eis to prōton Eukleidu stoicheion, Hypotyposis astronomicarum positionum, Stoicheiosis physikē (=Institutio physica), Stoicheiosis theologikē (=Institutio theologica, Elementatio theologica)*

**Works:** *The Existence of Evil, On Providence and Fate, On Plato's Theology, On the First Book of Euclid's Elements, Introduction to Astronomy, Elements of Physics, Elements of Theology*

## 078. *Eis tēn Platōnos theologian / On Plato's Theology*

This work in 6 books discusses Plato's theology and philosophy from a Neoplatonist perspective.

Proclus thinks that the origin of all being is the One. The First Oneness is before any multitude, the First Good is before any good or any value, and the First Cause is before any being. Oneness, the First Good and the First Cause are in fact the same, namely the One, which is higher than anything else. It is beyond description and produces all other things. The One produces the universe (the kosmos noētos, the intelligible world), but there is no direct way from the One to the diversity and multiplicity of the intelligible world. Thus it needs "henads" ("units") which connect the world and the One. Blending religion and metaphysical consideration, Proclus thinks that these mediating "henads" are the traditional gods. He tries to describe the layers of the universe and likewise classifies the gods according to certain categories.

# 欧基皮乌斯（约 465—535 AD）

大概来自一个罗马家庭，在 470 年代曾经是 Severinus 在 Noricum 地区（今天奥地利）的助手，后来加入了 Favianis 的隐修团体，但于 488 年回到意大利。

著作：《圣塞维林传》

## 079.《圣塞维林传》

本书是"Noricum 的宗徒/使徒"的传记（亦称 *Commemoratorium* "纪念书"），成书时间大约在 511 年。它描述 Severinus 的言行，同时也反映 Noricum 省在当时民族迁移时期的情况（Noricum 大约是今天奥地利东北部地区）。因为关于这段历史的资料非常稀罕，这部传记是相当珍贵的。

Severinus 来自意大利或罗马的贵族家庭，是一位基督徒（famulus Dei "神之仆人"）。他原来任高级官员，但 454 年匈奴人在 Noricum 的统治崩溃后，Severinus 被派遣到那里。他拥有社会和军事上的权力，他的任务是重新建立 Alpes（阿尔卑斯山）东部地区和 Danubius（多瑙河）地区（即 Noricum 省）的社会秩序。461 年他由于政治变化而被迫逃到埃及，但在 467 年他再次回到 Noricum 去，继续任职直到 476 年。476 年罗马人的管理制度解体了，此后 Severinus 主动试图组织整个地区，他平等地帮助罗马人和日耳曼人、公教徒和 Arius 派的基督徒。他在管理方面具有丰富的经验，多次与日耳曼人的领导者进行谈判（比如和 Rugii 人的君主们），此时也发挥了他的外交能力。

当时居住在 Danubius（多瑙河）的人民不断遭受日耳曼侵略者的干扰，各地有强盗，而很多人处于穷困无力当中。Severinus 成为这些人的世俗领导和精神支柱。他组织了一些隐修者的团体（称他们为 fratres 弟兄），但他自己既不是司铎，也不是隐修者。主要的隐修院建立在 Favianis（今天的 Mautern 城，在奥地利地区）。这些小型的隐修者团体也有管理中心的功能，他们是食品和衣服的仓库，又是简单的医疗所。有时候，这些隐修者担任外交官和使者，被派往一些部落。Severinus 多次试图从日耳曼侵略者的手中赎回被俘的人。在他去世后，Severinus 的骨灰被带到意大利——当时第一个外族的罗马王 Odoacer（476—493 年在位）于 488 年下令一切罗曼居民必须移民到意大利。902 年，Severinus 的遗体被迁到一个位于 Neapoli 附近的墓。

本书的 46 章表达了 Severinus 的美德（virtus）并为此提出很多鲜明的例子。他曾经治疗了一些人的病，而作者尽可能模仿《福音书》的治病故事。另一些奇迹（比如复

# Eugippius

**Opera:** *Vita Sancti Severini*
**Works:** *The Life of Saint Severin*

## 079. *Vita Sancti Severini* / *The Life of Saint Severin*

This biography (also called *Commemoratorium*—memorial book) of the "Apostle of Noricum" was written ca. in 511 AD. It describes the actions and words of Severin but also reflects the situation of the province of Noricum (roughly the north-eastern part of modern Austria) at the time of the tribal migrations. Since historical sources about that period are extremely rare, the *Vita* is very valuable.

Severin came from a noble family from Italy or Rome and was a Christian (famulus Dei "servant of God"). He held a high office before he was sent to Noricum in 454 AD, just after the collapse of the empire of the Huns in that area. He commanded civil and military authority and was supposed to reorganize the regions in the eastern Alps and Danube area (the province of Noricum). In 461 AD he had to flee to Egypt due to political changes, but in 467 AD he returned to Noricum again and continued to work there in an official post until 476 AD. After the collapse of the Roman administration he tried to organize the area on his own initiative, helping Romans and Germanic people, Catholics and Arianist believers alike. He had a strong background in administration and diplomacy, especially in dealing with Germanic leaders, for example, the kings of the Rugii.

The local population in the Danube valley suffering constantly from Germanic invasions, robbers and poverty, had Severin become their spiritual and secular leader. He organized communities of monks (fratres), but he himself was neither priest nor monk. The main monastery was set up in Favianis (today's Mautern in Austria). These small communities also served as administration centers, as storing places for food and clothes, and as simple hospitals. The monks were sometimes sent to some tribes on diplomatic missions. Severin repeatedly tried to redeem captives from the hands of the Germanic invaders. After his death Severin's bones were taken back to Italy in the year 488 AD, when Rome's first barbarian king (Odoacer, 476—493 AD) ordered the local Romanic population to emigrate to Italy. In the year 902 Severin's remains were transferred to a tomb in Naples.

The 46 chapters of the book try to present shining examples of Severin's virtue (virtus). The narratives of his healing the sick are shaped according to the Gospels.

活一些亡者或再次点燃已经熄灭的蜡烛)在其他的圣人传记中也能找到。第 11 到 26 章记录 Severinus 到一些 Danubius 上游地区的堡垒城市(castellum)的旅程,还有关于他的奇迹以及他对穷人的照顾的记载。第 27~31 章叙述他晚年的努力:他想组织人们从西部移民到东部。他的死亡被描述于第 43 章,而最后 3 章谈论后来的种种事件以及他在死亡以后行的奇迹(比如当一个患病的人在他寿床前祈祷时,病人的病被治好了)。

Other miracles (like the resurrection of a dead person or the candle-miracles) are also found in the biographies of other saints. Chapters 11~26 record Severin's travels to several fortified towns (castellum, castles) in the upper Danube area, his miracles, and his care for the poor. Chapters 27~31 narrate how he tried to organize the evacuation of the population from the west to the east in the last years. His death is described in chapter 43, and the last 3 chapters tell about further events and the miracles he worked after his death (for example the healing of a sick man who prayed at his death-bed).

# 小狄奥尼修斯（约 470—550 AD）

这位来自欧洲东部（Skythia）的隐修士曾前往罗马并翻译了许多希腊语的著作，因此他成为一位有影响的教会法学家和历史学家。他自称 Exiguus（"微小的"）。

著作：《教规集》（从希腊语译成拉丁语的会议文献和教会法文献，成书于 498—501 年间）、《复活节日期查订表》

## 080. 《复活节日期查订表》

在 525 年，Dionysius 回应了罗马教宗 Johannes I（约翰一世）的邀请并完成了这部著作，其中提供了一些计算基督教节日的方法。在这些节日中，复活节，即基督复活的节日，具有核心的地位。根据他的编年学资料，Dionysius 认定基督的诞生落到罗马建城后第 754 年。自从公元 532 年以来，罗马的公教会就使用 Dionysius 的编年方式，另一些学者和历史学家（比如英国的 Bede）也采纳和传播了这个编年法，所以这样就决定了基督宗教的"元年"。实际上，今天的大多数学者都认为，Dionysius 的算法有 4 到 7 年的误差。（换言之，基督不是诞生在公元元年的，而是大约在公元前 5 年诞生。）

# Dionysius Exiguus / Denis the Little

**Opera:** *Kanones, Liber de Paschale*
**Works:** *Regulations, The Book on Easter*

## 080. *Liber de paschale / The Book on Easter*

This book was written by Dionysius answering a request of Pope John I in the year 525 AD. The book provides the basic material for the computation of the Christian feast-days, among which Easter, the celebration of the resurrection of Christ, is of central importance. According to his chronological research Dionysius decided that Christ was born in the 754th year after the foundation of Rome. Since the year 532 AD the Catholic Church applied Dionysius' chronology, other scholars and historians popularized the new calendar (cf. Bede), and so this year became the turning point of the Christian chronology, although today it is generally assumed that Dionysius made a mistake of 4 to 7 years. (In other words, Christ was not born in the year 0 but probably ca. 5 years earlier.)

# 波伊提乌（476—524 AD）

出身于罗马 Anicius 贵族，获得了很好的教育（大概在 Alexandria），他可能是古代晚期最后精通古希腊语的拉丁作者；他在 Theodoricus 王的时代（493—526年）任执政官（510年），后享有 magister officiorum（等于"总理"）的崇高地位，但于 523 年遭诽谤，被捕入狱，524 年在 Pavia 附近被处死。有人怀疑他是一名叛徒，因为他和 Constantinopolis 政府有联系并有一些秘密文献。他想强化元老院的影响力，所以国王反对他。他曾想为拉丁语世界介绍 Plato 和 Aristoteles 的著作，后来通过他的翻译，这两位哲学家确实在中世纪产生了较大的影响。

**著作**：《哲学的慰藉》、《论音乐》、《论解释》（从 Aristoteles *Peri hermēneias* 翻译的）、《论三位一体的上主》、《注解〈导论〉》、《论数学》、《反驳 Eutyches 和 Nestorius》

## 081.《哲学的慰藉》

这部具有深远影响的杰作成书于 524 年；作者当时在监狱中面临死亡。全书 5 卷，作者在散文的叙述中前后插入 39 首诗。今天，本书和 Augustinus 的自传 *Confessiones* 一起是古代晚期最广为人知的著作。它结合了三个主题：义人必须孤独地受苦，只有美德和智慧陪同着他（参见 Socrates 和 Cicero, *Tuscul.* 5:13）；哲学是灵魂的治疗者（参见 Seneca）；一种教育过程：从最简单的原则一步步走向最难懂的伦理学问题（第 5 卷）。

在第 1 卷的开始有一首受文艺女神启迪的哀歌体诗。不幸的作者哀叹自己的命运。当他写这首诗时，他感觉到有一个高大的、威严的妇女走近他的床，她就是哲学的化身。她同时既是年龄很大的，又是很年轻的；有时候像一个普通的人，有时候她又非常高，似乎充满整个宇宙。在她的衣服下端绣有希腊字母"P"，而在其上端绣了一个"Th"，这两个字母代表"实践"和"理论"。她右手拿着一些书（libellos），左手握着一个权杖。她的面容令人感到敬畏，她的眼睛闪耀传神，她的精力是永不枯竭的。她驱逐那些文艺女神，因为她们仅仅要用甘甜的毒（dulcibus venenis）来干扰这个病人。这个不幸的人患有忧郁症，只有哲学才是这种病的真正良药（medicina）。哲学开始作诊断并发现 Boethius（即作者）的问题是一种昏睡症，一种病态的漠不关心。

作者问哲学她为什么来到监狱里，而她回答说她始终和那些受迫害的人在一起，她还提到了 Socrates、Seneca 和其他思想家。此后她转向 Boethius，请他说明他坐牢的原因。她说"如果你想获得治疗，你必须揭露你的伤口"（Si operam medicantis exspectas, oportet vulnus detegas）。Boethius 说他被控诉的原因大概是因为他接受了一些来自 Constantinopolis 的文献，而在 Ravenna 的 Gothones（哥特人）怀疑他是一个叛徒。他

# Anicius Manlius Severinus Boethius

**Opera:** *De consolatione philosophiae, De institutione musica, De interpretatione, De Sancta Trinitate, In Isagogen, (=Commentarius in Eisagogen Porphyrii), Institutio arithmetica, Liber contra Eutychen et Nestorium*

**Works:** *The Consolation of Philosophy, On Music, On Interpretation, On the Holy Trinity, Commentary to the Isagoge (of Porphyrios), On Mathematics, Against Eutyches and Nestorius*

## 081. *De consolatione philosophiae / The Consolation of Philosophy*

This influential masterpiece was written in 524 AD when the author was imprisoned and faced his execution. Altogether 39 short poems are inserted into the prose narrative of five books. Together with Augustine's *Confessions*, this book is the most well-known work of late antiquity today. It combines three motives: the just man suffering alone, only accompanied by virtue and wisdom (cf. Socrates, Cicero, *Tuscul.* 5,13); philosophy as healer of the soul (cf. Seneca); and a pedagogical progress from simple principles to the most difficult ethical issues (book 5).

Book 1 starts with an elegiac poem inspired by the Muses. The infortunate author mourns his own fate. As he writes his poem he senses that a dignified woman—the allegory of philosophy—approaches his bed. She is old and young at the same time, she appears sometimes like a human, but sometimes she is so tall that she fills the universe. On the bottom of her dress the Greek letter "P" is embroidered, and on top a "Th", symbolizing praxis and theory. In one hand she carries books (libellos), in her left a scepter. Her face is awe-inspiring, her eyes are sparkling, her strength is inexhaustible. She ousts the Muses who would only excite the sick man with their sweet poison (dulcibus venenis). Only philosophy can be the true remedy (medicina) for the patient's depression. Philosophy makes a diagnosis and finds out that Boethius' problem is lethargy, a kind of pathological dullness.

The author asks why philosophy is in prison, and she answers that she was always persecuted, mentioning the examples of Socrates, Seneca and other thinkers. Now she turns to Boethius and asks him to explain his imprisonment, saying "If you want healing, you must expose your wound". (Si operam medicantis exspectas, oportet vulnus detegas). Boethius tells why he was accused, probably because he had some documents from

最终的不幸是这一点：连他原来的朋友也会诅咒和蔑视他，他失去的将不仅仅是生命，还有名誉。

哲学谴责他，因为他不仅仅离开了物质上的家乡，而且也放弃了精神性的家园：他失去了内心的平静，现在反而感到痛苦、悲伤和愤怒。首先需要调节这些情绪（affectus），此后才能开始治疗他的病。哲学想进一步确诊他的疾病，因此她问5个问题：1) 宇宙中的一切行动是偶然的还是符合某种理性的安排（regimen rationis）？这是一个古典哲学的问题，Epicurus 派的人肯定"偶然性"，而在另一方面 Stoa、Plato 学派和基督徒会坚持"理性的计划"。Boethius 很快回答：世界中有一个计划。2) 第二个问题是：宇宙以什么方式被管理引导？Boethius 说他不知道答案，而这种无知似乎也和他的病态有关。3) 一切事物的目标是什么？Boethius 说他曾经知道答案，但因为现在感到很悲痛，他想不起来。4) 一切事物的来源是什么？Boethius 立刻回答：神（deus）。5) 哲学最后问：人是什么？Boethius 用古典的、来自 Plato 和 Aristoteles 的说法作答：人是一个"有理性的、会死的活物"（animal rationale et mortale）。然而，哲学说，这种回答还不够，而且恰恰因为 Boethius 忘记了他是谁、因为他想不起一切事物的目标，所以他感到如此悲伤。然而，他仍然相信神的理性和计划（divina ratio），所以这个小小的火花（scintillula）也许能够再次恢复他的生命力。

第2卷的开始是一种安慰讲演。哲学说 Boethius 应该知道命运女神 Fortuna-Tyche 的真实面貌。如果哲学的原则被保存，那么在描述 Fortuna 时可以使用修辞学的工具。Fortuna 是一个始终处于变化当中的妇女。她是不可靠的、无情的、残酷的。现在 Fortuna 自己出现并为自己进行辩护："人啊，你出生的时候是赤裸裸的，什么都没有，你所有的一切都是我给予你的；如果我现在收回这些东西，你有什么抱怨的理由？"（参见 *Job* 1）。Fortuna 是一个轮子（在西方文献中，这是最早使用这个比喻的章节之一）。如果 Fortuna 满足人们的一切渴望，人们还是会贪婪地追求更多。

哲学说，这还不是 Boethius 心灵的真正治疗，而仅仅是一种止痛药。她说 Boethius 的妻子和儿子们很安全和幸福，但 Boethius 不愿意接受这种安慰。这就引发更多考虑：没有一个人真正完全满足于自己的处境（nemo facile cum fortunae suae condicione concordat）。人们虽然很快乐但仍然想改变自己的境况。最终，真正的幸福和快乐不能在外面寻找，只能在内心寻求。

第二个疗程在于理解到一切财富的虚幻：1) 物质财富如果不被消耗，就没有用。2) 任何财富都将他人排除在外。3) 任何珍贵的物质财富的价值都不如一个活的人。4) 大自然的美丽本身是一种价值，但人无法掌握它、拥有它。5) 某些艺术品的美丽并不是艺术品的所有者的贡献。6) 拥有很多优秀的仆人，这不能归功于主人，而要归功于仆人们。7) 追求一些物质的东西等于是渴望一些低于自身尊严的东西，这就意味着一个人不认识自己，甚至堕落到一个比动物还要低的地步。8) 物质财富经常为所有者带来灾难。

Constantinople and the Goths in Ravenna suspected him to be a traitor. His ultimate calamity is that even his friends will curse him and despise him, he will not only lose his life, but also his reputation.

Philosophy rebukes him for not only leaving his physical but also his spiritual home. He has lost the calmness of heart and feels now pain, sorrow and wrath. First these emotions (affectus) need relief, then only can the healing process start. The further diagnosis of philosophy is based on 5 questions: (1) Is the universe left to chance or directed by a rational plan (regimen rationis)? This classical question divided Epicureans (chance) on the one side and Stoa, Platonists and Christians on the other (rational guidance). Boethius answers quickly: There is a plan in the world. (2) By which means is the universe governed? Boethius does not know the answer, and this seems to be one symptom of his illness. (3) What is the purpose of all things? Boethius once knew the answer, but now sadness impairs his memory. (4) What is the origin of all things? Boethius answers immediately: God. (5) Philosophy asks then: What is man? And Boethius answers with the classical Platonic-Aristotelian formula: "a rational and mortal living being" (animal rationale et mortale), but philosophy says this is not enough, and exactly because Boethius has forgotten who he is and cannot remember the purpose of all things, he feels so sad. However, because he still has faith in divine providence (divina ratio), this spark of fire (scintillula) can rekindle the warmth of life.

The second book starts with a speech of consolation. Philosophy says that Boethius has to know the true nature of Fortuna-Tyche, the goddess of fate. If the rules of philosophy are kept, rhetoric is an apt means for the description of Fortuna. Fortuna is a lady who always changes. She is unreliable, inexorable, cruel. Now the personification of Fortuna appears herself and defends her case: "Naked you were born, man, and everything you possess now was granted by me: how can you complain if I take it back?" (Cf. *Job* 1). Fortuna is like a wheel (this is one of the earliest texts for this metaphor). Even if Fortuna would always satisfy humans, they would be ever greedy for more.

Philosophy now points out that this is not yet the true remedy for Boethius' soul, but only a relief of pain. She says that Boethius' wife and sons are quite safe and happy, but Boethius refuses to be consoled. That induces more considerations: Nobody is really fully satisfied with his (her) lot (Nemo facile cum fortunae suae condicione concordat). Nobody is so happy that he would not like to change his situation. Finally, true happiness is not found outside, but in the heart of man.

A second therapy shows the futility of all riches: (1) Wealth is only useful when consumed. (2) Riches always exclude others. (3) The splendor of precious things is never as valuable as a living person. (4) The beauty of nature is a value of itself and cannot be possessed by man. (5) Beauty of artifacts is not a merit of the possessor. (6) To have many good servants is only an achievement of the servants, and not of their lord. (7) To strive for material goods is to long for things that are below one's dignity, it implies lack of self-awareness which brings about a fall even below the status of an animal. (8) Wealth is often detrimental to the possessor.

反对世俗权力与世俗荣誉的论点是:1)坏人掌权是一种灾难。2)人在宇宙中如此渺小,他追求权力是好高骛远的表现。3)政治权力只能控制身体,不能控制精神。4)政权变化无常,且不久就将面临挑战。5)最坏的人经常得到最大的荣耀和赞扬(比如Nero皇帝)。6)音乐使人有节奏感,但荣誉和权力并不使人们变得更节制,因此权力并不是一个值得追求的价值。7)从宇宙的庞大空间和悠久的时间范围来看,人们追求的荣誉都是虚伪的。Fortuna(命运女神)教导人们,通过种种灾难来认出真正的朋友。第2卷最后的诗歌赞扬友谊以及那种充满整个宇宙的爱。

在第3卷的开头,"病人"说他现在感觉到已经有足够的力量,他愿意服用那种能够完全治好他的苦药。因此哲学向他说明虚假的与真实的幸福分别是什么。幸福是一切人追求的目标,但人们在五个方面误认世俗的东西是最高的价值(summum bonum):1)人们追求自给自足(nihilo indigere)并搜刮财富(divitiae)。2)人们寻求尊荣(dignissimum venerationi)和社会上的地位(honores)。3)他们寻求权力(potentia)并想当王(regnare)。4)人们追求幸福的美好生活(claritas),用战争或和平手段来争取名誉(gloria)。5)人们想得到真正的喜乐(gaudium et laetitia),但他们又寻求物质上的快感(voluptates)。世俗的东西无法满足人的需要:财富不会导致自给自足,他们相反地还会产生更大的需求。社会上的地位并不一定意味着真正的尊严(比如Nero皇帝)。寻求权力是危险的(例子:被迫自杀的Seneca和被Caracalla皇帝处死的法律学家Papinianus)。只有那个能够控制自己欲望的人才是真正有力量的人。真正的光荣不建立在民众那些变化无常的谣言之上。感官上的娱乐和蜜蜂一样:它们先给予甜美的蜂蜜,后来却用刺蜇你。

无论如何,人的一切欲望都是对于幸福的渴望,也是对于至善的渴望,而最高的善实际上就是神(beatitudo=bonitas=summum bonum=deus,幸福=美善=至善=神)。至善的特征是"一"(unum)。一切活物都是灵魂和身体的整体,只有保持它们的合一性,它们才能够生活。植物也同样尽力保护它们的生命及它们种类的合一性。自我保卫最终是对于"一"和"善"的渴望,这就回答了第1卷中的问题:一切事物的目标是什么?一切都追求"一"(omnia unum desiderant)。上主管理这个世界的方式(gubernatio mundi)是他结合一切东西。他通过美善统治整个宇宙,因此一切万物很自由地服从于他,因为他们都追求"善"。第3卷的结尾是对Orpheus和Eurydice的神话的象征性解释:人心回顾世俗的东西就无法观看真理。

在第4卷的开始,Boethius提出异议:哲学的慰藉没有连贯性。如果神统治世界,恶人怎能占上风,好人则被迫害呢(参见Platōn, *Polit.* 361A~362C:义人受虐待)。现在哲学说她将要提升Boethius的心灵,使之上升到很高的地方(参见"精神的翅膀",*Phaedrus* 246B)。哲学说一切万物都渴望美善,尤其人心追求美善。如果人们没有达到或没有实现善(失败、罪恶、邪恶的意图),这都是软弱的表现。好的行动都是那些符

The arguments against secular power and honor are these: (1) Bad people who are in power are a disaster. (2) Man is so frail a part in the universe, his quest for power is arrogant. (3) Power can only control the body but not the spirit. (4) Power is changeable and faces rivals soon. (5) Usually the worst people are honored most (example: Nero). (6) Music brings rhythm to man and can make people more harmonious, but honor and power do not make men moderate, therefore power is not a desirable good. (7) Seen from the immense extension of the universe in time and space, all human honor is vain. Fortuna educates man, calamities show true friends. The last poem of book 2 praises friendship and the love that pervades the cosmos.

At the beginning of book 3 the patient declares that he feels strong enough to take the tough medicine that can fully cure him. Now Philosophia talks to him about false and true happiness. Happiness is the one aim which all pursue, but in five areas many people mistake earthly goods for the highest good (summum bonum): (1) They search for self-sufficiency (nihilo indigere) and heap up riches (divitiae). (2) They look for dignity (dignissimum venerationi) and desire social recognition (honores). (3) They want power (potentia) and try to become king (regnare). (4) They desire the brightness (claritas) of beatitude and pursue fame (gloria) by war or by peaceful means. (5) They intend to feel true joy (gaudium et laetitia), but they strive for physical gratifications (voluptates). The worldly values cannot satisfy the needs of man: riches will not lead to self-sufficiency but on the contrary generate more greed. Social recognition or high rank does not necessarily imply real dignity (example: Nero). The search for power is dangerous (examples: Seneca who was forced to commit suicide, and the jurist Papinian who was executed by Caracalla). Only one who can control his own desires is really powerful. True glory is not built upon the ever-changing rumors of the people. Sensual enjoyments are like bees that first give honey and then sting.

However, all human desires point to the search for happiness and to the desire for the highest good, which is in fact God (beatitudo=bonitas=summum bonum=deus). This highest good is characterized by "unity" (unum). All living beings are a unity of body and soul, and as long as this unity is preserved they can live. Even plants try to protect their existence and the unity of their species. Self-preservation is finally the desire for unity and for the good, which answers the question of book 1: What is the purpose of all things? All strive for unity (omnia unum desiderant). The way how God rules the world (gubernatio mundi) is that he keeps all things together, he rules the universe by his goodness, so that all things freely obey, striving for the good. The end of book 3 is an allegorical interpretation of Orpheus and Eurydice: If the mind turns back to the world, it will lose sight of the truth.

Book 4 starts with an objection presented by Boethius: Philosophy's consolations are not conclusive. How is it possible that in a world ordered by God the bad triumphs and the good is persecuted? (cf. Plato's just man who is tortured, *Polit.* 361A – 362C). Now Philosophy says she will take Boethius' mind up to lofty heights (cf. the wings of the spirit, *Phaedrus* 246B). Philosophy explains that all things desire the good, and especially the human will strives for the good. Wherever the good is not attained (=failure,

合本性的行动(比如用脚走路,而不是用手掌和手臂走路)。因此,邪恶仅仅是人们无法很自然地使用自己的能力。罪恶的行动来自无知,因为一个人让某些欲望征服自己或一个人知道邪恶的东西且真正愿意追求它(参见 Aristoteles、*Ethic. Nic.* 7 卷宗)。如果一个人让欲望征服自己,他就是一个愚蠢的人;如果他知道邪恶但仍然犯罪,他就是软弱的;而如果他追求恶,他就不再是一个有人格的存在。

因此,美德是幸福,也是具有神肖像的存在,因为神追求善并能够实践它。邪恶是自己的惩罚,因为他是人性的丢失。邪恶的人就和动物一样(参见 *Phaedo* 81E):贪婪的人是狼,爱争吵的人和狗一样。人也许会上升到神界或堕落到野兽那里(参见 *Eth. Nic.* 1145a 18~33)。此后加上魔术家 Circe(参见 *Odysseia*)的哲学性解释:"人面兽心"的情况比"兽身人心"更恶劣。因此,遭受不义比引起不义更好。然而,Boethius 感到不满意,所以哲学需要谈论五个概念:1)预先安排(providentia);2)信仰的联结,即一切事物的互相联系;3)偶然性;4)神的预知;5)人的决定的自由。宇宙的秩序因预先安排(providentia)而被保护,只是因为我们的无能我们看不到这种秩序,所以看来是一种不正义的秩序。第 4 卷的最后一首诗提醒 Boethius 说人必须通过长期的痛苦和辛劳才能够达到最终的目的(就像 Agamemnon、Odysseus、尤其是 Hercules 那样)。

第 5 卷谈论最难理解的问题:关于人类自由和神预知的问题。Boethius 问:如果神知道一切将来要发生的事,就没有自由,而诸如"善"、"恶"、"赏报"、"惩罚"的观念都将是没有意义的。哲学区分预知和必然性。人心并不是 Stoa 派所说的"白板"(tabula rasa),而是已经有了某些基本的观念,而感官印象将会激励这些基本观念(参见 Plato 的思想)。知识也有某些阶层,比如人的知识永远无法达到神性知识的阶层。对人来说,一切体验因时间而被分为"以前"、"现在"、"以后",但对神来说,一切事物存在于完美的"现在"当中(这是"永恒"aeternitas 的著名定义)。在神的眼中,那些必然发生的事件以及那些因自由选择发生的事件都同时存在。神也知道行动中的人的种种能力和可能性(omniscientia)。这种论点确保自由意志,所以"美"、"恶"、"赏报"和"惩罚"都保持其意义。一个正义的人向神做的祈祷是有意义的,而义人也能够怀有希望。最后几句话鼓励人们应该承认行善的义务,不可以在一种盲目的必然的束缚中回避人生:"你们要回避恶习,要培养美德,要怀着正当的希望,要向天发出谦卑的祈祷。如果你们不否认这些,你们就有行善的伟大义务,因为你们在一个理解一切的审判者眼前生活。"(Aversamini igitur vitia, colite virtutes, ad rectas spes animum sublevate, humiles preces in excelsa porrigite. Magna vobis est, si dissimulare non vultis, necessitas indicta probitatis, cum ante oculos agitis iudicis cuncta cernentis.)

sin, maliciousness), it is only a sign of human weakness. Good actions are actions according to nature (like walking on feet and not on arms and hands). Evilness therefore is only the inability to use one's talents in a natural way. Evil actions stem from ignorance, because a person lets himself/herself be overtaken by desires or because he/she knows and wants the evil (cf. Arist. *Ethic. Nic.* bk 7). In the first case the person is stupid, in the second weak, in the third case he/she ceases to exist as a person.

Virtue therefore is happiness and being in the image of God who wants the good and is able to realize it. Evilness is its own punishment because it is the loss of humanity. Sinful people are like animals (cf. *Phaedo* 81E): greedy people are wolves, those who quarrel are like dogs. Man can ascend to divinity or sink into bestiality (*Eth. Nic.* 1145a 18~33). A philosophical interpretation of Circe's sorcery (*Odyssey*) follows: it is even worse if people are in a normal physical condition but have the soul of a beast. Therefore it is better to suffer injustice than to cause injustice. However, Boethius is not satisfied, and Philosophy now discusses five more concepts: (1) providence, (2) the chain of faith, the interconnectedness of all things, (3) chance, (4) the pre-science of God, (5) the freedom of human decisions. The order of the universe is protected by providence, it is only our inability to perceive this order that makes it look like it would be unjust. The final poem of book 4 reminds Boethius that man can only achieve the final goal through long suffering and labor (like Agamemnon, Odysseus, and especially Hercules).

Book 5 treats the most difficult question of human freedom and divine prescience. Boethius asks: If God knows all future events, then there is no freedom, and the concepts of good and evil, reward and punishment lose their meaning. Philosophy discerns between prescience and necessity. The human mind is not a Stoic "tabula rasa" (blank slate), but has certain basic ideas which are activated by sensual impressions (Platonic). There is a certain hierarchy of knowing: Human knowledge can never attain to the level of divine knowledge. For humans, time divides all experience in a "before", "now" and "later", but for God all exists in perfect presence (the famous definition of "eternity"). In the eyes of God those things that happen out of necessity and those chosen in free decision are equally present. God also knows about the possibilities of the person doing an action (omniscience). This argument preserves the free will, and therefore good, evil, reward and punishment retain their meaning. The prayers of a just person to God are meaningful, and the just can have hope. The end of the work is an admonition that all should recognize the duty to be good and should not hide behind the shackles of a blind predestination: "Thus resist vices, be virtuous, lift up your mind in a good hope and send humble prayers to heaven. If you do not ignore this, you have the great duty of being good, since you act before the eyes of a Judge who discerns all." (Aversamini igitur vitia, colite virtutes, ad rectas spes animum sublevate, humiles preces in excelsa porrigite. Magna vobis est, si dissimulare non vultis, necessitas indicta probitatis, cum ante oculos agitis iudicis cuncta cernentis.)

# (伪)狄奥尼修斯（约 480—520 AD）

重要的希腊作者（可能生活在叙利亚？），生平不详。他使用 Paulus 的学生 Dionysios（参见《新约》Acts 17:34）的名字写作，因此中世纪的人普遍认为这个 Dionysios Areiopagita 曾是雅典第一位主教（参见 Eusebios, *Hist. eccl.* 3, 4），是使徒/宗徒时期的、具有权威性的神学家。但在 6 世纪已有人提出怀疑，而文艺复兴时期的学者（Valla 和 Erasmus）证明，这些著作来自第 5、6 世纪，不可能来自第 1、2 世纪。因此，该作者经常被称为"伪狄奥尼修斯"。他结合了 Proklos 的新柏拉图主义与基督信仰，这样不再视 Platōn 主义的传统为一种敌对于基督信仰的思想。他深远地影响了中世纪和近代思想。

**著作：**《天阶体系》（或译《天界的秩序》、《论上天的等级》，即诸天使的等级和教会的等级——主教、司铎、隐修者、平信徒——相符合）、《论神圣的名称》（或译《圣名》，即神超越一切名称和概念，指出《圣经》中有一种 theologia negativa"否定性神学"）、《教阶体系》（或译《教会的等级》）、《神秘神学》（都是希腊文写的，但早就被译成别的语言，影响非常深远，比如参见 Dante 的《神曲》。）

## 082.《教阶体系》

该论文编写于 485—520 年间，它深深地影响了中世纪人对于教会的理解。

本著作将教会分为三个领域，每一个领域又分为三个部分，这样就符合"九层的天阶"。第一个领域包括那些传达恩典的奥迹，即洗礼、感恩祭（亦称"圣餐"）以及坚振圣事（亦称"坚信礼"）。第二个领域是这三种恩典的中介人，即执事、司铎和主教。第三个领域是那些接受恩典的人：走向洁净的信徒（所谓 via purgatoriae 净化之途），即是慕道者（准备领洗者）和忏悔者：他们准备加入教会的团体。此后有那些走在"照明之途"（via illuminationis）上的平信徒（即那些没有圣职的基督信徒）。最后有那些处于"合一之途"（via unionis）的人，即隐修士和独修者。在整个圣统制的顶点有基督的宝座，他是可见的神。

本篇神学论文中对于圣事（sacramentum）的象征性解释后来启发了许多中世纪及近代神秘思想家的灵感。第一个圣事是"圣洗"（baptisma），它是"再生"的圣事，而在本文中，它被理解为"神在灵魂中的诞生"。"坚振圣事"（confirmatio）被视为不死的神圣涂油。关于感恩祭（弥撒、圣餐）的解释比较详细，这是神对于他的祭祀的邀请，也是接受基督的邀请。

# Dionysios Areiopagita / Dionysius the Areopagite, Pseudo-Dionysius

**Opera:** *De coelesti hierarchia (=Peri tēs ouranias hierarchias), De divinis nominibus (= Peri tōn theōn onomatōn), De ecclesiastica hierarchia (=Peri tēs ekklēsiastikēs hierarchias), De mystica theologia*

**Works:** *The Celestial Hierarchy, On Sacred Names, The Ecclesiastical Hierarchy, On Mystic Theology*

## 082. *Peri tēs ekklēsiastikēs hierarchias / The Ecclesiastical Hierarchy*

This treatise was written between 485 and 520 AD. It deeply influenced the medieval understanding of the Church.

This work divides the Church into three triads, similar to the divisions of the celestial hierarchy. The first triad comprises the three mysteries that mediate graces: baptism, the eucharist and confirmation. The second triad are the mediators of these graces: deacons, priests and bishops. The third hierarchy are those who share the graces: the believers on the way of purification (via purgatoriae), namely the catechumens and those doing penitence: they prepare themselves to join the community of the Church. Those following next are on the way of illumination (via illuminationis): the lay people (=believers without holy orders). Finally come those on the way of unity (via unionis), namely the monks and hermits. At the apex of the whole hierarchy, Christ, the manifest God, is enthroned.

The symbolic explanations of the sacraments given in this theological treatise have inspired medieval and later mystical thinkers. The first sacrament is baptism—the sacrament of rebirth—, and here it is understood as "birth of God" (in the soul). Confirmation is the sacred ointment of immortality, and the eucharist which is explained in more detail, is seen as God's invitation to His sacrifice, the invitation to receive Christ.

### 083. 《天阶体系》

在这篇神学性的论文中（成书时间在 485 年后），作者使用一些新柏拉图主义的理念来说明某些基督宗教的概念。

在新柏拉图主义中，"太一"（to hen）被视为非常崇高的存在，所以它不能当创造者。因此，"太一"委任一些比较低层的力量（dynameis）来完成创造的工作。然而，在 Dionysios 的著作中，唯独神是创造主。那些"力量"是天使们（共分为九种），而他们的功能主要是照亮人们。天使们能够根据他们在整个制度中的地位照亮一些灵魂。天使们的照亮在教会的圣统制中发挥作用。比如，一个主教可能需要一个 Seraph（"色拉芬"，高层天使）的照亮来施行坚振的圣事。天使们代表神圣者在世俗世界中的临在（parousia）。他们自己是净化的，同时也净化人，他们是被照亮的，同时也照亮人；他们是完美的，又使人走向完美。

"从上而下"的过程（参见新柏拉图主义的 emanatio"流溢说"）与另一个过程是对应的，即灵魂渴望接近神的动力（homoiōsis"与神相似"）。灵魂要走向神是一个灵修的进程。灵魂需要从认识自己开始，然后转向信仰，再走向默观（contemplatio），在合一与爱内感到神秘的精神超拔。灵魂的上升过程有净化、照亮与合一三个阶段，最终灵魂接近神，比较相似于神，甚至以某种方式被神化。灵魂一旦达到了顶点，它就参与纯粹精神的完美运动，即循环式的或螺旋式的运动。

## 083. *Peri tēs ouranias hierarchias / The Celestial Hierarchy*

In this theological treatise (written after 485) the author uses ideas from Neoplatonism to explain Christian concepts.

In Neoplatonism "the one" (to hen) is thought to be too sublime to be the Creator, therefore it delegates creation activities to subordinate levels of powers (dynameis). However, in Dionysius' treatise only God is Creator. The powers appear as three triads of angels, whose function is to illuminate. The angels can illuminate souls, according to their respective rank in the hierarchy. Their illumination is effective in the ecclesiastical hierarchy. For example, a bishop might need the illumination of a Seraph in order to administer the sacrament of confirmation. The angels symbolize the presence (parousia) of the divine in the temporal world. They purify and are purified; they illuminate and are illuminated; they make perfect and are perfected.

The movement from top to bottom (confer the Neoplatonic concept of the "emanatio") is balanced by the desire of the soul to be like God (homoiosis). This way of approaching the divine starts as a spiritual progress from self-knowing to faith, then to contemplation and to the mystic ecstasy (ecstasis) of unity and love. On this ascent through purgation, illumination and unification, the soul becomes similar to God, the soul is even somehow divinized. Once the soul reaches the top, it takes part in the perfect circular or spiral motions of the pure spirits.

# 本笃（本尼狄克）（约 480—547 AD）

意大利 Nursia 人，曾在罗马学习，但不久后离开世俗化的罗马城，在山区"独修"，曾组织一些小的隐修者团体，于 525 年后在罗马以南的地区建立了著名的 Monte Cassino 隐修院。这是一座规模很大的隐修院，成为本笃会的母修院（529 年正式成立），后来成为学术基地和非常重要的图书馆，保存许多手抄本。Benedictus 本人大概没有被祝圣司铎。关于他生活的资料来自 Gregorius Magnus 的 *Dialogi*（《对话集》）。

**著作**：《本笃会规》（对于隐修院生活制度的具体规定，影响了整个中世纪的修道文化。）

## 084. 《会规》

该《会规》是 Benedictus 晚年写下的，它分为 70 章并组织和规定了隐修士生活的方方面面。

在导论以后，第 1 章介绍 4 种类型的隐修者，并批评了那些没有固定居所的修士。第 2 章描述一个良好的隐修院长的特征：他有时候需要严格，但也要使人感到快乐，应该是一个严厉的老师，但也要表示父亲般的仁慈（miscens temporibus tempora, terroribus blandimenta, dirum magistri, pium patris ostendat affectum）。他也应该知道给予正义的惩罚，因为一个愚蠢的人不会仅仅因口头上的谴责而改过迁善（stultus verbis non corrigitur）。弟兄们（隐修者们）需要定期地为商榷问题而聚会（第 3 章）。第 4 章包含基督宗教伦理，比如十诫，对于上主的爱以及对别人的照顾。第 5 章解释服从的美德，第 6 章说明沉默的智慧和对说话的控制。第 7 章论述达到 humilitas（谦卑）的 12 个步骤：(1) timor Domini（敬畏神）；(2) 不爱恋自己的意愿；(3) 服从于上主；(4) 忍耐痛苦；(5) 承认自己的罪；(6) 满足于最低劣的待遇；(7) 认为自己是一条虫；(8) 遵守《会规》；(9) 控制舌头；(10) 控制自己的笑声（non sit facilis in risu）；(11) 语气要温和；(12) 姿势与外貌要谦虚。

第 8 到 20 章解释祈祷的秩序（每日赞礼），夜间要念多少 psalmi（圣咏），夏季的夜间祈祷、星期天的晚祷、晨祷、说"哈利路亚"的时期、白天的祈祷、一天应该念多少圣咏、歌唱《圣咏集》的顺序，以及在祈祷时该有尊敬的态度。

第 21 到 30 章包含一些关于遵守纪律的规则，比如犯规时应该受什么惩罚、不同程度的开除、院长对于那些被开除的人的照顾以及那些曾经被开除的人的再次接纳。此后有一些关于"公共生活方式"的特征的论述，从隐修院中管理酒窖的人开始（第

# Benedictus / Benedict of Nursia

**Opera:** *Regula (Regula Sancti Benedicti)*
**Works:** *Rule*

## 084. *Regula / Rule*

Written towards the end of Benedict's life, this *Rule* in more than 70 chapters organizes the different aspects of the monastic life.

After the prologue, chapter 1 introduces 4 types of monks, criticizing those who have no stable abide. Chapter 2 describes the positive qualities of a good abbot; he should be strict at times, able to threaten but also to please, should be a stern teacher but also show affection like a father (miscens temporibus tempora, terroribus blandimenta, dirum magistri, pium patris ostendat affectum). He also should know how to mete out just punishment, for a fool does not learn by verbal reproach only (stultus verbis non corrigitur). The brothers need to be summoned for counsel at times (chapter 3). Chapter 4 is a summary of Christian ethics, containing the Ten Commandments, love of God and concern for others. Chapter 5 expounds the virtues of obedience, and chapter 6 the wisdom of silence and restrained speech. Chapter 7 describes the 12 steps of humility: (1) timor Domini (fear of the Lord); (2) not to love one's own will; (3) obedience to God; (4) enduring suffering; (5) confession of sins; (6) be content with the lowest treatment; (7) believe that you are a worm; (8) keep the rule; (9) control one's tongue; (10) control one's laughter (non sit facilis in risu); (11) speak gently; (12) have a humble bearing and modest appearance.

Chapters 8 to 20 explain the prayers (Divine Office), the number of psalms of the night prayers, the night prayers in summer, the vigils on Sunday, the lauds (morning prayer), the times for saying "Alleluja", the prayers during the day, the number of psalms that should be prayed, the order and discipline of the psalmody, and the attitude of reverence in prayer.

Chapters 21 to 30 contain some rules for the preservation of discipline, for example punishment for faults, certain degrees of excommunication, the abbot's care for those excommunicated from the monastic community and the readmission of those who left. Then follow some chapters about the character of the "communitarian lifestyle", starting with

31章),进而谈论修院中的设备、工具和财产(32)。修士们共有一切事物(参见《新约》 *Acts* 4:32),并且没有个人财产(33)。各种东西应该按照需要而分配(34)。后来的章节针对厨房中的工作、患病的弟兄、年长的修士和年青人、饮食的恰当分配和数量(39、40),吃饭的时间和夜祷以后的沉默(41、42)。第43到46章针对修士们的一些缺点,比如怎么对待一个在祈祷或吃饭来迟的人,祈祷时的错误或其他方面的犯规。

第48章说明每天劳动的意义和秩序。闲暇对精神生活是有害的。下面几章规定了隐修生活的某些方面:四旬期的守斋(49)、在外面工作或旅行的弟兄(50、51)、隐修院的祈祷所(52)、接待客人(53)、给隐修士们送来的信件或礼物(54)、修士们的衣物和鞋子(55)、院长的餐桌(56)、隐修院中的工匠和艺术家(cum omni humilitate faciant ipsas artes"他们应该很谦卑地完成他们的种种职务",57)、接受新弟兄的过程(58)、贵族人士或穷人送来他们的儿子的情况(59)、允许司铎们进入隐修院(60)、接待一些路过的隐修者(61)。在早期阶段,大部分的隐修者并不是司铎,而第62章谈论团体中的司铎。虽然一些弟兄都是平等的,在团体中也存在着某些阶层和头衔:年老的人被称为"长上"、"前辈"(priores, maiores, seniors),年轻的修士被称为"小的"、"年轻者"(juniores, minores, nonnus)(63章)。第64章规定选择院长(abbas)的程序,而后来的章节涉及到长上(prior,65)、守门者(66)、被派遣到外面的弟兄(67)以及一些不可能完成的任务(68)。

一切规则需要以一种平等地尊敬所有人的精神完成。隐修院中不可以有争吵(69),没有人可以随意殴打一个隐修者(70),弟兄们应该互相服从(71),并且要很热心地完成他们的服务(72)。该*Regula*(《会规》)只是在达到完美的漫长道路上的第一步。

the monastery cellarer (chap. 31), the tools and goods of the monastery (32). The monks should have all things in common (cf. *Acts* 4:32), there are no private possessions (33). The goods are distributed according to need (34). The following chapters deal with the kitchen service, sick brothers, the elderly and children, the proper amount of food and drink (39, 40), meal time and the silence after compline (41,42). Chapters 43 to 46 are concerned with certain shortcomings of the monks, for example how to deal with tardiness at prayers or being late for meals, mistakes in the oratory, and faults in other matters.

Chapter 48 explains the meaning and the schedule of daily manual labor. Idleness is harmful for the spiritual life. The following chapters regulate certain aspects of monastic life: the observance of lent (49), brothers working far away or are travelling (50, 51), the oratory of the monastery (52), reception of guests (53), letters or gifts for the monks (54), their clothing and footwear (55), the abbot's table (56), the artisans of the monastery (cum omni humilitate faciant ipsas artes, "Let them work in their professions in all humility", 57), the procedure for receiving new brothers (58), the offering of sons by nobles or by the poor (59), the admission of priests to the monastery (60), the reception of visiting monks (61). In the early period most of the monks were not ordained, and chapter 62 explains the position of priests in the community. Although the brothers are equal, there are certain ranks and titles in the community (the elders are called "priores, maiores, seniores", the younger ones are "juniores, minores, nonnus", chapter 63). Chapter 64 gives instructions on the election of an abbot (abbas), and the following chapters are concerned with the prior of the monastery (65), the porter (66), brothers sent on a journey (67) and impossible tasks (68).

All of the regulations should be kept in a spirit of equal respect for all. There shouldn't be any fights (69), nobody must strike another monk at will (70), there should be mutual obedience (71), and the monks should show enthusiasm for their service (72). The *Rule* is only a first step on the long road to perfection (73).

第四篇

# 拜占庭的崛起与西欧的新型文人
## The Rise of Byzantium and the Emerging Scholars of Western Europe

(529 — 650 AD)

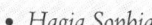
*Hagia Sophia*

# 优士丁尼（482—565 AD）

出生于 Dardania（原先的南斯拉夫地区，是说拉丁语的地区）的农民家庭，但他是 Iustinos（518—527 年）皇帝的侄子，在 Constantinopolis 接受了良好的教育（包括神学教育），521 年任执政官，525 年与演员 Theodora 结婚并于 527 年正式成为东罗马帝国的皇帝。在 532 年的 Nika 起义中，他下令屠杀那些聚集在 Constantinopolis 赛马场的群众。Iustinianus 恢复了对于北 Africa（阿富利加）、意大利和西班牙南部的统治，但因 Langobardi 和阿拉伯人后来的侵略，这些军事性的和政治性的成就也并不长久。皇帝于 537 年建立了 Hagia Sophia（圣智慧）大教堂，而在同时期也开始镇压 monophysitismus（基督一性论）。因为皇帝尽可能地支持正统的基督宗教并镇压异端、异教和犹太人，他的政策也曾引起了很多争论（比如 544 年后的"三章争论"）；他晚年很少过问朝政，一心研究神学。皇帝于 529 年关闭了雅典学院，这样就结束了 900 年的 Plato 主义传统（有的学者曾认为，这意味着"古代的终结"）。Iustinianus 成立了编纂帝国法律的委员会，而这些学者编写的法典在 11 世纪的意大利（Bologna 等地）被重新发现，成了欧洲法学以及世界法学的基础。

**著作**：《民法大全》（或译《优士丁尼民法大全》、《查士丁尼民法大全》），包括下列四个部分：《优士丁尼法典》（528—534 年间命令编写，529 年第一次颁布，534 年第二版）、《学说汇编》（50 卷，533 年颁布，包括古典罗马法学家著作的摘录）、《法学总论》（或译《法学阶梯》，是一种法学导论）、《新律》（565 年颁布，包含 534—565 年间的新法律）

## 085.《民法大全》

这部法律汇编（拉丁语），约成书于 528—534 年间，直到 569 年才有一些补充。

Iustinianus 皇帝曾经委任一批法学专家对罗马法学的传统文献进行汇编，其成果被分为四个部分：*Institutiones*（《法学总论》）、*Digestae*（《学说汇编》）和 *Codex Iustinianus*（《优士丁尼法典》）完成于 528 到 534 年间，而 *Novellae*（《新律》）在 534 年到 565 年间宣布。

《法学总论》[1]（4 卷）是民法方面的教科书，他符合罗马著名法学家 Gaius 约于 161 年写成的 *Institutiones*（《法学总论》）。Gaius 的著作分为 4 卷：第 1 卷介绍"法人"（personae）：人身法，家庭法；第 2、3 卷讨论"事物"（res），即财产法，继承法，债务法；第 4 卷：诉讼法，即法庭的程序规定。

被称为 *Digesta*（《学说汇编》，亦称 *Panedectae*，从 pandechomai＝digerere＝整理）的部分包含一些实用性的文献提要——这些文献是古典罗马法学时期（约公元前 100 年到公元 244 年）的律师所用的文献。《学说汇编》分为 7 个领域，共有 50 卷（大约 15

# Flavius Iustinianus / Justinian

**Opera:** *Corpus Iuris Civilis, Codex Iustinianus, Digesta (Pandectae), Iustiniani Institutiones, Novellae*

**Works:** *Code of the Civil Law, The Code of Justinian, Digest, Institutions, Novels*

## 085. *Corpus Iuris Civilis / Code of the Civil Law*

This collection of legal texts (in Latin) was compiled between 528 and 534 and continued to be expanded until 569.

The collection of the texts of the Roman legal tradition in 4 parts was elaborated by a group of legal experts commissioned by Emperor Justinian. The *Institutiones* [1], *Digestae* [2] and *Codex Iustinianus* [3] were completed in the years from 528—534, the *Novellae* [4] were issued in the years from 534 to 565.

The *Institutiones* [1] are a textbook of civil law in 4 books, based on the *Institutiones* of the Roman jurist Gaius. (Gaius' *Institutiones* date from ca. 161 AD. They are a basic introduction to jurisprudence in 4 books; book 1: "personae", law of persons, family law; books 2, 3: "res", property law, law of inheritance, debt law, etc.; book 4: law of procedure, proceeding of lawsuits.

The *Digesta* (or: *Pandectae*, pandechomai=digerere=to bring in order) are excerpts of practical texts used by lawyers in the classical Roman legal tradition (ca. 100 BC to 244 AD). The *Digesta* are divided into 7 areas; they comprise 50 books (150, 000 lines), but they are a condensed abridgement of circa 2000 books with 3 million lines. Each excerpt is signed with an inscription bearing the name of the jurist who made the excerpt, the title of the original book and the book's number.

万行),但实际上是2000本书(共300万行)的提要。每一个提要都有编写该提要的法学家的名字,也有原著的书名和书号。

《优士丁尼法典》是皇帝敕令(所谓的constitutiones)的汇编。它的基础是早期的法典,尤其是 *Codex Theodosianus*(《狄奥多修斯法典》,来自Theodosius II 皇帝,408—450年),该法典于438年颁布为东方的法律,439年由Valentinianus III 皇帝在罗马帝国西部宣布为法律。*Codex Iustinianus*(《优士丁尼法典》)则颁布于529年(当时的版本没有保存),而一个补充性的版本于534年代替了它(所谓的 *Codex repetitae praelectionis*《修订法典》)。内容分为12卷:第1卷:教会法,法律的来源、官职法;第2到第8卷:民法;第9卷:刑法,刑法中的程序规则;10~12卷:管理法、税法等等。

被称为 *Novellae*(《新律》)或 *Novellae constitutiones* 的文献是534年以后作的修改和增补,主要是以希腊语编写的。

由于经济的衰退,古代的法学(iuris prudentia)在250年后陷入了一个低谷,这就导致这样的转变:管理法和刑法逐渐比财产法和民法更受重视。民法的种种问题可能会促进更多法学研究,但从250年到500年间的法学著作相对较少。Iustinianus 的复兴运动的目标是让他的帝国与古典罗马的法律传统有联系。只有中世纪的人才为这些法学著作用了 *Corpus iuris civilis*(《民法大全》)的称呼;在11世纪的Bologna(意大利),Iustinianus 的伟大文集再次被发现,而它成为罗马法的长期复兴的基础——这个复兴很有创造力,因为它影响了欧洲所有国家的法律编写工作(进而也成了很多非欧洲国度的法学基础)。

The *Codex Iustinianus* is a collection of imperial edicts (the so-called constitutiones). It is based on earlier collections, especially on the *Codex Theodosianus* (of Emperor Theodosius II 408—450), promulgated for the East in 438 and enacted by Emperor Valentinianus III for the Western part of the Empire in 439. The *Codex Iustinianus* was promulgated as law in 529 (that version is not extant), but an enlarged version, the *Codex repetitae prælectionis*, replaced it in 534. It consists of 12 books: Book 1: ecclesiastical law, sources of law, law of magistrates; books 2~8: civil law; book 9: criminal law, law of procedure in criminal law; books 10~12: administration law, tax law etc.

The *Novellae* ( = *Novellae constitutiones* ) are "additions" made after 534 and mainly written in Greek.

Legal science (jurisprudence) had sunk down to a low standard after 250, due to a recession of the economy, which led to a shift from property law and civil law to administration and criminal law. Civil law could and would have inspired more academic work, but from the period of 250 to 500 rather few legal works have come down. Justinians restoration program intended to connect his empire with the legal tradition of classical Rome and the period of late antiquity. The title "Corpus iuris civilis" was only used since the Middle Ages, when the great work of Justinian was rediscovered in Italy (Bologna) in the 11th century and became the basis of the creative and lasting Renaissance of the Roman Law, which led to all European codifications of Law (and by extension it became the basis of jurisprudence in many non-European countries all over the world).

# 菲洛普诺斯（约 490—570 AD）

生活在 Alexandria，是一位基督徒学者，生平不详。他的著作非常多，涉及到哲学、神学、语文学、天文学、数学、医学诸领域。因为他是"基督一性论者"，又提出了"三神论"的说法，他于 570 年和 680 年曾两次被教会谴责。

**著作**：《驳亚里士多德》（残篇）、《驳普洛克鲁斯论宇宙的永恒》（529 年成书，证明物质的有限性和非永恒性；该著作已有中世纪经院思想的特征）、《世界的创造》、《论复活》、《论圣三》（约于 567 年成书，第一次提出"三神论"的说法）、《狄艾特特斯》

## 086. 《世界的创造》

本书的全名是 *Tōn eis tēn Mōyseōs kosmogonian exēgētikōn logoi*（《针对摩西宇宙形成论的注解》），但它经常被引用为 *Peri kosmopoiias*（《论宇宙的形成》，希腊语）、*De opificio mundi*（《论世界的形成》）或 *De creatione mundi*（《论世界的创造》，拉丁语）。成书时间大约在 550 年。

根据前言的记载，很多基督徒对 Philoponos 有一些不满，因为他编写了很多关于宇宙、创造和物质的局限性的著作，但在这一切书中他很少提到《圣经》。现在他想弥补这个缺陷并提供关于《创造记》第 1 章——《圣经》创造论的典型论述——的注解。他逐字解释《圣经》的创世说，同时引用了无数的来自《圣经》其他书卷的引言。他的典范是 Basileios 的 *Hexaemeron*，而和 Basileios 一样他也利用《圣经》的记载来展示出他在物理学、生物学、天文学、地理学和数学方面的渊博知识，这样他的论述也反映出这些学科在第 6 世纪的希腊世界中的研究水平。

Philoponos 的目标是说明《圣经》符合自然界的实际情况，同时他也想调和一些科学理论与《圣经》的记载，比如他认为 Ptolemaios 的世界观比"世界平面观"更符合《圣经》的论述——在当时的 Antiochia（安提阿）学派中有一些神学家坚持这种"世界平面观"。部分的人认为世界不是球形的而是一个正方形的房子，其中包括 Kosmas Indikopleustēs（生活约于 550 年），他在其 *Christianikē Topographia*（《基督徒风土志》）中也提到了中国（Tzinitza）和丝绸商人。在物理学史上，值得注意的是这一点：Philoponos 第一次提出了关于惯力的理论，他认为这个理论适用于所有的受造物，包括天体。这样，他的基督信仰要求他放弃 Aristoteles（亚里士多德）主义，这样准备了现代科学的路。Galileo Galilei（伽利略）看过他的著作的拉丁语译本。

# Iōannēs Philoponos / John Philoponus

**Opera:** *Contra Aristotelem, De aeternitate mundi contra Proclum, De creatione mundi, De resurrectione, De Trinitate, Diaitetes*

**Works:** *Against Aristotle, The Eternity of the World against Proclus, The Creation of the World, The Resurrection, The Trinity, Diatetes*

## 086. *De creatione mundi / The Creation of the World*

The full title of this book is *Tōn eis tēn Mōyseōs kosmogonian exēgētikōn logoi* (*Commentary to the Cosmogony of Moses*), but it is often quoted in Greek as *Peri kosmopoiias* and in Latin as *De opificio mundi* or *De creatione mundi*. The book was possibly written around 550.

According to the preface many Christians were dissatisfied with Philoponos who wrote books about the cosmos, about creation and about the limitations of matter, since in all these works he did not pay much attention to Holy Scripture. Now he wants to make up for this shortcoming and presents a commentary to *Genesis* 1, the classical text of the Biblical creation. He explains the cosmogony word for word, using innumerable quotations from other parts of the Bible. His model is Basilius' *Hexaemeron*, and like Basilius, he also uses the Biblical account of the Creation to display his immense knowledge in the areas of physics, biology, astronomy, geography and mathematics, thus reflecting the level of these sciences in the Greek world of the 6th century.

Philoponos' aim is to demonstrate the harmony between the Bible and the processes of nature in reality, and at the same time he tries to reconcile scientific theories with the Biblical account. For example, he thinks the Ptolemaic world view is more Biblical than the flat-earth-theory held by some of his contemporaries in the theological school of Antioch. One of those who perceived the earth not as globe but as a square building was Cosmas Indicopleustes (fl. around 550 AD), who in his *Christian Topography* also mentions China (Tzinitza) and silk trade. For the history of physics, it may be interesting to know that Philoponos was the first to formulate the theory of impetus, which he applied to all physical bodies in creation, including celestial bodies. It is remarkable that his Christian faith thus led him to a rejection of Aristotelianism and prepared the way to modern science. The Latin translations of his works were known to Galileo Galilei.

# 卡西奥多鲁斯（490—583 AD）

生于意大利的 Bruttium 地区，506—511 年任 quaestor 官，514 年在罗马任 Theodoricus 王的执政官，533—538 年间任 praefectus praetorio（皇宫卫队长）。他曾前往 Constantinopolis 一段时间，回意大利后（于 540 年或 550 年？）在南部的 Vivarium（Calabria, Bruttium 地区）建立了一所隐修院，其中包括庞大的图书馆，他致力于抄录和搜集古代经典的工作。他自己可能没有成为隐修士，但他成为修士们的精神领袖并教导他们抄写书籍，这样使隐修院成为古代文献的保存者和古代文化的培养者，因为 Benedictus（本笃）修会不久后也开始重视抄书的工作。

**著作**：《远古史》《世界史》，从 Adam 到公元 519 年）、《诸自由学科》（指"七艺"：grammatica, rhetorica, dialectica ［logica］; geometria, arithmetica, musica, astronomia，即整个中世纪的教育结构）、《哥特人的来源和历史》（中世纪第一部民族历史著作）、《拼写法》（包含一些古代著作）、《宗教文学与世俗文学的教学》（一部神学百科全书，包括圣经学、教父文献等，也介绍七个自由学科；Cassiodorus 强调，圣职人员也应该学习世俗的知识——"七艺"，影响了后人）、《杂录》（12 卷，包含 486 封信）

## 087. 《宗教文学与世俗文学的教学》

该两卷本著作的书名因不同的手抄本而异（*Institutio / Institutiones divinarum et humanarum litterarum / lectionum*《宗教文学与世俗文学的教学》）。写于 550 年，并成为中世纪教育的基本教科书之一。

在导论中 Cassiodorus 说在世俗文学方面有足够多的老师（mundani auctores, mundi prudentia, saeculares litterae），但在《圣经》知识方面缺少老师，虽然东方的学校曾经有很多这样的专家，比如 Alexandria、Edessa 和 Nisibis 的学院。由于 Justinus 皇帝的种种战役，Cassiodorus 无法实现他的计划——他本来想和 Agapitus（"罗马城的教宗"）一起在罗马建立一所基督宗教大学。因此，Cassiodorus 决定至少要编写一部对他的隐修者有用的"导论"（introductorios libros，这个词来自希腊语的 eisagōgē）。他希望这部著作一方面帮助修士们获得救恩，另一方面也提高他们的世俗教育水平。他的目标是提供一些古老的文献（priscorum dicta）以及对于《圣经》的正统解释（expositiones probabiles patrum）。

第 1 卷（33 章）是基督宗教文学的导论，从《旧约》和《新约》入手（第 1 到 9 章）。作者列出不同的《圣经》版本、译本、注解以及谈论有关解释《圣经》某些章节的问题。可以用 6 种方式来了解《圣经》（第 10 章）：1）阅读那些介绍《圣经》的作者（introductores scripturae 比如 Augustinus 的 *Doctrina Christiana*）；2）参考关于某些《圣经》书

# Flavius Magnus Aurelius Cassiodorus / Cassiodorus

...on (*Historia tripartita*), *De artibus ac disciplinis liberalium litterarum*, *De ...ctibusque Getarum,* (=*Getica*), *De orthographia*, *Institutiones* (*divinarum ...arum litterarum*), *Variae epistulae*

... *On the liberal arts*, *The Origin and History of the Getes*, *On Writing*, ..., *Various Letters*

### ...es / Institutions

... work in two books varies in different manuscripts (*Institutio/Institu-... humanarum litterarum/ lectionum*, *Introduction to Religious and Sec-... written in the 550s and became one of the basic textbooks of me-...

... Cassiodorus mentions that there are enough teachers for secular ...ctores, mundi prudentia, saeculares litterae), but there is a lack ...iences of the Bible, although the schools of Alexandria, Edessa ... such experts. Due to Emperor Justinian's military campaigns, ... realize his plans to set up a Christian university in Rome, to-... "Pope of the City of Rome". Therefore Cassiodorus decided to ...tion useful for his monks (introductorios libros, a term coming ...gē"). He hopes that this book aids both the salvation of their ...rudition. His aim is to present some ancient texts (priscorum ...xplanations of the Bible (expositiones probabiles patrum).

... chapters) is an introduction to the study of Christian litera-... s of the Old and New Testament (chapters 1~9) The author ...itions, translations, and commentaries and discusses certain ...terpretation of Biblical passages. There are six ways to un-...apter 10): 1). reading authors who introduce the Bible (in-...ctores scripturae, for example Augustine's *Doctrina Christiana*), 2) consulting the explanation of certain Biblical books (librorum expositores), 3) studying the orthodox authorities (catholici magistri), 4) reading the works of the Church Fathers (patres ecclesiae), 5) noting with great diligence passages of special importance in order to examine various orthodox writers, and 6) having conversations with experienced elderly Christians. Cassiodor thus divides orthodox authors (catholici) into "introductores, ex-

卷的解释(librorum expositores);3)研究正统学者的著作(catholici magistri);4)阅读教父们的书(patres ecclesiae);5)认真地注意到某些核心章节并根据它们研究不同正统作者的看法;6)与一些年老的、有经验的基督徒谈话。由此可见,Cassiodorus 将"正统的作者"(catholici)区分为四类:"introductores 教导者、expositores 解释者、magistri 老师、patres 教父",但他没有提供一个名单。在第 11 章中,Cassiodorus 论及"四个普遍被接受的主教会议",即在 Nicaea、Constantinopolis、Ephesus 以及 Chalcedon 召开的大公会议,作者也提到会议文献的拉丁译本。

就《圣经》书卷的分段问题,Hieronymus 曾将《旧约》分为 22 卷,《新约》分为 27 卷,如果在这个数字上加"一"(即圣三),就等于 50,而这又是"禧年"的数字(参见《旧约》*Lev* 25:10)。根据 Augustinus 的分法,《圣经》共有 71 卷,而这个数字(如果加"一")也同样达到一种"非常完善的状态"。Cassiodorus 提到这样的细节:《圣经》译本中的拉丁语并不都符合古典拉丁语的标准,但不应该纠正这些偏差。希伯来语的人名必须被保留;如果想纠正拉丁语的《圣经》译本必须参考希伯来语的文本:"那些残酷的士兵并没有撕裂我们救主的长衣,因此也不能让一个没有能力的修改者随意处置它"(参见 *Jn* 19:23)。然而,在文献中应该加入一些标点符号,因为这些符号是"思想的指南"。Cassiodorus 也说明基督宗教文献中的缩写符号,比如 AAA 指 *Actus Apostolorum*(《新约·使徒行传》)。

Cassiodorus 介绍一些教会史方面的作者以及"教父们"(patres ecclesiae)。历史学家包括 Iosephus Flavius、Eusebius 以及那些曾经扩充了 Eusebius 著作的人,还有 Orosius、Marcellinus 和 Prosper。Cassiodorus 也描写一些教父的生活、贡献、思想和文笔,比如 Hilarius、Cyprianus、Ambrosius、Hieronymus 和 Augustinus。他特别注重 Hieronymus,因为他结合了世俗的与宗教性的知识。最后,作者就隐修团体中的工作分类问题作了一些建议。

第 2 卷(共 7 章)是顺着"七个自由学科"的正统顺序写的。在 9 世纪后,前 3 个学科被称为 trivium,后 4 个被称为 quadrivium。前言说明数字"七"的象征意义并加上说上主"按照一定的尺度、数字与衡量制定了一切"(《智慧篇》11:21)。在中世纪的文献中,这句话是引用频率最高的《圣经》格言。从语源学上看,"书"(book)来源于"自由"(free),象征着从树上脱落下来的树皮可用作书写材料。

Cassiodorus 在"语法"的章节中推荐 Donatus 的语法书 *Artes*。关于修辞学的介绍基本上符合 Cicero 的著作 *De inventione*,比如讲演的五个部分是决定主题、结构、语言表达、背熟、讲演。Cassiodorus 比较 Cicero 和 Quintilianus 这两位伟大的修辞学家,并提到一个比较晚期的作者,即 Fortunatianus。

关于逻辑学的那一章包含一种"哲学导论",并区分哲学的领域为思辨性哲学(包括

positores, magistri, patres", but he does not provide a name list. In chapter 11 Cassiodorus records the "four accepted synods", i. e. the ecumenical councils of Nicaea, Constantinople, Ephesus, and Chalcedon, and he mentions the Latin translation of the synod documents.

As to the different ways of dividing the books of the Holy Scriptures, Jerome arranged the Old Testament in 22 books and the New Testament in 27 books, which—added the Holy Trinity—makes 50, the number of the the jubilee year(*Lev* 25:10). Augustine counts 71 Biblical books, and this number too—again, with the addition of the Holy Trinity—arrives at a "most glorious perfection". Cassiodor mentions that Biblical Latin does not always meet the standards of classical Latin, but these deviations must not be corrected. Hebrew names must be kept, and the Hebrew Scripture must be consulted if some Latin translations are to be emended: "The tunic of the Lord our Saviour, which the cruel soldiers were not allowed to cut, be not put in the power of unskilled emenders"(cf. *Jn* 19:23). However, punctuation marks should be added in every section of the text, since these marks are "paths for thought". Cassiodorus also explains the use of abbreviations in Christian literature, for example the sign AAA designates the *Actus Apostolorum*(*Acts of the Apostles*).

Cassiodorus introduces the authors who wrote works about Church history and the Fathers of the Church(patres ecclesiae). The historians include Josephus Flavius, Eusebios and those who elaborated Eusebios' work, Orosius, Marcellinus, and Prosper. Cassiodorus describes the biographies, contributions, thought and style of Hilarius, Cyprian, Ambrose, Jerome and Augustine, in particular focusing on Jerome who combined secular and religious knowledge. Finally, the author makes some suggestions concerning the division of tasks within a monastic community.

The second book (seven chapters) follows the canonical order of the seven liberal arts. After the 9th century the first three arts were called "trivium", the others "quadrivium". The preface explains the symbolic meaning of the number seven and adds that God has "ordered all things in measure, and number, and weight"(*Wisdom* 11:21). In the Middle Ages this quotation from the Old Testament was one of the most frequently cited words of the Bible. As to the etymology of "book", it comes from the word "free", denoting the removed and freed bark of a tree used as writing material.

In the chapter on grammar Cassiodorus recommends Donatus' *Artes*. The discussion of rhetoric is based on Cicero's *De inventione*, the five parts of rhetoric are invention, arrangement, proper expression, memorization, and delivery of the speech. Cassiodorus compares Cicero, Quintilianus, and a more recent author, Fortunatianus.

The chapter *De dialectica* contains an introduction to philosophy, dividing this science into speculative philosophy (natural, theoretical, and divine), and practical philosophy(moral, economic, political philosophy). Theoretical philosophy is again divided into the four arts of the "quadrivium". Cassiodorus presents six definitions of philosophy: 1)

自然哲学、理论哲学和宗教哲学),以及实践哲学(道德、经济和政治哲学)。"理论哲学"被分为四个自由学科(算术学、几何学、音乐、天文学)。Cassiodorus 提供了哲学的六种定义:哲学是 1)了解存有和种种存在的方式;2)理解属神的和属人的事务;3)一种准备死去的方式;4)人逐渐接近神的方式;5)"众艺之艺,众学之学"(ars artium et disciplina disciplinarum);6)爱好智慧。Cassiodorus 谈论十个范畴、三段论、15 种类型的定义、比喻和隐喻,以及论点——这些论点对演讲家、诗人和律师都是有用的。Cassiodorus 区分"技艺"(artes)和"科学"(disciplinae)并且介绍数学、算术学、音乐和天文学。

Cassiodorus 认为这些知识的"种子"可以在上主的永恒智慧以及《圣经》中找到(参见 Clemens 的思想)。世俗学问的专家原来从《圣经》那里获得了他们的知识,他们重新整理了这些内容。在他的 *Commentarius in Psalmis*(亦称 *Expositio psalmorum*)一书中,Cassiodorus 说明在 *Psalmi*(《圣咏》)中有 120 种比喻和隐喻方式,而古代的修辞学传统也使用了其中很多类型的比喻,将它们系统化。根据 Cassiodorus 的想法,世界上所有民族原来都普遍具有关于《旧约》的知识,这也是《圣咏》*Ps* 19:5 的深层意义:"他们的声音传到地极。""《圣经》非常渊博精深,同时用如此普遍的语言来表达以至于一切人毫不犹豫接受它。然而,《圣经》的意义隐藏在真理的奥秘内,所以需要以最认真的努力去研究其中的核心意义。"

the understanding of being and the ways of existence; 2) insight into divine and human matters; 3) a kind of preparation for death; 4) the imitation of God; 5) the "art of arts and science of sciences" (ars artium et disciplina disciplinarum); 6) love of wisdom. Cassiodor discusses the categories, syllogism, 15 different definitions, the figures of speech and arguments which are useful for orators, poets, and lawyers. Cassiodorus explains the distinction between arts (artes) and sciences (disciplinae) and then introduces mathematics, arithmetic, music, and astronomy.

Cassiodorus thinks that the seeds of the arts are to be found in the eternal wisdom of God and in the Bible (confer the thought of Clement). The teachers of secular knowledge have received their sciences from the Bible and just rearranged them. In his *Commentarius in Psalmis* (also known as *Expositio psalmorum*), Cassiodorus shows that 120 figures of speech are to be found in the Psalms, and many of them were also used in the classical schools of rhetoric, where they were brought into a system. According to Cassiodorus, the Old Testament was somehow universally known to all peoples, which is the hidden meaning of *Ps* 19:5: "their voice reaches to the ends of the earth." "The awesome depth of the Holy Scriptures has such a common language that all people accept it without hesitation. But the meaning of the Scriptures is hidden in the mystery of truth, so that one should investigate the vital meaning of it with greatest diligence." (Scripturae autem divinae sancta profunditas adeo communes sermones habet, ut eam universi incunctanter admittant. Sensus autem recondit veritatis arcano, ut in ipsa studiosissime vitalis sententia debeat indagari.)

# 罗曼努斯·梅洛多斯（约 500—560 AD）

可能来自 Syria（叙利亚）的 Emesa，在 Constantinopolis 去世，关于他的生活年代有一些争议。他可能曾在 Berytos 当执事，后到首都担任圣职人员。他是 Kontakion（"圣歌"）的最重要代表，也被称为东方基督教最伟大的诗人。

**著作:**《圣歌》

## 088.《圣歌》

所谓的 kontakion（"圣歌"）是一首基督宗教的赞美诗，分为 18 段或 24 段；这种诗等于是一种神学性的反思或诗歌式的讲道稿，其题目是《圣经》中的人物、殉道者、圣徒、一些比喻、基督徒的习俗、节日或宗教象征。根据传统的说法，Romanos Melodos 写了 1000 多首圣诗，保存的只有 90 首，而有 60 首被认为是来自他自己。34 首是对基督的赞美。其中最著名的圣歌是 *Akathistos hymnos*（"不可坐着唱的圣诗"），内容是对上主之母 Maria 以及基督诞生的赞美，共有 24 段，每一段是以一个希腊字母开始的，从 A 到 Ō。根据传统的说法，这首赞美诗的作者不是 Romanos，而是 Sergios 大主教，他在 Avari（阿瓦尔人）围攻 Byzantion 时（626 年）写下了这首诗。另一些学者曾认为这首诗来自 451 年以后的年代（参见 Chalkedon 的主教会议），但近来的学者更多地将它归于 Romanos。

# Romanos Melodos

**Opera:** *Kontakia*
**Works:** *Kontakia*

## 088. *Kontakia*

A Kontakion is a Christian hymn consisting of 18 to 24 stanzas, it can be understood as a theological reflection or homily (sermon) in verses about Biblical personalities, martyrs, saints, but also about parables, Christian customs, feasts or religious symbols. According to legend, Romanos Melodos wrote more than 1000 hymns, of which 90 are extant and 60 are considered to be authentic. 34 hymns of these praise Christ. The most famous hymn is the *Akathistos hymnos* (a-kathistos = "not to be sung while sitting"), which in 24 stanzas praises the birth of Christ and Mary, the mother of God. Each stanza begins with one letter of the Greek alphabet, from Alpha to Omega. Traditionally the hymn was not attributed to Romanos but to Patriarch Sergios who wrote it at the time of the Avars' siege of Byzanz (in 626). Some scholars have dated this hymn to a time shortly after 451 AD (synod of Chalcedon), but more recent opinion ascribes it to Romanos.

# 马丁（约 515—579 AD）

出生于 Pannonia（今天奥地利东部和匈牙利地区）并获得良好的教育（能阅读希腊语），550 年后在西班牙西北部的 Suebi 传教，并使他们从 Arius 派转向天主教。他在 Bracara / Braga 附近的 Dumium 建立一所隐修院，约于 556 年成为 Dumium 的主教。在他的著作中，他发挥了 Seneca 和 Johannes Cassianus 的思想。

**著作：**《马丁规章》（来自不同主教会议的 84 条规章，目标是强化教会内部的纪律）、《论纠正农民》、《论愤怒》、《论复活节》（关于复活节的日期）、《论贫困》、《论骄傲》、《关于三次浸水的信》（谈论圣洗的礼仪）、《劝人保持谦虚》、《荣誉生活的规则》（在中世纪被认为是 Seneca 的著作，但 Petrarca 确认他是 Martinus 写的书）、《埃及教父的名言》（一些埃及隐修者的警句）、《反对自夸》

## 089. 《论纠正农民》

本文是一篇讲道稿，有时被视为 Martinus 最独特的著作，因为它描述在 6 世纪的西班牙的流行迷信和异教徒的习俗。后来的作者曾使用本册子的内容来撰写一些反驳偶像崇拜的讲演。古代世界的迷信习俗有很多表现，包括相信魔术和算命，担忧不吉利的征兆、不吉祥的时日、动物、东西或行为，用咒语召唤精灵或崇拜各种男女神明的雕像。基督信仰试图使用礼仪和教会节庆来代替这些不健康的迷信习俗，而 Martinus 主教也编写一些与礼仪问题相关的著作。他的 *De pascha*（《论复活节》）说明复活节的日期，因为这个日期每年都不一样，而他的 *Epistula de trina mersione*（《关于三次浸水的信》）解释基督宗教的一个仪式，即在圣洗礼仪中要三次向受洗的人洒水或使他三次浸入水中。当时西班牙的某位 Bonifatius 主教曾向 Martinus 提出质问，因为他认为这种三次浸水的习俗来自 Arius 主义，而 Martinus 的信解释了这个问题。Arius 派的人是早期教会中的非正统派系。他们的名字来自埃及的长老 Arius，而他们没有接受 325 年的 Nicaea 会议所规定的关于基督神性的信仰。早期的主教会议或大公主教会议的决定经常成为有约束力的教会规定，即所谓的 canones（教规）。Martinus 也编写了一部教规集（*Capitula Martini*《马丁规章》，亦名 *Collectio orientalium canonum*）。该文集包含 84 条教规，大部分来自希腊，也有一些来自在西班牙和阿富利加地区举行的主教会议。一些教规管理司铎的祝圣和圣职人员的任务，其他的为平信徒的生活提供了一些指导规定。Martinus 的规章集成为一种基础性的文献，而这类文献为中世纪的教会法（jus canonicum）的发展创造了条件。

# Martinus de Bracara / Martin of Braga

**Opera:** *Capitula Martini, De correctione rusticorum, De ira, De pascha, De paupertate, De superbia, Epistula de trina mersione, Exhortatio humilitatis, Formulae vitae honestae, Patrum Aegyptorum Sententiae, Pro repellenda iactantia*

**Works:** *Chapters of Martin, On the Correction of Peasants, On Wrath, On Easter, On Poverty, On Pride, Letter on the Threefold Immersion at Baptism, Exhortation to Humility, Rules for an Honorable Life, Sentences from the Egyptian Fathers, Against Bragging*

## 089. *De correctione rusticorum / On the Correction of Peasants*

This treatise in the form of a homily is sometimes thought to be the most interesting of Martin's works, since it describes the different kinds of superstitions and pagan customs that were popular in 6th century Spain. Later authors used the booklet for their sermons against idolatry. The superstitious practices of the ancient world were manifold, among them were the belief in witchcraft, divination and the fear of bad omens, unlucky days, inauspicious animals, things, and actions, the incantation of spirits and the worship of statues of gods and goddesses. Christianity tried to use liturgical ceremonies and celebrations of Christian feasts to replace these unwholesome practices, and Bishop Martin dedicated some of his other writings to the clarification of liturgical issues. His *De pascha* (*On Easter*) explains the date of the celebration of Easter, which changes every year, and the *Epistula de trina mersione* (*Letter on the Threefold Immersion at Baptism*) shows that the Christian custom of sprinkling water on the baptized person three times has a deeper spiritual meaning. The occasion of this letter was the request of Boniface, a bishop from Spain, who thought that the custom of triple aspersion in baptism came from Arianism. The Arianists were a non-orthodox Christian group in the early Church. They had their name from the Egyptian presbyter Arius and did not accept the divinity of Christ as it was defined on the Council of Nicaea in 325 AD. Many of the resolutions of the synods and ecumenical councils of the early Church became obligatory ecclesiastical rules, so-called canons. Bishop Martin compiled a collection of canons(*Capitula Martini, Chapters of Martin*, also known under the title *Collectio orientalium canonum*). This collection contains 84 canons, most of them from Greece, some of them from synods held in Spain and Africa. Some of the canons govern the ordination of priests and the duties of the clergy, other canons provide guidelines for the life of the lay Christians. Martin's collection of canons became one of the basic texts from which the ecclesiastical law ("canon law") of the Middle Ages could develop.

# 维南蒂乌斯（约 535—600 AD）

出生于意大利北部的 Treviso，曾在 Ravenna 受教育，后到高卢地区的 Tours 和 Poitiers 工作，在这里和 Radegunde 女王有来往，也照顾女王建立的修女院的修女们。他成了司铎，大约在 595 年成了 Poitiers 的主教。他是一位很有才华并有灵感的拉丁语诗人，曾被称为"古代最后的以及第一位中世纪的拉丁语诗人"。

**著作：**《诗集》、《圣马丁的美德》、《圣格尔曼努斯传》、《圣希拉留斯传》、《圣拉德公德传》

## 090. 《诗集》

这部《诗集》共分为 11 卷，其内容是一些在不同场合写的诗、哀歌、赞美诗、婚姻诗以及墓志铭。

《诗集》中最著名的诗歌之一是 *Pange lingua gloriosi lauream certaminis*（《我的舌头，你要唱这次战争的光荣胜利》，2,2）以及 *Vexilla Regis prodeunt, fulget crucis mysterium*（《君王的旗子走在前面，十字架的奥迹闪耀发光》，2,6），这两首诗都赞美基督的十字架。在公元 569 年，Radegunde 女王要求作者写一首朝拜圣十字架的诗，因为 Justinos II 皇帝当时赠送给她十字架的一个小块，而这个圣物将要在 Poitiers 的"圣十字架隐修院"中受尊敬。女王举行一次隆重的迎接礼仪，所以她需要一首赞美诗，但 Venantius 的诗后来成为非常著名的圣诗，并在 9 世纪后普遍使用于十字架的朝拜（尤其在圣周的星期五）。另一首是 Vexilla Regis prodeunt，该赞美诗在圣周的游行活动被使用一直到今日。

另一个例子是长达 400 行的 *De virginitate*（《论贞洁》，8,3）。这首诗献给 Radegunde 领养的女儿 Agnes。当时 Agnes 被祝圣为 Poitiers 的圣十字架隐修院。Venantius 在诗中使用教父们在他们对《旧约·雅歌》的注解中提出对贞洁生活的劝勉，他也引用一些来自非基督教传统的婚姻诗歌（epithalamium）的元素。诗人描述新娘与其神圣配偶（基督）的神秘婚姻。新娘甚至向她的配偶写一封情书，而在一次天界圣人的大聚会中，基督向圣徒们宣读这封信。这就意味着 Venantius 以基督徒的精神和方式要恢复 Ovidius 的著作 *Heroides*（《女英雄》）所开创的传统。

# Venantius Fortunatus

**Opera:** *Carmina, De virtutibus S. Martini, Vita S. Germani, Vita S. Hilarii, Vita S. Radegundis*

**Works:** *Poems, The Virtues of St. Martin, Life of St. Germanus, Life of St. Hilarius, Life of St. Radegunde*

## 090. *Carmina / Poems*

This collection in 11 books holds poems written on various occasions, elegies, hymns, wedding songs, and epitaphs.

Among the most famous hymns are *Pange lingua gloriosi lauream certaminis* (*Sing, my tongue, the glorious battle*) (2,2) and *Vexilla Regis prodeunt, fulget crucis mysterium* (*The royal banners forward go, the mystery of the cross shines bright*) (2,6), both praising the Cross of Christ. In 569 AD Queen Radegunde asked the author to write a hymn for the adoration of Christ's Cross, since Emperor Justinos II had donated a particle of the Holy Cross to be sent to the "Holy Cross Monastery" in Poitiers. A hymn for the solemn welcoming ceremony of the particle was needed, and Venantius' hymn *Pange lingua gloriosi* became so famous that it has been widely used for the veneration of the Cross (especially at Good Friday) since the 9th century. The hymn *Vexilla Regis prodeunt* has been used at processions during the Holy Week even until today.

Another example is the poem *De virginitate* (*On virginity*, 8,3) extending over 400 lines. It was written for Agnes, the adopted daughter of Queen Radegunde, who was ordained abbess of the Holy Cross Monastery at Poitiers. Venantius uses the traditional exhortations to virginity of the Fathers of the Church in their interpretations of the *Canticum Canticorum* (*Song of Songs*), but the author also employs some elements of the pagan wedding songs (epithalamium). The poem describes the mystical marriage of the bride and her heavenly spouse, Christ. The bride even writes a letter to her spouse, and during an assembly of the saints in heaven, Christ reads out this letter to the inhabitants of the celestial spheres. In this way Venantius wanted to revive the tradition of Ovid's *Heroides* by imbuing it with a Christian spirit.

# 格列高利（538—594 AD）

生于法国 Clermont-Ferrant 地区的一个贵族家庭，563 年被祝圣执事，开始在 Lyon 的大教堂任职，于 573 年成为 Tours 的主教。由于当时的政治管理软弱，他的工作也包括一些公共职务，比如照顾病人、穷人、奴隶、孤儿以及进行司法工作。他当过法兰克王 Chilperich II 的顾问，曾重建 Lyon 的大教堂。

**著作**：《法兰克人史》、《奇迹之书》（包括 23 个圣人的传记以及圣 Martinus 所行的奇迹）

## 091.《法兰克人史》

本著作分为 10 卷，其书名原来是 *Decem libri historiarum*（《历史十卷》），但经常被引用为 *Historia / Historiae Francorum*（《法兰克人史》）。第一个部分（1 到 4 卷）成书于 575 年，第二个部分（5、6 卷）是在 585 年以前完成的，而第三个部分（7 到 10 卷）是在 585 到 591 年间编写的。本著作是第一部以基督徒的眼光写的民族史，同时也是关于第 6 世纪的种种历史事件的重要资料书。本著作的文笔简单，有时候其使用的拉丁语不符合语法规则，比如作者偶尔混淆介词后面应该使用的格。他抱怨文学修养（liberalium cultura litterarum）在高卢的城市中的缺乏，同时他请读者原谅如果他自己"违背一些语法规则"（si aut in litteris aut in sillabis grammaticam artem excessero）。他的借口是他希望那些没有受过高级教育的人也能够理解他："很少人能听明白一个讲哲学道理的演说家，但很多人能听懂农民的话。"（Philosophantem rethorem intellegunt pauci, loquentem rusticum multi）

第 1 卷是从世界的创造开始并结束于圣 Martinus（317—397 年）的逝世。Martinus 曾经是 Tours（法国图尔）的主教，也是第一个在罗马帝国西部建立隐修团体的人。根据作者的说法，本卷覆盖"5596 年"，因为他认为基督诞生是在世界被创造后 5200 年（参见 Oriosus 和 Augustinus 的编年方式）。第 2 卷继续论述 Tours 教区的历史并提到 Vandales、匈奴和法兰克人如何镇压基督宗教，一直到 Chlodowech（=Clovis，466—511 年）的逝世。这位国王约于 497 年接受了基督信仰。这是一个具有深远历史意义的时刻，因为这样他就引导了法兰克人接受公教信仰以及与罗马建立更密切的关系。第 3 卷继续叙述种种历史事件，一直到 Theudebert 王的逝世（547 年），而第 4 卷覆盖从 547 年到 Sigibert I 王逝世（575 年）的阶段。第 5、6 卷描述 Childebert II 王（570—596 年在位）和 Chilperich 王（539—584 年）的时期。

第三个部分覆盖从 585 年到 594 年的时代并描述在 Tours 发生的内战（第 7 卷）、Gunthramn 王隆重地进入 Orleans（奥尔良）城的情况、西班牙的 Leuvigild 王的逝

# Gregorius Turonensis / Gregory of Tours

**Opera:** *Historia Francorum, Libri miraculorum*
**Works:** *History of the Franks, Books of Miracles*

## 091. *Historia Francorum / History of the Franks*

The title of this work in 10 books is actually *Decem libri historiarum*, but it is often quoted as *Historia (e) Francorum*. The first part (books 1~4) was written in 575, the second section (books 5,6) before 585, and the third section (books 7~10) between 585—591. The work is the first national history written in a Christian spirit, and it is one of the most important source books for the events of the 6th century. The book is written in a simple and sometimes incorrect Latin style, e.g. the author sometimes confuses the cases after prepositions. He complains about the low level of literature (liberalium cultura litterarum) in the cities of Gaul, and at the same time he asks pardon from his readers if he "should happen to make grammpbe261atical mistakes" (si aut in litteris aut in sillabis grammaticam artem excessero). His justification is that he wants to be understood by the people who have less opportunity to receive a good education: "Few understand the philosophical theorizing of an orator, but many understand the words of a peasant" (Philosophantem rethorem intellegunt pauci, loquentem rusticum multi).

The first book starts with the creation of the world and ends with the death of St. Martin (317—397), the bishop of Tours and the first to found monastic communities in the West. According to the author this first volume covers "5596 years", since he supposed that Christ was born 5200 years after the world was created (confer Oriosus and Augustinus' chronology). The second book continues the chronicle of the Diocese of Tours and tells of the persecutions under the Vandals, Huns and Franks until the death of King Chlodowech (Clovis, 466—511). This king accepted Christianity ca. in 497, which was a moment of great historical significance, because he thus lead the Franks to the Catholic faith and to a closer contact with Rome. The third book leads the narrative up to the death of King Theudebert (547), and the fourth book covers the period from 547 to the death of King Sigibert I (575). Books 5 and 6 describe the reign of King Childebert II (570—596) until the death of King Chilperich (539—584).

The third part covers the years from 585 to 594 and gives an account of the civil war in Tours (book 7), the solemn entry of King Gunthramn in Orleans, the death of King Leuvigild in Spain (book 8), the delegation which Rekkared (the son of Leuvigild)

世（第 8 卷）、Leuvigild 的儿子 Rekkared 王向 Gunthramn 和 Childebert II 王派遣的使团。这件事引发了法国地区第一次迫害犹太人的运动(589 年)。第 9 卷也描述那一年的反常天气。第 10 卷报告关于 Gregorius Magnus 教宗当选的情况、法兰克人派遣使团到拜占庭以及 Childebert 如何侵略意大利。最后一章提供历代在 Tours 任职的主教们的总览。

sent to King Gunthramn and King Childebert II. This event triggered the first persecution of Jews in France (589). Book 9 also describes the abnormal weather of that year. The tenth book reports about the election of Pope Gregory the Great, of the Frankish delegation to Byzanz, and of Childebert's invasion of Italy. The last chapter gives a synopsis of the bishops of Tours.

# (大)格列高利(540—604 AD)

来自一个很富有的罗马家族,曾有一两名教宗(Felix III 和 Agapetus I)也属于他的家族。Gregorius 获得了语文学和法学的教育,于 572/573 年任罗马市长(praefectus urbis)并很成功地处理了当时的种种事务(食品供应、治安、建筑)。他退隐并建立了一个隐修团体。578 年他被祝圣执事并奉派到 Constantinopolis 朝廷,在那里任 apocrisiarius(教宗的代表)。585 年他回罗马隐居,但于 590 年被选为罗马主教。他改进了罗马教廷的组织形式,仅仅选择圣职人员和隐修者为他的助手。Gregorius 与一些执事一起着手管理罗马教会在意大利、西西里、高卢、达尔玛蒂亚(Dalmatia)和阿富利加(Africa)北部的教产并用那里的收入来进行慈善工作或解决罗马的难民问题。Gregorius 和西班牙王、法兰克王和 Langobardi 的女王 Theodelinde 保持良好关系,经常给他们写信或赠送礼物来巩固他们的信仰或影响他们接受基督信仰。在 597 年他派遣了 Augustinus 隐修士到英国并嘱咐这些传教士不要破坏当地的外教文化,但要逐渐以基督信仰取代旧文化。

**著作**:《对话集》(4 卷,包括许多圣人的传记,第 2 卷是 Benedictus 的传记,第 4 卷涉及到关于来世的神视,影响深远,参见 Dante 的《神曲》)、《信集》(847 封信被保存,但他大概写了几千封信)、《解释 Ezechiel 的讲道》《约伯传诠释》(《约伯伦理记》,第一部伦理神学著作)、《牧民守则》(《牧灵者规则集》,内容:如何当牧者、司铎,如何讲道,如何过纯朴的生活)、《额我略礼仪集》(《格列高利礼仪集》,涉及到弥撒礼仪的改革)

## 092.《对话集》

本书(共 4 卷)的全名是 *Dialogi de vita et de miraculis patrum Italicorum*(《关于意大利教父们生活和奇迹的对话集》)。这些叙述和传记约于 594 年以对话的形式记载下来。

作者与他的朋友 Petrus 执事谈话,而 Petrus 问他是否意大利的教父们也行了很多奇迹。因此,Gregorius 叙述了很多曾经在意大利教会中发生过的奇迹般的事件。这些故事也表明上主始终惩罚恶人并保护善良的人。意大利的圣人/圣徒们治疗了很多病人,正如东方的圣人/圣徒一样。(当时关于东方的圣人/圣徒的故事在西部也广泛流传,而 Gregorius 强调不仅仅东方产生了很多圣人/圣徒。)

第 2 卷描述 Nursia 的 Benedictus(480—547 年)并且这是关于这位圣人的生活的最重要研究资料。Benedictus 生于 Nursia(在罗马东北地区)一个"相当有地位的家庭"。他被派遣去罗马学习自由学科,但他因城市的道德腐败而感到厌恶。大约在 500

# Gregorius Magnus / Gregory the Great

**Opera:** *Dialogi de vita et miraculis patrum Italicorum, Epistulae, Homiliae in Ezechielem, Moralia in Job, Regula pastoralis (=Liber regulae pastoralis, Cura pastoralis), Sacramentarium Gregorianum*

**Works:** *Dialogues, Letters, Sermons on Ezekiel, Moralia in Job, Book of Rules for Pastors, Sacramentary*

## 092. *Dialogi / Dialogues*

The full title of this work in 4 books is *Dialogi de vita et de miraculis patrum Italicorum* (*Dialogues on the Life and Miracles of the Italian Fathers*). The narratives were written in 594 AD in the form of a dialogue.

The author talks to his friend, the deacon Petrus, who asks whether the Italian fathers worked miracles. Gregory tells of many miraculous events that happened in the history of the church in Italy. These stories also show that God always punishes evil people and protects the good. The Italian saints cured many sick people, just like the great saints of the Orient. (At that time there were many popular stories known in the West about Eastern saints. Gregory emphasizes that saintly people have not only been produced from the East.)

The second book is dedicated to Benedict of Nursia (480—547) and is the most important source for details about the life of this saint. Benedict was born in Nursia, northeast of Rome, into a "family of high station". When he was sent to Rome to study the liberal arts, he was repelled by the immorality he found in the city. So, around the year 500 he sought solitude and lived the life of a hermit at Subiaco in a hillside cave for three years. A nearby community of monks invited Benedict to become their abbot, but there were conflicts, and some of the monks even tried to poison him. After returning to Subiaco he founded twelve small monasteries in the area but in 525 migrated to Casinum, ca. 120 km south of Rome, where he built the famous monastery of Monte Cassino

年他开始追求独处的生活并在 Subiaco 的一个山洞里过一个独修者的生活达三年之久。附近的隐修者团体请他当他们的院长,但不久后出现了一些冲突,一些隐修者甚至试图毒死 Benedictus。回到 Subiaco 后,他在该地区建立了 12 个小的隐修院,但于 525 年迁到罗马以南 120 公里的 Casinum,在那里的山上建立了著名的 Monte Cassino 隐修院。他写了隐修会的《会规》,而这些规则对于后来的所有隐修院都有深远的影响。他和他的姐妹 Scholastica 一年见面一次——她生活在 Monte Cassino 附近的一个修女团体中。

第 3 卷继续第 1 卷的奇迹故事,而第 4 卷包含一些关于灵魂死后的生活的故事。Gregorius 谈论死亡以后的灵魂们。他认为 Nicaea 大公会议(公元 325 年)的《信经》中提到的圣人的共融这个概念应该包括活的和已亡的信徒。已亡的信徒为活的信徒祈祷,他们为信徒们祈求上主,正如在世的信徒们也应该为别的信徒以及为亡者的安息而祈祷。Gregorius 相信,基督徒们能够通过祈祷协助其他的基督徒,包括协助已亡的信徒,而这个基本的原则影响了他对于补赎的看法。告解的圣事(亦称和好圣事)和补赎有关系,即善功和虔诚的行为。当一个犯过罪的人宣告了自己的罪并进行补赎后,他再一次被允许参与基督徒们的团体。然而,部分的补赎者在完成补赎之前已经去世,而为了这些人 Gregorius 提出灵魂死后的第三条路:炼狱(purgatorium)。天堂和地狱是两个永恒的领域,但炼狱应该是灵魂在某段时间内被净化的地方。人间的基督徒们的祈祷、弥撒和施舍以及天上的圣人的祈祷都能够帮助炼狱中的灵魂们早一点达到他们的目的地——天堂。Gregorius 关于炼狱的教导基本上是正当的和公平的;他要解决这样的问题:一部分灵魂在死亡后既不适合马上升天,又不应该下地狱。在一些古代非基督教的宗教和哲学文献中也能够找到类似的观点。Gregorius 讲了很多关于那些在炼狱中受苦的灵魂们的故事,他还描述天堂和地狱。这些具有虔诚宗教情怀的故事影响了基督徒们的想象力(参见 Dante 的《神曲》),并且成为所谓的 Missa Gregoriana("额我略弥撒")的基础——这些礼仪的目标是拯救那些处于炼狱中的灵魂们。

### 093. 《约伯伦理记》

这是一部巨大的(35 卷!)关于 Job(《约伯传/约伯记》)的注解,Gregorius 应 Sevilla 的总主教 Leander 的要求编写了它,于 595 年完成了这部著作——它也被称为历史上第一部完整的"伦理神学大全"。

Gregorius 逐句解释《圣经》文献,先谈论历史意义,然后分析其精神性和比喻性的意义,最后提出每一句话的道德意义。Gregorius 选择了 Job 来解释很多灵修和伦理价值,因为 Job 的故事催促人们思考这样的问题:正义的人为什么要受苦?对 Gregorius 来说,"恶"的现象不是一种形而上学的问题;他认为上主允许恶、允许 Job 受苦,这是一项奥迹,而这个奥秘的目标是考验和强化信徒们的信仰。因为 Job 始终信赖上

on the top of a hill and wrote the rule for monks which had a lasting influence on all subsequent monastic orders. Once a year he visited his sister Scholastica who lived near Monte Cassino with a community of nuns.

Book 3 continues the miracle stories of book one, and book 4 contains narratives that try to show that the souls continue to live after death. Gregory understands the "communion of saints"—a doctrine stated in the Creed of Nicaea (325 AD)—as including the living faithful and the dead. The departed saints pray for the living, they intercede with God on their behalf, just as living Christians can and should pray for fellow believers and for the repose of the dead. Gregory believes that Christians can assist other Christians with their prayers in this life but also after death, and this basic principle influences his view of penance. The sacrament of penance is linked to satisfaction, namely good works or pious practices. After the confession of his sins and the completion of his satisfaction a sinner was readmitted to the Christian community. However, some penitents died before completing their satisfaction, and for these persons Gregory posits a third destination of the soul after death: the purgatory (purgatorium). Heaven and hell are timeless realms, but the purgatory is meant to be a temporal stage of purgation of the souls from sin. The prayers, masses, and almsgiving of Christians on earth and the prayers of the saints in Heaven can help the souls in purgatory to reach their final destination—Heaven—earlier. Gregory's teaching on purgatory basically is a just and balanced solution to the problem of a group of souls who do not fit into the other two alternatives of Heaven and Hell. The doctrine of the purgatory also has analogies in some texts of ancient non-Christian religions and philosophies. Gregory tells many stories about the souls who suffer in purgatory, and he describes heaven and hell. These pious legends influenced Christian imagination (cf. Dante) and became the basis of the so-called "Gregorian Masses", which are intended to save souls from the purgatory.

## 093. *Moralia in Job*

This extensive (35 books!) commentary to the *Book of Job* was written in response to a request from Archbishop Leander of Sevilla. Gregory finished this first compendium of moral theology in the year 595.

Gregory explains the Biblical text verse after verse, first discussing the historical meaning, then the spiritual and allegorical sense, and finally the moral implications of each sentence. Gregory chooses Job to explain spiritual and ethical values because Job's story raises the thought-provoking question of why the just man must suffer. For Gregory the problem of evil as a metaphysical reality is not interesting, he rather sees God's permission of evil and the suffering of Job as a mystery, which is designed to test and strengthen the faith of the believers. Always trusting in God Job could endure his afflictions, even though he did not know the saving grace of Christ's death and resurrection. If Job, a Jew, could unshakeably love God in all trials and temptations, then how much more should Christians do so, profiting from Job's example. In Gregory's explanations we find the theme of the seven capital sins (septem peccata capitalia, also "deadly sins"

主,他才能够忍受他的遭遇,虽然他还不知道基督死亡与复活带来的救恩。如果 Job 这个犹太人能够在一切困境和诱惑中坚定不移地爱慕上主,那么那些基督徒们更应该有这样的精神,而 Job 的榜样对他们有好处。在 Gregorius 的解释中出现了"七罪宗"(septem peccata capitalia,亦称"死罪")的论点;七个罪宗是 luxuria(迷色)、gula(贪吃)、avaritia(吝啬、贪婪)、acedia(懒惰)、ira(愤怒)、invidia(嫉妒)和 superbia(骄傲)。如果按照这个顺序理解七个大罪的严重性,精神性的罪恶比肉身上的罪恶还要严重。Gregorius 关于"七罪宗"的分析成为欧洲西部地区的基督宗教的核心概念,比如 Dante 在他的《神曲·地狱》中就使用了这七种罪来描述地狱的结构。

## 094. 《牧民守则》

教宗 Gregorius 在 590 年以后编写了这部牧灵者的手册(亦称 *Liber regulae pastoralis*)。早在 Gregorius 还活着的年代,这部书被译成希腊语。在中世纪这部著作对教区的圣职人员有很大的影响,就好比 Benedictus 的 *Regula*(《会规》)对隐修团体产生深远的影响一样。

在 Ambrosius 的 *De officiis ministrorum*(《论圣职人员的职务》)及 Augustinus 的 *De doctrina Christiana*(《论基督宗教的教导》)后,Gregorius 为他的圣职人员写了一部手册。他称照顾灵魂的工作为"众技艺之技艺"(ars artium),因为这种工作需要各种各样的能力和技巧。和 Ambrosius 一样,Gregorius 也强调在一切事物上的节制、礼貌以及一些在日常生活中能够实践的解决方案。圣职人员的主要任务之一是在共同的礼仪中解释福音书,即讲道(praedicare)。与 Augustinus 相似,Gregorius 建议一个讲道者应该适应他的听众,虽然这一点也许意味着他要忽略优雅的词藻或放弃高妙的修辞学手段。这样的原则暗示这样的事实:许多教会团体的教育水平下降了。Gregorius 也意识到他同时代的司铎们的文化修养低于 Augustinus 时代的圣职人员的教育背景。一个司铎在讲道时面对一些来自不同社会背景的人,而 Gregorius 使用很多实例来说明这种情况。通过其劝导和鼓励讲道者应该尽可能消除部分人的恶习,同时要避免惹起另一些人的相反恶习。听众可以根据他们的基本道德观念而区分为几个类型,而且人们的年龄、性别和职业不一定会影响他们的基本道德观念。讲道者应该很熟悉属于他的教会团体的人的情况和他们的需要。这样,他的讲道起一种道德教育的作用并帮助他们控制自己的过错。

就那些掌握权柄的人,Gregorius 提出这样的建议(2,1.6):"长上的行为必须远超过一般人的行为,正如牧人的生活也超过羊群的生活。长上的思想必须是纯洁的,他的行动应该是一种榜样,他的沉默必须是得体的,他的话必须是有用的。通过他的同情心他必须接近所有的人,而他应该具有默想的眼光,超过别人。对于那些行善的人,他应该是一个谦卑的朋友。正义是他热切追求的,所以他必须对罪人及其缺陷采取耿直的态度。他不可以因为需要照顾外在事务而忽略内心生活,同时也不可以因

or "mortal sins"), namely lust(luxuria), gluttony(gula), avarice(avaritia), sloth(acedia), wrath(ira), envy(invidia), and pride(superbia). This sequence of increasing seriousness treats sins of the flesh as less serious than sins of the intellect. Gregory's analysis of the seven main sins became a standard idea in the world of Christianity in western Europe, for example Dante used the seven capital sins to structure the layers of the hell (see his *Commedia, Inferno*).

## 094. *Regula pastoralis / Rules for Pastors*

Pope Gregory wrote this instruction for pastors(also entitled *Liber regulae pastoralis* or *Cura pastoralis, Book of Pastoral Rules*)after 590 AD. The book was translated into Greek already in Gregory's lifetime. In the Middle Ages the influence of this book on the secular (=diocesan)clergy was equal to the impact which Benedict's *Rule* had on monastic communities.

In the tradition of Ambrose's *De officiis ministrorum* (*On the Duties of the Clergy*) and Augustine's *De doctrina Christiana* (*On Christian Doctrine*), Gregory produces a manual for his clergy, calling the cure of souls the "ars artium"(art of arts), since pastoral work demands skills of many different kinds. Similar to Ambrose, Gregory emphasizes moderation in all things, decorum, and practical solutions that are viable in day to day life. Clerics must take on practical duties as to care for the believers entrusted to their care. One of their main tasks is the preaching of the Gospel at the common liturgical celebrations (praedicare). Similar to Augustine, Gregory suggests that a preacher should adjust his style to his audience, even if that implies the neglect of literary refinement or the omission of rhetorical subtleties. From this principle it is obvious that the educational level of many Church communities was declining. Gregory is aware of the fact that the priests of his age have a less thorough education compared to the clergy of Augustine's time. Gregory uses many examples to show how to preach to a congregation made up of people from different backgrounds. Through his admonitions and encouraging words the preacher should try to expurgate the vices of some without inflaming the opposing vices of others. The audience can be divided into different groups according to their basic moral attitudes, and these moral traits are not necessarily determined by age, sex, and occupation. The preacher should know well where the members of the church are and what they need. In this way his preaching should help them to control their excesses and thus educate them morally.

Concerning the use of power, Gregory offers the following advice(2,1.6): "The conduct of a person in authority must be so high above the conduct of the people as the life of a shepherd is above the life of his flock. His thinking must be pure, his actions a model, his silence must be tactful, his words must be useful. Through his compassion he must be close to all people, and he must be steeped in meditation more than anyone else. To those who do good works he should be a humble friend. In his zeal for justice he should be straightforward towards the sinner and toward his failures. He must not neglect the care for inner life because of outward duties, and for all his concentration on

为专务心灵的生活而放弃对外在事物的关心。

很多时候一位长上认为他因地位高而远远超过别人。他的属下在他成功的时候夸奖他,而在他失败的时候没有人敢谴责他,人们甚至在应该批评的时候也赞扬他,结果他让自己滑入欺骗并采取一种骄傲的态度。从外面他获得没有根据的赞美,而在心中他失去真理。他忘记他自己并仅仅聆听别人说的话。他真正相信自己是他们所描述的那位伟大人物,而不愿意相信他是自己的良心所控诉的那种人。他居高临下地蔑视他的部下并忘记,就共同的人性而言,他与他们是完全平等的。他认为他比别人都高尚,因为他掌握的权力更大,而因为他的权柄大他也相信他比别人更有智慧。

有权威的人必须始终在内心中控制权力意识,而如果他们在社会上是公共权威,更应该是这样的。一位长上在任何时候都不可以有虚荣心或对权力的空洞享受。因此那位明智的人正当地说:'当你是宴会上的主席时,你不要自傲,而要像客人中的任何人一样。'(*Sir* 32:1)而 Petrus 说:'不要视你们自己为上主的遗产的主人,但求做群羊的模范。'(1 *Petr* 5:3)永恒的真理也鼓励我们追求更大的美德:'你们知道外邦人的君主统治他们的人民,而权贵管辖他们。但你们不该那样。如果你们当中谁要做大的,他应先成为你们的仆人。你们中谁想位列第一,他就应该先做你们的奴仆。就像人子来不是为受人服侍,而是来为人服务一样的,他牺牲自己的生命,为众人作赎价。'(*Mt* 20:25–28)"

Gregorius 鼓励男青年成为司铎:"很多人拥有杰出的美德和当领导人的才能;他们爱慕贞洁和纯洁的生活,他们因无欲而刚强,他们从神圣的教导中汲取营养,他们忍耐且坚韧,有荣誉感并表现仁慈和同情,但他们也有很严格的正义精神。如果这样的人拒绝成为圣职人员,他们将失去他们所受到的种种恩赐,因为这些恩典是为了别人蒙受的,而不是为自己蒙受的。另一些人拥有非凡的能力,但他们仅仅注意到自己的默观生活,不愿意通过他们的讲道令别人受益。他们享受安静的独处和单独一个人的默想……另一些人则出于谦虚而回避当司铎的任务,因为他们不愿意引导那些比自己更大的或地位更高的人。然而,如果一个人意识到上主的旨意是要他当教会内的领导但仍然拒绝这种邀请,这样的人并不是真正谦虚的人。"(1,5~6)

Gregorius 始终支持那些平衡的、可行的观点。他描述一套价值观,而在这种价值观中,对于最高的价值(永福)的追求不应该导致对于比较低级的价值的忽略。Gregorius 意识到关于美好价值的不恰当教导也许不知不觉地会引起一些坏的后果。他使用很多具体的例子,语言简单,又多次重复他的教导,这样那些教育水平比较低的圣职人员也应该能够明白他的一切论点。

the inner life he must not give up the care for outward matters.

Very often the superior thinks he towers above the others because of his high position. Since his subordinates shower praises on him if he did well, and because nobody dares to blame him for a failure, and also because they praise him even when they should criticize him, he lets himself be deceived and adopts an attitude of presumption and arrogance. From the outside he receives unjustified praise, and inside he loses the truth. He forgets himself and only listens to what others say. He really believes he is the great man they describe and not the man who is accused by his own conscience. He looks down on his subjects and forgets that because of the one human nature he is equal to them. He thinks he is nobler than anyone else because he is more powerful than they are. And due to his power he also believes that he is wiser than the others.

The superior must always try to control the conscience of power in his heart, even more so if this power is manifest in public. A superior must never harbor vain delight in power. Thus the wise man says rightly: 'If you host a banquet, do not raise yourself above the guests, but be among them like one of them' (*Sir* 32:1), and Peter says: 'Do not be lords over God's heritage, but be examples to the flock' (1 *Petr* 5:3). The eternal Truth encourages us to strive for greater virtue: 'You know that the princes of the gentiles exercise dominion over them, and they that are great exercise authority upon them. But it shall not be so among you: whoever wants to be great among you, let him be your minister. And whoever wants to be chief among you, let him be your servant. Likewise, the Son of man did not come to be served but to serve and to give his life as ransom for many' (*Mt* 20:25-28)."

Gregory encourages able young man to become priests: "Many possess excellent virtues and the ability to lead others; they are chaste and love purity, they are strong through their self-control, they are nourished at the meal of the divine teachings, patient and enduring, they are honorable, show benevolence and compassion, but they also have a sense of strict justice. If such persons decline to follow the call to a clerical office, then they deprive themselves of the gifts which they have received, not for themselves but also for others. Others possess great gifts but they only care about their contemplative life and do not want to be useful for others by their preaching. They love to enjoy quiet solitude and loneliness in meditation… some, however, shy away from becoming a priest out of humility, because they do not want to lead others whom they consider as superior to themselves. But someone who understands that it is God's will for him to be a leader in the Church and still rejects this invitation is not truly humble." (1,5~6)

Always advocating balance and practicality, Gregory presents a value system in which the lesser values are not discarded even as one strives for the highest good (eternal happiness). Gregorius is aware that inappropriate preaching of good values might incidentally give rise to what is evil. He uses many example and a simple, reiterative language so as to make sure that also the less educated members of the clergy grasp his points.

# 科伦班（543—616 AD）

生于爱尔兰的 Leinster，长大后进入 Bangor 隐修院，于 590 年（或 591 年）与 12 位朋友一起前往欧洲大陆传教（即所谓的 peregrinatio propter Christum"因基督的缘故到国外去"）。他在高卢（今天法国地区）的 Luxeuil、Annegray、Corbie 和 Fontaine 建立了一些隐修院，但 20 年后被驱逐，因此他到瑞士地区传教并建立了 St. Gallen 隐修院，并大约于 612 年在意大利北部建立了 Bobbio 隐修院。在这些隐修院中，爱尔兰人提供了拉丁语和希腊语教育并制造了相当多的世俗文献和宗教文学的手抄本。Columba 的学生 Jonas 于 642 年编写了他的 vita（传记）。

**著作**：《忏悔书》、《隐修士会规》

## 095. 《隐修士会规》

该《会规》成书于 590—600 年间，他与 *Poenitentiale*（《忏悔书》）一同诞生。在法国地区，该《会规》曾流行一时，但在 650 年后，Benedictus（本笃）的 *Regula*（《会规》）逐渐代替了它。

Columba 的 *Regula*（《会规》）是一些比较一般性的原则的汇集。隐修者需要在服从中生活（第 1 章），他们必须保持沉默（2），在饮食方面要节制（3），必须放弃世俗的欲望（4），不可追求人间的荣誉（5），必须过一种克己的、有纪律的生活（6），他们应该是清醒的和明智的（8），又要舍弃自己（abnegatio sui，参见 *Mt* 16:24）（9）。这样，隐修者将会在他们的生活中达到一种完美的状态（10）。第 7 章包含一些规定共同祈祷和日课的规则。

Columba 的《会规》针对隐修者的某些不正当行为规定了一些惩罚：大声说话的人要受"打 6 杖"；在共同祈祷时迟到或进入房子时没有拿下帽子——"50 杖"；单独与一个妇女说话——"200 杖"。这种杖责的象征意义也许更甚于加诸肉身的疼痛，它在不同章节中也被称为"打击、殴打、鞭打"（plagae，percussiones，verbera）。其他惩罚包括：守斋、禁闭、禁言、唱一些 psalmi（圣咏）。对于惩罚的比较机械性的理解导致了这样的想法：30 杖等于唱 15 篇圣咏；200 杖等于两天守斋。因为《会规》中的惩罚规定提到了盗窃、杀人、鸡奸、醉酒等，我们可以认为当时的具体生活向 Columba 的隐修理想发起了相当大的挑战。他的 *Poenitentiale*（《忏悔书》）也提供了某些犯罪行为的惩罚标准。

# Columban / Columbanus

**Opera:** *Poenitentiale, Regula coenobialis*
**Works:** *Penitential, Monastic Rule*

## 095. *Regula coenobialis / Monastic Rule*

This *Rule* was written between 590 and 600 and accompanied the *Poenitentiale* (*Penitential*). The *Rule* was quite popular in France for some time, but after 650 it was gradually replaced by Benedict's *Regula*.

Columba's *Rule* is a collection of rather general principles. The monks should live in obedience (chapter 1), they must observe silence (2), be moderate in food and drink (3), they must abandon earthly desires (4), vanity and secular fame (5), they must observe continence and be disciplined (6), sober and prudent (8), and practice self-denial (abnegatio sui, cf. *Mt* 16:24) (9). In this way they will reach perfection in their life as monks (10). Chapter 7 contains rules concerning common prayers and the liturgy of the hours.

Columba's *Rule* metes out certain penalties to improper behavior of the monks: talking in a loud voice—six strokes; late arrival at a prayer or entering the house without taking off his hat—fifty strokes; private conversation with a woman—200 strokes; These strokes were perhaps more symbolic than painful; they are variously called "plagae, percussiones, verbera" ("blows, striking, flogging"). Other penalties included fasting, being locked up in a room, prohibition of talking, singing of psalms. The somewhat mechanical understanding of penalties led to such equations: 30 strokes equal the singing of 15 psalms, 200 strokes equal two days of fasting. Since the penal regulations mention sins like theft, murder, sodomy, drunkenness, it may be concluded that Columba's monastic ideals met a reality that posed considerable challenges. The *Penitential* likewise contains standard rules for the punishments of certain sins.

# 伊西多尔（约 560—636 AD）

来自一个西班牙罗马人家族，他们本来居住在 Cartagena 地区，但因 Byzanz 人的侵入迁到 Sevilla。Isidorus 的姐姐 Florentina 是修女，他的哥哥 Leander 曾是 Sevilla 的总主教，而另一个哥哥 Fulgentius 是 Ecija(Andalusia)的主教。在 Leander 去世后(600 年)，Isidorus 成为 Sevilla 的总主教并主持 619 年的 Sevilla 主教会议以及 633 年在 Toledo 举行的主教会议。他曾被称为"最后的拉丁教父"，著作等身。

**著作：**《世界史》(继续 Eusebius 和 Hieronymus 的《世界史》到 615 年为止)、《反驳犹太人》、《论教会的礼仪》(包括弥撒、庆日、祈祷文等)、《论自然》、《论受造物的秩序》、《论教会职位的来源》、《圣祖生平始末》(包括《圣经》中 86 个人的小传记)、《名人传记》(根据 Hieronymus 和 Gennadius 的著作)、《差异》(谈论一些语法问题，也是一部同义词词典)、《语源学》(20 卷，一种百科全书，影响很大)、《西班牙集》(《教令集》，也许并非 Isidorus 的作品；对中世纪教会法的发展有深远的影响)、《哥特人历史》(表达 Isidorus 对于西哥特人的兴趣及好感)、《哀叹之书》(人和理性之间的对话)、《旧约诸问题》、《隐修者会规》(为 Isidorus 建立的隐修院写的)、《诸命题》(3 卷，根据 Gregorius 的 *Moralia* 谈论各种教义和伦理问题)、《同义词》

## 096. 《语源学》

该百科全书分为 20 卷，也被称为 *Origines*（来自 *Originum sive etymologiarum libri XX*《来源或语源学 20 卷》），成为中世纪最受欢迎的手册之一（今天保存了 950 个手抄本）。本著作是由 Isidorus 的朋友 Braulio 完成并出版的。它不仅仅是一种语言学字典(参见书名《语源学》)，而且也是一种几乎包括所有古代知识领域的百科全书。在 Cato、Varro、Celsus、Plinius、Martianus Capella 与 Cassiodorus 以后，Isidorus 是古代最后的百科全书作家。他的著作对于古代知识向中世纪的传播具有深远的影响（其影响类似于 Martianus 的 *De nuptiis* 和 Cassiodorus 的 *Institutiones*）。Isidorus 的资料来源非常多，包括 Servius、Cassiodorus、Suetonius、Boethius、Hieronymus、Augustinus、Lactantius、Plinius、Vergilius、Columella、Petronius 等等。他多次引用《圣经》，而因为他记载很多古代诗人或学者的原话，他保存了很多宝贵的资料，尤其是早期罗马文学方面的文献。

20 卷的标题是：1 卷：论语法(*De grammatica*)、2 卷：修辞学和逻辑学(*De rhetorica et dialectica*)、3 卷：四个数学科（算术、几何、音乐、天文学）(*De quatuor disciplinis mathematicis: arithmetica, geometria, musica, astronomia*)、4 卷：医学(*De medicina*)、5 卷：诸法律和时代(*De legibus et temporibus*，包括简单的世界史)、6 卷：教会的书籍和职位(*De libris et officiis ecclesiasticis*)、7 卷：论神、天使和信徒的等级(*De Deo, ange-*

# Isidorus de Sevilla / Isidore

**Opera:** *Chronicon, Contra Iudaeos ad Florentinam sororem, De ecclesiasticis officiis, De natura rerum, De ordine creaturarum, De origine officiorum ecclesiasticorum, De ortu et obitu patrum, De viris illustribus, Differentiarum libri II, Etymologiae (Origines), Hispana, Historia Gothorum, Liber lamentationum, Quaestiones in Vetus Testamentum, Regula monachorum, Sententiarum libri III, Synonymorum libri II*

**Works:** *World History, Against the Jews, On the Liturgy of the Church, On Nature, On the Order of Creation, On the Origin of Ecclesiastical Offices, On the Life of the Fathers, On Famous Men, Differences, Etymologies (Origins), Hispana, History of the Goths, Lamentations, Questions pertaining to the Old Testament, A Rule for Monks, Sentences, Synonyms*

## 096. *Etymologiae / Etymologies*

This dictionary in 20 books is also quoted as *Origins* (from *Origines / Originum sive etymologiarum libri XX*). It became one of the most popular encyclopedic handbooks of the Middle ages (950 manuscripts are extant). The work was finished and edited by Isidore's friend Braulio. It is not only a linguistic dictionary, as the title suggests, but rather an encyclopedia of almost all areas of classical science. After Cato, Varro, Celsus, Plinius, Martianus Capella and Cassiodor, Isidore is the the last great encyclopedist of antiquity. His work was immensely influential in the transmission of classical education to the subsequent centuries (together with Martianus' *De nuptiis* and Cassiodor's *Institutiones*). Isidore's sources are very manifold and include works from Servius, Cassiodor, Sueton, Boethius, Jerome, Augustine, Lactantius, Plinius, Virgil, Columella, Petronius etc. He quotes the Bible very often, and his citations of classical poets and scholars have preserved precious passages, especially from early Roman literature.

The titles of the 20 books are: (1) *On grammar*, (2) *Rhetoric and Dialectics*, (3) *The four Mathematical Disciplines*, (4) *Medicine*, (5) *On Laws and Times* (containing a short world history), (6) *Ecclesiastical Books and Offices*, (7) *God, Angels and the Orders of the Faithful*, (8) *The Church and certain Sects*, (containing an account of pagan philosophy, poetry and mythology), (9) *On Languages, Peoples, Kingdoms, the Military, Inhabitants and Friendships*, (10) *Certain Etymological Explanations*, (11) *On Man and Portents*, (12) *Animals*, (13) *The Universe*, (14) *The World and the Elements*, (15) *Architecture and*

lis et fidelium ordinibus）、8 卷：教会和各种教派（*De ecclesia et sectis diversis*，介绍外教人的哲学、文学和神话）、9 卷：论诸语言、民族、统治、军事、市民、关系（*De linguis, gentibus, regnis, militia, civibus, affinitatibus*）、10 卷：语源学分析（*Vocum certarum alphabetum*）、11 卷：论人和预兆（*De homine et portentis*）、12 卷：论动物（*De animalibus*）、13 卷：宇宙和宇宙的部分（*De mundo et partibus*）、14 卷：大地及其元素（*De terra et partibus*）、15 卷：论房子和农地（*De aedificiis et agris*）、16 卷：矿学和金属（*De lapidibus et metallis*，包括衡量尺度）、17 卷：论农业（*De rebus rusticis*）、18 卷：论战争和表演（*De bello et ludis*，包括戏剧）、19 卷：论船、建筑、衣服（*De navibus, aedificiis et vestibus*，包括对于手工业的描述）、20 卷：论食品，论室内外用的工具（*De penu et instrumentis domesticis et rusticis*）。

*Geology*, (16)*Mineralogy and Metals* (containing different measures and weights), (17)*Agriculture*, (18)*War and Games* (including theatrical performances), (19)*Ships, Buildings and Dress* (containing descriptions of manufacturing and professional skills), (20)*Food, Household Tools and Agricultural Instruments*.

# 梯子约翰（约 575—650 AD）

出生地不详；他 16 岁时在 Sinai 山当隐修者，前后过独修生活 40 年，此后成为 Sinai 山的 St. Catharina 隐修院的院长（约 631 年到 650 年）。

著作：《天堂之梯》

## 097.《天堂之梯》

Iōannēs 这部道德性论文成书于 7 世纪初。

本书的目标是为读者提供一生可以阅读的训导。"梯子"的 30 个节代表着基督隐藏生活的 30 年。登上这个"梯子"的人应该达到一个很完美的状态，正如信徒们应该走的"窄门"。30 级台阶是这些：拒绝世俗的生活、远离七情六欲、放弃家乡和财富、严格的服从、感到羞愧和忏悔、默想自己的死亡、自愿地接受痛苦并使它在基督徒的希望内变成喜乐、温和与谦逊、和好与宽恕、控制自己的语言、沉默地接受一切、回避谎言和闲逸、节制与尺度、贞洁、克己和自律、慷慨、贫困、内在的刻苦、夜间的祈祷和守夜、勇气、放弃一切自豪、骄傲和虚荣心、谦卑、纯洁和纯净、感到自卑并谴责自己、反省自己的良心、内心的平安（hēsychia）、祈祷中的默观、与神合一、无限完美的喜乐、精神性的复活以及活出无所不包的爱——这就是达到完满的最后步骤。

这 30 个步骤有时被排成一对一对，其中也能看出基督徒精神生活的基本过程和结构：从远离世俗世界（apatheia）开始，人要净化自己的灵魂，才能获得内心的平安（hēsychia）以及与神的合一。作者引用《圣经》和"沙漠教父"（即埃及隐修者）的许多句子。他也加上了一些历史榜样和来自个人经验的观察，这样就很形象地表达了道德和宗教上的呼吁。作者第一次提到与呼吸技巧有关系的"耶稣祈祷"，这样已经指向 Gregorios Sinaites（1296—1359 年）的"静修主义"。

# Iōannēs Klimakos / John Climacus

**Opera:** *Klimax ton paradersou*
**Works:** *The Ladder of Divine Ascent*

### 097.  *Klimax tou paradeisou / Scala paradisi / The Ladder of Divine Ascent*

This moral treatise of John was written in the early 7th century.

The book wants to accompany the reader throughout his or her life. The 30 stairs of the "ladder" symbolize the 30 years of the hidden life of Christ, and they promise to lead a person to perfection like the "narrow gate" which a believer should pass(cf. *Mt* 7:13–14). The thirty stairs are: renunciation of secular life, detachment of affections, leaving back home and possessions, strict obedience, contrition and penitence, meditation of death, voluntary acceptance of sorrows that turn into joy in Christian hope, mildness and meekness, reconciliation and forgiving, control of one's words, taciturn acceptance of all things, avoidance of lies and of idleness, moderation and temperance, chastity, continence and self-control, generosity, poverty, inner mortification, prayer at night and vigilance, courage, renunciation of all conceit, vanity and pride, humility, innocence and purity, contrition and self-accusation, examination of conscience, inner peace (hēsychia), prayerful contemplation, unity with God, joy of unlimited perfection, the spiritual resurrection in this life, and the realization of comprehensive love as final step in the way of perfection.

These 30 steps are sometimes ordered in pairs of two and show the basic process and structure of Christian spirituality: detachment (apatheia) from the world, purification of the soul, inner peace (hēsychia) and unity with God. The author uses many quotations from the Bible and from the "desert fathers"(famous Egyptian hermits). Historical examples and moral insights from personal experience visualize his moral and religious exhortations. For the first time the author mentions the Jesus-prayer(the continual repetition of the name "Jesus")in connection with breathing techniques and so already points to the Hesychasm of Gregorios Palamas(1296—1359 AD).

# 马克西摩斯（580—662 AD）

他可能是一个 Samaria 人的儿子，生于巴勒斯坦地区，10 岁丧父，进入一所隐修院，在那里开始阅读 Ōrigenēs 的书，于 614 年来到 Constantinopolis 附近的 Chrysopolis 隐修院，又于 624 年到小亚细亚的 Kyzikos 隐修院，但因波斯人的入侵迁到北 Africa（阿富利加），于 645 年和 monotheletist（基督一志论者）Pyrrhos 进行了对话（记录被保存），于 646 年到罗马，参与 649 年的 Lateran 主教会议，在那里又反对 monotheletismus（基督一志论）的异端。因为东方皇帝认为 Maximos 的主张阻碍他的"协调政策"，Maximos 于 655 年被要求去 Constantinopolis 受审，此后被流放到 Thracia 的 Byzia，因为他拒绝在"合一文献"（Typos）上签名。662 年他再次被押送到首都，并因为坚持正统信仰而受折磨，不久死去。第 3 届 Constantinopolis 主教会议（680 年）肯定了他的教导的正确性并给他 Homologētēs（"宣认者"）的尊称。他是 7 世纪最渊博的神学家，著作等身，他也被称为"最后的希腊教父"。

**著作**：《疑问之书》、《论博爱 400 首》（=《警句集》）、《与 Pyrrhos 的辩论》、《信集》、《第 59 圣咏的解释》、《克修书》、《引入神秘》、《小作品集》、《主导文的诠解》、《向 Thalassius 解释的问题》、《向 Theopemptus 解释的问题》、《问题和疑问》、《Areopagita 文集的注解》（共有 90 部著作）

## 098. 《警句集》

本文集亦称 *Capitum de caritate quattuor centuriae*（《论博爱 400 首》），约于 626 年成书并包含其他教父著作的一些名言，尤其重视隐修者 Evagrios Pontikos（345—399 年）的著作。

Maximos 的文集专门谈论"爱神"和"爱近人"的问题。他以某种顺序排列了种种格言和警句。这部著作写给隐修者；作者要求人们活出完善的基督徒的博爱、无私的仁慈和对一切人的善意。"能平等地关爱一切人的人是有福的。能想到一切事物并始终因神的美丽而感到喜乐的心灵是有福的。"该著作曾被译成很多语言，在后来的几个世纪中是一部相当流行的著作。

在某一章中 Maximos 写道："博爱是心灵的神圣态度，就是不让任何东西超过对于神的爱。如果一个人的心受世俗事物的束缚，那么他就无法达到这种博爱。谁爱慕上主，谁就会恒心地追求这种神圣的知识，并且要珍惜关于神的知识，超过神所创造的一切事物。……能平等地关爱一切人的人是有福的。无论谁爱慕神，他肯定也会关爱邻人。这种人不会积累钱财，而会以神圣的慷慨去花钱，他会很自由地施舍给穷人。通过施舍效法神的人并不会区分好人和坏人，不会有差异地对待正义的人和不正直的人，而会根据每人的物质需要给予他。爱的表现不仅仅是施舍或给钱，而更多是传

# Maximos Homologētēs / Maximus Confessor

**Opera:** *Ambiguorum liber, Capitum de caritate quattuor centuriae (=Capita, Kephalaia), Disputatio cum Pyrrho, Epistolae, Expositio in Psalmum LIX, Liber asceticus, Mystagogia, Opuscula, Orationis dominicae expositio, Quaestiones ad Thalassium, Quaestiones ad Theopemptum, Quaestiones et dubia, Scholia in corpus Areopagiticum*

**Works:** Book of Ambiguities, Four-hundred Chapters on Charity (=Sentences, =Centuries on Charity), Disputation with Pyrrhos, Letters, Exposition of Psalm 59, Ascetic Exhortations, Mystagogy, Minor Works, Explanation of the Lord's Prayer, Questions to Thalassius, Questions to Theopemptus, Questions and Doubts, Commentary to the Works of the Areopagite

## 098. *Capita / Kephalaia / Sentences*

This collection is also entitled *Capitum de caritate quattuor centuriae* (*Four-hundred Chapters on Charity*), it was written circa in 626 AD and contains excerpts from the works of the Fathers of the Church, especially from the works of the monk Evagrios Pontikos (345—400 AD).

Maximos concentrates on the theme "love of God" and "love of neighbor". He presents the different proverbs and sentences in a certain order. The booklet was written for monks and demands perfect Christian love, selfless charity and benevolence towards all people. "Blessed is the man who can love all people equally. Blessed is the mind which, passing by all creatures, constantly rejoices in God's beauty." The work was translated into many languages and was very popular in the subsequent centuries.

In one chapter Maximus writes: "Love is a sacred attitude of the mind which does not prefer anything to the knowledge of God. Nobody whose heart is chained to any earthly good can obtain this love. Whoever loves God will constantly strive for this divine knowledge and will value the knowledge of God more than anything created by Him. (···) Blessed is the person who is able to love all men and women in the same way. Whoever loves God will certainly also love the neighbor. Whoever is of this kind cannot amass money and riches, but he will spend it in divine liberality and distributes it freely among the poor. Whoever imitates God by giving alms does not make a difference between good and evil people, between the just and the unjust, but he gives to everyone according to his physical need. Love is not only expressed by giving alms or money but even more by spreading the divine teaching and by serving bodily needs. Whoever gives

播神圣的教导或照顾人们的身体需要。无论谁诚心放弃世俗的财富并诚恳地为别人服务,他即将不再受欲望和罪恶的困扰,而会获得神爱以及关于神的知识。"

为了抵抗"基督一性论"(以及其分支"基督一志论"和"基督一能力论"),Maximos 试图理解自然为一种动态的、而非预定的原则,这样能够确保个人在行动上的自律。自然本性既是理性的又是被创造的,它没有必然性,而是动态的、充满能量的。某人的意志为这个人指导这种自然本性,因此意志并不违背自然的秩序,而引导其运动,因此包含某人在伦理上的责任。比如,我们的视力包含在自然本性内,但每一个人的意志需要决定如何使用这个基本的功能。

### 099. 《引入神秘》

该著作的书名是 *Mystagōgia peri tou tinōn symbola ta kata ten hagian ekklēsian*(《关于神圣教会的某些象征的神秘意志的解释》),即是关于基督徒礼仪的象征性解释,成书于 630 年或 634 年。作者说他的目标是对 Dionysios Areopagita 的 *Peri tēs ekklēsiastikēs hierarchias*(《教阶体系》)提供一些补充性的解释。

Maximos 从一个教堂的建筑结构开始谈起;教堂的楼房一般都有两个部分:长殿和前殿。他解释这两个部分为代表神的象征,又是世界的形象(物质宇宙和精神性的世界),以及代表人生和灵性生活的形象。针对神圣弥撒的礼仪,Maximos 解释"圣道礼仪"(直到宣读福音为止)为基督第一次来临的象征,也是教会到来的象征。他认为,礼仪的第二个部分可以解释为"基督第二次来临",或视之为"已复活的教会"。

up earthly possessions sincerely and serves other people with candour will soon be freed from any desire and sin, and he will attain divine love and knowledge of God."

In order to resist monophysitism (and its outgrowths monotheletism and monoergism) Maximos tries to conceive of nature as a dynamic, not determined principle and thus is able to safeguard the operational autonomy of the person. Nature is both noetic (rational) and created, it has no necessity, but implies movement and energy. The individual will directs nature for a person, it does not violate the order of nature but orientates its movement and therefore entails the ethical responsibility of a person. For example, our capacity to see is inherent in nature, but how we use this basic function depends on the person's will.

## 099. *Mystagōgia / Mystagogy*

The full title of this treatise is *Mystagōgia peri tou tinōn symbola ta kata tēn hagian ekklēsian* (*Mystagogy concerning some Symbols of the Holy Church*). This symbolic explanation of the Christian liturgy was written ca. 630 or 634 AD. The author states that his aim is to present some complementary observations to Dionysius Areopagita's *Peri tēs ekklēsiastikēs hierarchias* (*On the Hierarchy of the Church*).

Maximos starts from the architectural structure of a church building which usually consists of the nave and the choir. He interprets these two parts as the image of God, as symbol of the world (material and spiritual cosmos), and as an image of human existence and the life of the soul. As to the liturgy of the Holy Mass, Maximos interprets the liturgy of the word (until the reading of the gospel) as symbolic of the first coming of Christ and the advent of the Church community. He explains the second part of the liturgy as pointing to the second coming of Christ and as the resurrected Church.

# 附 录
Appendix

- *The Last Super*

# 无名作者

## 100. 《十二使徒/宗徒遗训》

该著作全名为 *Didachē tōn dōdeka apostolōn*(《十二使徒/宗徒遗训》),拉丁语书名是 *Doctrina apostolorum*。它是第一部包含某种形式的"教会制度"的著作,大约成书于公元 100 年(部分学者认为成书时间应该是 150 年或 180 年)。它可能是在叙利亚或巴勒斯坦写的(大概不在埃及)。在研究早期教会史方面,本文献提供了非常关键的资料。

前面几章(第 1 到 6 章)包含"两条路"的基督宗教式的描述:与"死亡之路"和"罪恶之路"对应的是"生命之路"和"真理之道"。文献几次引用《圣经·福音书》的一些章节。这个部分基本上是一种道德上的劝勉,也许在古代教会中是一种给那些还没有领洗的慕道者的教育资料。

第 7 到 10 章涉及圣洗(洗礼)和基督徒的生活,其中描述施洗用的圣水和洗礼中宣读的经文。在受洗之前,那些慕道者应该守一定时间的斋期(第 7 章)。基督徒们也要遵守某些守斋规定(每周有一个或一些守斋日),并且每天要念某些祈祷经文,其中包括"天主经/主祷文"(第 8 章)。第 9、10 章提供一些"感恩"经文(eucharistia),但这些经文是属于仁爱大餐(agapē)的祝福还是属于正式的感恩祭礼仪(弥撒)是一个有争议的问题。这种礼仪部分与当时的犹太礼仪形式也有某些相似之处。

第 11、12 和 13 章论述一些巡回式的老师、宗徒/使徒和先知。如果那些老师和先知们来到一个基督徒团体并想在那里居住一段时间,他们就享有被接待的权利。关于一个地方团体给予这些老师们什么样的照顾有很多具体规定。第 14 章包含一些关于忏悔自己的罪及和好过程的规律。第 15 章描述选择主教(episkopoi)和执事(diakonoi)的程序。这些教士们属于一个固定的地方并拥有某些义务和权利。其中一个任务是他们需要辨别什么人有纯正的神恩,什么人的精神是不能被接受的。一些章节谈论教会内的批评和对某弟兄的劝告或纠正(所谓的 correctio fraterna)。第 16 章包含一些指向未来和"最后的事"(即基督第二次来临、复活、审判)的劝勉。

## 101. 《谈论自然者》

这本小册子的希腊语版本包含 48 个主要与动物有关的小故事,大约在 150—170 年间写成于埃及的 Alexandreia。第一个引用它的作者是 Iustinos。它被译成很多东方语言,也有拉丁语译本,它是《圣经》以外被最广泛阅读的著作之一。

# Anonymus

## 100. *Didachē / Teaching of the Twelve Apostles*

The full title of this work in 16 chapters is *Didachē tōn dōdeka apostolōn* (*Teaching of the Twelve Apostles*), but it is also known as (Latin) Doctrina apostolorum. It is the first book containing an ecclesiastical constitution and was probably written around the year 100 (some have dated it to 150 or 180)in Syria or Palestine (rather than in Egypt). The unique text is very important for the study of early Church history.

The first chapters (1 to 6)contain a Christian version of the "two-ways" motif: the way of death and sin is compared to the way of life and truth. There are some quotations from the gospels. This part is basically an exhortation to a moral life and might have served as pre-baptismal teaching material in the early Church.

Chapters 7 to 10 are about baptism and Christian life. The baptismal water and the baptismal formula used at the baptism ceremony are described. Before receiving baptism the catechumens should keep a certain period of fasting (ch. 7). Christians should observe certain fasting regulations (some days of fasting every week)and they should say certain prayers every day, one of these prayers is the "Our Father" (chapter 8). Chapters 9 and 10 present several "thanksgiving" (eucharistia)prayers, but it is debatable whether the prayers were said as blessing at charity meals (agapē)or at formal liturgical eucharistic celebrations (Holy Mass). This liturgical part also shows similarities to contemporary Jewish celebrations.

Chapters 11, 12, and 13 tell about itinerant teachers, apostles and prophets. Teachers and prophets who come to a Christian community and plan to stay there enjoy the right of accommodation. There are detailed regulations as to how a local community should care for these teachers. Chapter 14 contains certain regulations concerning the confession of sins and the procedure of reconciliation. Chapter 15 presents the order according to which bishops (episkopoi)and deacons (diakonoi)should be chosen. These church ministers belong to a fixed place and have certain duties and rights. One of their tasks is to distinguish between genuine charisms and inacceptable spirits. Some passages are concerned with criticism and correction within the Christian community (the so-called correctio fraterna). Chapter 16 contains some exhortations pointing to the future and the "last things" (the coming of Christ, resurrection, judgment).

## 101. *Physiologos / Physiologus*

The Greek version of this small booklet contains 48 stories mainly about animals and was probably written in Egypt (Alexandria)between 150 and 170 AD. Justin the Martyr was the first author to quote from it. It was translated into many oriental languages and

大部分故事涉及真实的动物、植物和石头,但也有一些虚构的动物(如凤凰,独角兽)。不同动物的行为为基督徒提供一个值得学习的榜样,而每一个动物都有一种象征性意义。作者愿意对动物的世界作出一个完全宗教化的解释,又多次引用《圣经》的语句。大自然的有形世界指向信仰的无形世界。比如,《诗篇/圣咏》*Ps* 103:5 中说"你的力量被恢复,与鹰一样",而"论自然者关于老鹰说"当一只鹰感觉到自己衰弱时,它的眼力和双翼的力量衰退,所以鹰去找一个有清水的泉源,三次浸入水里,这样便再次变得很年青。那个仍然以"旧人"的样子生活的人也应该找活水的泉源(基督)并恢复他的精神生活,这样恢复自己的青春和力量(第6章)。

有一些关于其他飞鸟的故事:凤凰每 500 年一次从印度飞到黎巴嫩,在那里搜集一些香料,又飞到埃及的 Heliopolis(太阳城),在那里烧毁自己,第三天再一次起来,就像救世主(基督),它也带来了美好的"香味"(话语,圣言),它有权力自己杀死自己或复活自己(第7章)。鹈鹕代表自我牺牲,因为母鹈鹕打开自己的肋膀,流出来的血能够恢复小鹈鹕们的生命(第4章)。鸽子只有一个丈夫,它经常单独一个生活,远离群众,与耶稣一样,因为他也经常一个人独处。如果一只鸽子的雏鸟被夺走,它不抵抗,只好离开那个地方,在别处做一个新的巢,努力成立一个新的家庭(第28章)。鹤很聪明,它只有一个巢,不在陌生的地方找食物,也不吃腐尸的肉。基督徒也应该照样仅仅睡在一个床上,只有一个家乡(即神圣教会),不寻找那些"死亡的教导"(异端,第47章)。

基督徒甚至可以从蛇那里学到一些东西("蛇"=ophis 被解释为 ho phēs"那个说话的",即向 Eva 说话的,见第 11 章)。当一条蛇感觉到衰老或疲倦时,它守斋 40 天,找一个有狭窄缝隙的岩石,在那里蜕皮(=通过守斋恢复精力)。当一条毒蛇要去水泉喝水时,它把毒素留在家里;基督徒照样应该在去礼拜时将自己的恶习和怀恨留在家里。如果一条蛇受攻击,它准备放弃它的整个身体,仅仅保护自己的头。在受试探时,一个基督徒也同样得准备牺牲整个身体(殉道),但必须保存头(信仰)。鹿与大蛇(drakōn)的搏斗代表基督徒与恶和罪的搏斗(第 30 章)。

## 102. 《爱笑者》

这部"笑话集"在 4 世纪成书,共包含 265 个笑话。部分的笑话讽刺 Abdera 城、Sidon 城和 Kyme 城的居民,另一些笑话嘲笑某些职业或某些性格,比如医生、算命先生、阉人、吝啬的人、自夸者或懦夫。大约一半的故事描述所谓的 scholastikos(书呆子),他仅仅掌握书本上的知识但在实际的生活中表现很笨拙。这里有几个例子:一个书呆子告诉医生:"当我早上起来时,我每次发昏半个小时,此后就感到没事。"医生回答:"你就晚半个小时起床吧。"(第 3)一个书呆子陷入贫困并开始卖掉自己的书。他向父亲写信说:"父亲,你应该感到高兴,因为我的书已经为我赚得了一些钱。"

into Latin, and it became one of the most popular books of antiquity after the Bible.

Most stories in the book are about real animals, plants or stones, but fantastic animals (such as the phoenix and the unicorn) also appear. The behavior of animals should give a good example for the Christian, and each animal has a certain symbolic value. Many quotations from the Bible show that a thoroughly Christian interpretation of the animal world is intended. The visible world of nature is understood to express the invisible reality of faith. For example, *Psalm* 103:5 says "your youth is renewed like the eagle's", and "the Physiologus says about the eagle …" that when an eagle gets old, his eyesight and the strength of his wings decrease, the eagle looks for a source of clean water, dives into it three times and becomes young again. A person living in the ways of "the old man" should in a similar way look for the living water) of Christ) and renew his spiritual life, thereby regaining youth and strength.(chapter 6).

Stories about other birds are these: The phoenix arrives every 500 years from India in Lebanon, where it collects fragrant odors, goes to Heliopolis (Egypt), burns itself on a pyre but rises on the third day, like the Savior (Christ) who brought fragrant odor (good words) in his wings and who has the power to kill Himself and raise Himself (ch. 7). The pelican is a symbol of self-sacrifice, since the pelican mother opens her side and the blood flowing from her heart brings the dead pelican chicks back to life (ch. 4). The dove only has one husband, it is often alone and flees the crowds, like Jesus who looked for solitude. If a dove is bereaved of her children, she does not protest but leaves the place, makes a new nest and tries to produce new eggs (ch. 28). The crane is very smart, it only has one nest, does not look for food in strange places and does not eat carrion. A Christian should learn from it to sleep only in one bed, have one home (the holy Church) and show no interest for heresies (dead doctrines) (ch. 47).

A Christian can even learn from the snake (ophis = interpreted as "ho phēs", the one "who spoke" to Eve, see chapter 11). When a snake feels old and weak, it fasts for 40 days, then looks for a rock with a narrow opening and there molts (=rejuvenation through fasting). When a poisonous snake comes to the fountain to drink it leaves the poison at home, and when Christians go to a common service they should also leave malice (ta kakia) at home. When a snake is attacked it protects its head but is ready to sacrifice its whole body. Therefore in times of temptation a Christian should be ready to give up the whole body (martyrdom), but keep the head (faith). The fight of the deer against a snake (drakōn, dragon) symbolizes the fight of Christians against evil and sin (ch. 30).

## 102. *Philogelōs / Philogelus*

This collection of 265 jokes was compiled in the 4th century AD. Some of the jokes make fun of the inhabitants of Abdera, Sidon and Kyme, others ridicule certain character types or representatives of various professions, like doctors, astrologers, eunuchs, misers, boastful people or cowards. About half of the funny stories depict the "scholastikos", a bookworm whose theoretical learning seems to impair his practical intelligence. Here are some examples: A bookworm tells the doctor: "Whenever I get up in the morning, I am always dizzy for half an hour, and only then I feel better." The doctor responds: "Then get up half an hour later." (nr. 3) A bookworm needs money and sells his books. In a let-

（第55）一个书呆子航海时经历可怕的暴风。其他的乘客扔掉自己的行李，这样希望能减轻船只的负担。书呆子拿出一张值150万的支票（cheirographon），拿笔勾销50万并说："你看我放弃了多少东西来帮助我们的船。"（第80）有一天，一个书呆子购买一只乌鸦。当人们问他为什么这样做，他就回答："我听说这个动物经常活到200岁；我要研究这个说法是不是真的。"（第255）

### 103. 《艾格瑞亚的游记》

关于这位在4世纪末写下这部宝贵游记（亦称 *Peregrinatio Aetheriae*《艾格瑞亚朝圣记》）的妇女，我们几乎一无所知。她的名字在不同的文献中写成 Egeria、Eucheria 或 Aetheria。她写书时面向一批妇女读者，将她们称为 sorores（姐妹们），但这并不意味着她和那些妇女都是"修女"。她可能来自西班牙或法国（高卢）南部地区，并于381到384年间去以色列朝圣。

第1到23章描述到圣地（以色列）的旅途，Egeria 先到 Constantinopolis，然后到了耶路撒冷。她从耶城出发去埃及（Alexandria 和 Thebais 地区），去看看 Sinai 山和 Goshen 地区，又到 Jordan（约旦）河的东部地区和叙利亚。在回去时，她经过 Antiochia 城，又到了美索不达米亚，经过 Tarsos 回到 Constantinopolis。第24~49章是关于她在耶路撒冷体验到的礼仪形式的记录。这个部分是描述4世纪东方礼仪的最重要历史资料之一。

ter he writes to his father: "Father, rejoice with me, my books already earn a living for me." (nr. 55) A bookworm takes a ship and is caught in a terrible storm. As the other passengers throw their luggage overboard in order to alleviate the ship, the bookworm takes out a check (cheirographon) for 150 myriads (one myriad equals ten thousand). He crosses out 50 myriads and says: "See, how many things I gave up to relieve the ship." (nr. 80) One day a bookworm buys a raven. Asked for the reason, he answers: "I have heard that this animal frequently lives over 200 years, and now I want to see whether that is true." (nr. 255)

## 103. *Itinerarium Egeriae / Itinerary of Egeria*

Almost nothing is known about the woman who wrote this precious itinerary (also known as *Peregrinatio Aetheriae*) at the end of the 4th century. Her name is variously given as Egeria, Eucheria or Aetheria. She addresses a group of women whom she calls "sorores", but this does not necessarily mean that she and these women were nuns. She was probably from Spain or from southern France and undertook a pilgrimage to Israel in the years from 381 to 384 AD.

Chapters 1~23 describe the journey to the Holy Land, which led Egeria first to Constantinople, then to Jerusalem. From Jerusalem she traveled to Egypt (Alexandria and Thebais), visited Mt. Sinai and Goshen, and made journeys to the area east of the Jordan and to Syria. On the way back she passed by Antioch, journeyed to Mesopotamia, and returned to Constantinopolis via Tarsus. Chapters 24~49 report about the liturgical celebrations which she experienced in Jerusalem. This part is one of the most important documents concerning oriental liturgy in the 4th century.

# 拉丁语—希腊语—英语—汉语索引
## Latin–Greek–English–Chinese Index

拉丁语=L、希腊语=Gr、英语=E。拉丁语和英语的写法多数是一样的。
外文中的 ē 和 ō 指希腊语的长 ē 和长 ō。
根源符号"<"表示某词的来源。"？"表示不确定的解释。"=>"意为"请查阅……"

Latin = L, Greek = Gr, English = E. Sometimes the spelling of
the Latin and English version of a name is the same.
ē and ō denote the Greek letters Eta (long e) and Omega (long o).
The symbol "<" signifies the origin of a word or name."？" signifies doubtful or uncertain
explainations."=>" means "Please check..."

**作者缩写表：**

Aesch. = Aeschylus 埃斯库罗斯
Ambros. = Ambrosius 安博罗修斯
Apoll. = Apollonius 阿波罗尼俄斯
Ar. = Aristophanes 阿里斯托芬
Arist. = Aristoteles 亚里士多德
Arrian. = Arrianus 阿里安
Athanas. = Athanasius 亚大纳西
Aug. = Augustinus 奥古斯丁
Basil. = Basilius 巴西略
Bened. = Benedictus 本笃
Bibl. = Biblia 圣经
Boeth. = Boethius 波伊提乌
Caes. = Caesar 恺撒
Cass. = Cassiodorus 卡西奥多鲁斯
Chrysostom. = Chrysostomus 克里索斯托谟
Cic. = Cicero 西塞罗
Clem. = Clemens 克雷芒
Diog. Laert. = Diogenes Laertius 第欧根尼·拉尔修
Dion. Ar. = Dionysius Areopagites 狄奥尼修斯
Epict. = Epictetus 埃比克泰德
Eur. = Euripides 欧里庇得斯
Euseb. = Eusebius 优西比乌斯
Greg. = Gregorius 格列高利
Hdt. = Herodotus 希罗多德
Hes. = Hesiodus 赫西奥德
Hier. = Hieronymus 哲罗姆
Hom. = Homerus 荷马
Hor. = Horatius 贺拉斯
Ioh. Clim. = Johannes Climacus 梯子约翰
Ios. Flav. = Josephus Flavius 约瑟夫斯
Iren. = Irenaeus 依勒内
Isidor. = Isidorus 伊西多尔
Iuv. = Juvenalis 朱文纳尔

Lact. = Lactantius 拉克坦提乌斯
Liv. = Livius 李维
Lucr. = Lucretius 卢克莱修
Macrob. = Macrobius 马克罗比乌斯
Marc. Aurel. = Marcus Aurelius 马可·奥勒留
Maxim. Conf. = Maximus Confessor 马克西摩斯
Orig. = Origenes 奥利金
Ov. = Ovidius 奥维德
Paus. = Pausanias 保萨尼阿斯
Plat. = Plato 柏拉图
Plaut. = Plautus 普劳图斯
Plin. = Plinius 普林尼
Plot. = Plotinus 普罗提诺
Plut. = Plutarchus 普卢塔克
Polyb. = Polybius 波利比奥斯
Prud. = Prudentius 普鲁登蒂乌斯
Publ. Syr. = Publilius Syrus 普珀里琉斯
Quint. = Quintilianus 昆体良
Sall. = Sallustius 萨卢斯特
Sen. = Seneca 塞涅卡
Sext. Emp. = Sextus Empiricus 塞克斯都·恩披里柯
Soph. = Sophocles 索福克勒斯
Stat. = Statius 斯塔提乌斯
Suet. = Suetonius 苏埃托尼乌斯
Sulp. = Sulpicius Severus 塞维鲁斯
Tac. = Tacitus 塔西佗
Ter. = Terentius 泰伦斯
Tert. = Tertullianus 德尔图良
Theophr. = Theophrastus 泰奥弗拉斯托斯
Thuc. = Thucydides 修昔底德
Verg. = Vergilius 维吉尔
Vitr. = Vitruvius 维特鲁威
Xen. = Xenophon 色诺芬

# A

*Ab urbe condita,* E: *History of Rome from its Foundation,* a work by Livy《罗马通史》, 见 Livius, Aug. *De civ. Dei*（Romulus）

**abbreviatio,** E: abbreviation, 缩写, 见 Cassiod. *Inst.* （AAA）

**Abraham,** Gr: Abraam, one of the Jewish patriarchs, symbol of faith 亚伯拉罕、亚巴郎, 见 Biblia, *Gen* 12 (the "man of faith"), *Ioann.* 8 (Jesus is older than Abraham), Philo, *De opificio*; Ambros. *De off. ministr.*

**abstinentia,** Gr: askēsis, E: abstinence, ascetic life style; => ascesis, certamen, virtus 克己, 刻苦, 见 Clem. Alex. *Paedag.*

**Academia,** Gr: Akadēmia, Akadēmeia, Akadēmos, "of a silent district", E: Academy, (from a shrine in groves sacred to the hero Akademos near Athens), the place where Plato established his school (the Academy) in 387 BC; Plato and his successors directed the school until 529 AD, when emperor Justinian closed it; Cosimo de' Medici founded a new Platonic Academy in Florence in 1459 which existed until 1521 and hosted many Byzantine scholars who fled from the Turks to Italy 学园、学院、柏拉图学派, 见 Cic. *De fin.* 4, Lact. *Inst.* 3, Aug. *De beata vita* (the shortcomings of the school)

*Academica,* E: *Academics,* a work by Cicero《学院派哲学》, 见 Cic.

**accidens,** accidentia, Gr: to symbebēkon, to tychon, tychē, to automaton, symphora, ta kairia, E: accidental, accidentals 偶有属性, 见 Arist. *Org.*

**accusatio,** Gr: diōgma, E: accusation (against Christians), => persecutio 控告, 见 Plat. *Apol.,* Tert. *Apol.,* Minucius, *Oct.,* Aug. *De civ. Dei*

**acedia,** Gr: akēdia, E: sloth, laziness, neglect 懈怠、怠惰, 见 Cass. *De inst.,* Greg. Magn., *Moralia* (one of the seven cardinal sins)

**Acestes,** Gr: Aigestēs, "pleasing he-goat", founder of the city of Egesta (Segesta) in Sicily 阿塞斯特斯, 见 Verg. *Aen.* 5

**Achaea,** Gr: Achaia, E: Achaea, a region at the north coast of the Peloponnesus 阿克亚, 见 Achivi

*Acharniae,* Gr: *Acharniai,* E: *Acharnians,* comedy by Aristophanes《阿卡奈人》, 见 Ar.

**Achilleis,** E: *Achilleid,* a work by Statius《阿喀琉斯纪》, 见 Stat.

**Achilleus,** Gr: Achilleus, "Greek man", "sufferer", "lipless" (?), E: Achilles, son of Peleus and Thetis, main hero at Troy 阿克流斯、阿喀琉斯、阿基琉斯, 见 Hom. *Il.* 1~24, *Od.* 11; Plat. *Apol.,* Eur. *Iph. Aul.,* Ov. *Her.,* Statius *Achill., Peri hypsous*

**Achivi,** Gr: Achaioi, E: Achaeans, name of the people of Thracia or the northern part of the Peloponnesus, also a term denoting all Greeks (in Homer's works) 阿海亚人, 见 Graeci

**Acontius,** Gr: Akontios, "javelin-thrower", the lover of Cydippe, who wrote on an apple "I swear to Artemis to marry none but Acontius" and threw the apple to her; upon reading the inscription aloud Cydippe was bound to keep the oath, and Acontius won her. 阿孔提乌斯, 见 Ov. *Her.*

**Acragas** => Agrigentum

**acroama,** Gr: akroama, E: lectures for an audience 宣读的文献, 见 Arist. *Poiet.*

**Acropolis,** Gr: Akropolis, "upper town", citadel of a Greek town, especially the Acropolis of Athens, which was first built in 3000 BC, temples were built in the 6th ct. BC, but the whole area was destroyed by the Persians in 480 BC; Pericles rebuilt the Acropolis; the Parthenon was erected 448—432 BC; other sanctuaries are the tomb of Cecrops, altars of Poseidon and Erechtheus etc. 城堡、堡垒, 见 Aesch. *Eumen.,* Ar. *Lysistrate*

*acta diurna urbis,* E: *Daily Events of Rome,* a newspaper published daily since 59 BC, also distributed to the provinces《罗马日报》, 见 Tac., *Ann.*

**actio,** Gr: hypokrisis, E: performance (of a speech), => rhetorica 演出, 见 Cic. *Brutus*

**Actium,** Gr: Aktion, E: Actium, promontory at the west coast of Greece, where Octavian defeated the fleet of Antony and Cleopatra in 31 BC, marking the beginning of the Roman empire 阿克提翁, 见 Augustus

**actus,** actio, Gr: praxis, poiēma, ergon, E: action, praxis 行动、实践, 见 Arist. *Eth. Nik.,* Cic. *Cato de sen.,* Boethius, *De cons.* 1, (theory and praxis)

*Ad Pammachium* => Hieronymus, *Epist.* 57

**Adam,** Adamus, Gr: Adam, < Hebr. adamah, "earth", E: Adam, the first man, symbol of (fallen) mankind 亚当, 见 Bibl. *Gen,* Iren. *Adv. haer.,* Aug. *De civ. Dei* 13, 14（Adam's sin）

**Adelphoe,** Gr: *Adelphoi*, E: *Brothers*, play by Terence 《两弟兄》, 见 Terentius

**Admetus,** Gr: Admētos, "untamed", E: Admete, Admetus, son of Pheres and king of Pherae in Thessaly 阿德梅托斯, 见 Eur. *Alk.*, Apoll. *Arg.*

**administratio,** Gr: oikonomia, diokēsis, diacheirisis, E: administration 管理, 见 Xen. *Oik.*, Cic. *De off.* 1,92, Ambros. *De off. ministr.*, Greg. Magnus (administration talent)

**Adonis,** Gr: Adōnis, <Hebr adon "Lord", a beautiful youth, loved by Aphrodite, killed by a wild boar; his cult was probably oriental in origin 阿多尼斯, 见 Aphrodite

**adoratio,** Gr: proskynēsis, sebas, theosebeia, E: adoration, => idololatria 朝拜, 敬拜, 见 Bibl. *Jn* 4, Greg. Nys. *Peri parthen.*, Aug. *De civ. Dei* 10 (theosebeia = adoratio), Venantius, *Carmina* (adoration of the Cross of Christ)

**adulatio,** E: adulation, flattery 诌媚, 见 Ov. *Ars am.*, Martial (attitude to Domitian)

**adulterium,** Gr: moicheia, E: adultery 私通, 见 Aisch. *Orest.* (Clytemnestra), Eur. *Hippol.*, *Medea*, Plaut. *Amphitruo*, Aug. *Confess.* 1, *De civ. Dei* 2 (Jupiter the adulterer)

**Adversus haereses,** Gr: *Elenchos kai anatropē tēs pseudonymou gnōseōs*, E: *Against Heresies*, work by Irenaeus 《驳斥异端》, 见 Irenaeus

**agon** => certamen

**Aeaea,** Gr: Aiaiē, the island of Circe 埃埃亚, 见 Hom. *Od.* 10

**aedilis,** Roman magistrate in charge of public buildings; => cursus honorum 建筑官, 见 Cic. *De off.* 2,59

**Aeetes,** Gr: Aiētēs, "mighty", "eagle", king of Colchis, father of Medea 阿厄特斯, 见 Apoll. *Arg.*

**Aegeum mare,** Gr: Aigaios pontos, < aigos "storm", or < Aegeus, E: Aegean Sea, the sea between Greece and Asia Minor 爱琴海, 见 Hdt. *Hist.* 5, Ov. *Met.* 8

**Aegeus,** Gr: Aigeus, "goatish", King of Athens and father of Theseus 埃格乌斯, 见 Eur. *Med.*, Ov. *Met.* 8

**Aegisthus,** Gr: Aigisthos, "goat strength", E: Aegisthus, son of Thyestes, lover of Clytemnestra who helped her to kill Agamemnon, then became king of Mycene for seven years before he was killed by Orestes 埃格斯托斯, 见 Aesch. *Choephor.*, Soph. *Elektra*

**aegritudo,** Gr: lypē, E: sorrow, ailment, => dolor, medicina, morbus 痛苦, 疾病, 见 Cic. *De fin.* 3,35; Apuleius, *Met.* (sufferings of Psyche)

**Aegyptus,** Gr: Aigyptos, "he-goat" (?), E: Egypt, mythical king of Egypt, the land of Egypt; Egypt was under Persian rule (525—332 BC), then under the Greeks, from 30 BC until 640 AD it was a province of the Roman Empire, then conquered by the Arabs; => Alexandria 埃及, 见 Hom. *Od.* 4; Hdt. 2 (description of Egytian culture and customs), Philo Alexandrinus, Bibl. *Gen* 37~50 (story of Joseph), *Ex*, Arrian 3 (invasion of Egypt 332 BC), Clemens Alexandrinus, Origenes, Euseb. *Hist. Eccl.*, Athanas. *Vita Antonii*

**Aeneas,** Aeneus, Gr: Aineias, "praiseworthy", "terrified" (?), one of the legendary Trojan leaders, son of Anchises and Aphrodite/ Venus, father of Ascanius / Julus; he fled from Troy ca. in 1200 BC and became the ancestor of Romulus and of the Romans; especially through Vergil he was seen as a national hero, embodying Roman piety and dutifulness 埃涅阿斯, 见 Hom. *Il.* 5, 20, Verg. *Aen.*, Hor. *Carm. saec.*, Ov. *Her.*

**Aeneis,** E: *Aeneid*, epos by Vergilius 《埃涅亚特》, 见 Verg.

**Aeolis,** Gr: Aiolis, the territory in the northern part of the west coast of Asia Minor, including the islands of Lesbos and Tenedos; also the inhabitants of Thessaly were called Aeolians 埃俄里斯, 见 Aeolus

**Aeolus,** Gr: Aiolos, "earth destroyer" (?), 1) Greek god of the winds; 2) son of Hellen and legendary ancestor of the Aeolians, father of Sisyphus, Athamas etc. 埃俄洛斯, 见 Hom. *Od.* 10, Verg. *Aen.* 1

**Aequi,** an Italian tribe; they attacked Rome in 458 BC 厄奎, 见 Liv. 3

**aequus,** aequabilitas, Gr: isotēs, homoiotēs, homalotēs, E: balance, fairness, calmness 平衡, 见 Cic. *De re publ.* (balanced mixture of constitutions), Hor. *Carm.* 2,3 (aequam mentem), Sen. *Epist mor.* 4 (aequo animo vitam reliquere)

**Aeschines,** Gr: Aischinēs, E: Aeschines, 389—314 BC, Athenian orator who supported Macedonia and was thus attacked by Demosthenes; only 3 of his speeches are extant 埃斯克内斯, 见 rhetorica

**Aeschylus,** Gr: Aischylos, "sufferer", Greek tragedian, 525—456 BC; seven of his 79 (or 90) tragedies are extant 埃斯库罗斯，见 Aesch., Quint. *Inst.* 10

**Aesculapius,** Gr: Asklēpios, from askelēs ēpios "always merciful", E: Asclepius, Greek god of healing, son of Apollo; his symbol is the staff entwined with a snake; at his sanctuaries emerged schools of physicians, esp. on the island of Cos, in Cnidos, Epidarus, and Pergamum. The cult of Asclepius was introduced to Rome in 293 BC; => medicina 阿斯克勒庇俄斯，见 Soph., Lucian. *Theon dial.*

**Aeson,** Gr: Aesōn, "ruler" (?), father of Jason 阿厄松，见 Apoll. *Arg.*

**Aesopus,** Gr: Aisōpos, "happy eye", E: Aesop, Greek author of a collection of fables, ca. 550—500 BC, according to tradition he was a freed Thracian slave from Samos 伊索，见 Aes. *Myth.*

**aestimabile,** Gr: axios, timios, endoxes, E: valuable, value 有价值的、价值，见 Cic. *De fin.* 3,20, Sen. *De vita beata*

**aetas,** (iuvenis—senex), Gr: aion, hēlikia, (neanias—geron), gēras, presbeia, E: age (youth—old age); => puer, tempus 年龄，见 Arist. *Rhet.*, Cic. *Cato de sen.*, *De off.* 1,122, *Tusc.*, Hor. *Carm. saec.*, *De arte poet.*, Longos (four seasons and personal development), Prud. *Psych.* (four directions are symbols of childhood, youth, maturity, old age), Aug. *Confess.* 1 (childhood, youth), *Physiologus* (renewal of youth like the eagle)

**aetas aurea** = aurea aetas

**aeternitas,** Gr: aei, aiōn, athanasia, E: eternity, => vita aeterna 永恒，见 Thuc. 1 (ktēma eis aei), Plat. *Symp.* (love as to share immortality), Hor. *Carm.* 3,30 (monumentum aere perennius), Philo, *De opificio* (no eternal world), Bibl. *Ioann.* 3 (eternal life), *Peri hypsous* 7 (a great work is pleasing at all times), Orig. *De princ.* (eternity of the world, excluding divine providence), Aug. *De civ. Dei* 12 (the world is not everlasting), Boethius, *De cons.* 5 (definition of eternity)

**Aether,** Gr: Aithēr, "bright sky", E: Aether, the god of the bright atmosphere 光明的苍穹，见 Hes. *Theog.*

**Aethiopia,** Gr: Aithiopia, "burned face", E: Ethiopia 埃塞俄比亚，见 Hdt. *Hist.* 3, Heliodorus, *Aithiopika*

**affectus,** Gr: pathēma, pathos, E: emotion, feelings, affection; => cupiditas, epithymia, pathos 感受，见 Arist. *Rhet.*, Ov. *Her.*, Epict. *Enchir.* (control of passions), Boethius, *De consol.* (emotions need relief)

**Africa,** < a-frigus "not cold", or < apricus "sunny", the area surrounding Carthage, after 146 BC known as "province of Africa"; => Apuleius, Augustinus, Carthago, Cyprianus, Orosius, Tertullianus 阿富利加，见 Polyb., Aen. *Verg.*, Hieron. *Vulgata* (Itala and Afra versions)

**afterlife** => futura vita

**Agamemnon,** Gr: Agamemnōn, "very resolute", E: Agamemnon, King of Mycenae, leader of the Greeks at Troy, killed by his wife Clytaemnestra; son of Atreus, father of Orestes, Iphigenia, Electra 阿伽门农，见 Hom. *Il.* 1, 2, 3, 8, 9, 11, 14; *Od.* 1; Aesch. *Oresteia*, Soph. *Elektra*, Eur. *Iph. Aul.*, Boethius, *De cons.* 4 (symbol of patience)

***Agamemnon,*** Gr: *Agamemnōn*, Greek tragedy by Aeschylus, first part of the *Oresteia* 《阿伽门农》，见 Aesch.

**Agathon,** Gr: Agathōn, "good man", Athenian dramatic poet, ca. 445—401 BC, also a dialogue partner of Socrates 阿伽通，见 Plat. *Symp.*

**Agenor,** Gr: Agēnōr, "very manly", king of Tyre (Phoenicia), father of Cadmus and Europa 阿格诺尔，见 Ov. *Met.* 2

**Agesilaus,** Gr: Agesilaos, "lead the people", ca. 444—360 BC, king of Sparta after 399 BC who tried to resist Athen's influence after the Peloponnesian War; his army was defeated by Epaminondas in 371 and 362 BC 阿格西劳斯，见 Plut. *Bioi*

**Agis,** a legendary Dorian king who subjected the population of Sparta, => Cleomenes 阿格斯，见 Plut. *Bioi*

**Aglaia** => Gratiae

**Agnus Dei,** Gr: amnos tou theou, E: the Lamb of God (Jesus) 上主的羔羊，见 Bibl. *Ioann.* 1:29

**agōn** => certamen

**agora,** agorē, L: forum, market place, place of assembly, assembly; center of public life, surrounded by temples, statues, and public buildings; => forum 集议场，见 Hom. *Il.* 7, *Od.* 8

**agraphos nomos,** unwritten law 不成文法，见 Philo, *De opificio*

**agricultura,** Gr: geōrgia, geōrgikē, E: agriculture; => Demeter / Ceres, planta, rus 农业，见 Hes. *Erga*, Xen. *Oik.*, Cic. *De off.* 1,150; 2,89; Verg. *Georg.* (rural gods, labor improbus), Hor. *Sat.* 2.2

（rusticus）, Plin. *Nat. hist.* 12~19, Claudian. *De raptu Proserp.*, Isidor. *Etym.* 17

**Agrigentum,** Gr: Akragas, E: Acragas, town at the southern coast of Sicily, founded in 580 BC, after Syracuse the richest port of Sicily; the temple of Concord is one of the best preserved temples of antiquity 阿格瑞根特, 见 Sicilia

**Agrippa,** 1) Menenius Agrippa, Roman politician who persuaded the secessionists to return to Rome in 494 BC; 2) Marcus Vipsanius Agrippa, 64—12 BC, general of Augustus, builder of the Pantheon and other public edifices, who also organized the drawing of a map of the world 阿格瑞帕, 见 Liv. 2

**Aiax,** Gr: Aias, "of the earth", E: Ajax, 1) "Great Ajax", son of Telamon, king of Salamis, a great hero before Troy who went mad and killed himself; 2) "Little Ajax", son of Oileus, king of the Locrians, who fought at Troy and died on the way back 埃阿斯, 见 1) Hom. *Ili.* 7, 9, *Od.* 11, 14

**aidos** => L: pudor, E: shame 羞耻感, 见 Hes. *Erga*, 200

**Aigeus** = Aegeus

**Aigisthos** = Aegisthus

**Aineas** = Aeneas

**Aiolos** = Aeolus

**aiōn** => saeculum

**Aischylos** = Aeschylus

**Aisopos** = Aesopus

**aitia** => causa

**Aither** = Aether

**Aithiopia** = Aethiopia

***Aithiopika,*** E:*Ethiopian Stories*, a novel by Heliodorus 《埃塞俄比亚故事》, 见 Heliodorus

**Akropolis** = Acropolis

**Alba Longa,** ancient city in Latium at Mt.Alban, 20 km south-east of Rome, according to tradition founded by Ascanius in 1152 BC; the city was destroyed by Rome in the reign of Tullius Hostilius ca. 600 BC 阿尔巴, 见 Aug. *De civ. Dei* 3 (unjust aggression of Rome)

**Alcaeus,** Gr: Alkaios, "mighty one", E: Alcaeus, Greek lyric poet ca. 600 BC, who influenced Roman poets, especially Catull and Horace 阿尔开俄斯, 见 Hor. *Carmina*

**Alcestis,** Gr: Alkēstis, "might of the home", daughter of Pelias, wife of Admetus 阿尔克斯提斯, 见 Eur. *Alk.*

***Alcestis,*** Gr: *Alkēstis*, tragedy by Euripides 《阿尔克斯提斯》, 见 Eur.

**Alcibiades,** Gr: Alkibiadēs, Athenian politician, 450—404 BC; notorious for his ambition he initiated the disastrous campaign of Athens against Sicily in 415 BC; then he collaborated with Sparta, fled to Persia in 412 BC, was reconciled to the Athenians, led their fleet and defeated Sparta in 411 and 410 BC; exiled in 407 BC he was killed in Phrygia. 阿尔喀比亚德, 见 Plat. *Symp.*, Plut. *Bioi*

**Alcinous,** Gr: Alkinoos, "mighty mind", King of the Phaeacians, known for his wealth and hospitality, husband of Arete, host of Odysseus 阿尔喀诺斯, 见 Hom. *Od.* 6

**Alcumena,** Gr: Alkmēnē, "strong in wrath", "mighty of the moon" (?), E: Alcumena, Alcmena, Alcmene; wife of Amphitruo and mother of Hercules by Jupiter 阿尔克墨纳, 见 Plaut. *Amph.*

**Alecto,** (=Allecto), Gr: Alekto, "unnameable", one of the Furies; => Furiae 阿勒克托

**Alesia,** Celtic town in Gallia Lugdunensis (Alise-Sainte-Reine), where Vercingetorix was forced to surrender in 52 BC 阿雷西亚, 见 Caesar, *De bell. gall.*

**aletheia** => veritas

**Alexander,** Gr: Alexandros, "protector", "defender of men", E: Alexander the Great, 356—323 BC, son of Philip II and Olympias of Epirus, who led a Greek army into Asia in 334 BC, defeated the Persians, occupied Phoenicia, Palestine and Egypt in 332 BC, invaded India in 327 BC but died suddenly at the age of 32. 亚历山大, 见 Plut. *Bioi*, Arrian. *Alexandrou Anabasis*

**Alexandria,** Gr: Alexandreia, city in Egypt founded in 331 BC by Alexander the Great, center of Hellenist learning, industry and commerce, by 200 BC it was the largest city in the world (ca. 600,000 inhabitants, half of them free citizens); Ptolemy I Soter (reigned 323—283 BC) founded the Alexandrian Library, the biggest library of antiquity; the city was conquered by the Romans in 30 BC and fell to the Muslims in 642 AD; after that the city lost its important position 亚历山大里亚, 见 Philo, Arrian. 3, Clement of A., Origenes, Eusebios (bishops of Alex.), Athanasios (bishop of A.), *Vita Antonii*, Nestorios (attacked by Cyril of Alex.), Philoponos

***Alexandrou Anabasis***, E: *Expedition of Alexander*, by Arrian《亚历山大远征记》, 见 Arrianos

**Alkaios** = Alcaeus

**Alkestis** = Alcestis

**Alkibiades** = Alcibiades

**Allecto,** Alecto => Furiae

**allegoria,** Gr: allēgoria, symbolon, E: allegory, symbolic use of the language 比喻、隐喻, 见 Philo, *Legum allegoriae*, Aug. *De civ. Dei* 13 (allegorical understanding of the *Genesis*)

**alphabetum,** Gr: alpha, beta, <Hebr. aeleph = *bull*, beth = *house*; E: the alphabet, arrangement of dictionaries and encyclopedias according to the ABC 字母, 见 Publ. Syr. *Sent.*, Nonius

**Amalthea,** Gr: Amalthiē, "tender", E: Amaltheia, Amalthea, a legendary goat (or nymph) that raised Zeus; from the horn of the goat Zeus made the "horn of plenty" (cornu copiae) which could produce whatever its possessor wished 阿玛尔提亚, 见 Hes. *Theog.*

**Amasis,** Pharaoh of Egypt, 570—526 BC 阿马西斯, 见 Hdt. 2

**Amata,** "beloved", wife of Latinus and mother of Lavinia 阿马塔, 见 Verg. *Aen.* 7, 12

**Amazonae,** Gr: Amazōnes, "moon-women", "breastless" (?), E: Amazons, legendary women warriors under their queen Hippolyta; they only raised girls and had the custom of burning away their right breast in order to enable them to use the bow; in the Trojan War their queen Penthesilea supported Troy but was killed by Achilles 阿玛宗, 见 Apoll. *Arg.*, Ov. *Met.* 8

**ambrosia,** Gr: am-brosios, am-brotos, "immortal", E: ambrosia, the food and drink (nectar) of the gods, associated with immortality 神仙长生不老的食物, 见 Apuleius, *Met.*

**Ambrosius,** Gr: Ambrosios (<a-brotos), "immortal", E: Ambrose, 339—397 AD, bishop of Milan, Father of the Church 安博罗修斯, 见 *De off. ministr.*, *Epist.*, *Hymni*, Aug. *Confess.* 5, Greg. Magn. *Regula past.*

**amicitia,** Gr: philia, philotēs, hetaireia, xenia, E: friendship 友谊, 见 Hom. *Il.* (Achilles and Patroclos), Arist. *Eth. Nik.*, *Rhet.*, Cic. *De fin.* 1, 2, *De off.* 3,44 (amicitia et coniuratio); Sen. *Epist. mor.* 3 (vera amicitia), Plin. *Nat. hist.* 9 (friendship between dolphins and humans)

**amicus** => amicitia

**Ammianus Marcellinus,** ca. 330—395 AD, Roman historian, originally from Antiochia 阿米阿努斯, 见 *Rerum gestarum libri*

**amor,** Gr: erōs, philia, philotēs, storgē, agapē, E: love, tender affection; => eros, Eros (Hom., Hes., Apoll., etc.), => Aphrodite, Venus, dilectio, caritas 爱情, 见 Ter. *Adelph.*, *Heaut. Tim.*, Verg. *Aen.* 1, 4, (conflict of duty and love), *Buc.* 2, 3, 8, 9; Hor. *Carm.* (distance to passion), *Heroides*, Bibl. *Ioann.* 13 (agapate allelous), Apuleius, *Met.*, Longos (love novel), Heliod. *Aithiopika*, Claudian. *De raptu Pros.*, Aug. *De beata vita* (amore philosophiae succensus sum), *De civ. Dei* 14 (amor sui = earthly city, amor Dei = city of God), Venantius, *Carmina* (spiritual wedding)

**Amor,** Gr: Erōs, god of love; => Eros 爱情之神, 见 Verg. *Aen.* 1, Apul. *Met.*, Capella, *De nuptiis* (boy Amor carrying Philologia)

**amor patriae,** Gr: philopatria, E: patriotism, love for the fatherland, => patria 爱国, 见 Cic. *De off.* 1,57, Hor. *Carm.* 3,2 (pro patria mori)

**amore istorum verborum,** out of love for those words 因爱这些话, 见 Cic. *De fin.* 2,51

**Amphipolis,** Gr: Amphipolis, city in northern Greece, ally of Athens in the Peloponnesian War 安菲波里斯, 见 Thuc. 4

**amphitheatrum,** Gr: amphitheatron, E: amphitheater, place of performances, competitions or gladiatorial fights; early buildings were made of wood, in 29 BC the first amphitheater made of stone was constructed in Rome; the most famous is the Colosseum in Rome, which was opened in 80 AD; many amphitheaters have been preserved in Italy, France, Spain, Africa, and Asia Minor; => ludus, spectaculum, theatrum 露天剧场, 见 Sen. *Epist. mor.* 7, Tert. *De spec.*, Perpetua

**Amphitruo,** Gr: Amphitryon, "harassing on both sides", E: Amphitryon, husband of Alcumena 安菲特律翁, 见 Plaut. *Amph.*, Lucian. *Theon dial.*

***Anabasis***, Gr: *Anabasis*, < baino, "going inland", "marching up", work by Xenophon; => Arrianus, *Alexandrou anabasis*《远征记》, 见 Xen.

**Anacreon,** Gr: Anakreiōn, "ruler", E: Anacreon, Greek lyric poet ca. 570—520 BC 阿那克里翁, 见 Hor. *Carm.*

**anamnēsis,** L: recollectio, recordari, E: remembering, the epistemological theory of Plato 回忆, 见 Plat. *Men.*

**ananke** = necessitas

**anastasis** = resurrectio

**Anaxagoras,** Gr: Anaxagoras, "king of the market-place", 500—428 BC the first philosopher to reside in Athens; as he taught that the sun is a burning stone, he was accused of impiety and fled to Lampsakos in 431 BC 阿那克撒格拉斯, 见 Plat. *Phaid.*, Min. Felix, *Octav.*, Diog. Laert.

**Anaximandrus,** Gr: Anaximandros, "leader of men", E: Anaximander, ca. 610—545 BC, Greek philosopher, known for his theory that the apeiron (the Unbounded) is the origin of all things (archē) 阿那克西曼德, 见 Diog. Laert.

**Anchises,** Gr: Anchises, "living with Isis", a great-grandson of Tros and Trojan prince, loved by Aphrodite he fathered Aeneas, but as he boasted of the goddess' favor he was struck blind (or paralysed) by Zeus' thunderbolt; => Isis 安西塞斯, 见 Verg. *Aen.* 2, 5, 6; Longos

**Ancus Marcius,** the fourth king of Rome (640—617 BC), who built Ostia, bridges and aquaeducts 安库斯·马尔基乌斯, 见 Liv. 1

**andreia** => fortitudo, virtus

**Androclus,** Gr: Androkleios, "glory of men", name of a slave 安德若克鲁斯, 见 Gellius 5,14

**Andromache,** Gr: Andromachē, "manly fight", wife of Hector, who was given to Neoptolemus (the son of Achilles) after the fall of Troy and later married Helenus 安提若马赫, 见 Hom. *Il.* 6, 24; Verg. *Aen.* 3

**angelus,** Gr: angelos, "messenger", E: angel, God's messenger (esp. in Christian texts) 天使, 见 Irenaeus, *Adv. haer.*, Orig. *De princ.*, Dionys. Ar., *Peri tes ouran. hier.*, Isidor. *Etym.* 7

**anima,** spiritus, Gr: psychē, nous, thymos, E: soul, spirit 灵魂、精神, 见 Hom. *Od.* 11 (soul of Odysseus' mother), Plat. *Phaid.*, *Polit.*, Cic. *De fin.* 1, 2,114 (divine nature of the soul), *De off.* 1,11 (only man is "particeps rationis"), 1,96 (animals do not have "decus"), Lucr. *De rer. nat.*, Apuleius, *Met.* (Psyche and Amor), Tert. *Apol.* 17 (anima naturaliter Christiana), *De testimonio animae*, Plotin. *Enn.* (psyche, mediating the spiritual and material), Athanas. *Logos*, Greg. Nys. *Peri psyches*, Aug. *De beata vita* (spiritual hunger), *De civ. Dei* 14 (soul and body), Capella, *De nuptiis* (Psyche, a possible partner for Mercury), Macrobius, *Comm.* (Neoplatonist view of the soul)

**animal divinum,** E: divine being, man 神圣的活物, 即人, 见 Cic. *De fin.* 2,40

**animalia,** Gr: zōon, thēr, E: animal; => apes, aquila, asellus, avis, bos, bubo, centaurus, Cerberus, columba, draco, elephas, equus, gallus, leo, lupus, Minotaurus, Pegasus, phoenix, serpens; 动物, 见 Hom. (horse Xanthus), *Od.* (aquila; => Circe), Aesop, Eur. *Iphig.* (a hind sacrificed), Ar. *Ornith.*, Plat. *Phaid.* (reincarnation as wolf, vulture), Arist. *Hai peri ton zoon*, Cic. *De nat. deor.* 2,120~130, Verg. *Georg.* 3 (cows, horses, sheep, goats, animal products, animal diseases), Plin. *Hist. nat.* 8~11 (the elephant is "proximum humanis sensibus"), Plut. *Mor.*, Bibl. *Ioann.* 1 (lamb), 12 (donkey), Arrian 5 (Boukephalas), Lactantius, *Carmen de ave phoenice*, Basil. *Hexaem.* (symbols of moral values), Greg. Nys. *Peri kataskeues* (use of animals), Prud. *Perist.* (dove, symbol of the soul), Aug. *Confess.* 13 (human rule over animals as symbol of the spiritual power of the Church), Boethius, *De cons.* 4 (sin means to sink into bestiality), Isidor. *Etym.* 12, *Physiologus* (Christian interpretation of animals)

**animus,** Gr: nous, thymos, phronēsis, psychē, pneuma, E: spirit, will, mental energy 精神, 见 Lucr. *De rer. nat.*, Sen. *De vita beata* 4,3 (liber animus; concordia animi; bonum animi), *Epist. mor.* 4 (aequo animo vitam relinquere)

**Anna,** < Phoenician / Hebr. Hannah, "grace", E: Ann, 1) Hannah, the mother of Samuel in the Old Testament; 2) Anna, the sister of Dido, who (according to Ovid) left Carthage and came to Italy but had a conflict with Aeneas' wife Lavinia 安娜, 见 Verg. *Aen.* 4, Aug. *De civ. Dei* 17 (Hanna, mother of Samuel, is a model of the Church)

**annales,** E: annals, the first official historical records of the Romans, based on the white tables kept in the office of the priests ("annales maximi", or "tabulae pontificum"); the inscriptions recorded the high names of high magistrates, wars, eclipses and other important events of each year 年度记载

**Annales,** E: *Annals*, a work by Tacitus 《编年史》, 见 Tac.

**Antaeus,** Gr: Antaios, E: Antaeus, a giant, son of Poseidon and Gaia (Earth), who wrestled with

Heracles; the contact with his mother (the Earth) restored his strength, thus Heracles lifted him up and so killed him 安太乌斯，见 Heracles

**Antenor,** Gr: Antēnōr, "instead of a man", Trojan hero 安特诺尔，见 Hom. *Il.* 7

**Antichristus,** Gr: Antichristos, E: the Antichrist (mentioned in the *Book of Revelations*), 敌基督、反基督，见 Aug. *De civ. Dei* 18, 20

**Anticlea,** Gr: Antikleia, "in place of the famous one", "second glory", the wife of Laertes and mother of Odysseus 安提克雷亚，见 Hom. *Od.* 11

**Antigone,** Gr: Antigonē, "excellent by birth", "instead of a mother" (?), daughter of Oedipus, who tried to bury her brother Polynices and was therefore immured by king Creon 安提戈涅，见 Soph. *Ant.*, *Oid. epi Kol.*

*Antigone,* drama by Sophocles《安提戈涅》，见 Soph.

**Antilochus,** Gr: Antilochos, "lying in ambush against", Greek hero at Troy 安提洛赫斯，见 Hom. *Il.* 17

**Antinous,** Gr: Antinoos, "hostile mind", the most arrogant of Penelope's suitors, killed by Odysseus 安提诺斯，见 Hom. *Od.* 22

**Antiochia,** Gr: Antiocheia, the capital of ancient Syria, founded ca. 300 BC, it became an important center of trade and scholarship under Antiochus I the Great (223—187 BC); it was also the place where the name "Christians" appeared first (cf. *Acts* 11: 26) 安条克，见 Ignatius, Euseb. *Ekkl. Hist.* (bishops of Antioch), Ammianus, Philoponus, *De creatione mundi* (theological school of Antioch)

**Antiochus,** Gr: Antiochos, "standing firm against", "driver against", Seleucid King Antiochus III (223—187 BC) who tried to occupy Thrace in 196 BC but was defeated by the Romans 安提俄库斯，见 Ios. *Antiqu.* 12

**Antiphon,** Gr: Antiphōn, Attic orator, 480—411 BC, the first to write speeches for others to deliver at court; he was one of the 10 great Attic orators 安提风

**antiquitas,** Gr: presbeia, presbytēs, E: old age, (argument of) antiquity 古老，见 Irenaeus, *Adv. Haer.* 3, Orig. *Contra Cels.* (the Old Testament is older than any other scripture), Ambros. *De off. ministr.*

*Antiquitates Iudaicae,* E: *Jewish Archaeology,* a work by Josephus Flavius《上古犹太史》，见 Ios.

**Antoninus Pius,** Roman emperor AD 138—161, he was adopted by Hadrian and lead Rome in a time of prosperity 安托尼努斯·彼乌斯，见 Justin. *Apol.*,

**Antonius** => Marcus Antonius

**Antonius,** Gr: Antonios, E: Anthony, ca. 251—356 AD, hermit in Egypt, the "Father of monasticism" 安托尼，安东尼，见 Athanas. *Vita S. Antonii*

**Anytus,** Gr: Anytos, one of Socrates' dialogue partners and accusers 阿尼图斯，见 Plat., *Menon*

**apate** => Dios apate

**apatheia** => impassibilitas

**apes,** Gr: melissa, E: bee, symbol of diligence and good organization 蜜蜂，见 Verg. *Georg.* 4, Plin. *Nat. hist.* 11, Basil. *Hexaem.* (symbol of order in society), Boethius, *De cons.* 3 (sensual pleasures are like bees)

**Aphrodite,** (Venus), Gr: Aphroditē, "born of foam", "sea-born" (?), E: Aphrodite, Greek goddess of love and beauty, wife of Hephaestus, lover of Ares and Anchises; => Venus 阿佛洛狄特，见 Hom. *Il.*, 3, 5; *Od.* 8; Hes. *Erga*, Eur. *Hipp.*, Plat. *Symp.* (Aphrodite Pandemos), Apoll. *Arg.*, Lucian. *Theon dial.*, Longos

**apocrypha,** Gr: apokrypha, E: apocryphal books, deuterocanonical books (books which are not included in the Hebrew canon of the Old Testament) 旁经、次经、伪经，见 Biblia

**apokalypsis** => revelatio

**apokatastasis panton,** E: apocatastasis, the return of all things, final harmony of all, a (heretic) theory of Origen 万有复兴论，见 *De principiis*

**Apollo,** Gr: Apollōn, "destroyer", "apple-man" (?), E: Apollo, son of Zeus and Leto, brother of Artemis, born on Delos island, worshiped there and at Delphi; his attributes are bow, quiver, lyre, tripod; he was (1) god of agriculture, symbol tree: laurel; (2) god of medicine and of expiation (also sending diseases, conf. *Iliad*), his son Asclepius became the god healing; (3) god of divination; his oracle in Delphi was famous in the ancient world; (4) god of the arts and of science, the leader of the Muses; (5) god of the sun, identified with Helios and named "Phoebus Apollo" 阿波罗，见 Hom. *Il.* 1, 4, 5, 7, 16, 21, 22, *Od.* 20; Aesch. *Choeph.*, *Eumenid*, Soph., *Oed. Tyr.*, Eur. *Alk.*, Verg. *Buc.* 10, Hor. *Carm.* 1,12, *Carm. saec.* (leader of the nine Muses, healer), Ov. *Met.* 1 (lover of Daphne), 6 (Niobe), Lucian. *Theon dial.*, Tert. *De spect.* (games dedicated to him), Lactantius, *Carmen de ave phoenice*, Capella, *De nuptiis*

**Apollonius,** Gr: Apollōnios, "man from Apollo", Greek author, 295—215 BC 阿波罗尼俄斯，见 Apoll. *Argonaut.*

*Apologia,* Gr: *Apologia*, < apo-logeomai, "to defend oneself", E: *Apology*, Christian apologetic literature 《申辩篇》，见 Xen. *Apol.*, Plat. *Apol.*, Justin. *Apol.* (=*Apologeticus*), Lact. *Inst.*

*Apologeticus,* (=*Apologia*), => Apologia

**apotheosis,** Gr: apotheosis, E: deification, the worship of a hero or king as god; this custom came from Egypt and was accepted in Greece after the decline of the traditional religion; the Romans raised their emperors to the status of gods, calling them "divi"; => ascensio in caelum; Caesar, Augustus 奉为神，见 Verg. *Buc.* 5, Ov. *Met.* 15 (Caesar changed into a star), Apuleius, *Met.*, Capella, *De nuptiis*

**appetitus,** appetitio, Gr: hormē, orexis, epithymia, E: desire, appetite; => fames 渴望，见 Arist. *Eth. Nik.*, Cic. *De fin.* 3,22 (appetitio animi), *De off.* 1,100 (governed by ratio)

**Appius Claudius** => Claudius

**Apsyrtus,** Gr: Apsyrtos, "swept downstream", E: Apsyrtus, brother of Medea 阿普西尔图斯，见 Apoll. *Arg.*

**Apuleius,** Lucius, ca. 125—190, Carthaginian lawyer and orator, author of the only surviving Latin novel 阿普列乌斯，见 *Metamorphosae*

**aqua,** Gr: hydor, E: water, one of the elements, basic need 水，见 Cic. *De off.* 1,52 (not to be denied), Vitr. *De arch.* 8 (finding of fountains, water channels), Plin. *Nat. hist.* 31 (therapeutic effects of water), Front. *De aquis*, Bibl. *Gen* 6~9 (flood => diluvium), *Ioann.* 2 (water changed into wine), 4 (living water), Aug. *Confess.* 13 (the sea is a symbol of estrangement from God, dry land = good souls)

**aquaeductus,** E: aqueduct, structures built to supply cities (esp. Rome) with water; the Greeks had water supply systems since the 6th ct. BC, but they preferred underground channels 水渠，见 Vitr. *De arch.* 8, Front. *De aquis*

**aquila,** Gr: aetos, aietos, E: eagle, (symbol of Zeus); => avis 鹰、老鹰，见 Hom. *Od.* 2, Hes. *Erga* 202~212, Aesch. *Agamemnon*, *Physiologus* (Christian interpretation)

**Arabia,** E: Arabia, in antiquity the Arabs were famous for their trade connections, they imported goods from India and China; in late antiquity they preserved much of the Greek cultural heritage through their translation work 阿拉伯，见 Ptolemaios (*Almagest*), Athanasius, *Vita Antonii*

**Aratus,** Gr: Aratos, "wish", ca. 315—240 BC, Greek poet and scientist at the court of Macedonia; his only surviving work is *Phaenomena*, a didactic poem about astronomy 阿拉图斯，见 Plut. *Bioi*

**arbor,** Gr: dendron, E: tree => planta

**Arcadia,** region in the center of the Peloponnese, through Evander connected with the origins of Rome 阿尔卡狄亚，见 Verg. *Aen.* 8, *Buc.* 10

**archai, arche** => principium

**Archelaus,** Gr: Archelaos, "ruler of the people", 1) king of Macedonia 413—399 BC; 2) son of Herod the Great, king of Judaea from 4 BC to 6 AD 阿克劳斯，见 Ios. *Bell. Iud.*

**Archidamus,** Gr: Archidamos, "ruler and tamer", Spartan king 469—427 BC, who invaded Athens 阿基达摩斯，见 Thuc. 2,

**Archilochus,** Gr: Archilochos, Greek poet ca. 650 BC, who lived on the island of Paros; he was the first to express personal feelings in his poems, attacked private enemies, also mentioned the solar eclipse of 648 BC 阿基罗克斯，见 *Peri hypsous*

**Archimedes,** Gr: Archimēdēs, "eminent thinker", ca. 287—212 BC, Greek scientist and famous inventor, perhaps educated in Alexandria, he served the tyrant of Syracuse, Hieron II, and helped to defend Syracuse against Roman attackers 阿基米德，见 Liv. 21~23

**architectura**, Gr: architektonia, oikodomia, E: architecture 建筑学，见 Vitr. *De arch.*, Isidor. *Etym.* 15 (de aedificiis et agris), Maximus, *Mystagogia* (symbolic significance of the structure of a church),

**archōn,** "ruler", since the time of Solon the Athenians annually elected nine officials and called them "archontes"; they directed the public sacrifices and festive celebrations; => princeps 领导者

**Areopagita** => Dionysius Areopagita

**Areopagus,** Gr: Areios pagos, "hill of Ares", E: Areopagus, a hill near the Acropolis in Athens, the legendary place of the tribunal of Athens, where Orestes was tried; also connected with Solon; in the early period the Areopagus was the central government institution, since the 5th ct. BC it only dealt with murder cases; => Dionysius Areopagita 战神山，见 Aesch. *Eumen*., Cic. *De off.* 1,75

**Ares,** Mars, Gr: Arēs, "male warrior", E: Ares, child of Zeus and Hera, god of war; the Romans identified Ares with their own war god Mars; => Mars 阿瑞斯，见 Hom. *Il*.5, 21, *Od*. 8; Apoll. *Arg*.

**aretē** => virtus

**Arete,** Gr: Aretē, "virtue", wife of King Antinous 阿瑞特，见 Hom. *Od.* 7

**argenteum aetas,** Gr: aiōn argyros, E: silver age, the second age after the "golden age" 白银时期, 见 Hes. *Erga*, Ov. *Met.*, Orosius, *Hist.* (statue of gold, silver, etc. symbol of four ages)

**argo,** Gr: argō, the ship that led Jason and the other Greek heroes to Colchis 阿戈，见 Apoll., *Arg*

**Argolis** = Argos

***Argonautica*,** Gr: *Argonautika*, E: *Argonautica*, an epic by Apollonius of Rhodus《阿戈远征记》,见 Apollonius

**Argos,** also "Argolis", Greek city in the north-east of the Peloponnesus, area of Mycenae and Tiryns; after the rise of Sparta Argos tended to support Athens 阿尔格斯，见 Aesch. *Agam*., Pausanias

**argumentatio** => probatio

**argumentum,** Gr: mythos, E: plot, the structure of a play 情节, 见 Arist. *Poiet*.

**Argus,** Gr: Argous, "bright", 1) the builder of the Argo; 2) Argus Panoptes, a monster with many eyes 阿戈斯，见 Apoll. *Arg*.

**Ariadne,** Gr: Ariadnē, "most pure" (?), daughter of Minos and Pasiphae, who helped Theseus to escape from the labyrinth but was abandoned on the island of Naxos 阿里阿德内，见 Ov. *Her.*, *Met*.8

**Arianismus** => Arius

**Ariovistus,** chief of the Germanic tribe of the Suebi, defeated by Caesar in 58 BC 阿里奥维斯托，见 Caes. *De bello Gall*.1

**Aristaeus,** Gr: Aristaios, "the best", E: Aristaeus, the son of Apollo, god of husbandry and bee-keeping 阿瑞斯泰俄斯，见 Verg. *Georg*. 4

**Aristarchus,** Gr: Aristarchos, 1) Aristarchus of Samos, ca. 320—250 BC, astronomer, famous for his heliocentric theory; 2) A. of Samothrace, 217—145 BC, head of the library of Alexandria, grammarian and philologist who edited the works of Homer, Hesiod and other authors 阿里斯塔尔科斯

**Aristides,** Gr: Aristeidēs, "most beautiful", ca. 520—468 BC, Athenian statesman, general at Plataeae 479 BC 阿瑞斯德斯，见 Plut. *Bioi*

**Aristippus,** Gr: Aristippos "best horse", E: Aristippus of Cyrene, c. 435—355 BC, a friend and pupil of Socrates, famous for the doctrine that sensation and immediate pleasure are the only reality 阿里斯提波斯，见 Cic. *Tusc*.

**aristocratia,** Gr: aristokratiē, E: aristocracy; the "rule of the best", one of the forms of government in Greek political thought, it might turn into oligarchy or plutocracy 精英政治, 见 *Arist. Polit*., *Rhet*., Cic. *De re publica*

**Aristophanes,** Gr: Aristophanēs, "bright goodness", Greek writer of comedies, 445—386 BC, the most important poet of Attic Old Comedy, 11 of his works are extant 阿里斯托芬，见 Ar. *Acharnai*, *Eirene*, *Lysistrate*, *Nephele*, *Ornithes*, *Sphekes*, Plat. *Symp*., Quint. *Inst.* 10

**Aristoteles,** Gr: Aristotelēs, "noble", E: Aristotle, Greek philosopher, 384—322 BC, who founded the Peripatetic School and wrote numerous books in the areas of philosophy, ethics, politics, rhetoric, poetry, cosmology, biology, etc. 亚里士多德，见 Arist., Cic. *De fin.* 4,74, Quint. *Inst.* 10, Min. Felix, *Octav*., Diog. Laert., Lact. *Inst*., Basil. *Hexaem*., Philoponus, *De creatione mundi* (rejection of Aristotelianism, progress in the history of science)

**arithmetica,** Gr: arithmētikē, E: arithmetic 算术学, 见 Eucl.

**Arius,** Gr: Areios, E: Arius, ca. 260—336, a presbyter in Alexandria who propagated subordinationism, i.e. he denied the divinity of Christ; his views split the Church and led to the Council of Nicaea 325 AD 亚略、亚流，见 Euseb., Athanas. *Logos*, Chrysostom. *Hom*.

**arma,** Gr: hoplos, E: weapons, arms, symbol of war; => bellum 武器, 见 Hom. *Il.* 18 (new armour for Achill), Cic. *De off.* 1,77; Verg. *Aen.* 8 (armour for Aeneas)

**Arnobius,** ca. 260—310 AD, African orator, teacher of Lactantius; he converted to Christianity in 295 and attacked paganism 阿尔诺比乌斯，见 Lactantius

**Arpinum,** town in central Italy, the birthplace of Marius and Cicero 阿尔皮农，见 Cic.

**Arrianus,** Flavius Arrianus, Gr: Arrianos, E: Arrian, Greek author, ca. 90—160, author of *Alexandrou Anabasis* 阿里安

**Arruns,** hero in the *Aeneis* 阿任斯，见 Verg. *Aen.* 11

**ars,** Gr: technē, E: art, skill, => ars poetica 技术，见 Plat. *Gorg.*, Arist. *Eth. Nik.*, Ov. *Ars amatoria*, Plin. *Nat. hist.* 36 (artefacts, artists), Capella, *De nuptiis* (the seven arts appear as women), Cassiod.*Inst.*, Greg. Magn., *Regula past.* (pastoral care as "ars artium")

**Ars amatoria,** E: *The Art of Love*, poem by Ovid《爱的艺术》，见 Ov.

**Ars minor / Ars maior,** grammar books by Donatus《拉丁语法基础》/《拉丁语法中级》，见 Donatus

**ars poetica,** E: the art of poetry 诗艺，见 Hor. *De arte poet.*

**ars vivendi,** E: the art of a good life 生活的艺术，见 Cic. *De fin.*, Sen. *Epist.*

**Artaphernes,** Gr: Artaphernēs, Persian commander 490 BC 阿塔菲内斯，见 Hdt. *Hist.* 6

**Artaxerxes,** Gr: Artaxerxēs, name of Persian kings; Artaxerxes II defeated his brother Cyrus in 401 BC at Cunaxa 阿塔薛西斯，见 Xen. *Anab.*, Plut. *Bioi*

**Artemis,** Gr: Artemis, "the untouched, virgin", "high source of water" (?), L: Diana, daughter of Zeus and Leto, sister of Apollo, Greek goddess of hunting and childbirth 阿尔特弥斯，见 Hom. *Il.* 21; Aesch. *Agamemnon*, Eur. *Hipp.*, *Iph. Aul.*, Ov. *Met.*, Lucian. *Theon dial.*

**Artemisium,** Gr: Artemision, "temple of Artemis", place at the north-eastern coast of Euboea, scene of a sea-battle in 480 BC 阿特弥西翁，见 Hdt. *Hist.* 7

**artes** => septem artes liberales; ars

**artificium, artifex,** Gr: mēchanē, technēma, sophisma, dolos, E: artifice, trick 作品、技巧 Plin. *Nat. hist* 36 (artefacts, artists)

**Ascanius,** Gr: a-skenios "tentless", Ascanius = Iulus, the son of Aeneas, legendary ancestor of the Roman people (especially the gens Iulia, see Julii); according to Livy his mother was Lavinia and not Creusa 阿斯卡尼乌斯，见 Verg. *Aen.*1, 2

**ascensio in caelum,** E: ascent to heaven, a motive found in Greek and Latin literature; => apotheosis, caelum 升天，见 Heracles, Apuleius, *Met.* (Psyche accepted in heaven), Perpetua, *Passio*, Capella, *De nuptiis* (Apollo, Virtus, Mercury ascend to Jupiter's palace), Boeth. *De cons.* 4, Dionys. Areopag., *Cael. hier.* (purgatio, illuminatio, unificatio), Ioann. Klimakos,

**ascesis,** Gr: askēsis, E: ascesis, rigid practices to achieve freedom and perfection, => jejunium, virtus (asketikē aretē) 刻苦修炼，见 Basil. *Ascetica*, Greg. Nys. *Peri parth.* (fasting), Chrysost. *Peri parthen.* (forced abstinence might be sinful), Hieron. *Epist.* 22, 107 (ascetic life understood as a race, => certamen), Bened. *Regula*, Columban, *Regula coen.*

**Ascetica,** Gr: Askētika, E: *Ascetic Admonitions*, work by Basilius《修道生活教导》，见 Basilius

**Asclepius** = Aesculapius

**asebeia,** Gr: asebeia, < a-sebomai, "impious", E: impiety; in early times only the profaning or plundering of a temple was seen as "asebeia", but since 432 BC a law in Athens punished incorrect teachings about the gods; this law aimed at controlling the Sophists; according to this law Anaxagoras, Protagoras and Socrates were sentenced. In the Roman Empire many Christians refused to perform sacrifices to the emperors and thus were accused of impiety; => Anaxagoras, pietas, religio, Socrates 不敬神，见 Plat. *Apol.*, Iust. *Apol.*

**asellus,** Gr: onos, E: ass, donkey 驴，见 Aesop, Apuleius, *Met.*

**assimiliatio,** Gr: homoiōsis, E: approach, assimilation 接近，同化，见 Dionys. Ar. *Peri tes our. hier.* (desire of the soul to approach God)

**asteriscus,** E: asterisc, a diacritical mark; => abbreviatio 小星星，标点符号，见 Hieron. *Ep.* 57

**astrologia,** Gr: astrologia, E: astrology 占星术，见 Ptolem., Aug. *De civ. Dei* 5

**astronomia,** Gr: astronomia, E: astronomy; => septem artes liberales 天文学，见 Ptolemaeus, *Mathematike syntaxis*, Macrobius, *Comm.*, Philoponus, *De creatione mundi*

**Astyanax,** Gr: Astyanax, "leader of the city", son of Hector and Andromache 阿斯提阿纳克斯，见 Hom. *Il.* 6

**asyndeton,** Gr: asyndetos, "without connection", E: asyndeton 无连接词结构，见 *Peri hypsous* 19

**ataraxia,** Gr: ataraxia, "unshaken attitude", E: mental steadfastness, calmness, according to Epicurus a precondition of happiness (eudaimonia) 内心不动摇，见 Stoa

**Athamas,** "reaper on high", king of Thebes, father of Helle and Phrixus 阿塔马斯，见 Apoll. *Arg.*

**Athanasia** => immortalitas

**Athanasius,** Gr. Athanasios, "immortal", E: Athanasius, ca. 295—373 AD, theologian and Church leader, bishop of Alexandria 亚大纳西，见 *Logos, Vita Antonii*

**Athena,** (Minerva), Gr: Athēnē, "the flourishing" (from "anthos"?), inversion of Sumerian Anatha "Queen of Heaven" (?), also called Pallas "youth", E: Athena, Greek goddess, daughter of Zeus and Metis; born from Zeus' head, goddess of science and the arts who protected heroes like Odysseus and Heracles; she was usually depicted with a helmet, a spear and a shield (aigis, goat-skin shield); her sanctuary in Athens was the Parthenon; => bubo, Parthenon 雅典娜，见 Hom. *Il.* 5~8, 21~22; *Od.* 1~24; Hes. *Erga*, Aesch. *Eumen.*, Theophr. *Eth.* 16, Lucian. *Theon dial.* (born from Zeus' head)

**Athenae,** Gr: Athēnai, E: Athens, the main city of Attica, important center of Greek culture, connected with Aegeus, Theseus, Dracon, Solon, Peisistratus, Cleisthenes, Pericles, etc.; the oldest part of the city is the => Acropolis; in 480 BC the Persians destroyed the city, but Themistocles and Pericles erected many new buildings and set up a city wall; the time after the Persian Wars marked the political and cultural climax of Athens; since the disasters of the Peloponnesian War (431—404 BC) the city entered a long period of decline; Athens was conquered by Sulla in 86 BC, and the termination of the Academy in 529 AD implied that Athens lost its pre-eminence in culture and thought. 雅典城，见 Soph. *Oid. epi Kol.*, Hdt. *Hist.* 8, Thuc. 2; Cic. *De fin.* 5, Greg. Naz. *Carm.*

**athla,** athletic games, performed in honour of a deceased person; panhellenic athletic festivals were held in intervals of four years at Olympia, Corinth (Isthmian Games), Nemea (Nemean Games) and Delphi (Pythian Games, emphasizing musical competitons); => agon, ludus, Olympia 运动会，见 Hom. *Il.* 23, Verg. *Aen.* 5, Tert. *De spect.*

**Athos,** high mountain on one of the promontories of Chalcidice, (later site of monasteries) 阿托斯，见 Hdt. *Hist.* 6, 7

**Atlantis,** legendary island which (according to Plato's *Critias* and *Timaeus*) sank into the sea 阿特兰提斯

**Atlas,** Gr: Atlas, "he who suffers", "he who dares", a son of Iapetus, brother of Prometheus and Epimetheus; since he participated in the fight of the Titans against the Olympian gods he was sentenced to carry the vault of the sky on his shoulders; his daughters were the Hyades, Pleiades, and Hesperides 阿特拉斯，见 Hes. *Theog.*

**atomos,** Gr: atomos, <a-temno, "in-divisible", E: atom, cf. the atomist theory of the Epicurean school 原子、原子论，见 Cic. *De nat. deor.* 1,65, Lucr. *De rer. nat.* (primordia, inane; atomic structure of mind and body)

**Atossa,** Xerxes' mother 阿托撒，见 Aesch. *Persai*

**Atreus,** Gr: Atreus, "fearless", Greek king of Mycenae, son of Pelops, father of Agamemnon and Menelaus; his cruelty against his brother Thyestes brought calamity upon his clan. 阿特柔斯，见 Hom. *Od.* 3, Aesch. *Agamemnon*

**Atropos,** Gr: Atropos, "irresistible", "she who cannot be turned", one of the Fates who cuts of the thread of life; => Parcae, Clotho, Lachesis 阿特若普斯，见 Hes. *Theog.*

**Attica,** Gr: Attikē, E: Attica, the country around Athens; Cleisthenes divided the region into 10 counties (phylai) and 174 local communities (demoi) 阿提卡，见 Soph. *Oid. epi Kol.*, Pausanias

**Atticus,** Titus Pomponius, 110—32 BC, friend of Cicero and copyist of his works 阿提克斯，见 Cic. *Brutus, Cato de sen., De fin.*

**Augusta,** E: Augusta, since Domitian the official title of the wife of the Roman emperor 奥古斯塔

**Augustinus,** Aurelius Augustinus, E: Augustine, 354—430 AD, important thinker and author from Thagaste in Numidia (Africa), he became teacher of rhetoric, went to Rome and received baptism in 387 AD; later he became bishop of Hippo and wrote many important works; he is the most influential of the Latin Fathers of the Church 奥古斯丁、奥思定，见 *Confessiones, De beata vita, De civitate Dei, De vera religione, Soliloquia*

**Augustus,** Gr: sebastos, "reverend", E: Augustus, the title of Gaius Octavius, 63 BC—14 AD, the first Roman emperor, heir and adopted son of Caesar; having defeated Marcus Antonius, he controlled the whole empire since 31 BC; as "Augustus" and "Imperator" ("general", emperor) he implemented religious and moral reforms, encouraged poets to praise the virtues of the old Roman tradition and erected many splendid buildings. His wife Livia did not have children, therefore he adopted Tiberius and made him his successor. 奥古斯都，见 Verg. *Aen.* 6, *Buc.*1, Hor. *Carm.* 4,14, (prince of peace), Liv. 121~135, Tac. *Ann.*

**Aulis,** town of Boeotia, where the Greek fleet assembled before departing for Troy; according to legend Iphigenia was sacrificed here. 奥里斯，见 Aesch. *Agam.*, Eur. *Iph. Aul.*, Stat. *Achill.*

*Aulularia,* play by Plautus《一坛黄金》，见 Plaut.

**aurea aetas,** Gr: chryseos, E: golden age, a state of happiness 黄金时期，见 Hes. *Erga*, Verg. *Buc.* 4, *Georg.* 1,118~158, Ovid, *Met.*1, Orosius, *Hist.* (statue of gold, silver, etc. symbol of four ages)

**aurea mediocritas,** Gr: mesotēs, metrion, meson, E: the golden middle way 中庸之道，见 Hor. *Carm.* 2,10

**aureum vellus,** Gr: chrysomallos, E: Golden Fleece 金羊毛，见 Apoll. *Arg.*

**Aurora** = Eos

**Ausonius,** Decimus Magnus, ca. 310—393 AD, Latin poet from Bordeaux 奥索尼乌斯，见 *Epistulae*

**auspicium** => mantike

**autobiographia,** < Gr: autos "self", bios "life", graphē "record", E: autobiography 自传，见 Hor. *Saturae*, Marc. Aurel., Greg. Naz. *Carmina*, (*peri ton heautou bion*), August. *Confess.*

**autonomia,** Gr: autonomos, "having one's own law", E: autonomy 自律，见 Soph. *Ant.*

**autopathia,** Gr: autopathia, E: active participation in events 亲自参与，见 Polyb.

**autopsia,** Gr: autopsia, "seeing oneself", E: autopsy, own observations 亲自观察，见 Polyb.

**avaritia,** Gr: pleonexia, aneleutheria, philargyria, aischrokerdeia, E: avarice, greed, stinginess 贪婪，见 Theophr. *Eth.* 22, Cic. *De off.* 1,24 (cause of injustice), *Peri hypsous* 44 (avarice enslaves minds), Prud. *Psych.* (Avaritia strangled by Operatio), Cass. *De inst.*, Greg. Mag., *Moralia*, (one of the cardinal sins)

**Aventinus (mons),** E: Aventine hill, one of the seven hills in Rome 阿文提努斯，见 Liv. 1

**Avernus,** Gr: a -ornos, "without birds", lake near Cumae and Naples, close to the cave supposed to be the entrance to the Underworld 阿维努斯，见 Verg. *Aen.* 6

**avis,** Gr: ornis, ornithes, E: bird, => aquila, bubo, columba, gallus, phoenix 鸟类，见 Ar. *Ornith.*, Plinius, *Nat. hist.* 10, *Physiologus* (symbolic meaning of eagle, crane, dove, pelican, phoenix, etc.)

**axios** => aestimabile

# B

**Babrius,** Gr: Babrios, Greek author of a collection of Aesop's fables, the *Mythiamboi Aisopeioi*, ca. 150 AD 巴布瑞斯，见 Aes. *Myth.*

**Babylon,** city in Mesopotamia 巴比伦，见 Arrian. *Alex. anab.* 7

**Bacchae,** Gr: Bakchai, Mainades, Thyiades, E: Bacchants, female worshipers of Bacchus who performed ecstatic dances at night 酒神崇拜者

**Bacchis,** name of a prostitute in Terence's play 巴赫斯，见 Ter. *Heauton Tim.*

**Bacchus,** Gr: Bakchos, Dionysos, E: Bacchus, the god of wine; => Dionysus 酒神，见 Verg. *Georg.* 2, Ov. *Met.* 8, Tert. *De spect.* (as demon)

**Balbus,** "stammerer", Quintus Lucilius Balbus, Stoic thinker, nephew of the more famous Lucius Cornelius Balbus, who was born in Spain but received Roman citizenship in 72 BC and became consul in 40 BC 巴尔布斯，见 Cic. *De nat. deor.*

**baptismus,** Gr: baptisma, E: baptism, the first Christian sacrament 圣洗，洗礼，见 Biblia, *Didache*, Cyrillus, *Catecheses*, Aug. *Confess.* 9, Dion. Ar., *Eccl. hier.* (seen as birth of God in the soul)

**basileia tou Theou,** L: regnum caelorum, E: reign of God, announced by Jesus 天国，见 Biblia, *Kata Ioannen*

**Basileia,** Gr: Basileia, daughter of Zeus, symbol of world-domination 巴西勒亚，见 Ar. *Ornithes*

**basileus,** Gr: basileus, "ruler" => rex 王，见 Hes. *Erga*

**Basilius Magnus,** Gr: Basileios, E: Basilius the Great, 330—379 AD, Greek bishop and author, one of the Cappadocian Fathers 巴西略、巴西尔，见 *Ascetica, Hexaemeron*

**Bdelycleon,** Gr: Bdelykleōn, "hate Cleōn", figure in Aristophanes' comedy 布得里克勒翁，见 Ar. *Sphekes*

**beatitudo,** beata vita, beatum, Gr: eudaimonia, makariotēs, E: happiness 幸福，见 Arist. *Eth. Nik.*, Arist. *Polit.*7, *Rhet.*, Cic. *De fin.*, (only virtue is happiness, 3,11); *De nat. deor.* 1,45 (gods live in eternal joy), Hor. *Carm.* 2,16 (nihil est ab omne parte beatum), *Sat.* 2,6; Sen. *De beata vita*, Epict. *Diatr.* (eudaimonia), Chrysostom. *Peri parthen.* (virginity leads to happiness), Aug. *De beata vita*, Boethius, *De cons.* (beatitudo = bonitas = summum bonum = deus)

**Bellerophon,** Gr:Bellerophōn, Bellerophontēs, "bearing darts" (?), E: Bellerophon, ancient Corinthian hero, who tried to ride the winged horse Pegasus to heaven 贝勒若丰，见 Ar. *Eirene*

**bellum,** Gr: polemos, machē, E: war, fight, => vis 战争，见 Cic. *De off.* 1,35~38 (moral admissibility of war and rules in war), 3,107 (ius bellicum = keep a promise made to an enemy); Caes. *De bello Gall.* (bellum iustum), Prud. *Psychomachia*

***Bellum Catilinae,*** E: *The War of Catiline*, work by Sallust《喀提林判乱记》，见 Sall.

***Bellum Iudaicum,*** E: *The Jewish War*, a work by Josephus Flavius《犹太战争史》，见 Ios.

**benedictio,** Gr: eulogia, euphēmia, E: blessing; => maledictum 祝福，见 Soph. *Oed. Col.*, Hor. *Carm. saec.*, Biblia, *Gen.*

**Benedictus,** E: Benedict, 480—547 AD, monk in Italy, founder of the Benedictine Order 本笃，见 *Regula*, Greg. Mag., *Dialogi* 2 (biography of Benedict)

**beneficentia,** Gr: euergesia, chrēstotēs, E: benevolence 善意，见 Cic. *De off.* 1,42; 2,32 (beneficia)

**benevolentia,** Gr: eunoia, eumeneia, philanthropia, E: benevolence 善意，见 Aesch. *Orest. Eumen.*

**Biblia,** Gr: Biblia, ta biblia = "the scriptures", "books", < Byblos, E: Bible, the Holy Scripture, Old Testament and New Testament; => antiquitas《圣经》，即《旧约》和《新约》，见 Philo, Ios., *Antiqu.*, Biblia, Irenaeus, *Adv. haer.* (Bible as the standard of theology), Basil. *Hexaem.*, Chrysostom. *Hom.*, Hieron. *Vulgata*, Aug. *De civ. Dei, De doctrina christ.* (interpretation of the Bible), Cassiod. *Inst.* (number and arrangement of the books of the Bible), Greg. Mag., *Moralia in Job*

**biblion** => liber

**bibliotheca,** Gr: bibliothēkē, E: book shelf, library; the biggest and most famous library of antiquity was at Alexandria; during the fights of 48 AD a big part of the 700,000 scrolls was destroyed; Pergamum also had an important library. Asinius Pollio opened the first public library in Rome in 39 BC; in the subsequent centuries most bigger cities in Italy had public libraries 图书馆，见 Alexandria

**Biton,** "bison", "wild ox" => Cleobis

**bios** = vita (biography); =>autobiographia

**Boeotia,** Gr: Boiōtia, "cow-land", a region of central Greece, Thebes being the main city; the famous mountains Cithaeron and Helicon are in Boeotia; its inhabitants were ridiculed as being uncultured and clumsy 伯欧提亚，见 Eur. *Iph. Aul.*

**Boethius,** Anicius Manlius Severinus Boethius, Gr: boētheia = "help, protection", E: Boethius, 476—524 AD, Roman politician, philosopher, translator; he held high posts under king Theodoricus but later was accused of treason. 波伊提乌，见 *De consolatione philosophiae*

**bonum,** Gr: to kalon, to kalos, to philon, E: a good, a value, => summum bonum 美好的事物，价值，见 Plat. *Symp.*, Cic. *De fin.*, Sen. *De vita beata* 2,2, (bonum animi), Aug. *De civ. Dei* 19 (288 opinions concerning the supreme good), Boethius, *De cons.* 3 (summum bonum = deus), Greg. Magn. *Regula past.*

**bonum commune,** Gr: ta koina, E: the common good, => communis 公益，见 Cic. *De fin.*1, 3,64 (salus omnium, communis utilitas)

**bonum per se,** Gr: kalon, E: a value in itself 本身就是价值，见 Cic. *De fin.* 5,61 (virtus per se expetendum)

**Boreas,** Gr: Boreas, "North Wind", son of the Titan Astraios (Stars) and Eos (Dawn), his native land was said to be Thrace; father of Zetes and Calais 玻瑞阿斯，北风神，见 Apoll. *Arg.*

**bos,** taurus, Gr: bous, tauros, E: ox, bull, symbol of strength; => Centaurus, Europa, Minotaurus 牛，见 Hes. *Erg.*, Eur. *Hippol.*, Apoll. *Arg.* (two bulls with hooves of bronze), Verg. *Georg.* 3

**boule,** Gr: boulē, assembly; => comitium 开会商议，见 Hom. *Il.* 7, Capella (assembly of the gods)

**Brasidas,** Gr: Brasidas, Spartan general in the Peloponnesian War, who captured the city of Amphipolis in 424 BC but died two years later 布拉西达斯，见 Thuc. 4, Ar. *Eirene*

**Briareus,** Gr: Briareōs, "strong", also called Aegaeon, one of the three Hecatoncheires 布里阿瑞乌斯，

见 Hes. *Theog.*

**Briseis,** Gr: Brisēis, "she who prevails", Achilles' slave-concubine seized by Agamemnon which caused Achilles' wrath 布里塞伊斯, 见 Hom. *Il.* 1, 19, Ov. *Her.*

**Britannia,** E: Britain, England; the island was known to the traders of the Mediterranean, who imported tin from Britain; the area was first invaded by Caesar in 55 and 54 BC; the Roman province Britannia was founded in 43 AD under Emperor Claudius, who conquered the southern part of England. The Roman armies retreated in 407 AD, and after that the tribes from the north (Caledones, Picts, Scots) and from the continent (Saxons, Angles) mixed with the local Roman population. 布列颠, 见 Caes. *De bello Gall.* 4

**Brundisium,** modern Brindisi, a town and important harbour on the "heel" of Italy; the place where Virgil died 布伦迪西, 见 Hor. *Sat.* 1,5 (journey from Rome to B.)

**Brutus,** 1) Lucius Iunius Brutus, the traditional founder of the Roman republic and the first consul in 509 BC; he exiled Tarquinius Superbus; 2) Marcus Iunius Brutus, 85—42 BC, the prime assassin of Julius Caesar who was pardonned by Caesar after Pharsalis, 48 BC; Cicero dedicated many of his writings to him 布鲁图斯, 见 Cic. *Brutus*, *De fin.*, Hor. *Sat.* 1,7; Liv. 1, Plut. *Bioi*, Aug. *De civ. Dei* 3 (Brutus exiled his colleague)

**bubo,** Gr: glaukē, E: owl, symbol of Athena, => avis, 猫头鹰, 见 Theophr. *Eth.* 16, Apuleius, *Met.*

**Bucephalas,** Gr: Boukephalas, Alexander's beloved horse 布克法拉斯, 见 Arrian., *Alexandrou anab.* 5

**Bucolica,** (=*Eclogae*), Gr: boukoloi, "shepherd", E: *Eclogues*, a cycle of 10 poems by Virgil 《牧歌》, 见 Verg., Lact. *Inst.* (Christian interpretation of the fourth Eclogue)

**byblos** => liber

**Byblos,** town in Syria, trade center of paper, origin of the name "byblos" for "book", => liber 比布鲁斯, 见 Biblia

**Byzantium,** Gr: Byzantion, E: Byzantium, Greek city at the Bosporus on the European side, first founded in 660 BC as colony of Megara, destroyed by the Persians under Dareius I, the city was rebuilt and in 477 BC joined the Delian League (a naval league under Athenian leadership); in 330 AD Constantine the Great made it capital of the eastern part of the empire and renamed the city Konstantinou Polis = Constantinople; under Justinianus (527—565 AD) the city flourished, but the crusades (invasion in 1204) weakened its influence, and after the conquest of the Turks in 1453 AD the city lost much of its political and cultural significance; => Constantinus 拜占庭, 见 Xen. *Anab*.

# C

**Cadmus,** Gr: Kadmos, "from the east", E: Cadmus, brother of Europa and legendary founder of Thebes, who killed a dragon and sowed the dragon teeth from which the ancestry of the Theban nobility grew; Cadmus married Harmonia, daughter of Ares and Aphrodite. According to one tradition Cadmus is also credited with introducing the Phoenician alphabet to Greece. 卡德摩斯, 见 Ov. *Met.* 2, 3

**Caecilius,** E: Cecil, common Roman name 泽奇留斯, 见 Minucius, *Oct.*

**caelum,** Gr: ouranos, E: heaven, the afterlife; => elysium 天、天堂, 见 Cic. *De re publ.* (Somnium Scipionis), Apuleius, *Met.* (Psyche accepted in heaven)

**Caesar,** Gaius Iulius Caesar, Gr: Kaisar, E: Caesar, 100—44 BC, Roman statesman, general, author, who was consul in 59 BC and conquered Gaul 58—51 BC; he triggered the Civil War in 49 BC, could defeat his rival Pompey at Pharsalus (48 BC), made Cleopatra queen of Egypt, returned to Rome and became officially "dictator perpetuus"; he was assassinated in 44 BC but deified in 42 BC 恺撒、凯撒、该撒, 见 Cic. *De off.* 1,25 (his greed for power), Caes. *De bello gallico*, Sall. *Bell. Cat.*, Verg. *Aen.* 6, *Buc.* 5 (apotheosis of Daphis / Caesar), *Georg.* 1, Hor. *Carm.* 1,12, Liv. 106~120, Ov. *Met.* 15, 750 (Caesar is changed into a star), Quint. *Inst.* 10, Luc. *Phars.*, Plut. *Bioi*

**Caesar,** Gr: Kaisar, E: Caesar, emperor, title of the emperors of Rome 皇帝, 见 Suet. *De vita Caesarum*

**Caesarea,** Gr: Kaisareia, E: Caesarea, city in Palestine; in the ancient world several cities were named "Caesarea" 凯撒瑞亚, 见 Euseb.

**Cain,** Gr: Kain, E: Cain, figure of the Old Testament

(*Gen* 4), symbol of fratricide 加音，见 Aug. *De civ. Dei*（compared to Romulus）

**Calais,** Gr: Kalais, "of changing colour", one of the Argonauts, son of Boreas 卡来斯，见 Apoll. *Arg.*

**Calcedonense,** Concilium, < Gr: Chalkēdōn, E: Synod of Chalcedon of 451 AD, the last of the "four ecumenical councils" 卡尔西顿主教会议，见 Leo, *Tomus*, Cassiod. *Inst.*

**Calchas,** Gr: Kalchas, "brazen", seer of the Greeks at Aulis and Troy 卡尔卡斯，见 Hom. *Il.* 1, Eur. *Iph. Aul.*, Stat. *Achill.*

**Caligula,** "little boot", Gaius Julius Caesar Germanicus "Caligula", Roman emperor 37—41 AD 卡里格拉，见 Tac. *Ann.*, Suet. *De vita Caes.*

**Calipurnius,** Lucius Calipurnius Piso, consul in 15 BC 卡利普尼乌斯，见 Hor. *De arte poet.*

**Calipurnius,** Marcus Pupius Piso Frugi Calipurnius, ca. 115—50 BC, grandson of Calipurnius Piso Frugi 卡利普尼乌斯，见 Cic. *De fin.*

**Calipurnius Piso Frugi,** Roman statesman and symbol of frugality, consul in 133 BC 卡利普尼乌斯，见 Cic. *De fin.*

**Callicles,** Gr: Kalliklēs, "beautiful praise", a ruthless politician at Socrates' time 卡里克雷斯，见 Plat., *Gorg.*

**Callimachus,** Gr: Kallimachos, "fair fight", ca. 310—240 BC, Greek poet and scholar who made a catalogue of the books in the library of Alexandria (*Pinakes*), author of *Aitia* (origins of mythical lore); he possibly wrote 800 books, most of them are lost 卡利马科斯，见 Ov. *Fasti*

**Calliope,** Gr: Kalliopē, "nice words", one of the Muses, Muse of epic poetry, rhetoric and philosophy 卡利欧佩，见 Hes. *Theog.*

**Callisthenes,** Gr: Kallisthenēs, "handsome and strong", Greek historian, ca. 370—327 BC, put to death by Alexander 卡利斯特内斯，见 Arrian. *Alex. anab.*, 4

**Calypso,** Gr: Kalypsō, "hider", Greek nymph who held Odysseus back on her island Ogygia 卡吕普索，见 Hom. *Od.* 1, 5, 12, Lucian, *Alethe*

**Cambyses,** Gr: Kambysēs, son of Cyrus, king of Persia 530—522 BC, who conquered Egypt 坎比塞斯，见 Hdt. *Hist.* 2

**Camenae,** Italian goddesses, identified with the Greek Muses 卡梅内，见 Hor. *Carm.* 3,4 (Vester, Camenae)

**Camilla,** "attendant at a religious feast", a maiden-warrior of the Volsci and ally of Turnus, killed by Arruns; perhaps she is an invention of Virgil 卡弥拉，见 Verg. *Aen.* 7, 11

**Camillus,** Marcus Furius Camillus, ca. 430—365 BC, Roman statesman and general, a model of justice, who captured the Etruscan town of Veji in 396 BC and was dictator after the invasion of the Gauls in 390 BC 卡弥卢斯，见 Hor. *Carm.* 1,12, Plut. *Bioi*

**Canace,** Gr: Kanakē, the daughter of Aeolus and Enarete, who loved her brother Macareus and was killed for this incest 卡纳克，见 Ov. *Her.*

**canis,** Gr: kyōn, E: dog, symbol of uncleanliness, but also of loyalty, confer Cynics (school of thought) 狗，见 Aesop; Theophr. *Eth.* 29, (dog of the people), Lucian. *Vit. auct.* (Diogenes as dog), Boethius, *De cons.* 4 (quarrelsome people are like dogs)

**Cannae,** village in southern Italy (Apulia), where Hannibal disastrously defeated the Romans in 216 BC; around 50,000 Romans were killed, some 20,000 were taken captives 勘内，见 Liv. 21~23

**canon,** Gr: kanōn, "measure rod", norm, model, E: canon, 1) the authoritative collection of books, esp. of the Bible 2) ecclesiastical rules and regulations concerning the faith or practical and disciplinary matters; 1) 正经、正典, 2) 教规，见 Biblia; Aug. *De civ. Dei* 11, 18 (canonical Scriptures), Cassiodor. *Inst.*, Martinus de Bracara

***Canticum Canticorum,*** Gr: *Asma asmatōn*, E: *Song of Songs,* a book of the Old Testament, traditionally interpreted as expressing the love of the soul for God《雅歌》，见 Hieron. *Epist.*, Venantius, *Carmina*

**cantus** => musica

***Capita,*** Gr: *Kephalaia,* E: *Sentences,* a work by Maximus Confessor《警句集》，见 Maxim.

**Capitolinus** (mons), **Capitolium,** E: the Capitoline hill, the center and most sacred part of Rome, located at the west side of the Forum Romanum, site of the temple to Iuppiter Optimus Maximus, Juno Moneta (where the mint office was) and Minerva (Athena); => Jupiter, Manlius Capitolinus 卡皮托利努斯，见 Liv. 3 (Manlius Capitolinus)

**Cappadocia,** Gr: Kappadokia, E: Cappadocia, area in Asia Minor, the home of the "Cappadocian Fathers", i. e. Basilius, Gregory of Nyssa, Gregory of Nazianz 卡帕多西亚，见 Basilius, Gregorius

**caput,** Gr: kephalos, E: head; => Capitolium, Cephalos, Boucephalas 首, 见 Plat. *Polit.* (symbol of reason and leadership), Lucian. *Theon dial.* (Athena born from Zeus' head), Iren. *Adv. haer.* (recapitulatio, Christ the head of all things)

**Caracalla,** Marcus Aurelius Severus Antoninus, son of Septimius Severus, Roman emperor 211—217 AD; in 212 AD he granted all freeborn inhabitants of the empire Roman citizenship and thus made the provinces equal to Rome 卡拉卡拉

**cardinales virtutes,** E: cardinal virtues, => virtus

**caritas,** (=charitas), misericordia, gratia, Gr: philanthropia, chrēstotēs, eleēmosynē, agapē, E: charity 仁慈, 见 Cic. *De off.* 2,24 (metus absit, caritas retineatur), Epict. *Diatr.* (show compassion), Bibl. *Ioann.* 13 (agapate alleilous), Lact. *De ira*, Aug. *De civ. Dei* 14 (sign of the City of God), Sulpic. Sev. *Vita S. Martini* (sharing a coat with a poor man), Maximus Conf., *Capita*

***Carmen de ave phoenice,*** E: *Poem of the Phoenix*, a work by Lactantius 《凤凰之诗》, 见 Lact.

***Carmen saeculare,*** a poem written by Horace for the centennial celebration in 17 BC 《世纪之歌》, 见 Hor. *Carm.*

***Carmina,*** E: *Odes*, a collection of (Latin) poems by Horace 《歌集》, 见 Hor.

***Carmina,*** E: *Poems*, a collection of ca. 400 Greek poems by Gregorius Nazianzus 《诗集》, 见 Greg. Naz.

***Carmina,*** E: *Poems*, a collection of Latin poems by Venantius Fortunatus 《诗集》, 见 Venantius

**caro,** Gr: sarx, E: flesh 肉、肉身, 见 Bibl. *Ioann.* 1 (logos sarx egeneto), Aug. *De civ. Dei* 14 (the cause of sin is in the soul, not in the flesh), Greg. Magn. *Moralia* (sins of the flesh and of the intellect)

**Carthago,** Gr: Karchēdōn, < Phoen. Kart chadash = "new city", E: Carthage, city in northern Africa, a Phoenician colony, founded in 814 BC, since 600 BC Carthago dominated the Mediterranean and became a rival of Rome, the city was destroyed in 146 BC, renamed Colonia Iulia Carthago by Caesar in 44 BC, conquered by the Vandals in 439 AD, annexed by Byzanz in 533 AD and destroyed by the Arabs in 698 AD; before that it was an important center of Christianity 迦太基, 见 Arist. *Polit.*, Polyb., Cic. *De re publ.*, Verg. *Aen.*, Tert., Cyprian. *Epist.*, Aug. *Confess.*, Orosius, *Hist.* (Carthaginian Empire)

**Cassandra,** Gr: Kassandra, Kasandra, "she who entangles men", E: Cassandra, (also called Alexandra), prophetic daughter of Priam, loved by Apollo and granted the gift of prophecy but because she rejected Apollo she was punished by him with the curse that nobody should believe her words; she was killed at Mycene together with Agamemnon 卡珊德拉, 见 Aesch. *Agam.*

**Cassianus,** Johannes, E: John Cassian, 360—435 AD, monk and Christian author 卡西安, 见 Cass. *De institutis monachorum*

**Cassiodorus,** E: Cassiodor, 490—583 AD, Latin scholar, politician, educator 卡西奥多鲁斯, 见 Cassiod. *Institutiones*

**Cassius Dio,** (=Dio Cassius), Greek historian, c. 150—235 AD, born in Bithynia he went to Rome early and became a high official; author of a history of Rome (written in Greek) in 80 books, out of which books 36~60 have been preserved 卡修斯·迪欧

**castitas** => virginitas

**Castor,** Gr: Kastōr, "beaver", son of Zeus and Leda, brother of Pollux / Polydeukes 卡斯托尔, 见 Apoll. *Arg.*, Lucian. *Theon dial.*, Tert. *De spect.*, (connected to horse-riding)

**Catamites,** Gr: Ganymēdēs, "joy", E: Ganymede, symbol of beauty, carried off to Mt. Olympus to be the cup-bearer of Zeus 伽尼墨德斯, 见 Lucian. *Theon dial.*

***Catecheses,*** Gr: *Katēchēseis*, E: *Catecheses, Catechetical Lectures*, held by Cyril of Jerusalem 《教理讲授》, 见 Cyrillus

**categoriae,** praedicamenta, Gr: katēgoriai, E: categories 范畴, 见 Arist., *Org.*

**catharsis** => purificatio

**Catilina,** Lucius Sergius Catilina, E: Catiline, ca. 110—62 BC, Roman patrician whose revolutionary plans were discovered by Cicero in 63 BC 卡提利纳, 见 Cic., Sall. *Bell. Cat.*

**Cato maior,** Marcus Porcius Cato, E: the Elder Cato, 234—149 BC, Roman statesman, moralist, author of several works (mostly lost) 卡图, 见 Cic. *Brutus, Cato de sen., De off.* 2,89; Sen. *Epist. mor.* 11, Plut. *Bioi*

**Cato Uticensis,** Marcus Porcius Cato, (Cato minor), E: Cato of Utica, 95—46 BC, the great-grandson of Cato maior, symbol of Stoic virtue, who committed suicide in Utica (Africa) because he refused to surrender to Caesar 卡图, 见 Cic. *De fin.*, Sall. *Bell. Cat.*, Luc. *Phars.*, Plut. *Bioi*, Aug. *De civ. Dei* 1 (against suicide)

**Catullus**, "little dog", "puppy", Roman poet, c. 85—55 BC, famous for his love poems in praise of Lesbia 卡图卢斯, 见 Hor. *Carm.*, Ov. *Her.*

**causa**, (causa formalis, materialis, efficiens, finalis), Gr: aitia, archē, dia ti, E: cause, causes of historical events, the "four causes" 来源、原因, 见 Plat. *Tim.*, Thuc., Arist. Met., *Polyb.*, Cic. *De off.* 2,5, Verg. *Georg.* 2 (Felix qui potuit rerum cognoscere causas)

**Cecrops**, Gr: Kekrōps (kerk-ops = "tail-face"), E: Cecrops, mythological founder of Athens, first king of the city and culture hero, depicted as man with a dragon's tail 克刻洛普斯, 见 draco

**Celsus**, Gr: Kelsos, E: Celsus, 1) Roman encyclopedist in Tiberius' time (14—37 AD); 2) Platonist philosopher of the second century AD who attacked Christianity 凯尔索, 见 Origen, *Contra Celsum*

**Celtae**, Gallli, Gr: Keltoi, Galatai, E: Celts, a tribe that controlled big parts of central and northern Eruope since 600 BC; they invaded Rome in 387 BC; Caesar conquered their settlements in Gaul but was also interested in their culture. 克尔特人, 见 Caes. *De bell. Gall.*, Aug. *De civ. Dei* 1, Orosius, *Hist.*

**cena, cenare**, esca, Gr: brōsis, esthiō, E: food, to eat; => jejunium 食品, 吃, 见 Hom. *Od.* 6, (Phaeaces, famous for good food), Biblia, *Kata Iohann.* (bread of life), Tertull., *Spectac.* (watching performances is like eating dirty food), Nonius 18, Aug. *De vita beata* (spiritual hunger), Cassian. *De inst.* (diet of the monks)

**cenodoxia**, Gr: kenodoxia, E: vainglory, thirst for glory 虚荣心, 见 Aug. *De civ. Dei* 5 ("Lady Glory"), Cassian. *De inst.*

**centaurus**, Gr: kentauros, "empty bull", "one hundred strong" (?), E: centaur, half-man, half-horse, mythological figure; the most famous centaurs were Chiron, the tutor of Achilleus, and Nessus, connected with Heracles; => Chiro 人马, 见 Stat. *Achill.*

**Cephalus**, Gr: Kephalos, "head", a dialogue partner of Socrates; => Boucephalas, caput 克法卢斯, 见 Plat. *Polit.*

**Cerberus**, Gr: Kerberos, "demon of the pit", "destruction", E: Cerberus, a monstrous dog guarding the entrance to the Underworld 克尔伯若斯, 见 Verg. *Aen.* 6

**Ceres**, "gerens" = "the Fruit-bringer", Gr: Demētēr, E: Ceres, Roman goddess of agriculture and grain, identified with Demeter, the mother of Proserpine / Persephone; her feast, the cerialia, was celebrated on the 19th of April 泽瑞斯, 见 Plaut. *Aul.*, Cic. *De nat. deor.* 2,60~70, Hor. *Carm. saec.*, Tert. *De spect.* (games dedicated to her), Claudian. *De raptu Proserp.*

**certamen**, Gr: agōn, L: ludus, competitive performances; => athla 竞赛, 见 Hom. *Iliad* 23; *Od.* 8; Ar. *Acharn.*, *Nephel.*, *Sphekes* (oratorical competitions), Tert. *De spectaculis* (spiritual struggles), Hieron. *Epist.* 22 (stadium est haec vita), Prudent. *Psychomachia*, Venantius, *Carmina* (Pange lingua gloriosi lauream certaminis)

**Chaeronea**, Gr: Chairōnea, E: Chaeronea, town in Boeotia, site of the defeat of the Theban and Athenian forces by Philip of Macedonia in 338 BC; this victory ended the freedom of the cities of Greece and inaugurated Greek unity under Macedonian leadership 凯若内阿

*Chairephon*, Gr: Charephōn, "happy listener", one of Socrates' students 凯瑞丰, 见 Ar. *Nephel.*, Plat. *Gorg.*

**chaos**, Gr: chaos, "yawning", E: chaos, formlessness 无序、混沌, 见 Hes. *Theog.*, Ov. *Met.* 1, Aug. *Confess.* 13 (spiritual meaning of chaos and darkness)

*Characteres*, Gr: *Charaktēres ēthikoi*, E: *Characters*, a work by Theophrastus《品格论》, 见 Theophr.

**charaktēr** => natura, mores, animus, persona

**Charicleia**, Gr: Charikleia, E: Charicleia, main character of Heliodorus' novel *Aithiopika* 卡利克雷亚, 见 Heliod.

**charitas** = caritas

**Charites** => Gratiae

**Charon**, Gr: Charōn, "fierce brightness", the ferryman who sent the dead across the river Styx; the fee he was supposed to receive was a coin (obolos) put into the mouth of the deceased person; => Hades 卡容, 见 Verg. *Aen.* 6

**Cheirisophus**, Gr: Cheirisophos, "wise in the fists", Greek soldier in the *Anabasis* 克瑞索福斯, 见 Xen. *Anab.*

**Cheiron** = Chiro

**Cheops,** Pharaoh of Egypt, 2589—2566 BC, builder of pyramids 克欧普斯，见 Hdt. 2,

**China** = Sina

**Chiro,** Gr: Cheirōn,"hand", E: Chiron, centaur, who educated Jason and Achill 克若，见 Apoll. *Arg.*, Stat. *Achill.*

**Chloe,** Gr: Chloē,"green", E: Chloe, figure in Longos' novel 克洛亚，见 Longos

**choe** = libatio

***Choephoroe,*** Gr: *Choēphoroi,* "sacrificing women", Greek tragedy by Aeschylus, second part of the *Oresteia*《奠酒人》，见 Aesch. *Oresteia*

**chorismus,** separatio, Gr: chōrismos, E: separation (of the ideas and concrete things) 分离，见 Arist. *Met.*,

**chorus,** Gr: choros, "dance", "dancing place", E: chorus, the choir of public religious ceremonies; Pindar and other Greek poets wrote poetry to be sung by the choir; Greek drama developed from choir songs at the feast of Dionysus. Thespis arranged a single character responding to the choir, Aeschylus introduced a second speaker, and Sophocles a third person. After the 5th century BC the role of the choir at tragedies and especially comedies became less important. 歌舞队，见 Aesch. *Choephoroe,* Soph., Eurip., Ar.

**Chremes,** Gr: Chrēmēs, "wealth", figure in one of Terence's plays 克瑞梅斯，见 Ter. *Heaut. Tim., Phorm.*

**Christiani,** Gr: Christianoi, E: Christians, the believers of Christ, persecuted before 313 AD; => Christus 基督徒，见 Iustin., Iren., Tert., Cyprian., Hieron. *De viris ill.* (lives of educated Christians), *Epist.* (fiunt non nascuntur Christiani)

**Christus,** Gr: Christos, E: Christ, the "anointed one" (from Hebr./ Aram. Mashiah), the title of Jesus 基督，见 Biblia; Justin. *Apol.* (Christ as Logos); Iren., Perpetua, *Passio* (image of the shepherd), Tert., Lact., Euseb., Prud. *Psych.* (all virtues point to Christ), Aug. *De civ. Dei* 17, 18 (Christ foretold by the prophets), Leo, *Tomus* (two natures of Christ), Venantius, *Carmina* (cross of Christ)

***Chronica,*** Gr: *Chronikon,* E: *Chronicles,* a work on chronology《编年史》，见 Eusebius

**chronologia,** E: chronology, => annales, historia 编年史，见 Eusebius, Aug. *De civ. Dei* 18 (example of synchronist chronology: the Jews were freed from Babylon when the Romans exiled their kings), Orosius

**Chryseis,** Gr: Chrysēis, "golden", daughter of Chryses, captive of the Greeks 克吕塞伊斯，见 Hom. *Il.* 1

**Chryses,** Gr: Chrysēs, "golden", priest of Apollo 克吕塞斯，见 Hom. *Il.* 1

**Chrysippus,** Gr: Chrysippos, "golden horse", ca. 250 BC, Stoic philosopher; of his 705 books only fragments are extant 克吕西普斯，见 Epict. *Diatr.,* Lucian. *Vit. auct.,* Min. Felix, *Octav.,* Diog. Laert.

**Chrysostomus, Johannes,** Gr: Iōannēs Chrysostomos, "golden voice", E: John Chrysostom, 344—407 AD, Greek Father of the Church, famous for his eloquence 克里索斯托谟，见 *Logoi, Peri parthenias*

**Chrysothemis,** Gr: Chrysothemis, "golden justice", Electra's sister 克吕索特弥斯，见 Soph. *Elektra*

**cibus** => cena, cenare

**Cicero,** Lucius Tullius Cicero, ca. 90—68 BC, the cousin of Marcus Tullius Cicero 西塞罗，见 Cic. *De fin..*

**Cicero,** Marcus Tullius Cicero, 106—43 BC, Roman politician, orator and author of many important works, one of the greatest minds of antiquity. Cicero opposed Caesar and later attacked Marcus Antonius. His works (only few of them are lost) deeply influenced subsequent centuries, especially the Renaissance. 西塞罗，见 Cic. *Brutus, Cato de sen., De finibus, De nat. deor., De officiis,* Plut. *Bioi, Peri hypsous* (compared to Demosthenes), Minucius, *Oct.,* Lact. *De ira, Inst.* (Cicero Christianus), Ambros. *De off. ministr.,* Hieron. *Epist.* 22 (Ciceronianus, non Christianus), *Epist.* 57, Aug. *Confess.* 3 (Hortensius), *De beata vita* (magnus opinator), Macrobius, *Commmentarii in Somn. Scip.*

**Cicero,** Quintus Tullius Cicero, 102—43 BC, the younger brother of M. T. Cicero 西塞罗，见 Cic. *De fin.De div.*

**Cicones,** Gr: Kikones, a tribe in Thrace 克扣内斯，见 Hom. *Od.* 9

**Cimon,** Gr: Kimōn, Athenian statesman and military commander, 510—450 BC 克蒙，见 Plat. *Gorg.,* Plut. *Bioi*

**Cincinnatus,** Lucius Quinctius Cincinnatus, a Roman

hero, consul in 460 BC, he was made dictator in 458 BC in order to lead the fight against the Aequi; he was admired for his humility and diligence 辛辛纳图斯, 见 Liv. 3

**Circe,** Gr: Kirkē, "falcon", E: Circe, goddess with magical powers, daughter of Helios and Perse, living on Aeaea; she changed the friends of Odysseus into swine. 克尔克, 见 Hom. *Od.* 10

**circulus,** Gr: kyklos, E: circle, cycle 圆圈, 见 Eucl. *Stoich.*

**circumscriptio,** Gr: periphrasis, E: circumscription 委婉描述, 见 *Peri hypsous* 28

**circus** => ludus, spectaculum, theatrum

**Cithaeron,** Gr: Kithairōn, E: Mount Cithaeron, where Oedipus was exposed 克泰任山, 见 Soph. *Oid. Tyr.*

**civis,** Gr: politēs, astos, dēmotēs, E: citizen 城民、公民, 见 Arist. *Polit.*

**civitas,** Gr: polis, asty, E: city, city-state, society, citizenship 城邦、社会、公民权利, 见 Ar. *Ornith.*, Arist. *Polit.*, Cic. *De fin.* 3,40 (civitatem dare), Vitr. *De arch.* 1 (city planning), Iuv. *Sat.* 3 (the dangers of living in Rome), Prud. *Psych.* (civitas sancta, a spiritual civilization), Aug. *De civ. Dei* 14 (amor sui = civitas terrena, amor Dei = civitas Dei), 19 (sinful origin of the state against the naturalism of Plato and Aristotle)

**Claudianus,** E: Claudian, ca. 370—404 AD, Latin poet 克劳狄安, 见 *De raptu Proserpinae*

**Claudius,** Appius Claudius, one of the decemvirs of 450 BC, he tried to seduce Virginia 克劳狄乌斯, 见 Liv. 3

**Claudius,** Tiberius Claudius Nero Germanicus, Roman emperor 41—54 AD 克劳狄乌斯, 见 Tac. *Ann.*, Suet. *De vita Caes.*

**Cleanthes,** Gr: Kleanthēs, "flowering glory", ca. 331—232 BC, Stoic philosopher, famous for his hymn to Zeus 克勒安特斯, 见 Cic. *De nat. deor.* 2, Epict. *Diatr.*, Min. Felix, *Octav.*, Diog. Laert.

**Cleisthenes,** Gr: Kleisthenēs, E: Cleisthenes, Athenian politician, the founder of a democratic system; in 508 BC he divided Attica into 10 phylai (counties) and more than 100 local communities (demoi) in order to break the power of the aristocracy; the council of the 500 became the highest executive institution 克勒斯特涅斯

**Cleitus,** Gr: Kleitos, "famous", a cavalry commander of Alexander, killed by Alexander at a drinking party 克雷托斯, 见 Arrian. *Alex. anab.* 4

**Clemens Alexandrinus,** E: Clement, ca. 150—215 AD, important early Christian philosopher and theologian in Alexandria 克雷芒, 见 *Paedagogus, Protrepticus, Stromateis,* Euseb.

**Clemens Romanus,** E: Clement of Rome, Pope ca. 90—100 AD, author of a remarkable epistle to the church of Corinth (96 AD), an early document of papal authority 克雷芒, 见 Euseb. 3,

**clementia,** Gr: epieieia, oiktos, eleos, philanthropia, E: clemency, mildness, => severitas, odium 温和, 见 Cic. *De off.* 1,88, Sen. *De clem.*, Orig. *De princ.* (mercy of God)

**Cleobis, Biton,** Gr: Kleobis, "famous life", Bitōn, "wild ox", two Greek brothers, praised as the happiest of men 克勒欧比斯, 比通, 见 Hdt. *Hist.* 1

**Cleomenes,** Gr: Kleomenēs, "famous strength", ca. 520—490 BC, a Spartan king of the Agian line (=> Agis); he expelled the tyrant Hippias from Athens in 510 BC 克勒欧梅内斯, 见 Plut. *Bioi*

**Cleon,** Gr: Kleōn, "famous", Athenian politician and general, who promoted war and died in 422 BC; often caricatured by Aristophanes 克勒翁, 见 Thuc. 4, Ar. *Acharn.*, *Sphekes*, *Eirene*

**Cleopatra VII,** Gr: Kleopatra, "father's glory", E: Cleopatra, 69—30 BC, daughter of Ptolemaeus Auletes, queen of Egypt, her power was restored in 48 BC by Caesar, married Antonius in 37 BC but committed suicide after the battle of Actium 克娄巴特拉, 见 Caesar, Marcus Antonius

**clericus** => sacerdos

**Climacus** => Johannes Climacus

**Clio,** Gr: Kleiō, "proclaimer", E: Clio, one of the Muses, Muse of history 克雷欧, 见 Hes. *Theog.*

**Cloelia,** a Roman heroine at the time of Lars Porsenna 克洛厄利亚, 见 Liv. 2

**Clotho,** Gr: Klōthō, "spinner", E: Clotho, one of the Fates 克洛托, 见 Hes. *Theog.*

**Clovis,** (=Chlodwig, Clodwig, Ludwig, Louis), king of the Franks, baptized in 497 AD, he led the Franks to Roman Catholicism 克洛维, 见 Severus, *Vita Martini*, Greg. Turon. *Hist. Franc.*

**Clytaemnestra,** Gr: Klytaimnēstra, "suitor-fame", E: Clytemnestra, wife of Agamemnon, mother of Orestes, Chrysothemis, Electra, Iphigenia; together with her lover Aegisthus she killed her husband Agamemnon 克吕泰内斯特拉, 见 Aesch. *Oresteia*, Soph. *Elektra*, Eur. *Iph. Aul.*

**Cnemon,** Gr: Knēmōn, main character of the *Dyscolus* 克内孟, 见 Men. *Dysc.*, Heliodor., *Aithiopika*

**Cnossus,** Gr: Knōssos, E: Cnossos, old city at Crete, center of the Minoic Culture (ca. 2000—1400 BC) 克诺苏斯, 见 Creta

**Cocles,** Publius Horatius Cocles, a Roman hero around 500 BC 科克勒斯, 见 Liv. 2

**Coeus,** Gr: Koeos, "intelligent", one of the Titans, father of Leto 克厄欧斯, 见 Hes. *Theog.*

**cogitatio,** Gr: dianoia, noēma, phronema, ennoia, meletē, merimna, E: thinking, thought (an element of a dramatic performance) 思想, 见 Arist. *Poiet.*; *Peri hypsous* 7 (a work evokes thought = anatheoresis), August. *De beata vita* (cogitationes)

**cognitio,** Gr: gnōmē, gnōsis, epistēmē, synesis, E: insight, knowledge 认识, 理解, 见 Plat. *Polit.*

**Colchis,** Gr: Kolchis, a country at the eastern end of the Black Sea 克尔希斯, 见 Apoll. *Arg.*

**Colonus,** Gr: Kolōnos, a district (demos) close to Athens, the home of Sophocles 科罗努斯, 见 Soph., *Oidipus epi Kol.*

**Colosseum** => amphitheatrum

**columba,** Gr: peristera, E: dove, symbol of Aphrodite, also symbol of the Holy Spirit, and of the soul; => avis 鸽子, 见 Apoll. *Arg.*, Prud. *Peristeph.* (symbol of the soul), *Physiologus* (symbol of solitude)

**Columbanus,** E: Columban, ca. 543—616 AD, Irish missionary and founder of monasteries 科伦班, 见 Columban, *Regula coenobialis*

**comitium,** E: assembly (of the Roman people) on the Comitium (north-west side of the Roman Forum), in order to vote on matters proposed by the magistrates; the senate ratified the resolutions. 聚会, 见 Liv. 1 (the Comitium was founded by Tullus Hostilius)

**Commodus,** Lucius Aelius Aurelius C., E: Commodus, 161—192 AD, son of Marc Aurel 克摩都斯, 见 Marcus Aurelius

***Commentarii in Somnium Scipionis***, E: *Commentaries on the Dream of Scipio*, 《评注〈西皮欧的梦〉》, 见 Macrobius

**communis,** communitas, vita communis, Gr: koinōnia, E: communitarian life, cf. bonum commune 共同生活, 见 Plat. *Polit.* 5, Cic. *De fin.* 3,64 (communis utilitas), *De off.* 1,153 (sapientia as knowledge about the communitas et societas of men and gods), 2,14 (life is always vita communis); 3,23 (coniunctio civium); 3,28 (communis societas humani generis); Basil. *Ascet.*, Bened. *Regula* 33 (no private property)

**comoedia,** Gr: kōmōidia, kōmos = festive procession or party, E: comedy; the development of Greek comedy is divided into "Old Comedy" (= Aristophanic comedy, often higly political), "Middle Comedy" (c. 400—323 BC, some of the late works of Aristophanes belong to this type), and "New Comedy" (323—263 BC), Menander and Philemon (361—263 BC) are the main exponents of the last type; Plautus and Terence imitated the unpolitical style of the "New Comedy". 喜剧, 见 Aristophanes, Menandros, Hor. *De arte poet.*, Tatian. *Logos* (critical of theatrical performances)

**comprehensio** => perceptio

**conciliare,** Gr: prosagōgē, E: reconcile 和好, 见 Cic. *De off.* 2,17 (task of virtue is to conciliare animos), Aug. *Confess.* (reconcile faith and science), Ioann. Klimakos, *Klimax* (reconciliation)

**concilium,** synodus, Gr: synodos, E: synod, council, assembly of bishops, esp. the four ecumenical councils of 325 (Nicaea), 381 (Constantinople), 431 (Ephesus) and 451 (Chalkedon) 主教会议, 见 Cyrillus, Athanasius, Eusebius, Nestorios, Leo, Tomus, Cassiod. *Inst.*

**conclusio,** Gr: syllogismos, synkleisis, E: conclusion, syllogism 结论, 见 Arist. *Org.*, Boethius, *Consolatio* (reasoning leads to the conclusion that life is meaningful)

**concordia,** Gr: homonia, homophrosynē, harmonia, E: unity, cooperation, concord, => ordo, 合一, 见 Cic. *De nat. deor.* 2,60 (Concordia as goddess), *De off.* 1,85 (discordia, seditio), Sen. *De vita beata* 8,6 (concordia animi), Tatian. *Diatess.* (harmonization of the gospels), Clemens Alex. (emphasizes harmony), Prud. *Psych.* (allegory, attacked by Discordia), Aug. *De civ. Dei* 2 (temple of Concordia in Rome was built on the site of massacres)

**concupiscentia** => cupiditas

**conditio humana,** E: the human situation 人的条件, 人生的情况, 见 Sen. *De clem.*, Aug. *Confess.* (sinfulness of mankind)

***Confessiones***, E: *Confessions*, an autobiography by Augustine 《忏悔录》, 见 Aug.

**confirmatio,** E: confirmation, a Christian sacrament

坚振，见 Cyrillus, *Catecheses*, Dionysius Ar., *Eccl. hier.*

**conjuratio,** Gr: mageutikē, manganeia, E: conspiracy 阴谋，见 Cic. *De off.* 3,44（friendship is not conspiracy）, Sall. *Bell. Cat.*

**conscientia,** Gr: synnoia, syneidēsis, daimonion, E: conscience 良心，见 Aesch. *Orest.* (Eumenides), Plat. *Apol.* (daimonion, divine voice)

**consolatio,** Gr: paraklēsis, E: consolation 安慰，见 Boethius, *De consolatione phil.*

**constantia,** Gr: bebaiotēs, E: constancy, firmness (of character) 坚定不移，见 Cic. *De off.* 1,70 (feature of a politician)

**Constantinopolis,** (=Byzantium), Gr: Konstantinou polis, (=Byzantion), E: Constantinople, (=Byzanz), the imperial residence in the East since 330 AD; it also became the see of a patriarch (bishop) 君士坦丁堡，见 Athanas., Greg. Naz. (Council of C. in 381), Greg. Turon. *Hist. Franc.* 10 (delegation to Byzanz)

**Constantinus,** Flavius Valerius Constantinus Augustus, E: Constantine the Great, ca. 285—337 AD, emperor of Rome after 312; his Edict of Milan (313) granted complete freedom for Christians; in 330 he formally established the imperial residence at Byzantium, renaming the city Constantinople 君士坦丁，见 Lact. *De mortibus*, Euseb.

**constitutio,** Gr: politeia, E: constitution (of a state) 政治制度，见 Hdt. *Hist.* 3, Plat. *Polit.*7~8, Arist. *Polit.*, Polyb.

**consules,** (consul), E: consuls, the supreme civil and military magistrates at Rome during the time of the republic (since ca. 510 BC); two consuls were annually elected by the assembly of the people; => cursus honorum 执政官，见 Cicero, Livius (Brutus)

**contaminatio,** Gr: miasma, E: combination of several (Greek) plays into a new (Latin) play 混合写作方法，见 Ter. *Heauton Tim.*,

**contemplatio,** E: contemplation (of the highest being or God), blissful vision of God; => visio 默观，见 Plot. *Enn.*, Greg. Naz., *Logoi* (theologians need contemplation)

**continentia,** Gr: enkrateia, sōphrosynē, anechein, askēsis, E: continence, self-control, => ascesis, modus, moderatio 自制，克己，见 Arist. *Eth. Nik.*, Hor. *Carm.* 3,1 (satis), 2,10; *Sat.* 1,2, Epict. *Diatr.* (askesis), Tatianus, Tert., Hieron. *Epist.*

***Contra Celsum,*** Gr: *Kata Kelsou*, E: *Against Celsus*, a work by Origen《驳凯尔索》，见 Orig.

**convenientia,** Gr: homologia, epitēdeiotēs, eukairia, E: congruence（with the order of nature）符合，见 Cic. *De fin.* 3,22

**conversio,** Gr: metanoia, E: conversion 皈依，见 Aug. *Confess.*

**copia,** multitudo, Gr: plēthos, E: bounty, wealth 富饶，见 Hor. *Carm. saec.* (goddess of bounty)

**cor,** Gr: kardia, E: heart, => mens, anima, animus, pectus 心，见 Aug. *Confess.* 1 (cor inquietum)

**Corcyra,** Gr: Kerkyra, E: Corfu, island in the Ionian Sea, allied to Athens since 435 BC 克克拉，见 Thuc. 3

**Corinthus,** Gr: Korinthos, E: Corinth, city on the Isthmus situated at important trade-routes; the city was destroyed c. 2000 BC and rebuilt by Dorians in 900 BC. The city founded colonies (Syracuse, Cercyra); it flourished under the tyrants Cypselus (657—625 BC) and his son Periandrus (625—585 BC); since 583 BC the city had an oligarchic constitution. In the following conflicts Corinth often sided with Sparta. The city was occupied by Macedonia in 338 BC and destroyed by the Roman consul Mummius in 146 BC, becoming the capital of the Province of Achaia. Probably in 50 AD St. Paul organized an important community of Christians in Corinth. 格林多，见 Soph. *Oid. Tyr.*, Eur. *Med.*, Ar. *Lysist.*, Vitr. *De arch.* 3~4 (Corinthian style)

**Coriolanus,** Gnaeus Marcius Coriolanus, legendary Roman hero, who captured the Volscian town Corioli in 493 BC but then led troups against Rome 科利欧兰努斯，见 Liv. 2, Plut. *Bioi*

**cornu copiae,** Gr: keras, E: horn of plenty 魔角，见 Amalthea

**corpus,** Gr: sōma, E: body, => caro, spirit, resurrectio (resurrection of the body) 身体、肉身，见 Plat. *Phaid.* (soma - sema), Cic. *De fin.*, *De nat. deor.* 2,133~153, Apuleius, *Met.* (change of physical appearance), Orig. *De princ.* (punishment for sin), Greg. Nys. *Peri kataskeues anthropou*, *Peri parthen.* (the spirit should control the body), *Peri psyches* (separation of soul and body), Macrob. *Sat.* 7 (discussion of physiological questions)

***Corpus Iuris Civilis*,** E: *Code of the Civil Law*, a collection of legal texts《民法大全》，见 Justinianus

**coryphaeus**, Gr: koryphaios, E: chorus-leader (at a dramatic performance) 歌舞队领导，见 Aesch. *Choeph.*

**Cosmas Indicopleustes**, Gr: Kosmas Indikopleustes "Cosmas, navigator to India", ca. 550, author of *Christianike Topographia* 克斯马斯，见 Philoponus

**cosmogonia**, Gr: kosmogoniē, E: cosmogony, => creatio 宇宙生成论，见 Hes. *Theog.*, Plat. *Tim.*, Lucr. *De rer. nat.*

**cosmos**, mundus, Gr: kosmos = 1) cosmos, universe, 2) order, 3) ornament, cosmetics; E: cosmos, the universe 宇宙、秩序、布置，见 Xen. *Oik.*, Plat. *Tim.*, Arist. *Met.*, Lucr., Verg. *Georg.* 1 (nature and human action are connected), Ov. *Met.* 1, Plin. *Nat. hist.* 2, Bibl. *Gen* (creation), *Job* (God talks in a thunderstorm), Clem. Alex. *Protrept.* (cosmic harmony), Plot. *Enn.* (mundus intelligibilis = kosmos noetos), Basil. *Hexaemeron*, Proclus, *Plat. theol.* (kosmos noetos)

**Cotta**, Gaius Aurelius Cotta, Roman orator, consul in 75 BC 科塔，见 Cic. *De nat. deor.*

**Cottus**, Gr: Kottos, one of the Hecatoncheires 克图斯，见 Hes. *Theog.*

**Crassus**, Lucius Licinius Crassus, 140—91 BC, outstanding Roman orator 克拉苏斯，见 Cic. *Brutus*

**Crassus**, Marcus Licinius Crassus, 115—53 BC, Roman statesman, famous for his riches, one of the triumvirs (with Caesar and Pompey) 克拉苏斯，见 Cic. *De off.* 1,25, Plut. *Bioi*

**Crassus**, Publius Licinius Crassus, a lieutenant of Caesar in Gaul in 57 BC 克拉苏斯，见 Caes. *De bello Gall.* 2

**Cratinus**, Gr: Kratinos, ca. 450 BC, one of the three Athenian writers of Old Comedy 克拉提努斯，见 Quint. *Inst.* 10

**creatio**, Gr: ktisis, genesis, E: creation, esp. the creation of the world by the Jewish-Christian God 创造，见 Bibl. *Gen.*, Philo, *De opificio*, Ios. *Antiqu.* 1, Justin. *Apol.* (link between *Timaios* and *Genesis*), Orig. *De princ.*, Basil. *Hexaem.*, Aug. *De civ. Dei* 11 (no infinite time before the world, no infinite space outside it)

**credere** => fides

**Creon** [1], Gr: Kreōn, "ruler", E: Creon, brother of Jocasta and ruler of Thebes 克瑞翁，见 Soph. *Ant.*, *Oid. epi Kol.*

**Creon** [2], Gr: Kreōn, "ruler", E: Creon, king of Corinth, who received Jason and Medea 克瑞翁，见 Eur. *Med.*

**Creta**, Gr: Krētē, < wine-krater for mixing new wine, "new", "young", "strong" (?), E: Crete, island south of Greece; the old Minoan culture of Crete (pictorial script under Egyptian influence, palaces at Cnossus and Hagia Triada) was conquered by the Achaeans (Mycene) since 1500 BC, then again invaded by the Dorians c. in 1150 BC; the Dorians founded many independent cities (Gortyn and Cnossus) but did not accept the indigenous culture; before the Romans occupied the island in 67 BC it was a refuge place for pirates; => Minos 克里特岛，见 Arist. *Polit.*, Polyb., Verg. *Aen.* 3, Ov. *Met.* 2, 8 (Europa, Minos)

**Creusa**, Gr: Kreousa, (female form of Creon, "ruler"), name of several heroines, esp. the daughter of Priam, wife of Aeneas and mother of Ascanius 克瑞乌萨，见 Verg. *Aen.* 2

**Critias**, Gr: Kritias, E: Critias, ca. 460—403 BC, Athenian politician, sophist, writer, an uncle of Plato; he had radical ideas and was one of the Thirty Tyrants in 404 BC 克里提亚斯，见 Plato

**Critobulos**, Gr: Kritoboulos, "judge in the assembly", figure in Xenophon's *Oeconomicus* 克瑞托布罗斯，见 Xen. *Oik.*

**Crito**, Gr: Kritōn, E: Crito, friend and student of Socrates who visited his teacher in prison and tried to persuade him to flee; Plato mentions him in the *Crito* and *Phaedo* 克力同，见 Plato

**Crius**, Gr: Krios, one of the Titans 克瑞乌斯，见 Hes. *Theog.*

**Croesus**, Gr: Kroisos, the wealthy king of Lydia, ca. 560—546 BC, who was defeated by Cyrus in 546 BC but became a provincial governor (Satrap) of Persia 克瑞索斯，见 Hdt. *Hist.*

**Cronus**, Gr: Kronos, "crow", "time" (?), son of Uranus, husband of Rhea and father of Hestia, Demeter, Hera, Hades, Poseidon, Zeus 克洛诺斯，见 Hes. *Theog.*

**crux**, Gr: stauros, E: cross, (crucifixion) 十字架，见 Bibl. *Ioann.* 19, Athanas. *Logos*, Venantius, *Carmina* (adoration of the Cross of Christ)

**Ctesias**, Gr: Ktēsias, E: Ctesias, Greek historian, ca. 400 BC, author of *Persika*, *Indika* 克特修斯，见 Loukianos, *Alethe diheg.*

**cubus**, Gr: kybos, E: cube, one of the five regular

solids 立方体, 见 Eucl. *Stoich.*

**cultus,** a cultivated appearance, religious worship, => kosmos, religio 美容, 见 Ov. *Ars am.* 3, *Fasti*, Lact. *Inst.* 6 (de vero cultu), Aug. *De civ. Dei* 10 (latreia = servitus, cultus)

**Cumae,** Gr: Kymē, E: Cumae, oldest Greek colony in southern Italy, founded by Chalcis (Euboea) c. in 750 BC; after being conquered by the Samnites in 420 BC the decline became inevitable 库梅, 见 Sibylla

**Cunaxa,** Gr: Kounaxa, place in Persia, scene of the defeat of Cyrus the Younger against his brother Artaxerxes II in 401 BC 库纳撒, 见 Xen. *Anab.*

**Cupido,** "desire", Gr: Erōs, E: Cupid, the Roman boy-god of love with wings and arrows, more a literary figure than an object of cultic worship 库皮得, 见 Plat. *Symp.*, Ov. *Met.* 1, Apuleius, *Met.*

**cupiditas,** desiderium, Gr: epithymetikon, epithymia, E: desire, longing, => amor, avaritia, voluptas 欲望, 见 Plat. *Polit.* 4, Cic. *De fin.* 1, *De off.* 1,66 (cupiditas gloriae), Sen. *Epist. mor.*, Epict. *Diatr.*, Tac. *Ann.* 1,10 (cupido dominandi), *Peri hypsous* 44 (epithymia), Greg. Nys. *Peri parthen.*, Chrysostom. *Peri parthen.* (marriage as remedium concupiscentiae), Aug. *Confess.* 2, *De civ Dei* 14 (conjugal love without concupiscence)

**cura,** Gr: merimna, meletēs, phrontis, pronoia, E: care (for others) 照顾, 见 Cic. *De off.* 1,12, Greg. Magn. *Regula past.* (cure and care of souls)

**curia,** E: senate-house (in Rome), first built by king Tullus Hostilius ("Curia Hostilia"); Caesar set up a new building at the Forum Romanum ("Curia Julia"), which serves as church building (S. Adriano) and has been preserved 元老院, 见 Liv. 1 (first established by Tullus Hostilius)

**cursus honorum,** E: the sequence of offices, the order of the various political offices at Rome (in the period of the late republic); after having served in the army a candidate could become quaestor, aedile, praetor, consul, and censor; the minimum age for consulship was around 42 years 职位的程序, 见 Cicero

**Cybele,** Gr: Kybelē, Kybēbē, Megalē Mētēr, E: Cybele, fertility goddess, identified with Rhea, the mother of Zeus; her cult was introduced to Rome in 204 BC 克贝勒, 见 Rhea

**Cyclopes,** Gr: Kyklōps, Kyklōpes, "round-eye", giants on an island (Sicily), one of them is Polyphemus 库克罗普斯, 圆眼巨人, 见 Hom. *Od.* 9, Hes. *Theog.*, Ar. *Sphekes*, Verg. *Aen.* 3, (country of the Cyclopes = Sicily)

**Cydippe,** Gr: Kydippē, "glorious horse", an Athenian girl loved by Acontius 基迪佩, 见 Ov. *Her.*

**Cynici,** Gr: kynikoi, "dog-like", E: Cynics, those following the principles of Diogenes of Sinope, ca. 400—325 BC and Antisthenes, ca. 445—360 BC, famous for a "natural", austere and unconventional life style 犬儒派, 见 Cic. *De off.* 1,128, Sen. *Epist. mor.* 5 (critique of Cynics), Lucian. *Vitarum auct.*, Diog. Laert.

**Cyprianus,** Caecilius, Gr: Kyprianos, "from Cyprus", E: Cyprian, bishop of Carthage, ca. 200—258 AD 西普利安, 见 Cypr., *Epist.* Prud. *Peristeph.*

**Cypselus,** Gr: Kypselos, the tyrant of Corinth, in power from ca. 657—625 BC 克普塞洛斯, 见 Liv. 1

**Cyrene,** Gr: Kyrēnē, "sovereign queen", capital of the Cyrenaica (modern Libya) in north Africa; originally a colony of Crete, then new founded by Greek settlers in 630 BC, also center of a philosophical school (Aristippus); since 322 BC the area belonged to Egypt, and since 96 BC to Rome. 库瑞内, 见 Hdt. *Hist.* 4

**Cyrillus,** Gr: Kyrillos, E: Cyril of Jerusalem, 313—381 AD, bishop and patriarch of Jerusalem, one of the Fathers of the Church 基里洛斯, 见 *Catecheses*

**Cyrus I,** Gr: Kyros, Cyros I, 559—529 BC, founder of the Persian empire, father of Cambyses, he defeated the Medes in 550 BC, conquered Lydia (Croesus) in 546 BC and Babylon in 539 BC. 居鲁士, 见 Hdt., *Hist.*

**Cyrus Minor,** Gr: Kyros, E: Cyrus the Younger, king of Persia 424—405 BC, who tried to oust his brother Artaxerxes, led an army (with Greek mercenaries) to Babylon but was defeated at Cunaxa in 401 BC and killed himself (小) 居鲁士, 见 Xen. *Anab.*

# D

**Daedalus,** Gr: Daidalos, "bright", famous Athenian architect, father of Icarus 代达罗斯, 见 Ov. *Met.* 8

**daemon,** Gr: daimōn, E: spirit, demon; => spiritus 精灵, 见 Hes. *Erga*, Plat. *Apol.*, *Symp.*, Tert. *De spect.* (theater is a place of demons, Venus and Bacchus are demons), Orig. *De princ.*, Lact. *Inst.*,

Aug. *De civ. Dei* 2 (evil spirits incite men to evil deeds)

**daimonion,** Gr: "inner spirit", L: con-scientia, Socrates' conscience 良心，见 Plat. *Apol.*

**Damasus,** Pope, 366—384 AD, who encouraged the translation of the *Vulgate* by Jerome 达玛苏斯，见 Hieron. *Epist.*

**Damon,** "subduer", philosopher from Syracuse who stood surety for his friend Phintias, saved by Phintias' last-minute return; symbol of trust and friendship 达蒙，见 Cic. *De off.* 3,50

**Danai,** Gr: Danaoi, E: Danaans, name for the Greeks 达纳伊

**Danaus,** Gr: Danaos, E: Danaus, in Greek myth the son of Belus and brother of Aegyptus; he fought against his brother 达纳乌斯

**Daphne,** Gr: Daphnē, "laurel", a nymph, daughter of Peneus, who rejected Apollo's love 达弗内，见 Ov. *Met.* 1, 452~567

**Daphnis,** legendary Sicilian shepherd, the originator of bucolic song, sometimes said to be the son of Hermes and a nymph who exposed him under a laurel tree (daphne); figure in Longus' novel 达弗尼斯，见 Verg. *Buc.* 5, Longos

***Daphnis kai Chloe,*** Gr: *Poimenika ta kata Daphnin kai Chloēn*, E: *Daphnis and Chloe*, a novel by Longus《达夫尼斯和赫洛亚》，见 Longos

**Dardanus,** Gr: Dardanos, "burner" (?), son of Zeus and Electra, founder of Dardania, father of Ilos 达尔达诺斯

**Darius,** Gr: Dareios, king of Persia 521—485 BC who reorganized the huge kingdom with the capitals Susa, Persepolis, Ecbatana, and Babylon; his campaigns against the Scythes (in 514 BC) failed; he suppressed the insurrection of the Ionian cities 499—494 BC and attacked Greece in 492—490 BC but was defeated 达瑞乌斯，见 Aesch. *Persai*, Hdt. *Hist.* 3, 7

**Darius III Codomanus,** Gr: Dareios III, 380—330 BC, defeated by Alexander 达瑞乌斯三世，见 Arrian. *Alexandrou anab.*

**David,** Hebr. "darling", Jewish king 1004—965 BC who established a kingdom around the city of Jerusalem, father of Solomon 大卫，见 Ios. *Antiquit.* 7, Ambros. *De off. ministr.*, Aug. *De civ. Dei* 17

***De aquis urbis Romae,*** E: *On the Water Supply of Rome*, a work by Frontinus《论罗马城的供水问题》，见 Front.

***De architectura,*** E: *On Architecture*, a work by Vitruvius《建筑学》，见 Vitr.

***De arte poetica,*** E: *The Art of Poetry*, a work by Horace《诗艺》，见 Horatius, Hieronymus, *Ep.* 57

***De beata vita,*** E: *On a Happy Life*, a dialog by Augustine《论幸福生活》，见 Aug.

***De bello Gallico,*** E: *The War in Gaul*, a work by Caesar《高卢战记》，见 Caes.

***De civitate Dei,*** E: *The City of God*, a monumental critique of Roman culture by Augustine《上帝之城》，见 Aug.

***De clementia,*** E: *On Clemency*, a work by Seneca《论宽和》，见 Sen.

***De compendiosa doctrina,*** E: *Handbook of Instruction*, a work by Nonius《教育手册》，见 Nonius

***De correctione rusticorum,*** E: *On the Correction of Peasants*, a work by Martin of Braga《论纠正农民》，见 Martinus de Bracara

***De doctrina christiana,*** E: *On Christian Doctrine*, a work by Augustine《论基督宗教的教导》，见 Aug.

***De finibus bonorum et malorum,*** E: *On the Greatest Goods and Evils*, a work by Cicero《论至善》，见 Cic.

***De ira Dei,*** E: *On God's Wrath*, a treatise by Lactantius《论上主之愤怒》，见 Lact.

***De lingua Latina,*** E: *On the Latin Language*, a work by Varro《论拉丁语》，见 Varro

***De mortibus persecutorum,*** E: *On the Deaths of the Persecutors*, a treatise by Lactantius《论迫害者之死》，见 Lact.

***De natura deorum,*** E: *On the Nature of the Gods*, a dialog by Cicero《论诸神的本性》，见 Cic.

***De officiis,*** E: *On Moral Obligations*, a work by Cicero《论义务》，见 Cic.

***De officiis ministrorum,*** E: *On the Duties of the Clergy*, a work by Ambrosius《论圣职人员的职务》，见 Ambros.

***De opificio mundi,*** E: *The Creation of the World*, a work by Philo《世界的创造》，见 Philo

***De principiis,*** Gr: *Peri archōn*, E: *On First Principles*, a work by Origen《论基本的原理》，见 Orig.

***De raptu Proserpinae,*** E: *The Rape of Proserpine*, an epic by Claudian《珀尔塞福涅的掠夺》，见 Claudianus

***De re publica,*** E: *On the State*, a work by Cicero《论国度》，见 Cic.

***De spectaculis,*** E: *On the Games*, a work by

Tertullian《论斗兽场的表演》，见 Tert.

***De sublimitate*** => Peri hypsous

***De testimonio animae,*** E: *The Witness of the Soul*, a work by Tertullian《灵魂的见证》，见 Tert.

***De vera religione,*** E: *On True Religion*, treatise by Augustine《论真实的宗教》，见 Aug.

***De viris illustribus,*** E: *On the Lives of Famous Men*, a work by Jerome《诸名人传》，见 Hieron.

***De vita beata,*** E: *On a Happy Life*, a work by Seneca《论幸福的人生》，见 Sen.

***De vita Caesarum,*** E: *Lives of the Caesars*, a work by Suetonius《诸恺撒传》，《十二恺撒传》，见 Suet.

**Decalogus,** Gr: deka logia, dekalogos, E: the Decalog, Ten Commandments 十诫，见 Bible, *Exodus* 20; Philo, *De opificio*

**Decelea,** Gr: Dekeleia, an Attic deme ca. 20 km from Athens, occupied by the Spartans in 413 BC, which led to the Decelean War, lasting from 413—404 BC 得克勒亚，见 Thuc. 8

**decemviri,** E: decemvirs, "ten men", a council of 10 men set up for special purposes, for example in 451 BC for a codification of the laws 十人会，见 Liv. 3

**Decius,** Messius Quintus Decius, Roman emperor 249—251 AD, persecutor of Christians 得西乌斯，见 Cyprianus, Lact. *De mortibus*, Euseb. 6,7

**Decius Mus,** Publius Decius Mus, consul in 340 BC who fought against the Latins 德修斯·姆斯，见 Liv. 8

**decus,** decorum, Gr: prepon, E: propriety, respect for the feelings of others, => honor; 礼貌，见 Cic. *De off.* 1,93; 1,126（the fourth role）

**definitio, definire,** Gr: horos, horismos, E: definition 定义，见 Arist. *Org.*, Cic. *De fin.* 2

**Deianira,** Gr: Dēianeira, "stringing together spoil", the wife of Heracles 得伊阿内拉，见 Ov. *Her.*

**Deidamia,** Gr: Dēidameia, "spoil taker", the wife of Achilleus 得伊达梅亚，见 Stat. *Achill.*

**Deipara,** Gr: theotokos, E: Mother of God, a title of Mary, rejected by Nestorius 上主之母，天主之母，见 Nestorius

**Deiphobus,** Gr: Dēiphobos, "scaring the spoiler", son of Priam, hero at Troy 得弗布斯，见 Hom. *Il.* 22

**delectare,** delectatio, Gr: terpsis, euphrosynē, hēdonē, chara, E: entertainment, entertainment value of a speech; => dilectio 使喜欢，见 Cic. *Brutus, De off.* 1,105,（good entertainment nourishes the mind by learning）, Hor. *De arte poet.* 333（aut prodesse aut delectare）

**Delos,** Gr: Dēlos, "manifest, clear", island in the Aegean Sea, the birthplace of Artemis and Apollo and thus an island of the worship of Apollo; in 478 BC the island was the center of the Delian League, until the league treasure was moved to Athens; in 166 BC the Romans made it a free port, but in 88 BC the Soldiers of Mithridates of Pontus sacked the island; a sharp decline followed. 得洛斯，见 Verg. *Aen.* 3

**Delphi,** Gr: Delphoi, "brother-mountain"（?）, city in the Greek state of Phocis and the site where Apollo killed the dragon Python; since the 8th ct. BC it was a cult-center, the temple dedicated to Apollo was built in the 7th ct. but was destroyed by fire in 548 BC; all Greeks cooperated in the reconstruction beginning in 513 BC. Since inside the temple was the navel-stone（omphalos）it was seen as the mid-point of the earth. Alongside the road leading to the temple many city-states had their treasury-houses for storing valuable offerings to Apollo. In antiquity many people（even non-Greeks）sought help from the famous oracle of Apollo. On the front of the temple were the inscription "know yourself"（gnothi seauton）and "nothing in excess"（meden agan）. The priestess Pythia lived at the sanctuary. The Pythian Games were held every fourth year since 582 BC. After 450 BC the sanctuary gradually declined, and in 391 AD it was closed by emperor Theodosius. => athla（Pythian Games）, Python, 得尔菲，见 Aesch. *Eumen.*, Hdt. *Hist.* 1, Plat. *Apol.*

**Demeter,** Gr: Dēmētēr, "barley mother", L: Ceres, goddess of agriculture and corn, mother of Persephone; => Ceres 得梅特尔，见 Hes. *Theog.*

**Demetrius,** Gr: Dēmētrios, "of Demeter", Athenian statesman, ca. 350—283 BC 得梅特利乌斯，见 Plut. *Bioi*

**demiurgus,** creator, Gr: dēmiourgos, "worker", E: demiurge, creator god 造物神，见 Plat. *Tim.*

**democratia,** Gr: archia tou dēmou, dēmokratiē, dēmokratia, E: democracy; => civitas, polis 民众的统治，见 Hdt. *Hist.* 3, Plat. *Polit.* 8, Arist. *Polit., Rhet.*, Theophr. *Eth.* 25, Cic. *De re publica*

**Democritus,** Gr: Dēmokritos, "judge of the people", ca. 460—371 BC, Greek philosopher and prolific writer, famous for his theory of atoms; only a few fragments of his works are extant. 德谟克利特，

见 Cic. *De fin.*1, Lucian, *Vit. auct.*, Clem. Alex. *Strom.* (some texts preserved), Diog. Laert.

**Demodocus,** Gr: Dēmodokos, "glory of the people", bard at Antinous' court 得摩多科斯, 见 Hom. *Od.* 8

**Demophon,** Gr: Dēmophōn, "voice of the people", E: Demophoon / Demophon, son of Theseus and Phaedra, lover of Phyllis 得摩丰, 见 Ov. *Her.*

**dēmos,** L: tribus, E: demos, district; a region and its inhabitants, "the people", the self-governing community in the system of Cleisthenes; => Cleisthenes, populus, gens 某地区, 其人民, 见 Colonus

**Demosthenes,** Gr: Dēmosthenēs, "strength of the people", famous Greek orator, 384—322 BC; after 355 BC he held political speeches aiming at a unification of Greece against the Macedonian king Philipp; he also opposed the rule of Alexander; => orator 狄摩西尼, 见 Quint. *Inst.* 10, Plut. *Bioi; Peri hypsous* 12 (compared to Cicero), Hieron. *Ep.* 57

***Deorum dialogi,*** Gr: *Theōn dialogoi*, E: *Dialogues of the Gods*, a work by Lucian《诸神对话》, 见 Loukianos

**descriptio,** Gr: ekphrasis, E: description 描述, 见 elocutio

**deserta,** Gr: erēmos, E: desert, the regions where monks (hermits) lived, especially in Egypt 沙漠, 见 Athan. *Vita Anton.*

**desiderium** => cupiditas

**Deucalion,** Gr: Deukaliōn, "=deikelos", "mirroring image" (?), who was warned by his father Prometheus to prepare a boat for the flood which was sent by Zeus as punishment for a corrupted world; in response to an oracle from Themis, Deucalion and his wife Pyrrha threw stones over their shoulder, and the stones grew into men and women; Deucalion and his wife became the parents of Hellen, ancestor of the Greeks 丢卡利翁, 见 Ov. *Met.* 1

**deus, dea, di,** Gr: theos, E: god, godess, godhead, gods; => apotheosis, religio, theologia, penates, lares, Zeus/Jupiter, Hera/ Juno, Athena/ Minerva, Apollo, Aphrodite/ Venus, etc. 神, 神明, 神灵, 见 Cic. *De nat. deor.* 3,39 (deifications of Love, Fear etc. are to be rejected), Verg. *Aen., Georg.* 2, 490 (dei agrestes), Hor. *Carm.* 1,17 (di me tuentur), *Carm. saec.* (prayers to many Roman gods), Ov. *Met.* (many stories about gods), Philo, *De opificio* (critical of polytheism, atheism), Sen. *Epist. mor.* 10 (tamquam deus videat), Luc. *Phars.*, Tatian. *Logos*, Tert. *Apol.* (euhemerism), Aug. *De civ. Dei* (pagan gods are immoral, were ridiculed; worship of divine gifts: Segetia, Pomona, Virtus, Concordia etc.), Macrob. *Sat.* (monotheist interpretation of mythology), Proclus, *Plat. theol.* (gods are henads to connect the world with the One)

**Deus,** Gr: theos, E: God, the strictly monotheist concept of God as Creator and Law-giver, expressed in the Jewish-Christian canon of the Bible, => Logos, monotheismus, Spiritus Sanctus 神、天主、上帝, 见 Biblia, Gen, Tert. *Apol.*, Aug. *De beata vita* (Deum quaerere / habere), Boethius, *De cons.* 3 (Deus = summum bonum), Joh. Climac. *Scala* (contemplation of God)

**deus ex machina,** "a god coming out of a machine", the sudden appearance of a god (lowered from above by a theater-crane) in order to bring a miraculous solution to a difficult situation "解决困难的神", 见 Eur. *Iph. Aul.*, vv. 1532~1626; Hor. *De arte poet.* 191 (nisi dignus vindice nodus)

**devotio,** the "devoting" of oneself and the enemy to the gods below so as to gain victory 奉献自己, 见 Liv. 8 (Decius Mus)

**di** => deus

**di consentes,** E: superior gods (whose statues stood in the Roman Forum) 核心的神明, 见 Aug. *De civ. Dei* 4

**diabolus** => Satana

**diaconus,** Gr: diakonos, "servant", E: deacon, an early office in the Church; => episcopoi 执事, 见 Didache, Dionys. Areop. *Eccl. hier.*

**diadochoi,** gr: diadochoi, E: "successors", the name of the Greek rulers who ruled the huge empire of Alexander the Great after his death in 323 BC, namely the Attalids (in Pergamum), Ptolemies (in Egypt), Antigonids (in Macedonia), and the Seleucids (in Syria). 继承者, 见 Antiochus, Ptolemaeus

***Dialogi,*** E: *Dialogues*, a work by Gregory the Great《对话集》, 见 Greg. Mag., *Dial.*

***Dialogus de anima et de resurrectione*** = *Peri psychēs kai anastaseōs*

**Diana,** Gr: Artemis, E: Diana, Italian goddess of the moon, and of wild nature, protector of women, identified with Artemis 狄安娜，见 Cic. *De nat. deor.* 2,60~70, Hor. *Carm.* 1,12, *Carm.* saec., Ov. *Met.* 6（Niobe）, Claudian. *De raptu Proserp.*

**Diatessaron,** Gr: *Diatessarōn*, a work by Tatian《四部福音合参》

**diatheke** => testamentum

***Diatribai,*** E: *Lectures*, a work by Epictetus《论集》, 见 Epict.

**dictator,** E: dictator; dictatorship was a magistracy for emergencies; during a crisis the consuls could choose a former consul to be dictator for at most 6 months; the dictator had extraordinary power. Sulla and Caesar made use of this old title in order to justify their intentions of lasting rule. 独裁者，见 Cincinnatus

**dictionarium** => encyclopaedia

***Didache,*** Gr: *Didachē tōn dōdeka apostolōn*, E: *Teaching of the Twelve Apostles*, anonymous work of the second century《十二使徒/宗徒遗训》, 见 Didache

**didaskalos** => magister

**Dido,** originally named Elissa, the legendary wife of Sychaeus who was murdered by Pygmalion, king of Tyre; Dido fled from Tyre to Libya and founded Carthage on the land which the local king Iarbas had granted her. According to Virgil she killed herself after Aeneas had left her. 狄多，见 Verg. *Aen.*, Ov. *Her.*

**dignitas,** gravitas, Gr: timē, axia, semnotēs, baros, E: dignity; => imago Dei 尊严，见 Cic. *De off.* 1,130, Greg. Nys. *Peri kataskeues*

**Dikaiopolis,** "just citizen", figure in Aristophanes' comedy "正义的公民"，见 Ar. *Acharn.*

**dikaiosynē** = justitia

**dikē** => 1) mos, 2) jus, lex, justitia, 3) sententia, judicium, 4) poena, 5) vindicatio; E: justice, punishment; also personified as virgin（parthenos Dike）, daughter of Zeus and Themis 正义，见 Hes. *Erga*

**dikē en chersin,** "justice in the fists", E: might is right 权力就是正义，见 Hes. *Erga*, 192

**dilectio, diligere,** Gr: philia, philein, hēdonē, chara, E: delight in, love, appreciate 爱好，喜欢，见 Cic. *De fin.* 3,16（se diligere）

**diligentia** => industria

**diluvium,** Gr: epirrhoē, kataklysmos, E: flood 洪水，见 Bibl. *Gen.* 6~9（Noah is saved in the flood）; Ov. *Met.* 1,253~345（the great flood which destroys mankind, => Deucalion）

**Diocletianus,** Gaius Aurelius Valerius Diocletianus, Gr: Dioklēs, "praise of god", E: Diocletian, son of a freedman, Roman emperor 284—305 AD, he tried to reorganize the empire, dividing it into four parts（Gallia, Italia, Illyria, the East）and triggered a severe persecution of Christians in 303 AD; he retired in 305 and died in Dalmatia in 313（or 316）AD. 戴克里先，见 Lact. *De mortibus*

**Diogenes,** Gr: Diogenēs, "son of Zeus", E: Diogenes of Sinope, Greek philosopher, ca. 400—325 BC, founder of the Cynic school of thought 狄奥根尼，见 Arrian. *Alex. anab.*, 7,（meeting with Alexander）, Lucian. *Vitarum auctio*

**Diogenes Laertius,** Gr: Diogenēs Laertios, E: Diogenes of Laerte, ca. 220—280 AD, Greek author 第欧根尼·拉尔修，见 *Philosophon bion kai dogmaton synagoge*

**Diomedes,** Gr: Diomēdēs, "divine cunning", E: Diomede, son of Tydeus and Deipyle, legendary king of Argos who raided the Trojan camp and did not even fear the encounter with Ares and Aphrodite. 狄俄梅得斯，见 Hom. *Il.* 5, 9, 10, 14, Stat. *Achill.*

**Dion,** 1）409—353 BC, since 388 BC friend of Plato and tyrant of Syracuse who wanted to realize Plato's ideas but was exiled; in 357 BC he obtained the rule of Syracuse but was assassinated in 353 BC; 2）Stoic philosopher, ca. 40—111 AD 狄翁，见 Plut. *Bioi*

**Dionysius,** Gr: Dionysios, "of Dionysus", E: Dionysius, tyrant of Syracuse 405—367 BC 狄欧尼修斯，见 Cic. *De off.* 2,25; 3,50

**Dionysius,** Gr: Dionysios, E: Dionysius of Halicarnassus, ca. 50—10 BC, Greek rhetor and historian living at Rome, author of *Roman Antiquities* 狄欧尼修斯，见 Ios. *Antiquitates*

**Dionysius Areopagita,** Gr: Dionysios Areopagita, E: Dionysius the Areopagite, Pseudo-Dionysius, ca. 480—510 AD, author and theologian 狄奥尼修斯，（或译丢尼修）见 *Peri tes ekklesiastikes hierarchias, Peri tes ouranias hierarchias*

**Dionysophanes,** a figure in Longus' *Daphnis and Chloe* 狄欧尼修法内斯，见 Longus

**Dionysus,** Gr: Dionysos, "child of Zeus", "lame god", E: Dionysus, also called Bacchus, the god of wine and ecstasy, son of Zeus and the Theban princess Semele;（Semele had to die since she wanted to see the splendor of Zeus who appeared to her as lightning.) Dionysus was accompanied by Sileni and Satyrs, and the plants dedicated to him were the vine and ivy. In Athens the festival of the Great Dionysia in March was crowned with dramatic performances. => Bacchus 狄欧尼苏斯, 见 Soph. *Ant.*, Lucian. *Theon dial.*, Tert. *De spect.*

**Dios apatē,** the deception of Zeus by his wife Hera, so that the gods can secretly help the Greeks at Troy 宙斯受骗, 见 Hom. *Il.* 14

**Dioscuri,** Gr: Dioskouroi, "sons of Zeus", E: Dioscures, two sons of Zeus and Leda, namely Castor (famous as tamer of horses) and Pollux (boxer). 宙斯的两个儿子, 见 Apoll. *Arg.*

**Diotima,** Gr: Diotima, "fear god", a mysterious priestess who told Socrates about the meaning of love 狄俄提马, 见 Plat. *Symp.*

**disciplina,** Gr: mathēsis, syntaxis, E: discipline, branch of knowledge 学科, 见 Cic. *De fin.* 3,74 (structure of Stoic teaching), *De fin.* 5,7, (disciplines of the Peripatos), Aug. *De vera religione*, Cassiod. *Inst.*

**discipulus,** Gr: mathētēs, E: disciple, follower, student 学生、门徒, 见 Bibl. *Ioann.* 6,

**discordia** => concordia

**dispositio,** Gr: taxis, diathesis, diataxis, E: arrangement, disposition (of a speech) 排列、编写, 见 Cic. *Brut.*, Quint. *Inst.*

**divinatio,** Gr: mantikē, hieroskopia, cheiromanteia, E: divination, fortune telling, soothsaying; Greeks had their oracles at Delphi and other sanctuaries; Romans performed auspices (auspicium, from "aves spicere") by observing birds or interpreting the intestines of sacrificial animals; => magus, oraculum 算命, 见 Cic. *De nat. deor.*1,55, *De div.*, Mart. *Epigr.*

**divinitas,** Gr: theiotēs, to theion, E: divinity, divine being; => apotheosis, deus, religio 神性, 见 Cic. *De nat. deor.* 2,16 (heavenly bodies share divinity)

**divitiae** => opes

**docere,** to teach, provide information 教导, 见 Cic. *Brutus*

**doctrina,** disciplina, Gr: mathēsis, mathēma, didaskalia, didachē, E: teaching, doctrine 教导, 见 Cic. *De fin.* 3,74, Tert. *De spect.* ("scaenica doctrina" of Christianity), Orig. *Contra Cels.*, Aug. *De doctrina christ.*

**dogmatici,** Gr: dogmatikoi, E: dogmatists, (in skeptic theory) those who believe in reliable knowledge 独断论者, 见 Sext. Emp. *Skept.*, Minucius, *Oct.*

**Dolon,** Gr: Dolōn, "ensnarer", Trojan hero 多伦, 见 Hom. *Il.* 10

**dolor,** Gr: algos, lypē, ponos, pathos, E: pain, suffering; acceptance of pain; => labor, morbus, mors; Hercules, Regulus, Scaevola 痛苦, 见 Cic. *De fin.* 1, Sen. *De vita beata* 22, (readiness to accept pain), Bibl. *Gen* (aetiology of human suffering), *Job* (suffering of the just), Perpetua, *Passio*, Chrysostom. *Peri parthen.* (hardships of conjugal life), Boethius, *Cons.*

**dominus,** Gr: kyrios, Hebr. adonay, E: Lord, (in the Old Testament used for God, later also for Jesus) 主, 见 Bibl. *Ioann.* 20:28 (kyrios mou)

**Domitianus,** Titus Flavius Domitianus, E: Domitian, son of Vespasian, brother of Titus, Roman emperor 81—96, the last of the Flavian emperors 多弥贤, 见 Mart. *Epigr.*, Tac. *Ann.*, Iuv. *Sat.* 4, Lact. *De mort.*

**domus,** Gr: oikos, oikia, domos, E: house, household, family, dynasty 家、房屋, 见 Xen. *Oik.*, Cic. *De off.* 1,138

**Domus aurea,** E: Golden House, the huge palace in Rome, projected by Nero after the fire of AD 64 金宫, 见 Suet. *De vita Caes.*

**Dores,** Gr: Dōrides, E: Dorians, a people from Thessaly who occupied the Peloponnesus and parts of Asia Minor after 1150 BC (the so-called Dorian Invasion); from their bases in Greece (Corinth) the Dorians founded colonies in Sicily and in southern Italy 多里斯人, 见 Creta

**Doricus stylus,** Gr: Dōrikos, E: Doric style (of architecture) 多里斯人风格, 见 Vitr. *De arch.* 3~4

**doxai** = notiones

**drachma,** Gr: drachmē, E: drachma, a Greek coin 德拉克马, 见 Ar. *Acharn.*

**draco,** serpens, Gr: drakōn, "glancing", "looking", (from derkomai), ophis, sauros, E: dragon, snake, usually a symbol of evil powers 龙, 见 Aesch. *Choeph.*, Arist. *Rhet.*, Apoll. *Arg.* (seed of dragon teeth; serpent guarding the fleece), Ov. *Met.* 3 (Cadmus kills a snake), Bibl. *Gen* 3 (the snake, ophis, induces sin), Physiologus, Apuleius, *Met.*, Perpetua, Passio

**Draco,** Gr: Drakōn, "dragon", E: Dracon, the first lawgiver of Athens, ca. 620 BC who ordered the codification of the law; his laws were notoriously harsh. 德拉孔, 见 Arist. *Polit.*, Arist. *Rhet.*

**Drepanum,** place in Sicily 得瑞帕农, 见 Verg. *Aen.* 3

**druides,** E: druids, the religious leaders and priests of Gallic tribes 司祭, 见 Caes. *De bello Gall.*

**Dryades,** Gr: Dryas, Dryades, (drys = tree), E: Dryads, nymphs of trees 树神, 见 Verg. *Georg.* 4

**Dryas,** Gr: Dryas, "tree", name of a shepherd in Daphnis kai Chloe 得瑞亚斯, 见 Longos

*Dyscolus,* Gr: *Dyskolos,* E: *The Misanthrope,* the only extant comedy of Menander《恨世者》, 见 Men.

# E

**ecclesia,** Gr: ekklēsia, "the convoked (assembly)", E: 1) the assembly and sovereign body of Athens which met 40 times a year; all adult male citizens over the age of 18 could vote and address the assembly; 2) the Church, the community of Christians; => Christians, Christ, persecutio 公民大会, 教会, 见 *Didache* (the first ecclesiastical constitution), Iren., Cyprian. (sectarians), Lact. *De mortibus,* Aug. *De civ. Dei,* 15, 17, 18 (symbols of the Church: Noah's ark, Hannah, Jerusalem), Dionysius Ar., *Eccl. hier.*, Maximus Conf., *Mystagogia* (deeper meaning of Church liturgy)

**ecclesia catholica,** Gr: katholikē ekklēsia, E: the universal Church, an expression first used by Ignatius 大公教会, 见 Ignatius, Ep.

*Ecclesiastica historia,* Gr: *Ekklēsiastikē historia,* E: *Church History,* the first history of the Church《教会历史》, 见 Eusebius

**Eclogae,** Gr: Eklogai, E: Eclogues => Bucolica

**Echecrates,** Gr: Echekratēs, "hold–fast", friend of Socrates 厄赫克拉特斯, 见 Plat. *Phaid.*,

**Echo,** Gr: Ēchō, "echo", name of a nymph who loved Narcissus 厄科、回声女神, 见 Ov. *Met.* 3

**educatio,** Gr: paideia, paidagōgia, mathēsis, scholē, maieutikē, trophē, didaskalia, E: education, instruction, learning, teaching, pedagogy, "midwifery"; => institutio, disciplina, discipulus, doctrina, eruditio, magister, schole 教育、培养、教育方式, 见 Ar. *Nephel.*, Xen. *Oik.* (maieutike), Plat. *Gorg., Polit.,* Arist. *Polit.*7, Theophr. *Eth.* 27 (opsimathia), Ter. *Adelph.*, Cic. *Brutus*, Vitr. *De arch.*1, Sall. *Bell. Cat.* (textbook), Publ. Syr. (textbook), Verg. *Aen.* (textbook), Ov. *Ars am.* 3, Quint. *Inst.,* Stat. *Achill.* (Chiron), Plut. *Mor.* (*Peri paidon agoges*), Iuv. *Sat.* 14; *Peri hypsous* 8, Clem. Alex. *Paed.*, Lact. *Inst.*, Hieron. Epist. 107 (*de institutione filiae,* fiunt non nascuntur Christiani), Aug. *De doctrina christiana* (education of preachers), Capella, *De nuptiis* (used as textbook), Greg. Magn., *Regula pastoralis* (moral education; declining education level)

**effectio recta,** Gr: kathorthoma, E: right action 正当的行动, 见 Cic. *De fin.* 3,45

**egestas,** E: need, lack 匮乏, 见 Aug. *De beata vita* (animi egestas)

**Egypt** = Aegyptus

**eidōla** => spiritus

**eidos** => forma, idea

*Eidyllia,* Gr: *Eidyllia,* E: *Idylls,* poems by Theocritus《写景短诗》、《牧歌》, 见 Verg. *Buc.*

**Eirenaios** = Irenaeus

**eirene** => pax

*Eirene,* Gr: *Eirēnē,* E: *Peace,* comedy by Aristophanes《和平》, 见 Ar.

**Eis tēn Platōnos theologian,** E: *On Plato's Theology,* a work by Proclus《论柏拉图的神学》, 见 Proclus

**ekklesia** = ecclesia

**Electra,** Gr: Ēlektra, "bright", "amber", E: Electra, daughter of Agamemnon, sister of Orestes who assisted him in his revenge; tragedies by Aeschylus, Sophocles and Euripides on the theme are extant. 厄勒克特拉, 见 Aesch. *Choeph.*, Soph. *Elektra*

*Electra,* Gr: *Ēlektra,* drama by Sophocles《厄勒克特拉》, 见 Soph.

**elegia,** Gr: elegos, E: elegy, a poem written in elegiac couplets (alternating lines of hexameters and pentameters); in Greece elegies covered a wide variety of themes (lament, politics, meditation, dedication to a god, love); the Romans accepted the elegy only in the first century BC and used it for love–poems and laments; => Gallus, Catullus, Tibullus, Propertius, Ovid 哀歌, 见 Hor. *De arte poet.*

**elementa,** Gr: stoicheia, E: elements, usually earth, water, fire, air; => aqua, aer, ignis, terra 元素, 见 Plat. *Tim.*, Plin. *Nat. hist.* 2, 33 ~37, Basil. *Hexaem.*

*Elementa Geometriae,* Gr: *Stoicheia,* E: *Elements of Geometry,* a work by Euclid《几何原本》, 见 Eucl.

**elephas,** Gr: elephas, E: elephant 大象, 见 *Plin. Nat. hist.* 8 (elephants have human features)

**eleutheria** => libertas

**elocutio,** Gr: lexis, phrasis, E: diction, verbal expression, elaboration of style 表达，见 Arist. *Poiet.*, *Rhet.*, Cic. *Brutus*, Quint. *Inst.*, *Peri hypsous* 8（phrasis）

**eloquentia,**（negative: loquacia, jactantia）, Gr: euepeia, euglossia,（negative: adoleschia, lalia, alazoneia）, E: eloquence;（garrulity, bragging）; => silentium 口才、爱闲谈、夸耀，见 Theophr. *Eth.* 3, 7, 23; Hieron. *Ep.* 57（verbosa rusticitas）, Aug. *De doctrina christiana*（critique of empty words）, Gregor. Magn., *Reg. past.*（eloquence is not important）

**elysium,** Gr: ēlysion, makarōn nēsoi, E: Elysium, the Isles of the Blest, in later myth（Virgil）a part of the Underworld 冥土的一个岛、冥乡乐土，见 Hom. *Od.* 11, Hes. *Erg.*, Verg. *Aen.* 6, Lucian, *Alethe diheg.*

**emanatio,** E: emanation, the Neoplatonic view that the lower levels of being flow out from higher levels 流溢说，见 Dionys. Ar., *Peri tes our. hier.*

**Empedocles,** Gr: Empedoklēs, ca. 495—435 BC, Greek philosopher born in Agrigentum（Sicily）, famous for his theory of the four elements as the origin of all things; his many students worshiped him like a god 恩佩多克勒斯，见 Clem. Alex. *Strom.*（quotations preserved）

**empeireia** => experientia

**Empiricus** = Sextus Empiricus

**encyclopaedia,** Gr: en kyklo paideia "circular teaching", E: encyclopedia; compilations or handbooks for instruction, usually arranged according to subject matter, sometimes according to the alphabet, => alphabetum 百科全书，见 Cato, Varro, Publ. Syrus, Plinius, *Hist. nat.*, Gellius, Nonius, Capella, *De nuptiis*, Cassiod. *Inst.*, Isidorus, *Etymol.*

**energeia,** Gr: energeia, E: energy 能力，见 Arist. *Met.*

***Enneades,*** E: *Enneads*, work by Plotin's student Porphyry《九章集》，见 Plotinus

**ennoia** => notio

**Ennius,** Quintus Ennius, 239—169 BC, early Roman poet of whose works only fragments survive; author of the *Annales*, a history of Rome from Aeneas until the first Punic War 恩尼乌斯，见 Cic. *De nat. deor.* 2,93, Quint. *Inst.* 10, Nonius Marcellus, *De compend.*

**enthymema,** E: persuasive rhetorical means, metaphors 修辞学手段，见 Arist. *Rhet.*

**Eos,** Gr: Eōs, Ēōs, "dawn", L: Aurora, dawn-goddess, sister of Helios and Selene 厄俄斯、晨光女神，见 Hes. *Theog.*

**Epaminondas,** Gr: Epameinōndas, ca. 400—362 BC, Theban statesman and general 厄帕门能达斯，见 Plut. *Bioi*

**Ephesus,** Gr: Ephesos, "dream-town", important city in Asia Minor, inhabitated by Greeks since 1100 BC; coins were minted in the 7th ct. BC, and after the fall of Miletus（494 BC）Ephesus became the wealthiest and most powerful of all Ionian cities; the famous temple dedicated to Artemis was destroyed by fire in 356 BC but was rebuilt and became one of the Seven Wonders of the ancient world; in 190 BC the city fell to Pergamum and in 133 BC to the Romans. St. Paul was in Ephesus in 56—58 AD. In 391 AD the emperor Theodosius suppressed all pagan worship, and the temple of Artemis / Diana was closed. 厄弗所，以弗所，见 Plaut. *Miles*, Ignatius, *Ep.*, Nestorius（his teachings were condemned at the Council of 431 AD）, Leo, *Tomus*（Synod of 449 AD）, Cassiod. *Inst.*（Ecumenical Council of 431 AD）

**Epictetus,** Gr: Epiktētos, "bought slave", Greek Stoic author, ca. 50—135 AD; Arrianus edited his lectures. 埃比克泰德，见 Epict. *Diatrib.*, *Encheir.*

**Epicurus,** Gr: Epikouros, E: Epicurus, 341—271 BC, Greek philosopher, founder of the Epicurean school emphasizing individual happiness（eudaimonia）and freedom from pain. Many Romans rejected the hedonist tendencies of Epicurus' thought, and Christian authors attacked him for abandoning religious reverence and the afterlife. 伊壁鸠鲁，见 Cic. *De fin.*, *Tusc.*, Lucr. *De rer. nat.*, Sen. *De vita beata*, Lucian. *Vit. auct.*, Clem. Alex. *Strom.*（the only school to be rejected）, Diog. Laert., Lact. *De ira Dei*, *Inst.*

**epigramma,** Gr: epigramma, E: epigram, a verse inscription, originally on a building, gate, artifact, tombstone or monument; Greek epigrams were written first in hexameters, later in elegiacs; since the 6th ct. BC epigrams were written as literature and served to cover an unlimited variety of themes: expression of feelings, maxims, love, art criticism, politics, glorification of gods or heroes etc. The first famous epigrammatist was Simonides of Ceos（556—468 BC）. Among Roman authors Ennius, Catull and especially Martial are famous for their epigrams 警句, 见 Martial, *Epigr.*

***Epigrammata,*** E: *Epigrams,* a work by Martial《警句诗集》, 见 Mart.

**epilogus,** peroratio, Gr: epilogos, E: conclusion of a speech, epilogue 结语, 见 Arist. *Rhet.*,

**Epimetheus,** Gr: Epimētheus, "afterthought", "slow learner", brother of Prometheus 厄皮梅特斯, 见 Hes. *Erga, Theog.*

**episcopus,** Gr: episkopos, "supervisor", E: bishop, leader of a Christian community 主教, 见 Didache (episkopoi and diakonoi), Iren. *Adv. haer.* (succession of bishops), Cyprian. *Epist.*, (bishops of Rome, Carthage), Basilius, Greg. Naz. (patriarch of Constantinople), Greg. Nys., Dionys. Areop., *Eccl. hier.*, Greg. Turon. *Hist. Franc.* (bishops of Tours)

**epistēmē** => scientia, cognitio, notio, intellectus

**epistula,** Gr: epistolē, E: letter, (love letter) 书信、情书, 见 Eur. *Hippol., Iphigen.,* Cic. Ov. *Ars amat., Her., Sen., Ep. mor.,* Biblia (Novum Testamentum), Cyprian. *Ep.,* Hieron. *Ep.,* Auson. *Ep.*

***Epistulae,*** E: *Letters,* by Ausonius《书信集》, 见 Ausonius

***Epistulae,*** E: *Letters,* by Cyprianus《书信集》, 见 Cyprianus

***Epistulae,*** E: *Letters,* by Jerome《信集》, 见 Hieron.

**epitaphius,** Gr: epitaphios, "added to the tomb", E: funeral oration 讣词, 见 Thuc. 2

**epithymia** => cupiditas

**epoche,** Gr: epochē, "holding back", E: refraining from judgment 不作判断, 见 Sext. Emp. *Skept.*

**epos,** Gr: epos, E: epic, a long narrative poem in majestic style; Greek epics were usually written in hexameter verses; since the time of Peisistratus the epics of Homer were recited at public festivals; later epics imitated Homer, for example Apollonius' *Argonautika,* Nonnus' *Dionysiaka,* Musaeus' *Hero kai Leander*; Latin epic poetry started with the translation of the *Odyssey* by Livius Andronicus, ca. 240 BC. Other Roman epic poets were Naevius, Ennius, and Lucretius; Vergil created the most influential national epic of Rome. 史诗, 见 Homeros, Apollonios, *Arg.,* Lucretius, *De rerum nat.,* Vergilius, *Aeneis*

**equus,** Gr: hippos, E: horse 马, 见 Hom. *Il.* 19 (Xanthus), Plat. *Phaedrus* (symbol of the forces of the soul), Verg. *Aen.* 2 (equus ligneus, wooden horse), *Aen.* 10 (Rhaebus), *Georg.* 3 (raising of horses), Suet. *De vita Caes.* (Nero's passion for horses), Arrian. 5 (Bucephalas), Prud. *Psych.* (Superbia falls from the horse)

**Er,** Gr: Er, a legendary man who reports about the after-life 厄尔, 见 Plat. *Polit.* 10, Cic. *De re publ.* (*Somnium Scipionis*)

**Erato,** Gr: Eratō, "passionate", one of the Muses, Muse of lyrics 俄拉托, 见 Hes. *Theog.*

**Eratosthenes,** Gr: Eratosthenēs, "strength of Erato", E: Eratosthenes of Cyrene, 285—205 BC, head of the Library of Alexandria after 235 BC, poet, grammarian, mathematician, geographer, astronomer, who described himself as "philologos". He calculated the earth's circumference with amazing accuracy. His works are lost. 厄拉托斯特内斯, 见 Alexandria

**Erebus,** Gr: Erebos, E: Erebus, the darkness of the Underworld 厄瑞布斯, 见 Hes. *Theog.*

**Erechtheum,** Gr: Erechtheion, E: Erechtheum, the temple at Athens which housed the cult of Athena and Erechtheus, a mythical king of Athens; it was constructed 421—406 BC and is the second most important building after the Parthenon 厄瑞克特翁, 见 Acropolis

***Erga kai hēmerai,*** *Works and Days,* a work by Hesiod《农作与时日》

**ergon,** Gr: ergon, => ponos; E: hard work; => labor 劳动, 见 Hes. *Erga*

**Erinyes** = Furiae

**eris,** quarrel, strife, also personified as Eris, goddess of discord; at the wedding feast of Peleus and Thetis she threw an apple with the inscription "for the most beautiful" among the guests and so triggered the quarrel between Hera, Athena and Aphrodite; Paris decided to give the apple to Aphrodite (the "judgment of Paris") 艾瑞斯, 见 Hes. *Erga*

**Eros,** Gr: Erōs, "erotic love", E: Eros, god (or spirit) of love, son of Aphrodite and Ares (according to Plato son of Ponos and Penia); according to Plato's explanation Eros would lead to the contemplation of the idea of beauty; => amor, Amor, Cupido 爱欲之神, 见 Hes. *Theog.,* Eur. *Hipp.,* Ar. *Lysistr.,* Plat., *Symp.,* Apoll. *Arg.,* Lucian. *Theon dial.,* Longus

**eschatologia,** Gr: eschaton, "the last", E: eschatology, the Christian doctrines concerning the "last things", such as death, resurrection, judgment, eternal life 终末论，末世论，见 Iren., Orig. *Peri archon*, Greg. Nyss., *Peri psyches kai anastaseos*, Aug. *De civ. Dei* 20~21, Greg. Magn. *Dialogi* 4

**esse, ens,** Gr: einai, ousia, E: being 存在，见 Arist. *Met.*, Greg. Naz. *Logoi* (two names of God: ho ōn, hē ousia), Aug. *De beata vita* (frugalitas = esse, nequitia = non esse)

**Eteocles,** Gr: Eteoklēs, "perennial glory", son of Oedipus, brother of Polyneices 厄特俄克勒斯，见 Soph. *Ant.*, *Oid. epi Kol.*

***Ethica Nicomachia,*** Gr: *Ēthika Nikomacheia*, E: *Nicomachian Ethics*, work by Aristotle《尼各马可伦理学》，见 Arist.

**ethos** = mores

**Etrusci,** Tusci, Gr: Thyrrenioi, E: Etruscans, a pre-Roman people of central Italy, they probably migrated to Italy in the 9th ct. BC and came from Asia Minor; since the 6th ct. BC they were repeatedly defeated by the Latins, in 424 BC they lost Capua, 396 BC they lost the city of Veji to the Gauls; among the things which the Romans inherited from the Etruscans were gladiatorial fights, divination practices (augury) and the name system (first name, clan name, nickname); => Tarchon 伊特鲁斯基人，见 Verg. *Aen.* 10;

**etymologia,** Gr: etymologia, E: etymology, the explanation of the origin of words 语源学/词源学，见 Varro (etymology as science), Cic. *De nat. deor.* (explanations of the names of Roman gods), Gellius, Aug. *De civ.* 10, Isid. *Etymologiae*

***Etymologiae,*** E: *Etymologies*, an encyclopedia in 20 books by Isidore of Sevilla《语源学》，见 Isidorus

**Euagrios** = Evagrius

**Euandros** = Evander

**euangelion** = evangelium

**Euangelion kata Ioannen** => Evangelium secundum Johannem

**Euboea,** Gr: Euboia, "bull-land", after Crete the second largest island of Greece; its most important cities were Eretrea and Chalcis 希腊东部的岛屿

**eucharistia,** Gr: eucharistia, "giving thanks", E: eucharist, a Christian sacrament 感恩祭，见 *Didache*, Cyrillus, *Catecheses*, Dion. Areop., *Eccl. hier.*, Maximus Conf. *Mystagogia*

**Euclides,** Gr: Eukleidēs, "glorious", E: Euclid, Greek mathematician 320—280 BC 欧几里得，见 Eucl. *Stoicheia*, Capella, De nuptiis

**Euclio,** an old stingy man in Plautus' play *Aulularia* 欧克留，见 Plaut. *Aul.*

**eudaimonia** = beatitudo

**eudoxia** = fama bona

**Euelpides,** Gr: Euelpidēs, "good hope", figure in Aristophanes' *Birds* "乐观者"，欧厄尔皮得斯，见 Ar. *Ornithes*

**Eugippius,** E: Eugippius, ca. 465—535 AD, Latin author 欧格彼乌斯，见 *Vita Sancti Severini*

**Euhemerus,** Gr: Euēmeros, E: Euhemerus, ca. 300 BC, Greek author; he thought that the gods of mythology were originally great kings who were deified by their people. This theory is known as "euhemerism" and quoted by Christian apologists to show the irrational nature of the Greek gods. 欧厄梅鲁斯，见 Tert. *Apol.*, Lact. *Inst.*, Aug. *De civ. Dei* 6

**eulogia** => benedictio

**Eumaeus,** Gr: Eumaios, "of good endeavour", E: Eumaius, the faithful swineherd of Odysseus 欧迈乌斯，见 Hom. *Od.* 14~17

**Eumelus,** Gr: Eumelos, "nice melody", son of Admetus and Alcestis 欧梅卢斯，见 Eur. *Alk.*

**Eumenides,** Gr: Eumenides, "well-meaning", euphemism for the godesses of wrath and revenge; => Furiae, Erinyes 慈悲女神（指复仇女神），见 Aesch. *Eumen.*

***Eumenides,*** Gr: *Eumenides*, "well-meaning goddesses", the third part of the Oresteia《慈悲女神》，见 Aesch. *Eumen.*

**Euphrates,** Gr: Euphratēs, "bringer (phora) of good" (?), river in Mesopotamia 幼发拉底河，见 Xen. *Anab.*

**Euphrosyne** => Gratiae

**Eupolis,** ca. 460—410 BC, "good citizen", one of the three famous Athenian writers of Old Comedy, only fragments of his 14 comedies are preserved; => Cratinus, Aristophanes 欧波里斯，见 Quint. *Inst.* 10

**Euripides,** Gr: Euripidēs, "fresh", "energetic", Greek tragedian, 484—425 BC; his tragedies convey new and quite modern views and thus stimulated fierce discussions among his contemporaries. For the first time in the history of drama he gave women the central roles. 欧里庇得斯，见 Eur. *Alkestis, Hipp., Iphigen., Medeia*, Ar. *Acharn., Nephel.*, Quint. *Inst.* 10

**Europa,** Gr: Europē, "far-seeing", "broad faced" (?), daughter of Agenor, king of Tyre

(Phoenicia), sister of Cadmus, she was loved by Zeus, who took her to Crete, where she gave birth to Minos and Rhadamanthys 欧罗巴，见 Hdt. *Hist.* 1, Ov. *Met.* 2

**Euryalus,** Gr: Euryalos, "wide wanderer", Trojan hero, friend of Nisus 欧瑞阿鲁斯，见 Verg. *Aen.* 9

**Eurycleia,** Gr: Eurykleia, "wide glory", the old nurse of Odysseus 欧瑞克雷亚，见 Hom. *Od.* 19

**Eurydice,** Gr: Eurydikē, "wide justice", 1) the wife of Creon who killed herself; 2) a nymph, the wife of Orpheus, who was pursued by Aristaeus, bitten by a snake and died; Orpheus almost brought her back from the Underworld; => Orpheus 欧吕狄克，见 Soph. *Ant.*, Verg. *Georg.* 4, Boeth. *De cons.* 3

**eusebeia** => religio, pietas

**Eusebius,** Gr: Eusēbios "well-respected", E: Eusebius, Greek Christian historian, ca. 265—339 AD 优西比乌斯，见 *Ekklesiastike Historia*, Hieron. *De viris ill.*

**Eustochium,** Gr: Eustochion, "good target", E: Eustochium, a Christian virgin, friend of St. Jerome 欧斯托克翁，见 Hieron. *Epist.*

**Euterpe,** Gr: Euterpē, "rejoicing well", the Muse of music (flute) and of tragic choir songs 欧特尔佩，见 Hes. *Theog.*

**Eutyches,** Gr: Eutychēs, "good fate", E: Eutyches, 378—454 AD, abbot in Asia Minor, proponent of monophysitism 欧提克斯，见 Leo, *Tomus*

**Eva,** Heva, Gr: Heua, < Hebr. hawwa, "life", E: Eve, the first woman, created by God and in His image like Adam; => femina 厄娃、夏娃，见 Bibl. *Gen*, Chrysostom. *Peri parthen.*

**Evagrius Ponticus,** Gr: Euagrios Pontikos, "rural goodness", E: Evagrius Ponticus, ca. 345—400 AD, monk in Asia Minor and Egypt; his spirituality was very influential 埃瓦格利乌斯，见 Cassianus, *De inst.*, Maximus, *Capita*

**Evander,** Gr: Euandros, "good man", E: Evander, a deity associated with Pan and worshipped in Arcadia, esp. at Pallantion; in Roman legend he led a small colony from Arcadia to Italy and was the first to settle at the site of the future city of Rome, naming his city Pallanteum (=> Palatine Hill); the Lupercalia festival was instituted by him; his son Pallas was killed by Turnus 埃万德尔，见 Verg. *Aen.* 8

**evangelium,** Gr: euangelion, "good news", E: gospel, especially one of the four gospels of the New Testament 福音，见 Biblia, Tatian. *Diatess*.

***Evangelium secundum Johannem,*** Gr: *Euangelion kata Iōannēn*, E: *Gospel according to John*《约翰福音》，见 Biblia, *Euangelion*

**exegesis,** Gr: exēgēsis, "guide", "explanation", E: exegesis, the explanation of Biblical texts; => Biblia 圣经解释学，见 Philo, *De opificio*, Orig. *De princ.* 4 (spiritual interpretation)

**exempla,** E: examples, models 榜样、典范，见 Philo, *De opificio* (Abraham, Isaac, Jacob), Sen. *Epist. mor.* 11

**existentia,** Gr: ōn, einai, E: to be, being, => substantia 存在，见 Greg. Naz. *Logoi* (a name of God is "ho ōn")

**exodus,** Gr: exodos, "way out", E: the Exodus, the emigration of the Jews from Egypt ca. 1250 BC 出埃及的过程，见 Ios. *Antiqu.* 3, Biblia (the book *Exodus*)

**experientia,** Gr: peira, empeireia, E: experience, practical knowledge 经验，见 Plat. *Gorg.*

# F

**Fabius Maximus,** Quintus Fabius Maximus Cunctator (= "delayer"), ca. 275—203 BC, Roman general, consul and dictator in the Second Punic War 法比乌斯，见 Liv. 21~23, Plut. *Bioi*

**fabula,** Gr: mythos, logos, mythologēma, E: fable, short narrative, usually about animals, => novella, 寓言，见 Aes. *Myth.*, Arist. *Rhet.*

***Fabulae Aesopiae,*** *Aesop's Fables*, a work by Phaedrus from ca. 30—50 AD; => animalia《伊索寓言》，见 Aes. *Myth.*

**fama** => rumor

**fama bona,** Gr: eudoxia, E: a good reputation 美好名声，见 Cic. *De fin.* 3,59, Sen, *Ep.*, Greg. Magn. *Reg. past.*

**fames** => cena, cenare

**familia,** < famulus "servant", Gr: oikos, genos, E: family, household; => penates, lares 家庭，见 Xen. *Oik.*, Plat. *Polit.* 5, Arist. *Polit.*, Cic. *De off.* 1,53~60 (=> seminarium; graded relationships), Biblia (tribes of Israel, children of God), Plut. *Mor.*, Suet. *De vita Caes.* (ancestry of the emperors), Nonius, *De compend.* 20 (family relationships), Justinian. Codex (family law)

**fasces,** E: "rods bound together", a symbol of power carried by the servants (lictors) of Roman magistrates, origin of the word "fascism", "捆的木

条",权力的象征,见 potentia

**fasti,** the old Roman calendar, indicating dies fasti and dies nefasti (days suitable or unfit for public transactions) 罗马日历,见 Ov. *Fasti*

***Fasti,*** E: *Feastdays,* a work by Ovid《岁时记》,见 Ov.

**Fata** => Parcae, Moirai

**Fathers of the Church** => patres ecclesiae

**fatum, fortuna,** Gr: tychē, heimarmenē, moira, moros, daimōn, E: fate, destiny, coincidence; => necessitas, providentia 命运,见 Polyb., Cic. *De fin.* 5,24; Biblia *Job,* Epict. *Diatr., Peri hypsous* 28 (Plato calls death heimarmene poreia), Heliodor. *Aithiopika,* Aug. *De civ. Dei,* Boethius *De consol.*

**Faunus,** old Roman god of fertility, protector of the herds, agriculture and the forests; later he was identified with Pan; his feast were the Lupercalia on Febr. 15th 法乌努斯,见 Pan

**Felicitas,** common Roman name, also goddess of felicity 费里奇塔斯,见 *Passio Perpetuae et Felicitatis,* Aug. *De civ. Dei* 3 (why is Felicity not among the 12 superior gods?)

**femina,** Gr: gynē, gynaikes, E: woman, women and feminine features, men and women; => Eva 妇女、男女差别或冲突,见 Hom. (Helena, Andromache, Hecuba, Penelope), Hes. *Erga* (Pandora), Soph. *Antig.,* Eur. *Med.* (the dire fate of women), Ar. *Lysistrate,* Xen. *Oik.* (respect for the wife), Plat. *Polit.* 5, Verg. *Aen.* 4, Ov. *Ars am., Her.* (the various affections of a woman's heart), Tac. *Germ.* (the virtues of German women), Iuv. *Sat.* 6 (the vices of Roman women), Bibl. *Gen* 1 (creation of man and woman), *Job* (wife of Job), Apuleius (envy of Venus), Greg. Nys. *Peri kataskeues* (image of God and sexual differentiation), Prudentius, *Psychomachia* (virtues and vices as female warriors); Aug. *De civ. Dei* 5 (virtues enslaved by Queen Pleasure and Lady Glory), Capella, *De nuptiis* (allegories of the sciences), Boethius (Lady Philosophy)

**festum,** Gr: heortē, daitē, E: feast day; => religio, Saturnalia 纪念日、节庆,见 Eur. *Med.* 1383, Ar. *Eirene*(performed at a festival), Ov. *Fasti,* Biblia *Ioann.* (feastdays of the Jews), Dionysius Exiguus, *Liber de paschale*

**fides,** Gr: pistis, E: faith, trustfulness 信仰、信用,见 Theophr. *Eth.* 18 (apistos), Plaut. *Aul.* (personification: Fides), Cic. *De nat. deor.* 2,60 (goddess of faith), *De off.* 1,15; 1,22 (fides from "fiat"), 2,33 (justice wins trust), 2,85; Hor. *Carm. saec.* (goddess of faith), Sen. *Epist. mor.* 3 (trust in friendship), Bibl. *Gen* 12 (Abraham = "man of faith"), Ioann., Clem. Alex. *Strom.* (faith is the standard of truth), Prud. *Psych.* (allegory)

**figura,** Gr: tropos, schēma, metaphora, parabolē, E: figure of speech, =>praefiguratio 寓言,见 *Peri hypsous* 8, 30~39; Sextus Emp. *Skept.* (tropai, ways of argumentation)

**finis,** Gr: telos, "aim, perfection", E: aim, limit 目的,见 Cic. *De fin.,* 3,26 (finis ultimus), Aug. *Confess.* (destination of the soul)

**firmitudo,** Gr: bebaiotēs, ataraxia, E: firmness, stability 稳定,坚定,见 Sext. Emp. *Skept.*

**Flaminius,** Titus Quinctius Flaminius, ca. 230—174 BC, a Roman general who fought against Macedonia and was hailed as "saviour" at the Isthmian games of 196 in Corinth 弗拉梅纽斯,见 Plut. *Bioi*

**Flavius,** E: Flavian, the emperors of Rome who belonged to the gens Flavia and reigned from 71—96 AD; => Vespasianus, Titus, Domitianus 弗拉维亚家族,见 Suet. *De vita Caes.*

**Flavius Josephus** = Iosephus Flavius

**flos, flores,** Gr: anthos, E: flower, flowers; => Hyacinthus, Narcissus 花,见 Basil. *Hexaemeron* (symbol of transiency), Claudian. *De raptu Proserp.* 2

**fons,** Gr: pēgē, E: source 泉源,见 *Peri hypsous* 8 (five sources of sublimity)

**forma,** idea, ratio aeterna, Gr: eidos, eidē, morphē, schēma, typos, E: form, idea, => Metamorphosae 观念、形式、永恒的理念,见 Plat. *Phaid.,* Arist. *Phys.*

**formido** => timor

**fortitudo,** Gr: aretē, andreia, "manliness", E: fortitude, strength, courage; => virtutes cardinales 勇气,见 Plat. *Polit.,* Arist. *Polit.* 8, Theophr. *Eth.* 25 (deilos)

**fortuitus,** fortuito, Gr: tychaios, automatos, E: random, by chance 偶然,见 Cic. *De nat. deor.* 2,93 (concursione fortuita)

**fortuna** => fatum

**Fortuna, Fors Fortuna,** < ferre, "to bring", Gr: tychē, daimōn, E: Fortuna, Italian goddess of good fortune 佛尔图纳,命运女神,见 Polyb., Liv. 26~

30 (favoring Scipio), Aug. *De civ. Dei* 4 (only worshipped by wicked people), Boethius, *De cons.* 2 (Fortuna's wheel)

**forum,** Gr: agora, E: forum, market-place, the center of public life in every large Roman town; the Forum Romanum was the market-place, political, commercial and religious center of Rome with the temples dedicated to Saturn, Castor, and Concordia; orators held their speeches at the rostra (speaker's platform) 集议场, 见 agora

**Franci,** E: Franks, a tribe that migrated to Gaul after 250 AD and resisted Rome, thus they were able to establish their own dynasty (Merowingian kings); their king Clovis accepted Christianity in 497 AD, => Clovis 法兰克人, 见 Sulpicius Sever., Greg. Turon. *Hist. Franc.*, Venantius Fort.

**frater,** Gr: adelphos, E: brother 弟兄, 见 Hom. *Il.* (Agamemnon and Menelaos, Hector and Paris), Eur. *Iphigenia* (Agamemnon and Menelaos), Ter. *Adelphoe*; Bibl. *Gen* 4 (Cain and Abel), 37~50 (Joseph and his brothers), Aug. *De civ. Dei* 15 (fratricide of Cain and Romulus), Benedictus, *Regula* (brotherly community)

**fraus,** Gr: apatē, klemma, parakrousis, E: fraud, deceit 欺骗, 见 Cic. *De off.* 3,52 (aliud est celare aliud tacere), Prud. *Psych.* (allegory)

**Frontinus,** Sextus Julius Frontinus, ca. 35—104 AD, Latin author 弗朗蒂努斯, 见 Front. *De aquis*

**Fronto,** Marcus Cornelius Fronto, ca. 100—170 AD, Roman teacher of rhetoric, tutor to Marcus Aurelius 弗伦托, 见 Marcus Aurelius

**frugalitas,** Gr: euteleia, pheidōlia, E: frugality, simple life style 朴素、节俭, 见 Sen. *Epist. mor.* 5, Tac. *Germ.*, Iuv. *Sat.* 11, Prud. *Psych.* (Frugi, the appearance of Greed), Aug. *De beata vita*

**frui (Deo),** E: to enjoy (God) 享受神, 见 Aug. *De vita beata* (deum habere est deo perfrui)

**Furiae,** Gr: Erinyes, E: Furies, the three goddesses of vengeance: Megaera, Tisiphone, Alecto/Allecto; => Eumenides 厄里尼斯, 复仇女神, 见 Aesch. *Choephoroe*, Soph. *Oid. epi Kol.*, Verg. *Aen.* 7 (Allecto)

**furor,** Gr: mēnis, mania, mainomai, lyssa, E: fury, wrath; => ira 愤怒, 见 Hom. *Il.* 1 (wrath of Achilles), Cic. *De off.* 3,95; Tac. *Ann.* 1,1 (sine ira et studio)

**futura vita,** Gr: zōē erchomene, to mellon, E: future life; => eschatologia, vita aeterna 来世的生命, 见 Plat. *Polit.* 10, Cic. *De re publ.* (Somnium Scipionis), Cic. *Cato de sen.*

# G

**Gaea,** Gr: Gaia, Gē, E: Earth, goddess of the earth; => Ceres, Demeter 大地女神, 见 Hes. *Theog.*

**Gaia** = Gaea

**Galatae,** Gr: Galatai, E: Galatians, Gallic (Celtic) tribes that invaded Asia Minor in 278 BC and settled in Phrygia; Attalus I of Pergamum checked their further expansions in 235 BC; in 188 BC they were subdued by Rome and formed a Roman province in 25 BC; the apostle Paul passed through the area on his second missionary journey 伽拉达, 见 Asia Minor

**Galba,** Servius Sulpicius Galba, Roman emperor for six months (68—69 AD) after Nero's death 格尔巴, 见 Plut. *Bioi*, Suet. *De vita Caes.*

**Galenus,** Gr: Galēnos, E: Galen, 129—199 AD, Greek physician and voluminous writer, => medicina 盖伦, 见 *Peri ton idion biblion*

**Galerius Maximianus,** named Caesar in 293 AD; he was emperor of the East from 305—311 AD and continued the persecution of Christians triggered by Diocletian 伽勒瑞乌斯

**Galli,** E: Gauls, people of Gaul; => Celtae 高卢人, 见 Caes. *De bell. Gall.*, Orosius, *Hist.* (invasion of Rome in 390 BC)

**Gallia,** E: Gaul, divided into Gallia Transalpina (roughly modern France) and Gallia Cisalpina (the northern part of Italy); Gallia Cisalpina was Roman province since 200 BC, and Caesar granted citizenship to the inhabitants in 48 BC; Gallia Transalpina was conquered by Caesar in the years 58—51 BC. Since the 3rd ct. AD more and more Germanic tribes migrated to Gaul, and since the 5th ct. they formed the kingdoms of the Burgundians, Franks and Visigoths. 高卢, 见 Caes. *De bell. Gall.*, Sulpic. Severus, *Martin.*

**gallus,** Gr: alektōr, E: cock, rooster 公鸡, 见 Ambros., *Hymni*

**Gallus,** Cornelius Gallus, 69—26 BC, Roman poet, a friend of Virgil; he was the creator of Roman elegy; after a conflict with Augustus he committed suicide. 高卢斯, 见 Verg. *Buc.* 10

**Ganymede** = Catamites

**gaudium** => laetitia

**Gaugamela,** village in Assyria, site of Alexander's

victory over Darius III in 331 BC 高伽梅拉, 见 Arrian. *Alexandrou anab.*

**Ge** = Gaea, => terra

**Gellius,** Aulus Gellius, 130—180 AD, Latin author 格利乌斯, 见 *Noctes Atticae*

**genesis,** Gr: genesis, E: genesis, emergence, becoming 形成, 见 Arist. *Phys.*

***Genesis,*** Gr: *Genesis*, "emergence", E: *Genesis*, *Gen.*, the first book of the Old Testament《创世记》, 见 Philo, *Legum alleg.*, Biblia, *Gen.*, Basil. *Hexaem.*, Philoponus, *De creatione mundi*

**Genitalis** => Lucina

**genius,** Roman god, a man's guardian spirit protecting the ability to have children; later it was developed into the idea that places and corporations had their own genius; Christians were sentenced because they refused to sacrifice to the genius of the emperor; => ingenium, natura, studium 保护神, 见 persecutio

**Gennadius de Massilia,** E: Gennadius of Marseille, ca. 430—490 AD, Latin author who enlarged Jerome's *De viris illustribus* 格纳丢斯, 见 Hieron. *De viris*

**gens** => familia

**genus,** species, Gr: genos, E: species 种类, 见 Arist. *Org.*

**genus deliberativum,** Gr: genos symbouleutikon, E: advisory type (of oratory) 顾问式的讲演, 见 Arist. *Rhet.*

**genus demonstrativum,** Gr: genos epideiktikon, g. panēgyrikon, E: praise, ceremonial type (of oratory) 赞美的讲演, 见 Arist. *Rhet.*

**genus judiciale,** Gr: genos dikanikon, E: forensic type (of oratory) 法院式的讲演, 见 Arist. *Rhet.*

**geographia,** Gr: geōgraphia, E: geography 地理学, 见 Hdt., Polyb., Caes. *De bello gall.*, Plin. *Nat. hist.* 3~6, Tac. *Germ.*, Arrian., Ptolemaios, Pausanias, Loukian. *Alethe diheg.*, Philoponus, *De creatione mundi*, Itinerarium Egeriae

**geometria,** Gr: geometriē, E: geometry, its origin discussed by Herodotus 几何学, 见 Hdt. *Hist.* 2, Plat. *Men.*, Eucl. *Stoich.*

***Georgica,*** E: *Georgics*, a poem by Virgil《农事诗》, 见 Verg.

**georgos** = agricola => agricultura, gaea

**Germani,** E: Germanic tribes in northern Europe; Caesar was the first to distinguish them from the Celts (Galli); Augustus tried to conquer the area up to the Elbe but met resistance, and after 16 AD the Romans tried to keep the Rhine as borderline, founding cities like Cologne (Colonia Agrippinensis) and Trier (Augusta Treverorum); since the first century the German tribes repeatedly raided the area of the Roman Empire until the political structure collapsed in 476 AD 日耳曼人, 见 Caes. *De bello Gall.*, Tac. *Germania*, Eugipp. *Vita S. Severini*

***Germania,*** a work by Tacitus《日耳曼志》, 见 Tac.

**Germanicus,** Julius Caesar Germanicus, 15 BC—19 AD, son of Drusus and Antonia, adopted by Tiberius; he led successful campaigns against the Germanic tribes (thence his title "Germanicus") but was sent to the East in 17 AD and died in Antioch 格尔曼尼克斯, 见 Germani

**Gigantes,** Gr: Gigas, Gigantes, "of tough lands" (<vis ge) ?, E: giants, son of Gaia, the Earth; the giants fought against the Olympian gods ("gigantomachia"), a motive of many artifacts of antiquity 巨人, 见 Hes. *Theog.*

**gladius,** Gr: machaira, E: sword, symbol of fight, violence; gladiatorial fights and hunting performances (venationes) were organized in Rome since 264 BC in the amphitheaters; the Greeks felt these massacres were abominable. 剑, 见 Tert. *De spect.* (munus gladiatorium), Perpetua, *Passio*

**Glaucon,** Gr: Glaukōn, E: Glaucon, a brother of Plato 格劳孔, 见 Plat. *Polit.*

**Glauke,** Gr: Glaukē, "owl", daughter of Creon, king of Corinth; => bubo 格劳克, 见 Eur. *Med.*

**gloria,** => honos, Gr: timē, kleos, eudoxia, doxa, E: honors, glory 好声誉, 光荣, 见 Theophrast. (mikrophilotimos), Cic. *De off.* 2,31~52, Plin. *Nat. hist.* 8 (elephants have a sense of honor), Aug. *De civ. Dei* 5 (Roman love of glory prevented greater vices), Benedict. *Reg.* (renunciation of secular glory), Greg. Magn. *Reg. past.* (care for reputation)

**gnosis,** E: insight, understanding, => intellectus, 知识, 见 Clem. Alex. *Strom.* (insightful faith), Iren. *Adv. haer.* (gnosticism)

**gnothi seauton,** know yourself, one of the inscriptions at the oracle of Delphi 认识你自己, 见 Soph. *Oid. Tyr.*, Aug. *Conf.* 8

**Gordianus nodus,** E: Gordian knot, cut by Alexander 格迪翁的结, 见 Arrian. *Alexandrou Anabasis*, 2

**Gorgias,** Gr: Gorgias of Leontinoi (Sicily), 483—385

BC, the main representative of the rhetorical skill of the sophists at Socrates' time 高尔吉亚, 见 Plat., *Gorg.*

***Gorgias,*** a dialogue by Plato《高尔吉亚》, 见 Plat.

**Gorgones,** Gr: Gorgōn, "grim one", E: Gorgo, Gorgons, three female monsters 蛇发三女妖, 见 Medusa

**Gotones, Gothones,** E: Goths, the main ethnic group of the eastern Germanic tribes; their origins are in the south of Sweden, but ca. in 150 AD they moved to the north of the Black Sea and split into Ostrogoths and Visigoths; the Visigoths repeatedly raided the Roman empire until Constantine pacified them as allies and gave them settlements north of the Danube river in 332 AD; Bishop Wulfila introduced Arianism to them; in 378 AD they defeated Valens at Adrianople, and in 395 AD Alarich led them to Italy, in 410 AD they sacked Rome; in 415 AD they founded a kingdom in Spain which fell to the Arabs in 711 AD. The kingdom of the Ostrogoths in Russia was conquered by the Huns in 375 AD; after Attila's death the Ostrogoths settled in Pannonia (453 AD) but in 488 AD founded the kingdom of the Ostrogoths under Theodoric the Great; Byzantium ended their reign in Italy in 552 AD; => Visigothones 哥特人, 见 Aug. *De civ. Dei* 1, Boethius (connections to Byzanz), Isidorus (history of the Goths)

**Gracchi,** two Roman statesmen and reformers: Tiberius Sempronius Gracchus, 164—133 BC, and his brother Gaius Sempronius Gracchus, 153—121 BC; the latter suggested to convey citizenship to all allies (socii) of Rome, but these and similar reforms triggered bloody riots and the social and political struggles of the following century 格拉希, 见 Cic. *Brutus*, Plut. *Bioi*, Aug. *De civ. Dei* 3

**Graecia,** Gr: Hellas, E: Greece, an area of the Balkan peninsula, namely: (1) the Peloponnese, (2) the land north of the Isthmus of Corinth, ("mainland Greece"), and (3) the northern regions cut off from the rest by high mountains (Epirus, Thrace, Macedonia); => Magna Graecia 希腊, 见 Pausanias

**grammatica,** Gr: grammatikē, E: grammar 语法, 见 Varro, Donatus, Priscianus, Capella, *De nuptiis* (personification as old lady from Egypt), Isidor. *Etym.*

**gratia,** misericordia, Gr: charitas, eleēmosynē, E: mercy 仁慈, 见 Lact. *De ira*, Aug. *De civ. Dei* 15 (grace produces inhabitants of the City of God)

**Gratiae,** Gr: Charites "joyful ones", E: the Graces, three daughters of Zeus, Euphrosyne, Aglaia, Thalia; being personifications of grace and beauty, they accompany the Muses and Aphrodite 美惠三女神, 见 Capella, *De nuptiis*

**gravitas,** Gr: semnotēs, baros, E: seriousness, dignity, authority; =>dignitas 权威性, 见 Cic. *De off.* 1,70 (a feature of a politician), 1,103 (ad studia graviora et maiora)

**Gregorius,** Gr: Grēgorios, "vigilant", "shepherd", E: Gregory 希腊、罗马人名

**Gregorius Magnus,** E: Gregory the Great, 540—604 AD, Pope from 590—604, one of the Latin Fathers of the Church (大) 格列高利, 见 Greg. Mag., *Dialogi, Moralia, Reg. past.*

**Gregorius Nazianzus,** Gr: Grēgorios Nazianzos, E: Gregory of Nazianz, ca. 331—390 AD, Greek Christian author, one of the Cappadocian Fathers 格列高利, 见 *Carmina, Logoi*

**Gregorius Nyssenus,** Gr: Grēgorios Nyssēnos, E: Gregory of Nyssa, ca. 335—394 AD, Greek Christian author, bishop of Nyssa, one of the Cappadocian Fathers 格列高利, 见 *Peri kataskeuēs anthrōpou, Peri parthenias, Peri psychēs*

**Gregorius Turonensis,** E: Gregory of Tours, ca. 538—594 AD, Latin historian 格列高利, 见 *Historia Francorum*

**gubernatio mundi,** providentia, Gr: heimarmenē, basileia, E: government of the world (by divine reason) 宇宙的统治, 见 Hom., Hes. (Zeus), Ar. *Ornith.* (basileia), Cic. *De nat. deor.* 1,4; 2,154~167, Aug. *De civ. Dei* 5, Boethius, *De cons.* 3

**gula,** E: gluttony, one of the main vices 饕餮, 贪吃, 见 Cass. *De inst.*, Greg. Magn., *Moralia*

**Gyes,** Gr: Gyēs, one of the Hecatoncheires 格艾斯, 见 Hes. *Theog.*

**Gyges,** Gr: Gygēs, (=gē-genēs, "earthborn"), a shepherd who became a criminal because of the gift of invisibility 格格斯, 见 Cic. *De off.* 3,38~39

**gynē** => femina

# H

**habere,** Gr: echein, E: to have 拥有, 见 Aug. *De beata vita* (habere deum; => frui)

**Hades,** Gr: Haidēs, Aidēs, < a –ides, "invisible", "sightless", also known as Pluto (Gr: Ploutōn) or Dis, one of the three sons of Cronus and Rhea, brother of Zeus and Poseidon, husband of Persephone, lord of the Underworld; => Cerberus, Charon, Styx, Tartarus, Elysium, Lethe 哈得斯、冥土的主神, 见 Hom. *Od.* 11, Hes. *Theog.*, Eur. *Alc.* (Heracles entering the lower world), Plat. *Gorg.* (judges of the lower world), *Phaid.*, Verg. *Aen.* 6, *Georg.* 4 (Orpheus), Ov. *Met.* 2 (Minos and Rhadamanthys, judges in the lower world), 8 (Theseus and Pirithous entering Hades), Apuleius, *Met.* (Psyche in the Underworld), Claudius

**Hadrian,** Publius Aelius Hadrianus, Roman emperor 117—138 AD, born in Spain, later adopted by Trajan, he became the most cultivated of the Roman emperors; the only war he led was against the Jews under Bar-Kochba (132—135 AD); he ordered the construction of the Olympieion in Athens, the Villa in Tivoli and his mausoleum in Rome (Castel d'Angelo); he replaced and enlarged Agrippa's Pantheon on the Campus Martius. 哈德良, 见 Suet. *De vita Caes.*

**Haemon,** Gr: Haimōn, "skilful", or "making blood", E: Haemon, son of Creon, lover of Antigone 海蒙, 见 Soph. *Ant.*

**haereses,** <Gr: haireo "take out", E: heresy, heresies, unorthodox teachings and sectarian movements (in the early Church) 异端, 见 Iren. *Adv. haer.*, Euseb., Basil. *Hexaem.* (weeds are symbol of heresies), Leo

**Haimon** = Haemon

**Hannah** => Anna

**Hannibal,** <Phoen. "God is graceful", 247—183 BC, son of Hamilcar Barca and general of the Carthaginians in the Second Punic War (218—202 BC) 汉尼拔, 见 Cic. *De off.* 1,107; Liv. 20~30

**harmonia,** Gr: harmonia, symphōnia, "concord", E: harmony, => ordo, concordia 和谐, 见 Plat. *Phaid.*

**Harmonia,** Gr: Harmonia, mother of the Amazons, daughter of Ares and Aphrodite 哈尔摩尼亚, 见 Apoll. *Arg.*

**Harpya,** Gr: harpai, "snatchers", E: Harpy, Harpies, frightful birds 怪鸟, 见 Apoll. *Arg.*, Verg. *Aen.* 3

***Heauton Timoroumenos,*** Gr: "self-tormentor", E: *Self-Tormentor*, a play by Terence 《自责者》, 见 Terentius

**Hebe** => Juventus

**Hebraica lingua,** => lingua Hebraica

**Hecabe** = Hecuba

**Hecatoncheires,** Gr: Hekatoncheires, "one-hundred arms", three giant sons of Uranus and Gaia, who helped Zeus to fight the Titans 百手巨人, 见 Hes. *Theog.*

**Hector,** Gr: Hektōr, "keeper, protector", the oldest son of Priam and Hecuba, husband of Andromache, the outstanding protector of Troy; he killed Patroclus and was in turn killed by Achilles 赫克托尔, 见 Hom. *Il.* 5, 6, 7, 9, 10, 11, 14~24

**Hecuba,** Hecabe, Gr: Hekabē, "go far", E: Hecuba, chief wife of Priam and mother of 19 children, including Hector, Paris, Cassandra, Creusa 赫卡贝, 见 Hom. *Il.* 6, 24

**hedone** => voluptas, laetitia

**heimarmene** => fatum

**Hekabe** = Hecuba

**Hekatoncheires** = Hecatonchires

**Hektor** = Hector

**Helena,** Gr: Helenē, "ship-destroyer", "shining", "moon" (?), E: Helen, daughter of Zeus and Leda, wife of Menelaus, symbol of beauty; she fled with Paris and so brought about the Trojan War 海伦娜, 见 Hom. *Il.*, 3, 24; *Od.* 4, Ov. *Her.*, Stat. *Achill.*

**Helenus,** Gr: Helenos, "of the moon", son of Priam and Hecuba, gifted with prophecy, who married Andromache and became king of Chaonia (Epirus) after the fall of Troy 赫勒诺斯, 见 Verg. *Aen.* 3

**Helicon,** Gr: Helikōn, E: Mount Helicon, the home of the Muses 赫里孔, 见 Hes. *Theog.*, 1~103

**Heliodorus,** Gr: Hēliodōros, "gift of the sun-god", E: Heliodorus, Greek novelist, ca. 200—250 AD 赫利奥多鲁斯, 见 *Aithiopika*

**Helius,** Gr: Hēlios, "sun", god of the sun, son of Hyperion and Theia, brother of Selene and Eos, father of Phaeton; his main sanctuary was at Rhodos; => Sol 赫利乌斯, 见 Hes. *Theog.*, Eur. *Med.*, Cic. *De off.* 3,94; *Peri hypsous* 15; Lucian. *Theon dial.*

**Helle,** Gr: Hellē, "bright", daughter of Athamas and Nephele, who fell into the sea which was called "Hellespont" later 赫勒, 见 Apoll. *Arg.*

**Hellen,** Gr: Hellēn, E: Hellen, son of Deucalion, ruler

in Phthia, legendary ancestor of the Greeks (Hellenes); his three sons (Aiolos, Doros and Xythos) became the ancestors of Aeolians, Dorians and Ionians 赫伦,见 Graecia

**Hellespontus,** Gr: Hellēspontos, "sea of Helle", E: Hellespont, the Dardanelles, the strait which divides Europe from Asia, bridged by boats in the Persian War; => Helle 赫勒海,见 Aesch. *Persai*, Hdt. *Hist.* 7, Apoll. *Arg.*

**Hemere,** Gr: Hēmerē, E: bright day 白天,见 Hes. *Theog.*

**hemitheoi,** E: half-gods, 半神半人,见 Hes. *Erga*

**hen,** to, L: unum, E: the One, the first principle of being in Neoplatonism 太一,见 Plot. *Enn.*, Procl. *Plat. theol.* (henades), Dionys. Ar., *Peri tes our. hier.*

**Hephaestus,** Gr: Hēphaistos, (=hemera phaestos), "shining by day", son of Hera (and Zeus), Greek god of fire and of crafts, together with the Cyclops he produced elaborate tools and artifacts and thus his wife was Aphrodite (symbol of beauty); in Rome he was identified with Vulcanus 赫菲斯托斯,见 Hom. *Il.* 18, 21; Hes. *Erga*, Lucian. *Theon dial.*

**Hera,** Gr: Hēra, "protectress", L: Juno, Greek goddess, daughter of Cronus and Rhea, sister and chief wife of Zeus, mother of Ares, Hephaestus, and Hebe; she protected marriage and childbirth, her symbol animals were the cow and the peacock; her sanctuary was called "Heraion", the most important of them were in Olympia, Samos, Paestum, Corinthus, Argos, and Delos. 赫拉,见 Hom. *Il.* 8, 14, 21; Hes. *Theog.*, Apoll. *Arg.*, Lucian. *Theon dial.*

**Heracles, Herakles** = Hercules

**Heraclitus,** Gr: Hērakleitos, "glory of Hera", E: Heracleitus, Greek philosopher, ca. 540—480 BC, famous for his teaching that all things are changing; he influenced the sophists, Plato, and the Stoa (fire as the origin of all) 赫拉克利特,见 Lucian. *Vit. auct.*, Clem. Alex. *Strom.* (quotations preserved)

**Hercules,** Gr: Hēraklēs, "praise of Hera", E: Heracles, son of Zeus and Alcumena, hero and model of virtue, who completed the "Twelve Labours of Heracles" (killing the Nemean Lion, the Hydra, catching alive the Erymanthian Boar, the Cerynitian Hind, the Cretan Bull, the Horses of Diomedes, driving away the Stymphalian Birds, cleaning the stables of King Augeas, obtaining the Girdle of the Amazon Queen Hippolyte, the Cattle of Geryon, the Golden Apples of the Hesperides, and finally capturing Cerberus from the Underworld, thereby freeing Theseus). Heracles married Deianeira but was later accidentally killed by her through a poisoned robe. One of the many stories tells that in a fit of madness (caused by Hera) Heracles killed the children of his wife Megara, => Sen. *Hercules furens*.赫拉克勒斯,见 Hes. *Theog.*, Eur. *Alk.*, Ar. *Ornithes*, Plaut. *Amphitruo*, Apoll. *Arg.*, Plaut. *Amph.*, Cic. *De fin.* 2,117, *De nat. deor.* 3,39 (Hercules is not divine), *De off.* 1,118 (choice between voluptas and virtus), 3,25; Hor. *Carm.* 1,12, Ov. *Her.*, *Met.* 8 (Theseus and Hercules), Lucian, *Theon dial.* (parody), Tert. *De spect.* 11 (games ad Neme dedicated to Hercules), Boeth. *De cons.* 4 (symbol of patience)

**Hermes,** Gr: Hermēs, "pillar", E: Hermes, Mercury, son of Zeus and Maia, god of travellers, messengers, merchants, interpreters; => Mercurius 赫尔梅斯、赫尔墨斯,见 Hom. *Il.*, 24; *Od.* 5, 10; Hes. *Erga*, *Theog.*, Ar. *Eirene*, Apoll. *Arg.*, Lucian, *Theon dial.*

**Hermes Trismegistus,** Gr: Hermēs Trismegistos, E: Hermes the 'thricegreatest', a name given to the Egyptian god Thoth who was identified with Hermes, the patron of all knowledge, allegedly the author of some Greek and Latin religious and philosophical writings dated at ca. 250 AD 三大的赫尔梅斯,见 Aug. *De civ. Dei* 8

**Hermione,** Gr: Hermionē, "pillar-queen", daughter of Menelaus and Helena, wife of Neoptolemus and (later) of Orestes 赫尔弥奥内,见 Ov. *Her.*

**Hero,** a priestess of Aphrodite at the west coast of the Hellespont, she was loved by Leander, who swam over to her; upon seeing his dead body on the shore she killed herself. 赫若,见 Ov. *Her.*

**Herodes,** Gr: Hērōdēs, "song of Hera"(?), E: Herod, Herod the Great, 73—4 BC, tyrannical ruler in Judaea, who ruled Jerusalem since 37 BC and set up many buildings there; he managed to stay in power under Augustus and is said to have ordered the slaughter of male infants in Behtlehem. 赫若多特,见 Ios. *Antiqu.*

**Herodotus,** Gr: Hērodotos, "gift of Hera", Greek

historian, 485—425 BC, Cicero respectfully called him the "Father of Historiography" 希罗多德, 见 Hdt. *Hist.* Arist. *Poiet.*, Quint. *Inst.*10, *Peri hypsous* 12, Lucian, *Alethe diheg.* (parody),

**Heroides,** E: *Letters of Heroines*, a collection of fictive letters by Ovid《女英雄》, 见 Ov.

**heros,** Gr: hērōs, hērōes, E: hero, => Achilleus, Aeneas, Heracles, Theseus, etc. 英雄, 见 Hes. *Erga*

**Hesiodus,** Gr: Hēsiodos, "directing the way", E: Hesiod, Greek poet from Boeotia, ca. 750—650 BC, similar to Homer in language and metre he describes the life of farmers and gives the first systematic account of the gods and their origin. 赫西奥德, 见 Hes. *Erga, Theogonia,* Xen. *Oikon.*, Verg. *Georgica,* Minucius, *Octav.*

**Hesperides,** Gr: Hesperides, the four (or seven) daughters of Atlas who guarded the golden apples of life in the garden of the gods in the far west; Heracles had to obtain three of these apples 赫斯佩瑞德斯, 见 Hercules

**Hestia,** L: Vesta, Gr: Hēstia, "hearth", daughter of Cronus, goddess of the hearth 赫斯提亚, 灶火女神, 见 Hes. *Theog.*

**hēsychia** => pax

**hetaerae,** Gr: hetairai "female companions", E: courtesans, prostitutes, who often were musicians or dancers and entertained dinner parties; prominent hetaerae were Aspasia, loved by Pericles, Lais, loved by Demosthenes, Thais, loved by Alexander, and Phryne, loved by Praxiteles. Many plots of the New Comedy are centered on the hetaerae who are often depicted as having a good heart. 女伴, 伴妓, 见 Plautus, Terentius

**Heva** = Eva

**Hexaemeron,** Gr: *hexa-hēmera* "six days", E: *Hexaemeron*, works on the creation of the world in six days《论六天创造》, 见 Basil. *Hex.*, Philoponus

**hexameter,** Gr: hexametron, E: hexameter, a metre consisting of six dactyls (or spondees), the metre of Homer's and Hesiod's works and thus imitated by most epics of antiquity 六音步, 见 Hom. *Il. Od.*, Hes., Apollod., Lucr., Verg. *Buc., Aen.*, etc.

**Hexapla,** Gr: *Hexapla* "six-folded", E: *Hexapla*, a scholarly edition of the Old Testament in Hebrew and Greek《六文本合参》, 见 Origenes, Hieron. *Vulgata*

**hierarchia,** Gr: hierarchia "sacred order", E: hierarchy 秩序, 神圣的制度, 见 Dionysius Areopagita

**Hieron,** Gr: Hierōn, tyrant of Syracuse 478—467 BC, who defeated the Etruscans at Cumae in 474 BC; he attracted the most famous contemporary poets (Aeschylus, Pindar, Simonides) to come to his court 赫润, 见 Syracusae

**Hieronymus,** Eusebius, Gr: Hieronymos "holy name", E: Jerome, 347—420, one of the Church fathers, famous for his love of classical literature and translation work 哲罗姆, 见 *De viris illustribus, Epistulae,* Vulgata, Cassiod. *Inst.*

**Hilarius de Poitiers,** E: Hilary of Poitiers, ca. 315—367 AD, theologian and bishop in Gaul 希拉利乌斯, 见 Sulp. Sev. *Vita Martini*

**Hipparchus,** Gr : Hipparchos, "horse-tamer", E: Hipparchus, ca. 190—120 BC, astronomer and mathematician at Alexandria, founder of trigonometry, he divided the circle into 360 degrees and made a list of 850 stars 赫巴克斯, 见 Alexandria

**Hippocrates,** Gr: Hippokratēs, "horse-tamer", Hippocrates of Cos, ca. 460—370 BC, the greatest physician of antiquity, founder of scientific medicine; some 53 of his 130 writings are collected in the *Corpus Hippocraticum* (the authorship of some is debated) 希波克拉底, 见 medicina

**Hippolyta,** Gr: Hippolyta, "charioteer", "of the stampeding horses", E: Hippolyte, the legendary queen of the Amazons, married by Theseus, mother of Hippolytus 希波吕塔, 见 Ov. *Met.* 8

**Hippolytus,** Gr: Hippolytos, "charioteer", "torn by horses"; E: Hippolytus, son of Theseus and the Amazon queen Hippolyta; he was loved by Phaedra but did not return this love and died a tragic death. 希波吕托斯, 见 Eur. *Hipp.*, Ov. *Her.*

**Hippolytus,** E: Hippolytus, ca. 170—235 AD, theologian in Rome, antipope for some time, martyr and saint 依波里托, 见 Prud. *Peristeph.*

***Hippolytus,*** Gr: *Hippolytos*, tragedy by Euripides《希波吕托斯》, 见 Eur.

**hippos** = equus

**Hirtius,** Aulus Hirtius, one of Caesar's officers in Gaul and consul in 43 BC 希提乌斯, 见 Caes. *De bello Gallico*

**Hispania,** E: Spain, important trade ports and Phoenician colonies existed since 1100 BC, the Greeks arrived in Spain ca. in 700 BC, but the

Carthaginians dominated the peninsula until the end of the Second Punic War (202 BC); the Romans divided the area into Hispania citerior, Hispania Baetica, and Hispania Lusitania. After 400 AD the Alans and Vandals invaded the area, and in 415 AD the Visigoths established their kingdom which lasted until the Arab invasion (711 AD) 西班牙, 见 Polyb., Martinus de Bracara, Isidorus

**historia,** = 1) inquisitio, 2) cognitio, 3) relatio, Gr: historia, historiē, "inquiry", E: history, historical studies, chronology, 历史, 见 Hdt., Thuc., Arist. *Poiet.*, Polyb., Cic. *Brutus* (history of oratory), Sall., Liv., Iosephus, Plut., Tac., Suet., Lucian, *Alethe diheg.* (parody of historiography), Euseb. (the first history of the Church), Hieron. *De viris ill.* (the first history of Christian literature), Aug. *De civ. Dei* (the first great "philosophy of history"), Orosius, *Histor.* (chronology: "six days", "four world powers"), Gregor. Turon., *Hist. Franc.*

***Historia Francorum,*** E: *History of the Franks*, a work by Gregory of Tours《法兰克人史》, 见 Greg. Turon.

**historia pragmatica,** Gr: pragmatikē historia, E: pragmatic historiography, a factual history of events 实际上的历史记载, 见 Polyb.

**historia universalis,** universal history 世界史, 见 Polyb., Euseb. (*Chronikon*)

***Historiae,*** Gr: *Historiai* (=Histories apodexis), E: *Histories*, work by Herodotus《历史》, 见 Her.

***Historiae,*** Gr: *Historiai*, E: *History*, a compilation by Polybios《通史》, 见 Polyb.

***Historiae adversus paganos,*** E: *Histories against the Pagans*, a work by Orosius《反驳异教徒的世界史》, 见 Orosius

***Histories apodexis*** = *Historiae*

**Homerus,** Gr: Homēros, "hostage", "blind" (?); E: Homer, Greek poet ca. 800—700 BC, the author of the *Iliad* and *Odyssee*, he was immensely influential on literature and thought 荷马, 见 Hom. *Il.*, *Od.*, Arist. *Peri poiet.* (comparison of epic and tragedy), Hor. *De arte poet.* (imitation of Homer), Quint. *Inst.* 10, Plut. *Mor.* (discussion of the interpretation of Homer), *Peri hypsous*, Minucius, *Octav.* (respect for monotheist elements), Macrob. *Sat.* (dependence of Virgil on Homer)

**homilia,** E: homily, Hector's exhortation to the Trojan women 劝说, 见 Hom. *Il.* 6

***Homiliae,*** Gr: *Logoi*, E: *Homilies*, a collection of sermons《讲道集》, 见 Chrysostomus

**homo,** Gr: anthrōpos, E: man, human being, person 人, 见 Ter. *Heauton Tim.* (homo sum), Bibl. *Gen* (man created as image of God), Aug. *De vera rel.* (homo interior, the inner man)

**homoiosis** => assimiliatio

**homologia** => convenientia

**homousios,** Gr: homo-ousios, E: "one in being", the central tenet of the Nicene creed of 325, defining Jesus Christ as "one in being" with God the Father 同性同体, 见 Athanasius, Cyrillus

**honos,** honor, honestum, reputatio, decus, Gr: timē, timia, axiōma, doxa, agalma, E: reputation, honor; => gloria 名誉, 见 Theophr. *Eth.* 21 (mikrophilotimia), Cic. *De fin.*2, Hor. *Carm. saec.* (god of honor), Aug. *De civ. Dei* (a sense of honor prevents greater sins), Boeth. *De cons.* 2,3 (worldly glory cannot satisfy)

**hoplites,** Gr: hoplitai, E: hoplits, Greek heavy-armed infantry, victorious at Marathon 士兵, 见 Hdt. *Hist.* 6

**Horatii et Curiatii,** Roman legend about three Roman brothers (the Horatii) fighting three brothers from Alba Longa (the Curiatii) so as to decide the war between the two cities; one of the Horatii survived the duels, therefore Rome had won 赫拉提伊与库利亚提伊, 见 Liv. 1

**Horatius,** E: Horace, 65—8 BC, eminent Latin poet, member of the circle around Maecenas 贺拉斯, 见 Hor. *Carm.*, *De arte poetica*, *Serm.* Quint. *Inst.* 10, Hieron. *Ep.* 57

**horkos** => jus jurandum

**Hortensius,** Quintus Hortensius Hortalus, 114—50 BC, Roman orator; Cicero dedicated a book to him (*Hortensius*) which inspired Augustine but has not come down to us. 霍滕修斯, 见 Cic. *Brutus*, Aug. *Confess.*

**hortus,** E: garden, symbol of the soul etc. 花园, 见 Biblia *Gen* (paradise), Perpetua, *Passio*, Aug. *Conf.* 8 (conversion in a garden), *Conf.* 13 (spiritual meaning of the paradise)

**hospes,** hospitalitas, Gr: xenos, xenia, E: stranger, hospitality 陌生人、好客的态度, 见 Hom. *Od.* 6

**humanum,** humanitas; Gr: philanthropia, chrēstotēs, E: humanism, philanthropy, clemency 人道主义、仁风, 见 Xen. *Oik.*, Cic. *De off.* 1,50 (reason, justice and language), Sen. *De clem.*, *Epist. mor.*

7 (inhumanior quia inter homines fui), Hier. *Epist.* 22 (tension between humanism and Christian faith)

**humilitas,** Gr: tapeinotēs, tapeinōsis, E: powerlessness, humility 无力，谦卑，见 Marc Aurel., Prud. *Psychom.* (Mens humilis), Bened. *Regula* (12 steps of humility), Columban, *Regula* (abnegatio sui), Ioann. Klimakos

**Hunni,** E: Huns, a people coming from central Asia, they invaded Europe in 375 which led to migrations 匈奴人，见 Ammianus, *Rerum gest.*, Eugipp. *Vita S. Severini*, Greg. Turon. *Hist. Franc.*

**Hyacinthus,** Gr: Hyakinthos, E: Hyacinthus, a Dorian god, loved by Apollo but mistakenly killed by the same god, flowers grew from the blood of Hyacinthus 希亚金多斯，见 Claudian. *De raptu Proserp.*

**hybris** = superbia

**hydor** = aqua

**hydra,** Gr: hydra, "water creature", E: hydra 水蛇 Aesop

**Hylas,** Gr: Hylas, "of the woods", friend of Heracles 希拉斯，见 Apoll. *Arg.*

**Hymenaeus,** Gr: Hymenaios, the god of weddings; wedding-song; 婚姻歌，婚姻神，见 matrimonium

*Hymni,* E: *Hymns,* a work by Ambrose 《赞美诗集》，见 Ambrosius

**hymnus,** Gr: hymnos, E: hymns, songs sung in honor of a hero or a god, usually in hexameter or elegiac verses; famous hymns include those of Homer, Alcaeus, Pindar, Callimachus, the invocation of Venus at the beginning of Lucretius' *De rerum natura*, and the *Carmen saeculare* of Horace 赞美诗，见 Homerus, Lucretius, Horatius

**hyperbola,** Gr: hyperbolē, E: hyperbole 夸张，见 *Peri hypsous* 22

**Hyperion,** Gr: Hyperiōn, sun god, son of Uranos, father of Helios, one of the Titans 许佩里翁，见 Hes. *Theog.*

**Hypermestra,** (=-mnestra), "excessive wooing", daughter of Danaus, who loved Lynceus 许佩梅斯特拉，见 Ov. *Her.*

**Hypnos,** L: Somnus, god of sleep, son of Nyx (Night), brother of Thanatos (Death), both are depicted as winged youths in art 睡眠之神，见 Hom. *Il.* 14

**Hypsipyle,** Gr: Hypsipylē, "of the high gate", daughter of King Thoas; she lived at Lemnos island and loved Iason, bearing twin sons to him 许普西皮勒，见 Ov. *Her.*

# I

**Iakobos** = Jacobus

**iambus,** E: iamb, one of the metres, => metrum 短长律，见 Publ. *Sent.*

**Iapetus,** Gr: Iapetos, "hurrier", one of the Titans, father of Prometheus, Epimetheus and Atlas 伊阿佩托斯，见 Hes. *Theog.*

**Iarbas,** king of Libya, who gave land to Dido but was rejected by her 伊阿巴斯，见 Verg. *Aen.* 4

**Iason** = Jason

**Icarus,** Gr: Ikaros, "dedicated to the moon goddess Kar" (?), the son of Daedalus 伊卡若斯，见 Ov. *Met.* 8

**idea,** Gr: eidos, noesis, E: idea 理念，见 Arist. *Met.*

**idololatria,** (=idolatria), Gr: eidōla "images", latria "worship", E: idolatry, the adoration of idols 偶像崇拜，见 Tatian. *Logos*, Lact. *Inst.* 2, Athanas. *Logos* (psychology of idol worship), Prud. *Psych.*, Aug. *De civ. Dei* (the inconsistencies of polytheism)

**ieiunium** = jejunium

**Ierosolyma, Hierosolyma, Ierusalem,** Gr: Ierousalēm, E: Jerusalem, capital of Judaea, conquered by the Romans in 70 AD 耶路撒冷，见 Ios. *Bell. Iud.* 5~7, Bibl. *Ioann.* 2 (Jesus expels merchants from the temple), Tert. *De spect.* (the New Jerus.), Euseb., *Ekkl. hist.* (destruction of the city, bishops of Jerusalem), Aug. *De civ. Dei* 17 (symbol of the Church), *Itinerarium Egeriae* (liturgy in Jerusalem)

**Ignatius,** Gr: Ignatios, E: Ignatius, Bishop of Antiochia, martyr, saint, author of letters, 50—110 AD 依纳爵，见 Ig. *Epist.*

**ignis,** Gr: pyr, (Sanskrit: agni), E: fire, one of the elements; basic need 火，见 Cic. *De nat. deor.* 3,35 (Stoic doctrine of eternal fire); Cic. *De off.* 1,52 (not to be denied), *Peri hypsous* 12 (Cicero compared to fire), Iren. *Adv. haer.* 5 (eternal fire as punishment), Basil. *Hexaem.* (the most pure element, equated with heaven), Greg. Nys. *Peri psyches* (post-mortal purgation), Hieron. *Epist.* 107 (flamma libidinis)

**Ikaros** = Icarus

*Ilias,* E: *Iliad,* epic by Homer 《伊利亚特》，见

Homeros; Verg. *Aen.*

**Ilion** = Troia

**Ilium,** Gr: Ilion, "moss-mountain", = Troia

**illuminatio,** Gr: phōtismos, E: illumination, enlightening 照亮，见 Dionys. Ar., *Peri tes our. hier.*

**imago,** Gr: eikon, eidōlon, E: image => figura

**imago Dei,** creation of man as image of God, => dignitas 上主的肖像，见 Bibl. *Gen.*, Hes. *Erga* 63 (woman created in the image of goddesses), Tert. *De spect.* (violence as deformation of), Greg. Nys. *Peri kataskeues*, *Peri psyches* (purification after death to restore the original likeness to God), Aug. *Confess.* 13 (the gift of reason is likeness to God), *De civ. Dei* 11 (image of the Trinity in mind, intellect and will)

**imitatio,** Gr: mimēsis, E: imitation, the basis of all human arts 模仿，见 Arist. *Poiet.*, Hor. *De arte poet.*, Sen. *Epist. mor.* 7 (imitation of vices), Iuv. *Sat.* 14 (children imitate parents), *Peri hypsous* 13 (mimesis kai zelosis = imitation of antiquity)

**immortalitas,** perpetuitas, aeternitas, Gr: athanasia, ambrosia, E: immortality, => vita aeterna 不死，永恒生命，见 Plat. *Menon* (anamnesis), *Phaid.*, *Symp.*, Capella, *De nuptiis* (Athanasia)

**impassibilitas,** Gr: apatheia, E: impassibility, a Stoic ideal 内心平静，见 Aug. *De civ. Dei* 14, Joh. Climac. *Scala* (apatheia = detachment from the world)

**imperator,** E: general, emperor, originally a title granted by the Roman Senate to a victorious general; the power (imperium) of a general was only effective outside Rome, he could command the army and had the right to coinage in the provinces. As soon as the general entered Rome his authority ceased to exist. In 45 BC Caesar received the title Imperator, and since then it was a hereditary title of the Roman rulers ("emperors"); => Alexander, Augustus, Caesar 皇帝，见 Sueton., Arrian. (proskynesis)

**imperium** => imperator

**impudentia** => pudor

**incarnatio,** Gr: ensarkeia, "in the flesh", enanthrōpesis, "in humanity", E: incarnation, (the doctrine about) Christ becoming man, central to the Christian faith 基督降生成人，道成肉身，见 Orig., *Contra Cels.*, Athanas. *Logos*, Leo, *Tomus*

**India,** Alexander reached India in 326 BC 印度，见 Arrian. *Alex. anab.* 5,6; Cosmas Indicopleustes

**Indikopleustes** => Cosmas Indicopleustes

**indifferens bonum,** praeposita, Gr: proēgmenon, E: preferable values, indifferent things 应取的价值，见 Cic. *De fin.* 3,52

**inductio,** Gr: epagōgē, E: induction, inductive method 归纳法，见 Arist. *Org.*

**industria,** diligentia, Gr: meletē, philergia, philoponia, E: diligence 勤奋，见 Cic. *Brutus*, Philoponus

**informatio** => notio

**ingenium,** Gr: physis, phrēn, dynamis, E: talent, genius 才华，见 Cic. *De off.* 1,114, Hor. *De arte poet.* 408 (needs refinement = studium, ars)

**Ino,** Gr: Inō, 1) sea-goddess, daughter of Cadmus and Harmonia; 2) wife of Athamas who wanted to get rid of Helle and Phrixus 伊诺，见 Hom. *Od.* 5; Apoll. *Arg.*

**inspiratio,** Gr: epipnoia, E: inspiration (of the Bible), the Biblical texts are seen as "inspired" by the Holy Spirit, they are divine revelation through human authors and human words (《圣经》的)默启，见 Biblia, Iren. *Adv. haer.* 4, Orig. *De princ.*

**instauratio** = recapitulatio

***Institutio oratoria,*** E: *The Education of an Orator*, a work by Quintilian《演讲家的培训》，见 Quint.

***Institutiones,*** E: *Institutions*, an introduction to jurisprudence by Gaius, written in 161 AD《法学总论》，见 Justinianus

***Institutiones divinae,*** E: *Divine Institutions*, a work by Lactantius《神圣教规》，见 Lact.

***Institutiones divinarum et humanarum litterarum,*** E: *Introduction to Religious and Secular Texts*, important textbook by Cassiodorus《宗教文学与世俗文学的教学》，见 Cassiod. *Inst.*

**intellectus,** intelligere, Gr: nous, dianoia, logistikon, gnōmē, phrēn, E: reason, intellect, understanding 理性，见 Plat. *Polit.* 4, Clem. Alex. *Strom.*, Minucius, *Oct.*, Orig. *Contra Celsum* (rationalism and faith), Aug. *De civ. Dei* 11 (mind, intellect, will, image of the Trinity), Capella (Mercury, symbol of quick intellect), Greg. Magn. *Moralia* (sins of the intellect more serious)

**interpretatio,** interpres, Gr: hermeneia, hermeneus, E: interpretation, => translatio 解释，见 Arist. *Org.*, Hier. *Ep.* (theory of translation), Capella (Mercury / Hermes is the interpreter of the gods)

**introductio,** introductorius liber, Gr: eisagōgē, E: introduction, introductory literature 导论，见 Cassiod. *Inst.*

**inventio,** Gr: heuresis, E: finding a topic（for a speech）找题目，见 Cic. *Brutus*, Quint. *Inst.*

**invidia,** Gr: phthonos, zēlos, E: envy 嫉妒，见 Hor. *Sat.* 1,1, Chrysostom. *Peri parthen.*（envy in marriage life）, Greg. Mag., *Moralia*（one of the cardinal sins）

**Io,** Gr: Iō, "moon", daughter of Inachus, the first king of Argos, she was loved by Zeus and changed into a cow by him but was harassed by Hera; finally she went to Egypt, gave birth to Epaphus and later was worshipped as Isis 伊俄，见 Hdt. *Hist.* 1

**Iōannēs** => Johannes

**Iocasta** = Jocasta

**Ion,** Gr: Iōn, "native", E: Ion, 1) ancestor of the Ionian Greeks, son of Apollo and Creusa, the wife of Xuthus, => Hellen; 2) Ion of Chios, ca. 490—421 BC, Greek poet; none of his tragedies is extant 伊翁，见 *Peri hypsous* 39（Ion compared to Sophocles）

**Ionia,** Gr: Iōnia, a part of the west coast of Asia Minor, from Smyrna to Miletus, including adjacent islands; the area was inhabitated by the Ionian Greeks（Ionians）who had migrated there ca. 1000 BC; the legendary origin of their name is => Ion 伊俄尼亚，见 Hdt. *Hist.* 2, Vitr. *De arch.* 3~4（Ionian style）, Diog. Laert.（Ionian philosophers）

**Ioseph** = Joseph

**Iosephos Flavius** = Josephus Flavius

**Ioudaike archaiologia** = *Antiquitates Iudaicae*

**Iphicles,** Gr: Iphiklēs, "glory of might", son of Amphitruo and Alcumena 伊菲克勒斯，见 Plaut. *Amph.*

**Iphigenia,** Gr: Iphigeniē, Iphigeneia,（iphi = vis）"mighty since birth", "mother of a strong race", E: Iphigenia, daughter of Agamemnon, sacrificed by her father at Aulis but taken to Tauris by Artemis, where she became a priestess in the sanctuary of Artemis 伊菲格尼亚，见 Aesch. *Agamemnon*, Eur. *Iph. Aul.*, Lucr. *De rer. nat.*

**Iphigenia in Aulis,** Gr: *Iphigeneia hē en Aulidi*, tragedy by Euripides《伊菲格尼亚在奥利斯》，见 Eur.

**ira,** Gr: mēnis, mania, E: wrath, fury, => furor, 愤怒，见 Prud. *Psych.*（allegory）, Cass. *De inst.*, Greg. Mag., *Moralia*,（one of the cardinal sins）

**ira Dei,** E: the wrath of God; => caritas, gratia 上主的愤怒，见 Tert. *Apol.*（provoked by pagan worship）, Lact. *De ira*

**Irenaeus,** Gr: Eirēnaios, "peaceful", E: Irenaeus, bishop of Lyon, ca. 135—202 AD 依勒内，见 *Adversus haereses*

**Iris,** "rainbow", Greek goddess of the rainbow, messenger of the gods 伊里斯，见 Hom. *Il.* 15, 24

**ironia,** Gr: eirōneia, E: irony 讽刺，见 Theophr.

**Irus,** Gr: Iros, "rainbow", beggar at Odysseus' court 伊若斯，见 Hom. *Od.* 18

**Isaac,** Gr: Isaak, E: Isaac, one of the Jewish patriarchs 伊撒格，见 Philo, *De opificio*, Ios. *Antiqu.* 1, Bibl. *Gen*

**isagoge,** Gr: eisagōgē "guide into", E: introduction, literature for beginners; => introductio 导论，见 Cassiod. *Inst.*

**Ischomachus,** Gr: Ischomachos, "forceful fighter", a farmer in Xenophon's *Oeconomicus* 伊斯克马克斯，见 Xen. *Oik.*,

**Isidorus,** E: Isidore of Sevilla, ca. 560—636 AD, bishop and Latin author 伊西多尔，见 *Etymologiae*

**Isis,** "she who weeps", Egyptian goddess, sister and wife of Osiris, mother of Horus, symbol of fertility, later identified with Aphrodite, cf. Anchises = "with Isis"; her symbol was the cow, grain and the horn of plenty 伊西斯，见 Plut. *Mor.*, Apuleius, *Met.*

**Ismene,** Gr: Ismēnē, E: Ismene, sister of Antigone 伊斯梅内，见 Soph. *Ant.*, *Oid. epi Kol.*

**isonomia,** Gr: isonomiē, E: equal access to the laws, balanced laws 法律上的平等，见 Hdt. *Hist.* 3

**Isocrates,** Gr: Isokratēs, Attic σrator, 436—338 BC, famous for his panegyrics 伊索克拉底，见 orator

**Issos,** coastal city in Cilicia（Asia Minor）, site of a battle in 333 BC, where Alexander defeated the Persians 伊索斯，见 *Alexandrou anabasis*, 2

**Isthmus,** Gr: Isthmos, E: the Isthmus of Corinth, important trade route; the Isthmian games were held in honor of Poseidon every two years 伊斯特摩斯地岬，见 Corinthus

**Italia,** < vitulus, "land of cows", E: Italy, early settlers included the Umbrians, Ligurians, Sabines, Samnites and the Oscians; Latium in central Italy was the place where the Greek culture of Magna Graecia and the Etruscan traditions met; in the 6th ct. BC the Etruscans dominated central Italy, but since ca. 250 BC Rome could control all tribes in Italy; in 89 BC all Italics were granted the rights of the Latin allies; => Roma, Latium, Neapolis 意大利，见 Verg. *Aen.*, *Georg.*2, Plin. *Nat. hist.* 37, Diog.

Laert. (Italian philosophers), Aug. *Confess.* (arrival in and departure from Italy)

**Ithaca,** Gr: Ithakē, island west of Greece, home of Odysseus 伊塔刻, 见 Hom. *Od.* 1, 14~24

***Itinerarium Egeriae,*** E: *Itinerary of Egeria*, a work by a woman (Egeria or Aetheria), from the end of the 4th century《艾格瑞亚的游记》, 见 Itinerarium

**iudex** = judex

**Iulus** = Ascanius

**Iuno** = Juno

**iustitia** = justitia

**Iuvenalis** = Juvenalis

**Ixion,** Gr: Ixiōn, "strong native", ruler of the Lapiths and father of Pirithous, traditionally the first Greek to murder a kinsman; he tried to seduce Hera but was deceived by Zeus who formed Nephele ("cloud"); by this cloud Ixion fathered the centaurs; he was punished in the Underworld 伊克西翁, 见 Lucian. *Theon dial.*

## J

**Jacob,** Gr: Iakōb, E: Jacob, James, also called "Israel", one of the Jewish patriarchs, father of 12 sons, the ancestors of the 12 tribes of Israel (Judah, Reuben, Levi, Benjamin etc.) 雅各伯, 见 Philo, *De opificio*, Ios. *Antiqu.* 2, *Bibl.* Gen

**Jacobus,** Gr: Iakōbos, E: James, one of Jesus' disciples 雅各, 见 Biblia

**jactantia** => eloquentia

**Janus,** Roman god of gates and doorways, who gave his name to the first month (Januarius); his temple was at the Forum in Rome 雅努斯、门神, 见 Cic. *De nat deor.* 2,60

**Jason,** Gr: Iasōn, "healer", son of Aeson, leader of the Argonauts, husband of Medea 伊阿宋, 见 Eur. *Med.*, Apoll. *Arg.*, Ov. *Her.*

**jejunium,** E: fasting, an ascetic practice 守斋, 见 Didache (weekly fasting days), Greg. Nys. *Peri parthen.*, Hieron. *Epist.* 107 (fasting not for children, but for adults), Bened. *Regula* 49, *Physiologus* (rejuvenation through fasting)

**Jerome** = Hieronymus

**Jerusalem** = Ierosolyma

**Jesus,** Iesus, Gr: Iēsous, < Hebr: Jehoshuah "God saves", E: Jesus, the Christ, the Messiah, ca. 5 BC to 33 AD, the origin of the Christian movement 耶稣, 见 Ios. *Antiqu.* 18,3, Bibl. *Ioann.*, Iren. *Adv. haer.* (recapitulatio), Euseb. 1

**Job,** Gr: Iōb, E: *Job*, one book of the Old Testament《约伯传》, 见 *Bibl.*, Ambros. *De off. ministr.*

**Jocasta,** Gr: Iokastē, E: Jocasta, wife of Laius and mother (wife) of Oedipus 伊俄卡斯特, 见 Soph. *Oid. Tyr.*

**jocus,** risus, Gr: gelos, gelōs, E: joke, laughter, ridicule 玩笑, 见 Cic. *De off.* 1,103; Hor. *De arte poet.* 246 (no shameless jokes)

**Johannes Evangelista,** Gr: Iōannēs, <Hebr: Johanan, "God is merciful", E: John, important theologian and evangelist, author of the *Gospel of John* 若望、约翰, 见 Biblia, Ioann. Chrysostom. *Hom.* (88 homilies expound the *Gospel of John*)

**Johannes Cassianus** => Cassianus

**Johannes Climacus,** Gr: Ioannes Klimakos, E: John Climacus, ca. 575—650 AD, Greek hermit, author 梯子约翰, 见 *Scala paradisi*

**Josephus,** Gr: Iōsēph, <Hebr. "to add", "enrich", E: Joseph, the son of Jacob, who came to power in Egypt and sought reconciliation with his brothers 若瑟、约瑟, 见 Bibl. *Gen* 37~50, Philo, *De opificio*, Ambros. *De off. ministr.*

**Josephus Flavius,** Gr: Iōsephos, < Hebr "enrich", "add", E: Josephus Flavius, 37—100 AD, Jewish author who wrote in Greek 约瑟夫斯, 见 Ios. *Antiquitates, Bellum Iudaicum,* Euseb. 3, Hieron. *De viris*

**Judaea,** Gr: Ioudaia, E: Judea in Palestine, kingdom of the Jews with the capital in Jerusalem, a Roman province since 6 AD 犹大地区, 见 Ios. *Antiqu., Bell. Iud.*

**Judaei,** Gr: Ioudaioi, E: Jews, => Judaea 犹太人, 见 Chrysostom. *Hom.* (eight homilies against Jews in Antioch), Greg. Turon. *Hist. Franc.* (the first persecution of Jews in France)

**judex** = iudex, Gr: dikastēs, E: judge 审判员, 见 Aesch. *Eumen.*, Ar. *Sphekes*, Plat. *Apol.*, Hor. *De arte poet.* (a poet must know the duty of a judge), Aug. *De civ. Dei* 19 (even a good judge resorts to torture)

**judicium,** sententia, Gr: dikē, krisis, E: judgment 见 Aesch. *Eumen.*, Bibl. *Ioann.* 3 (krisis), 8 (adulterous woman), Iren. *Adv. haer.* 5 (last judgment), Sext. Emp. *Skept.* (epoche, refraining from judgment), Tert. *Apol.* (God's judgment above earthly courts), Lact. *De ira* (God's continual judgment), *Inst.* 7, Aug. *De civ. Dei* 20 (last judgment)

**Jughurta,** c. 160—104 BC, king of Numidia, grandson

of Massinissa 尤古达, 见 Sallust

**Julianus,** Flavius Claudius Julianus Apostata, E: Julian, Roman emperor 361—363 who received Christian and classical education but later turned against Christianity and was hence named "the Apostate"; he demanded the restoration of the pagan temples 尤利安努斯, 见 Ammianus, Greg. Naz. *Logoi*

**Julii,** E: Julians, the Julian clan, the family of Caesar, an old patrician family from Alba Longa whose (legendary) ancestry went back to Aeneas' son Iulus (=Ascanius) and thus even to Aphrodite 尤利阿家族, 见 Caesar

**Juno,** (=Iuno), Gr: Hēra, E: Juno, wife of Jupiter, as Juno Lucina she protected childbirth, and as Juno Moneta she gave advice; close to her temple on the Capitol was the Roman mint (stamping of coins, confer the words "money" and "mint"); => Hera 尤诺, 见 Plaut. *Aul.,* (Juno Lucina), Cic. *De nat. deor.* 2,60, Verg. *Aeneis* 4, 5, 7, 10, Liv. 6(Juno Moneta), Aug. *De civ. Dei,* 4, Capella, *De nuptiis* (welcomes Philologia)

**Jupiter,** (=Iupiter, Iuppiter) < dios-pater, "father of the day", or: < iuris pater "father of justice", Gr: Zeus, E: Jupiter, Jove; the highest Roman god, god of thunder (Jupiter tonans), lightning, weather (thus worshipped on hills); his most famous temple was on the Capitoline Hill in Rome; the Romans thought he granted power to them; => Zeus 朱庇特、尤皮特, 见 Plaut. *Amph.,* Cic. *De nat. deor.* 2,64 (name explained as "iuvans pater"), Verg. *Aen.* 4, 5, *Georg.* 1,118 (Jupiter ended the Golden Era), Hor. *Carm.* 1,12, Ov. *Met.* 2 (lover of Europa, father of Minos and Rhadamanthys), Claudian. *De raptu Pros.*, Capella, *De nuptiis,* Aug. *De civ. Dei, Confess.* (Jupiter the adulterer)

**jus,** Gr: dikē, nomos, E: law, lawfulness, justice; => dike 法律、公道, 见 Cic. *De fin.* 3,67(jus civile), *De off.* 2,15; 3,23 (jus gentium)

**jus jurandum,** jurare, sacramentum dicere, Gr: horkos, E: oath 誓言, 见 Cic. *De off.* 1,39~40; 3,99~101 (example of Regulus), 3,104 (oath = affirmatio religiosa); *Peri hypsous* 16 (horkos)

**Justinianus,** Gr: Iustinianos, E: Justinian, 482—565 AD, emperor in Constantinople 527—565 AD, who tried to restore the greatness of the Roman Empire and regained areas in Africa, Sardinia, Sicily, Italy and southern Spain; he erected many buildings (among them the Hagia Sophia) and codified the law, which became the basis for European law.优士丁尼, 见 *Corpus Iuris Civilis*

**Justinus,** Gr: Iustinos, E: Justin the Martyr, Christian author, ca. 100—165 AD 犹斯丁, 见 *Apologia*; (Logos), Euseb. 4

**justitia** = iustitia, Gr: dikē, dikaiosynē, epieikeia, E: justice, 正义, 见 Hom. *Il.* (justice and the fate of Troy), *Od.* 22~24 (just revenge), Hes. *Erga* (Dike), Plat. *Gorg., Polit.,* Arist. *Eth. Nik., Polit., Rhet.,* Cic. *De fin.* 3,70, *De off., De re publ.* 3, Bibl. *Job* (suffering of the just), Tert. *Apolog.* (unfair treatment of Christians), Ambros. *De off. ministr.,* Aug. *De civ. Dei* 4 (without justice kingdoms are groups of robbers)

**Juvenalis** (= Iuvenalis), Latin author, 60—130 AD, famous for his satirical criticism of Roman society 朱文纳尔, 见 Iuv. *Sat.*

**Juventus,** Gr: Hēbē, E: Hebe, daughter of Zeus and Hera, the personification of Youth, together with Ganymede cup-bearer of the gods; she married Heracles after he was elevated to the gods 尤文图斯, 见 Catamites

# K

**Kadmos** = Cadmus
**kairos** => tempus, occasio
**kakon** => malum
**Kalchas** = Calchas
**Kallikles** = Callicles
**Kalliope** = Calliope
**kakon,** kakia => malum, vitium, turpitudo
**kalon eidos eperaton,** a beautiful and lovable resemblance (of the goddesses), woman 美丽可爱的形象, 见 Hes. *Erga,* 63
**kalos,** to kallos => pulchritudo, bonum
**Kalypso** = Calypso
**Kassandra** = Cassandra
**Kastor** = Castor
*Kata Kelsou* = *Contra Celsum*
*Katecheseis* = *Catecheses*
**kathekon** => officium
**Kebes,** Gr: Kēbēs, dialogue partner of Socrates 克贝斯, 见 Plat. *Phaid.*
**Kekrops** => Cecrops
**Kephalaia** => Capita
**Kerkyra** = Corcyra
**Kikones** = Cicones
**Kirke** = Circe

**Kithairon** = Cithaeron
**Kleio** = Clio
**klimax** => scala
**Klytaimnestra** = Clytemnestra
**Knemon** = Cnemon
**Koeos** = Coeus
**koinobion** = monasterium
**koinonia** => communitas
**koryphaios** = choryphaeus
**Korinthos** = Corinthus
**Kosmas** = Cosmas
**kosmos** => cosmos, mundus, ordo, ornamentum
**Kottos** = Cottus
**Kreon** = Creon
**Kreousa** = Creusa
**Krios** = Crius
**Kritoboulos** = Critobulos
**Kroisos** = Croesus
**Kronos** = Cronus
**kybos** = cubus
**Kyklopes** = Cyclopes
**kyklos** = circulus
**Kyrene** = Cyrene
**Kyrillos** = Cyrillus
**kyrios** = dominus
**Kyros** = Cyrus
***Kyrou anabasis*** = *Anabasis*

# L

**labor,** Gr: ergon, ponos, E: hard work, toils 辛劳, 见 Hes. *Erga*, Ter. *Heaut. Tim.*, (field work as self-punishment), Cic. *De off.* 1,66; 1,150; Verg. *Georg.* (labor improbus), Bibl. *Gen* 3 (work as punishment imposed by God), Claud. *De raptu* (Jupiter decides that Ceres should spread agriculture), Capella, *De nuptiis* (the boy Labor carrying Philologia), Bened. *Regula* 48

**Lacedaemonia,** Gr: Lakedaimōn, "happiness", (= Sparta), town and area in the southern Peloponnesus, the area around Sparta 拉科代门, 见 Pausanias

**Lachesis,** Gr: Lachesis, "apportioner", "measurer", one of the Fates; => Fata 命运女神, 见 Hes. *Theog.*

**Laconia,** Gr: Lakōnikē = Lacedaemonia

**Lactantius,** Lucius Caelius Firmianus Lactantius, ca. 250—325 AD, Latin Christian author, known as "Cicero Christianus" 拉克坦提乌斯, 见 *Carmen de ave phoenice, De ira Dei, De mortibus, Institutiones divinae*

**Laelius,** Gaius Laelius, ca. 190—129 BC, soldier under Scipio in the Third Punic War and member of the philhellenic circle of Scipio, consul in 140 BC 勒流斯, 见 Cic. *Cato de sen.*

**Laertes,** Gr: Laertēs, "ant", the old father of Odysseus 拉厄尔特斯, 见 Hom. *Od.* 24

**Laestrygones,** Gr: Laistrygones, E: Laestrygonians, cannibal giants 莱斯特律贡人, 见 Hom. *Od.* 10

**laetitia,** gaudium, Gr: hēdonē, chara, terpsis, charmonē, euphrosynē, E: joy, happiness 快乐, 见 Cic. *De fin.* 3,35, *Peri hypsous* 7 (greatness gives joy), Tert. *De spect.* (spiritual joys), Boethius, *De cons.* 3 (true joy = gaudium, laetitia, versus physical gratification = voluptates)

**Laius,** Gr: Laios, "left-hand" (?), king of Thebes, father of Oedipus 拉伊俄斯, 见 Soph. *Oid. Tyr.*

**Langobardi,** E: Lombards, a Germanic people which migrated to northern Italy in 568 AD; their kingdom was conquered by Charlemagne in 774 AD 隆巴底人, 见 Germani, Justinian

**Lakonike** = Laconia

**Lamachus,** Gr: Lamachos, "fighter", Athenian general, strategos ca. 435 BC, caricatured by Aristophanes 拉马克斯, 见 Ar. *Acharn.*

**Laocoon,** Gr: Laokoōn, "very perceptive", E: Laocoon, a Trojan priest of Apollo who warned the Trojans not to accept the Trojan horse (=> equus ligneus), but he and his two sons were killed by two serpents 拉奥孔, 见 Verg. *Aen.* 2

**Laodamia,** Gr: Laodameia, "tamer of people", the wife of Protesilaos who killed herself when her husband left her the second time 拉俄达美亚, 见 Ov. *Her.*

**Laomedon,** Gr: Laomedōn, E: Laomedon, king of Troy, father of Priam; he did not want to reward Poseidon and Apollo for building the city walls and thus was asked to sacrifice his daughter Hesione. 拉俄墨冬, 见 Troia

**Lapithae,** Gr: Lapithai, E: Lapiths, a mythical tribe from Thessaly; among their heroes were Ixion and king Pirithous, the friend of Theseus; they fought against the centaurs 拉比泰, 见 Ixion

**lapsi,** E: fallen, lapsed (Christians), Christians who renounced their faith under pressure 背教的信

徒，见 Cyprian. *Epist.*

**lar familiaris,** E: family god, => penates 家庭的保护神，见 Plaut. *Aul.*

**Latinus,** king of Latium, who gave his daughter Lavinia in marriage to Aeneas; according to Vergilius he was the son of Faunus, the grandson of Picus and so descended from Saturnus 拉丁努斯，见 Verg. *Aen.* 7

**Latium,** the area around the Alban Mount, ca. 20 km. south-east of Rome, between the Etruscan culture in the north and the Greek culture of Magna Graecia in the south; the area was inhabitated by the Latini, and it gave the name to the Latin language; the main towns were Rome, Tibur, Praeneste, Tusculum, Alba Longa, Lavinium, Aricia; the Romans defeated a league of the Latins in 496 BC and finally confirmed their control over the area in the Latin War (340—338 BC); => Italia, Lingua Latina 拉丁地区，见 Verg. *Aen.*

**Latona** => Lētō

**laurea,** Gr: daphnē, E: laurels, symbol of Apollo, worn by triumphant generals and by poets 桂树，见 Ov. *Met.* 1

**Laurentius,** E: Lawrence, deacon in Rome, martyred in 258 AD 劳伦佐，见 Prud. *Peristeph.*

**Lausus,** son of Mezentius 劳苏斯，见 Verg. *Aen.* 10

**Lavinia,** daughter of Latinus, betrothed to Turnus, but later she became the wife of Aeneas 拉维尼亚，见 Verg. *Aen.* 7

**Lazarus,** Gr: Lazaros, E: Lazarus, a friend of Jesus 拉匝禄，见 Bibl. *Ioann.* 11

**Leander,** Gr: Leandros, "lion-man", a young man from Abydus (Asia Minor) who loved Hero, the priestess on the other shore of the Hellespont, so he swam across the sea every night but eventually drowned in the darkness. 勒安德，见 Ov. *Her.*

**Leda,** Gr: Lēda, E: Leda, the daughter of Thestius, king of Aetiolia, wife of Tyndareus, king of Sparta, mother of Clytaemnestra; Zeus loved her and approached her in the shape of a swan, whereupon she gave birth to Helena and to Castor and Pollux (Dioscuri) 勒达，见 Helena

**legere,** Gr: krinein, E: select, distinguish, examine, according to Cicero the common root of religio, diligens, elegans and intelligens 选择，见 Cic. *De nat. deor.* 2,72

**leges** => lex

**Leges,** Gr: *Pentateuchos*, E: *Pentateuch*, the books of the Law, i.e. *Genesis, Exodus, Leviticus, Numeri, Deuteronomium*《法律书》、《律法》，见 Biblia

**legio,** E: legion, the biggest unit within the Roman army, consisting of about 5000 soldiers and 300 riders 兵团，见 Caesar, *De bell. gall.*

**Legum allegoriae,** E: *Allegories of the Laws*, a work by Philo《法律的比喻》，见 Philo

**Lemnos,** Gr: Lēmnos, Greek island 勒姆诺斯，见 Apoll. *Arg.*

**leo,** Gr: leon, => Leander, Leonidas, E: lion 狮子，见 Aes., Ov. *Met.* 4 (Pyramus, Thisbe)

**Leo Magnus,** E: Leo the Great, ca. 400—461 AD, Pope from 440—461, one of the Latin Fathers of the Church 利奥，见 Leo, *Tomus*

**Leonidas,** Gr: Leōnidas, "lionheart", Spartan king who commanded the Greeks at the battle of Thermopylae in 480 BC and died heroically 勒俄尼达斯，见 Hdt. *Hist.* 7

**Lesbos,** a Greek island off the coast of Asia Minor, birth place of the poets Sappho and Alcaeus; the main city is Mytilene 勒斯波斯，见 Longos

**Lethe,** Gr: Lēthē, "forgetfulness", one of the five rivers of the Underworld; the souls of the deceased had to drink from its water so as to forget their former life; => Hades, Styx 勒特，见 Verg. *Aen.* 6

**Leto,** Latona, Gr: Lētō, "stone", "lady" (?), daughter of Coeus, mother of Artemis and Apollo; since Hera chased her from one place to another she fled to the island of Delos to give birth to her children; => Delos 勒托，见 Hes. *Theog.*, Ov. *Met.* 6, Lucian. *Theon dial.*

**lex,** leges, legislatio, Gr: nomos, nomoi, E: law, legislation 法律、立法，见 Soph. *Ant.*, Plat. *Gorg.*, Arist. *Rhet.*, Cic. *De off.* 1,33 (malicious interpretation of a law: summum ius, summa iniuria), 2,40 (leges latronum esse dicuntur), 3,23 (lex divina et humana); Hor. *Carm.* 3,24 (leges sine moribus vanae), Liv. 3 (Leges XII Tabularum), Philo, *De opificio*, (Mosaic Law), Biblia (Pentateuch), Gellius, Justinianus, *Corpus Iur. Civ.*, Martinus de Bracara (canon), Isidor. *Etym.* 5

**lex naturae,** Gr: nomos agraphos, E: law of nature 自然法，见 Soph. *Ant.*, Cic. *De off.* 3,23 (lex divina = ratio naturae); Philo, *De opificio* (agraphoi nomoi), Basil. *Hexaem.*

**lexis** = elocutio

**libatio,** Gr: choē, E: libation, sacrifices（at a tomb）奠酒礼，见 Aesch. *Choeph.*

**liber,** Gr: biblion, byblos, papyrus, syngraphē, E: book, scroll; => bibliotheca 书卷、书本，见 Caes. *Bell. gall.*（textbook）, Sall. *Bell. Cat.*（textbook）, Publ. Syr.（textbook）, Sen. *Epist. mor.* 2（reading of good books）, Biblia, Capella, *De nuptiis*（Philologia vomits books）

**Liber,** Italian god of fertility, identified with Dionysus, his festival（March 17）were the Liberalia, also the time for young men to assume the toga virilis（man's toga）利柏尔，见 Hor. *Carm.* 1,12, Tert. *De spect.*（liberalia）

***Liber Heraclidis,*** Gr: *Pragmata Herakleidou Damaskenou,* E: *Essay of Heracleides* 《赫拉克勒伊德斯之书》，见 Nestorius

**liberalitas,** Gr: eleutheria, E: generosity; => avaritia 慷慨，见 Theophr. *Eth.* 22（aneleutheria）, Cic. *De off.* 1,42; 2,53~71

**libertas,** Gr: eleutheria, parrhēsia, E: freedom 自由，见 Arist. *Polit.* 6, Theophr. *Eth.* 28, Cic. *De nat. deor.* 2,60（personified goddess Libertas）, *De off.* 2,24; Bible *Exodus, Ioann.* 8（truth will liberate you）, Sen. *De vita beata,*（liberum animum）, Epict. *Enchir.*, Tac. *Ann.*, *Germ.*（Germanorum libertas）, *Peri hypsous* 44（only freedom nourishes great spirits）; Basil. *Ascet.*（liberation of the soul）, Chrysostom. *Peri parthen.*, Aug. *De civ. Dei* 5（virtues enslaved by pleasure）, *De vera rel.*, Boethius, *De cons.* 5（human freedom and divine providence）

**libido,** Gr: epithymia, lagneia, E: lust, sexual desire 欲望，见 Cic. *De fin.* 3,35, Tert. *De Spect.*（Venus, the demon of libido）, Prud. *Psychom.*（killed by chastity）, Aug. *De civ. Dei* 19（libido dominandi）

**Libya,** Gr: Libyē, "dripping rain", land in north Africa; => Cyrene 利比亚，见 Hdt. *Hist.* 4, Verg. *Aen.*

**lingua,** Gr: glossa, E: language, tongue 语言，见 Varro, *De lingua Lat.*, Tert. *De spect.* 2, Hieron. *Ep.* 107（language learning）, Aug. *Conf.* 1（mother tongue and other languages）, Isidor. *Etym.* 9（de linguis, gentibus, regnis）

**lingua Graeca,** litterae Graecae, Gr: Hellēnikē glōssa, E: Greek language and literature; => lingua Latina 希腊语，见 Quint. *Inst.* 1, Hieron. *Epist.* 107（children should learn Greek early）, Aug. *Conf.* 1（he fails to learn Greek well）

**lingua Hebraica,** Gr: Hebraikē glōssa, E: Hebrew, the language of the Old Testament; => Vetus testamentum 希伯来语，见 Origen. *Hexapla*, Hieron. *Ep.* 57（Hebraica veritas）, *Vulgata*, Aug. *De civ. Dei* 15（the Hebrew text more reliable than the Greek）

**lingua Latina,** litterae Latinae, Gr: Rhōmaikē glōssa, E: Latin language and literature 拉丁语，见 Varro, *De lingua Latina*, Cic. *De fin.* 1, *De off.* 1, Hor. *De arte poet.* 268（Greek and Latin poets）, Bibl. *Ioann.* 19（trilingual inscription on the cross）, Donatus, Aug. *Confess.* 1（learning Latin as mother tongue）, Cassiod. *Inst.*（biblical Latin different from classical Latin）

**lingua Syria,** Gr: Syria glōssa, E: Syrian language 叙利亚语，见 Aug. *De civ. Dei* 15

**litterae,** Gr: grammata, logoi, E: letters, texts, literature 文学，见 Cic. *Brutus*（a history of oratory）, Hor. *Carm.* 1,1, 3,30（meaning of literature）, Hor. *Arte poet.*, Ov. *Met.* 3（Cadmus and the Phoenician alphabet）, *Peri hypsous*, Gellius, Hieron. *Ep.* 57（translation ad sensus or ad litteram）, *Ep.* 107（teaching children the ABC）

**liturgia,** Gr: leitourgia, E: liturgy, ceremonial rites of the Christian community, => eucharistia 礼仪，见 Didache, Cyrillus, *Catech.*, Maximus Conf. *Mystagogia*（symbolic meaning of the Holy Mass）, Egeria, *Itinerarium*

**Livius,** 1）Livius Andronicus, ca. 260—200 BC, the founder of Latin literature, he translated the *Odyssee* into Latin（*Odusia*）, and created the Latin drama; 2）Titus Livius, E: Livy, Roman historian, 59 BC—17 AD 李维，见 Liv. *Ab urbe*, Quint. *Inst.* 10

**loci communes,** Gr: koinoi topoi, E: commonplaces, topics（for a speech）通用的话题

**logica,** Gr: logikē（technē）, E: logic, the rules of reasoning 逻辑学，见 Arist. *Organon*, Cic. *De fin.* 1; 5,22

***Logoi*** => *Homiliae, Orationes*

***Logoi theologikoi,*** E: *Five Theological Orations*, a work by Gregory of Nazianz 《神学讲道稿》，见 Greg. Naz.

**logos** => fabula, oratio, proverbium, ratio, sententia

**Logos,** Verbum Dei, Gr: Logos, E: the Logos, the

Word of God, Christ 逻各斯，见 Bible, *Jn* 1; Justin. *Apol.* (logos spermatikos), Clem. Alex. *Paed.*, Orig. *De princ.* (personal understanding of the Logos), Athanas. *Logos* (enanthropesis, incarnation of the Logos), Greg. Nys. *Peri parthen.* (spiritual birth of the Word)

***Logos kata ton Hellenon*** => *Oratio contra gentes*

***Logos pros Hellēnas***, E: *Oration to the Greeks*, a work by Tatian《反驳希腊人》

**Longinus,** Cassius Longinus, 212—273 AD, a rhetor and the (supposed) author of *Peri hypsous* 伦基努斯，见 *Peri hyps.*

**Longus,** Gr: Longos, E: Longus, Greek novelist, ca. 200—250 AD, author of *Daphnis and Chloe* 朗格斯，见 *Poimenika ta kata Daphnin kai Chloen*

**loquacia** => eloquentia

**Lotophages,** Gr: Lōtophagoi, "lotus-eaters", a mythical people 以洛托斯为食的人，见 Hom. *Od.* 9

**Loukianos** = Lucianus

**Lucanus,** Marcus Annaeus Lucanus, E: Lucan, Latin author, 39—65 AD; he was a nephew of Seneca and a friend of Nero, but was forced to commit suicide by Nero. 卢坎，见 Pharsalia

**Lucas,** Gr: Loukas, E: Luke, one of the four evangelists, => *Novum Testamentum* 路加，见 Chrysostom. *Hom.* (16 homilies expound the gospel of Luke)

**Lucianus,** Gr: Loukianos, E: Lucian of Samosata, Greek author, ca. 120—180 AD 卢奇安（或译琉善、路吉阿诺斯），见 *Alethe dihegemata, Theon dialogoi, Vitarum auctio*

**Lucilius,** Gaius Lucilius, ca. 180—102 BC, Latin satirical poet 卢基利乌斯，见 Hor. *Sat.*, Quint. *Inst.* 10

**Lucina,** Juno Lucina, "who brings the child to the light", Roman goddess of mothers; her feastday, the Matronalia, was celebrated on March 1st. 卢基娜，见 Hor. *Carm. saec.*

**Lucius** => Cicero, Lucius Tullius

**Lucius Apuleius** => Apuleius

**Lucretia,** Roman woman, symbol of virtue; she committed suicide after being raped by Sextus Superbus, the elder son of Tarquinius Superbus, the last Roman king. Her death helped to overthrow the monarchy in Rome. 卢克莱夏，见 Aug. *De civ. Dei* 1 (not to be imitated)

**Lucretius,** Titus Lucretius Carus, Latin poet, 99—55 BC 卢克莱修，见 Lucr. *De rer. nat.*, Quint. *Inst.* 10

**Lucullus,** Lucius Licinius Lucullus, 114—57 BC, Roman general and statesman, whose wealth and hedonism became proverbial 卢库鲁斯，见 Cic. *De fin.*3, Plut. *Bioi*

**ludus,** ludi, Gr: agōn, athla, E: games, especially the public games at Rome held at religious festivals; they included sports, theatrical performances, competitions, chariot-races (ludi circenses), => theatrum 游戏，见 Hom. *Il.* 23, Cic. *De off.* 1,103, Verg. *Aen.* 5, Sen. *Epist. mor.* 7 (depraving influence of cruel games), Suet. *De vita Caes.*, Tert. *De spect.*, Hieron. *Epist.* 107 (lusus, playful learning), Isidor. *Etym.*

**lumen** => lux

**luna,** Gr: selēnē, E: moon 月亮，见 Cic. *De nat. deor.* 2,4, Lucian. *Alethe diheg.* (sailing to the moon), Basil. *Hexaem.* (symbol of transitoriness)

**Luna,** Gr: Selēnē, E: Luna, goddess of the moon, identified with Diana 卢娜，见 Hor. *Carm. saec.*

**lupus,** Gr: lykos, E: wolf, symbol of violence or shrewdness; => animalia 狼，见 Plat. *Phaed.* (reincarnation as wolf), Boethius, *De cons.* 4 (avaricious people are like wolves)

**lusus,** E: play, entertainment 玩耍，见 Hieron. *Epist.* 107 (et lusus et eruditio)

**lux,** Gr: phōs, E: light, => Lucina, Luna, Phoibos, Sol 光明，见 Bibl. *Ioann.* 1 (phos - skotia), 8 (phos tou kosmou), Aug. *Confess.* 13 (spiritual meaning of light)

**luxuria,** E: lust, one of the cardinal sins; => luxus 迷色，见 Greg. Mag., *Moralia*

**luxus,** E: luxury, licentiousness, indulgence 奢侈豪华的表现，见 Tert. *De spect.* (Liber, symbol of luxury), Prud. *Psych.* (Luxuria weakens all virtues but is defeated by the cross), Aug. *De civ. Dei* 1 (weakened Roman virtue)

**Lycomedes,** Gr: Lykomēdes, "bright thinker" (?), king of Scyrus 吕克梅德斯，见 Stat. *Achill.*

**Lyconides,** lover of Phaedria in Plautus' play *Aulularia* 吕克尼德斯，见 Plaut. *Aul.*

**Lycurgus,** Gr: Lykourgos, "bright work", 1) legendary legislator of Sparta, ca. 800 BC; 2) Athenian politician and orator, ca. 390—324 BC, he supported Demostenes against Macedonia. 吕库尔格斯，见 Plat. *Symp.*, Plut. *Bioi*

**Lydia,** Gr: Lydia, a country in the western part of

Asia Minor, ruled by king Croesus until 546 BC, then became a Persian province; the capital was Sardis; the Lydians allegedly invented the mint of coins.吕蒂亚, 见 Hdt. *Hist.*

**lykos** = lupus

**Lynceus,** Gr: Lynkaios, "sharp-eyed as a lynx", a son of Aegyptus, king of Argos, married to Hypermestra 林开欧斯, 见 Ov. *Her.*

**Lysandrus,** Gr: Lysandros, "freed man", E: Lysander, a Spartan naval commander, who died in 395 BC at the siege of Haliartus Boeotia 吕三德, 见 Plut. *Bioi*

**Lysias,** Gr: Lysias, 445—380 BC, Attic orator, famous for forensic oratory; 34 of his speeches are extant 吕西阿斯, 见 orator

**lysis Hektoros,** the release of Hector, the last part of the *Iliad* 赫克托尔的释放, 见 Hom. *Il.* 24

**Lysistrata,** Gr: Lysistratē, "disband the army", a figure in Aristophanes' comedy 吕西斯忒拉忒, 见 Ar. *Ornith.*

**Lysistrata,** Gr: *Lysistratē*, E: *Lysistrata*, comedy by Aristophanes《吕西斯忒拉忒》, 见 Ar.

# M

**Maccabaei,** Gr: Makkabaioi, Jewish leaders who resisted the oppression of the Seleucids, esp. Judas Maccabaeus (166—160 BC) and Jonatan Maccabaeus (160—142 BC)玛加伯弟兄, 见 Ios. *Antiqu.* 12, Biblia

**Macedonia,** Gr: Makedonia, < makros, "wide land", the central area of the Balkan Peninsula; after 400 BC the Macedonians sought more contact to the Hellenic world; king Philipp II (359—336 BC) defeated Athens and Thebes in the battle at Charioneia (338 BC) and dominated almost all of Greece, except Sparta; his son Alexander (336—323 BC) expanded Macedonian rule and established a huge empire; the Antigonides established their dynasty in 277 BC; King Philipp V was defeated by the Romans in 197 BC ad Cynoscephalae, and his son Perseus in 168 BC ad Pydna; Macedonia became a Roman province in 148 BC and in 395 AD fell to Byzanz. 马其顿, 见 Hdt. *Hist.* 6, Polyb.

**machina,** Gr: mēchanē, E: machine 机械, 见 Vitr. *De arch.* 9, 10, (clockworks, crane)

**Macrina,** Gr: Makrina, "blessed", E: Macrina, sister of Gregorius of Nyssa 马克瑞纳, 见 Greg. Nys. *Peri psyches*

**Macrobius,** Ambrosius Theodosius Macrobius, ca. 380—440 AD, proconsul of Africa in 410 AD; scholarly Latin author 马克罗比乌斯, 见 *Commentarii in Somnium Scipionis, Saturnalia*

**Maecenas,** Gaius Maecenas, ca. 80—8 BC, the most famous Roman literary patron who supported Virgil, Horace, Propertiius and Varius 迈克纳斯, 见 Verg. *Georg.* 1, 3, Hor. *Sat.* 1,5~8, 2,6

**magae artes** => magus

**magister,** praeceptor, Gr: didaskalos, E: teacher, => discipulus 老师, 见 Ausonius (and his student Paulinus), Hieron. *Epist.* 107 (pride of teaching a bride of Christ)

**Magna Graecia,** Gr: Megalē Hellas, E: Greater Greece, the wealthy and influential Greek cities of southern Italy and Sicily, where the Greeks had founded colonies since 800 BC; => Cumae, Neapolis, Paestum, Tarentum; Agrigentum, Syracusae;"大希腊", 见 Vitr. *De arch.* 3~4

**magnanimitas,** Gr: megalopsychia, E: magnanimity 慷慨的心, 见 Cic. *De off.* 1,17; 1, 66~69; *Peri hypsous* 8 (megalophrosyne = greatness of spirit)

**magus,** maga, magae artes, Gr: magos, mageia, E: sorcerer, sorceress, magic skills; => divinatio, medicina, Circe, *Medea*, Sibylla 巫术、魔术, 见 Hom. *Od.* (Circe changes humans into animals), Eur. *Medeia*, Apollod., Cic. *De div.*, Plin. *Hist. nat.* 30, Apuleius, *Met.* (changing humans into animals), Macrob., *Sat.* (Virgil as magus)

**Maia,** Gr: Maia, "grandmother", daughter of Atlas, mother of Hermes 麦亚, 见 Hes. *Theog.*, Lucian, *Theon dial.*

**maieutikē,** "midwifery", Socratic pedagogy, Socrates' way of teaching 助产术, 见 Xen. *Oik.*

**makarōn nēsoi,** E: Isles of the Blest; => elysium 幸福之岛, 见 Hes. *Erga,* 171

**maledictum,** maledictio, Gr: ara, kateugma, E: curse; => benedictio 诅咒, 见 Soph. *Antig., Oid. Tyr.,* Eur. *Hippolyt., Medeia,* Verg. *Aen.* 4, Ov. *Met.* (Echo, Daedalus), Bibl. *Job*

**malum,** malitia, turpitudo, Gr: kakon, kakia, kakotēs, E: evil, maliciousness, vice, suffering 恶, 见 Hes. *Erga,* (pleie men gaia kakon), Cic. *De fin.* 3,38, *De off.* 3,106 (minus malum); Bibl. *Gen.* 3, Aug. *Confess.* 7, *De vera rel.* (evil = perversion of the will, not a substance), Boethius, *De cons.* 4 (question of evil)

**Mani,** a sectarian in Persia ca. 215—275, founder of Manichaeism 摩尼, 马尼, 见 Aug. *Confess.* 3, *De vera rel.* (problem of evil)

**Manlius Capitolinus,** Marcus Manlius C., Roman hero who held the Capitol against the attacking Gauls in 390 BC 曼利乌斯·卡皮托利努斯, 见 Liv. 6

**Manlius Torquatus,** Titus Manlius Torquatus Imperiosus, Roman hero in the 4th ct BC 曼利乌斯·托夸图斯, 见 Liv. 8

**manteion,** mantike => oraculum, divinatio

**Mantua,** town in northern Italy, close to the birth place of Vergil 曼托瓦, 见 Verg.

**manus,** Gr: cheir, E: hand 手, 见 Iren. *Adv. haer.* (God's two 'hands' are the Word and the Spirit)

**Marathon,** Marathōn, region on the north-east coast of Attica, where the Greeks under Miltiades defeated the invading Persians in 490 BC 马拉松, 见 Aesch., Hdt. *Hist.* 6, Ar. *Lysistr.*

**Marcellus,** Marcus Claudius Marcellus, Roman general, who became consul 5 times between 222 and 208 BC; he captured Syracuse in 211 BC and brought the city's artifacts to Rome. 马塞卢斯, 见 Plut. *Bioi*

**Marcion,** Gr: Markion, heretic, died ca. 160 马西翁, 见 Iren. *Adv. haer.*, Orig. *Peri archon*;

**Marcus,** Gr: Markos, E: Mark, a disciple of Jesus, evangelist 马尔谷, 马可, 见 Euseb.

**Marcus Antonius,** E: Mark Anthony, 1) 143—87 BC famous Roman orator, grandfather of 2) Mark Anthony 82—30 BC, Roman statesman whose eloquence after the assassination won over the people in 44 BC; he ruled in a triumvirate with Octavian and Lepidus and after 42 was made ruler of the East; he had three children with Cleopatra but was defeated at the battle of Actium in 31 BC and took his life the following year. 马克·安托尼, 见 Cic. *Brutus*, Plut. *Bioi*

**Marcus Aurelius,** E: Marc Aurel, orig. Marcus Annius Verus, 121—180, Roman emperor from 161 to 180 马可·奥勒留, 见 *Ta eis heauton*, Euseb. 5 (persecutions of Christians in his reign)

**Mardonius,** Gr: Mardonios, Persian general, nephew of Darius, killed at Plataea in 479 BC 马多尼乌斯, 见 Hdt. *Hist.* 6, 9

**mare,** Gr: thalatta, thalassa, pontos, E: sea; cf. Pontus, Pontus Euxenus, Hellespontus 海, 见 Xen. *Anab.*

**Mare nostrum,** Gr: mesogeios pontos, E: Mediterranean Sea 地中海, 见 Apoll. *Arg*

**Maria,** Gr: Mariam, E: Mary, mother of Christ, thus "Deipara" (Theotokos, Mother of God), model of Christians; => incarnatio 玛利亚, 见 Greg. Nys. *Peri parthenias* (fruitful virgin), Hieron., Leo, *Tomus*, Romanus Mel. *Kontakia*

**Marius,** Gaius Marius, 157—86 BC, Roman general, he fought against Jugurtha (105 BC) and was consul from 104—100 BC; he reorganized the army; together with Cinna he fought against his rival Sulla. 马利乌斯, 见 Liv. 61~75, Plut. *Bioi*, Aug. *De civ. Dei* 3 (accused for cruelty)

**Maro** = Vergilius Maro

**Mars,** Mavors, Gr: Arēs, E: Mars, Roman god of war, father of Romulus; => Ares 马尔斯, 战神, 见 Cic. *De nat. deor.* 2,60~70 ("magna verteret", the great converter), Tert. *De spect.* (patron of horse races), Aug. *De civ. Dei* 3 (committed adultery)

**Martialis,** Latin author of epigrams, 40—103 AD 玛尔提阿里斯, 见 Mart. *Epigr.*

**Martinus,** E: Martin of Tours, 317—397 AD, bishop and founder of monastic communities; => *Vita Sancti Martini* 马丁, 见 Severus, *Vita*, Greg. Turon. *Hist. Franc.*

**Martinus de Bracara,** E: Martin of Braga, ca. 515—579 AD, Latin author 马丁, 见 *De correctione rusticorum*

**martyr,** Gr: martys "witness", E: martyr, Christians put to death because of their faith; => persecutio, sanctus 殉道者(基督徒), 见 Perpetua, *Passio*, Tert. *Apol.* 49 (sanguis martyrum semen Christianorum), Lact. *Inst.* 5 (the steadfastness of martyrs is a proof of the truth of the gospel), Athanas. *Logos*, Prud. *Peristeph.*, Physiologus (snakes protect their head like martyrs)

**Masada,** Jewish fortress whose fall in 72 AD marked the end of the Jewish state 玛撒达, 见 Ios. *Bell. Iud.*7

**Masinissa,** a Numidian prince who led a Roman army in 203 during the Second Punic War 马西尼撒, 见 Cic. *De re publ.* (Somnium Scipionis), Liv. 26~30

**Massagetes,** Gr: Massagetai, a people conquered by Cyrus 马撒格太, 见 Hdt. *Hist.*1

**materia,** Gr: hylē, E: matter 物质, 见 Arist. *Phys.*, Justin. *Apol.* (amorphos hylē), Orig. *De princ.*, Plotin. *Enn.* (hyle)

**mathematica,** Gr: mathematikē, E: mathematics,

geometry; => septem artes 数学，见 Eucl. *Stoich.*, Macrob. *Comm.*, Isidor. *Etym.* 3

*Mathēmatikē syntaxis,* E: *System of Mathematics, Almagest*《天文学大成》，见 Ptolemaeus

**mathesis, mathema** => disciplina, doctrina

**matrimonium**, Gr: gamos, E: marriage, conjugal relationship; => adulterium, amor, femina, nuptiae 婚姻，见 Eurip. *Medea*（marriage oath）, Cic. *De off.* 1,54（basis of the state）, Apuleius（Amor and Psyche）, Longos, Greg. Nys. *Peri parthen.*, Chrystostom. *Peri parthen.*（instituted as remedium concupiscentiae, marriage is not an eternal value）, Hieron. *Epist.* 107（sponsa Christi）, Aug. *De civ. Dei* 14（marriage in paradise would be without concupiscence）, Claud. *De raptu Proserp.*（Pluto in search of a wife）, Capella（Mercury in search of a wife, formal wedding celebration in heaven）

**Matthaeus**, Gr: Matthaios, E: Matthew, one of the four evangelists, => Novum Testamentum 玛窦、马太，见 Chrysostom. *Hom.*（90 homilies about Matthew）

**Maximus Confessor**, Gr: Maximos Homologētēs, E: Maximus Confessor, ca 580—662 AD, Greek author 马克西摩斯，见 *Capita, Mystagogia*

**Medea**, Gr: Mēdeia, "meditating, scheming woman", daughter of king Aeetes, niece of Circe, wife of Jason 美狄亚，见 Eur. *Med.*, Apoll. *Arg.*, Cic. *De nat. deor.* 3,69, Ov. *Her.*

*Medea,* Gr: *Mēdeia,* tragedy by Euripides《美狄亚》，见 Eur.

**media via**, Gr: mesotēs, E: the middle way, avoidance of extremes 中间的道路，见 Arist. *Eth. Nik.*, Cic. *De fin.* 3,39; 3,59（media, res mediae, neutral values）, Hor. *Carm.* 2,10（aurea mediocritas）, *Sat.* 2,1（middle way between polemic and adulation）, Greg. Magn. *Reg. past.*（exhortation without exciting passions）

**medicina, ars medica**, Gr: iatrikē technē, therapeia, therapeutikē methodos, E: medicine, healing; => magus 医术、医学，见 Eur. *Medea*, Plat. *Gorg., Tim.*, Apollod., Sen. *De clem.*（a ruler is like a physician）, Plin. *Nat. hist.* 20~27（pharmaceutic plants）, 29（history of medicine）, Mart. *Epigr.*（quackery）, Bibl. *Ioann.* 4, 5, 9,（Jesus heals sick, lame, blind people）, Galenus（most influential author of medical literature）, Gellius, Clem. Alex. *Paed.*（Christ heals wounds of the heart）, Athanas. *Vita Ant.*（healing powers of a saint）, Eugipp. *Vita S. Severini*（monasteries as hospitals, healing powers of the saint）, Boethius, *De cons.*（philosophy is healing the soul）, Greg. Mag., *Dialogi*（saints cure the sick）, *Reg. past.*（cura animarum）, Isidor. *Etym.* 4

**medicus**, Gr: iatros, E: doctor, physician; => medicina 医生，见 *Philogelos*

**Mediolanum**, It.: Milano, E: Milan, important city in northern Italy 米兰，见 Lact. *De mortibus*（Edict of Milan）, Aug. *Confess.* 5~9

*Meditationes,* Gr: *Ta eis heauton,* E: *Meditations,* a work by Marc Aurel《沉思录》，见 Marcus Aurelius

**medium, mediocritas** => media via

**Medusa**, Gr: Medousa, "cunning", E: Medusa, one of the three Gorgons whose snaky head was so ugly that anyone who looked at her would die; she was killed by Perseus 墨杜萨，见 Perseus

**Megabazus**, Gr: Megabaouz, Persian general 迈伽巴苏斯，见 Hdt. *Hist.* 5

**Megalē Hellas** = Magna Graecia

**megalēgoria**, "big talk", accusation brought up against Socrates 见 Plat. *Apol.*, Xen. *Apol.*

**megalophrosyne** => magnanimitas

**megalopsychia** => magnanimitas

**Megara**, Gr, ta megara = "the temples", main city of the Megaris, close to Salamis and Athens, since the 8th ct. BC it was an independent city and a traditional rival of Athens; since 460 BC under Athenian protection but after 447 BC in conflict with Athens; Athens' embargo against Megara（432 BC）contributed to the Peloponnesian War 梅格拉，见 Ar. *Acharn., Eirene*

**Melanthius**, Gr: Melanthios, "black flower", goatherd of Odysseus 梅兰修斯，见 Hom. *Od.* 17

**Melantho**, Gr: "black flower", maid at Odysseus' court 梅兰托，见 Hom. *Od.* 18~19

**Melchisedech**, < Hebr. melki "my king", zedek "justice", a figure from the Old Testament（*Gen* 14:18–20）, symbol of priesthood 默基瑟德，麦基洗德，见 Prud. *Psychomachia*

**Melpomene**, Gr: Melpomenē, Muse of tragedy 梅尔波梅内，见 Hes. *Theog.*, Hor. *Carm.* 4,3（prayer to her）

**memoria**, Gr: mnēmē, mnemosynē, mneia, E: memorization（of a speech）记忆、背诵，见 Cic. *Brutus*, Quint. *Inst.*

**Menandrus**, Gr: Menandros, E: Menander, the

greatest writer of Attic New Comedy, 342—291 BC 米南德，见 Men. *Dysk.*, Quint. *Inst.* 10

**Menedemus,** Gr: Menedēmos, "stay with the commoners", figure in Terence's play 梅内得姆斯，见 Ter. *Heaut. Tim.*

**Menelaus,** Gr: Menelaos, "stay with the people", brother of Agamemnon, husband of Helena, king of Sparta; after the fall of Troy he wandered around for 8 years (even to Egypt) before arriving at home. 梅内劳斯，见 Hom. *Il*, 3, *Od.* 4; Aesch. *Agamemnon*, Eur. *Iph. Aul.*

**mēnidos aporrhēsis,** the relinquishing of the wrath of Achilles 愤怒的熄灭，见 Hom. *Il.* 19

**mēnis,** L: furor, E: wrath, especially the wrath of Achilles 愤怒，见 Hom. *Il.* 1,1

**Menon,** Gr: Menōn, a dialogue partner of Socrates 美诺，见 Plat. *Men.*

***Menōn,*** E: Meno, a dialogue of Plato《美诺篇》，见 Plat.

**mens,** Gr: nous, phrēn, thymos, dianoia, phrontis, psychē, E: mind, spirit, thinking 精神，记忆力，见 Cic. *De nat. deor.* 1,4, (mente et ratione deorum), 2,60 (personification: goddess Mens), Hor. *Carm.* 2,3 (mens aequa), Prudentius, *Psychomachia* (Mens Humilis), Aug. *De civ. Dei* 11 (unity of mind, intellect, will)

**Mentes,** Greek prince, one of the appearances of Athena 门忒斯，见 Hom. *Od.* 1

**Mentor,** Gr: Mentōr, "patient" (?), father-like protector of Telemachus, one appearance of Athena 门托尔，见 Hom. *Od.* 2~4

**Mercurius,** Gr: Hermēs, E: Mercury, Roman god of trade and merchants, early identified with Hermes; => Hermes 梅库利，见 Plaut. *Amph.*, Hor. *Sat.* 2,6, Apuleius, *Met.*, Claudian. *De raptu Pros.*, Capella, *De nuptiis* (looks for a wife)

**meretrix,** Gr: pornē, hetaira, E: prostitute, music-girl, dancer, usually enslaved women 妓女、娱乐小姐，见 Ter. *Adelph.*, *Heauton Tim.*, Cic. *De fin.* 2, Chrysostom. *Peri parthen.*

**Merope,** Gr: Meropē, "eloquent", wife of Polybos 梅若佩，见 Soph. *Oid. Tyr.*

**Messapus,** one of the Italian leaders that resisted Aeneas 梅撒普斯，见 Verg. *Aen.* 7

**Messenia,** a region in the south-west of the Peloponnese, conquered by Sparta in 740—720 BC; in 146 BC the region fell to Rome. 梅瑟尼亚，见 Pausanias

**Messias,** (Unctus), Gr: Christos, "the anointed", E: Messiah, the expected redeemer of the Jews; => Christus 弥赛亚，见 Verg. *Buc.* 4, Origen. *Kata Kelsou*, Athanas. *Logos*

***Metamorphosae,*** Gr: *meta morphe* "changing form", E: *Metamorphoses*, 1) collection of myths by Ovid; 2) novel by Apuleius《变形记》，见 Ov. *Met.*, Apuleius, *Met.*

**metaphora,** Gr: metaphora, "carry over", E: metaphor; => figura 转义用法/比喻，见 Arist. *Rhet.*, Donatus (use of metaphors), Ammianus (metaphor of Rome as a person)

***Metaphysica,*** Gr: *Ta meta ta physika*, E: *Metaphysics*, a work by Aristotle《形而上学》，见 Arist.

**methexis,** participation, the partaking of certain phenomena in one idea 分享，见 Plat. *Men.*, *Phaid.*

**Metis,** Gr: Mētis, "counsel", the wisest of the gods, daughter of Tethys and Oceanus, the first wife of Zeus 梅提斯，见 Hes. *Theog.*

**Meton,** Gr: Metōn, "measurer", name of an astronomer, a figure in a comedy 梅通，见 Ar. *Ornithes*

**metrum,** Gr: metron, E: metre, the rhythm of a poem, => iambus, hexameter 格律、韵律，见 Hor. *De arte poet.* 73~118, (discussion of the proper metre)

**metus,** Gr: phobos, deima, E: fear; => timor 害怕，见 Cic. *De off.* 1,24 (cause of injustice), 2,22~24 (the worst means to secure cooperation), *Tusc.* (fear of death), Sen. *De vita beata* 4,3 (animus extra metum)

**Mezentius,** a cruel tyrant of Etruria, father of Lausus; both are killed by Aeneas 梅增提乌斯，见 Verg. *Aen.* 7

**Midas,** Gr: Midas, mythical king of Phrygia; Dionysus granted that everything he touched changed to gold 米达斯，见 Phrygia

**Milan** = Mediolanum

***Miles gloriosus,*** E: *Braggart Soldier*, play by Plautus《吹牛的军人》，见 Plaut.

**Miletus,** Gr: Miletos, "yew-tree", E: Miletus, city in Asia Minor, founded by Ionians in the 11th ct. BC; since the 8th ct. BC it was the most powerful Greek city of Asia Minor, reaching a cultural climax under the tyrant Thrasybulus (ca. 600 BC). It was destroyed by the Persians in 494 BC but rebuilt according to the plans of Hippodamus. The city was conquered by Alexander in 334 BC and came under Roman control in 78 BC. 米利

都,见 Herodotos

**millennium,** Gr: chilias "1000 years", E: chiliasm, millennium 一千年(的统治),见 Iren. *Adv. haer.* 5

**Miltiades,** Gr: Miltiadēs, "red view", Greek military commander 550—489 BC who led the Greeks to the victory at Marathon 弥尔提阿得斯,见 Hdt. *Hist.* 6, Plat. *Gorg.*

**mimesis** => imitatio

**Minerva,** Gr: Athēna, E: Minerva, the Latin name of Athena; Minerva was worshiped on the Capitoline Hill together with Jupiter and Hera; her main temple was on the Aventine Hill, where she was venerated as protectress of craftsmen, teachers and artists; since 207 BC the association of poets and actors held assemblies in this temple (Livius Andronicus); => Athena 弥内尔瓦,见 Cic. *De nat. deor.* 2,60 ~70（her name derived from "minueret" or "minaretur"), Claudian. *De raptu Proserp.* Aug. *De civ. Dei* 4

**minister,** E: servant, minister, administrator, clergyman; => sacerdos 服务者,圣职人员,见 Ambros. *De off. ministrorum*

**Minos,** Gr: Minōs, "the moon's creature" (?), son of Zeus and Europa, king of Crete; he was the lawgiver of Crete. After his son Androgeos had been killed in Attica he conquered Athens and demanded an annual tribute of 7 Athenian young men and women who were devoured by the Minotaurus until Theseus killed this monster. Minos became judge in Hades, together with Rhadamanthys and Aeacus. 弥诺斯,见 Hom. *Od.* 11, Ov. *Met.* 2 (Europa), 8 (Daedalus)

**Minotaurus,** Gr: Minōtauros, "Minos' bull", a monstrous bull, half man, half bull, living in a labyrinth built by Daedalus at Cnossus (Crete); the monster was killed by Theseus. 弥诺陶鲁斯,见 Ov. *Met.* 8

**Minucius Felix, Marcus,** E: Minucius, ca. 170—240 AD, Latin Christian apologist, author of *Octavius* 米努其乌斯,见 *Octavius*

**minus malum** => malum

**miraculum,** signum, Gr: thauma, dynamis, sēmeion, E: miracle, sign, wonder 奇迹,见 Bibl. *Ioann.* 6, Lact. *Inst.* 2, Aug. *De vera relig.* (miracles no longer needed), Eugipp. *Vita S. Severini,* Greg. Mag. *Dialogi*

**misericordia,** Gr: sympathein, E: sympathy, empathy; => gratia 怜悯,见 Sen. *De clem.,*

**missio,** missio ad gentes, apostolatus, Gr: => apostolos, E: mission work, the apostolate of missionaries 传教,宣教,见 Euseb., Greg. Magn.

**Mnemosyne,** Gr: Mnēmosynē, "memory", one of the Titans, mother (by Zeus) of the Muses 谟内摩绪内,记忆女神,见 Hes. *Theog.*

**Mithras,** Gr: Mithras, name of a god, originally from Persia, as "invincible god of the sun" ("Sol invictus") he became one of the most popular deities of the Roman empire; its cult centered on the slaughter of a sacred bull; the faith included the ideas of an immortal soul, resurrection and judgment of the dead 米特拉斯,见 religio

**Mithridates,** Gr: Mithradatēs Eupator, E: Mithridates IV, 120—63 BC, king of Pontus who fought three wars against Rome; in 88 BC conquered most of Asia Minor and ordered Romans and Italian residents in Asia Minor to be killed (allegedly 80000 died); he was defeated by Sulla. 米特瑞达特斯,见 Sulla

**modus,** moderatio, modestia, Gr: metron, mesotēs, eutaxia, sōphrosynē, E: self-control, moderation; => via media, temperantia, finis, continentia 自制,节制,见 Plat. *Polit.* 4, Cic. *De off.* 1,142, Hor. *Carm.* 2,10, *Sat.* 1,2, Aug. *De beata vita* (summus modus = beatitudo), *De civ. Dei* 5 (*Wisd.* 11:20, everything arranged according to number)

**Moirai** = Parcae

**monarchia,** Gr: mounarchiē, monarchiē, E: monarchy; cf. constitutio 君主制/王政,见 Hdt. *Hist.* 3, Arist. *Polit*., Polyb., Cic. *Brutus* (monarchy excludes oratory), *De re publica* 42~71

**monachus,** Gr: monachos, E: monk, hermit or a religious living in a community of monks (monastery) 隐修者,见 Athanas. *Vita Antonii,* (Ant. = "Father of monasticism"), Basilius, Hieron. *Epist.,* Dion. Ar., *Eccl. hier.*

**monasterium,** Gr: koinobion, E: monastery, 隐修院,见 Basil. *Ascetica,* Cassian. *De inst.,* Eugipp. *Vita S. Severini,* Bened. *Regula,* Cassiod. *Inst.,*

**Moneta** = Juno Moneta

**Monica,** mother of Augustine 默尼加,见 Aug. *Confess.*

**monologus,** < Gr: mono "single", logos "talk", E: monologue 自言自语,见 Marc. Aurel., Greg. Naz. *Carmina* (*Peri ton heautou biou*), Aug. *Soliloquia*

**monotheismus,** < Gr: monos theos, "one god", E: monotheism, the basic tenet of the Bible; => deus 一神论, 见 Bibl. *Gen.*, Tert. *Apol.*, Macrobius, *Sat.* (monotheist tendencies of Neoplatonism)

*Moralia in Job,* E: *Moralia*, a work by Gregory the Great《约伯伦理记》, 见 Greg. Mag.

**morbus,** Gr: nosos, E: disease, physical weakness, => medicina 疾病, 见 Plat. *Tim.*, Cic. *Cato de sen.*, Plin. *Nat. hist.* 26

**mores** => mos

**morphē** => forma, Metamorphosae

**Morpheus,** Gr: Morpheus, the son of Hypnos, god of dreams 摩尔夫斯, 见 Hypnos

**morphologia,** <Gr: morphe, logos, E: morphology, flective forms of words 形态学, 见 Donatus

**mors,** timor mortis, Gr: thanatos, moros, teleutē, E: death, mortality; often discussed: fear of death; => aeternitas, Hades, immortalitas, Stoa, suicidium, vita aeterna 死亡, 见 Hom. *Il.* (death, mourning, funeral), Soph. *Oed. Col.* (dignified death), Eur. *Alk.* (Thanatos, personification of death), Plat. *Apol.*, *Phaid.* (after–life), Cic. *Cato de sen.*, *Tusc.*, Lucr. *De rer. nat.* (fear of death), Hor. *Carm.* 1,24 (perpetuus sopor), 4,7 (pulvis et umbra), Ov. *Met.* 3 (Narcissus), 6 (Niobe), Sen. *Epist. mor.* 61, 70, Epict. *Enchir.*, Suet. *De vita Caes.* (last words of emperors), Bibl. *Ioann.* 19 (death of Jesus), *Peri hypsous* 28 (death = "way of destiny"), Marc. Aurel., Lactantius, *Carmen de ave phoenice* (mors genitalis), Athanas. *Vita Antonii* (foretelling one's death), Greg. Nys. *Peri psyches*, Prud. Peristeph. (martyrs pray when facing death), Aug. *De civ. Dei* 13, Boethius, *De consol.* (unjust execution), Johannes Climac. *Scala* (meditation of death)

**mos,** mores, Gr: ēthos, dikē, E: custom, moral values; => virtus, ethos 习俗、道德, 见 Hor. *Carm.* 3,24 (leges sine moribus vanae), Sen. *Epist. mor.* 5 (bonos mores), 6 (plus ex moribus quam ex verbis), Iuv. *Sat.* (moral decay), Tatian., Tertull., August., (superiority of Christian morality), Greg. Magn., *Regula pastoralis* (preaching as moral education)

**Moses, Moyses,** Gr: Mōyses, E: Moses, Jewish patriarch, ca. 1250—1200 BC, associated with the Exodus from Egypt and with the Jewish law 摩西, 见 Biblia, *Gen.*, Philo, *De opificio*, Ambros. *De off. ministr.*

**motus,** Gr: kinēsis, E: movement 运动, 见 Arist. *Met.*

**Mousai** = Musae

**movere,** motus, Gr: kinein, E: to move (the audience) 推动, 见 Cic. *Brutus*, Hor. *De arte poet.* 102 (si vis me flere, dolendum est tibi), Greg. Magn. *Reg. pastor.* (element of a good homily)

**mundus,** universum, Gr: kosmos, to pan, ta hola, physis, E: world, the cosmos, universe; => cosmos, saeculum 世界, 见 Plat. *Tim.*, Arist. *Phys.*, Cic. *De nat. deor.* 2,21 (the universe as divine and rational), Philo, *De opificio* (only one world exists), Plot. *Enn.* (mundus intelligibilis), Aug. *Cf.* 11~13 (creation of the world), *De vera rel.* (non diligamus mundum), Proclus, *Plat. theol.* (kosmos noetos), Philoponus, *De creatione mundi*, Isidor. *Etym.*

**munus,** E: service, contribution 服务、贡献, 见 Tert. *De spect.* (service to the deceased)

**mus,** Gr: mys, E: mouse 老鼠, 见 Hor. *Sat.* 2,6 (town mouse and country mouse)

**Musae,** Gr: Mousai, (<monsa < mens = "thinking", "inventing"), E: Muses, daughters of Zeus and Mnemosyne, originally nymphs, then the nine (or ten) patron goddesses of the arts of poetry, music etc., see Calliope, Clio, Erato, Euterpe, Polyhymnia, Thalia, Melpomene, Terpsichore, Urania 文艺女神, 见 Hom. *Il.* 1; *Od.* 1; Hes. *Erga*, *Theogon.*, Hor. *Carm.*3,4, (Vester, Camenae), 4,3 (Melpomene), *Carm. saec.*; Boethius, *De consol.* (Philosophy expels the Muses)

**musaeum,** Gr: mouseion, E: "museum", sanctuary dedicated to the Muses, later a place of the cultivation of the arts and sciences; the most famous musaeum was founded in the 3rd ct. BC in Alexandria which had a big library and housed ca. 100 scholars; the director of the instituted was also tutor to the prince; it was destroyed in the 3rd ct. AD.文艺神庙, 见 Alexandria

**musica,** Gr: mousikē, E: music 音乐, 见 Arist. *Poiet.*, (one element of a dramatic performance), Verg. *Georg.* 4 (Orpheus), *Peri hypsous* 39 (words can have an effect like music), Cass. *De inst.* (singing of psalms), Capella, *De nuptiis* (one of the seven arts), Boethius, *De cons.* 2 (music makes rhythmic)

**Mycale,** Gr: Mykalē, a town in Asia Minor, scene of a Greek victory in 479 BC 弥卡勒, 见 Hdt. *Hist.* 9

**Mycenae,** Gr: Mykēnē, Mykenai (<mykes = corner?), E: Mycenae, a city on the Peloponnes in the plain of Argos, according to myth founded by Perseus, it was the residence of Pelops, Atreus, and Agamemnon. In 1876 H. Schliemann discovered royal tombs dating from the 16th ct. BC; the golden era of the culture of Mycenae was from 1500—1350 BC; Mycenae conquered Crete in 1400 BC and was itself destroyed by the Dorians in 1200 BC. 迈锡尼, 见 Agamemnon

**Myrmidones,** Gr: Myrmidones, E: Myrmidons, the people under Achilles' command 米尔弥多内斯, 见 Achilleus

*Mystagōgia,* E: *Mystagogy*, a work by Maximus Confessor《引入神秘》, 见 Maxim.

**mysterium,** Gr: mystērion, E: mystery, secret; Greece had some mystery cults since 600 BC; the participants were obliged to keep silence about the worship ceremonies; important cults were those of Demeter in Eleusis, of Dionysus and of Orpheus; other secret cults came from the East and were very popular in Rome, for example the cults of Mithras, Isis, Cybele etc. 奥迹, 见 Clem. Alex. *Strom.* (deeper wisdom of Christianity)

*Mythōn synagōgē,* L: *Fabulae Aesopiae*, work of Aesop, a later Latin edition was made by Phaedrus《寓言集》, 见 Aes. *Mython*

**mythus,** Gr: mythos (= "word, speech, narrative"), E: myth, => argumentum, sermo, fabula 神话, 见 Ov. *Met.*, Tatian. *Logos* (critical of Greek mythology)

**Mytilene,** Gr: Mytilēnē, a city on the island of Lesbos; birthplace of Pittacus, Alcaeus, and Sappho; => Lesbos 米特累内, 见 Longus

# N

**Naevius,** Gnaeus Naevius, ca. 260—201 BC, creator of Roman drama (fabula praetexta, fabula togata); he wrote the epic *Bellum Punicum*. 内维乌斯, 见 Punicum Bellum

**Narcissus,** Gr: Narkissos, "paralyzed", "without feeling", E: Narcissus, a young man loved by Echo, changed into a flower 那尔克索斯, 见 Ov. *Met.* 3, Claud. *De raptu Proserp.*

**natura,** ingenium, indoles, Gr: physis, ousia, E: nature, talent, genius 天赋、自然本性, 见 Cic. *Brutus*, *De fin.* 3,20 (status naturae), Cic. *De off.* 1,107; 3,21 (to harm others is contra naturam); 3,23 (natura = ius gentium); Verg. *Georg.* 1, 2, Hor. *De arte poet.* 408, (natura = ingenium), Ov. *Met.* 8 (Daedalus "novat naturam" by making wings), Sen. *De vita beata* 8,2 (secundum naturam vivere est beate vivere), Plin. *Nat. hist.* 37 ("mother Nature", salve parens natura), Iuv. *Sat.* 9 (homosexuality, an unnatural vice), *Peri hypsous* 8 (ideas and pathos are a gift of nature), Tert. *De test. anim.* (maiestas naturae), Basil. *Hexaem.* (law of nature), Leo, *Tomus* (two natures of Christ)

*Naturalis historia,* E: *Natural history*, an encyclopedia by the Elder Pliny《博物志》, 见 Plin.

**Nausicaa,** Gr: Nausikaa, "arriving ship", daughter of King Alkinous who led Odysseus into her father's palace 瑙西卡, 见 Hom. *Od.* 6

**navis,** Gr: naus, E: ship, navy, sailing 船只, 见 Bibl. *Gen* 6~9 (Noah's ship), Hom. *Il.* 2 ("catalogue of ships"), *Od.*, Aesch. *Pers.* (the ponton bridge across the Hellespont arouses Poseidon's anger), Hdt. 7, Theophr. *Eth.*, 25, Apoll. *Arg.*, Verg. *Aen.* 1, 3, 5 (ship race), Hor. *Carm.* 1,14 (metaphor of the nation), Ov. *Met.* 8 (Theseus sailing home), Lucian. *Alethe diheg.* (sailing to sun and moon), Aug. *De beata vita* (thinking is like sailing), *De civ. Dei* 16 (Noah's ark, a symbol of the Church), Isidor. *Etym.* 19

**Neapolis, Parthenope,** Gr: Neapolis, "new city", E: Naples, city in south Italy, founded ca. 600 BC by Cumae; important trade port and center of Greek-Roman cultural exchange; the place where Virgil wrote his *Georgica* 那不勒斯, 见 Verg.

**necessitas,** Gr: anankē, E: necessity; => fatum, providentia, libertas 必然性, 见 Plat. *Tim.*, Cic. *De nat. deor.* 1,50 (fatalis necessitas)

**nekyia,** (Odysseus') journey to the nether world 下阴间之旅, 见 Hom. *Od.* 11

**Nemea,** valley in the west of Corinthus; once in two years the Nemean Games took place here in honor of Zeus; Heracles killed the mythical lion of this area. 内梅亚, 见 athla, ludi

**nemesis,** Gr: nemesis, "due measure", "divine enactment", "anger for wrongdoing"; E: nemesis, personified as Nemesis, goddess of revenge 正义感, 见 Hes. *Erga*, 200; *Theog.*

**Neoplatonismus** => Macrobius, Plotinus, Augustinus, Proclus, Dionys. Areop.

**Neoptolemus,** Gr: Neoptolemos, "new war", (also called Pyrrhus, "red-haired"), E: Neoptolemus, son of Achilles and Deidamia, he went with Odysseus to bring Philoctetes to the siege of Troy; Neoptolemus killed Priam and his daughter Polyxena at Achilles' tomb. 内俄普托勒摩斯, 见 Achilleus

**neoterici**, (=novi poetae), Gr: neōterikoi "moderns", E: neoterics, a school of poets in Rome who avoided epic and drama and imitated the Hellenist style of the Alexandrians (Callimachus); they wrote a more individualistic and romantic kind of poetry in a mannered style (elegy, love song); only the poems of Catullus survive, other poets were C. Gallus, C. H. Cinna, Calvus. They influenced Virgil, Tibullus, Propertius, and Ovid. 青年派诗人, 见 Catullus

*Nephelae*, Gr: *Nephelai*, E: *Clouds*, comedy by Aristophanes 《云》, 见 Ar.

**Nephele**, Gr: Nephelē, a cloud goddess, mother of Phrixus and Helle 云雾女神, 见 Apoll. *Arg*.

**Nephelococcygia**, Gr: Nephelokokkygia, "cloud-cockoo-city", E: Land of Cockaigne 云中鹁鸪国, 见 Ar. *Ornithes*

**Nepos**, Cornelius Nepos, 100—25 BC, Roman historian, friend of Cicero, Atticus, and Catullus, author of a world history (*Chronica*) and a collection of biographies (*De viris illustribus*, 16 books) 内波斯, 见 historia

**Neptunus**, Gr: Poseidōn, E: Neptune, god of the sea, since 400 BC identified with Poseidon; he was worshiped at fountains, rivers, bridges and coasts. 尼普顿, 见 Liv. 26~30, Tert. *De spect*. (Isthmian games dedicated to him)

**nequitia**, E: nothingness, lack 匮乏, 见 Aug. *De beata vita* (animi egestas = the mother of vices)

**Nereus**, Gr: Nēreus, "wet one", sea-god, son of Pontus and Gaia, father of Thetis and the other Nereids; under pressure he told Heracles the place of the apples of the Hesperides. The Nereids (among them Amphitrite and Galatea) were thought to be benevolent and were thus worshiped by seamen; they were depicted as riding on dolphins. 内柔斯, 见 Hom. *Il*. 1

**Nero**, Claudius Drusus Germanicus Caesar Nero, 37—68 AD, Roman emperor 54—68, son of Cn. Domitius Ahenobarbus and Agrippina, adopted by emperor Claudius as son and heir, notorious for his extravagance, cruelty, and for the persecution of Christians 尼禄, 见 Seneca, Luc. *Phars*., Tac. *Ann*., Suet. *De vita Caes*., Tert. *Apol*., Lact. *De mortibus*, Euseb., Boethius, *De cons*.

**Nestor**, Gr: Nestōr, (= neostoreus? "newly speaking"), mythical king of Pylos, Greek leader at Troy, respected for his old age, experience and wisdom; he participated in the struggle of the Lapiths against the Centaurs, in the journey of the Argo, and in the siege of Troy. 内斯托尔, 见 Hom. *Il*. 2, 11; *Od*. 3

**Nestorius**, Gr: Nestorios, E: Nestorius, ca. 381—452 AD, patriarch of Constantinople 聂斯托里乌斯, 见 Liber Heraclidis

**Nicaea**, Gr: Nikaia, E: Nicaea, town in Asia Minor, place of an important ecumenical council in 325 AD; => concilium, homoousios 尼西亚, 见 Cyrillus

**Nicias**, Gr: Nikias, E: Nicias, Athenian politician and general, who managed to bring about the Peace of 421 BC, which suspended the Peloponnesian War for some time, in 413 BC he led the Athenians in the disastrous campaign against Syracuse. 尼克亚斯, 见 Thuc. 4, Plut. *Bioi*

**Nicodemus**, Gr: Nikodēmos, "stronger than the people", E: Nicodemus, a dialogue partner of Jesus 尼苛德摩, 见 Bibl. *Ioann*. 3,

**Nikē** => victoria

**Nilus**, Gr: Nilos, E: Nile, main river of Egypt 尼罗河, 见 Hdt. *Hist*. 2

**Nioba**, Niobe, "snowy", Gr: Niobē, daughter of Tantalus, wife of Amphion, king of Thebes, the proud mother of many children who insulted Leto and was thus punished by Apollo and Artemis with the sudden death of all her children. 尼俄贝, 见 Ov. *Met*. 6

**Nisus**, Gr: Nisos, "brightness", a Trojan hero, friend of Euryalus 尼苏斯, 见 Verg. *Aen*. 9,

*Noctes Atticae*, E: *Attic Nights*, an anthology by Gellius 《雅典之夜》, 见 Gellius

**nomen**, Gr: onoma, E: name; => verbum 名字, 见 Hom. *Od*. 9 (Odysseus' name is "nobody"), Ios. Flav. (changes his name), Bibl. *Gen*. 11 (longing for a great name), Greg. Naz. *Logoi* (names of God: ho ōn, hē ousia)

**nomos** => mos, principium, regula, lex, jus

**nomos agraphos**, the unwritten law (of the gods), => lex naturae 不成文的法律, 见 Soph. *Ant*., Arist. *Rhet*., Philo, *De opificio*

**Nonius Marcellus**, ca. 300—350 AD, author of an encylopedic work 诺尼乌斯, 见 *De compendiosa* *doctrina*

**Noricum,** area of the Alps south of the Danube River, Romanized since the 1st ct. AD; Roman rule collapsed around 480 诺瑞孔，见 Eugippius, *Vita Sancti Severini*

**notio,** Gr: ennoia, noēma, gnōmē, E: insight, idea 认识，见 Cic. *De fin.* 3,22, *De nat. deor.* 1,44（informatio）

**notiones verae,** Gr: doxai alētheis, E: right notions 本有的正确观念，见 Plat. *Menon,*

**nous, nus** => 1) sensus, prudentia, intellectus, ratio; 2) cor, animus, mens, spiritus; 3) cogitatio, opinio, voluntas

**Novatianus,** E: Novatian, ca. 200—258 AD, schismatic bishop in Rome in 251 AD, advocate of rigorism 诺瓦提安，见 Cyprian. *Epistulae*, Hieron. *De viris*

**novella,** Gr: mythos, E: novel, short story, => fabula 小说，见 Apuleius, Longos, Heliodoros

**novum praeceptum,** Gr: entolē kainē, E: new commandment 新诫命，见 Bibl. *Ioann.*

**Novum Testamentum,** Gr: Kainē diathēkē, E: New Testament, the "new covenant"《新约》，见 Biblia, Chrysostom. *Hom.*

**Nox** = Nyx

**nudus,** nuditas, Gr: gymnos, E: nakedness 赤裸，见 Bibl. *Gen* 3

**Numa Pompilius,** the legendary second king of Rome (715—673 BC), who introduced many religious institutions, festivals, sacrifices, priests (pontifices, Vestal Virgins etc.) 努马，见 Cic. *De nat. deor.* 3,5, Hor. *Carm.* 1,12, Liv. 1, Plut. *Bioi*, Tert. *De spect.*

**numen,** Gr:to daimonion, E: divine power, god; 神力
**numerus,** Gr: arithmos, E: number, symbolic value of 数字、数字神秘主义，见 Plat. *Tim.*, Philo, *De opificio*

**Numidia,** coastal area in Africa, roughly equal to modern Algeria; Masinissa founded the kingdom of Numidia in 200 BC, Hippo was the capital; king Jughurta fought against the Romans (111—105 BC); the area became a Roman province in 46 BC and fell to the Vandals in 439 AD 努米底亚，见 Masinissa

**nuptiae,** Gr: hymenaios, E: wedding, marriage; => matrimonium 结婚，见 Tert. *Heaut.*, Longus, Hieron. *Epist.* 107（sponsa Christi）, Capella

**nymphae,** Gr: nymphai, E: nymphs, goddesses of trees, rivers, fountains etc., they were thought to be the daughters of Zeus or of river gods; they were mortal and basically benevolent towards humans; popular worship of the nymphs included sacrifices of flowers, fruits, oil, milk, goats at fountains, in groves and in caves. 女神，仙女们，见 Longus

**Nyx,** L: Nox, E: Night, goddess of night 黑夜女神，见 Hes. *Theog.*

# O

**oboedire,** Gr: peithomai, E: obey 服从，见 Verg. *Aen.* 4, Bened. *Regula*, Columban, *Regula coenob.*,

**occasio** => tempus

**Oceanus,** Gr: Ōkeanos, "of the swift queen", E: Oceanus, Ocean, the biggest river god, son of Uranus and Gaia, husband of his sister Tethys, father of the 3000 sea nymphs and the river gods; he was imagined to be a river encircling the whole plain of the earth 欧克阿诺斯，见 Hom. *Od.* 11; Hes. *Erga*, 171, *Theog.*,

**Octavianus** => Augustus

*Octavius*, E: *Octavius*, work by Minucius《奥大维乌斯》，见 Minucius

**oculus,** Gr: omma, ophthalmos, E: eye, human eye 眼睛，见 Plat. *Tim.*（ommata phosphora）, Cic. *De nat. deor.* 2,133~150, Tert. *De spec.*

*Odi* => *Carmina*

**odium,** Gr: odyssomai, misēma, misos, E: hatred, hate; => amor, clementia 憎恨，见 Cic. *De off.* 1,88（politicians should not hate bitterly）, Suet. *De vita Caes.*（Caligula: oderint）, Bibl. *Ioann.* 15（hatred of the world）

**Odoacer,** (=Odovacer), the first barbarian king of Italy, 476—493 AD 欧多阿克，见 Eugipp. *Vita S. Severini*

*Odysseia*, E: *Odyssey*, epic by Homer《奥德赛》，见 Homeros; Verg. *Aen.*, *Buc.*

**Odysseus,** L: Ulixes, Ulysses, Gr: Odysseus, "hated", "angry", (=> odium), E: Ulysses, King of Ithaca and hero at Troy, famous for his resourcefulness in dangerous situations 奥德修斯，见 Hom. *Il.*, 2, 9, 10, 11, 14; *Od.* 1~24; Cic. *De off.* 3,97~98（symbol of prudence, not of honor）; Stat. *Achill.*, Lucian, *Alethe diheg.*

**oeconomia,** Gr: oikonomia, < oikos, nomos, "house-rule", E: economy, in Xenophon's work it is the administration of goods and management of a farm "管理家庭"，见 Xen. *Oik.*

***Oeconomicus,*** Gr: *Oikonomikos*, "housekeeping rules", E: *Oeconomicus*, a work by Xenophon《管理家庭》, 见 Xen.

**oecumenia,** Gr: oekeomenē, E: the inhabited world, the world as know to antiquity 普世, 见 Hdt. *Hist.* 3

**Oedipus,** Gr: Oidipous, "swollen foot", E: Oedipus, son of Laios and Jocasta, king of Thebes 俄狄浦斯, 见 Soph. *Ant., Oid. tyr., Oid. epi Kolono*

***Oedipus Coloneus,*** Gr: *Oidipous epi Kolōnō*, E: *Oedipus at Colonus*, tragedy by Sophocles《俄狄浦斯在科罗诺斯》, 见 Soph.

***Oedipus Tyrannus,*** Gr: *Oidipous Tyrannos*, E: *Oedipus the King*, tragedy by Sophocles《俄狄浦斯王》, 见 Soph.

**Oenone,** Gr: Oinōnē, "queen of wine", a nymph of mount Ida (near Troy) who loved Paris and persuaded him not to sail to Greece 俄诺内, 见 Ov. *Her.*

**officium,** Gr: kathēkon, katorthōma, archē, exousia, E: duty, responsibility, dutiful action, office 任务, 见 Cic. *De fin.* 3,20, Cic. *De off.* 3,14 (officium perfectum, officia media); Epict. *Diatr.* (kathekonta), Ambros. *De off. ministrorum*

**Ogygia,** island of Calypso 欧格基亚, 见 Hom. *Od.* 5, 12

**Oidipous** = Oedipus

**oikonomia** = oeconomia

**oikos** = familia

**Okeanos** = Oceanus

**oligarchia,** Gr: oligarchiē, "rule of a few", E: oligarchy 寡头政治, 见 Hdt. *Hist.* 3, Plat. *Polit.* 7,8, Arist. *Polit., Rhet.*, Theophr. *Eth.* 26, (oligarchos)

**Olympia,** Gr: Olympia, "all bright", town near the west coast of the Peloponnesus (Elis) with the main sanctuary of Zeus, where the famous Olympian / Olympic games were held every four years in honor of Zeus (first recorded in 776 BC and used in chronology); the temple of Hera (Heraion) was built in the 7th ct. BC. 奥林匹亚城, 见 Polybios, *Hist.* 7, Pausanias

**Olympias,** Gr: Olympias, wife of Philippus II, king of Macedonia, mother of Alexander the Great 欧林皮亚斯, 见 Alexander

**Olympus,** Gr: Olympos, mount in northern Greece, home of the Olympian gods 奥林波斯, 见 Hom. *Il.* 5, 21 etc. *Od.*; Verg. *Aen.* 10, Lucian, *Theon dial.*, Capella, *De nuptiis*

**opera,** Gr: erga, E: works, good works (demanded from Christians) 善功, 见 Prud. *Psych.* (Operatio strangles Avaritia)

**opes,** Gr: ploutos, chrēmata, euporia, E: wealth, riches 财富, 见 Arist. *Polit., Rhet.*, Cic. *De off.* 2,86; Sen. *De vita beata* 16~28 (a defense of riches), *Epist. mor.* 5 (pati posse divitias), Iuv. *Sat.* 6 (wealth is the root of moral decay), Bibl. *Job* (the rich man who loses his wealth), Clem. Alex. *Paedag.* (wealth does not exclude from salvation), Boethius, *De cons.* 2 (riches are futile), Bened. *Regula* (no private property), Joh. Climac. *Scala* (give possessions away)

**ophthalmos** = oculus

**opinio,** aestimatio, Gr: doxa, E: opinion 想法、猜测, 见 Plat. *Polit.* 5

**Opora,** Gr: Opōra, E: Opora, goddess of harvest 丰收女神, 见 Ar. *Eirene*

**Ops,** Gr: Opōra, E: Wealth, Riches, Roman goddess of wealth; => opes 财富女神, 见 Cic. *De nat. deor.* 2,60

**optimates,** "the best", a political party in Rome since ca. 130 BC; in response to the party of the "populares"(Gracchi) they defended the interests of the aristocracy ("nobiles") 贵族派, 见 Cicero, Caesar, Gracchi

**oraculum,** Gr: manteion, chrēstērion, omphē, phēmē, E: oracle, prediction or command of a god; famous places for asking a god to give a hint were the oracles of Zeus at Dodona and of Apollo in Delphi; => Calchas, Cassandra, Teiresias 神谕, 见 Soph. *Oid. Tyr.*, Cic. *De nat. deor.* 2,163, *De div.*, Verg. *Aen.* 3, 7, Arrian. *Alex. anab.* 7

**oratio** => logos, rhetorica, preces

***Oratio contra gentes,*** Gr: *Logos kata tōn Hellēnōn*, E: *Speech against the Gentiles*, an apologetic treatise by Athanasius《反驳外邦人》, 见 Athanas.

***Orationes,*** Gr: Logoi, E: Sermons, a collection of sermons by Gregory of Nazianz《讲道文集》, 见 Greg. Naz.

**orator,** Gr: rhētōr, E: orator; the ten canonical orators of ancient Greece were Antiphon (480—411 BC), Andocides, Lysias (ca. 445—380 BC, famous for forensic oratory = speeches at court), Isocrates (436—338 BC, the greatest epideictic orator = panegyric speeches of "display"), Isaeus, Demosthenes (384—322 BC, the outstanding political orator), Aeschines (390—315 BC), Lycurgus, Hypereides, and Deinarchus 讲演家,

见 Arist. *Techne rhetorike*, Cicero, *Brutus*, Quintilian

**oratoria** => rhetorica

**orchestra,** Gr: orchēstra, "dancing place", E: orchestra, the "dancing-floor", a circular area between the stage and the auditorium in a Greek theater; the choir (chorus) stood or danced on the orchestra 歌舞场, 见 theatrum

**ordo,** concordia rerum, Gr: taxis, eutaxia, eunomia, kosmos, harmonia, E: order, harmony (of the universe) 秩序, 见 Cic. *De fin.* 3,22, *De rer. nat.* 2,13 (origin of the idea of god), 2,73~153 (ordo naturae), Vitr. *De arch.* 3~4, (three orders of architecture), Hor. *De arte poet.* 41 (lucidus ordo, clear structure), Bibl. *Gen.* 1 (order of creation), *Peri hypsous* 39 (harmonia, synthesis logōn)

***Oresteia,*** E: *Oresty*, the only extant Greek trilogy by Aeschylus, see *Agamemnon*, *Choephoroe*, *Eumenides*《俄瑞斯特斯》, 见 Aesch. *Oresteia*

**Orestes,** Gr: Orestēs, "mountaineer", E: Orestes, son of Agamemnon and Clytemnestra, brother of Electra and Iphigeneia, who avenged his father's murder; he married Hermione, the daughter of Menelaus, and ruled Mycene, Argos, and Sparta. 俄瑞斯特斯, 见 Hom. *Od.* 3, Aesch. *Oresteia*, Soph. *Elektra*, Eur. *Iph. Aul.*, Ov. *Her.*

**Origenes,** Gr: Ōrigenēs, "mountain-born", E: Origen, ca. 185—254 AD, outstanding Greek scholar, exegete and theologian in Alexandria, later condemned for some special doctrines, => apokatastasis panton 奥利金, 见 *Hexapla, Kata Kelsou, Peri archon*, Euseb. 6, Aug. *De civ. Dei* 21 (denial of eternal punishment)

**Orion,** Gr: Ōriōn, a giant hunter of Boeotia in Greek myth; changed into a star by Zeus 俄里翁, 见 stella

***Ornithes,*** Gr: *Ornithes*, E: *Birds*, a comedy by Aristophanes《鸟》, 见 Ar. *Ornith.*

**Orosius,** E: Orosius, ca. 390—440 AD, Christian historian 奥罗修斯, 见 *Historiae adversus paganos*

**Orpheus,** Gr: Orpheus, mythical hero and musician, husband of Eurydice who tried to regain her from the realm of Hades but lost her again because he turned his head and looked back at her. 俄耳菲斯, 见 Apoll. *Arg.*, Verg. *Georg.* 4, Hor. *Ars poet.*, Clem. Alex. *Protrepticus* (Christ a new Orpheus), Boethius, *De cons.* 3 (the mind must not turn back)

**Osiris,** Egyptian god, incarnated in the sacred bull Apis, cut in pieces by his brother Set, but avenged by his sister and wife Isis 奥西里斯, 见 Plut. *Mor.* (*Peri Isidos kai Osiridos*), Apuleius, *Met.*

**Ostia,** the harbor city of Rome at the mouth of the Tiber river 欧斯提亚, 见 Liv. 1 (built by Ancus Marcius), Minucius, *Oct.*, Aug. *Confess.* 9 (Monica dies here)

**ostracismus,** Gr: ostrakismos, E: ostracism, an institution in Athens established by Cleisthenes in 507 BC in order to protect the constitution of the state; an unpopular but prominent person could be banished by the vote of at least 6000 citizens who wrote the name of a dangerous person on a potsherd (ostrakon); the ostracism was abolished in 417 BC; prominent men who were ostracized included Aristeides, Themistocles, Cimon. 陶片放逐, 见 Themistocles

**Otho,** Marcus Salvius Otho, Roman emperor for a short time after Nero's death, he committed suicide in 69 AD 欧托, 见 Plut. *Bioi*, Suet. *De vita Caes.*

**otium,** Gr: scholē, E: leisure, otiosity, idleness 休闲, 见 Cic. *De nat. deor.* 3,79~90 (gods are otiose beings), *De off.* 3,1 (otium et solitudo); Bened. *Regula* 48 (idleness is harmful), Joh. Climac. *Scala* (avoidance of idleness)

**Ouranos** = Uranus

**ousia** = esse

**Outis,** L: nemo, E: nobody, "name" of Odysseus 乌提斯, 见 Hom. *Od.* 9

**Ovidius,** Roman poet, 43 BC—18 AD, famous for his poetry focussing on love and on mythology; he was married three times and suddenly banned from Rome in 8 AD, died in exile in Pontus at the Black Sea. 奥维德, 见 Ov. *Ars amat., Fasti, Heroides, Met.* Quint. *Inst.* 10

# P

**pactum,** contractus, E: contract, promise => promissum

**paedagogia** => educatio

***Paedagogus,*** Gr: *Paidagōgos*, E: *The Instructor*, a work by Clement《教导者》, 见 Clemens Alexandrinus

**paena** = poena

**pagani,** gentes, Gr: ethnē, E: pagans, heathens, non-Christians 非基督徒，见 Clem. Alex. *Protrept.*, Lact. *Inst.* 2

**paideia** => educatio

**pais, paidion** => puer

**palaestra,** Gr: palaistra, "wrestling place", the place where Greek boys were instructed in wrestling and gymnastics 摔跤学校，见 Palaestrio

**Palaestrio,** (=> Gr: Palaistra, "wrestling place"), name of a slave 帕勒斯特瑞欧，见 Plaut. *Miles*

**Palatinus mons,** Palatium, Palantine hill, one of the seven hills of Rome, traditionally the site of the earliest settlements; since the time of Augustus the Roman emperors had their residence here (origin of the word "palace"); => Evander 帕拉提努斯，见 Verg. *Aen.* (Evander)

**Palinurus,** Aeneas' helmsman who fell overboard, was washed up on the shore of Italy and there murdered but remained unburied and so could not cross the river Styx; Aeneas met his ghost and later erected a tomb for him. 帕里努如斯，见 Verg. *Aen.* 5,6

**Pallas,** "maiden", "youth", 1) title of Athena; 2) name of Greek Titans and heroes, esp. the founder of the city Pallanteion and grandfather of Evander; 3) the son of Evander 帕拉斯，见 Verg. *Aen.* 10, Hor. *Carm.* 1,12

**palma,** Gr: phoinix, E: palm tree 棕榈树，见 Lactantius, *Carmen de ave phoenice*

**Pan,** Gr: Pan, "all", "pasture", Greek god of shepherds and flocks, depicted with goat's legs, ears and horns; he was born in Arcadia as the son of Hermes, identified with Faunus by the Romans; the story (by Plutarch) about a voice shouting "Pan is dead" was understood as the death of all the pagan (non-Christian) gods. => Arcadia 潘，见 Verg. *Buc.* 10, Lucian. *Theon dial.*, Longus

**Panaetius,** Gr: Panaitios, "(searching for) the causes of all things", E: Panaetius, Panaitius, ca. 185—109 BC, Greek Stoic philosopher 潘艾提乌斯，见 Cic. *De fin.* 4,80, *De off.* 1,9; 3,12

**Panathenaea,** Gr: Panathēnaia, E: Panathenaea, the main festival of Athens, held once in 4 years in summer, its climax was a solemn procession in which a newly woven piece of cloth (peplos) for Athena was brought to the Erectheion; musical and gymnastic competitions accompanied the festival which lasted for several days. 泛雅典娜节，见 Athena

**Pandarus,** Gr: Pandaros, "he who flays all", leader in the Trojan War who wounds Menelaus 潘达若斯，见 Hom. *Il.* 4, 5

**Pandora,** Gr: Pandōra, "all gifts", "all-giving", the woman created by the gods and sent to Epimetheus, equipped with attractivity but also carrying with her all evils as a punishment for Prometheus' theft of fire. 潘多拉，见 Hes. *Erga*

**panis,** Gr: artos, E: bread 面包，见 Iuv. *Sat.* 10, 80 (panem et circenses); Bibl. *Ioann.* 6 (bread of life)

**Pantheon,** Gr: pantheon, "all gods", E: Pantheon, a temple consecrated to all gods, the largest dome structure of antiquity and the best preserved building of Roman antiquity; in 609 AD it was changed into a Christian church. 万神殿，见 religio

**papyrus,** Gr: papyros, E: papyrus, ("paper"), the writing material of antiquity, produced in Egypt since c. 3000 BC; since this type of paper could not be folded it was preserved in scrolls; => Byblos, Pergamum 纸草纸，见 Biblia

**parabole,** Gr: parabolē, E: parable, symbolic narratives; => figura 比喻，见 Arist. *Rhet.*, *Peri hypsous* 37

**Paraclitus,** Gr: paraklētos, "helper", E: paraclete, the Holy Spirit 协助者，见 Bibl. *Ioann.* 14

**paradisus,** Gr: paradeisos, "garden", E: paradise, the garden of Eden 伊甸乐园，见 Bibl. *Gen*

**Parcae,** Fata, Gr: Moirai, E: Fates, goddesses of fate, namely: Clotho ("spinner"), Lachesis ("apportioner"), Atropos ("inevitable") 命运女神，见 Hes. *Theog*, Hor. *Carm. saec.*

**Paris,** Gr: Paris, "adventurer" (<peira), sometimes called Alexandros (Alexander); son of Priam and Hecuba, who was exposed as child and raised by shepherds on Mount Ida, where Oenone loved him; through his victory at a competition in Troy he was recognized as Priam's son; in Sparta Menelaus' wife Helena fell in love with him, they fled together and so brought about the Trojan War. 帕里斯，见 Hom. *Il.* 3, 6, 7, Ov. *Her.*, Stat. *Achill.*, Lucian. *Theon dial.*, Aug. *De civ. Dei* 3 (his adultery remainded unpunished)

**Parmenides,** Gr: Parmenidēs, E: Parmenides, Greek philosopher from Elea, ca. 515—450 BC 巴门尼德，见 Clem. Alex. *Strom.* (quotations from P.), Diog. Laert.

**Parnassus,** Gr: Parnassos, a mountain north of Delphi, associated with the worship of Apollo and of the Muses 巴尔纳索斯，见 Musae

**parodos,** Gr: "way in", the entrance song of the chorus at a Greek drama 进场歌，见 Aesch. *Persai*

**parthenia** = virginitas

**Parthenon,** Gr: Parthenōn, "temple of the maiden", the temple of Athena Parthenos in Athens, rebuilt ca. 447—438 BC; => Acropolis 雅典娜神殿，见 Vitr. *De arch.* 3~4,

**parthenos** = virgo

**Parthenos Dike,** virgin Dike = Dike

**Parthenope,** "maiden face", a name for Neapolis

**Pasiphae,** Gr: Pasiphaē, "she who shines for all", daughter of the sun god, wife of Minos, mother of Ariadne and of the Minotaurus 帕西费，见 Ov. *Met.* 8

**passio,** Gr: pathē, pathēma, pathos, E: passion, suffering, esp. the violent death of a Christian martyr 受难，遇难，见 *Passio Perpetuae*

***Passio Perpetuae et Felicitatis,*** E: *The Passion of Perpetua and Felicitas,* the earliest Latin text written by a woman《培培图阿与菲里契塔斯遇难录》，见 Perpetua

**pastor,** Gr: poimēn, E: shepherd, symbol of pastoral life and bucolic idylls; in the Christian era symbol of Christ and of priests; => *Eidyllia* 牧人，见 Hom. *Od.*14（Eumaios），Verg. *Buc.*，Bibl. *Ioann.* 10（Jesus, the good shepherd），Perpetua, *Passio*, Longus（life of shepherds），Greg. Magn. *Regula pastoralis*

**pater,** Gr: patēr, E: father 父亲，见 Hom. *Il.*（Priamus, father of Hector），*Od.*（Odysseus, father of Telemachus），Hes. *Theog.*（Ouranos–Cronus–Zeus），Hdt.（pater historiae），Verg. *Aen.*（Anchises–Aeneas–Ascanius），Bibl. *Ioann.* 5（Jesus calls God His father），Marc. Aurel.（thanking his father），Greg. Naz. *Carmina*（difficult relationship to his father），Bened. *Regula*（the abbot should be like a father）

**pathē, pathos** => affectus, passio, perturbatio

**pathos,** E: pathos, a pathetic style 激情，见 *Peri hypsous* 3（pathos kenon = empty pathos），8（enthousiastikon pathos）

**patientia,** Gr: makrothymia, E: patience, long-suffering 忍耐，见 Prud. *Psych.*（allegory）

**patres ecclesiae,** E: Fathers of the Church, Christian authors of the early Church whose writings are considered as orthodox or very important in the development of theology 教父，见 Ambrosius, Athanasius, Augustinus, Basilius, Clemens Alex., Gregor. Naz., Gregor. Nys., Gregor. Magnus, Ioann. Chrystostomos, Irenaeus, Isidorus, Maxim. Conf., Leo, Tertullianus

**patria,** amor patriae, Gr: patris, E: fatherland, patriotismus 祖国、爱国，见 Cic.（called "pater patriae"），Hor. *Carm.* 3,2（pro patria mori），Aug. *De civ. Dei* 1（supernatural fatherland），Columba（peregrinatio），

**patriarcha,** Gr: patriarchēs, E: patriarch, the forefathers, especially of the Jewish people, => Abraham, Isaac, Jacob 原祖、元祖，见 Bibl. *Gen* 12, Philon, *De opif.*, Aug. *De civ. Dei* 15, 16, 17（Adam, Cain, Enoch, Noah, Shem, Ham, Japhet, Abraham, Lot, Hagar, Sarah, Isaac, Esau, Jacob, Joseph, Moses, Joshuah, Samuel, Hannah, David, Solomon）

**patricii,** E: patricians, members of the privileged class at Rome; after the reign of the kings all political power and the magistracies were in their hands until the rise of the plebeian class since the end of the second century BC（罗马）贵族，见 plebeii

**Patroclus,** Gr: Patroklos, "glory of the father", close friend of Achillēs, killed by Hector 帕特若克洛斯，见 Hom. *Il.* 11, 15, 16, 18

**patrologia,** Gr: patrēs, logia, E: patrology, patristic studies, the academic efforts aiming at a better understanding of the Greek and Latin Fathers of the Church 教父学，见 patres ecclesiae

**Paulinus de Nola,** ca. 353—431 AD, Latin poet and bishop of Nola（near Naples），pupil of Ausonius 保利努斯，见 Ausonius, Hieron. *Epist.*

**Paullus,**（=Paulus），Lucius Aemilius Paullus, ca. 230—160 BC, Roman general, victor at Pydna 鲍卢斯，见 Ter. *Adelph.*, Hor. *Carm.* 1,12, Plut. *Bioi*

**Paulus,** Gr: Paulos, E: Paul, ca. 5—67 AD, important theologian and author of many letters of the New Testament 保禄/保罗，见 Biblia; Lact. *De mortibus*, Euseb.（martyred in Rome），Chrysostom. *Hom.*（explanation of the Letter to the Romans），Prud. *Peristeph.*, Aug. *Conf.* 8

**pauper,** Gr: ptōchos, E: poor, beggar 穷人，乞丐，见 Sulpicius Sev., *Vita Martini*

**Pausanias,** 1）Spartan general and politician who led Greece to victory at Plataeai in 479 BC; he was immured in a temple in 468 BC because of contacts to Persia; 2) Greek traveller and geographer, author of a "Description of Greece", ca. 112—180 AD 保萨尼阿斯，见 *Periēgēsis*

**pax,** Gr: eirēnē, hēsychia, E: peace 和平，见 Ar. *Acharn. Eirene, Lysistr.*, Cic. *De off.* 1,75, (achievements in peace are greater than those in war), Verg. *Aen.* 11 (truce), Hor. *Carm.* 4,14 (Augustus as prince of peace), *Carm. saec.* (goddess of peace), Prud. *Psych.* (allegory), Aug. *Conf., De beata vita* (inner peace), Joh. Climac. *Scala* (hesychia = inner peace)

**peccatum,** scelus, crimen, nefarium, turpitudo; Gr: anomia, hamartia, E: sin, crime, sinful behavior; => vitium 罪行，见 Hom., Hes., Aesch., Soph., Eur., Plat., Arist. *Rhet., De off.* 2,77; Hor. *Sat.* 1,3 (not all crimes are equally serious), Bibl. *Gen* 3 (fall of mankind), Tert. *De spect.*, Orig. *De princ.* (physical bodies as punishment for sin), Aug. *De civ. Dei* (Adam's sin), *De vera rel.* (de-emphasized sinfulness), Cassian. *De inst.* (eight main sins), Greg. Magnus, *Moralia* (seven cardinal sins)

**pecunia** => opes

**Pegasus,** Gr: Pēgasos, "of the fountain", a mythical winged horse, born of the head of Medusa; Bellerophon mounted the horse and thus could overcome the Chimaera; a stamp of Pegasus' hoof produced the sacred fountain Hippocrene on Mount Helicon, sacred to the Muses. 佩伽索斯，见 Ar. *Eirene*

**pēgē** = fons

**Peiraeios** = Piraeus

**Peirithoos** = Pirithous

**Peisetairus,** Gr: Peisetairos, < peitho hetairos, "persuader", Peisetairos, figure in Aristophanes' *Birds* "说服者"，佩塞泰若斯，见 Ar. *Ornithes*

**Peisistratus,** Gr: Peisistratos, "persuade the army", E: Peisistratus, ca. 600—527 BC, tyrant in Athens after 560 BC and according to tradition a benevolent ruler 佩西斯特拉托斯，见 Aes. *Myth.*

**Pelagius,** Gr: Pelagios "seaman", E: Pelagius, ca. 360—420 AD, monk at Rome since ca. 380, he emphasized the importance of human freedom and will, thus disparaging divine grace; his views were attacked by Augustine and Jerome 贝拉基，见 Cass. *De inst.* ("semi-Pelagianism")

**Peleus,** Gr: Pēleus, "muddy", husband of Thetis and father of Achilles 佩流斯，见 Hom. *Il.* 1, Apoll. *Arg.*

**Pelias,** Gr: Pelias, "black and blue", half-brother of Aeson who usurped the throne of Iolcus 佩里阿斯，见 Apoll. *Arg.*

**Pelopidas,** "muddy face", ca. 410—364 BC, Theban general who fought against Sparta 佩罗皮达斯，见 Plut. *Bioi*

**Pelops,** Gr: Pelops, "pale face", son of Tantalus, father of Atreus and Thyestes; he was killed by his father in order to test the gods but revived by them; In Elis he won Hippodamia, daughter of king Oenomaus, later he ruled Elis and the whole peninsula, giving his name to the area: Peloponnesus 佩罗普斯，见 Aesch. *Agam.*

**Peloponnesus,** Gr: Peloponnēsos, "island of Pelops", the peninsula that forms the southern part of Greece 伯罗奔尼撒半岛，见 Pausanias

**Peloponnesiorum bellum,** Gr: Peloponnēsiōn polemos, the Peloponnesian War 431—404 BC between Athens and Sparta and their allies 伯罗奔尼撒战争，见 Thuc.

**penates,** di penates, lares et penates, "penum" = pantry, "the gods of the store cupboard", Roman protector gods, especially of the house; they were brought to Italy from Troy by Aeneas 家神，见 Verg. *Aen.* 2

**Peneus,** Gr: Pēneios, "of the thread", the main river of Thessaly, passing between Mt. Olympus and Mt. Ossa, in myth the father of Daphne 佩内俄斯，见 Ov. *Met.* 1, 452

**Penelope,** Gr: Pēnelopē, "unravelling leaves", "veiled face" (?), the wife of Odysseus who waited loyally for her husband to return 佩内罗佩，见 Hom. *Od.* 1, 2, 16~23, Hor. *Her.*

**Penia,** Gr: penia, Penia, E: poverty, personification of poverty, mother of Eros 穷困，见 Plat. *Symp.*

***Pentateuchos,*** Gr: *pentateuchos* (biblos), "five vessels", E: *Pentateuch*, the Five Books (of Moses)(摩西)五书，见 Biblia

**Pentekontaetie,** Gr: pentekonta-etiē, "fifty years", E: five decades (of Athenian power), 480—431 BC 五十年繁荣期，见 Thuc. 1

**Penthesilea,** Gr: Penthesileia, daughter of Ares, queen of the Amazons, who fought for Priam but was killed by Achilles 彭特西勒亚，见 Achilleus

**perceptio,** comprehensio, Gr: katalēpsis, E: perception, insight; => intellectus 理解，见 Cic. *De fin.* 3,20

**peregrinatio,** E: pilgrimage, the traveling to holy places or (Christian) *monuments* 朝圣, 见 *Columbanus, Itinerarium Egeriae*

**Pergamum,** Gr: Pergamon, E: Pergamum, city in Mysia (Asia Minor), capital of the Kingdom of Pergamum under the Attalids (founded 283 BC); the city was famous for its splendid buildings and for its library, second only to Alexandria; in 133 BC the city became capital of the Roman province of Asia; because Alexandria prohibited the export of papyrus to Pergamum in the 3rd ct. BC, the city developed a different type of "paper" made of animal skin (charta Pergamena = parchment); parchment led to the switch from scrolls to our modern type of books ("codex") 珀尔伽蒙

*Peri archon* = *De principiis*

*Peri hypsous,* E: *On the Sublime*, work of unknown authorship《论崇高》

*Peri kataskeuēs anthrōpou,* E: *On the Equipment of Man*, treatise by Gregory of Nyssa《论人的准备》, 见 Greg. Nys.

*Peri parthenias,* E: *On Virginity*, treatise by Gregory of Nyssa; also by Chrysostom《论贞洁》, 见 Greg. Nys., Chrysostom.

*Peri psychēs kai anastaseōs,* E: *Dialog on the Soul and Resurrection*, philosophical dialog by Gregory of Nyssa《关于灵魂和复活的对话》, 见 Greg. Nys.

*Peri tēs ekklēsiastikēs hierarchias,* E: *The Ecclesiastical Hierarchy*, a work by Dionysius the Areopagite《教阶体系》, 见 Dion. Ar.

*Peri tēs ouranias hierarchias,* E: *The Celestial Hierarchy*, a work by Dionysius the Areopagite《天阶体系》, 见 Dion. Ar.

**Pericles,** Gr: Periklēs, Perikleios, "surrounding glory", E: Pericles, 495—429 BC, Athenian politician, supporter of democracy; he built the Acropolis and developed Athens into the cultural center of Greece. 伯里克利, 见 Soph., Thuc. 2, Plat. *Gorg.*, Cic. *De off.* 1,107, Plut. *Bioi*

**periculum,** Gr: peirasmos, E: danger 危险, 见 Cic. *De off.* 1,66

*Periēgēsis tēs Hellados,* E: *Description of Greece*《希腊志》, 见 Pausanias

**Peripatus,** Gr. Peripatos, "walking around", E: Peripatetic school, the Aristotelian school of philosophy in Athens 散步学派, 亚里士多德学派, 见 Arist., Cic. *De fin.* 3,41; 5,7; Aug. *De civ. Dei* 9

**periphrasis** => circumscriptio

**Periplectomenus,** Gr: Periplektomenos, "plaited all around", friend of Pleusicles in Plautus' play 佩瑞普勒克托梅努斯, 见 Plaut. *Miles*

*Peristephanon,* E: *Crowns of Martyrdom*, a collection of hymns by Prudentius《殉道士行传》, 见 Prud.

peristera = columba

**Perpetua,** "the lasting", name of a Christian martyr, 182—202 AD 培培图阿, 见 *Passio Perpetuae*

*Persae,* Gr: *Persai*, E: *Perses*, tragedy of Aeschylus《波斯人》, 见 Aes.

**persecutio,** Gr: diōgmos, (<diōkein), E: persecution (of Christians); => martyr 迫害, 逮捕, 见 Tert. *Apol.*, *De spect.*, Lact. *De mortibus persecutorum*

**Persephone** = Proserpina

**Persepolis,** the residence and burial place of the Persian kings, built by Darius I; Alexander sacked the city in 330 BC 波斯波里斯, 见 Persia

**Perses,** Gr: Perses, "destroyer", brother of Hesiod 佩尔塞斯, 见 Hes. *Erga*

**Perseus,** Gr: Perseus, "adventurer" (<peira), "destroyer", E: Perseus; 1) a legendary Greek hero, son of Zeus and Danae; king Polydectes asked him to obtain the head of Medusa, which Perseus achieved; his son Perses became ruler of the Persians; 2) king of Macedonia 179—168 BC, son of king Philipp V; he was beaten by the Romans at Pydna 168 BC. 珀耳修斯, 见 Medusa

**Persia,** Gr: Persai, Persis, E: Persia, => Cyrus, Cambyses, Dareius, Xerxes 波斯, 波斯人, 见 Aesch. *Pers.*, Hdt. *Hist.*

**Persius,** Aulus Persius Flaccus, 34—62 AD, Latin satirical poet 佩尔修斯, 见 Quint. *Inst.* 10,

**persona,** Gr: charaktēr, demas, sōma, phyē, eidos, E: character (in a drama), person 人物, 见 Arist. *Poiet.*, Cic. *De off.* 1,107~150, (four persons: natura, ingenium, modus vitae, decus), Mart. (Parcere personis), Orig. *De princ.* (personal understanding of the Logos)

**persuasio,** Gr: pistis, peithō, E: persuasion, the essence of rhetoric 说服, 见 Arist. *Rhet.*

**perturbatio,** Gr: tarachē, pathos, E: perturbation, tribulations 烦恼, 见 Cic. *De fin.* 3,35

**Petronius,** Petronius Arbiter, ca. 10—65 AD; author of the novel *Satyricon*, of which a part survives, (*the Cena Trimalchionis*) 彼特隆纽斯

**Petrus,** Gr: Petros, "rock", E: Peter, one of the disciples of Jesus, leader of the church in Rome and thus revered as the first Pope, martyred ca. in

67 AD 伯多禄、彼得，见 Bibl. *Ioann.* 2, Iren. *Adv. haer.* (successors of Peter in Rome), Lact. *De mortibus*, Euseb. (martyred in Rome), Prud. *Perist.* (description of his tomb, => sepulcrum)

**Phaeaces,** Gr: Phaiakes, "bright arrival" (?), E: Phaeacians, inhabitants of the island of Scheria, whose king Alcinous received Odysseus 菲亚克斯人，见 Hom. *Od.* 6

**Phaedo,** Gr: Phaidōn, friend of Socrates 斐多，见 Plat. *Phaid..*

*Phaedo,* Gr: *Phaidon*, a dialogue about immortality 《斐多篇》，见 Plat. *Phaid..*

**Phaedra,** Gr: Phaidra, "bright one", second wife of Theseus who loved Hippolytus 菲德拉，见 Eur. *Hipp.*, Ov. *Her.*

**Phaedria,** daughter of Euclio, loved by Lyconides; also name of a figure in a play by Terence 菲德里亚，见 Plaut. *Aul.*, Ter. *Phorm.*

**Phaedrus,** Gaius Iulius, ca. 15 BC—50 AD, Thracian slave who came to Rome and wrote *Fabulae Aesopiae* 菲德鲁斯，见 Aes. *Mython*

**Phaeton,** Gr: Phaethōn, "shining", E: Phaeton, the son of Helius, the sun-god; he asked his father to let him drive the chariot of the sun but scorched the ground and thus was killed by Zeus. 法厄同，见 Cic. *De off.* 3,94; *Peri hypsous* 15; Lucian. *Theon dial.*

**Phalaris,** Gr: Phalaris, ca. 580 BC, tyrant of Acragas in Sicily, notorious for his cruelty; => tyrannus 法拉瑞斯，见 Cic. *De off.* 2,25; 3,32

**phantasia,** Gr: phantasiai, E: images and impressions, illusions 印象、幻想，见 Epict. *Diatr.*, *Peri hypsous* 14 (phantasia, eidolopoiia)

*Pharsalia,* a work by Lucan 《法尔萨利亚》，见 Lucan

**Phaon,** Gr: Phaon, a legendary boatman in Lesbos; Aphrodite restored his youth 法翁，见 Ov. *Her.*

*Pheidias,* E: Pheidias, (Phidias), outstanding Athenian artist, ca. 490—432 BC, adorning the Acropolis, his master-pieces were the statues of Athena and the Zeus of the temple in Olympia 菲迪亚斯，见 Pausanias

**Pheidippides,** Gr: Pheidippidēs, "spare horses", (or: Philippides), famous runner at Marathon, 490 BC; also the name of a figure in Aristophanes' comedy 菲迪皮得斯，见 Hdt. *Hist.* 6, Ar. *Neph.*

**Pheres,** Gr: Pherēs, "bearer", father of Admetus 菲瑞斯，见 Eur. *Alk.*

**philargyria** => avaritia

**philedonia** => voluptas, cupiditas

**Philemon,** Gr: Philēmōn, "friendly slinger", E: Philemon, an old man, husband of Baucis, who showed hospitality to Zeus and Hermes in disguise; therefore Philemon and Baucis were saved from a deluge 菲勒蒙，见 Deucalion

**philia** => dilectio, amor, amicitia

*Philippicae,* a series of speeches of Cicero against Marcus Antonius 《菲利皮克》，见 Cic.

**Philo,** Gr: Philōn, Jewish author in Alexandria who wrote in Greek, 10 BC—45 AD 斐洛，见 Phil. *De opificio mundi, Legum alleg.* Hieron. *De viris*

**Philocleon,** Gr: Philokleōn, "love Cleon", figure in one of Aristophanes' comedies 菲洛克勒翁，见 Ar. *Sphekes*

**Philocomasium,** Gr: Philokomasion, "love long hair", girl loved by Pleusicles 菲洛克马西翁，见 Plaut. *Miles*

**Philoctetes,** Gr: Philoktētēs, "love of possessions", who owned Heracles' bow and arrows; he was left back by the Greeks at Lemnos; later Odysseus and Diomedes (or Neoptolemos) went there and tried to bring him back, since only by his help Troy could be conquered. Later Philoctetes was healed by Machaon and killed Paris with his arrow. 菲罗克特特斯

*Philogelos,* E: *Philogelōs*, a collection of funny stories 《爱笑者》，见 Appendix

**philologia,** Gr: philologia, E: philology, the arts connected with the languages 语文学，见 Capella, *De nuptiis* (personification of philology, married to Mercury)

**Philopoemen,** Gr. Philopoimēn, "good shepherd", ca. 250—182 BC, a general from Megalopolis (Arcadia) who defeated the Spartans 菲洛普门，见 Plut. *Bioi*

**Philoponus,** Johannes, Gr: Iōannēs Philoponos "lover of toil", E: Philoponus, ca. 490—570 AD, Greek scholar 菲洛普诺斯，见 *De creatione mundi*

**philosophia,** ars recte sapiendi, Gr: philosophia, "love of wisdom", E: philosophy, => sapientia 哲学，见 Arist. *Poiet.*, Cic. *De fin.* 3,40, *De off.* 2,5; Sen. *Epistulae morales*, Clem. Alex. *Strom.* 1 (philosophy a gift from God), Minuc. *Octav.* (philosophos esse Christianos), Aug. *De beata vita* (thinking is like sailing), *De vera rel.* (Christianity is the perfect heir of classical philosophy), Boethius, *De consolat.* (appearance as a woman), Cassiod. *Inst.* (definitions of phil.)

***Philosophōn biōn kai dogmatōn synagōgē,*** E: *A Collection of the Lives and Teachings of the Philosophers*, a work by Diogenes Laertius 《著名哲学家的生平和学说》(或译《名哲言行录》),见 Diogenes Laertius

**Phineus,** Gr: Phineus, "sea-eagle" (?), seer who was punished by Zeus 菲纽斯,见 Apoll. *Arg.*

**Phinthias** => Damon

**phobos** => terror, formido

**Pho cion,** Gr: Phōkion, Athenian statesman who advocated peace with Macedonia and was sentenced to death in 318 BC 佛基翁,见 Plut. *Bioi*

**Phocis,** Gr: Phōkis, small country of central Greece containing Delphi 佛克斯,见 Pausanias *Periegesis*

**Phoebe,** Gr: Phoibē, "shining", "bright moon", one of the Titans 菲贝,见 Hes. *Theog.*

**Phoebus,** Gr: Phoibos, "shining", one name of Apollo 弗波斯,见 Apollo

**Phoenicia,** Gr: Phoinikē, Phoinikeia< phoinix, "palm-tree-land", or "purple-land", E: Phoenicia, a country along the coast of Syria with the important towns of Sidon and Tyre (Tyros); between 1200 and 900 BC the Phoenician merchants controlled the trade between Spain and Syria, thus they played a crucial role in the cultural exchanges between Greece and the East; Carthago was a Phoinician colony, its inhabitants therefore called "Poeni" or "Punici", => Cadmus, Carthago, Europa, Punicum bellum 菲尼基亚,见 Hdt. *Hist.* 1, Lactantius, *Carmen de ave phoenice*

**phoenix,** Gr: phoinix, 1) red color; 2) palm tree; 3) phoenix, mythical bird which appears once in 500 years 凤凰,见 Hdt. *Hist.* 2, Lactantius, *Carmen de ave phoenice*, Physiologus (Christian interpretation)

**Phoenix,** Gr: Phoinix, "phoenix, palm-tree", Greek hero at Troy 菲尼克斯,见 Hom. *Il.* 9

**Phoibos** = Phoebus

***Phormio,*** play by Terence 《福尔米翁》,见 Ter. *Phorm.*

**Phrixus,** Gr: Phrixos, "bristling", son of Athamas and Nephele; => Helle 佛里克索斯,见 Apoll. *Arg.*

**phronesis** => prudentia

**phrontisterium,** Gr: phrontistērion, "thinking hall", school (or monastery) "思想屋",见 Ar. *Neph.*

**phylaces,** Gr: phylakes, guardian spirits 保护神灵,见 Hes. *Erga*

**Phyllis,** "leafy", daughter of king Sithon in Thrace, loved by Demophoon 菲里丝,见 Ov. *Her.*

**physike arete** => virtus

***Physiologus,*** Gr: *Physiologos*, E: *Physiologus*, a popular work from the second century AD 《谈论自然者》,见 Physiologus

**physis** => 1) ortus, 2) natura, ingenium, 3) ordo naturae, 4) mundus, universum

**pictura,** Gr: graphē, pinax, E: picture, painting 画图,见 Hom. *Il.* 18 (scenes on the shield), Hor. *De arte poet.* 361 (poetry is like a painting), Claudian. *De raptu Proserp.* (scenes on the cloth), Capella, *De nuptiis* (rhetorical figures on a dress)

**pietas,** Gr: hosiotēs, sebeia, eusebeia, theosebeia, E: piety, respect for gods, ancestors and the community 虔敬,见 Cic. *De nat. deor.*, *De off.* 3,28 (impii adversus deos), Verg. *Aen.* 2, Apuleius, *Met.*, Marc. Aurel., Heliodor. *Aithiop.*, Tert. *Apolog.* (pagan piety is not sincere), Aug. *De civ. Dei* 10 (eusebeia = pietas)

**Pindarus,** Gr: Pindaros, E: Pindar, Greek lyric poet, 522—446 BC, author of four books of E*pinician Odes*, in which he glorified the victors of the competitions at Olympia, Delphi, Nemea and Isthmos. 品达,见 Hor. *Carm.*, Quint. *Inst.*

**Piraeus,** Gr: Peiraieos, harbour (city) of Athens, enlarged by Themistocles in 493 BC; Sulla destroyed the city in 86 BC. 皮瑞欧斯,见 Hdt. *Hist.* 8

**Pirithous,** Gr: Pirithous, Pirithous, king of the Lapiths, a friend of Theseus, who was detained in Hades 皮里图斯,见 Ov. *Met.* 8

**Piso** => Calipurnius

**pistis** => fides, persuasio

**Pittacus,** Gr: Pittakos, E: Pittacus of Mytilene (Lesbos), ca. 650—570 BC, statesman and one of the Seven Sages 皮塔库斯,见 Lesbos

**planta,** Gr: phyta, E: plants, => agricultura, animalia, flos, medicina, palma 植物,见 Hom. *Od.* 9 (lotophagoi), 10 (herb moly), Verg. *Georg.* 1, 2, *Aen.* 6(ramus aureus), Ov. *Met.* (Daphne; Pyramus: mulberry tree), Plin. *Nat. hist.* 12~27, Bibl. *Gen* 2 (creation of plants, tree in the paradise), Ioann. 15 (vine), Lactantius, *Carmen* (palma), Basil. *Hexaem.* (grafting as symbol of conversion), Aug. *Conf.* 13 (spiritual meaning of plants)

**Plataea,** Gr: Plataiai, E: Plataea, city in Boeotia, scene of a great Greek victory over the Persian invaders in 479 BC 普拉泰阿，见 Aesch. *Persai*, Hdt. *Hist*.6, 9, Thuc. 3

**Plato,** Gr: Platōn, E: Plato, Greek philosopher and important author, 427—347 BC, student of Socrates since about 407 BC, he travelled widely after the death of his respected teacher, visiting Egypt and learning from the Pythagoreans in Tarentum; in 387 BC he founded the Academy in Athens and taught there until his death. His works present the basic questions to almost all areas of philosophy. 柏拉图，见 Plat. *Apolog., Gorg., Men., Phaid., Polit., Symp., Tim..*, Cic. *De fin., De nat. deor.*, Philo, *De opificio* (assumed that Plato knew the Old Testament), Quint. *Inst.* 10, *Peri hypsous*, Clem. Alex. *Protrepticus* (Plato in search for truth), Plotin. *Enn.*, Diog. Laert., Lact. *Inst.*, Athanas. *Logos*, Aug. *Confess.* 1, *De civ. Dei* 8 (Plato closest to Christianity), *De vera rel.* (Platonists easily converted), Macrob. *Sat.* (Neoplatonism and monotheism)

**Plautus,** Titus Maccius Plautus, 254—184 BC, Umbrian author of Latin comedies, 20 of his 130 plays have survived. 普劳图斯，见 Plaut. *Amphitruo, Aulularia, Miles*

**plebs,** Gr: laos, hoi polloi, E: plebeians, the common people; Roman citizens other than the patricians of the upper class 平民，见 patricii

**Pleiades,** Gr: Pleiades, E: Pleiad, the seven daughters of the Titan Atlas and Pleione, among them Maia and Merope; pursued by Orion they were changed into stars by Zeus 普雷阿德，见 Orion

**Pleusicles,** Gr: Pleusiklēs, "glorious sailor", figure in one of Plautus' plays 普勒西克勒斯，见 Plaut. *Miles*

**Plinius,** (maior), Roman author, encyclopedist, 23—79 AD; he died at the eruption of the Vesuv.(老)普林尼，见 Plin. *Hist. nat.*

**Plinius,** (minor), nephew of Plinius maior, author of ten books of letters, 61—113 AD, governor of Bithynia since 111 AD. He is known for his correspondence with Trajan concerning the treatment of Christians.(小)普林尼

**Plotinus,** Gr: Plotinos, E: Plotin, Plotinus, Greek philosopher, ca. 205—270 AD 普罗提诺，见 *Enneades*, Aug. *Confess.* 1, *De civ. Dei* 9

**ploutos** => opes

**Plutarchus,** Gr: Ploutarchos, E: Plutarch, Greek author, 46—120 AD 普卢塔克，见 Plut. *Bioi, Moralia*

**Pluto,** Gr: Ploutos, "wealth", E: Plutus, god of wealth; => Hades 普路同，见 Claudian. *De raptu Proserp.*

**pneuma** => spiritus

**pneuma hagion** = Spiritus Sanctus

**pneumatikoi,** E: inspired believers 属灵的信徒

**poena,** Gr: dikē, poinē, E: punishment, => severitas, clementia, iustitia 惩罚，见 Hom. *Od.* 11 (punishment in Hades), Soph. *Oed. Tyr.* (self-imposed punishment), Ter. *Heaut.* (self-imposed punishment), Cic. *De off.* 1,89, Bibl. *Ioann.* 8, Aug. *De civ. Dei* 13, 20, 21, 22, (eternal punishment)

**Poeni** => Punicum

**poenitentia,** E: penitence, expiation practice after a sin (fasting etc.); => poena 补赎，见 Cyprianus, Columban, *Regula coen.*(penal regulations, beating)

**poeta,** Gr: poiētēs, E: poet 诗人，见 Plat. *Polit.*, Hor. *De arte poet.* 295~322 (he should have a healthy world view), Iuv. *Sat.* 1 (pseudo-poets)

**poetica,** Gr: (technē) poiētikē, E: poetry 诗、诗学，见 Arist. *Poiet.*, Hor. *De arte poet.*, *Peri hyps.*

**poimen** = pastor

*Poimenika ta kata Daphnin kai Chloēn* = *Daphnis kai Chloe*

**Polemos,** Gr: polemos, "war", E: war, personification of the war, god of war; => Ares, Mars 战争（之神），见 Ar. *Eirene*

**polis,** Gr: polis, E: city, city-state, political community, => civitas, cives, res publica,城、城邦、国度,见 Ar. *Ornithes*

*Politeia, Res Publica,* Gr: *Politeia,* E: *The Republic,* one of Plato's major works《理想国》，见 Plat.

**polites** = civis

**politica** (scientia), ars regnandi, Gr: ta politika, politikē (technē, epistēmē), E: politics, political science 政治、政治学，见 Plat. *Gorg.*, Arist. *Polit.*, Cic. *De off.* 1, 60~90, Philo, *De opificio* (Joseph = aner politikos), Plut. *Mor.* (*Ei presbytero politeuteon; Peri monarchias kai demokratias*), Ambros. *Ep.*

**Pollio,** Gaius Asinius Pollio, 76 BC—4 AD, Roman statesman and literary patron, consul in 40 BC, founder of the first public library in Rome 波里欧，见 Verg. *Buc.*

**Pollux,** Gr: Polydeukēs, son of Zeus and Leda, brother of Castor 波吕丢克斯，见 Apoll. *Arg.*, Lucian.

*Theon dial.*

**Polos,** one of Gorgias' students 波罗斯，见 Plat. *Gorg.*

**Polybius,** Gr: Polybios, "long life", Greek author of a history of the rise of Rome, 200—118 BC 波利比奥斯，见 Polyb. *Hist.*

**Polybus,** Gr: Polybos, "many oxen", king of Corinth 波吕布斯，见 Soph. *Oid. Tyr.*

**Polycarpus,** Gr: Polykarpos "many fruits", E: Polycarp of Smyrna (in Asia Minor), 69—155 AD, important leader of the Church, martyr 波利加，见 Euseb. 4

**Polycrates,** Gr: Polykratēs, "powerful", E: Polycrates, tyrant of Samos from ca. 540—522 BC 波吕克拉特斯，见 Hdt. *Hist.* 3

**Polydeukes** = Pollux

**Polydorus,** Gr: Polydōros, "many gifts", E: Polydorus, the youngest son of Priam, murdered by the Thracian king Polymestor 波吕多洛斯，见 Verg. *Aen.* 3

**Polyhymnia,** Gr: Polyhymnia, (Polymnia), "many songs", one of the Muses, Muse of hymns; => Musae 波吕姆尼亚，见 Hes. *Theog.*

**Polyneices,** Gr: Polyneikēs, "killing many", E: Polyneices, son of Oedipus, rival of Eteocles 波吕内克斯，见 Soph. *Ant.*, *Oid. epi Kol.*

**Polyphemus,** Gr: Polyphēmos, "famous", one of the Cyclopes, son of Poseidon 波吕菲摩斯，见 Hom. *Od.* 9

**polytheismus,** Gr: "many gods", E: polytheism; => deus 多神论，见 Hes. *Theog.*, Philo, *De opificio* (critical of polytheism), Iustinos, *Apol.*, Lact. *Inst.* (original monotheism lost later)

**Pomona,** Roman goddess of orchards, loved by the god Vertumnus 波摩纳，见 Aug. *De civ. Dei* 4

**Pompeii,** port and town near the Vesuvius, covered by pumice and ash during the eruption of the volcano in 79 AD, together with the cities of Herculaneum and Stabiae; rediscovered in 1748 most of it has been excavated. 彭佩乌斯，见 Vesuvius

**Pompeius, Gnaeus Pompeius Magnus,** E: Pompey, 106—48 BC, Roman general and statesman, opponent of Caesar, he retreated to Greece when Caesar entered Italy in 48 BC; he was defeated at Pharsalus in the same year and fled to Egypt, where he was assassinated 庞培，见 Cic., Liv. 90~105, Luc. *Phars.*, Plut. *Bioi*

**Pompilius** => Numa Pompilius

**ponos** = labor

**Pontus,** Gr: Pontos, E: Sea, god of the sea 大海，见 Hes. *Theog.*

**Pontus Euxenus,** Gr: Pontos Euxenos, "friendly sea", E: Black Sea 黑海，见 Xen. *Anabasis*, Apoll. *Arg.*

**populares,** E: populares, "those on the side of the people", a party in Rome demanding more participation of the people in government; they opposed the optimates; outstanding representatives were the Gracchi, Marius, and Caesar 民众派，见 optimates

**populus,** gens, plebs, natio, turba, vulgus, Gr: dēmos, laos, ethnos, hoi polloi, plēthos, E: people, population, the crowds 人民、民众，见 Arist. *Polit.*, Cic. *De res publ.* (definition of populus), Sen. *Epist. mor.* 7 (turba; inhumanior quia inter homines), Iuv. *Sat.* 10 (panem et circenses, the concern of the people), Aug. *De civ. Dei* 19 (the new definition of "populus" also includes non-Roman peoples)

**Poros,** Gr: poros, "way", Poros, E: inventiveness, according to Plato the father of Eros 能干，见 Plat. *Symp.*

**Porphyrius,** Gr: Porphyrios, E: Porphyry, ca 233—305 AD, Neoplatonist philosopher, his introduction (*Isagōgē*) to Aristotle's categories was translated by Boethius and became an important textbook 波菲利，见 Plotinus, *Enn.*, Aug. *De civ. Dei* 10 (he rightly rejects reincarnation)

**Porsenna,** (=Porsena), Lars Porsenna, an Etruscan king who attacked Rome after 510 BC; Horatius Cocles and Mucius Scaevola fought against him. 波塞纳，见 Liv. 2

**Poseidon,** Gr: Poseidōn, "mighty lord", or "sea-god" (potis-dyas), L: Neptunus, god of the sea, also of earthquakes, and of horses; son of Cronus and Rhea, brother of Zeus, husband of the Nereid Amphrite; the Isthmian Games were dedicated to him; he competed with Athena for the possession of Attica, sending the Athenians the horse and a fountain on the Acropolis; => Neptunus 波塞冬，见 Hom. *Il.* 14, *Od.* 5, 9, Hes. *Theog.*, Aesch. *Persai*, Eur. *Hipp.*, Ar. *Ornithes*

**Posidonius,** Gr: Poseidōnios, E: Posidonius, ca. 135—50 BC, Greek historian and Stoic philosopher at Rhodos, who influenced Cicero, Lucretius, Virgil and Plinius (the Elder), his books are lost 波西多

尼乌斯，见 Philo, *Legum alleg.*, Basil. *Hexaem.*

**potentia, potestas,** Gr: kratos, archē, dynamis, E: power, reign; => rex, regnare 权力，见 Boethius, *De cons.* 3, Dionys. Areop., *Peri tes our. hier.* (dynameis = angels)

**praeceptum,** Gr: entolē, E: precept, commandment 诫命、规律，见 Bibl. *Ex* (dekalogus), *Ioann.* (commandment of love), Aug. *De civ. Dei* 2 (pagan gods never issued moral precepts)

**praedicare,** Gr: kērygma, kēryssein, E: preaching (of the Gospel), one of the main duties of the clerics; => rhetorica 讲道、布道，见 Aug., *De doctrina Christ.*, Greg. Magn. *Regula past.*

**praedictio** => divinatio

**praefiguratio,** Gr: antitypos, typos, E: prefiguration, symbol 预先的暗示，见 Aug. *De civ. Dei* 17 (Jerusalem is symbol of the Church)

**praepositum,** Gr: proēgmenon, E: preferable values 应取得的价值，见 Cic. *De fin.*,3,52; 4,74

**praetor,** the second highest magistrate after the consul; they were in charge of jurisdiction and after one year of office became governors of a province.裁判官，见 cursus honorum

**pragma** => res

**Praxiteles,** Gr: Praxitelēs, "perfect performance", E: Praxiteles, ca. 390—330 BC, famous Greek sculptor, among his best works are the Aphrodite of Cnidus and the Hermes found in Olympia 普拉克西特勒斯，见 Pheidias

**preces,** prex, adoratio, oratio, Gr: euchē, eugma, proseuchomai, proskynēsis, E: prayer (to the gods), adoration 祈祷、祈求，见 Hom. *Il.* 6, *Od.* 4, Aesch. *Choeph.*, Soph. *Antig.*, Verg. *Aen.* 5, Hor. *Carm.* 4,3 (prayer to Melpomene), *Carm. saec.* (prayer to the gods; "may Diana turn to the prayers of the children"), Sen. *Epist. mor.* 10 (pray as if people would hear it), Iuv. *Sat.* 10 (pray for health), Bibl. *Ioann.* 4 (adoration in spirit and in truth), Didache (daily prayers, the Our Father), Aug. *Confess.* (written in form of a prayer), Cass. *De inst.* (time of prayers), Bened. *Regula* 8~20

**presbyter** => sacerdos

**Priamus,** Gr: Priamos, "redeemed", E: Priam, son of Laomedon, King of Troy, husband of Hecuba and father of fifty sons and many daughters, including Hector, Paris, Cassandra, Creusa 普里阿摩斯，见 Hom. *Il.* 3, 24

**Priapus,** Gr: Priapos, "pruner of the pear-tree", E: Priapus, a god of fertility originally from Asia Minor, later in Italy worshipped as a god of gardens (as scarecrow with a phallus) 普里亚普斯，见 Hor. *Sat.* 1,8

**prima philosophia,** Gr: prōtē philosophia, E: first philosophy, metaphysics, basic principles 第一哲学，见 Arist. *Met.*

**princeps,** Gr: archōn, anax, kreiōn = kreōn, dynastēs, koiranos, E: ruler, statesman, king; => rex 统治者，见 Plat. *Polit.*

**principatus,** E: principate, the rule of Roman emperors (from 31 BC to 284 AD) 罗马皇帝的统治，见 Tac. *Ann.*

**principium,** elementum, Gr: archē, archai, hypothesis, E: first principles, beginnings, origins (of historical events), 原始，基本原则，见 Arist. *Met.*, Polyb., Bibl. *Gen* 1, Origenes, *Peri archon*

**Priscianus Caesariensis,** E: Priscian, ca. 480—520 AD, grammarian at Constantinople, author of the Latin *Institutio de arte grammatica* (a grammar with copious quotations from classical authors) in 18 vols.普瑞斯泽利安努斯，见 Donatus

**probatio,** probare, argumentatio, Gr: elenchos, sēmeion, deigma, martyrion, tekmērion, E: proof, argumentation (of a speech) 论证，证据，见 Arist. *Rhet.*, Cic. *Brutus*, *De nat. deor.* 1,61

**Proclus,** Gr: Proklos, E: Proclus, ca.412—485 AD, Greek philosopher, Neo-platonist 普洛克鲁斯，见 *Eis tēn Platōnos theologian*

**procreatio,** Gr: gennaein, genesis, E: procreation, childbearing 生育，见 Greg. Nys. *Peri parthen.* (spiritual birth; virginity interrupts chain of procreation)

**Procrustes,** Gr: Prokroustēs, E: Procrustes, a robber near Eleusis who tortured his victims by forcing them into a small bed and cutting off their feet; he was killed by Theseus 普洛克估斯特斯，见 Theseus

**Prometheus,** Gr: Promētheus, "quick learner", "forethinker", the clever son of the Titan Iapetus and Themis, brother of Epimetheus and Atlas; Zeus punished him for stealing a spark from heaven; => Pandora 普罗米修斯；见 Hes. *Erga*, 42~105; *Theog.*, Ar. *Ornithes*, Apoll. *Arg.*, Lucian, *Theon dial.*

**promissum,** Gr: horkos, hyposchesis, epangelma, E: promise, => ius iurandum 承诺，见 Cic. *De off.* 1,31, (fulfilment of promise under certain circumstances),

*De off.* 3,94; 3, 107（keep promise towards enemy）; Tac. *Germ.* (keeping of promises)

**pronuntiatio,** Gr: ekphōnesis, E: delivery（of a speech）, => actio 演讲，见 Quint. *Inst.*

**Propertius,** Sextus Propertius, 50—15 BC, Italian elegiac poet, born at Asisium in Umbria 普罗佩提乌斯，见 neoterici

**propheta,** Hebr: nabi, Gr: mantis, prophētēs, "one who speaks in the name of", E: prophet, esp. of the Old Testament; => vates 先知，见 Biblia; Didache, Iustinos, *Apol.*, Orig. *Contra Cels.*, Athanas. *Vita Anton.*（foretelling the hour of one's death is a sign of holiness）, Aug. *De civ. Dei* 17（Old Testament prophecies relating to Christ）

**propositio,** Gr: protasis, thesis, E: proposition, a statement 命题，见 Arist. *Org. Rhet.*

**propylaea,** Gr: propylaia, E: propylaea, gateway and entrance to public buildings or temples, esp. at the Acropolis in Athens 前门，见 Acropolis

**Proserpina,** Gr: Persephonē, "fearful one", E: Proserpine, also Korē, "daughter", the daughter of Zeus and Demeter / Ceres, who was suddenly abducted by Hades and became queen of the Underworld, thus causing the grief of Demeter 普罗塞皮纳，珀尔塞福涅，见 Ov. *Met.* 8, Apuleius, *Met.*, Claudian. *De raptu Proserp.*

**proskynēsis,** E: reverential kneeling, demanded by Alexander, =>adoratio 跪拜礼，见 Arrian. *Alex. anab.*, 4

**Protagoras,** Gr: Prōtagoras, E: Protagoras from Abdera, ca. 485—415 BC, famous sophist, opponent of Socrates in Plato's dialogue *Protagoras*, being an atheist he was banned from Athens 普洛塔格拉斯，见 Diog. Laert.

**prote philosophia** = prima philosophia

**Protesilaus,** Gr: Prōtesilaos, "first of the people", a Thessalian prince who was the first Greek killed at Troy; since his wife Laodamia was grieving so much, the gods allowed him to return to her for three hours, but when he left again she killed herself.普洛特西劳斯，见 Ov. *Her.*

**Proteus,** Gr: Prōteus, "first man", a Greek sea god, symbol of change and impredictability 普若特乌斯，见 Verg. *Georg.* 4

***Protrepticus,*** Gr: *Protreptikos*, E: *Exhortation*, work by Clement《劝说》，见 Clemens Alexandrinus

**proverbium,** Gr: paroimia, epos, logos, gnōmē, E: proverb, maxim 格言 Arist. *Rhet.*, Publ. *Sent.*, Maximus Conf. *Capita*

**providentia,** Gr: pronoia, promētheia, E: divine care for the world, the plan of the godhead for history and for individuals, => fatum, gubernatio mundi 天佐论，见 Cic. *De nat. deor.*, Verg. *Aen.*, Philo *De opificio*, Luc. *Phars.* (the gods do not care about men), Aug. *De civ. Dei* 5（everything arranged according to measure, *Wisd.* 11:20）, Boethius, *De cons.*

**prudentia,** Gr: phronēsis, sōphrosynē, pronoia, euboulia, E: prudence 明智，见 Cic. *De off.* 1,153, Ambros. *De off. ministr.*, Capella, *De nuptiis*（Phronesis = mother of Philologia）

**Prudentius,** Aurelius Clemens Prudentius, ca. 348—405 AD, Latin poet 普鲁登蒂乌斯，见 *Peristephanon, Psychomachia*

**psyche** => 1）anima, vita, 2）spiritus, persona, 3）intellectus, cor, 4）appetitus

**Psyche,** a girl loved by Amor in Apuleius' *Metamorphosae*, an allegory of the soul 普叙克，见 Apuleius

**psychikoi,** E: "ensouled" believers 有灵魂的信徒，见 Iren. *Adv. haer.*

**psychogonia,** E: the creation of the soul 灵魂的创造，见 Plat. *Tim.*, Plut *Mor.*（*Peri tes Timaiou psychogonias*）

**psychologia,** G: psychē–logos "teaching of the soul", E: psychology; => anima, virtus, temptationes 心理学，见 Galen（works on psychology）, Longus（maturing process）, Lact. *Inst.* 2（attraction of miracles）, Athanas. *Logos*（psychology of idol worship）, Macrobius, *Sat.* 7, Prud. *Psychomachia*, Aug. *Confess.* 2（passions of youth; God created the heart）, Cassian. *De inst.*（understanding of human weakness）, Greg. Magn. *Reg. past.*（pastoral guidance, understanding the feelings of listeners）

***Psychomachia,*** E: *Contest of the Soul*, didactic poem by Prudentius《灵魂之战》，见 Prud.

**Ptolemaei,** Gr: Ptolemaioi, E: Ptolemies, Macedonian Greek dynasty that ruled Egypt from 323 BC until the Roman conquest and the death of Cleopatra in 30 BC; especially influential were Ptolemy I Soter（ruled 323—283 BC）and his son Ptolemy II Philadelphus（in power 285—246 BC）; they fostered art and literature and established the library of Alexandria.托勒密，见 Aegyptus

**Ptolemaeus ,** Claudius Ptolemaeus, Gr: Ptolemaios, E: Ptolemy, Greek astronomer, mathematician, geographer, ca. 100—170 AD 托勒密，见 *Mathematike syntaxis*, Capella, *De nuptiis*; Philoponus, *De creatione mundi*

**Publicola,** a politician of ancient Rome 普布里克拉，见 Plut. *Bioi*

**Publilius Syrus,** ca. 80—20 BC, author of a collection of proverbs 普珀里琉斯

**pudicitia** => pudor

**pudor,** Gr: aidōs, aischyne, atimia, E: feeling of shame, sense of decency, modesty 羞耻感，见 Hes. *Erga* 200, Theophr. *Eth.* 19, 20, (aēdēs), Cic. *De off.* 1,128; Hor. *Carm. saec.* (god of shame), *Sat.* 1,2 (impudent dress), Tatian, *Logos*, (shameless pagan arts), Lucian, *Theon dial.*, Tert. *De spect.* (insolent performances), Prud. *Psych.* (pudicitia)

**puer,** infans, Gr: pais, paidion, teknon, E: boy, child, infant, baby 小男孩，见 Hom. *Il.* 6 (Astyanax), Eurip. *Med.*, Verg. *Aen.* 2 (Ascanius), 6 (children in the Underworld), Buc. 4, Hor. *De arte poet.* Quint. *Inst.* 1—2, Iuv. *Sat.* 14, Bibl. *Gen* 3 (pain of childbirth), Iren. *Adv. haer.* (Jesus was a child), Aug. *Conf.* 1 (reflection on childhood)

**pulchritudo,** Gr: to kallos, E: beauty 美丽，见 Plat. *Symp.* (pelagos tou kalou), Tert. *Apolog.* (beauty of universe witness to the Creator), Lact. *Inst.* (beautiful but empty expressions), Boeth. *De cons.* (beauty of artifacts), Greg. Magn. *Reg. past.* (eloquence less important than content)

**Punicum bellum,** Punicus; => Gr: Phoinikia, E: Punic War (Wars), the wars of Rome against Carthage 264—241 BC, 218—201 BC, and 149—146 BC 普尼克战争，见 Polyb., Liv., Aug. *De civ. Dei* 3 (the wars were a disaster)

**purgatorium,** E: purgatory, a place where souls are purified after death 炼狱，见 Greg. Nyss. *Peri psyches*, Gregorius Magnus, *Dialogi*,

**purificatio,** Gr: katharsis, E: purification, purgation, catharsis 净化，见 Arist. *Poet.* (the effect of dramatic performances), Greg. Nys. *Peri psyches* (souls need purgation from sins after death), Dion. Ar., *Eccl. hier.* (via purgatoriae), Joh. Climac. *Scala*

**Pydna,** city in Macedonia, scene of the battle in 168 BC, in which the Romans under Aemilius Paullus defeated the Macedonian king Perseus 皮得纳，见 Polyb.

**Pygmalion,** Gr: Pygmalion, "fighter", E: Pygmalion; 1) legendary king of Tyre, the brother of Elissa/Dido; he killed Sychaeus; 2) legendary king of Cyprus who fell in love with a beautiful statue; Aphrodite answered his prayers and gave the statue life; Pygmalion married the woman 皮格马利翁，见 Verg. *Aen.* 1

**Pylades,** Gr: Pyladēs, "gate-keeper", "gate of Hades" (?), friend of Orestes 皮拉得斯，见 Aesch. *Choeph.*

**Pylos,** Greek town in the SW of the Peloponnesus 皮罗斯，见 Hom. *Od.* 3

**pyr** = ignis

**pyramis,** Gr: pyramis, E: pyramids (in Egypt), their construction was discussed by Herodotus 金字塔，见 Hdt. *Hist.* 2

**Pyramus,** lover of Thisbe 皮拉姆斯，见 Ov. *Met.* 4

**Pyrgopolyneices,** Gr: Pyrgopolyneikes, "fortress-many-killed", the "braggart soldier" in Plautus' play 皮格波里内克斯，见 Plaut. *Miles*

**Pyrrha,** "fiery red", the wife of Deucalion, who survived the flood, => diluvium 皮拉，见 Ov. *Met.*1

**Pyrrhon,** E: Pyrrhon of Elis, 365—275 BC, founder of Greek scepticism 彼浪，见 Lucian. *Vit. auct.*, Sext. Emp. *Skept.*, Diog. Laert.

**Pyrrhus,** Gr: Pyrrhos, "fiery red", 319—272 BC, a Greek king who defeated the Roman armies in southern Italy in 280 and 279 BC, but nevertheless was forced to withdraw 皮罗斯，见 Plut. *Bioi*, Orosius, *Hist.*

**Pythagoras,** "counselor", Greek scholar, philosopher, ca. 580—500 BC, who lived in Italy (Croton), his teachings on reincarnation, on the numbers and proportions and the harmony of the heavenly spheres influenced Plato and subsequent philosophy 毕达歌拉斯，见 Philo, *De opificio*, Lucian. *Vit. auct.*, Diog. Laert.

**Pythia,** Gr: Pythia, 1) the priestess of Apollo at Delphi; 2) the Pythian Games held once in four years at Delphi in honor of Apollo; => Delphi 皮提亚

**Python,** Gr: Python, "seeking counsel", <pynthanomai, or "snake", the snake killed by Apollo near Delphi 皮通，见 Apollo

# Q

**quaerere,** Gr: zētein, E: search for, ask for 寻求，见 Aug. *De beata vita* (quaerere Deum),

**quaestor,** Roman magistrate; => cursus honorum 财政

官,见 Cic.

**qualitas,** Gr: poiotēs, to poion, E: quality 品质,见 Cic. *De fin.* 3,34 (special quality of virtue)

**quies,** Gr: galēnē, eirēnē, hēsychia, E: silence, rest, tranquility; => sabbatum 宁静,见 Aug. *Conf.* 1 (restless heart), *De civ. Dei* 4 (temple of Quies, unquiet mind),

**Quintilianus,** E: Quintilian, Latin author, teacher of rhetoric at Rome, 35—96 AD 昆体良,见 Quint. *Inst.*, Sall. *Bell. Cat.*

**Quirites,** an old name of the inhabitants of Latium, later meaning "Romans", or "populus Romanus" 奎瑞特斯,见 Verg. *Georg.* 4 (bees are "parvi Quirites")

# R

**ramus aureus,** E: golden bough; => planta 金枝,见 Verg. *Aen.* 6

**ratio,** Gr: logos, logismos, logistikon, nous, dianoia, gnōmē, E: reason, understanding, intellect 理性、理智,见 Plat. *Polit.* 4, Arist. *Met.*, Cic. *De nat. deor.* 1,4 (government of the world "mente atque ratione deorum"), *De off.* 1,11 (man = particeps rationis), 3,23 (ratio naturae); Epict. *Diatr.* (nous is the guiding principle), Prud. *Psych.* (Ratio protects the virtues), Aug. *De vera rel.* (rationalism), *Soliloquia*, (dialog with reason), Boethius, *De cons.* 1 (regimen rationis = divina ratio = providentia; man = a rational animal)

**Rea Silvia,** (Rhea), E: Rea Silvia, daughter of Numitor, king of Alba, who was ousted by his brother Numitor; Amulius made Rea a Vestal virgin but by Mars she became mother of Romulus and Remus; thus Amulius threw her into the Tiber River but she was saved by the river god 瑞阿,见 Romulus

**recapitulatio,** instauratio, Gr: anakephalaiosis, E: recapitulation, a Christocentric theory 总归基督论,见 Iren. *Adv. haer.*

**regula,** E: rule (for monastic life) 会规,见 Basilius, *Ascet.*, Bened. *Reg.*

***Regula,*** E: *Rule,* the rule of St. Benedict 《会规》,见 Benedict

***Regula coenobialis,*** E: *Monastic Rule,* written by St. Columban《隐修士会规》,见 Columban

***Regula pastoralis,*** E: *Rule for Pastors,* a handbook for pastors《牧民守则》,见 Gregorius Magnus

**Regulus,** Marcus Atilius Regulus, Roman consul in 265 and 256 BC, symbol of honesty and self-sacrifice in order to keep an oath 瑞格鲁斯,见 Cic. *De fin.* 2,70, *De off.* 3,104; Hor. *Carm.* 1,12; 3,5; Aug. *De civ. Dei* 1 (Christians excel Regulus), 2

**reincarnatio,** Gr: metempsychōsis, E: reincarnation 轮回说,见 Aug. *De civ. Dei* 10 (rightly rejected by Porphyry)

***Relationes,*** E: *Reports,* a work by Symmachus《报告》,见 Symmach.

**religio,** cultus, Gr: eusebeia, therapeia, thrēskeia, latreia, hosiotēs, (thysia, pompē, agōn), E: religion, worship, cult; => deus, pietas, preces, sanctitas, superstitio 敬拜、宗教,见 Cic. *De nat. deor.*, esp. 2,72 (etymology of "religio"), *De div.* 2,148, *De off.* 3,104 (oath = affirmatio religiosa); Lucr. *De rer. nat.* 1,102 (tantum religio potuit suadere malorum), Vitr. *De arch.* 3 (construction of religious buildings), Sen. *Epist.*, Plut. *Mor.* (Egyptian religion), Tac. *Germ.* 6~15 (religion of the German tribes), Suet. *De vita Caes.* (attitude of emperors towards religion), Tatian. *Logos,* Tert. *Apol.* (polytheism leads to irreligiousness), Lact. *Inst.* 1, 4, (de falsa religione, de vera religione), Ammianus (religio absoluta et simplex), Symmachus, *Relat.* (defense of old customs), Aug. *De civ. Dei* 4 (religion used by kings as a tool of control), 10 (analysis of words like latreia, theosebeia, threskeia)

**Remus,** brother of Romulus 瑞穆斯,见 Romulus

***Rerum gestarum libri,*** E: *History,* a work by Ammianus《历史》,见 Ammian.

**res,** Gr: pragma, chrēma, E: thing, matter, reality 实务、事情,见 Cic. *De fin.* 4,54 (res - vocabulum), Aug. *De doctrina christ.* (signs and things)

**res publica,** civitas, Gr: polis, politeia, dēmokratia, E: state, society; in theory all classes of Roman society participated in the functions of magistracy, Senate and popular assembly; in difference to the unlimited sovereignty of the people in Greek democracy the Roman system combined monarchy, aristocracy and democracy; the constitution of the republic lasted from 509 BC until 27 BC. 国家,见 Cic. *De off.* 1,85, *De rep.*, 38~41, (definition of the state), Aug. *De civ. Dei* 19 (even at its best, the state will cause fear and pain, it is linked to sin)

***Res publica*** = *Politeia*

**resurrectio,** Gr: anastasis, egersis, E: resurrection 复活,见 Bibl. *Ioann.* 11:25; *Didache,* Iren. *Adv. haer.* 5, Orig. *Contra Cels.*, Lact. *Carmen de ave* *phoenice*, *Inst.* 7, Greg. Nys. *Peri psyches*, Aug. *De civ. Dei*

**revelatio**, Gr: apokalypsis, phanerōsis, E: revelation, the revealing of some secret knowledge, sometimes through visions, 启示，见 Biblia, *Rev.*, Iren. *Adv. haer.* 4

**reverentia**, verecundia, Gr: aidōs, sebas, therapeia, E: respect 尊敬，见 Cic. *De off.* 1,97

**rex**, Gr: tyrannos, basileus, anax, monarchos, E: king; => potestas, princeps, tyrannus 王，见 Arist. *Polit.*, Liv 1（seven semi-legendary kings of Rome）, Sen. *De clem.*（rules for the king）, Bibl. *Ioann.* 19（king of the Jews）, Boethius, *De cons.* 2（usually the worst people are honored most）

**Rhadamanthys**, "diviner"（?）, son of Europa and Jupiter, judge in the Underworld; => Minos 拉达曼提斯，见 Ov. *Met.* 2

**Rhaebus**, horse of Mezentius 瑞布斯，见 Verg. *Aen.* 10

**Rhea**, Gr: Rhea, Rheia, "earth", Titan, wife of Cronus and mother of six Olympian gods 瑞亚，见 Hes. *Theog.*

**Rhea Silvia** = Rea Silvia

**Rhenus**, E: Rhine, the main river of Germany 莱茵河，见 Caes. *De bello Gall.* 4, 5

**Rhesus**, Gr: Rhēsos, "breaker", King of Thrace who came to help the Trojans but was killed by Odysseus and Diomedes 瑞索斯，见 Hom. *Il.* 10

**rhema** => verbum

**rhetorica**, rhetorice, ars oratoria, Gr: rhētoreia,（technē）rhetorikē, E: rhetoric, the art of oratory; => orator 修辞学，见 Plat. *Gorg.*, Arist. *Rhet.*, Cic. *Brutus*, *De off.* 2,48（a good speech earns admiration）, Hor. *De arte poet.*,（usus est norma loquendi）, Quint. *Inst.*（education of an orator）, Aug. *De doctrina christ.*,（new purpose of oratory）, Capella, *De nuptiis*（rhetoric personified as a well-armed woman）, Cassiod. *Inst.*, Greg. Magn., *Regula pastoralis*（rules for preaching）

**rhetorike** => rhetorica

**Rhodus**, Gr: Rhodos, "land of roses", E: Rhodes, most easterly of the Aegean islands, occupied by Dorians ca. 1000 BC; it became an important trade and literary center; around 300 BC the inhabitants erected the Colossus of Rhodes which was destroyed in 227 BC by an earthquake; Panaetius, Posidonius and Molon taught here, and many Romans went to Rhodes to study（Cicero, Caesar, Tiberius）. 罗得岛，见 Apollonius, Cicero, Posidonius

**risus**, ridere, Gr: gelaō, E: to laugh, laughter 笑，见 Bened. *Regula* 10（control one's laughter）, Philogelos（jokes）

**Roma**, <Etruscan "Romu", Gr: Rhōmē, "strength", E: Rome, city in Latium（Italy）; early settlements date from 1500 BC, the official date of the founding of Rome（given by Varro）was 753 BC; the Gauls destroyed the city in 387 BC; after the sack of Rome of 410 AD（and again in 455 AD）the city lost its paramount influence for the western part of the mediterranean world. 罗马，见 Polyb.（Roman constitution）, Cic. *De re publ.*（teleology of Roman history）, Caes., Sall., Verg. *Aen.*6（vision of future greatness of Rome）, Iuv. *Sat.* 3（city life of Rome）, Iren. *Adv. haer.*（special authority of the church in Rome）, Cyprian. *Epist.*, Euseb.（bishops of Rome）, Symmachus, *Relat.*（old Lady Rome wants to keep old customs）, Hieron. *Epist.*（mourning the fall of Rome in 410）, Aug. *De civ. Dei*（the Fall of Rome, review and new evaluation of Roman history, Rome is not the embodiment of justice）

**Romanus Melodus**, Gr: Romanos Melodos, ca. 500—560 AD, Greek Christian poet 罗马努斯，见 *Kontakia*

**Romulus**, son of Rea Silvia and Mars, brother of Remus, as child nourished by a she-wolf, raised by the shepherd Faustulus; Romulus became the legendary founder of Rome, who reigned as the first king（753—715 BC）罗姆卢斯，见 Cic. *De nat. deor.* 3,5,（Romulus as the first to introduce divination）, *De off.* 3,41; Verg. *Aen.* 6, Hor. *Carm.* 1,12, Liv. 1, Plut. *Bioi*, Aug. *De civ. Dei* 15（compared to Cain, his fratricide remained unpunished）

**rosa**, E: rose, a flower, => flos 玫瑰花，见 Apuleius, *Met.*（eating roses has magic effect）

**Roxana**, Gr: Roxanē, the wife of Alexander 若克萨内，见 Arrian. *Alex. anab.*, 4

**Rubicon**, "reddish", a river marking the border between Cisalpine Gaul and Italy; by crossing the Rubicon in 49 BC Caesar declared war on Pompey and the senate 鲁比孔，见 Luc. *Phars.*

**rumor**, fama, Gr: phēmē, akoē, logos, E: rumor 谣言，见 Verg. *Aen.* 4

**rus**, Gr: agros, chthōn, chōra, E: countryside; =>

**agricultura** 乡下，见 Hom. *Od.* 14（Eumaios），Hor. *Carm.* 2,6（mihi angulus ridet），*Sat.* 2,6, Iuv. *Sat.* 3, Martinus de Braca, *De corr. rusticorum*

**Rutuli,** E: Rutulians, an Italian tribe led by Turnus 儒图里人，见 Verg. *Aen.* 7~12

# S

**sabbatum,** <Hebr. Shabat, "rest", Gr: sabbaton, E: Sabbath; => quies 安息日，见 Aug. *Conf.* 13（eternal Sabbath），*De civ. Dei* 22

**Sabini,** E: Sabines, an Italian people north-east of Rome, who waged wars against Rome before 450 BC 萨比尼人，见 Liv. 1（Rape of the Sabines）

**sacerdos,** clericus, Gr: presbyteros, "elder", E: priest, moderator of the liturgy in a Christian community 司铎，见 Iren. *Adv. haer.*, Ambros. *De off. ministr.*, Dionys. Ar., *Eccl. hier.*, Greg. Magn. *Regula pastoralis*

**sacramentum,** <Gr: mystērion, E: sacrament; => baptismus, eucharistia 圣事，见 Didache, Dion. Ar. *Eccl. hier.*

**sacrificium,** Gr: thysis, ta hiera, E: sacrifice; => libatio, religio, pietas 祭祀，见 Hom. *Od.* 11, Aesch. *Choephor.*, Ar. *Ornithes*, Cic. *De nat. deor.* 3,5（placatio deorum），Verg. *Georg.* 4（sacrifice of expiation by Aristaeus）

**saeculum,** Gr: aiōn, kosmos, E: world, secular society; => mundus 世俗的世界，见 Tert. *De spect.*（exire de saeculo），Orig. *De princ.*, Hieron. *Epist.* 22, 70（secular literature）

**Saguntum,** modern Sagunto, city in Spain, ally of Rome, captured by Hannibal in 219 BC after eight months of siege. 萨翁图姆，见 Liv. 21~23

**Salamis,** "eastern"（?），Greek island near Athens, scene of the naval defeat of Persia by the Greeks in 480 BC 撒拉米斯，见 Aesch. *Pers.*, Hdt. *Hist.* 9

**Sallustius,** Gaius Sallustius Crispus, E: Sallust, Roman politician and historian, 86—34 BC 萨卢斯特，见 Sall. *Bellum Cat.* Quint. *Inst.* 10, Tac. *Ann.*

**Salomon,** Gr: Solōmōn, E: Solomon, son of David, King in Jerusalem, ca. 960 BC, famous for his justice 所罗门，撒罗满，见 Ambros. *De off. ministr.*, Hieron. *Epist.* 70, Aug. *De civ. Dei* 17

**salus,** Gr: sōtēria, hygieia, eudaimonia, E: wellbeing, health, beatitude;（Christianity: salvation）益处、救恩，见 Cic. *De nat. deor.* 2,60（Salus = goddess of wellbeing），Iren. *Adv. haer*

**Samos,** Greek island, famous for wine and for an old temple dedicated to Hera 撒摩斯，见 Hdt. *Hist.* 3,

**sanctitas,** sanctum, Gr: hagiotēs, hosiotēs, E: sanctity, holiness; => religio, pietas 圣性，见 Cic. *De nat. deor.*1,4

**sanctus,** Gr: hagios, E: saint, a Christian saint, usually leading an outstanding life of virtue and piety, or a martyr 圣人，圣徒，见 Athanas. *Vita Ant.*（the first biography of a saint），Sulp. Severus, *Vita Sancti Martini*

**sapientia,** Gr: sophia, phronēsis, synesis, E: wisdom, insight, reason 智慧、明智，见 Plat. *Apol., Polit.*, Arist. *Eth. Nik., Met.*, Cic. *De fin.* 1, *De off.* 1,15（sapientia as virtue），1,153（wisdom different from prudence），Hor. *De arte poet.* 404（wisdom of poetry），Bibl. *Gen.* 37~50（Joseph = man of wisdom），*Job* 42（to keep silence is wisdom），Clem. Alex. *Protrept., Strom.*（wisdom of the peoples），Lact. *Inst.* 3, 4,（de *falsa sapientia*, de *vera sapientia*），Ambros. *De off. ministr.*, Aug. *De vita beata*（sapientia = modus animi），Capella, *De nuptiis*（personification of wisdom: Sophia）

**Sappho,** Gr: Sapphō, Greek lyric poetess from Lesbos, ca. 600 BC 萨福，见 Hor. *Carm., Her., Peri hypsous*

**Sardanpall,** king of Syria, symbol of wealth 撒丹帕尔，见 Cic. *De fin.* 2,106

**Sardis,** Gr: Sardeis, town in Asia Minor, capital of Lydia 撒迪斯，见 Hdt. *Hist.* 1

**Sarpedon,** Gr: Sarpēdōn, "rejoicing in a wooden ark", son of Zeus and Laodamia, ally of the Trojans who is killed by Patroclus 萨尔佩顿，见 Hom. *Il.* 16

**sarx** => caro

**Satana,** diabolus, Gr: Satanas, Satana, "enemy", diabolos "subverter", E: Satan, the devil 撒旦，见 Bibl. *Job*, Athanas. *Vita S. Ant.*（temptations）

**satura,** satira, Gr: iamboi, E: satire, => Horatius, Iuvenalis, Lucilius, Persius 讽刺诗，见 Hor. *Sat.*, Quint. *Inst.* 10（satire seen as Roman invention），Mart. *Epigr.*, Iuv.

***Saturae,***（=*Sermones*），E: *Satires*, a work by Horace《讽刺诗集》，见 Hor.

***Saturae,*** E: *Satires*, a collection of satires by Juvenal《讽刺诗集》，见 Iuv.

**Saturnalia,** a Roman feast held in December, where presents were exchanged and the slaves had more freedom 萨图尔那里亚，见 Hor. *Sat.* 2,7,

Macrobius, *Sat.*

**Saturnalia,** E: *Saturnalia*, a work by Macrobius《农神节说》,见 Macrob.

**Saturnus,** Gr: Kronos, E: Saturn, old Roman god, sometimes identified with Cronus 萨图尔努斯,见 Cic. *De nat. deor.* 2,60, Aug. *De civ. Dei* 4 (why was he not adequately honoured?)

**Satyr,** Gr: satyros, satyroi, E: Satyr, Satyrs, servants of Dionysus, youthful spirits with some bestial aspects (tails, legs of a goat), in Rome identified with the Fauni; in the Greek semi-comic satyr-plays the chorus was made up of satyrs; => Silenus 羊人,见 Verg. *Buc.* 6

**Scaevola,** Gaius Mucius Scaevola, a Roman hero who tried to kill Porsenna 斯凯沃拉,见 Liv. 2, Aug. *De civ. Dei* 2 (Romans are descendants of the Scaevoli)

**scala,** Gr: klimax, E: ladder, symbol for the journey of life 梯子,见 Perpetua, *Passio*, Iohannes Klimakos

***Scala Paradisi,*** Gr: *Klimax tou paradeisou*, E: *Ladder to Heaven*, a work by John Climacus 《天堂之梯》,见 Johannes Climacus

**Scamander,** Gr: Skamandros, "crooked man", a river near Troy and its river-god 斯卡曼德若斯,见 Hom. *Il.* 21

**scelus** => peccatum

***Sceptica,*** Gr: *Skeptika*, E: *Outline of the Skeptical School*, a work by Sextus Empiricus《怀疑学派》见 Minucius, *Oct.* (refutation of scepticism)

**Scheria,** Gr: Scheriē, island of the Phaeacians 斯克瑞亚,见 Hom. *Od.* 5

**scholasticus,** Gr: scholastikos, "scholar", E: bookworm, ridiculed in antiquity 书呆子,见 *Philogelos*

**scholē** => otium, educatio

**scientia, scire,** intellectus, intellegere, Gr: epistēmē, gnōsis, noēsis, mathēsis, eidein, E: knowledge, science 知识,见 Plat. *Apol.*, *Menon*, *Polit.*, Arist., Cic. *De fin.* 5 (disciplines of the Peripatetic School), Sextus Empiricus, *Skeptika*, Hieron. *Ep.* 57 (Scio quod nesciam), Aug. *De doctrina christ.* (scientia et sapientia), Cassiod., *Inst.* (secular knowledge)

**Scipio maior,** Publius Cornelius Scipio Africanus Maior, 236—183 BC, Roman general in the Second Punic War, since 211 BC in charge of Roman forces in Spain, consul in 205 BC, he defeated Hannibal at Zama in 202 BC and thus received the honorary title "Africanus"斯基比欧,西皮欧,见 Cic. *De re publica* (*Somnium Scipionis*), Liv. 26~30, Plut. *Bioi*, Aug. *De civ. Dei* 2 (Romans can be proud to be descendants of Scipio), Macrobius, *Commentarii in Somnium Scip.*

**Scipio Africanus minor,** Publius Cornelius Scipio Aemilianus, ca. 185—129 BC, Roman general and statesman, adopted grandson of Scipio maior, consul in 147 BC; he destroyed Carthage in 146 BC; being an admirer of Greek culture he counted among his friends Polybius, Panaetius, Lucilius, Terence. 斯基比欧,西皮欧,见 Cic. *Cato de sen.*, *De off.* 3,1, *De re publica* (*Somnium Scipionis*), Liv. 61~75

**scriba quaestorius,** Gr: grammateus, E: secretary 秘书,见 Hor.

**scribere,** Gr: graphein, E: write 写字,见 Hieron. *Epist.* 107 (children learn to write)

**scriptura,** Gr: he graphē, grapha, E: scripture, esp. the Holy Scripture 书卷,见 Biblia (Hagiographa)

**Scylla, Charybdis,** monsters at Messina that threatened passing ships 斯克拉,见 Hom. *Od.* 2

**Scythia,** Gr: Skythia, the lands to the north and east, the area from the Danube to the Don, Volga and Caucasus, the lands north of the Black Sea 西徐亚,见 Hdt. *Hist.* 4

**Sebastos** => Augustus

**Seirenes** = Sirenes

**Selene,** Gr: Selēnē, "moon", L: Luna, goddess of the moon, sister of Helios and Eos 塞勒内,见 Hes. *Theog.*, Lucian. *Theon dial.*

**Seleucides,** Gr: Seleukidai, E: Seleucids, Macedonian dynasty in Syria, founded by Seleucus I who reigned in Babylonia 321—281 BC, cf. Antiochus III 色莱基德,见 Ios. *Antiqu.*

**Semele,** Gr: Semelē, "moon", the daughter of Cadmus, king of Thebes; she became the mother of Dionysos but was killed when she wanted to see her lover Zeus 塞墨勒

**seminarium,** Gr: didaskaleion, E: basic cell 基本的团体,见 Cic. *De off.* 1,54

**Semiramis,** name of a queen of Assyria, she supposedly built the Hanging Gardens at Babylon, one of the Seven Wonders of the ancient world 色米拉米斯

**senatus,** Gr: boulē, synklētos, ekklēsia, gerousia, E: senate, the legislative council of ancient Rome, which originated from the time of the kings (before 510 BC) and had important functions even under the empire 元老院，见 Liv. 1, 2; Symmachus, *Rel.*

**Seneca,** "the aged", 4 BC—65 AD, a politician and author from Spain who lived in Rome and became one of the leading men under Nero but was finally forced to commit suicide. 塞涅卡，见 Sen. *De beata vita, De clem., Epist.* Quint. *Inst.* 10, Lact. *De ira,* Aug. *De civ. Dei* 6（respect for Jews）, Boethius, *De cons.*

**senex,** Gr: gerōn, E: old man, => aetas 老人，见 Hor. *De arte poet.*

**sensus,** Gr: aisthesis, noēma, dianoia, E: sense, feeling, perception, meaning 感觉、直觉，见 Philo, *Legum alleg.* (sensus literalis), Hieron. *Ep.* 57 (translation of the meaning: sensum de sensu), Aug. *Confess.* 6（non-literal meaning）

**sententia,** Gr: dikē, logos, rhēma, gnōmē, krisis, E: sentence, judgment, proverb, opinion, meaning 审判，见 Aesch. *Eumen.*, Ar. *Sphekes,* Plat. *Apol.*, Publ. Syr. *Sent.*, Hieron. *Ep.* 57 (meaning, sententia, as opposed to littera)

**septem artes liberales,** E: seven liberal arts; => ars 七个自由学科，见 Capella, *De nuptiis,* Cassiod. *Inst.*

**septem miracula,** Gr: hepta theamata, E: Seven Wonders of the Ancient World, listed as a canon in Hellenistic times; the seven places included the Pyramids of Egypt, the Hanging Gardens of Babylon (=> Semiramis), the Mausoleum at Halicarnassus; the Artemisium at Ephesus, the statue of Zeus at Olympia (=> Pausanias), the Colossus of Rhodes, and the Pharos (lighthouse) of Alexandria 古代世界七大奇观

**septem sapientes,** Gr: hepta sophoi, E: the Seven Sages, the alleged authors of a collection of maxims; they were Thales, Solon, Periandros, Cleobulos, Chilon of Sparta, Bias of Priene, and Pittacus; also some other men were counted among the Seven Sages 七贤

***Septuaginta,*** E: *Septuagint,* the Greek translation of the Hebrew Old Testament, according to tradition elaborated by 70（or 72）scholars ca. 250 BC; the canon of the *Septuagint* includes apocryphal texts.《七十贤士译本》，见 Biblia, Orig. *Hexapla,* Hieron. *Ep.* 57, *Vulgata,* Aug. *De civ. Dei* 18

**sepulcrum,** Gr: taphos, E: tomb 墓，见 Prud. *Peristeph.* (description of the tombs of martyrs)

**seraphim,** Hebr: saraphim, E: seraph, a kind of angel, mentioned in the Old Testament（for example *Is* 6）色拉芬，见 Dionys. Areop., *Peri tes ouranias hier.*

**sermo,** Gr: logos, rhēma, E: speech, sermon, => oratio, rhetorica 讲演，见 Hor. *De arte poet.*

***Sermones*** = *Saturae*

**serpens,** Gr: ophis, E: snake, => draco 蛇，见 Physiologus（Christian interpretation）

**Sertorius,** Quintus Sertorius, ca. 120—73 BC, a Roman soldier who became praetor in Spain in 83 BC 塞尔托里乌斯，见 Plut. *Bioi*

**servitus,** Gr: latreia, E: cult, worship 崇拜，见 Aug. *De civ. Dei* 10

**Servius Tullius,** the sixth king of Rome（578—535 BC）, who organized the centuria and the tribus 塞尔维乌斯·图利乌斯，见 Liv. 1

**servus,** Gr: doulos, pais, hypēretēs, diakonos, therapōn, E: slave, servant; already Homer describes different types of unfree subjects (captives, servants); slaves could be bought on the market; slaves could purchase their freedom or be set free (freedmen); the influence of philosophy (Seneca) and religion (Christianity) led to a more humane approach to slaves. 奴隶，见 Arist. *Polit.*, Ter. *Adelph., Heaut. Tim.*, Cic. *De off.* 1, 41 (fairness towards slaves), Sen. *De vita beata* 24 (the fool is a slave of wealth), Loukian. *Vitarum auctio*

**Sestus,** Gr: Sestos, a city in Asia Minor 塞斯图斯，见 Hdt. *Hist.* 9

**Seven Wonders,** => septem miracula

**severitas,** Gr: chalepotēs, deinotēs, pikrotēs, E: severity, strictness; => vis 严厉要求，见 Ter. *Adelph., Heauton Tim.*, Cic. *De off.* 1,89 (needed for governing a state), Sen. *De clem.*, Bibl. *Ioann.* 8

**Severus, Sulpicius,** Latin historian, ca. 360—420 AD 塞维鲁斯，见 *Vita Sancti Martini*

**Sextus Empiricus,** Gr: Sextos Empeirikos, ca. 160—220 AD, Greek physician whose books are the main source of information on the Sceptical school of philosophy 塞克斯都·恩披里柯，见 *Skeptika*

**sibylla,** Gr: sibylla, E: Sibyl, prophetesses and priestesses, esp. the Sibyl of Cumae in Campania, who was visited by Aeneas; her oracles ("libri Sibyllini") were written on palm-leaves, and offered to the last king of Rome, Tarquinius Superbus; => Cumae 西彼拉，见 Verg. *Aen.* 6

**Sicilia,** Gr: Sikelia, < sika = pig, "pig-land", E: Sicily, island in the south-west of Italy, variously colonized by Greeks, Phoenicians and Carthaginians since the 8th century BC 西西里岛，见 Thuc. 6, 7, Ar. *Eirene*, Polyb., Cic., Verg. *Aen*.3, 5

**sidereon genos,** E: race of iron 黑铁之人，见 Hes. *Erga*, 176

**sigē** => silentium

**signum,** Gr: sēmeion, sēma, symbolon, tekmērion, hypodeigma, E: sign 记号，见 Bibl. *Ioann.*, Aug. *De doctrina christiana*, (theory of signs and things)

**Silenus,** Gr: Seilēnos, "moon-man", E: Silenus, a spirit of wild life, half-man, half-animal (=> satyr), in contrast to the young satyrs, sileni are depicted old and are supposed to be wise; Socrates was compared with Silenus 羊人，见 Verg. *Buc*.6

**Sikelia** = Sicilia

**silentium,** tacere, Gr: sigē, sigaō, E: silence, to be silent; => eloquentia 沉默，安静，见 Bened. *Regula* 6, 41, Columban, *Regula coen.*, Joh. Climac. *Scala* (taciturn acceptance of all things)

**Silvanus,** Gr: Seilēnos, Satyr, Pan, E: Silvanus, Silenus, Roman god of the forests, sometimes identified with Pan and the satyrs 西尔瓦努斯，见 Plaut. *Aul*.

**Simmias,** one of the dialogue partners of Socrates 西米亚斯，见 Plat. *Phaid*.

**Simonides,** Gr: Simōnidēs, "flat-nosed", E: Simonides of Ceos, 556—468 BC, Greek lyric and elegiac poet, writer of hymns and tomb epigrams 西摩尼得斯

**Sina,** Gr: Sēr, Sēres, E: China 中国，见 Hieronymus, *Epist.* 107 (Serum vellera), Philoponus (Cosmas Indicopleustes mentions China)

**Sirenes,** Gr: Seirēnes, "those who bind with a rope", E: Sirens, mythical female creatures who could destroy men by their songs; they lived on an island near Scylla 塞壬，见 Hom. *Od*. 12

**Sisyphus,** Gr: Sisyphos, from "soph-sophos" = "very wise", E: Sisyphus, founder and king of Corinth, the most cunning of men, punished by the gods in Hades; he had to perpetually roll up a rock to the top of a hill 西西福斯

**Skamandros** = Scamander

**Skeptica** = Sceptica

**societas humana,** Gr: synousia anthrōpōn, E: human race, mankind 人类，见 Cic. *De off.* 1,45

**Socrates,** Gr: Sōkratēs, < sozein - kratos, "strong in saving"; Athenian thinker, accused of misleading young people he was accused and died famously by drinking hemlock in 399 BC; his method of discussion was to lead others to the acknowledgment of their limitations. 苏格拉底，见 Ar. *Nephelai*, Platon, *Menon, Phaidon, Symposion*, Xen. *Oikon.*, Cic. *De nat. deor.* 3,82, (Socrates' death as argument against divine providence), Sen. *De vita beata* 28, Lucian. *Vit. auct.* (parody), Diog. Laert., Lact. *Inst.*, Hieron. *Ep.* 57 (Scio quod nesciam), Boethius, *De cons.* (wise men imprisoned)

**Sōkratēs** = Socrates

**sol,** Sol, Gr: hēlios, E: sun, god of the sun, 太阳，见 Hes., *Theog.*, Plat. *Polit.* 5, 6, 7, (parable for the highest idea), Cic. *De nat. deor.* 2,4, (symbol of the existence of gods), Hor. *Carm. Saec.*, Bibl. *Gen.* (creation of sun and moon), Basil. *Hexaem.* (sol iustitiae = Christ), Macrob. *Sat.* (solar origin of mythology)

***Soliloquia,*** E: *Soliloquies*, a dialog by Augustine 《独语》，见 Aug.

**solitudo,** Gr: erēmia, monōsis, E: solitude; => monachus 独处，见 Cic. *De off.* 3,1, Athan. *Vita Anton*.

**Solomon** = Salomo

**Solon,** Gr: Solōn, ca. 640—561 BC, Athenian politician and reformer of the legal system after 594 BC, famous for his wisdom and moderation 梭伦，见 Hdt. *Hist.*, Plat. *Symp.*, Arist. *Polit.*, Cic. *De off.* 1,75, Plut. *Bioi*, Diog. Laert.

**soma** = corpus

**somnium,** Gr: oneiros, onar, enypnion, horama, E: dream, often a message from the gods; => visio; revelatio 梦，见 Hom. *Od.* 4, Aesch. *Choeph.*, Plat. *Apol.* (mors = somnium), Cic. *De div*.1,34; 2,119, *De re publica* 6 (*Somnium Scipionis*), Philo, *Legum alleg.* (discussion of different types of dreams), Sulp. Sev. *Vita Martini*

**sophia** => peritia, intellectus, scientia, sapientia, prudentia

**sophistae,** Gr: sophistai, "wise men", itinerant teachers who gave lectures and private instruction for a fee, pretending also to teach virtue (arete) 智者、诡辩派，见 Ar. *Nephel.*, Plat. *Apol.*, *Menon*

**Sophocles,** Gr: Sophoklēs, "famous wise man", Greek tragedian, 497—406 BC; seven of his 130 dramas have survived. 索福克勒斯，见 Soph. *Antig., Elektra, Oidipous tyr., Oidipous epi Kolono*, Quint. *Inst.* 10, *Peri hypsous* 39

**sōphrosynē** = moderatio, intellectus

**Sosia**, "saviour", figure in Plautus' Amphitruo, the servant of Amphitruo 索西亚, 见 Plaut. *Amph.*

**soul** => anima, psyche

**Sparta**, Gr: Spartē, "rope", "plumb line", ( = Lacedaemon), town in the south of the Peloponnesus, occupied by the Dorians in 1100 BC; the education of the youth in Sparta emphasized the virtues of courage, steadfastness, obedience, austerity and military skills. 斯巴达/斯帕尔塔, 见 Hom. *Od.* 3, 4; Hdt. *Hist.* 3, 6, Ar. *Lysistr.*, Arist. *Polit.*, Polyb., Plut. *Mor.* (Apophthegmata Lakonika)

**Spartacus**, Gr: Spartakos, E: Spartacus, a slave-gladiator who escaped from a gladiatorial school at Capua, he organized an army of 60,000 men and triggered a war 73—71 BC; after defeating them Pompey had 6000 of the captives crucified at the Via Appia. 斯巴达克斯, 见 Orosius, *Hist.*

**spatium**, Gr: chōra, E: space 空间, 见 Plat. *Tim.*,

**species**, Gr: genos, eidos, E: kind, species, theme 种类, 见 Suet. *De vita Caes.* (thematic arrangement)

**spectaculum**, Gr: theōria, theama, horama, opsis, E: spectacle (at a dramatic performance), => ludus, theatrum 景色表演, 见 Arist. *Poiet.*, Tatian. *Logos*, Tert. *De spectaculis*

**spes**, Gr: elpis, E: hope, => vita aeterna 希望, 见 Sen. *Epist. mor.* 10, Ambros. *De off. ministr.* (hope and moral superiority), Prud. *Psych.* (allegory)

***Sphēkes***, E: *Wasps*, comedy by Aristophanes 《黄蜂》, 见 Ar.

**Sphinx**, Gr: Sphinx, < sphingein "bind fast", "strangler", E: Sphinx, monster with the head of a woman and the (winged) body of a lion 人面狮身女妖, 见 Soph. *Oid. Tyr.*

**spiritus**, ratio, Gr: nous, psychē, pneuma, menos, phronēsis, E: spirit, soul, thought; => anima, animus, vita interior 心神、思想, 见 Hom. *Od.* 11 (eidola = souls of the dead), Soph. *Oed. Col.* (spirit of Oedipus), Plat. *Tim.*, Arist. *Eth. Nik.*, Verg. *Aen.* 6 (reincarnation of souls), Sen. *Epist. mor.* 8 (spiritual life), Bibl. *Ioann.* 3 (spiritual rebirth), 19 (giving up the spirit), Plotin. *Enn.* (nous contains all things), Athanas. *Logos*

**Spiritus Sanctus**, Gr: pneuma hagion, E: the Holy Spirit; Christians believe in the Triune God, the Father, Son and Holy Spirit, => Deus, Logos 圣灵、圣神, 见 Iren. *Adv. haer.*, Tert. *Apol.*, Aug. *De civ. Dei* 12 (will = symbol of the Spirit), 13

**sponsa** => nuptiae

**stadium** => athla, certamen

**Statius**, Roman poet 45—96 AD 斯塔提乌斯, 见 *Achilleis*

**status naturae** => natura

**stella**, Gr: astron, E: star 星星, 见 Aug. *De beata vita* (faith is like a polar star), Aug. *De civ. Dei* 5 (against astrology)

**Stoa**, Gr: Stoa poikilē, E: Stoic school of thought, Stoicism; => Chrysippus, Cleanthes, Zeno 斯多亚派, 见 Cic. *De fin.*, Hor. *Sat.* 1, 3, Sen., Lucan, Epictetus, Plut. *Mor.* (Peri Stoikon enantiomaton), Marc. Aurel., Diog. Laert., Lact. (God incapable of wrath), Ambros. *De off. ministr.* (Stoa lacks hope), Aug. *De civ. Dei* 9, 14

**stoicheia** => elementa

**Strabon**, Gr: Strabōn, from Amaseia (Pontus), 63 BC—20 AD, Greek historian and geographer, author of *Geographica* (17 vols.) 斯特拉彭, 见 historia

**strategos**, L: dux, imperator, E: army commander 将军, 见 Hdt. *Hist.* 6, Thuc.

**Strepsiades**, Gr: Strepsiadēs, figure in Aristophanes' comedy 斯特瑞普西亚得斯, 见 Ar. *Neph.*

***Strōmateis***, E: *Stromateis* 《杂论》, 见 Clemens Alexandrinus

**studium**, Gr: spoudē, epimeleia, E: pursuit (of knowledge), diligence; => educatio 追求、学习, 见 Cic. *De off.* 1, 157 (studium cognitionis), 2, 5 (studium sapientiae), Hor. *De arte poet.* 408 (studium, ars are as important as genius)

**stultus**, stultitia, Gr: mōros, E: fool, foolishness 愚蠢, 见 Aug. *De beata vita*

**Styx**, Gr: Styx, Stygios, "abhorrent", "hated", the principal river of the Underworld; => Hades 斯提克斯, 见 Verg. *Aen.* 6

**sublimitas**, Gr: to hypsos, hyperphyes, E: sublimity, ingenuity, greatness 崇高, 见 *Peri hyps.*

**substantia**, Gr: ousia, E: substance 本体, 见 Greg. Naz. *Logoi* (name of God: he ousia)

**Suetonius**, Gaius Suetonius Tranquillus, Roman biographer, 69—122 AD, probably from Africa (Hippo Regius). 苏埃托尼乌斯, 见 Suet. *De vita Caesarum*, Hieron. *De viris ill.*

**suicidium**, Gr: autocheiria, E: suicide, => Aegeus, Antigone, Cato Uticensis, Decius Mus, Dido, Eurydice, Haemon, Hero, Jocasta, Lucretia, Marcus Antonius, Pyramus, Seneca, Socrates,

Thisbe 自杀，见 Sen. *Epist. mor.* 70, Aug. *De civ. Dei* 1 (Christians must not commit suicide)

**Sulla,** Lucius Cornelius Sulla, 138—78 BC, Roman general, dictator from 83—80 BC, who killed many without trial using the device of proscription 苏拉，见 Cic. *De off.* 2,25, Liv. 76~90, Plut. *Bioi*, Aug. *De civ. Dei* 3 (accused for cruelty)

**Sulpicius Severus** = Severus

**summum bonum,** finis, Gr: telos aristos, E: the highest good 至善，见 Cic. *De fin.* 4, Sen. *De vita beata*

**superbia,** Gr: hybris, hyperēphania, < hyper "above", authadeia, onkos, E: pride, conceit 自高自大，见 Aesch. *Persai*, Soph. *Ant.*, Theophr. *Eth.* 15, Hor. *Carm.*, Prud. *Psych.* (allegory, she rides on a horse), Cassian. *De inst.*, Greg. Mag., *Moralia* (the most serious one of the cardinal sins)

**superstitio,** Gr: deisidaimonia, E: superstition 迷信，见 Theophr. *Eth.*16, Cic. *De nat. deor.* 2,70 (etymology of "superstitio"), *De div.*, Plut. *Mor.* (*Peri deisidaimonias*), Aug. *De civ. Dei* 4 (Cicero could not separate superstition from religion), Martin de Bracara, *De correctione rusticorum*

**Sychaeus,** Gr: Sychaios, E: Sychaeus, husband of Dido 西开欧斯，见 Verg. *Aen.* 1

**symbebekos** = accidens

**symbolon** => allegoria

**Symmachus,** Quintus Aurelius Symmachus, ca. 340—402 AD, prefect of Rome in 384, orator and defender of ancient Roman religion, author of *Relationes* 徐马克斯，见 Ausonius, Macrob. *Sat.*

**sympathein** => misericordia

**symphilein,** E: to join in love, famous word of Antigone "一起爱"，见 Soph. *Ant.*

**Symplēgades,** Gr: "syn-plētto" = clashing together, a dangerous rock 危险的海峡，见 Apoll. *Arg.*

***Symposium,*** Gr: *Symposion*, "drinking together", E: *Symposium* 《会饮》，见 Plat.

**synodus, synodos** => concilium

**synthesis,** Gr: synthesis, "putting together", 结构，见 *Peri hypsous* 39 (synthesis logōn)

**Syracusae,** Gr: Syrakousai, "swamp-city", E: Syracuse, the main city of Sicily, founded in 733 BC by Corinthians; after the conquest in 212 BC many artifacts were brought to Rome; => Agrigentum, Archimedes 叙拉古，见 Thuc. 6, 7, Liv. 21~23

**Syria,** Gr: Syria, "swamp-land", E: Syria 叙利亚，见 => Antiochia, lingua Syria,

**Syrus,** Gr: Syros, name of slaves (coming from Syria) 叙卢斯，见 Ter. *Heaut. Tim.*

# T

***Ta eis heauton*** = *Meditationes*

**tacere** => silentium

**Tacitus,** "the silent one", Roman historian, 56—117 AD, studied in Rome, consul in 97 AD; his works show that he had penetrating insight into character and sober understanding of the important themes of his time. 塔西佗，见 Tac., *Annales*, *Germania*, Sall. *Bell. Cat.*

**Tantalus,** Gr: Tantalos, < talanteuo "in suspense", "most wretched" (?), father of Pelops, punished in Hades for his evil deeds 坦塔罗斯，见 Hom. *Od.* 11, Aesch. *Agamemnon*

**taphos** = sepulcrum

**Tarchon,** king of the Etruscans 塔孔，见 Verg. *Aen.* 10

**Tarquinius,** E: Tarquin, two Roman kings, 1) Tarquinius Priscus, in power 616—579 BC, and 2) Lucius Tarquinius Superbus, "the Proud", in reign from 534—510 BC 塔克文，见 Hor. *Carm.* 1,12, Liv.1

**Tartarus,** Gr: Tartaros, "far west" (?), E: the Underworld, the part of Hades where the wicked (e.g. Tantalus) are punished; =>Hades 阴间，地狱，见 Hes. *Theog.*

**Tatianus,** Gr: Tatianos, E: Tatian, Christian scholar and ascet, ca. 120—190 AD 塔提安努斯，见 *Diatessaron*, *Logos pros Hellenas*, Hieron. *De viris ill.*

**techne** => ars

**teichomachia,** "fighting at the wall", a passage in the Iliad 墙边之战，见 Hom. *Il.* 12

**teichoskopia,** "view from the city-wall", a passage in the *Iliad* 城墙之观，见 Hom. *Il.* 3

**Teiresias,** Gr: Teiresias, "he who delights in signs" (from teras = sign), a blind Theban seer who received from Zeus the gift of unerring prophecy, consulted by Odysseus in Hades 特瑞西亚斯，见 Hom. *Od.* 11; Soph. *Ant.*, *Oid. Tyr.*, Hor. *Sat.* 2,5 (gives advice on how to obtain a fortune)

**Telamon,** Gr:Telamōn,"he who supports (or suffers)", one of the Argonauts 特拉孟，见 Apoll. *Arg.*

***Telemachia,*** the first part of the *Odyssee* 《特勒马科斯记》，见 Hom., *Od.*

**Telemachus,** Gr: Tēlemachos, "final battle", son of Odysseus 特勒马科斯，见 Hom. *Od.* 1~4, 15~24

**teleologia,** from Gr: telos, E: teleology (of Roman

history）目的论，见 Cic. *De re publ.*, Verg. *Aen.* 6

**Tellos**, a honorable Athenian 特罗斯，见 Her. *Hist.* 1

**telos** => finis

**temperantia**, Gr: enkrateia, sōphrosynē, E: moderation, self-control, one of the main virtues 节制，见 Cic. *De fin.* 1, *De off.* 1,93 (ornatus vitae), Sen. *De clem.* 2,3 (clementia est temperantia animi), Ambros. *De off. ministr.*, Aug. *De beata vita*

**templum**, Gr: hieron, naos, temenos, E: temple, sanctuary 圣所、圣殿、神庙，见 Aesch. *Eumen.*, Cic. *De nat. deor.* 3,90, Vitr. *De arch.* 3 (construction of temples)

**temptatio**, Gr: peirasmos, E: temptation 试探，考验，见 Aug. *Confess.* 10

**tempus**, occasio, Gr: chronos, kairos, hōra, scholē, E: time, occasion, timeliness, => aeternitas, occasio 时间，见 Cic. *De off.* 1,142 (occasio = eukairia), Hor. *Carm.* 2,14 (labuntur anni), Sen. *Epist. mor.* 1, *Peri hypsous* 25 (change of time), Aug. *Confess.*11 (time a phenomenon of consciousness; creation = beginning of time)

**tenebrae**, Gr: skotia, E: darkness 黑暗，见 Plat. *Polit.* 7, (Parable of the Cave), Bibl. *Ioann.* 1 (phos - skotia)

**terateia**, (Gr), sensational ways of expression (as opposed to good historiography) 谈奇，见 *Polyb.*

**Terentius**, E: Terence, Roman writer of comedy, 190—159 BC 泰伦斯，见 Ter. *Adelphoe, Heauton tim., Phorm.*

**Tereus**, Gr:Tēreus, "watcher", mythical king of Thrace who betrayed his wife Procne and was changed into a Hoopoe 特柔斯，见 Ar. *Ornithes*

**Terpsichore**, Gr: Terpsichorē, "rejoicing in dance", one of the Muses, Muse of dance 特尔普西科瑞，见 Hes. *Theog.*

**terra**, Gr: ge, gaia, E: the earth 土地、领域，见 Basil. *Hexaem.*

**terribilis**, Gr: deinos, phoberos, E: terrible, awe-inspiring 可怕的，见 Soph. *Ant.*

**terror**, metus, formido, Gr: phobos, E: fear, terror 恐惧，见 Cic. *De nat. deor.* 1,56

**Tertullianus**, Florens Quintus Septimius Tertullianus, E: Tertullian, ca. 160—230 AD, Carthaginian lawyer and author of many apologetic and ascetic works, the "Father of Latin theology" 德尔图良，见 *Apologeticum, De spectaculis, De testimonio animae*

**testamentum**, Gr: diathēkē, E: testament, last will; the covenant (of God with His people), => Novum testamentum, Vetus testamentum 遗嘱，见 Suet. *De vita Caes.* (last will of emperors), Bibl. *Gen* 6, 15

**testis**, Gr: martys, E: witness 见证人，见 Arist. *Rhet.*, Tert. *De testimonio animae*

**Tethys**, Gr: Tēthys, "disposer", one of the Titans, wife of Oceanus and mother of the water-nymphs 特提斯，见 Hes. *Theog.*

**thalassa**, mare, Gr: thalassa = thalatta, E: the sea 大海、海洋，见 Xen. *Anab.*

**Thales**, Gr: Thalēs, ca. 600 BC, Greek philosopher, the first to propose a natural principle (water) as origin of all things. 泰勒斯，见 Cic. *De nat. deor.* 1, Min. Felix, *Octav.*, Diog. Laert.

**Thalia**, Gr: Thalia, "festive", one of the Muses, Muse of comedy 塔利亚，见 Hes. *Theog.*

**Thanatos** = mors

**theatrum**, Gr:theatron,E:theater,dramatic performances, => ludus, spectaculum 剧场，见 Tatian, *Logos*, Tert. *De spect.* (place of demons), Isidor. *Etym.* 18

**Thebae**, Gr: Thēbai, E: Thebes, main city of Boeotia in Greece, according to legend founded by Cadmus, connected with the myths of Hercules, Laius and Oedipus; a Mycenian palace was erected in 1400 BC:底比斯、忒拜，见 Hes. *Erga*, Soph. *Oid. Tyr., Oid. epi Kol.*, Polyb. (constitution), Ov. *Met.* 1~5 (stories connected with Thebes)

**Theia**, Gr: Theia, "divine", one of the Titans 特亚，见 Hes. *Theog.*

**Themis**, Gr: Themis, "order", "justice", one of the Titans, goddess of justice and wife of Zeus 特弥斯，见 Hes. *Theog.*

**Themistocles**, Gr: Themistoklēs, "praise of Justice", Athenian statesman and fleet commander, 524—459 BC; founder of the Athenian fleet in 482 BC who defeated the Persians at Salamis; he rebuilt Athens which had been destroyed by Persia.特弥斯托克勒斯，见 Plat. *Gorg.*, Cic. *De off.* 1,75, Plut. *Bioi*

**Theoclymenus**, Gr: Theoklymenos, "famous like a god", seer at Odysseus' court 特欧克吕梅诺斯，见 Hom. *Od.* 20

**Theocritus**, Gr: Theokritos, "divine judgment", ca. 300—250 BC, Greek poet, the originator of pastoral (bucolic) poetry 特俄克里托斯，见 Verg. *Buc.*

***Theogonia***, *Theogony*, a work of Hesiod《神谱》

**theologia**, Gr: theologia, "god-talk", E: theology 神

学，见 Plat. *Polit*.3, Greg. Naz. *Logoi* (logoi theologikoi: first distinction between theology and philosophy), Aug. *De civ. Dei* 6 (Varro's three kinds of theology: mythical, natural, political; Pythagoras, Thales, Plato developed a kind of natural theology)

***Theon dialogoi*** = *Deorum dialogi*

**Theophrastus,** Gr: Theophrastos, "interpreter of the divine", Greek author, successor of Aristotle, 370—287 BC 泰奥弗拉斯托斯，见 Theophr., *Ethikoi char.*

**theoria** => 1) visio, 2) adspectus, participatio, 3) inquisitio, speculatio, 4) festum

**Theoria,** Gr: Theōria, E: Theoria, Greek goddess of "attendance at festivals", holiday goddess 节庆女神，见 Ar. *Eirene*

**theos** => deus

**theosebeia** => adoratio

**theotokos** => Deipara

**thera** = venatio

**therapeia** => medicina

**Thermopylae,** Gr: Thermopylai, "warm gate", narrow pass between Thessaly and Locris, where the Greeks fought a heroic battle in 480 BC, cf. Leonidas 温泉关，见 Hdt. *Hist*. 7

**thesaurus,** Gr: thēsauros, E: treasure house; => Delphi 宝库，见 Hdt. *Hist*. 1

**Theseus,** Gr: Thēseus, "founder", "he who lays down", national hero of Athens, son of Aegeus (or Poseidon), who was loved by Ariadne, killed the Minotaurus in Crete, later was freed from Hades by Hercules 特修斯，见 Soph. *Oid. epi Kol.*, Eur. *Hipp.*, Ovid. *Her.*, *Met.*, Plut. *Bioi*

**Thessalia,** Gr: Thessalia, E: Thessaly, a district of north-eastern Greece 特撒利亚，见 Eur. *Alk.*, Xen. *Anab.*, Stat. *Achill.*

**Thetis,** Gr: Thetis, "disposer", daughter of the sea-god Nereus, wife of Peleus and mother of Achilles 特提斯，见 Hom. *Il*.1, 18, 19, 24, Stat. *Achill.*

**Thisbe,** Gr: Thisbē, lover of Pyramus 提斯贝，见 Ov. *Met*. 4

**Thracia,** Gr: Thrakē, Thrēkē, E: Thrace, the northern area of Greece between Macedonia and the Black Sea 色雷斯，见 Hdt. *Hist*. 5, Verg. *Aen*. 3

**Thrasymachus,** Gr: Thrasymachos, advocate of a "might is right" theory 特拉西马库斯，见 Plat. *Polit.*

**threskeia** => religio

**Thucydides,** Gr: Thoukydidēs, Greek historian, 454—399 BC 修昔底德，见 Thuc. *Ho polemos*, Sall. *Bell. Cat.*, Quint. *Inst.* 10, Tac. *Ann.*, *Peri hypsous*

**Thyestes,** Gr: Thyestēs, "pestle", son of Pelops, brother of Atreus 提厄斯特斯，见 Aesch. *Agamemnon*

**thymos** => voluntas

**Tiberis,** (=Tibris, Tybris), E: Tiber, the main river of central Italy; ancient Rome was located on its left bank 台伯河，见 Verg. *Aen*. 8 (river god)

**Tiberius,** Tiberius Claudius Nero Caesar, Roman emperor 14—37 AD 提贝里乌斯，见 Tac. *Ann.*, Suet. *De vita Caes.* (scandalous stories about his cruelty)

**Tibullus,** Albius Tibullus, 55—19 BC, Roman elegiac poet, friend of Horace and Ovid, whose focussed on romantic love and the joys of country life 提布卢斯，见 Ov. *Her.*,

**Tigris,** "tiger", river in Persia 底格里斯河，见 Xen. *Anab.*

**Timaeus ,** Gr: Timaios, "honored", a Pythagorean philosopher, main figure in Plato's dialogue *Timaeus* 蒂迈欧、提麦奥斯，见 Plat. *Tim.* Plut. *Mor.* (Peri tes Timaiou psychogonias), Min. Felix, *Octav.*

***Timaeus,*** Gr: Timaios, E: *Timaeus*, a dialogue of Plato 《蒂迈欧》、《提麦奥斯》，见 Plato, Aug. *De civ. Dei* 8 (semblance to the *Book of Genesis*)

**timocratia,** Gr: timokratia, E: timocracy 荣誉政治，见 Plat. *Polit*. 8

**Timoleon,** Gr: Timoleōn, "honoured lion", ca. 400—336 BC, Corinthian statesman who in 345 fought on the side of the people of Syracuse against their tyrant Dionysius II 提摩勒翁，见 Plut. *Bioi*

**timor,** metus, formido, terror, Gr: phobos, deima, E: fear, respect, terror 害怕、畏惧、敬畏，见 Cic. *De nat. deor.* 2,13; 3,10

**Tissaphernes,** Gr: Tissaphernēs, Persian satrap who was decisive in Artaxerxes' victory over Cyrus at Cunaxa in 401 BC 提撒菲内斯，见 Xen. *Anab*.

**Titanes,** Gr: Titanes, < titainontas "over-extension", E: Titans, (twelve) giant children of Earth and Sky 提坦、巨人，见 Hes. *Theog.* 209

**titanomachia,** the wars between Zeus and the Titans 巨人战争，见 Hes. *Theog.*

**titillatio sensus,** Gr: => terateia, E: titillation of the senses 感官的刺激，见 Cic. *De fin.*

**Titus,** Titus Flavius Vespasianus, Roman emperor 79—81 AD, famous for the capture of Jerusalem

提图斯, 见 Plin. *Nat. hist.*, Ios. *Bellum Iud.*, Suet. *De vita Caes.*

**toga,** the outer garment of a Roman citizen, also a symbol of peace, => pax 罗马人外衣, 见 Cic. *De off.* 1,77 (cedant arma togae)

***Tomus ad Flavianum,*** E: *Letter to Flavianus*, by Leo the Great《致佛拉维安的信》, 见 Leo

**Torquatus,** Lucius Manlius Torquatus, Roman thinker who committed suicide in 46 BC 托夸图斯, 见 Cic. *De fin.*

**Torquatus,** Titus Manlius Torquatus, Romana hero and symbol of Roman virtue, consul in 340 BC 托夸图斯, 见 Cic. *De fin.*

**tragoedia,** Gr: tragōdia, E: tragedy, a serious or tragic play 悲剧, 见 Aeschyl., Soph., Eurip., Hor. *De arte poet.*

**Traianus,** Marcus Ulpius Traianus, E: Trajan, Roman emperor from 98—117 AD 图拉真

**tranquilitas** => quies

**translatio,** transferre, vertere, mutare, E: translation; => lingua Graeca, Hebraica, Latina 翻译, 见 Cic. *De finibus*, *De off.* (translation of Greek terms), Hor. *Ars poet.*, Tatianus, Origenes *Hexapla*, Physiologus, Athanas. *Vita S. Antonii*, Hieron. *Epist.* 57 (theory of non-literal translation), *Vulgata*, Aug. *De civ. Dei* 15 (Syriac, Greek, Latin translations of the OT), 18 (translation of the Septuaginta by 72 scholars), Boethius, Dionysius Exiguus

**transubstantiatio,** Gr:metaballesthai, E: transubstanti-ation 变体说, 见 Cyrillus, *Catecheses*

**tribunus,** (tribuni plebis), E: tribune, tribunes of the people, Roman magistrate who protected the plebeians; they were elected annually and could impede decrees and laws of the senate 护民官, 见 Liv. 2 (institution of the tribuni in 494 BC)

**trinitas,** E: trinity, a basic tenet of the Christian faith: the Trinity of the Father, Son and Spirit 三位一体, 见 Cyrillus, *Catech.*, Aug. *De civ. Dei* 11 (human mind, intellect and will are an image of the Trinity), Nestorios

**Trismegistos** => Hermes Trismegistos

**tristities,** = tristitia, E: sadness 悲伤, 忧郁, 见 Apuleius, *Met.* (allegory), Cass. *De inst.* (one of the main vices), Boethius, *Cons.*

**triumphus,** E: triumph, victory parade, granted by the senate to a victorious general 凯旋游行, 见 Ios. Flav. *Bell. Iud.*, Tert. *De spect.*

**Troia,** Gr: Troiē, (=Ilion), E: Troy, town in Asia Minor, settlements since ca. 3000 BC, destroyed ca. 1200 BC (1184 BC according to Eratosthenes); the heroes who defended the city in the Trojan War were Hector, Paris, Aeneas 特洛伊, 见 Hom. *Il.*, *Od.*, 4; Hes. *Erga*, Aesch. *Agamemnon*, Hdt. *Hist.*, Verg. *Aen.*, Hor. *Carm.* 3,3 (Troiae renascens Fortuna clade iterabitur), Ov. *Met.* 6~13 (stories related to Troy), Aug. *De civ. Dei* 1 (fall of Troy compared to Fall of Rome: the gods did not protect their temples)

**Troianus equus,** equus ligneus, Gr: hippos xylinos, E: Trojan horse, the wooden horse built by the Greeks as a device to conquer Troy 木马, 见 Verg. *Aen.* 2

**tropos** => figura

**Tros,** Gr: Trōs, son of Dardanus, brother of Ilus, who gave his name to Troy and the Trojans 特洛斯, 见 Troia

**Troy** = Troia

**Trygaius,** Gr: Trygaios, "grape-harvester", figure in Aristophanes' comedy *Eirene* 特瑞格乌斯, 见 Ar. *Eir.*

**Tullia,** 79—45 BC, the much-loved daughter of Cicero 图利亚, 见 Cic. *Tusc.*

**Tullus Hostilius,** the third king of Rome (672—641 BC), he attacked Alba Longa and founded the senate-house (Curia Hostilia) 图卢斯, 见 Liv. 1

**Turnus,** king of the Rutulians, who killed Pallas, the son of Evander; he was the main rival of Aeneas and finally killed by the latter 图尔努斯, 见 Verg. *Aen.* 7~12

**turpitudo,** turpis => peccatum

***Tusculanae Disputationes,*** E: *Discussions at Tusculum*, a work of Cicero《图斯库卢姆谈话录》, 见 Cic.

**Tusculum,** Italian town ca. 25 km south-east from Rome, where Romans had their villas 图斯库卢姆, 见 Cic. *De fin.*3, *Tusculanae Disp.*

**tyche** => fortuna, Fortuna

**typus,** Gr: charaktēr, E: character, type of person 性格, 见 Arist. *Rhet.*

**tyrannis,** dictatura, Gr: tyrannis, E: tyranny, dictatorship 专制君主政治, 见 Plat. *Polit.* 7,8, Arist. *Polit.*, *Rhet.*, Cic. *De off.* 2,25~30 (Dionysius, Phalaris, Sulla)

**Tyrus,** Gr: Tyros, E: Tyre, old trade port of the Phoenicians who produced Glass, metal and textile products; => Europa, Phoenicia 提洛

# U

**Ulixes** = Odysseus

**ultio,** Gr: timōra, ekdikēsis, nemesis, E: revenge, => nemesis, Eumenides, 报复、复仇，见 Aesch. *Orest.*, Eur. *Medeia*, Tac. *Ann.*(sine ira et studio), Iuv. *Sat.* 13 (infirmi animi est voluptas ultio)

**Ulysses** = Ulyxes = Odysseus

**universum** => kosmos, mundus

**unum,** unitas, Gr: to hen, E: one, the unity (of the universe); => concordia; 一，见 Arist. *Met.*, Proclus, *Plat. theol.*, Boethius, *De cons.* 3 (unum = the highest good), Dionys. Ar., *Cael. hier.* (unificatio = homoiosis theo), Joh. Climac. *Scala* (contemplation and unity with God)

**Urania,** Gr: Ourania, "heavenly", the Muse of astronomy 乌拉尼亚，见 Hes. *Theog.*

**Uranus,** Gr: Ouranos, E: Uranus, Sky, god of the sky 天神，见 Hes. *Theog.*

**urbs,** Gr: polis, E: city, urban society 城市，见 Cic. *De off.* 2,15

**usus,** E: use, custom, =>mos 使用，见 Hor. *De arte poet.* 72 (usus est norma loquendi)

**Utica,** oldest colony of the Phoenicians in Africa, founded in the 9th ct. BC; after 146 BC it was the capital of the province of Africa => Cato Uticensis 乌提卡

**utile,** Gr: chrēsis, ōpheleia, E: utility 用处，见 Cic. *De off.* 1,9; 2,9; Hor. *De arte poet.* 323 (comparison of Greek genius and Roman utilitarianism)

# V

**Valentinos,** influential heretic in the 2nd cent. 瓦伦提努斯，见 Iren. *Adv. haer.* 1

**valetudo,** valere, Gr: hygieia, E: health; => medicina 身体健康，见 Cic. *De fin.* 4, *De off.* 2,86 (is a useful value), Sen. *De vita beata*, Plut. *Mor.* (*Hygieina parangelmata*)

**Vandales,** E: Vandals, a Germanic people who invaded Spain in 409 AD and Africa in 429 AD; their king Gaiseric captured Rome in 455 AD 旺达尔人，见 Greg. Turon., *Hist. Franc.*

**Varius Rufus,** Lucius Varius Rufus Roman poet and friend of Virgil and Horace 瓦利乌斯·鲁夫斯，见 Hor. *Sat.* 1,5

**Varro,** Marcus Terentius Varro, 116—27 BC, philologist, antiquarian and librarian, the most learned among the Romans of antiquity; most of his works are lost 瓦罗，见 Varro; Plin. *Nat. hist.*, Nonius, Aug. *De civ. Dei* 6 (three types of theology), 19 (280 opinions concerning the supreme good)

**vates,** Gr: mantis, E: seer, soothsayer, prophet, => Calchas, Cassandra, Teiresias 先知，见 Cic. *De div.*

**Veii,** an Etruscan town captured by Camillus in 396 BC 维伊，见 Liv. 1

**Velleius,** Gaius Velleius, Epicurean philosopher in Cicero's dialogue 维勒乌斯，见 Cic. *De nat. deor.*

**Venantius Fortunatus,** ca. 535—600 AD, Latin author, bishop of Poitiers 维南蒂乌斯，见 *Carmina*

**venatio,** venator, Gr: thēra, thēreutēs, E: hunting, hunter 狩猎，见 Plat. *Symp.*, (Eros as hunter), Verg. *Aen.* 4, 7

**Venus,** "charm", "beauty", Gr: Aphroditē, E: Venus, Italian goddess identified with Aphrodite, goddess of love 维纳斯，见 Cic. *De nat. deor.* 2,69 (Venus from "venire"), *De off.* 1,130 (dress of women expresses venustas), Lucr. *De rer. nat.* 1,1, (alma Venus), Verg. *Aen.* (mother of Aeneas), Ov. *Met.* 15,750—870 (Venus changes Caesar into a star), Apuleius, *Met.* (envious and vengeful), Tert. *De spect.* (performances dedicated to Venus), Lactantius, *Carmen de ave phoenice* (Veneris foedera), Aug. *De civ. Dei* 3 (Venus committed adultery)

***Verae historiae,*** Gr: *Alēthē dihēgēmata*, E: *True Stories*, a work by Lucian 《真实的故事》

**verbum,** vocabulum, nomen, Gr: logos, epos, mythos, E: word 话、言词，见 Varro (types of words), Hor. *De arte poet.* 70 (verba renascentur, creation of new words), Ov. *Ars am.*, (love-letters should use verba blanda), Sen. *Epist. mor.* 6 (plus ex moribus quam ex verbis), Epict. *Enchir.* (rather act than talk), Bibl. *Ioann.*1 (Logos = Verbum Dei), 6 (rhemata = words of eternal life), *Peri hypsous* 30 (choice of words = onomatōn eklogē), Orig. *De princ.* (negative or superlative expressions concerning the divine), Hieron. *Epist.* 57 (translation verbum e verbo, sensum de senso), Aug. *De doctrina christ.* (critical of empty words)

**Verbum Dei** => Logos

**Vercingetorix,** king of the Gallic tribe of the Averni who in 52 BC tried to unite Gaul to resist Roman rule, he was executed at Caesar's triumph in Rome in 46 BC 维辛格托瑞克斯，见 Caes. *De bell. Gall.* 7

**Vergilius,** Publius Vergilius Maro, E: Virgil, Vergil,

70—19 BC, the greatest Latin poet of antiquity 维吉尔，见 Verg., *Buc.*, *Georg.*, *Aeneis*, Quint. *Inst.* 10, Macrob. *Sat.* (Vergil as scholar, poet, prophet, magician)

**Verginia** = Virginia

**Verginius,** Lucius Verginius, Roman hero 维尔格尼乌斯，见 Liv. 3

**veritas,** verum, Gr: alētheia, E: truth 真理，见 Plat. *Apol.*, Cic. *De off.* 1,13 (veri inquisitio), Bibl. *Ioann.* 4:23 (adorabunt in spiritu et veritate), Lucian, *Alethe diheg.* (parody of truthfulness), Tert. *De spect.* (theater performances are not truthful), Lact. *Inst.* (vera religio, vera sapientia, verus cultus), Ammianus, Aug. *De beata vita* (more than opinion), *De vera rel.* (indubitable truth; God is summa et intima veritas)

**verum** => veritas

**Vespasianus,** Titus Flavius Sabinus Vespasianus, E: Vespasian, Roman emperor 69—79 AD 维斯帕芗，见 Ios. *Bellum Iud.*, Suet. *De vita Caes.*

**Vesta** = Hestia

**Veturia,** mother of Coriolanus 维图利亚，见 Liv. 2

**Vetus Testamentum,** E: Old Testament, OT《旧约》，见 Biblia; *Peri hypsous* 9 (*Gen.* 1 as example of powerful pathos); Iren. *Adv. haer.* 3, Athanas. *Logos* (prophecies announce the coming of the Messiah), Aug. *De civ. Dei* 8 (Plato probably read the OT)

**via,** Gr: hodos, E: way 道路，见 Bibl. *Ioann.* 14:6 (I am the way), Didache (two ways), Dionys. Ar., *Eccl. hier.* (via illuminationis, via unionis)

**via media** = media via

**Via Sacra,** E: sacred way, the street in the Forum in Rome 神路，见 Hor. *Sat.* 1,9

**via vitae** => vita

**victoria,** Gr: nikē, E: (goddess of) victory 胜利(的女神)，见 Cic. *De nat. deor.* 2,60 (Victoria)

**videre** => visio

**vinum,** vinea, Gr: oinos, ampelos, E: wine, vine trees; => Bacchus, Dionysus, Liber 葡萄酒、葡萄树，见 Verg. *Georg.* 2 (growing vine), Hor. *Carm.* 1,4; Bibl. *Ioann.* 2 (water changed into wine), 15 (ampelos alethinē), Tert. *De spect.* (Bacchus = daemon ebrietatis), Hieron. *Epist.* 107

**violentia** => vis

**Virbius,** Gr: hierobios "holy life", Italian god of the forests, later associated with Diana or identified with Hippolytus 维尔比乌斯，见 Verg. *Aen.* 7 (as son of Hippolytus and local chieftain)

**Virgil** = Vergilius

**virginitas, castitas,** Gr: parthenia, agneia, E: chastity, virginity; goddesses of virginity were Hestia / Vesta, Artemis / Diana, Athena / Minerva; => parthenon 童贞、贞洁，见 Eur. *Hipp.*, Virg. *Aen.* 4, Liv. 3 (Verginia), Tac. *Germ.*, Heliod. *Aithiopika* (chastity for the first time as an ideal), Lactantius, *Carmen*, Greg. Nys. *Peri parthen.*, Hieron. *Epist.* 107, Aug. *De civ. Dei* 1 (suicide in order to protect one's virginity is wrong), Venantius, *Carmina* (spiritual wedding)

**virgo,** Gr: parthenos, E: virgin, maiden, the image of certain goddesses, especially Athena, Artemis, Dike; => virginitas 童贞女、少女，见 Hes. *Erga* (Parthenos Dike), Eur. *Hipp.*

**virtus,** < vir "manliness", or < vis "strength", or < ars "skill", Gr: aretē, < aristos "perfect, outstanding", andreia, to kalon; E: virtue, esp. the four cardinal virtues: wisdom (sapientia, prudentia), fortitude (fortitudo), temperance (temperantia), justice (justitia), => mos, pietas, humanitas 美德，见 Plat. *Apol.*, *Menon*, *Polit.*, Arist. *Eth. Nik.*, *Polit.*, Rhet., Cic. *De fin.*, *De nat. deor.* 2,60~70 (Virtus = goddess of virtue), *De off.* 1,9 (virtus = honestum), 3,17 (progress in virtue), *Tusc.* (virtue brings happiness), Hor. *Carm.* 1,22, *Carm. saec.* (goddess of virtue), Philo, *De opificio* (didaskalikē aretē, physikē aretē, asketikē aretē), Sen. *De clem.*, *De vita beata*, Plut. *Mor.* (Ei didakton hē aretē), Iuv. *Sat.* (moral decay), Suet. *De vita Caes.* (virtues and vices of emperors), Bibl. *Ioann.* 13 (love each other = entolē kainē); Iustinos, *Apol.* (Christian virtue exceeds pagan virtue), Ambros. *De off. ministr.* (cardinal virtues; hope and moral superiority), Prud. *Psychomachia* (allegories of the virtues and vices), Capella, *De nuptiis* (allegory), Boethius, *De cons.* 5 (virtues are meaningful even in frustration)

**vis,** violentia, E: violence, => bellum 暴力，见 Cic. *De off.* 1,34; 1,81 (immane, "inhuman"), Sen. *De vita beata* 3,4 (omnis feritas ex infirmitate), Bibl. *Gen* 4 (murder), 6 (violence)

**Visigothones,** E: Visigoths, west Goths, a Germanic tribe which invaded Greece after 378 AD and sacked Rome in 410 AD (the "Fall of Rome"); => Gothones 西哥特人，见 Aug. *De civ. Dei*

**visio,** Gr: opsis, phasma, phantasma, horama, dokēma, E: vision, sometimes the revelation of secret knowledge, => contemplatio, somnium 神视，见 Plat. *Polit.* (mental vision = perceiving ideas), *Symp.*, Cic. *De re pub.* (Somnium Scipionis), Verg. *Aen.* 6, Ov. *Met.* 3 (stories about seeing forbidden things), Sen. *Epist. mor.* 10 (act as if "deus videat"), Biblia, *Rev.*, *Peri hypsous* 15 (visions of a poet inspire the audience), Apuleius, *Met.* (Psyche is denied the vision of her lover), Perpetua, *Passio*, (vision of a garden and Jesus as shepherd), Plot. *Enn.* (contemplation of "the One"), Athanas. *Vita Antonii* (visions), Sulpic. Severus, *Vita Martini*

**vita,** Gr: bios, zōē, E: life, life-style 生活，见 Cic. *De off.* 1,116 (modus vitae), Hor. *De arte poet.* 404 (vitae via), Sen. *De vita beata*, Lact. *Inst.* 7 (de vita beata)

**vita,** Gr: bios, E: biography, literary form; => 'autobiographia' 传记，评传，见 Sueton., Plutarch, *Bioi*, Diog. Laert., Athanas. *Vita Ant.* (the first vita of a Christian saint), Hieron. *De viris ill.*, *Epist.* (some letters contain biographies), Prud. *Perist.*, Aug. *Confess.* (the first detailed autobiography)

**vita aeterna,** Gr: zōē (aiōnios), E: eternal life, => aeternitas, spes 生命，永生，见 Bible, *Kata Ioannen*, Justin. *Apol.* (eternal bliss and eternal punishment), Lact. *Inst.*, Ambros. *De off. ministr.* (hope for eternal life and moral superiority), Aug. *Confess.* 13

**vita interior,** Gr: bios endoteros, E: inner life, spiritual life 内心生活，见 Sen. *Epist. mor.* 7 (recede in te ipse), Epict. *Diatr.*, Aug. *De beata vita*

*Vita Sancti Antonii,* Gr: Ho bios kai hē politeia tou Antoniou, E: Life of Saint Anthony, the biography of St. Anthony《圣安托尼传》，见 Athanasius

*Vita Sancti Martini,* E: *Life of Saint Martin*, a work by Severus《圣马丁传》，见 Severus, Sulpicius

*Vita Sancti Severini,* E: *Life of Saint Severin*, a biography by Eugippius《圣塞维林传》，见 Eugippius

*Vitarum auctio,* Gr: *Biōn prasis*, work by Lucian《拍卖诸生命》

**Vitellius,** Aulus Vitellius, Roman emperor who ruled briefly in 69 AD (after Galba and Otho) 维特利乌斯，见 Suet. *De vita Caes.*

**vitium,** Gr: kakia, kakotēs, ponēria, E: vice, bad habits; => virtus 恶习，见 Cic. *De fin.* 3,35, Hor. *Sat.* 1,3 (all have vices), Mart. (Parcere personis, dicere de vitiis), Suet. *De vita Caes.* (vices of emperors), Aug. *De beata vita* (nothingness is the mother of vices), Boethius, *De cons.* 4 (vices are a loss of humanity)

**Vitruvius,** Roman engineer and author, 90—30 BC 维特鲁威，见 Vitr., *De arch.*

**Volsci,** E: Volscians, a tribe of central Italy who threatened Rome but were subject to Rome since 300 BC; => Camilla, Coriolanus 沃尔斯基，见 Verg. *Aen.* 11, Liv. 2 (Coriolanus)

**voluntas,** Gr: boulē, thelēma, prothymia, thymos, thymoeidēs, E: will, willingness 志愿，见 Plat. *Polit.* 4, Aug. *Cf.* 7 (evil is a perversion of the will), *De civ. Dei* 11 (will as symbol of the Holy Spirit; perversion of the will is the origin of sin)

**voluptas,** Gr: hēdonē, philēdonia, terpsis, E: pleasure, crave for enjoyment; => dilectio, laetitia 享乐，见 Arist. *Rhet.*, Cic. *Cato de sen.*, *De fin.*, *De off.* 3,116~120 (condimenta); Hor. *Sat.* 2,4 (pleasure of good cuisine), *Peri hypsous* 44 (philedonia), Tert. *De spect.*, Boethius, *De cons.* 3 (opposed to true joy, laetitia)

**Vulcanus,** Volcanus, early Roman deity, later identified with Hephaestus, god of fire and of blacksmiths 伏尔甘、火神，见 Verg. *Aen.* 8

*Vulgata,* E: *Vulgate*, the Latin Bible translation by Jerome which became the authoritative version throughout the Middle Ages《圣经通行译本》，见 Hieron.

**vulgus** => populus

# X

**Xanthus,** Gr: Xanthos, "yellow", horse of Achilles; => equus 克散托斯，见 Hom. *Il.* 19

**Xenophanes,** Gr: Xenophanēs, early Greek philosopher, ca. 570—480 BC, teacher of Parmenides, known for his attacks on the polytheism and anthropomorphism of Greek religion 色诺法内斯，见 Tert. *Apolog.*, Min. Felix, *Octav.*, Diog. Laert.

**Xenophon,** Gr: Xenophōn, "foreign voice", Greek author, 428—354 BC, joined the campaign of Cyrus against his brother in 401 BC; he was one of the most versatile and sourceful authors of antiquity. 色诺芬，见 Xen., *Kyrou anabasis*, *Oikonomikos*, Quint. *Inst.* 10

**Xerxes,** Gr: Xerxēs, son of Darius, king of Persia 486—465 BC, who was defeated by the Greeks at Salamis (480 BC) and Plataea (479 BC) 薛西斯, 见 Aesch. *Persai*, Hdt. *Hist.* 7

# Z

**Zama,** place in Numidia (Africa), where Scipio defeated Hannibal in 202 BC and ended the Second Punic War 萨玛, 见 Liv. 26~30

**Zeno,** Gr: Zēnōn, 1) Zeno of Elea, ca. 490—445 BC, Greek philosopher; 2) Zeno of Citium, ca. 333—262 BC, founder of the Stoic school 芝诺, 见 Cic. *De fin.* 4, Epict. *Diatr.*, Diog. Laert., Min. Felix, *Octav.*

**Zetes,** Gr: Zētēs, "searcher", one of the Argonauts 泽特斯, 见 Apoll. *Arg.*

**Zeus,** Gr: Zeus, "bright sky", L: Jupiter, Greek god, son of Cronus and Rhea, brother of Hades, Poseidon, Hestia, Demeter, and Hera; king of Mount Olympus, "Father of gods and men", his main functions were: 1) god of the weather, in command of rain, thunder and lightning; 2) protector of the house and possessions; 3) guarantor of justice and law, contracts, oaths and hospitality; 4) god of prophecy who revealed his will through dreams, thunder, birds and oracles; his main temples were in Dodona and Olympia; => Jupiter 宙斯, 见 Hom. *Il.*, *Od.*, Hes. *Erga*, *Theog.*, Ar. *Ornithes*, Plat. *Symp.*, Pausanias (statue of Zeus by Pheidias), Lucian, *Theon dial.* (parody), Tert. *De spect.* (games at Olympia dedicated to Zeus)

**zōē** => vita

# 出版后记

对于受到启蒙运动史学影响的大多数中国读者来说,西方现代之前的历史,印象最深刻的当属古希腊—罗马的光辉灿烂与中世纪的黑暗幽深了,而处于这二者之间的转换过渡阶段——古代晚期(Late Antiquity),则往往了解不多,总觉得它像蒙了一层纱一样色调暧昧。

关于这一时期的具体时间界限,史学界仍有争论。这一研究领域的翘楚 Peter Brown 在他的名著《古代晚期的世界》(*The World of Late Antiquity: AD 150—750*, 1971/1989)中将这一时期大体划在公元 2 至 8 世纪。在这六百年间,罗马帝国由"黄金时代"走向衰落,最终分裂成东、西两部分,476 年 Odoacer 废黜西罗马帝国皇帝 Romulus Augustulus,标志着西罗马帝国的结束以及蛮族王国统治时代的开始,而东罗马帝国(即拜占庭帝国)则一直延续到 1453 年。在这个阶段的精神领域,最重大的事件莫过于基督教的兴起以及基督教文明逐步取代古希腊—罗马文明占据主导地位,本书作为《西方经典英汉提要》的第二卷,主旨即在于以 100 部左右的作品提要勾勒这个时期的精神变迁。由于这一时期最为活跃的写作群体为基督教教父,他们的活动时期大约为公元 2 至 6 世纪,因此本书的下限截止为 650 年。

基督教在 1 世纪时缓慢发展,2 世纪在罗马帝国扎下了根,到了 3 世纪则迅速发展广泛传播。基督教为什么能吸引那么多的追随者?总结起来大约有三点原因。第一,基督教通过耶稣的死而复生传达了救赎的讯息,这对遭受着帝国境内四处充斥的痛苦与不义的罗马人来说,具有极大的吸引力,它为生命提供了一种超越物质现实的意义与目的。第二,对于罗马人来说,基督教并非是完全陌生的事物,他们完全可以把它视作与那些通过向救主祭献牺牲而获得永生的其他东方神秘宗教类似的宗教。但是,基督教具有其他神秘宗教缺乏的优点。耶稣基督是以人的形象展现于世人面前的,而非一个神话人物,这与当时流行的 Mithras(源于波斯拜火教中的光明神,罗马人将之与太阳神等同起来)崇拜相比,具有独特的亲和力。另外,基督教不需要痛苦的或昂贵的入教仪式(Mithras 入教仪式繁复多达七级),只需要施洗就能完成,通过圣水的净化建立起个人与耶稣的联系。更重要的是基督教给了罗马国教所不能给的东西,即个人与神的联系以及更高级的生命意义。第三,基督教能满足人的归属感。基督教徒建立的社团通过互相帮助以及援助鳏寡孤独贫病无依者表达仁慈的爱,这种归属感是庞大、遥远、冷漠的罗马帝国无法给予的。

基督教向所有的阶层开放,对永恒生命的允诺也是面向所有人的,富与贫、贵族与奴隶、男人与女人,所有这些自然与社会属性上的差异在基督教面前全都没有意义,这种平等意识对于建基在等级秩序之上的古代社会无疑是一种精神革命。它不仅在底层民众中广受欢迎，也吸引着上层阶级，为坚持基督信仰而在Cathago的斗兽场中殉道的Perpetua——天主教有纪念她的传统节日——就是一位罗马贵族妇女。

随着基督教的壮大，3世纪的一些皇帝进行了几次更为系统的大规模迫害，但是这未能奏效。当Diocltian在4世纪初进行迫害时，他认识到基督教已经强大到无法用武力铲除了。313年，第一位基督教皇帝Constantine大帝颁布米兰敕令，宣布基督教合法。392年，Theodosius大帝将基督教立为国教，基督教至此获得了最终的胜利。

与基督教在政治与社会层面取得胜利的曲折相比，基督教神学思想发展的复杂性毫不逊色。欧洲神学是2世纪护教士将基督教与希腊诺斯替派哲学调合起来，在Alexandria城的海道学校中孕育出来的。当时，为了说明基督是上主的首生者，真正的logos，一切民族都分享这个logos，在基督教兴起之前的古代哲学家与基督教信仰也是一致的，这种初期神学几乎把基督教信仰化为理性主义，化为人的内心生活的伦理。这些神学家是古代晚期的文化精英，他们只是按自己的理解去捕捉基督教思想内容，使用的概念和语言则是古典文化提供的，他们不以基督教与异教的混杂为忤，反而认为基督教教义是充实了希腊哲学的智慧。在这些神学家中，Justin首当其中，其后有Clement of Alexandria、Origen和在他们之后的三位Cappadocia教父——Basil of Caesarea、Gregory of Nyssa、Gregory of Nazianzen，他们是基督教人本主义的第一批代言人；此后再经Jerome、Abéland、Petrarch、Erasmus、Budé和Leibniz，一直到19世纪，都强调异教和基督教的传统与智慧终将在圣洁之中联结为一体。

但是，基督教与异教之间的扞格也不是能够置之不理的。*Genesis*中上帝无中生有（creatio ex nihilo）的创世叙事对异教自然崇拜的暗中贬斥，基督教有始有终的历史观与罗马古谚Nil novi sub sole（太阳底下没有什么新鲜事）所表达的古代世界循环历史观之间的差异，诸此种种无不刺激着早期基督教会不同于理性主义的另一方面。Justin的弟子，叙利亚人Tatian就极力反对把基督教溶解为哲学和理念，并且写作《驳希腊人》对古希腊哲学与宗教进行全面否定和抨击，这是基督徒学者彻底批评希腊文化的最早先例。这种情绪与思考往往以被归于"拉丁神学之父"Tertullian的话"因为荒谬，所以信仰"以及《护教篇》中的名言——"雅典与耶路撒冷何干？学院与教会何干？异教徒与基督徒何干？"——为典范，这种强调灵性的对立偶句，既光辉诱人，又充满危险，其后每一个世纪都有学者沉醉于其中（如20世纪俄国著名思想家舍斯托夫）。一定程度上可以说，调和了基督教理性主义和灵性追求的是非洲人St. Augustine。他的精神经历之丰富令人吃惊，他的著作几乎无所不包，在他之后的一千五百多年间，基督教的各种流派、各种不同的发展方向都能从中获得启发，无论是正统还是异端。

St. Antony开创了隐修的传统，被称作"隐修运动之父"。"隐修者"的拉丁语写法为monachus，意为"独自生活的人"。早期的隐修者抛弃文明社会离群索居，这种灵性操练树立了一种新的基督徒典范，原来的圣徒是指那些为了信仰牺牲生命并在此过程中获得永恒生命的人，而新的圣徒是指那些通过遁世、禁欲和对上帝神秘体验以求灵性生活的人。

很快,早期隐修者发现他们的隐修生活很难再继续下去,因为他们圣洁的声名吸引了大批慕名而来的追随者。随后,一种隐修者在一起共同生活的隐修院文化形式发展起来并迅速占据了主导地位。隐修团体被视作理想的基督教社团,它为它周边的社团提供了一种道德榜样。St. Benedict of Nursia 修建的 Monte Cassino 隐修院非常有名,他为修会写的《会规》可视作西欧的第一部宪章。《会规》将隐修士的日常生活分割成一系列的活动,其中最主要的活动是祷告和体力劳动。修道士们的生活完全是一体的,他们共同吃饭、工作、睡觉、做礼拜。就这样,靠着作息时间的规律化和环境的单纯化,隐修士们的心灵和肉体都得以安静下来,使他们既有精力工作,也有精力享受闲暇。修道院在中世纪早期文明中扮演着不可或缺的重要角色,隐修士们抄写拉丁文献,为欧洲传承了古代世界的文明遗产,另外,隐修士在把基督教传播到整个欧洲世界的过程中也将要扮演越来越重要的角色。

以上是对古代晚期基督教文化的一些重要方面进行的简要概括和介绍,它远远不能涵括本书中所涉及著作代表的所有文化现象,希望它能为读者提供一些背景性的知识,以方便读者更为有效地阅读本书。

欢迎采用本书做教材的教师与本编辑部联系,我们将为您提供相关服务。

**世界图书出版公司北京公司**

服务热线:139-1140-1220　133-6631-2326　010-81616534

投稿邮箱:teacher@hinabook.com

服务信箱:onebook@263.net

**世图北京公司"大学堂"编辑部**
2010年3月

## 图书在版编目(CIP)数据

西方经典英汉提要.第2卷,古代晚期经典100部/雷立柏著.—北京:世界图书出版公司北京公司,2010.4

(读书会)

ISBN 978-7-5100-2068-1

Ⅰ.①西… Ⅱ.①雷… Ⅲ.①著作—内容提要—西方国家—英、汉 Ⅳ.①Z835

中国版本图书馆 CIP 数据核字(2010)第 058564 号

# 西方经典英汉提要(卷二):古代晚期经典100部

| | | | | | |
|---|---|---|---|---|---|
| 著 者: | (奥)雷立柏 | 筹划出版: | 银杏树下 | 责任编辑: | 张 鹏 |

出　　版:世界图书出版公司北京公司
发　　行:世界图书出版公司北京公司(北京朝内大街 137 号 邮编 100010)
销　　售:各地新华书店
印　　刷:北京盛兰兄弟印刷装订有限公司(北京市大兴区黄村镇西芦城 邮编 102612)
开　　本:787×1092 毫米 1/16
印　　张:25 插页 4
字　　数:500 千
版　　次:2010 年 6 月第 1 版
印　　次:2010 年 6 月第 1 次印刷

教师服务:teacher@hinabook.com　139-1140-1220
投稿邮箱:onebook@263.net
编辑咨询:133-6631-2326
营销咨询:133-6657-3072　010-8161-6534

ISBN 978-7-5100-2068-1/H·1091　　　　　　　　　　　　定　价:42.00 元

(如存在文字不清、漏印、缺页、倒页、脱页等印装质量问题,请与承印厂联系调换。联系电话:010-61232263)

**版权所有　翻印必究**

# 韦洛克拉丁语教程
## （插图第6版）

张卜天 译 （奥）雷立柏 审阅

雷立柏 彭小瑜 沈 弘 推荐

ISBN 978-7-5062-9310-5/G·323

定价：99.00元　2009年4月出版

### 为什么要学习拉丁语？

★ **拉丁语是了解欧洲文化的"大门"**。无论是在文学、历史学、哲学、法学、宗教学、伦理学，还是心理学、医学、自然科学或教育学，西方许多经典著作都是用拉丁文写成的，要想深入了解西方文化，学习拉丁语是最好的途径之一。

★ **了解拉丁语有助于学习英语**。60%的英语词汇都源于拉丁语。学过拉丁语的学生对SAT的词汇部分会更加得心应手。拥有较大词汇量也通常预示着管理方面的潜力和成功。

★ **在一个国家，古典语言是否受到足够的重视，是其综合实力的重要标志**。像拉丁语这样一门重要的语言，目前在我国远没有受到应有的重视。但随着我国综合国力的增强，拉丁语越来越热，必定是大势所趋。

### 学习拉丁语，人必称"韦洛克"

听说韦洛克（Wheelock）的著名拉丁语教程将要在中国出版，我感到非常兴奋与欣慰。2002年以来，我在北京教授拉丁语和古希腊语，但始终没有找到令我满意的拉丁语语法教材、文选和拉汉词典。《韦洛克拉丁语教程》终于能满足这个迫切需要。对学习西方哲学、文学、法律、历史或宗教的大学生和学者来说，这部教科书的出版是一件重大的事，因为拉丁语是一切西方知识的"大门"，而韦洛克也算是自学拉丁语的最好资料之一……我很高兴可以推荐它，希望它成为很多大学生的读物。

——雷立柏，奥地利古典学家，中国人民大学文学院教授

**内容简介**

《韦洛克拉丁语教程》是20世纪后半期以来英语世界最受欢迎的拉丁语教材，初版于1956年，很快就因其严密的组织结构、清晰的叙述讲解、循序渐进的设计安排、适中的难易程度以及其中收录的丰富的古代文献而被誉为"拉丁语学习的标准著作"，其"拉丁语学习首选教材"的地位无可撼动。

全书共分四十课，以简洁而不学究气的语言，系统讲解了拉丁语的基本词形、句法，并通过丰富的词汇学习、众多的英语词源研究、英拉句子互译和古典拉丁语作家原文赏读，来锻炼拉丁语学习者使用单词的灵活性和精确性，培养其观察、分析、判断和评价的能力，加强对语言形式、清晰性和美的感受；并通过探讨战争、友谊、未来、生老病死等发人深省的主题来学习古典作家的思想和技艺，分享他们的人文主义传统。